Inside LightWave 3D v10

Book 1

Dan Ablan

Inside LightWave 3D v10
by Dan Ablan

New Riders
1249 Eighth Street
Berkeley, CA 94710
510/524-2178
510/524-2221 (fax)

Find us on the Web at: www.newriders.com
To report errors, please send a note to: errata@peachpit.com

New Riders is an imprint of Peachpit, a division of Pearson Education.

Senior Editor: Karyn Johnson
Development Editor: Stephen Nathans-Kelly
Copy Editor: Scout Festa
Technical Reviewer: Jack Bennett II
Production Coordinator: Myrna Vladic
Compositor: David Van Ness
Proofreader: Bethany Stough
Indexer: James Minkin
Cover Design: Charlene Charles-Will
Front Cover Image: ©2010 NewTek, Inc. Artist, Leigh Bamforth.
Back Cover Images: Dan Ablan

ISBN-13: 978-0-321-76661-8
ISBN-10: 0-321-76661-X

9 8 7 6 5 4 3 2 1

Printed and bound in the United States of America

Contents at a Glance

Introduction xiii

1 LightWave Modeler 1

2 LightWave Layout 43

3 Texture Creation 83

4 Lighting 119

5 3D Cameras 143

6 3D Animation 173

7 Motion Graphics 215

8 Modeling Everyday Things 231

9 Particle Animation 267

10 Dynamics in Motion 289

11 Bones and Rigging 313

12 The LightWave Render Engine 339

A Plug-ins and Additional Resources 351

What's on the DVD 359

Index 361

Table of Contents

Introduction **xiii**

1 LightWave Modeler **1**

Understanding Modeler 2
Key Areas of Modeler 2
- 3D Modeling in LightWave 3
- LightWave v10 Modeler Interface 4

Tabs and Menus 15
- Create Tab 16
- Modify Tab 18
- Multiply Tab 19
- Construct Tab 20
- Detail Tab 22
- Map Tab 24
- Setup Tab 26
- Utilities Tab 28
- Selection Tab 29
- View Tab 30

Points, Edges, and Polygons 32
- Selection Modes 32
- Modeler General Commands 35
- Using and Understanding W, T, M, C, S 39
- Modeler Options 40

The Next Step 42

2 LightWave Layout **43**

Understanding Layout 44
- LightWave Layout Interface 44

Menus and Tabs 54
- File Menu 55
- Edit Menu 56
- Windows Menu 60
- Help Menu 60
- Surface Editor 60
- Image Editor 62
- Graph Editor 62
- Virtual Studio 63
- Scene Editor 64

Parent in Place 66
Items Tab 67
Modify Tab 68
Setup Tab 72
Utilities Tab 73
Render Tab 74
View Tab 76
Modeler Tools Tab 78
Preferences 79
The Next Step 81

3 Texture Creation **83**

Using the Surface Editor 85
Organizing Surfaces 85
Selecting Existing Surfaces 87
Working with Surfaces 88
Working with VIPER 94
Common Surface Settings 100
Introducing the Node Editor 110
The Next Step 118

4 Lighting **119**

Working with Lights 120
Light Color 122
Light Intensity 122
Adding Lights 123
Clone Lights 124
Mirror Lights 125
Ambient Light and Ambient Color 125
Lens Flares 126
Volumetric Lights 126
Global Illumination Options 126
Global Light and Lens Flare Intensity 127
Radiosity and Caustics 127
Applying Lights in LightWave 128
Simulating Studio Lighting 128
Enhanced Lighting with HDR 133
Using Projection Images on Lights 135
Using Area Lights 138
The Next Step 141

5 3D Cameras 143

Focus on Cameras ... 144
- Setting Up a Camera ... 144
- Motion Effects ... 158
- Stereo and Depth of Field (DOF) ... 160
- Camera Concepts ... 164
- Additional Camera Types ... 168

The Next Step ... 171

6 3D Animation 173

Creating Motion with Keyframes ... 174
- Automatic Keyframing ... 175
- Manual Keyframing ... 180
- Control Curves with the Move TCB Tool ... 187

Navigating the Graph Editor ... 189
- Working with Channels ... 191
- Working with the Graph Editor ... 193
- Adjusting Timing in the Graph Editor ... 194
- Copy Time Slice ... 198
- Navigating the Curve Window ... 202
- Exploring Additional Commands in the Graph Editor ... 202
- Footprints ... 203
- Using the Curves Tab ... 205
- Editing Color Channels ... 211

The Next Step ... 213

7 Motion Graphics 215

Modeling 3D Text ... 216
- Working with Backdrops in Modeler ... 217
- Building Over Images ... 219
- Pivot Points in Modeler ... 227
- Importing EPS Files ... 228
- Animating Text ... 228
- Lighting, Motion, and Backgrounds ... 228

The Next Step ... 229

8 Modeling Everyday Things 231

Modeling Fruit 231
- Begin with Bananas 232
- Orange You Glad You Got This Book? 243
- Create a Cluster of Grapes 249

Building a Fruit Bowl 256
Building a Set for the Still Life 261
The Next Step 265

9 Particle Animation 267

Particles In LightWave 268
- Creating a Basic Particle-Motion Scene 268
- Working with Particle Wind 274
- Introducing Particle Collisions 278
- Surfacing Particles 281
- Using Images on Particles 285
- Editing Particles 286

The Next Step 288

10 Dynamics in Motion 289

Dynamics in LightWave 290
- Understanding Dynamic Controls 290
- Hard-Body Dynamics 291
- Soft-Body Dynamics 309

The Next Step 312

11 Bones and Rigging 313

Understanding Bones 314
Creating Hierarchies 318
- Creating Multiple Hierarchies 321
- Bone Weights 325
- Applying Weight Maps 327

Skelegons 332
The Next Step 338

12 The LightWave Render Engine 339

Working in the Render Globals Panel 340
    Setting Up an Animation to Render 341
    General-Purpose Rendering 342
    Saving Renders 346
    Thoughts on Rendering 349
The Next Step 349

A Plug-ins and Additional Resources 351

Exporting Scenes and Objects 352
Package Scenes 352
Working with Plug-ins 353
    Where to Find LightWave's Plug-ins 354
    Loading Plug-ins 355
    LScripts 356
    Learn Your Tools 356
More References You Can Use 356
Reading References 356
Audiovisual References 357
Web Resources 358

What's on the DVD 359

    Technical Support Issues 359
    DVD Contents 360
    Using the Video Files 360
    System Requirements 360
    Loading the DVD Files 360

Index 361

Acknowledgments

I've said it before, and I'll say it again: I cannot express my gratitude to my friend Jack "Deuce" Bennett. He, in many ways, has made this book possible. Without his help and sincere friendship, this book would be nothing more than a paperweight. Thanks, Deuce, for all of your help and direction. But it goes further, maybe even more than Deuce (just kidding!)—thank you so much, William Vaughan, for your insight, help, and models. Your expertise, years in the field, and general good nature have made working on these books a tolerable task. A big thank you also to Leigh Bamforth, who created the cover image. To an old friend, Michael Kornet at NewTek, thank you for your help not only getting this cover image together for us, but getting the book off the ground.

Of course, I'd probably still be writing this tome at this very moment if it weren't for Karyn Johnson at Peachpit Press, and Stephen Nathans-Kelly. You both really lit the fire under my you-know-what to get this book done. Thank you for your support and words of encouragement! Thank you to Myrna Vladic and David Van Ness, as well as copyeditor Scout Festa and the rest of the talented editorial and production team for putting the polish on this book.

To the entire team at NewTek—you guys have been a tremendous help with not just this book, but all the previous *Inside LightWave* books and others.

To my wonderful wife, Maria. Your support while writing this book, creating video training, traveling, creating 3D animations all while we run our portrait business has been amazing. I can't thank you enough for everything you do. You're the best. And to not-so-little Amelia, thanks for being the best daughter anyone could ask for.

Finally, to all LightWave users around the globe who read my books and use my 3D Garage training materials—thanks. Your feedback, on all levels, is greatly appreciated. All of you are the reason I lose sleep writing these books, so keep in touch and let me know what you're doing with your newfound knowledge.

About the Author

People often ask me how I juggle the many different things I do. I've never been one for a typical 9 to 5 job. Even in grade school, I loved those days when class was interrupted because of a snowstorm, or a guest speaker, or perhaps a school assembly. I like to break the routine from time to time, but every once in a while it's good to come back to something you're not just familiar with, but comfortable with as well. For me, it's writing these *Inside LightWave* books. This is my sixth *Inside* book for New Riders Publishing (my 14th overall), and it feels like I'm visiting an old friend. Our first *Inside LightWave* book for version 5.5 was in 1997!

My daily routine is composed of 3D animation, training, and photography. After graduating from Valparaiso University in 1989 with a B.A. in Broadcast Journalism and a minor in Photojournalism, I boldly started my career at a tiny little CBS affiliate in the middle of Indiana. Without boring you with each step of the ladder I've climbed over the past 20 years, I'll keep it brief. It was about a year after college that I discovered 3D animation, and I was hooked. My photography, which I began at the ripe old age of 13 and studied in college, was my side thing. Video production was my main thing, and 3D was quickly finding its way into the mix. By 1992, I was animating regularly as part of my job as a corporate video producer. By 1994, I had started my own fledgling animation business and was working for myself—mostly because I got fired from the Video Toaster/LightWave dealership I was working for. But I was on my way into the small, yet quickly growing world of 3D. My 3D business is AGA Digital Studios, Inc., and you can see more at www.agadigital.com. I've created 3D animations for hundreds of clients over the years, most recently for United Airlines, NASA, the American Dental Association, and Johnson & Johnson.

In 1995, I started writing articles for *LightWave Pro* magazine, as well as *Video Toaster User*. I began teaching 3D at various trade shows and local user groups. By 1996, writing expanded to my first book, *LightWave Power Guide*, which was for version 5.0. My 3D animation business was building, with corporate work being the main focus, from animated logos, to odd robots, and the occasional medical animation and television commercial. My photography at this time was used for texturing work in 3D, and as a personal hobby.

Flash forward to today, and while the world is continually changing and 3D is everywhere, I still do all the same things I've been doing for the past 20 years. I create 3D animations for product shots, architecture, and medical uses. I continue to create training material for 3D software through a site I founded in 1993 called 3D Garage. 3D Garage offers downloadable and DVD-based high-quality 3D and photography software training. You can visit www.3dgarage.com to see all of our training offerings. However, sometimes it's good to spread things around, so you'll also find training from me on LightWave v10 over at www.lynda.com.

But sometimes people want to ask questions, so I'm on the road regularly, teaching people 3D or photography at trade shows, or often at companies such as Hallmark Cards, NASA's Jet Propulsion Laboratory, APCO Worldwide, and many others over the past 12 years. I also give one-on-one photography workshops. We shoot one day, and then process the photos with Adobe Lightroom and then Photoshop the next. It's a busy and fun two days! And when I'm not doing those things, my wife and I run a portrait photography studio in the Chicago area. In 2008, after 25 years of having a camera hanging around my neck, I felt it was time to add it to the professional mix. Much of my photography work over the years has been more photojournalistic in nature and for 3D work, but our new studio focuses on children, pets, high-school seniors, and families. You can visit www.ablangallery.com to see what it's all about.

So there you have it! I write books and articles, and I have a 3D-animation business, a training business, and a full-time photography studio. What's funny is that I'm always looking for more to do. And if managing three Web sites isn't enough, how about a fourth? Visit www.danablan.com for specific book-related posts and further information on the new CORE technology from NewTek.

Introduction

Welcome to yet another installment of *Inside LightWave*. This book represents more than… well, more than a lot of years of LightWave® books written and published by me, a few good friends, and New Riders. *Inside* books—a staple in the ever-growing digital-image creation industry and your own personal library—are found in bookstores and online retailers around the globe. I personally want to thank you for your continued support, suggestions, and comments, which have helped make this new version of *Inside LightWave* the best the series has ever seen. Sure, we said that in the last book, and probably the one before that, but really, this is the best one!

To give you the most complete and up-to-date information, *Inside LightWave* was written in conjunction with the development of the LightWave 10® software (including CORE) from NewTek, Inc. No other book can offer you as much comprehensive information. With *Inside LightWave*, you will take this classic 3D application to the next level. LightWave 10 is a major release for NewTek, Inc., and I've tried to put as much information in this book as possible while keeping it organized and to the point. Every project you'll create is straightforward so you can get up to speed with this powerful program quickly. Every exercise will give you a clear and concise understanding of the powerhouse of tools LightWave 10 has to offer through simple and easy-to-follow tutorials.

What's the deal with CORE?

I know what you're thinking. I've thought the same thing too. A third application included with LightWave 10? It's supposed to get simpler and easier to use. Adding a brand new third application kind of complicates things, right? Well, the answer to that is yes, and no. Simply put, LightWave 10 includes Modeler, for well, modeling! Then there's Layout, for lighting, animation, and rendering. And then there's CORE. CORE is the future technology of LightWave, and it will continue to be developed by the team at NewTek for enhanced modeling, better animation, dynamics, and more. It's an entirely new program, but it's designed to integrate with LightWave's existing applications, the newly updated Layout and Modeler. You'll be able to learn about CORE with a chapter that's not found in this book, because the application wasn't finalized at press time, but posted online. Visit www.3dgarage.com and go to the book's page. Click the *Inside LightWave 10* cover and you'll find the latest information on CORE training to accompany this book. In order to access the additional chapter(s), you'll need a password. The password will change often and be a specific word on one of these pages, so you'll always need this book to get access.

Getting the Most from *Inside LightWave*

Although we have a set format for the *Inside* books, I had a situation while planning the *Inside LightWave [8]* book in 2004 that forced me to change how I approached these books. I was at my favorite Borders bookstore in Chicago, looking for ideas to create a cool and modern Web site. Using my suite of tools from Macromedia and Adobe Photoshop 7, I had built a decent Web site but I still needed some excitement. Perhaps some of those cool animated Macromedia Flash header bars, some animated buttons, and a few little gizmos to spice up the site. But I found that there wasn't a book that showed me how to do what I wanted. All the books I looked at were good, informative, well thought-out, and so on. But I just wanted to get going! I didn't want to sift through page after page of making curves and animating little clip-art bumblebees and the like. This experience got me thinking! Afterward, I went back to the office and jotted down some notes on how I wanted to refocus the *Inside LightWave* books.

The formula for the *Inside* books has worked well since the first *Inside LightWave* edition in 1997, and I don't want to change that. Many of the longtime readers look for this same format because of its proven track record. However, I did not want you to find yourselves in the situation I was in, especially when trying to learn a complex 3D application, not just a simple Web-creation program. Therefore, I've added a series of topic-specific videos to the book's DVD to enhance various chapters. This is a not-too-involved type of tutorial that will get you up and running with LightWave 10.

About the Creation of This Book

Inside LightWave was written entirely on a MacBook Pro Core 2 Duo laptop computer. That I was able to build the projects for this book on a mainstream consumer system—and a laptop at that—is a testament to the performance of computer systems in today's marketplace, as many desktop systems couldn't support 3D applications a few years ago. There are few differences between LightWave on the Mac and LightWave on Windows. The biggest difference is the use of a two-button mouse. If you are a Mac user, you probably know that Macs shipped with single-button mice for years and only recently started shipping with the two-button Mighty Mouse. Many programs, and the Mac OS X operating system itself, employ right-mouse-button functions, however, and I highly recommend you get a two- or three-button mouse if you're working on the Mac. This will benefit you greatly working in LightWave 10 as well as other programs. Logitech-brand optical mice work well, from my experience. For you Mac users who cannot part with the one-button mouse, simply hold your Control key in conjunction with the mouse button to achieve right-mouse-button functions. We'll provide reminders to you throughout this book.

Your choice of using Mac or Windows is strictly up to you. There is no benefit or drawback to either. It's merely a matter of preference.

Using the LightWave 10 Software with This Book

LightWave 10 has many differences from LightWave 9. I recommend that you use the latest revision of LightWave with this book to maximize your learning. Many of the tutorials in this book use tools only available in version 10. Consequently, some of these tutorials won't work with previous versions of LightWave. However, if you happen to have the *Inside LightWave 6, Inside LightWave 7,* or *Inside LightWave [8]* or *v9* books, you can take advantage of the tutorials in those books with the LightWave 10 software. Although some buttons and panels may have changed, the primary workflow and key functions of LightWave 10 operate the same as with previous versions. Additionally, you can change LightWave's menus back to v9 series mode through the Edit Menu Layout panel, found in the Edit drop-down lists in the program.

Always Use the LightWave 10 Manual

People always criticize software manuals. I think it's almost a preconceived notion that they are not the best learning tools; and in some cases, they are not. However, they do serve a strong purpose: to introduce and offer reference material on the current version. The LightWave manuals are included with LightWave 10 in electronic form and provide great reference information when you need to find out about a key function or tool. The current manuals from NewTek are the best they've been in years, so refer to them often for specific technical information. For learning beyond what you find in the manual, use *Inside LightWave*. This book is not intended to replace the manual or the reference function it serves, but it takes you to the next level by walking you through the toolset with projects and tasks.

Where Should You Start?

As I mentioned earlier, it kills me to buy a big new book on a software application and be forced to sift through page after page of information that doesn't provide the answer I'm looking for. In the past, I've written the *Inside LightWave* books as "start to finish" guides. With this version, I've tried to make a collection of little books, with each chapter being self-contained. But, there might be some overlap as the new CORE application tends to blend in with Layout and Modeler from time to time, as you'll find when you download the CORE chapter posted online. When you're comfortable with the workflow of LightWave 10 and ready to go further, pick up this book and do one of two things. You can either start at the beginning with Chapter 1, learning about Modeler, and then move to Chapter 2, Chapter 3, and so on. Or you can hop over to a chapter of your choice and start working through a project right away. The benefit of this is time efficiency—if you're short on time, you can get in, learn something, and get out, then come back later for more. It's totally up to you. Some chapters will use projects from other chapters. For example, you might model in one chapter and then animate that object in another. If you would like to just learn about animation, you can load the finished object from this book's DVD without having to complete the modeling chapter first.

Explore the Software

When learning LightWave, or any other software application, technical skill, keen insight, forethought, and clever deduction are always helpful, but there's another ingredient that's far more important to your success: experimentation. As you work through the exercises in this book, don't get hung up on being a mathematical wizard or a serious traditional artist. These skills may help, but they are not necessary to create beautiful 3D animations and graphics. Explore the software on your own terms. Experiment with buttons and tools, and don't be intimidated. There is no substitute for practice, whether it's a musical instrument, athletic ability, or 3D animation. I've said it before, and I'll say it again: Don't wait until you have a paid project or assignment to work in LightWave! All the extra time you spend modeling and animating will give you an extra edge.

No Method Is the Best Method

If you've ever read any of the 3D forums on the Internet, you might have seen some discussions about what is "the best" modeling method, or "the best" renderer, and so on. Do yourself a favor: Read those posts and then forget them. They are nothing more than opinion. What matters is what works for you. Perhaps you like to model with splines. Great. Perhaps you would never like to see a spline curve for the rest of your life. That's great, too.

Have you ever watched the Fox television show *American Idol*? If you've heard its judges tell young hopefuls to take a song and "Make it your own," you've heard some good advice—advice that applies to 3D design and animation as well as pop stardom. When a prospective Idol sings her guts out on live television with a rendition of a popular tune, raw talent can make a performance stand out, but to really wow the judges, she must invest the song with her own personal feeling, style, and creativity. In other words, make it her own. You can do the same with 3D modeling and animation. Find what works for you and run with it.

Use Other Books with This Book

People often ask me how I write these books. Sometimes, I ask myself the very same question! Whether I'm completing my daily animation work, writing another book, or creating courseware for 3D Garage, I find that using other books is a huge help. Books on topics such as architectural design, photography, anatomy, and many other subjects can be significant resources for 3D modeling, texturing, lighting, and animation. Don't limit yourself to only books and magazines focused on LightWave, computers, or 3D. Go beyond the scope of what you're doing by referencing other books. You can find many resources for character study, sculpture, and even drawing that will help you understand the foundations 3D models and animations are based on—or that will simply inspire you to create.

The Organization of This Book

Inside LightWave 10 is organized similarly to our previous versions. This book starts with the basics, then moves to intermediate projects, and then walks you through a few advanced concepts.

In the book, you'll find a chapter overview on the new tools and enhancements available in LightWave 10 for both Modeler and Layout (Chapters 1 and 2). From here, you can learn about texturing, following that up with an overview of working with cameras, lights, and motions. You'll see first-hand the new VPR mode, or virtual preview render.

In the next part of this book, you'll model with just about all possible methods, allowing you to decide which method is right for you. You'll start with simple modeling using text, then move to the intermediate with real-world objects, and more. These chapters will instruct you in the process, tools, and organization needed to create literally anything you can think of.

After you have modeling mastered, along with some texturing and animation, you can educate yourself on more powerful texturing and lighting techniques, while learning how to put everything in motion.

Toward the end of this book, you'll learn to get your animations rendered and into playable formats. You'll see how easy it is to use real-world physics to collide objects, push them around, and make smoke. You'll learn about LightWave's powerful rendering engine and render options.

At the end of the book, you'll find details about where you can go for further learning as well as important information on using this book's DVD. Please read this before you insert the DVD into your computer.

As you read this book, you'll find helpful Notes. These will be noticeably marked with a small icon.

Control areas throughout the program will be referred to as panels. Fields in which you enter values are called requesters, and buttons that have downward-pointing triangles are drop-downs. Be sure to go through Chapters 1 and 2 for clear overviews of Modeler and Layout control areas.

When working in LightWave 10, be sure Caps Lock is off. Keyboard shortcuts are first programmed in lowercase keys, whereas more complex, less-used commands are programmed with uppercase keys. Should you be following a tutorial in this book, be instructed to press a keyboard function, and not see results, there's a good chance you've got your Caps Lock on.

System Considerations

LightWave 10 has had a boost in performance over previous versions. In addition, a good amount of display options have been added, which can be great for your animation setup but taxing on your system. Obviously, the better your video card, the better the performance that you'll see, and more memory is always good. But you don't need to have a multithousand-dollar system to run LightWave efficiently. On the contrary, LightWave can run exceptionally well on systems costing just a few hundred dollars. Of course, this is all dependent on the type of work you're doing. Simply put, the more detail you put into a 3D model and animation, the more system resources you'll need. If there is one thing I cannot stress enough, it's memory. Do not go out and get the fastest processor and skimp on the memory. You are better off with a 2 GHz processor and 4 GB of RAM than a 3.6 GHz processor and only 1 GB of RAM. You may render a little slower, but you'll be able to work faster. Many system crashes are attributed to lack of memory, so try to make your absolute minimum 256 MB. Your NewTek manual can also instruct you on the optimal system requirements. You can also work directly with your LightWave dealer or computer dealer.

One thing to remember when working in a computer-based field: Don't wait. There will always be an upgrade, always a faster system and cheaper parts. But if you wait too long, you'll put aside valuable hours in which you could have been creating and learning, as well as earning! Buy a computer that is comfortably within your budget but as powerful as it can be, Mac or PC, and get to work.

Video Memory

Don't think that because you have the latest PC processor on the market, or the fastest Mac available, you'll have the best computer for animation. Processing power is only one part of the computing process when it comes to creating with LightWave. Your system memory—in this case, 256 MB of RAM or more—is important to a productive system. However, your video memory is just as important.

With LightWave 10's expansive interface enhancements, you should have a decent OpenGL-compatible video card with at least 256 MB of DDR Memory. Personally, I wouldn't go less than that. LightWave's Modeler and Layout allow great control over viewports, shading, and interface color, and there are brand-new OpenGL controls in Layout, all of which will rely heavily on your video memory. This matters even more with the new VPR interactive render. The better your video card, the better LightWave will run.

You can view images projected through lights, fog, reflections, and multi-textures, and view them more directly in Layout. Because of the popular video-game market, graphics cards have become ridiculously fast and cheap. And, the Macintosh market finally has some powerful graphics cards. It's highly recommended that you get a decent video card.

Any video graphics card you use should be fully OpenGL-compliant. Also, video cards change often, so be sure to check with NewTek about any new card recommendations the company may have.

Installing LightWave 3D®

Installing LightWave 3D is as easy as putting the software disc into your PC or Mac. Follow the instructions that NewTek, Inc. has provided in its software manual. If you have any LightWave 3D installation problems, please direct those questions to

NewTek's Technical Support (www.newtek.com). However, it's often best to let the installer do its job—that is, don't be clever and try to install different parts of the application to different parts of your hard drive.

Using the Book's DVD

The DVD that comes with this book contains all the project files you'll need to follow along with the examples. Additionally, you can load finished project scenes and dissect them for your interest and reference.

What's on the DVD?

In addition to the project files on the book's DVD, you'll find materials to take your LightWave 10 learning further than you can with any other LightWave book. You'll find the following:

- Free video tutorials from 3D Garage, which will take you further with many of the book's chapters
- High-quality color JPEGs of the book's screen shots
- All the scene files for the book's projects and tutorials
- Royalty-free textures and backgrounds from Dan Ablan's very own portrait studio, www.AblanGallery.com

See "What's on the DVD," after the appendix, for more detailed information.

Installing and Using the Practice Files

Too often, readers install a book's DVD into their drive and then try to open scenes. Sure enough, an error appears. In this case, that error message will tell you that LightWave "can't find" a necessary object or image. This is not because your DVD is defective; rather, it has to do with LightWave's content directory. You'll learn more about this as the chapters progress.

This DVD contains all the files you need to complete the exercises in *Inside LightWave 3D v10.* These files can be found in the root directory's Projects folder. To properly access the project files, do the following:

1. In LightWave Layout, press the **o** key to call up the Preferences panel.
2. At the top of the panel, click the Paths tab and then select the Content Directory button.
3. A system file dialog box titled Set Content Directory opens. Select your DVD/CD-ROM drive, go to the 3D_Content folder, and click Open.

If you'd like to use the files directly from your own hard drive, simply copy the 3D_Content folder from the book's DVD to your drive.

4. Your content directory is now set for working through the exercises. The content directory path should look something like \X:\3D_Content\, where X is your DVD/CD-ROM drive.

When you select Load Scene, LightWave opens the Projects folder. There, you'll see folders named Scene, Objects, and Images. Within these folders are the individual chapter folders. Selecting Load Object within LightWave points to the Objects folder within the Projects folder.

Basically, the content directory tells LightWave 3D where to look for files. If you press the **o** key (not zero) in LightWave Layout or Modeler, you'll get the Preferences panel. Click the Paths tab. At the top of that tab, you can click the Content Directory button. If you ever have difficulty accessing files, set the content directory to point to your DVD drive://3D_Content. That's it!

Within the Projects folder is an Images folder for necessary textures and images, an Objects folder containing LightWave 3D objects, and finally a Scenes folder that is home to this book's LightWave scenes. When you load a scene into LightWave Layout (you cannot load scenes into Modeler, only objects), the Scene file looks to the content directory for the necessary objects. The objects loaded look to the content directory for the necessary images. It sounds complicated, but it's not. All you're doing is telling LightWave where to find its files.

Throughout these chapters, if you're called upon to "load an object," simply selecting the Load Object command in Layout or Modeler automatically opens the Objects folder within your set content directory. The same goes for images or scenes, so be sure to keep this set while working through the projects.

Words to Work By

The 3D market has changed since I got into this business. I mean really, it's been 20 years! In the beginning, it was like a little club, and everyone got along. Anything we did, and I want to stress anything, was just cool as hell. In a small LightWave user group in Chicago that met monthly, each month's 3D creations were crude and generally of poor quality, but great to look at nonetheless. Now, it's a different world. 3D is everywhere—in movies, television, video games, the Internet, even cell phones. Our likes and dislikes have changed, and the market has grown beyond belief. Not everything is cool to look at anymore, but that's OK. No matter what, it's always great to see someone's work because you can learn from it. The 3D world we live in is no longer a small club of enthusiasts, but rather a planet full of 3D artists all working toward that ultimate render. It has become a competitive industry, but an industry built on passion and the love of 3D art. To this day, I've never met anyone that just "had" to do 3D. They "wanted" to, and I'm pretty sure you are one of those people. That hunger for 3D animation is what makes your digital creations better each time you sit down in front of the computer. You're striving to learn more and to make it better, perhaps convey a message and portray your artistic style. That's what it's all about, after all.

The tools you have at your fingertips seemed inconceivable 14 years ago, or even 6 years ago. Some of you are students; some of you are professionals; and some just hobbyists, young and old. You have the ability to create anything you can imagine. Do not feel that you need additional plug-ins, or other four-lettered software applications to do "better" work. You don't. LightWave, like any other application, is nothing more than code. It is buttons and an interface. It is simply a machine that you are driving, and your job is to finish the race. Now, turn the page and start working as I help you steer down the course.

Chapter 1
LightWave Modeler

I used to think there were two types of people who create 3D imagery. But over the past 18 years or so, I've realized that there are really three types. The first two types are modelers and animators. The third is that person who has no clue as to what it takes to create a 3D model, texture it, light it, or bring it to life. To this type, creating 3D imagery means pushing a button and waiting for the computer to do it. For the purposes of this book, we're going to forget about the push-button types, because no matter what you say or do, they simply won't get it. Some of these people are your clients or bosses, which leaves the real work of creating 3D imagery up to you.

It also raises the question: Which of the remaining two types of people are you—a modeler or an animator? I'm not saying you can't be both, but in my experience the 3D modeler is left-brain oriented—logical, sequential, and rational. The 3D animator is more right-brained—random, intuitive, and subjective. The animator also enjoys and understands timing, lighting, and textures.

But these two approaches—like 3D animation and modeling themselves—don't have to be mutually exclusive. What I'd like to do is mix the left and right brain and have you not only enjoy what you're doing but also understand it. When I started creating 3D imagery in LightWave, it took me longer to get into a groove with Modeler, whereas with Layout, I felt right at home. Other guys I knew were just the opposite due, in large part, to differences in our backgrounds. With all of that being said, I want to dive right into LightWave Modeler to get you up and running, no matter which side of the brain you favor.

NOTE

If you plan to only animate, and never plan to model, you might wonder if you should even read this chapter. The answer is yes! Even if you don't expect to model in your career, it's still important to understand LightWave Modeler for a couple of reasons. You may at some point need to import a model from another program. Or, at the very least, you'll need to assign a surface to parts of your model. You can do that only in Modeler.

Imagine that LightWave is a virtual television studio and 3D models are your actors. Although some animations can be created with animated textures or photographs, most include 3D models. These models are made up of points, edges, and polygons. This chapter takes you on a tour of LightWave Modeler. Along the way, I'll explain points, edges, and polygons, and show you how to use them to create 3D objects—which you will then animate and render in LightWave Layout.

LightWave Modeler is where your original 3D animations begin. That's not to say you can't start animating right away. NewTek, Inc., the makers of LightWave, have included a terrific amount of prebuilt content for you to use and explore. In fact, you can load a sample scene in LightWave v10 Layout and click the Render button to create your very first animation without ever launching Modeler. But to really know your software, you must first understand what a 3D model is all about.

Understanding Modeler

When you open LightWave 10 Modeler for the first time, you'll see a big blank interface with lots of buttons, panels, and menus tucked neatly around the outer edges of the program. Where do you begin? It can be quite intimidating, but it's easy to stay focused on any task you want to accomplish once you understand the workflow. All the tools are useful, but many modeling jobs require only a few of the tools at once. You've probably heard this before: You'll use only 20 percent of the tools 80 percent of the time. As with any fully equipped software program, some of LightWave's general-purpose tools get used every day; more specialized ones get pulled out only once in a while, but you'll find them essential for specific tasks. So you should always know what's in your toolbox.

NOTE

Please, by all means, before you go any further, grab the DVD out of the back of this book. Stick it in your computer and watch the video about the content directory. Seriously… go do it. Now.

Key Areas of Modeler

There are practically no limits to what you can create using 3D animation, which means a virtually unlimited number of variables to manage—and a vast number of tools within LightWave to control them all. However, I want you to ignore the overall cluster of buttons in LightWave and concentrate instead on the tools and what you are trying to do.

In other words, don't get overwhelmed by the buttons. I can't stress this enough. I've trained hundreds of people over the years and this is the first thing I tell them. Don't just start clicking buttons hoping something will happen, like my Mom does (sorry, Mom, it's true). There are times when you'll use only half a dozen buttons and tools for an entire project. Often, your particular type of work may never even unwrap some of the tools and panels LightWave has to offer, and there's nothing wrong with that.

The goal of this book, and more specifically this chapter, is to help you understand how to use LightWave Modeler and work with its toolset. Even with so many improvements in LightWave over the years, version 10 includes some of the most complex changes to date. LightWave Modeler has been touted as one of the best 3D modelers in the industry, and the latest update makes it a more efficient, powerful tool, with a much-enhanced workflow. This chapter introduces you to that workflow. Here are some of the key areas discussed in this chapter:

- LightWave v10 Modeler interface navigation
- Viewports
- Simple objects
- Points, edges, and polygons
- Selection and deselection
- Subdivisional surfaces

Proper construction of 3D models and animations takes discipline, focus, and a keen sense of direction. And, just as if you were building a cabinet in your garage or redoing the tile in your own bathroom, it also requires careful planning and a full understanding of the tools involved. This is because you want your 3D models to be efficient. You have to construct the models properly so that you can animate them correctly. When you know your tools and methods, the goal is not difficult to accomplish. Your focus should be clear and your work environment should be comfortable. There's nothing worse than working on a complex model without a plan and in an uncomfortable workspace. Be prepared, both mentally and physically.

3D Modeling in LightWave

Before you start using Modeler, you should become familiar with the medium that is 3D animation. You should understand how the X, Y, and Z axes relate to one another and your LightWave workspace. If you don't, please refer to the QuickTime movie "3D Animation Basics" on this book's DVD for a primer.

3D modeling is like interactive geometry. You can begin creating models with simple points and connect them with curves or straight lines. LightWave also gives you a slew of basic geometric shapes such as boxes and spheres to work with, and you'll see throughout this book just how those basic shapes can be used to create complex 3D models. Before you concern yourself with building complex 3D models, however, let's take a look at how the LightWave interface is laid out.

NOTE

Too often, when people work in 3D, either in modeling or animation, they consider only what they see on the flat screen in front of them. Do not make this mistake! Remember that your 3D models are more than just what's visible in front of you—they have sides, a top, a bottom, and a back, even if you can't see them.

LightWave v10 Modeler Interface

If you're new to LightWave with version 10, the interface (**Figure 1.1**) will obviously look unfamiliar. Initially, working through the interface might be frustrating, but if you understand the tools and their arrangement and keep in mind what you want to do, you'll find using the program simpler than you might expect.

Figure 1.1 The LightWave 3D Modeler interface.

If you're an experienced LightWave user and have just upgraded to LightWave v10, you'll notice at first a similarity to previous versions. With version 10, LightWave adds some great new tools and rearranges some preexisting ones to bring them closer to the surface. Both LightWave Layout and Modeler have been significantly streamlined, and navigation has never been easier, but the changes may require some adjustment. In addition, you'll notice a shift in color for the interface. While it might appear dark at first, research has shown that this neutral gray and blue combination will be very pleasing to the eyes, especially on long projects!

Although much of this book focuses on the modeling tools in action, this section highlights the features of LightWave 10 Modeler. You'll be able to try them out in just a few steps to gain a strong working knowledge of their functions.

Modeler Viewports

To begin working with LightWave Modeler, you should understand the viewports first. These four windows are the areas that will be your work environment, and by default, they show all sides of your 3D model.

Take a look at **Figure 1.2**, which shows the same full Modeler interface as Figure 1.1, but this time with a 3D model loaded. By default, LightWave Modeler assigns the viewports Top, Back, and Right views of your model, along with a Perspective view. Each is a little awkward at first, but try to remember this:

- Top view (XZ) provides a view along the Y-axis. You are looking down at the top of your object.
- Back view (XY) looks down the Z-axis. You are looking from the back of your object toward its front.
- Right view (ZY) looks down the X-axis. You are looking at the left side of your object, toward its right.

Figure 1.2 A 3D model of an airplane loaded into LightWave Modeler can be seen from all sides, and the default layout also shows a solid color version.

This may sound confusing, but after you get used to the concept, it will make more sense. And eventually, it'll even become familiar. For instance, when you get to Layout later, you'll find that the Back view you see in Modeler is the default view that the LightWave camera sees. The LightWave camera looks toward the back of the object, forward in the scene.

Don't let this layout of viewports make you feel constrained. You can change any viewport to look any way you like. Check out **Figure 1.3** (on the next page), where a close-up of the top-left viewport is shown.

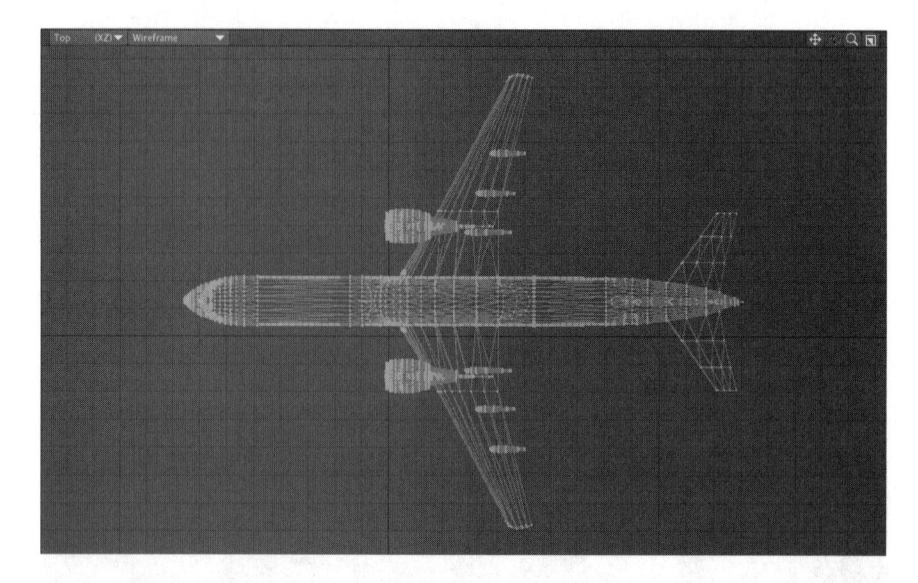

Figure 1.3 A close-up of the top-left viewport, showing a 3D object from above.

This top-left viewport is called Top by default, and it shows the 3D object from above—you're looking at the "top" of the object. Notice that at the top of the viewport there are buttons labeled Top (XZ) and Wireframe. This tells you that the particular viewport is set to Top. The XZ means these are the two axes you have control over. Because you're looking down the Y-axis, you can't move your object along that axis in this view.

At the top right of the viewport, you'll see four small icons. These are your viewport position controls. **Figure 1.4** shows the buttons up close.

NOTE

Depending on viewport settings, certain position control icons may be dimmed to indicate they are unavailable. In the Top viewport, for instance, the Rotate icon is dimmed because you can only rotate in a Perspective view, not an orthogonal (X, Y, Z) view.

Figure 1.4 The four small icons at the top right of each viewport enable you to move, rotate, zoom, and maximize the viewport.

Click, hold, and drag these buttons to use them. Too often, people click them and release, but that's not how they work. Click and hold to use! The first button (starting from the left) is Move, the next is Rotate, the third is Zoom, and the last is the Maximize viewport button. Click Maximize, and your viewport will become full screen. This is great for getting up close to your model for fine-tuning point position or measurements. To return from a full-screen viewport, just click that icon again.

NOTE

If your keyboard has a numeric keypad (most non-laptop models do, and some laptops sport them too) you can use its 0 key in place of the Maximize viewport button. (That's 0 as in zero, and in the numeric keypad only; you'll use the number keys at the top of your keyboard to change layers.) Be sure your mouse cursor is in the viewport you want to maximize before pressing the 0 key. Press 0 again to return from full-screen mode.

Viewport Customization

You can customize each of the four viewports in Modeler any way you like. **Figure 1.5** illustrates that you can assign any or all viewports a Back, Top, Right, or Perspective view. You can make all four viewports Top views if you like, although it might not help your modeling process too much.

Figure 1.5 Each viewport can be set to any view you like.

Something you might change more often than the viewport view is the viewport *style*—its method of drawing the objects it depicts. Choosing any of the ten settings from the drop-down menu shown in **Figure 1.6** (on the next page) lets you visualize models using styles, including Wireframe, Smooth Shade, and Textured Wire. Different styles are better suited to various modeling tasks, as we'll see later in the book.

NOTE

Although LightWave v10 is extremely customizable, the projects in this book will use the default configurations for Modeler and Layout, for the sake of consistency.

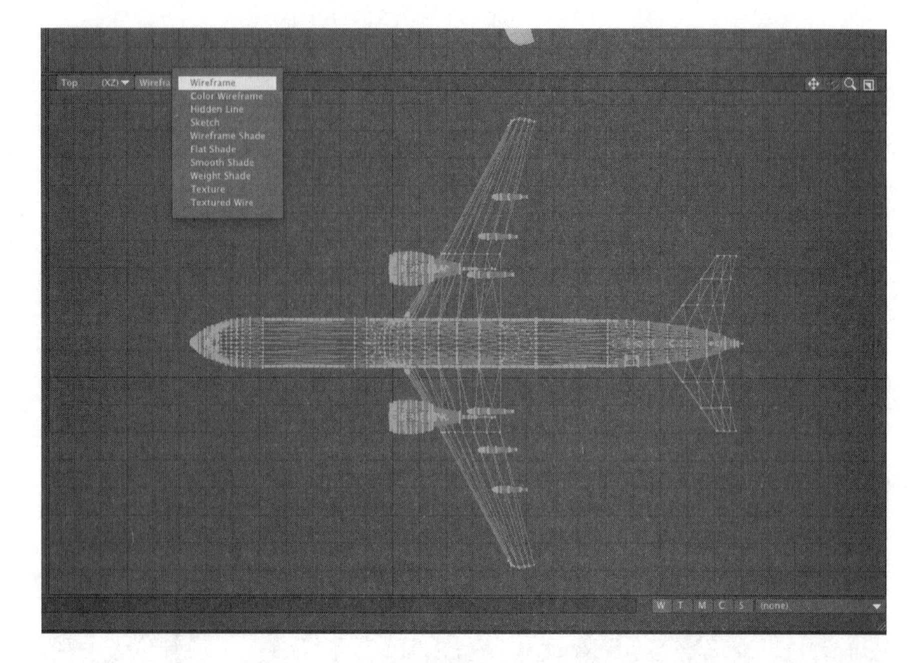

Figure 1.6 Each viewport can also have a unique viewport style, such as Wireframe or Textured Wire.

Figure 1.7 shows each viewport set to a different style with the same model loaded, so you can see how flexible the options are.

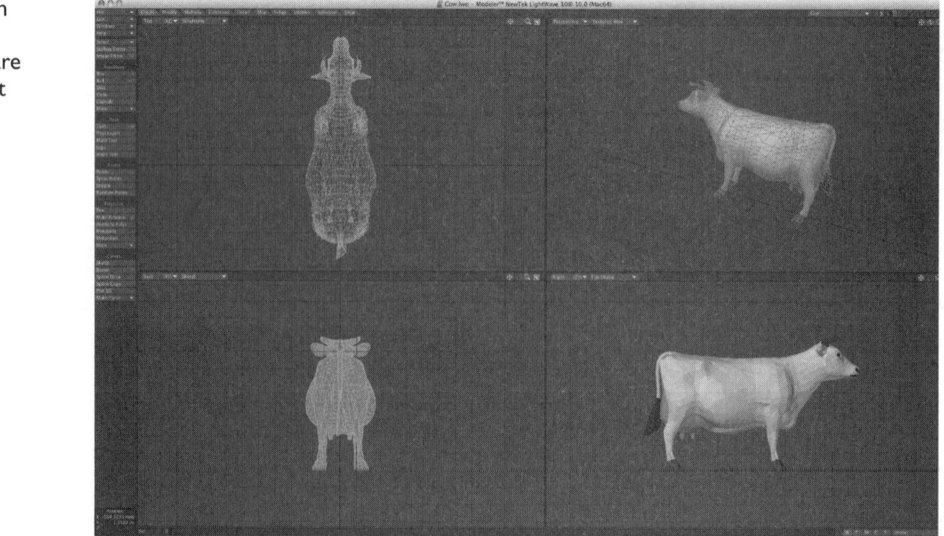

Figure 1.7 Here, each viewport is set to a different style. There are a total of ten viewport style choices.

NOTE

Your choice of viewport style will be based on the model you are creating. Often, a good way to work is with the default settings—Wireframe style in the X, Y, and Z viewports, while using a Smooth Shade or Textured Wire style in a Perspective view. It's totally up to you.

Working with Objects and Layers

Now you'll take a look at how LightWave works with objects. From there, you'll learn about points, edges, polygons, selection, and deselection, while creating a few simple objects along the way. LightWave objects are unique to the program, and have the file extension .lwo. You can load existing objects from LightWave's content directory simply by pressing Control+O for open (that's the letter o). But also take a look at the File drop-down menu at the top left of the Modeler interface. Click it, and you'll see all your common load and save functions, plus a few extras. **Figure 1.8** shows the panel.

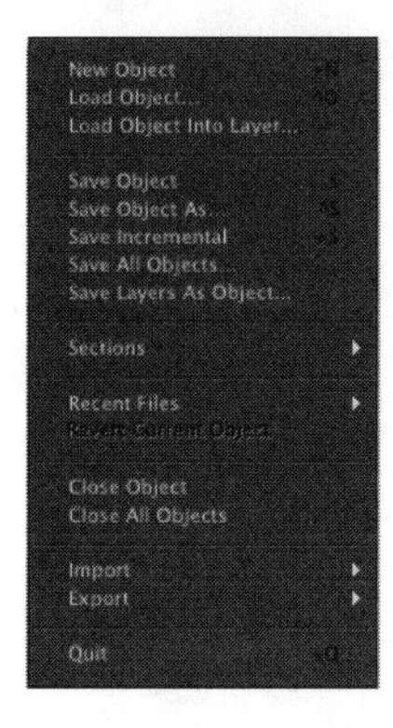

Figure 1.8 Using the File drop-down menu in Modeler, you can load, save, and perform similar operations.

If you use Photoshop, you are probably familiar with the concept of layers and how they are used if, say, you're building a billboard ad: You might put a color gradient in the background layer, add text in a new layer, place a picture in another, and so on. Why do you do all this in layers? So that each layer's contents can have its own set of parameters, such as size, position, effect settings, and so on. If all the components lived on the same layer, you'd have a tough time applying effects to any individual element. LightWave Modeler works in much the same way. Each item that you need to control individually, for purposes of modeling or animation, should be in its own layer.

NOTE

An object can have multiple layers. You can work with multiple layers at one time if you like (just hold the Shift key to select multiple layers). By the same token, you can also have multiple objects loaded at once.

This means that if your car model has four wheels (and I hope it does), and you want each wheel to be able to roll separately, each wheel must live on its own layer. If a wheel were placed in the same layer as the rest of the car, you'd have to animate the entire layer to make the wheel turn. You will also learn later in the book how layers are used to perform various modeling actions. For now, take a look at the top right of the Modeler interface, and you'll find a set of ten buttons (**Figure 1.9**), each representing a layer within a model. Layers within an object translate to actual objects in Layout. A car object with a separate layer for a door, for example, would show up in Layout as CAR:DOOR. The wheel layer would appear as CAR:WHEEL and so on.

Figure 1.9 At the top right of the Modeler interface are the layer buttons.

At first glance, if you start clicking the layer buttons, they look like they do nothing. However, they are crucial to properly setting up and building certain types of models. And don't think that because there are ten buttons you're limited to ten layers; you can have an unlimited number of layers in a LightWave project. Press **F7** and the Layers panel opens (**Figure 1.10**).

You can also open this panel from the Windows drop-down menu in Modeler, as shown in **Figure 1.11**.

Figure 1.10 Pressing F7 opens the Layers panel, which gives you access to Modeler layers. Here you see a blank Layers panel, because no objects are loaded.

Figure 1.11 Use the Windows drop-down menu to access the Layers panel if you don't like the F7 key.

NOTE

If you're working on a Mac laptop and nothing happens when you press a function key such as F1 or F9, you need to open System Preferences and tell your computer to allow software applications (rather than the system) to use the function keys. If you're on a desktop Mac, select Keyboard & Mouse in System Preferences, and under Keyboard Shortcuts uncheck the function keys, such as F9, that you wish to use in LightWave. F9 on a desktop Mac defaults to Exposé's All Windows command. F9 in LightWave is Render Current Frame. Note that you can change the shortcut for render in LightWave, but the tutorials in this book will use the default settings.

NOTE

One more plea: Before you do anything else, learn about the content directory! It will save you from lots of headaches. This is the number one problem reported by new LightWave users.

To demonstrate how LightWave Modeler handles existing 3D models, you'll work with simple models that are included with this book. These will be located in the Objects folder. Be sure you have set up the content directory as instructed in the "Content Directory" movie on this book's DVD (3D_GarageVideos\CH1\CH1_ContentDirectory.mov), and make sure to read the Read Me section of the disc contents.

Loading Objects and Naming Layers

The procedure for loading single-layer and multiple-layer objects is the same. Layer information is stored within each LightWave object file, and it's not something you need to worry about. LightWave object files retain data about changes you apply to them, such as colors and textures.

NOTE

The sample content included with LightWave v10 comes on a DVD that's separate from the program installer CD. Look for it in your LightWave software case, and install these files as instructed. You'll use them in this chapter.

Exercise 1.1 Loading Objects and Naming Layers

1. Press Control+O (Windows or Mac) or Command+O (Mac), or choose Load Object from the File drop-down menu and load the Hammerhead.lwo shark object from the Objects/CH1 folder from the book's DVD. Once it loads, press **a** to maximize the object within the window. You'll use this keyboard shortcut quite a bit throughout this book.

NOTE

When working with keyboard equivalents, it's best to always keep your Caps Lock off. Many basic LightWave functions are assigned to lowercase keyboard shortcuts, while more complex functions are set to capital letters. These complex functions can create problems if you use them accidentally. For example, pressing **q** as lowercase allows you to set a surface name. Pressing **q** with Caps Lock on will quit the program!

2. **Figure 1.12** shows the object-selection pull-down and the layer buttons as they appear after the model is loaded into LightWave Modeler. You'll see that the first layer button is depressed by default, and it contains a small dot.

Figure 1.12 Modeler's object-selection pull-down shows the name of the loaded object, Hammerhead, and the layer buttons indicate that just one layer is associated with this object.

These dots inform you that there is geometry in that layer, such as points, edges, or polygons. Open the Layers panel (**F7**) and look at what the listings show. You'll see the name of the object, and if you click the small white triangle to expand the object's layers, you'll see a listing that reads "unnamed." Unnamed refers to the geometry in the layer, which you've yet to name.

3. Double-click the last "unnamed" listing, and the Layer Settings panel pop-up will open. If you had multiple layers—that is, objects in other layers—selecting any one of these layers would instantly change your view to that selection.

NOTE

Just to the left of the ten layer buttons at the top left of Modeler is a number with left- and right-arrow buttons. When you open a model, you'll see the number 1. This means that you're working with the first set of ten layers. You can click the right arrow to get to another set of ten, and the number changes to 2. Click again, and you're in the third tier of layer buttons, and so on. However, this approach is cumbersome, and working with the Layers panel is often a better way to go. Open the panel and put it aside while you work. Unlimited layers, baby!

4. In the Layer Settings panel, enter **Shark** in the Name field. If you had another layer with geometry, you could also tell one layer to be "parented" to another. Parenting means that the selected object becomes a child and "belongs" to the parent. Whenever you move, rotate, or scale a parent object in LightWave Layout, objects in its child layers will follow. You'd use this for wheels on a car, letters in a logo, and more. **Figure 1.13** shows the operation.

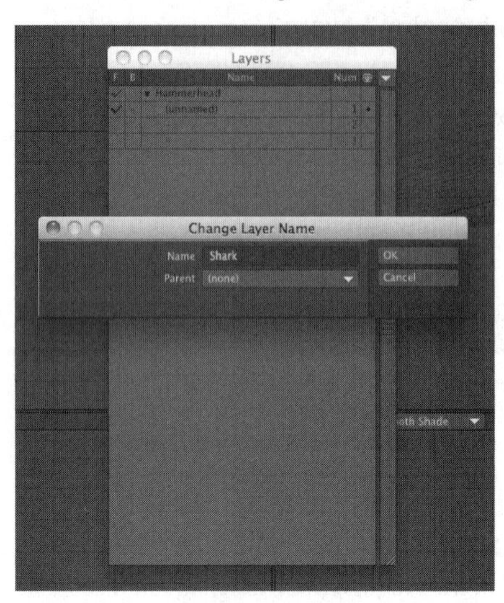

Figure 1.13
By double-clicking a chosen layer in the Layers panel, you can rename it and parent it to other layers.

NOTE

You can load multiple objects into Modeler at the same time. However, unless you specifically cut and paste those objects together in some fashion, you can view only one object at a time. Figure 1.12 shows the layer buttons at the top right of the interface, and to the left of the layer buttons is the Current Object selection list. Any objects loaded into Modeler can be selected from this drop-down list. It's important to note that each loaded object retains its own layers. Choosing to load multiple objects will not load them into individual layers within the same model.

When you loaded the Hammerhead shark object, you saw that the layer 1 button was selected. If you wanted to add parts to the model, or perhaps build a set of some sort, you would do so in another layer. To accomplish this, you select another layer by clicking it. And as you did earlier, simply double-click the layer listing in the Layers panel to name that layer.

So, what's the point of all this, you ask? Even though this is a simple object, all of your 3D objects will be handled in this way. The purpose of naming each layer is to ensure that when you're animating later, you won't have to guess which layer is which. Naming your object layers is not necessary, but it's an efficient way to work and organize. When you save your object, its layers and their names are saved with it. What's great about this is that you can send a single object to a coworker or client, and all of its parts (such as the wheels), as well as the parenting hierarchy, are contained within.

Foreground and Background Layers

There are a few more things to note about the Layers panel. Looking at **Figure 1.14**, you can see some additional labels in the Layers panel. The F at the top left of the panel stands for Foreground, while the B stands for Background. Additionally, the Num category displays the layer number and the eyeball hides the model from appearing in Layout. You'll learn more about this shortly.

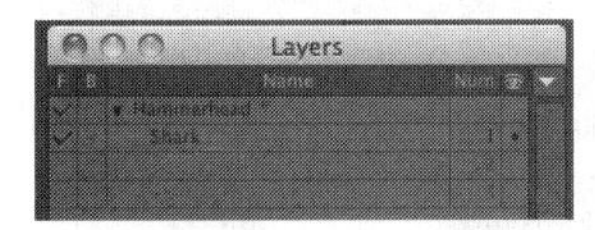

Figure 1.14 Additional controls are available in the Layers panel.

As you get into more-complex projects, you'll use these commands in the Layers panel to place objects in both the foreground and the background. To try this out, follow these steps:

1. Load AirMailPlane.lwo object from the book's DVD, found within the 3D Content folder. This object has three layers, and when first loaded, all are seen in the foreground, as in **Figure 1.15**.

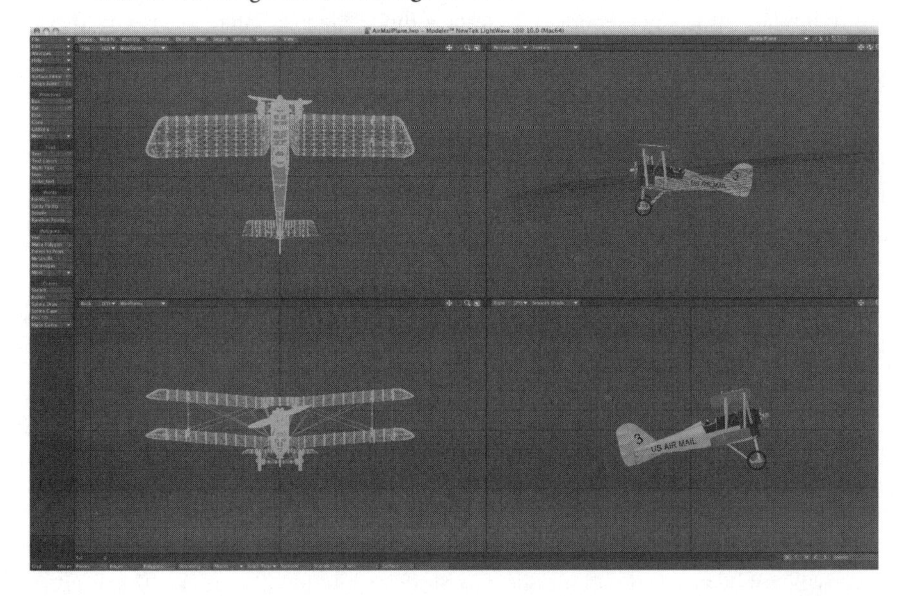

Figure 1.15 Selecting a layer in the Layers panel brings that layer to the foreground.

2. Press **F7** to open the Layers panel. Don't click any individual layer itself, but click the check box beneath the B column (B for background) next to the Plane layer. If you see only the name of the model, click the white expansion triangle to the left of its name to reveal all the layer names. **Figure 1.16** (on the next page) shows the model with the plane now as a background layer, signified by a black wireframe.

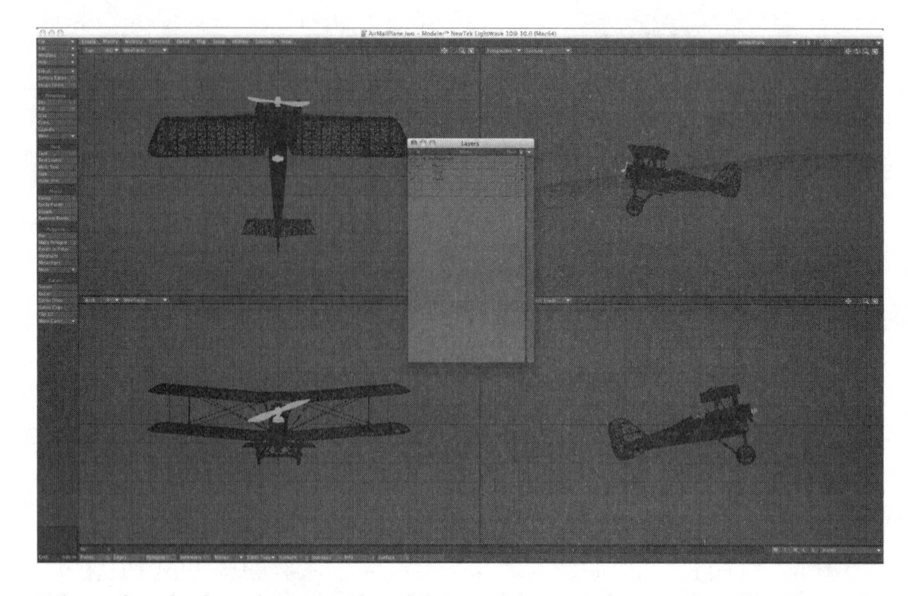

Figure 1.16 By selecting a layer under the B column in the Layers panel, you can put layers in the background for reference.

NOTE

Layer order becomes important when you use foreground and background layers as modeling tools. This topic will be covered later in the book.

Take a close look at the top right of the Modeler interface, and you'll still see the body fuselage of the plane, but in a dark outline. You'll see the wheels and other parts still in a foreground layer. You've now defined foreground and background layers. The reason for this is threefold: Objects in background layers are used for reference, as separate animation elements, or as modeling tools.

You can hold the Shift key and select multiple background layers as well. On the right side of the Layers panel, you'll see numbers. These are the layer numbers for each layer, and unlike Photoshop layers their order does not affect the appearance of the model.

Layer Visibility

To the right side of the Layers panel, at the top, is a small eyeball icon. Beneath that, next to each layer is a little dot. Let's say you've placed an object in a background layer and used it as a reference to build a new object. If you save your LightWave object and load it into Layout, all layers will be visible. However, if you click that little dot in the Layers panel in Modeler, when the object is loaded into Layout the layer will not be visible. Load it back into Modeler, and it will be there. This is great when you use objects as modeling tools.

Finally, there's one more area you should be aware of in the Layers panel: the Hierarchy view option. It's easy to miss, but at the top-right corner of the Layers panel, there's a small drop-down arrow. Select it and you see the option for List or Hierarchy. So far, you've been seeing the Layers panel in List view. **Figure 1.17** shows the Layers panel in List view. This is useful for more complex objects such as characters or mechanical creations.

Figure 1.17 You can choose to view your object layers as a List or a Hierarchy.

There are many more panels in LightWave Modeler, but it's important to understand how to navigate before you get more involved. Working with the layers is essential to any model you create, which is why it's covered first in this chapter. Now, to the menus!

Tabs and Menus

Across the top of the Modeler screen you'll see ten tabs, each representing a different group of modeling tools. This section guides you through the different tabs and explains how they're organized. **Figure 1.18** shows the tabs across the top of Modeler.

Figure 1.18 The LightWave menus are tabbed across the top of the interface. Selecting any of these brings up various tools on the left side of the screen.

When you select different tabs, different toolsets become available. Think of a toolset simply as a group of tools. Years ago, tools were just floating around in LightWave Modeler, some of them hidden deep within menus. Now, NewTek has significantly streamlined the tools and grouped them quite well. The LightWave Modeler toolset works similarly throughout the program, with slight variations depending on which tool you are using. This next section guides you through the toolset categories within each of the Modeler tabs.

NOTE

On the top left of the Modeler interface, you'll find a set of drop-down menus that will always appear, no matter what tab you've clicked. These include File, Edit, Windows, Help, Select, Surface Editor, and Image Editor. These selections are the same in Layout and are covered in detail in Chapter 2, "LightWave Layout."

When working in LightWave Modeler, really think about the process, and you'll have a much easier time locating the proper tool. For example, say you've just started up Modeler and want to build a 3D television set. You want to create something and need basic geometry to get started. OK, head on over to the Create tab. Choose the Box tool, and go. Then, let's say you want to change it in some way, perhaps rotate it or move it. What are you doing? You're modifying it, right? You'd go to the Modify tab to find the necessary tools. What if you need to add to this, perhaps by beveling it a bit? Think about a bevel and you might realize that this operation will add to the geometry of your object, so look under the Multiply tab. Many tools in LightWave v10 have been rearranged in ways that make even more sense than in previous versions. If some tools are no longer where you're used to finding them, keep the task at hand in mind and you'll probably see that they've been moved to a location that makes more sense.

Create Tab

The Create tab calls up the basic tools you need to create geometric shapes such as boxes, balls, discs, and more. Additionally, you'll find tools to create points and curves. **Figure 1.19** shows the tools under the Create tab.

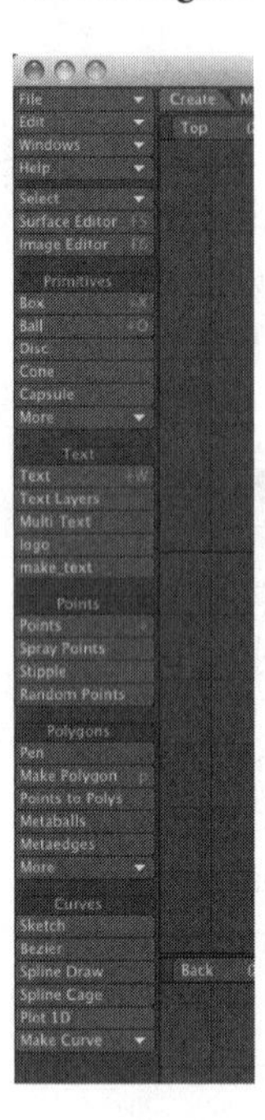

Figure 1.19 The Create tab is home to many basic tools that you'll need in the course of most modeling projects.

The first thing you'll see when you click the Create tab is that the toolset starts at the top of the screen on the left side and pretty much runs down the entire left side of the interface! The first seven buttons at the top will always be there, no matter what menu you've chosen (unless you customize your interface and change their location, as described later in the book). These key tools are the File menu, Edit menu, Windows menu, Help menu, Select menu, Surface Editor, and Image Editor. These are important areas that you will access often, which is why they're always accessible from every tab in Modeler.

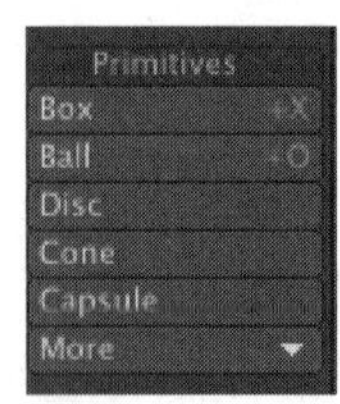

Figure 1.20 The Primitives category within the Create tab offers a wide range of basic (and some not-so-basic) shapes you can use to create 3D models.

Primitives

At the top of the toolset under the Create tab is the Primitives category, as shown in **Figure 1.20**. Here you'll find the tools for creating geometric shapes such as a box, ball, gemstone, and capsule. These basic (and some not-so-basic) geometric shapes are key building blocks for just about anything you want to create. Think about it—the forms of nearly everything around you are based on geometric shapes: a television, a couch, a kitchen sink! A vast number of 3D models start out as primitives, which are multiplied, cut, shaped, and formed into final objects.

Text

LightWave is famous for generating spaceships and animated characters but, believe it or not, 3D text is one of its most popular and in-demand applications. As you'll see in Chapter 7, "Broadcast Animation," you can make some pretty outstanding broadcast-style animations and graphics with these tools. But what's more, text objects can also be used as building blocks. For example, you can take the letter C, turn it on its side, extrude it, and you have a slide you can put into a 3D playground. Or how about using the letter E as a building block for creating a 3D maze?

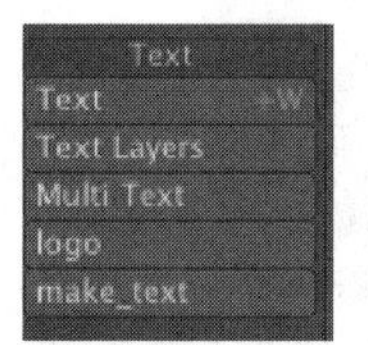

Figure 1.21 The Text tool category is where you'll find the Manage Fonts command, the Text Layers tool, the Multi Text tool, as well as the Text creation tool.

In previous versions of LightWave, to use the text tools properly you needed to first select the Manage Fonts button. Now you have a variety of text tools, shown in **Figure 1.21**. This tool enables you to load fonts into Modeler. But LightWave v10 has made text creation even easier: It allows you to choose any font on your system by opening the numeric panel for the Text tool. The Text Layers tool in LightWave v10 is so easy to use, it's just silly. Here, you can instantly create a string of text or a simple logo and have the program instantly add surfaces, while putting each word or letter on its own individual layer. This means you get to animating even faster!

Points

Often you'll need to build an object from scratch, starting not with a box or a ball, but with a point. Later in this chapter, you'll read about points, edges, and polygons, but essentially, points make up polygons, sort of like connect the dots. The Points category gives you the tools to create points one at a time, in clusters with the Spray Points tool, or with the Random Points generator. **Figure 1.22** shows the category.

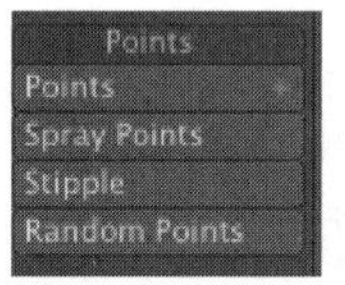

Figure 1.22 The Points category offers tools to create single points or clusters of points. Points, as you know, make up objects.

Polygons

Many 3D shapes you'll create in Modeler begin as simple 2D polygonal shapes. And just because primitive shapes make basic objects and points create individual points doesn't mean that you can't create simpler polygonal objects. For example, the Polygons category has a tool called Pen, which is similar to the Points tool except that as you create with the Pen tool, polygonal lines are automatically generated between each point; the dots are connected automatically. You can convert selected points to polygons or use the Make Polygon command, which you can apply after you've used the Points tool from the previous category. Additionally, you can create some organic objects with the Metaedges and Metaballs tools. **Figure 1.23** shows the category.

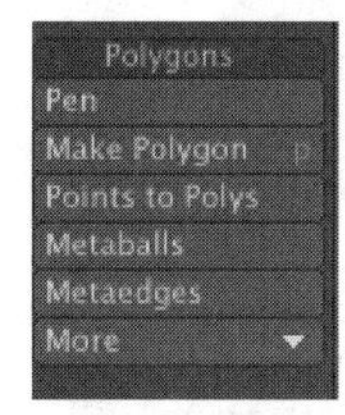

Figure 1.23 The Polygons category offers polygonal creation tools.

Curves

The last category in the Create tab is Curves. This category includes tools for generating curves from points you've created. Curves are used for many things, such as motion paths and extrusion paths as well as shaping models. The Sketch tool

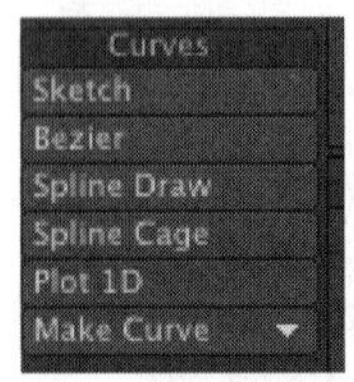

Figure 1.24 You can use curves for text, characters, motion paths, and more.

enables you to just click and draw, and when you release the mouse button you have a 3D curve! You can use curves to build objects with splines. As you'll learn later in this book, splines are useful for building organic objects such as boats, curtains, or sometimes characters. Another key tool in this category is Spline Draw, with which you can precisely create curves, not only for models but also for text or custom shapes. **Figure 1.24** shows the tools in this category.

Modify Tab

The Modify tab—sounds simple enough, right? Well, it is. Anytime you want to modify your object in some way that does not require adding or removing points or polygons, you need to use a modify function. Click this tab and at the top left you'll see the seven tools available in every tab. Below them, you'll see three toolset categories: Translate, Rotate, and Transform (**Figure 1.25**).

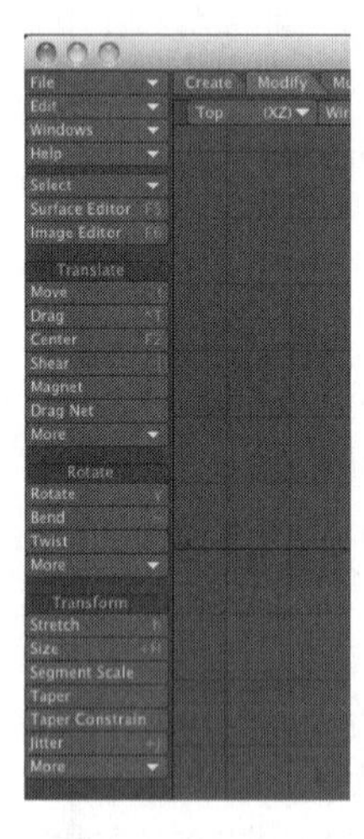

Figure 1.25 The Modify tab is used when you need tools to move, rotate, or size your object.

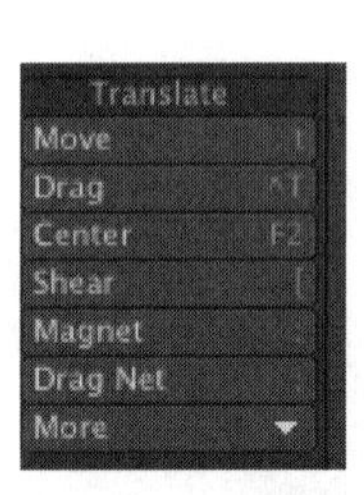

Figure 1.26 Tools in the Translate category let you move your geometry around—both points and polygons.

Translate

No, this category doesn't contain tools to make objects fluent in foreign languages. Its tools are used to move objects in 3D space (**Figure 1.26**). Typically, the 3D industry calls a move function a *translation*. The Translate category contains tools like Move, Drag, Magnet, and a few others. Each tool repositions your object in some way.

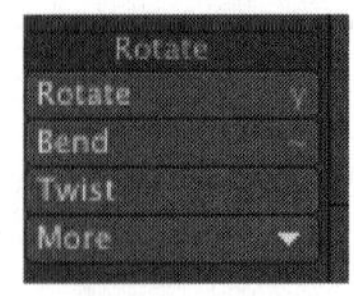

Figure 1.27 The Rotate category contains your basic rotation tools, as well as some cool extras like Vortex.

Rotate

This category (**Figure 1.27**) is almost self-explanatory. Of course, you can rotate points or polygons with the Rotate tool, but there's much more you can do with it. You can also bend, twist, and even use the cool Vortex tool (in the category's More drop-down). Other tools like Rotate to Ground or Rotate to Normal provide extra control for precise rotations.

Transform

Transform is a sizing function, so anytime you hear seasoned animation veterans talk about "transforming the object," they're not talking about a Saturday morning cartoon. The Transform category includes modification tools such as Size, Stretch, Pole, and others (**Figure 1.28**). Every tool in this category controls object size in some way. For example, Size scales your object or selection equally on all sides. Stretch sizes your object or selection on a specific axis. Use the Transform tools when you want to scale or distort objects or selections.

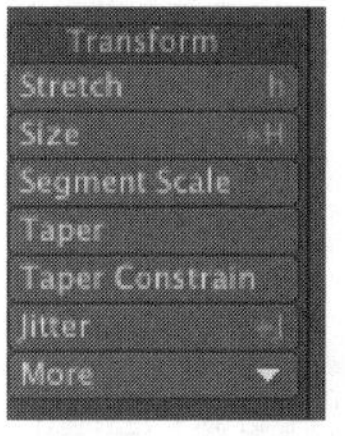

Figure 1.28 The Transform toolset is the place to find size/scale tools.

Multiply Tab

Tools in the Create and Modify tabs are generally easy to wrap your brain around. When you get into the Multiply tab (see **Figure 1.29**), things get more complex. Within LightWave, *multiply* means to add onto a selection, and the tools within this tab do so in a variety of ways. You'll use these tools often in later chapters. For now, read on to find out what the categories in the Multiply tab can do for you.

NOTE

Some tools throughout LightWave v10, especially those within the Multiply tab, are not available until there is geometry in a specific layer.

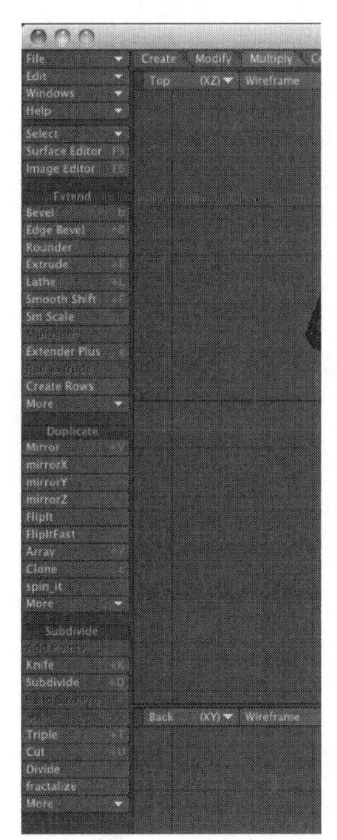

Figure 1.29 The Multiply tab contains some complex tools that enable you to build up your object in a variety of ways.

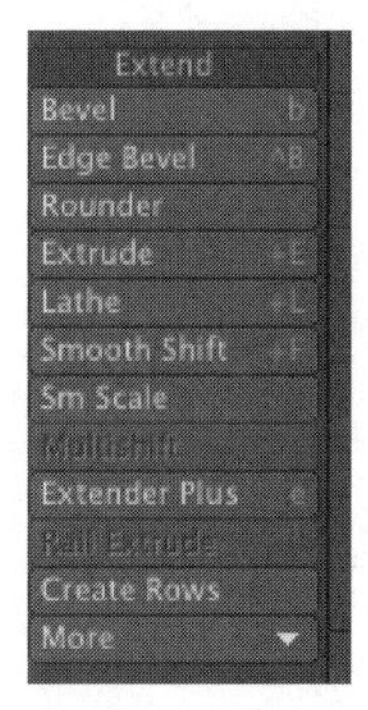

Figure 1.30 The Extend category within the Multiply menu tab offers tools, such as bevel tools, to add to your objects or selections.

Extend

Extend is the first category of the Multiply tab, and it contains tools you'll probably use often (**Figure 1.30**). The Extend tools "grow" your selection in different ways. The Extrude and Bevel tools, for example, provide different ways of "stretching" polygons into 3D shapes. The category also includes more complex tools, such as Rail Bevel (located in the More drop-down), which enable you to build a bevel from a curve placed in a background layer. When discussing layers earlier, it was mentioned that foreground and background layers are used for modeling as well as reference. Rail Bevel takes advantage of this.

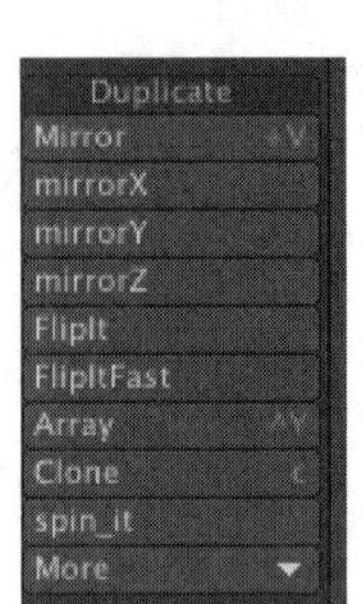

Figure 1.31 Duplicate tools add to your object or selection by mirroring, cloning, or otherwise copying it.

Duplicate

You might think that Duplicate tools (**Figure 1.31**) would be under the Modify tab, but think again! Creating a new object by mirroring, cloning, or otherwise copying another one is a form of multiplication. The Duplicate tools create variant copies of selections or objects, but these copies are not attached to your original object or selection, the way that points and polygons created with the Extend tools are.

Subdivide

Ah, the Subdivide category—a deep, dark, secret set of tools that can enhance your object or selection in a variety of ways. The Subdivide tools (**Figure 1.32**) perform very cool operations to slice up your object or selection, add to it, or split it up in some way. Let's say you built a cool character and soon realize that you can't bend the character's leg because it's just one long "solid" object. To make the leg bend at the knee, you would use the Knife tool in this category to slice the leg and add a segment so it can bend. Another cool set of Subdivide tools is the QuickCut tools in the category's More drop-down. These enable you to quickly slice up an object evenly, which helps you create additional detail for animation.

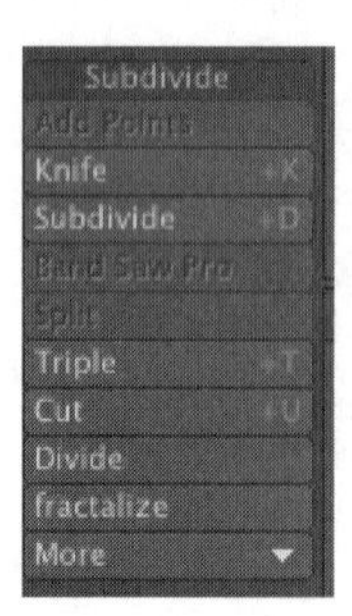

Figure 1.32 The Subdivide tools enable you to break up your model for added detail and animation control.

Construct Tab

When you have geometry that needs to be changed in terms of structure, you'll work with the Construct tab. Its tools handle tasks such as Boolean operations (which you'll perform later in the book) and reducing or converting various types of geometry. When you're building 3D models, it's easy to confuse the tools in the Construct tab with those in the Detail tab. The main difference between them is one of scale; when you're working with multiple objects or sizable portions of objects, Construct is the tab you want. Use the Detail tab for fine-tuning at the level of individual points, curves, and polygons. **Figure 1.33** shows the Construct tab tools.

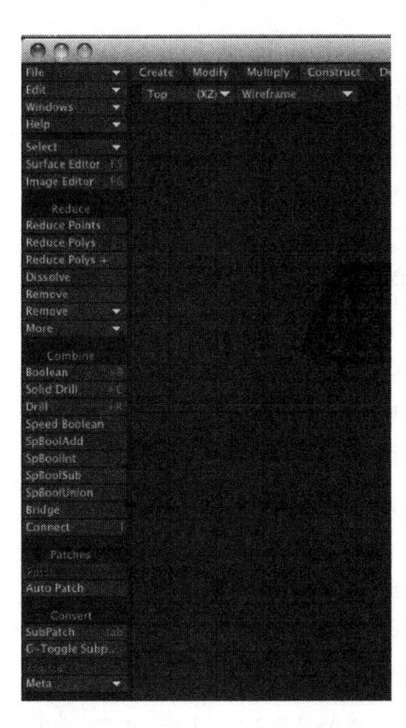

Figure 1.33 Using the Construct tab tools, you can add points and polygons to, or subtract them from, your models.

Reduce

The Reduce category contains tools that enable you to take away geometry (points or polygons) from your model without changing its appearance (**Figure 1.34**). Why would you do this? You could be creating a model for a video game that requires a low number of polygons for speedy animation. Or perhaps you realize you've overbuilt a model and added more detail than you need. Why not just leave it detailed? Simple—the more detail you have in an object, the longer it takes LightWave to calculate and render. As mentioned at the beginning of this chapter, you need to work efficiently from the ground up. Planning is key, and making models that are not too simple but not too complex is essential to 3D animation. The Reduce category enables you to reduce or remove points or polygons from models while keeping them intact with tools like Bandglue (found in the category's More drop-down).

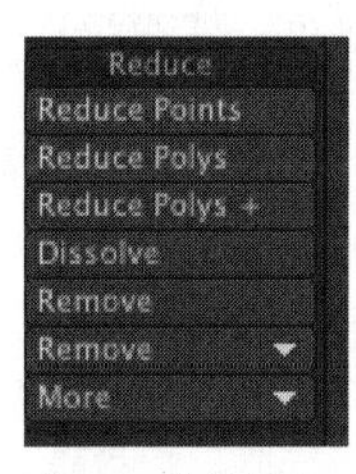

Figure 1.34 You can use tools in the Reduce category to decrease the number of points or polygons in an object or selection.

Combine

From time to time, it's useful to merge objects or to "subtract" the shape of one object from another to create a hole or cavity. These operations, called *Boolean functions*, are performed using Combine tools (**Figure 1.35**), and they are another example of how foreground and background layers are used for modeling purposes. Typical Boolean operations involve placing an object you want to add or subtract in a background layer so that it overlaps the foreground object. LightWave v10 also features new Speed Booleans, clever tools that permit Boolean operations between objects within a single layer. The Combine tools also include Bridge, which lets you select points on two objects and "bridge" or connect them.

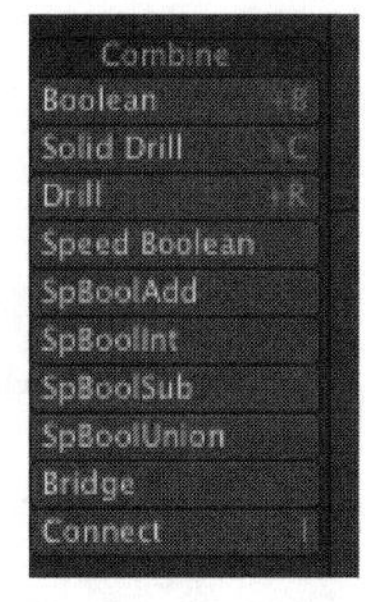

Figure 1.35 The Combine tools offer ways to cut holes in objects, merge and stencil objects, and bridge connections between them.

Figure 1.36 Use the tools in the Patches category to build a skin over a group of curves.

Patches

The tools in the Patches category (**Figure 1.36**) are useful for applying surfaces, or skins, to curves called *splines*. Splines are curves that can be put together in multiple ways to build objects. After you group enough curves together, you can patch them to create a surface. Think of an umbrella's ribs as splines, and its cloth covering as a skin. Patching joins splines together and controls skin characteristics.

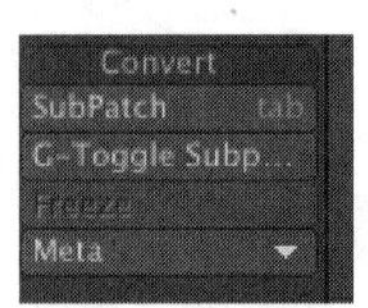

Figure 1.37 The Convert tool category within the Construct tab gives you the freedom to change—including the ability to change curves to polygons and vice versa.

Convert

The Convert tools (**Figure 1.37**) turn curves into polygons, and polygons into curves—a function that's more helpful than you might think. Let's say you've built the ultimate 3D logo, using curves to surround the client's name. All is cool until you're ready to render it out. Curves do not render, but polygons do. So, head on over to the Convert tools and use Freeze to convert your curves into polygons. Other tools here include the popular SubPatch command, which converts three- or four-point polygons into curves, to help create smooth organic objects. There's also the G-Toggle Subpatch, which works primarily in Layout as a way to turn a model's subpatch subdivisions on and off. In Modeler, it works like the normal Subpatch mode, which you access by pressing the Tab key. You'll use this feature extensively in various modeling sections of this book.

Detail Tab

It's all about the details, isn't it? The Detail tab provides the tools that are useful for, and sometimes essential to, creating decent 3D models (**Figure 1.38**).

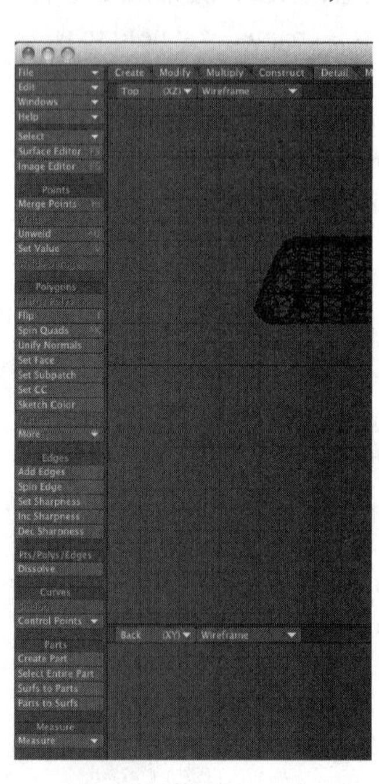

Figure 1.38 The Detail tab provides quite a few tools that let you make specific changes to points and polygons within your models.

Tools in the Detail tab are typically used to tweak a model once it's constructed, by fine-tuning one or more points or polygons. Their specific uses include adding and removing edges from models, adjusting the "grain" or "flow" of object surfaces, and cleaning up extra points that sometimes appear along the seams where objects are merged or mirrored.

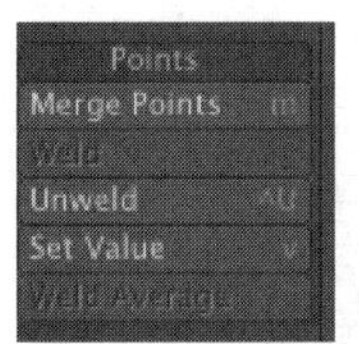

Figure 1.39 Tools in the Points category give you the power to control the detail of selected points within your models.

Points

Not to be confused with the Points tools in the Create tab, which are used to create points, the Detail tab's Points tools are used to adjust point details within an existing model (**Figure 1.39**). For example, the Weld tool lets you reduce a cluster of points down to one, in the position of the last point you selected, and the Weld Average tool joins irregular groups of adjacent points into smooth seams. The category's Set Value command lets you precisely reposition groups of selected points.

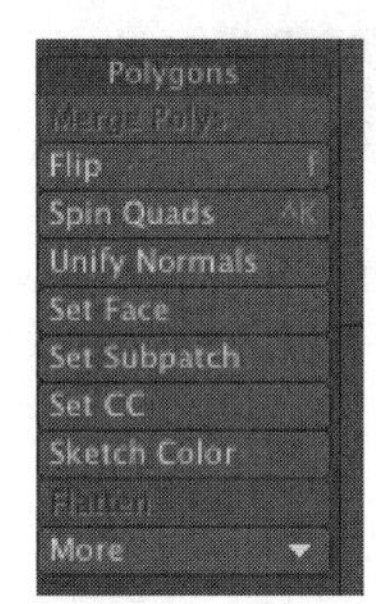

Figure 1.40 Tools in the Detail tab's Polygons category, such as Fix Poles (found in the category's More drop-down), give you great control over those nasty polygons.

Polygons

The Detail tab's Polygons category contains smart tools you can use to add polygons to models in spots where you need finer detail, merge polygons where you don't, and flip or perhaps just align them (**Figure 1.40**). Again, these are detail controls that help you fine-tune your models. So anytime you need to make detailed, specific polygon changes, this is the place to be.

Edges

Tools in the Edges category (**Figure 1.41**) help you control fine polygon detail within your model or selection. The Add Edges tool, for example, lets you divide a polygon precisely by creating a new edge within it. Click a point on one edge of a selected polygon, then a point on another edge, and a new edge segment is added, connecting the clicked points. Don't confuse this command category with the Edges button at the bottom of the Modeler interface, which is used in Edges-selection mode.

Figure 1.41 Tools for creating detailed polygon edges can be found in the Edges category of the Detail tab.

Curves

There are just a few tools in the Curves category (**Figure 1.42**). They enable you to quickly smooth out curves or control a curve's start and end points. When spline modeling, for instance, you'll probably use the Smooth function often to massage curves before skinning them, to make sure the resultant surface is clean and even.

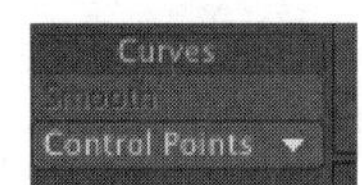

Figure 1.42 Tools for creating details for curves can be found in the Curves category of the Detail tab.

NOTE

Curves and splines can be used interchangeably for many tasks, and the choice of which to use is often a matter of user preference. Note that neither curves nor splines can be rendered in Layout, so curves and splines used in model construction must be converted to polygons for final output. Splines and curves are used in Layout for motion control, modeling, and deformation.

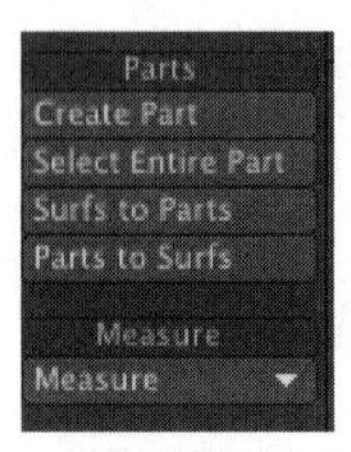

Figure 1.43 When you need to measure an object, find its center point, or generate a bounding-box representation, use the Measure tools.

Parts and Measure

The last tool categories in the Detail tab are Parts and Measure (**Figure 1.43**). These categories contain several organization and measurement tools. You can select various "parts" of a model and create a part for later selection and use. In the Measure category, you can click and drag within selections for precise measurement readouts in the lower left info panel. You can measure angles, object lengths, and perimeters. But wait, there's more! You can use other Measure tools to locate the centers of objects or create *bounding-box* representations, which can act as placeholders for complex objects within a model.

Map Tab

The Map tab is home to all the tools you'll need for working with vertex and weight maps in Modeler. Vertex maps control attributes of vertices, or points, in your models, and LightWave uses them to characterize the weights of different objects, control morphs, and more. You'll learn about setting these later in the book. In **Figure 1.44**, you can see that there are a lot of tools, but don't worry, they're not all used all the time, and they are easy to understand when you break them down into categories. When you begin working with vertex maps, you can edit and control them through the tools in the Map tab.

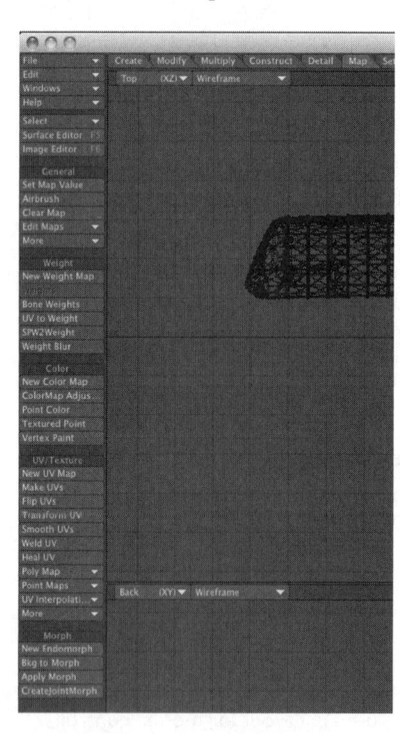

Figure 1.44 The Map tab group of tools is home to a lot of interesting commands, some of which are very powerful.

General

Multiple vertex maps may be applied to any given model, and the Map tab's General tool category (**Figure 1.45**) is useful for setting or adjusting map values for any point or set of points. You can also use its Airbrush tool to create new vertex maps.

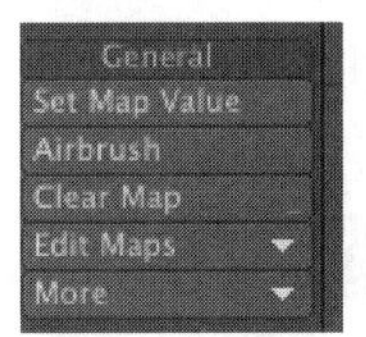

Figure 1.45 The General category of the Map tab.

Weight

Weights are a big deal in LightWave, and not just because you gain weight sitting in front of the computer while adding weights to your 3D models. You work with weights throughout the modeling process to control the flow of curves, and you can also use them in Layout during animations. You'll use the tools in the Weight category to create new weight maps, to apply weights to bones for character animation, and to generate weights from certain UV maps, which are described later in the Texture tool category. **Figure 1.46** shows the Weight tool category.

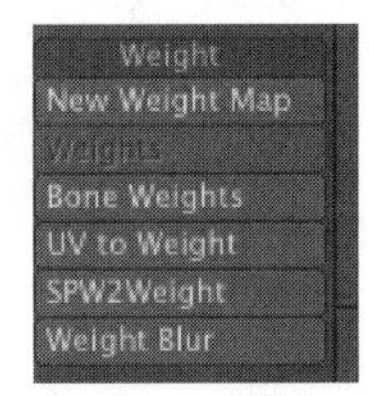

Figure 1.46 To control weights in LightWave Modeler, head on over to the Map tab's Weight tools.

Color

Don't confuse this category with the surface color of your object. Be aware of what you are doing and which panel and button you're working with. You're in the Map tab, which governs points, not the Surface Editor, which controls, well, surfaces. The Color tools within each have distinctly different applications. You use the Map tab Color tools to create color vertex maps, which you can then use for specific surface control later in Layout. These tools also include Vertex Paint, which lets you paint color onto your model's vertices. Vertex colors blend with any polygonal surface textures you apply separately, and they are great for skin, landscapes, or just about anything. **Figure 1.47** highlights the tools.

Figure 1.47 The Color category gives you access to tools that manipulate the color of an object's vertices, or points.

Texture

Tools in the Texture category are used for creating and working with UV maps, which you can think of as the unwrapped skins of 3D models, flattened out on a grid with coordinate axes *U* and *V*. You can "paint" colors and textures onto a UV map in third-party programs such as Adobe Photoshop, and then rewrap the model with it. UVs are often used in video games because one image can be used to surface an entire object.

Did you ever put together a model car when you were a kid? Do you remember that huge sheet of stickers that you would apply to the model after building it? In a way, a UV map is like that big sheet of stickers. It's your entire model's texture maps, laid out. However, the map contains data unique to the specific model, and it will apply itself around the model the way you specify.

Later in this book, you'll learn about working with UVs and create them yourself. When you do, you'll be guided to this Texture category of the Map tab. Here, you can edit or create UVs, set UV values, and more. **Figure 1.48** shows the category of tools.

Figure 1.48 The Map tab's Texture tools don't affect the actual surface textures of your models, but control UV maps, which "wrap around" your model and anchor at the points on its surface.

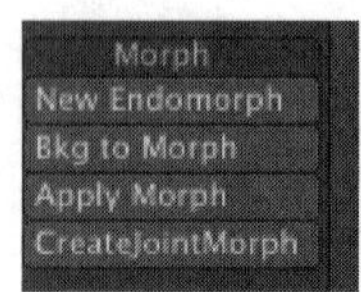

Figure 1.49 The Morph tools within the Map tab let you change an object's shape by repositioning points on its surface.

Morph

LightWave morphs are much misunderstood. People often think they change one object into another at the push of a button. In fact, a morph (technically called an *endomorph*) is an operation that changes the position of one or more points in an object. Moving points changes an object's shape without adding new polygons or geometry. You'll use morphs later in the book to make a character move. LightWave uses vertex maps to store the point-position information used in morphs, and the Map tab's Morph tools (**Figure 1.49**) control those maps. Also note the M button down at the bottom right of the Modeler interface, which is where you can access any morphs that might be applied to your model.

Setup Tab

This tab is where you'll find all the necessary tools to create Skelegons. What's a Skelegon? No, it is not an evil cartoon character (that's Skeletor), it's a deformation tool. Skelegons are skeletal structures that you build along with your model to define how it bends and moves. Later, when you take the model into LightWave Layout, you convert the Skelegons to bones and use them to deform and animate your object.

The Setup tab also includes tools for creating Luxigons and Powergons. Luxigons are polygons you turn into lights. Powergons are even more powerful. These are polygons to which you attach tiny command scripts, which will be executed when the model is moved into LightWave Layout for animation and rendering. You might use a Powergon to instantly add lights to a polygon for placement, like the headlights on a car. You can also define the properties for the light. **Figure 1.50** shows the tab and its tools.

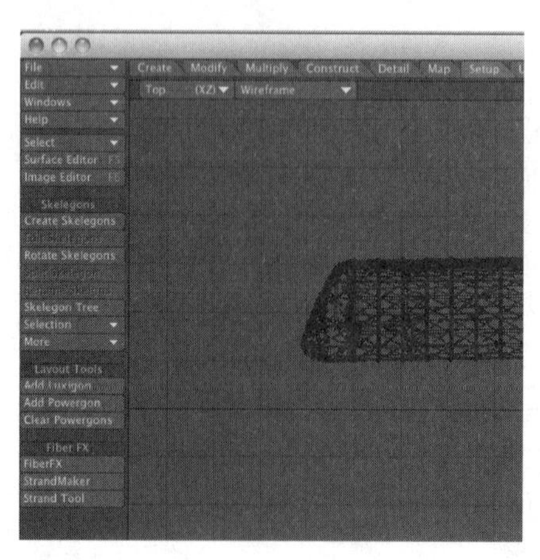

Figure 1.50 The Setup tab contains the tools you need for working with Skelegons as well as Luxigons and Powergons.

Skelegons

Naturally enough, the Skelegons category (**Figure 1.51**) is the area where you'll find all the Skelegon tools. Here, you can create Skelegons, edit them, rotate them, and so on.

Figure 1.51 The Skelegons category houses all the tools you need to create and edit Skelegons, which you'll convert to bones in the LightWave Layout application.

Layout Tools

Layout tools are the tools that you set up in Modeler whose direct effect comes to light (pun intended) in LightWave Layout. Since Layout is the portion of LightWave in which you render and see your final image, the Luxigons and Powergons tools won't show their effects right away. Luxigons and Powergons are tools that allow you to create multiple lights and lights from polygons, for things like stage lighting, large architectural interiors, or even disco balls. John Travolta, watch out!

Because the end result of creating Luxigons and Powergons in Modeler happens in Layout, commands for creating them are found in the Layout Tools category.

FiberFX

With the FiberFX category, you have access to the hair creation module in LightWave Modeler. Click the first button and a panel will open allowing you to add fibers to your 3D models, which you can later render in Layout to create hair and grass (**Figure 1.52**).

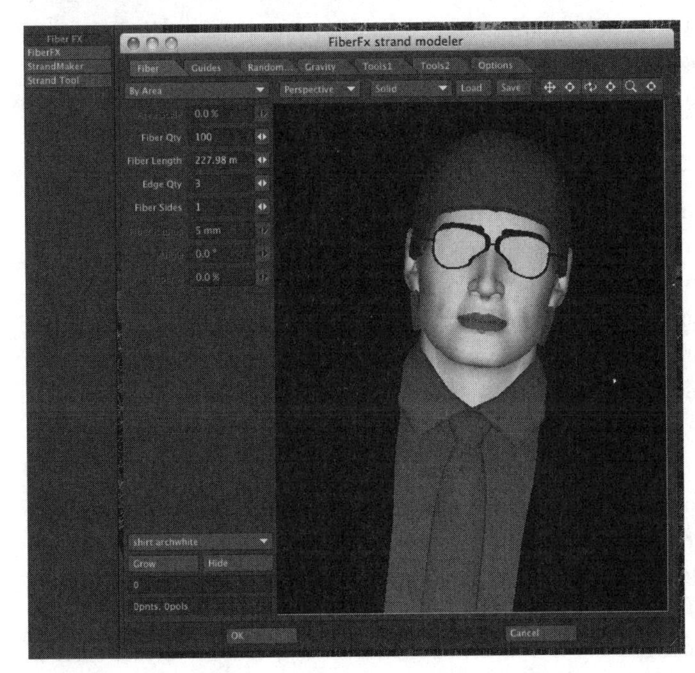

Figure 1.52 You can add fibers to your 3D models in the FiberFx strand modeler.

Utilities Tab

The Utilities tab contains tools for extending Modeler's features and giving you greater control over them (**Figure 1.53**). These tools are used to install and access third-party plug-ins. This tab is also home within Modeler to LightWave's custom scripting language, LScript. If you've added a third-party plug-in but don't know where it went, just look at the Additional drop-down list within this tab.

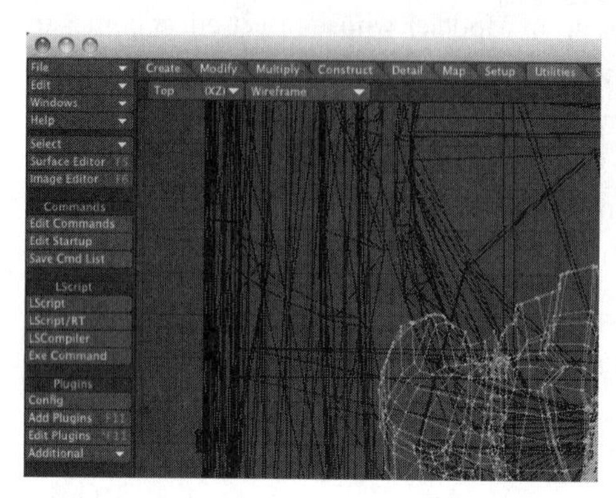

Figure 1.53 The Utilities tab is home to various commands, LScript tools, and plug-in controls.

Commands

Figure 1.54 The Commands tool category lets you create your own custom actions for Modeler.

You use tools in the Commands category (**Figure 1.54**) to create and edit instructions, or commands, for LightWave Modeler. Say you want to always perform the same string of events on an object. You can create a custom command to do so with the Edit Commands tool. Or perhaps upon startup you want to have a Luxigon created from a ball. You can do this and much more with the Edit Startup tool.

LScript

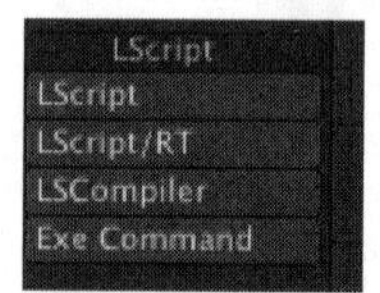

Figure 1.55 The LScript category gives you the tools to load and compile LScripts.

LightWave's custom scripting language enables you to create your own plug-ins and scripts, and the tools in the LScript category (**Figure 1.55**) let you create scripts of your own and manage ones you make or obtain elsewhere. Even if you never write a line of script, you may need these tools occasionally in order to tweak LScripts generated automatically by other LightWave tools or plug-ins, or to compile and load LScripts you exchange with friends.

Plugins

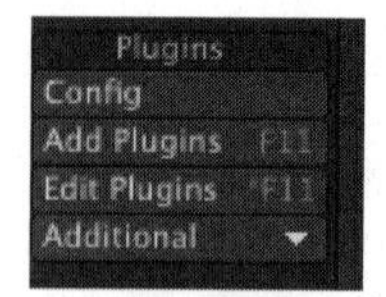

Figure 1.56 Use the tools in the Plugins category to manage software add-ons to LightWave.

Last in the Utilities tab is the Plugins category (**Figure 1.56**). Here, you can add a single plug-in or edit your existing plug-ins. You'll also find the Additional list, which contains LightWave's plug-ins, many of which are already assigned to buttons and keyboard equivalents with the default configuration. If you choose to add third-party plug-ins, you can find them here as well. You can also create custom buttons for those added plug-ins using the Edit Menu feature in LightWave's Edit drop-down lists.

Selection Tab

Without being able to select, you really couldn't function in Modeler. NewTek has brought the Selection tab to LightWave 10 along with a plethora of selection tools (**Figure 1.57**).

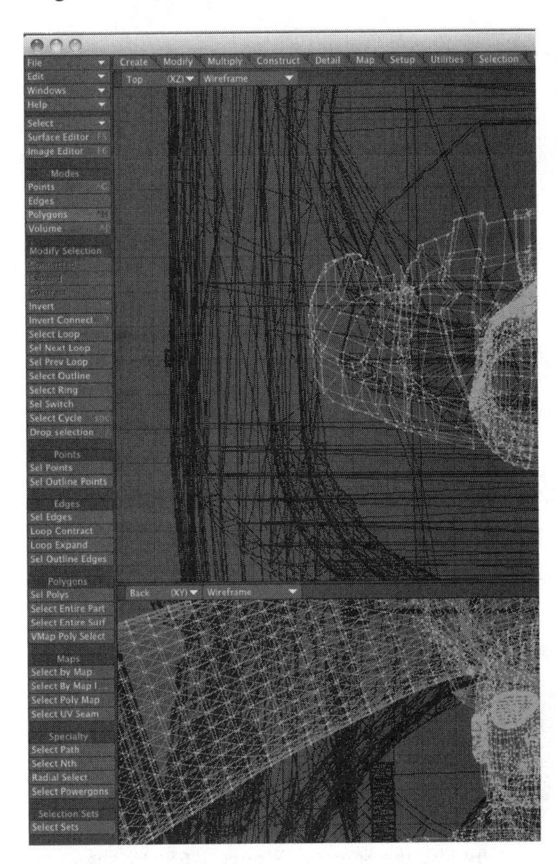

Figure 1.57 The Selection tab is home to a plethora of tools to enhance your selection pleasure.

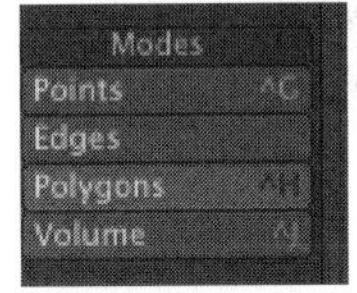

Figure 1.58 If you don't care to change selection modes at the bottom of Modeler, use this category.

Modes

Normally only visible at the bottom of the Modeler interface, the Points, Edges, Polygons, and Volume buttons are now available in the Modes category (**Figure 1.58**).

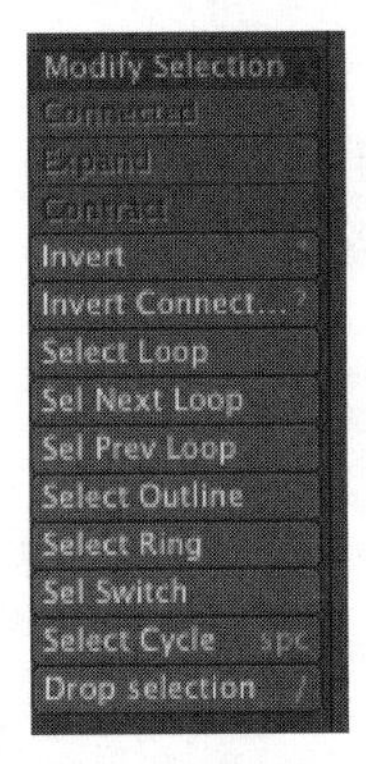

Figure 1.59 Use the Modify Selection category to change one type of selection to another.

Modify Selection

Once you've selected some polygons, edges, or points, what are you going to do with them? Perhaps you want a different variation of your selection. If so, the tool for you might just be within the Modify Selection category. Here you can invert a selection, select an outline, select a loop, and more (**Figure 1.59**).

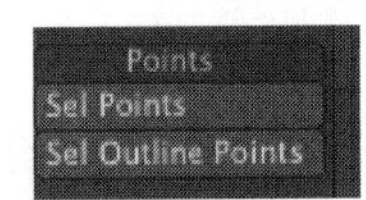

Figure 1.60 Use the Points category to select points or outline points.

Points

The Points category allows you to select specific points within a model (**Figure 1.60**).

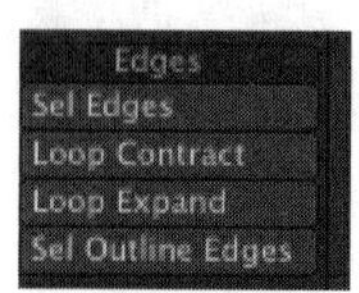

Figure 1.61 The Edges category allows you to select edges, loop select, or outline edges.

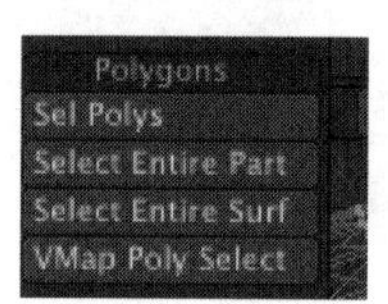

Figure 1.62 The Polygons tab is where you can select polygons or parts of polygons.

Edges

The Edges category allows you to select edges, as well as edge loops, within a model (**Figure 1.61**).

Polygons

The Polygons category allows you to select specific polygons, or parts of polygons, within a model (**Figure 1.62**).

Maps

You may have created morph maps or specific weight maps within your model. If so, you can use the Maps category to select specifically mapped areas (**Figure 1.63**).

Specialty

You can use the Specialty category to select paths or Powergons within a model (**Figure 1.64**).

Selection Sets

Selection sets are often overlooked by animators, but they are quite helpful. Tools in this category (**Figure 1.65**) make it easy to select groups of points or polygons and combine them as selection sets. The benefit of this is twofold—not only can you easily select those same points or polygons again whenever you need them, you can also use them as specific controls in LightWave Layout.

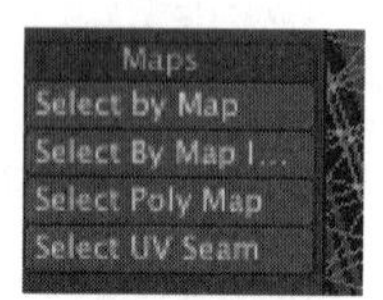

Figure 1.63 Use the Maps category to select any type of vertex map in Modeler.

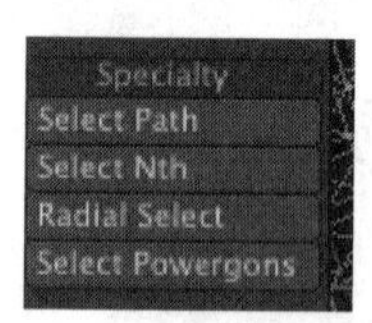

Figure 1.64 Use the Specialty category to select paths, select Powergons, and even radial select.

Figure 1.65 Use the Selection Sets category to create or delete selection sets.

View Tab

Earlier in this chapter, we discussed LightWave's viewports, but we have not yet talked about the other view options available to you. In the View tab (**Figure 1.66**), you'll find many tools designed to help you maximize your modeling experience, including Magnify tools, various Layers tools, and cool selection tools.

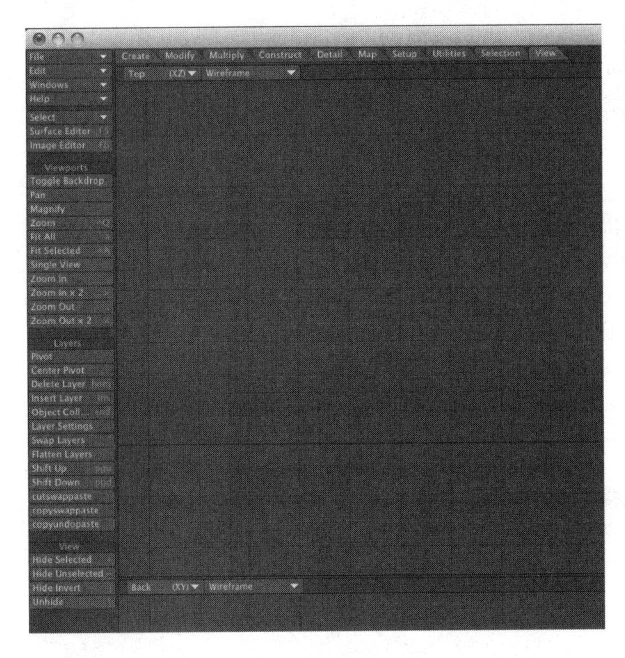

Figure 1.66 LightWave Modeler offers a wide range of selection tools, all found under the View tab.

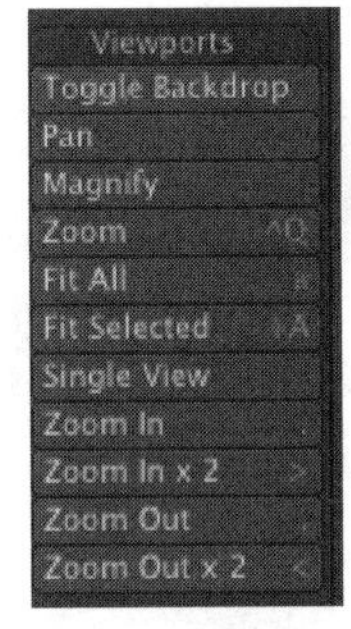

Figure 1.67 Take control of what you see with tools in the Viewports category.

Viewports

Much of the viewport control you'll access on a regular basis is done through the keyboard (like pressing **0** for maximize) or directly within each view. However, the Viewports tool category (**Figure 1.67**) gives you all those controls and more, such as Fit Selected and Fit All, as well as various zoom controls. So anytime you want to adjust what you're seeing in your viewports, look here.

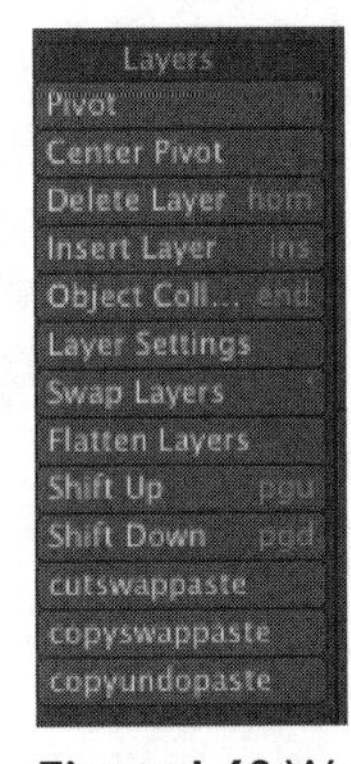

Figure 1.68 Work with your layers effectively by employing the Layers category tools in the View tab.

Layers

We talked about layers and the Layers panel (which you access by pressing **F7**) at the beginning of this chapter. The Layers tools within the View tab (**Figure 1.68**) complement the panel. Use these tools to add and remove layers, swap layers (foreground to background), or even flatten all layers into one. Look to this category for specific layer control in addition to the Layers panel.

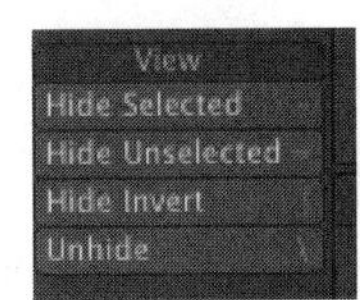

Figure 1.69 Find your way to the View category of the View tab, and you can hide or unhide selections.

View

Last in the View tab is the View category (**Figure 1.69**). Use these tools to hide and unhide items you've selected. They're handy when you want to work on a specific part of a model without touching neighboring parts, or to better see what you're doing when working in Wireframe mode. Just remember that if you hide some geometry, you'll need to unhide it again—don't forget it's there!

So, there you have it: all the LightWave v10 Modeler menus in a quite big nutshell. Now that you understand how they are organized, when it comes time to crack them open it will be much easier to find them and to understand what they do. The next section shows you how to work more specifically with geometry in Modeler through the point and polygon selection and deselection processes.

Points, Edges, and Polygons

For everything you create in Modeler, you'll need to select or deselect points, edges, and polygons. As mentioned earlier, you create points to make polygons. A polygon can't exist without at least three points. (It's like connect the dots, remember?) When points are connected to form polygons, the lines between the points become edges. With that said, take a look at **Figure 1.70**. Here you can see the Points, Edges, and Polygons selection and modeling modes.

Figure 1.70 At the bottom of the Modeler interface are the Points, Edges, and Polygons selection and modeling modes. Select the appropriate mode you want to work with.

Choose a selection mode by simply clicking it, or you can rotate among them by pressing the spacebar. Essentially, all you need to do is think about what you want to extend, move, rotate, and so on, and then choose the appropriate mode.

Selection Modes

Let's say you have a project you've created for your best client. They come to you and say it's great, but they would like you to move some of the model slightly. For something like this, you might want to move points, or perhaps adjust the edges. Whichever the case, selection and deselection work the same no matter what mode you're in. This next project will help you understand further.

Exercise 1.2 Selecting and Deselecting in Modeler

Follow these steps to get a feel for selection, deselection, and the various options available to you when working with points, edges, and polygons.

1. From the CH1 directory on this book's DVD, load the Briefcase.lwo object.
2. **Figure 1.71** (on the next page) shows the object loaded into Modeler. Notice that the briefcase is of ordinary size. Select the Points mode at the bottom of the interface in the Back view. The Back view is the bottom-left quadrant of the interface, and looks toward the back of the object. The Back view is an XY view, meaning that you have control only over those two axes; the Z-axis is not a factor in that viewport.

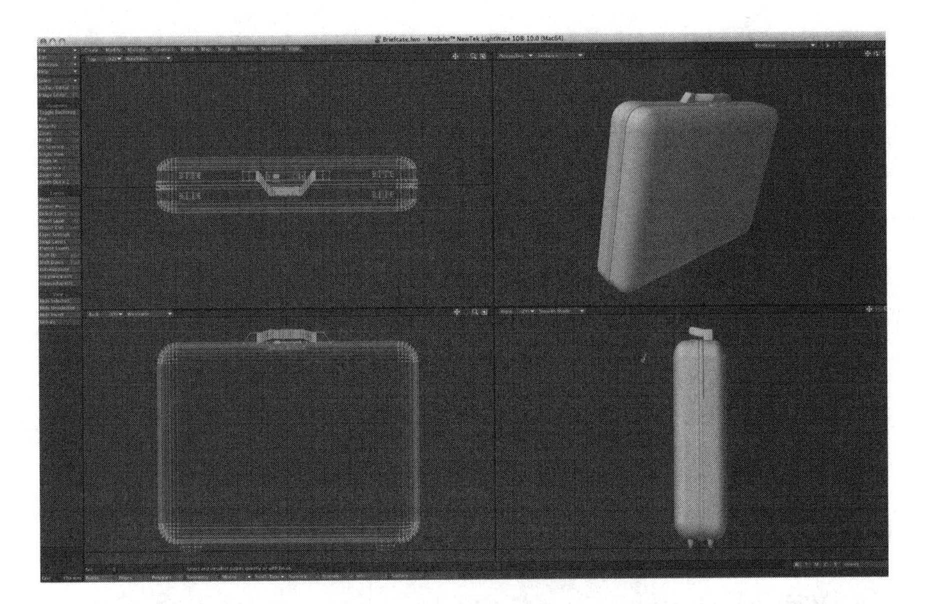

Figure 1.71 The ordinary briefcase object loaded into Modeler.

Note that you should be working with the Wireframe viewport style. Doing so will allow you to select the points in the front and back of the object. You can choose the viewport style from atop each individual viewport.

3. With Points selection mode enabled, you can select points of the object. You can do this in one of two ways. The first option is to click any point directly to select it, so click around the side of the case. Your point should become highlighted as in **Figure 1.72.**

Figure 1.72 Directly clicking a point with the left mouse button selects it. To deselect, let go of the mouse and click again.

When you release the mouse button, you automatically enter Deselect mode. Click the point again and it will be deselected. This is exactly how the Polygons selection mode works. Now that there is nothing selected, you can begin selecting points again. If you click a point and then realize you want to select more, just hold the Shift key down and continue your selection.

4. The second option for selecting points uses Lasso select mode, which is a better choice for selecting all of the points around the side of the briefcase. Press the slash key (/) to deselect the points. With the right mouse button held down, run your mouse around the points on the side of the case, as in **Figure 1.73** (on the next page).

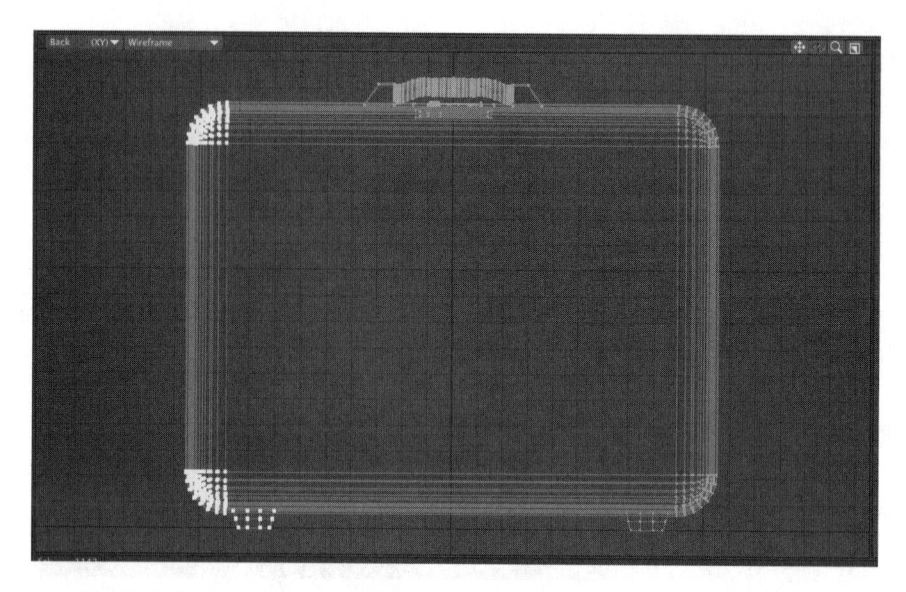

Figure 1.73 Use the right mouse button to select a range of points in Lasso mode.

NOTE

Mac users, if you're not working with a two-button mouse (even though you should be), use Control-click to accomplish right-mouse-button functions in LightWave 3D. But go get a two-button mouse already, OK?

5. With the points on the left side of the case selected, press **t** to select the Move tool from the Modify tab. Click and drag the points to the left in the Back view. You can hold the Control key as you move to constrain the movement to an axis. You can do the same to the right side, and now your ordinary briefcase is ready to carry a guitar. **Figure 1.74** shows the change.

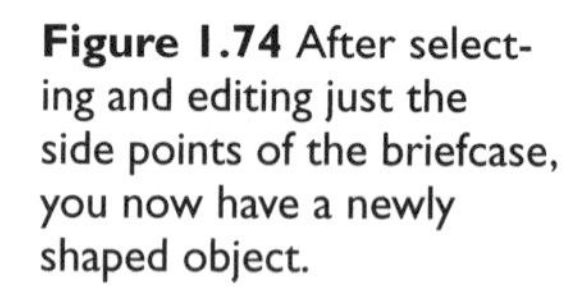

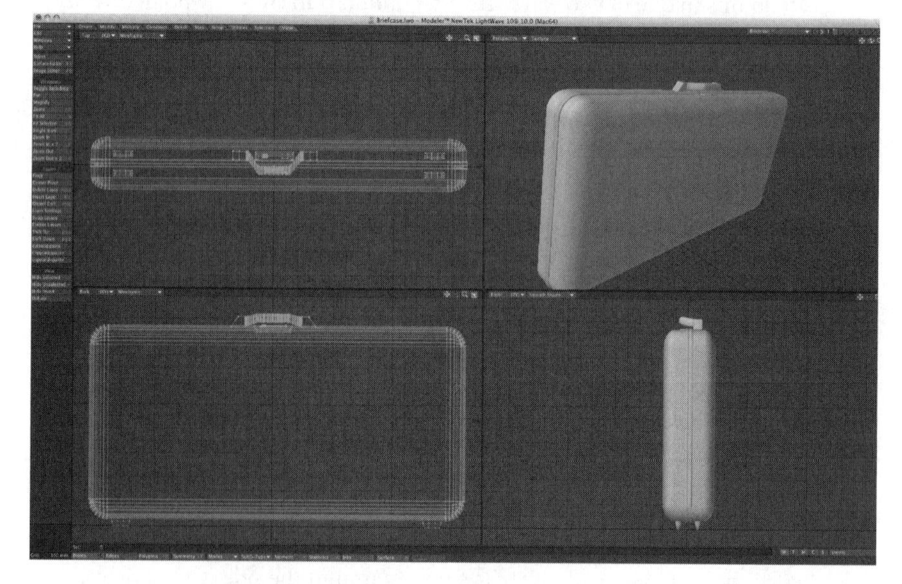

Figure 1.74 After selecting and editing just the side points of the briefcase, you now have a newly shaped object.

Congratulations! You just edited points. That's all there is to it! After the points are adjusted to your liking, deselect them by pressing /.

NOTE

To properly deselect points, edges, or polygons, first turn off any tool you're using by clicking its button in the LightWave toolset or simply press the spacebar. Then, press / to deselect. It's important to get in the habit of performing this process. Know what you're actually doing before you click the mouse or press a button. You can use only one tool at a time. Your process should be as follows. First, select points, edges, or polygons. Turn on a tool. Use the tool. Turn off the tool. Deselect the geometry. It sounds like a lot of steps, but learning this process will save you time in the long run.

Too often, people learning LightWave (or even those who already know it) jump the gun and forget to deselect their points or polygons and move on, only to accidentally get unwanted results in their model. And remember that the selection methods are identical whether you're working with points, edges, or polygons.

Symmetry Mode

Every once in a while, you might find that working on the same thing twice is a real pain. Perhaps you're building a character—why build one side of the body and then do it again for the other side? Sure, you could build half and then mirror it over. But there are times when creativity suffers because you can't see how your entire model is coming along. If you turn on Symmetry mode, using the button to the right of the Points, Edges, and Polygons mode-selection buttons, LightWave will apply whatever action you perform on the positive X-axis on the negative X-axis as well. Note, however, that whatever point, edge, or polygon you modify on the positive X-axis must live in the same space on the negative X-axis.

NOTE

If you have no need for Symmetry, turn it off. Keeping it on can really mess you up because actions are mirrored across the X-axis!

Modeler General Commands

Now take a look at the rest of the buttons along the bottom of the interface, shown in **Figure 1.75**. Here you can see a series of buttons and tools. These are key to working in Modeler, which is why they are always visible on the interface.

Figure 1.75 The LightWave Modeler interface keeps key tools accessible along the bottom of the screen, no matter which tool tab is selected.

At the bottom left of the interface is a small information area (**Figure 1.76**). This is the "info" area to which I'll refer you throughout this book. It shows you many properties, depending on the tool at hand, such as the size of objects, point position, and more.

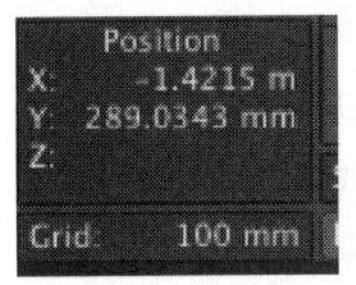

Figure 1.76 The info area at the bottom left of the Modeler interface shows key information about your tools.

You'll use the info area sometimes just as a reference and at other times to measure and control the movement of objects.

Modes: Action Center

To the right of the Symmetry button is another button, a drop-down list labeled Modes, which is used to set the *Action Center* for tools in Modeler. Settings in this list (**Figure 1.77**) determine how tools behave with respect to the mouse pointer, and you'll use them often in Modeler.

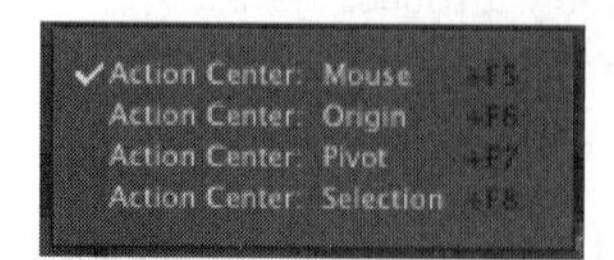

Figure 1.77 The Modes selection area enables you to change how tools react to the mouse.

The Modes options enable you to change how certain tools work with the mouse or how their "action" is centered. The Action Center for your mouse is where a tool action happens. For example, by default the mode is set to Action Center: Mouse. This means that if you select the Rotate tool from the Modify tab, you can click and rotate in any viewport and the spot you click will be the point around which your object or selection will rotate. If you change the Action Center to say, Selection, the selected object, polygon, or point will become the center around which other objects rotate.

You'll use these varying modes depending on what you're creating. If you're sizing an object within another object, it can be difficult to size perfectly in place using the Action Center: Mouse setting. Instead, set the Action Center to Selection and the Size tool works perfectly, with the object or selection sized without shifting toward the mouse location.

NOTE

The Catmull–Clark algorithm is used in computer graphics to create smooth surfaces by subdivision surface modeling. It was devised by Edwin Catmull and Jim Clark in 1978 as a generalization of bi-cubic uniform B-spline surfaces to arbitrary topology. In 2005, Edwin Catmull received an Academy Award for Technical Achievement together with Tony DeRose and Jos Stam for their invention and application of subdivision surfaces. Edwin Catmull is also the current president of Pixar.

SubD-Type

SubD-Type stands for subdivision type. A subdivided object is one in which each polygonal patch is subdivided *x* number of times. You can tell Modeler (and Layout) how much subdivision to apply. The benefit of this feature is that you can create very simple geometry, manipulate it in the software, and then render it out as a detailed high-resolution model. There are two SubD-Type options in Modeler: the original Subpatch mode that existed in earlier versions of LightWave, and a new option called Catmull-Clark.

To work in Subpatch mode, select it from the SubD-Type drop-down and press the Tab key. You'll see your model change into curved surfaces, and a representative cage will appear around it. To revert to standard model view, press the Tab key again. In order to use the Subpatch SubD-Type, your object must have three or four vertices. That means a polygon can't be made up of five sides or more. For that matter, it can't be made up of one or two sides either.

Every once in a while, however, there's no way to reduce your entire model to polygons with just three or four vertices. It's for just those occasions that LightWave v10 added the SubD-Type called Catmull-Clark. Because this SubD-Type allows you to subdivide objects with more than three or four vertices, why even bother with the original Subpatch method at all? Backward compatibility is one reason. Those of you who have used LightWave in the past will appreciate that you can still use your existing models. Another reason is that the Catmull-Clark SubD-Type is more complex and a bit more demanding of your system resources. Applying it to one or more complex models might bring your system to its knees. That's not to say Catmull-Clark is bad; I just recommend that you use it only when needed and not as a default.

Numeric Panel

Vital to most modeling tools is the Numeric panel. Although many tools will be used just by turning them on and clicking and dragging, most tools have added control through the Numeric panel. **Figure 1.78** shows the Numeric panel open with the Capsule tool selected. You can press **n** on your keyboard or just click the Numeric button at the bottom of the interface to open the panel.

NOTE

The Numeric panel can stay open all the time. Adjust your interface to give the Numeric panel its own space on your screen. It's useful for determining whether a tool is active. If the Numeric panel is blank, no tool is active.

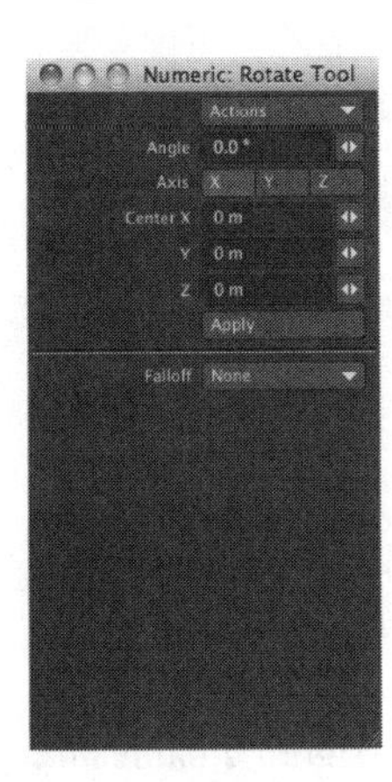

Figure 1.78 The Numeric panel, accessible by pressing n on the keyboard or by choosing it from the bottom of the interface, is useful for specific tool control.

Use the Numeric panel often, as both a reference and a control center for your tools.

Statistics

The Statistics panel (**Figure 1.79**) is another key panel you should keep open. It lets you view information about your points, polygons, surfaces, and much more. You'll employ this panel throughout the book. Note that it will change statistical information for both points and polygons based on which selection mode you're working in. You can also use this panel to select specific surfaces you've set up, even subpatched polygons.

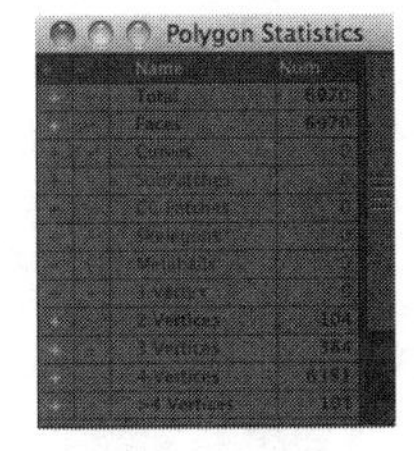

Figure 1.79 The Statistics panel, accessible from the bottom of the LightWave Modeler interface (or by pressing the w key), holds key information for points, polygons, surfaces, and more.

Info Panel

The Info panel (**Figure 1.80**) was a little-known feature in early versions of LightWave. Now you'll find this panel at the forefront, with an access button at the bottom of the LightWave interface. This panel displays specific information about the points or polygons you have selected; the panel does not work in Edges selection mode. You can color wireframes with this panel, view surface names and groupings, and more.

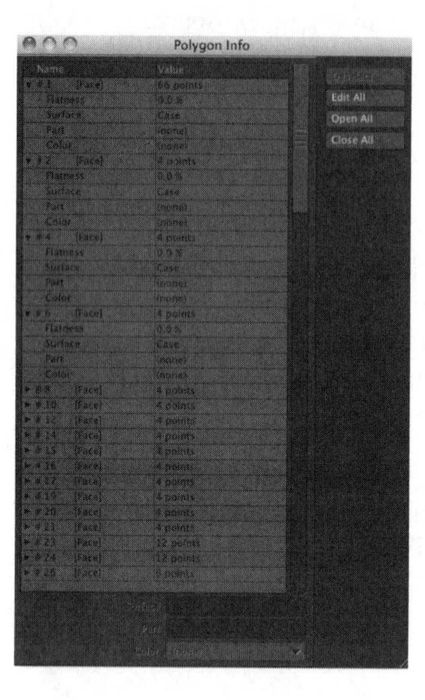

Figure 1.80 The Info panel, accessible from the bottom of the Modeler interface, shows you information about point and polygon selections (but not edges).

Surface

Another important button in Modeler is the Surface button, located at the bottom of the interface. Be sure not to confuse this with the Surface Editor. Clicking the Surface button opens the Change Surface requester panel, which lets you define any polygon selection as a distinct *surface* within your model and assign it a name and a basic color. You'll do most of your surfacing and texturing in Layout, but you use this panel to tell LightWave that the eyeballs on your character are white, that the polygons that make up the fingernails are green, and so on. If you don't use this panel, your object will have only one surface to which colors and textures can be applied. **Figure 1.81** shows the Change Surface panel.

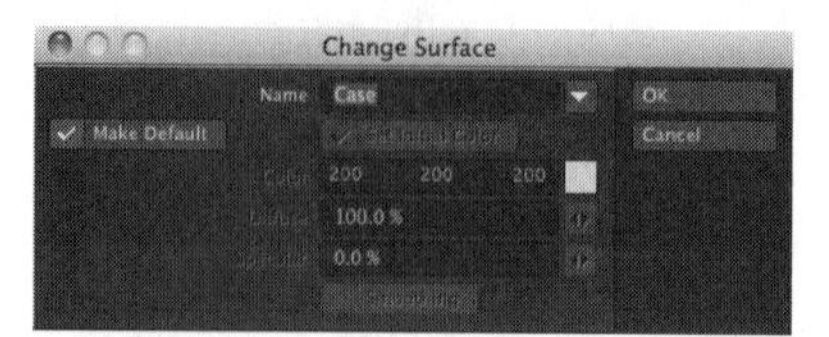

Figure 1.81 The Change Surface panel, accessible from the bottom of the Modeler interface (or by pressing q), enables you to name and assign colors to polygonal regions.

Make

The Make control does not have a panel but just a single button at the bottom of the Modeler interface. Say you created a few points to build an object. After laying your points down, you can click the Make button (or press the Enter key on your keyboard) to "make" the polygon.

Using and Understanding W, T, M, C, S

To the far right of the bottom of the interface is a set of tool buttons with single-letter labels W, T, M, C, and S, plus an associated drop-down list (**Figure 1.82**). These tools are part of LightWave's vertex map system, and you'll use them regularly as your work progresses in Modeler.

Figure 1.82 The W, T, M, C, and S function controls.

The vertex map tools all work in a similar fashion, but each has a different function. To use one of these tools, click its button and select New from the drop-down list to the right; the appropriate panel will appear. But what are these tools? They are simpler than you might think.

W, for Weights

The Weights tool's main job, which we'll discuss later in the book, is to assign information to points or polygons in your model so that you can apply specific controls later in Layout. When you're first learning to create 3D models, you won't have much need for these functions. However, you can apply a SubPatch Weight to subpatched objects as well to change the shape of its curves. To do this, first select the W button for Weights. Then from the drop-down list to the right, choose SubPatch Weight. Go the Map menu tab at the top of the interface, and then on the left toolbar, select the Weights tool from the Weight category. Simply click and drag a point of your subpatched object, and you can sharpen or smooth the curve. You'll use this feature later during the modeling chapters.

T, for Texture

The Texture mode enables you to create a new UV map for your objects. By first clicking the T button and then selecting New from the drop-down list, you can access the Create UV Map panel. UV maps are great for texturing complex objects, especially those with curves. Later in the texturing tutorials in this book, you'll see this panel in action.

M, for Morph

Morph (or endomorph) is a powerful feature in LightWave that enables you to move a point or set of points from one position to another over time. By first clicking the M button and then choosing New from the drop-down list to the right, you'll be able to create a new endomorph. This endomorph simply records the position of points or polygons. You can make multiple endomorphs and then use the Morph Mixer in Layout to access this data, which is saved with the object. You'll use this feature to change the shape of an object over time, such as a character talking or a car suddenly crashing and bending.

C, for Create Vertex Color Map

Create a new color vertex map with the C button. Vertex color maps tell Modeler to label specific point (vertices) selections so you can access them in Layout to apply additional surfacing and details. If you press **F8** or go to the Edit drop-down menu, you can open the Vertex Map panel and see which vertex maps are applied to your objects.

S, for Selection Set

Finally, the last button in the row at the bottom of the Modeler interface is S, for Selection Set. This handy option enables you to select any collection of points and define them as group—a selection set. It's like taking a bunch of points you've selected and giving them a group name. This group name can be accessed later in Layout for things like animated dynamics, cloth, and more. It's also handy for creating selection sets around areas of your models to create endomorphs. For example, you can create a selection set of points around the eye area of a character. By opening the Statistics panel (press **w**), you can quickly select this group anytime and adjust it, changing the shape of the eye for example, and then move on. This is a handy feature. Don't confuse it with the Surface button, which affects appearance and surfacing.

Modeler Options

There's one final area you should be aware of in LightWave Modeler: the Display Options panel (**Figure 1.83**), which you access by pressing **d** on your keyboard.

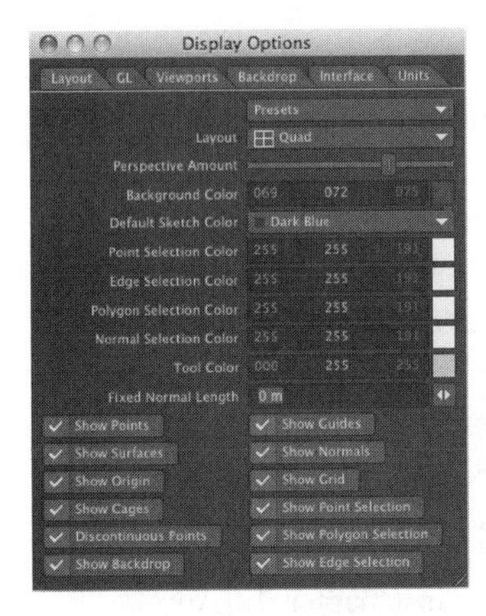

Figure 1.83 Pressing d calls up the Display Options panel, which controls settings that determine how the LightWave interface is organized.

Here, you can tell Modeler to change the way the layout of the viewports looks or change what's visible in the views. You can also use this panel to hide all your tools from view. What's more, in this panel you can specify background images and place them in Modeler's backdrop. Doing this enables you to work over a template, helping you build 3D models to real-world objects. You'll do this in the character modeling section of the book. Also in the Display Options panel, you can tell Modeler to work in English, Metric, or SI. The default is SI (System International), a common unit of measurement. This book uses all default settings for tutorials.

Now, if you press **o** on your keyboard (that's the letter o), you get the General Options panel (**Figure 1.84**). Here, you can set LightWave's content directory as well as Subpatch level and the number of undo operations you would like.

NOTE

The maximum number of undo operations available is 128. It's a good idea to set this value to the max and leave it. The only reason to lower it is if you have limited system resources and are working with very large amounts of polygons. Undoing too many times on large objects can bring down even the best of systems.

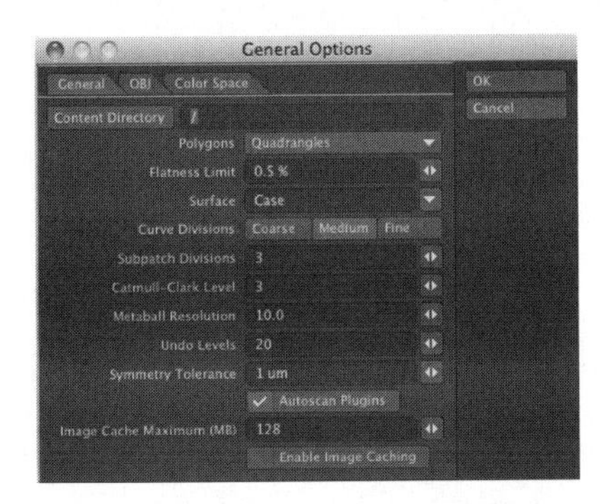

Figure 1.84 The General Options panel lets you set the number of undos, the content directory location, and more.

Any value you set in the General Options panel will become the default once you quit Modeler because the program writes that information to LightWave's configuration file.

The Next Step

This chapter has taken you on a tour through LightWave Modeler. And although it's not the most exciting chapter in this book, it is a chapter you can come back to often when you ask yourself, "What was that tool for?" Throughout this chapter, I've noted that certain tools are used later in the book. Be sure to go through every chapter so that you can see how all these tools come together and so that you can learn just why they are included with your 3D software. There are a few other customizable areas that you should be aware of, but these tools work the same way in LightWave Layout, so we'll cover them in that discussion. We'll look at tools that enable you to edit your menus and set up custom keyboard shortcuts.

The next step is to take a tour of LightWave Layout in Chapter 2. (Another key new component of LightWave, CORE, will become available shortly after the release of the production and the publication of this book. You can introduce yourself to LightWave's next generation with CORE via a bonus chapter that will be available for download in PDF form at www.danablan.com.) As the book progresses, we'll ramp up the complexity and get you into even bigger and cooler projects.

Chapter 2
LightWave Layout

Along with Modeler, which we met in the previous chapter, LightWave 10 includes another application called Layout. Layout is where all of your hard work in Modeler pays off. In Layout, you apply textures to models; assemble scenes, complete with lighting and motion; and see the final animated results.

Just about everything in Layout can be animated, from textures to lights to cameras to (of course) objects. There are plenty of tools for you to harness; in fact, many people spend more time in Layout than they do in Modeler. This chapter guides you through a tour of the LightWave 3D Layout interface and its workflow, panels, and possibilities. You'll learn about these topics:

- LightWave Layout interface navigation
- Simple motions
- Viewports
- New cameras
- Surfacing enhancements
- Render Globals basics

Understanding Layout

3D animation is about geometry and movement. Modeler is where you create 3D geometry, and Layout is where you put things in motion. LightWave's animation program is appropriately referred to as Layout, because that's where you lay out your scene. A scene consists of 3D models, lights, and cameras. Think of Layout as your stage. The 3D models you build in Modeler are your actors. You are the director. Oh, and if you haven't figured it out yet, you're also the gaffer, the lighting coordinator, and the production designer. Keep this in mind as you learn about navigating the Layout interface.

LightWave Layout Interface

When you first start up Layout, you see a large, empty workspace. This workspace is a three-dimensional space, rather than a flat grid as in most other programs. The view you're looking through is a Perspective view—sort of a bird's-eye view of your virtual set. After all, Layout is your virtual television studio, and there is a camera and a light already in place for you. **Figure 2.1** shows the Layout interface upon startup.

Figure 2.1 The LightWave v10 Layout interface.

This view is the default, and there is always one light and one camera. The interface will look familiar, because it resembles LightWave Modeler in its organization and workflow.

To understand how the LightWave 3D world works, consider this: LightWave Layout is a big 3D space. When you're working in Layout, you're inside a big invisible sphere, and everything you do in that sphere can cause reactions in various ways with everything else, such as reflections, shadows, and even dynamics such as gravity.

Across the top of the interface are tabbed menus, each containing key tools for object editing, animating different items, compositing, and more. Before you learn about the different menus, take a look at the bottom of the Layout interface. Here, you'll find your timeline.

The Timeline

Animation is all about timing. It's about telling items such as lights, cameras, objects, or even textures to occupy a specific point in space at a specific time. **Figure 2.2** shows the LightWave Layout timeline.

Figure 2.2 The LightWave Layout timeline.

By default, Layout measures time in frames rather than seconds or minutes. This is because 3D animation, and even 2D animation, is a frame-by-frame process. Although the computer automatically interpolates motions, it's still up to you to create the "key" frames. A *keyframe* is nothing more than a marker in time. At the left side of the timeline, the value is 0, representing the first frame of the animation.

NOTE

Just because the front of the timeline defaults to 0, you are not locked into this value. You can start an animation at frame 6 or frame 40. You can also start an animation before 0 by entering a negative value. You would do this for certain animations that need a head start, for example. Let's say your object needs to already be in motion by the time your viewers see it. If it starts at frame 0 and then ramps up to speed, you could start the animation at the point when it's in full motion. Similarly, you could keyframe the motion before frame 0, and then when your animation starts at 0, the item is already in full motion. It's all about control!

At the right side of the timeline is the ending frame number, which defaults to 60. Because LightWave defaults to the National Television System Committee (NTSC) video standard, 60 frames is 2 seconds, at a 30 frames per second rate. You can change this easily by pressing **o** (that's the letter o) and opening the General Options panel. Here, you can change the Frames Per Second setting to anything you like. Later in this chapter, you'll learn about all of LightWave Layout's preferences.

The last frame of your animation can be changed just like the first frame. Most likely, many of your animations will go well beyond 60 frames, or 2 seconds. To change your current animation's overall time, it's just a matter of changing one value:

1. Double-click the end frame window, which should read 60 by default. You can also just click and drag over the number.
2. Enter a new value—for example, *250*—and press the Enter key (Windows) or the Return key (Mac).

After you enter the value, you'll see that the timeline looks a little different—this one's busier because it's now displaying keys for 250 frames instead of 60. If you need more frames for your animation, just change that value. Now, with all of that being said, you don't have to be animating to use Layout! Thousands of users just render still images in LightWave for illustrations, compositing with other programs such as Photoshop, or simply creative art.

Selecting Items

You'll see that beneath the timeline on the left are four interesting buttons labeled Objects, Bones, Lights, and Cameras. Above the buttons is a drop-down list called Item. When an object is loaded and the Objects button is selected, you'll see the selected item here. You can also choose different items with this list, as well as bones, lights, and cameras. To the right of the Item list is a tiny button. If you click this, you'll be presented with Layout's Current Item selector. **Figure 2.3** shows the item selection.

Figure 2.3 The item selection buttons allow you to choose which type of item you want to work with.

The Current Item selector will be your friend in complex scenes because it allows you to easily organize your items, especially when you're using numerous objects in your scene. You'll employ this feature later in the book.

Here's your goal: Do not be confused by the buttons. Think about what you're doing before you click. Too often, animators click the mouse, press the spacebar, or press the Esc key until something happens. Usually, something does happen, but not what they intended. Do yourself a favor and think about your actions just as you do in Modeler. Select an item, turn on a tool, use it, and turn off the tool. Think about the process. Then, by paying attention to the buttons at the bottom of the interface, you'll know whether you are working with Layout's objects, bones, lights, or cameras. After you've selected an item category, simply choose the Current Item from the drop-down list. Then pick a tool, such as Move, and have at it.

NOTE

Never judge your animation entirely by the Layout playback buttons. This applies to motions, timing, shadows, textures, and so on. Always reserve judgment until the animation has been properly rendered out.

Of course, there's more to animation than point, click, move—so much more! What's great about LightWave's vast toolset is that some things, such as the timeline, stay the same no matter what you're doing. Take a look at the bottom right. Those VCR-like buttons you see are your playback buttons (**Figure 2.4**). Don't confuse these with a final animation or real-time reference. These give you a pretty good idea of how your animation will play back.

Figure 2.4 The playback controls in LightWave v10 Layout.

Keyframes

The best way to understand timing is to work with it every day, all day. Timing is truly the hidden art of animation. Without it, nothing works. Sure, you can make pretty images, print ads, and the like. But if you're putting anything in motion, the timing needs to be dead on. It needs to "work." With that said, follow this next simple tutorial to set up some keyframes of your own, and see how LightWave interpolates motion.

Exercise 2.1 Creating Keyframes

1. Open LightWave Layout and make sure that nothing is in the scene. The scene is like your current project, so if you've loaded any objects, or sample scenes, be sure to save your work and then choose Clear Scene from the File drop-down menu (or press Shift+N).
2. With a nice new default blank scene, all you're going to do is animate the camera. Click Cameras at the bottom of the Layout interface, as shown in **Figure 2.5**.

Figure 2.5 Tell LightWave Layout that you want to work with cameras by selecting the Cameras button at the bottom of Layout.

3. Because there is only one camera in the scene, it is automatically selected and highlighted after you choose to use cameras. If you had multiple cameras in the scene, you would select which camera you want from the Current Item drop-down list, just above the Cameras button.
4. Make sure that the Auto Key button, beneath the timeline, is on.

   Layout's Auto Key function provides a great way to get started with keyframing. When activated, it creates a keyframe to mark the position and rotation of an object, camera, or light any time you move it within a scene. As your animations get more sophisticated, you won't always want this turned on, but it's great for blocking out a basic scene.
5. You can grab the slider in the timeline to make sure it's at frame 0, all the way to the left. This is the start of your animation.
6. Make sure the camera is still selected (it should be highlighted in yellow) and press **t**. This calls up the Move tool from the Modify tab. Move the camera slightly to test.

NOTE

To add multiple cameras to a scene, go to the Items tab at the top of Layout; then from the tools on the left side of the interface, choose Add > Camera. You can name this camera anything you like. Multiple cameras are great for scenes in which you need to show your client different views. Rather than always moving the camera, it's better to switch between multiple cameras.

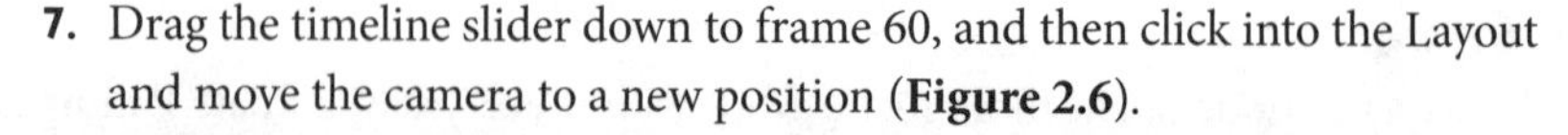

7. Drag the timeline slider down to frame 60, and then click into the Layout and move the camera to a new position (**Figure 2.6**).

Figure 2.6 When the Auto Key button beneath the timeline is active, moving the frame slider automatically creates a new keyframe for the camera.

8. Click the Rewind button at the bottom right of the Layout, beneath the timeline, as shown in **Figure 2.7**. This quickly jumps your timeline slider back to 0.

Figure 2.7 Click the Rewind button at the bottom right of Layout to set the timeline back to 0.

9. Press the Play button in the timeline, and you'll see your camera move from its 0 keyframe position to its 60 keyframe position.

   Layout calculates frames 1 – 59, and you might notice that after a keyframe at 60 is created (automatically with Auto Key), a motion path appears. That's the white line you see connecting the camera's first- and last-frame positions. LightWave has interpolated the motion of the frames in between. If you do not see the motion path, press **d** to open the Display Options panel and, under the OpenGL tab, make sure Show Motion Paths is selected. Of course, this motion path is just a straight line. So, try what is suggested in this next step.

10. Move your timeline slider to frame 30. Then move the camera in some way, perhaps off to the side. You should see the motion path now curve, to accept the new keyframe. LightWave interactively updates the motion path, as shown in **Figure 2.8**.

NOTE

A good way to keep track of your keyframes is to simply look at the timeline. When a keyframe is created, LightWave puts a small yellow dash at that point in time, like a marker. If you're wondering how many keyframes you've created, look to see how many markers are in the timeline.

Figure 2.8 With the Auto Key button on, moving the camera at any frame will automatically create a keyframe.

This example shows keyframing in the simplest form. Throughout this book, you'll be creating more advanced keyframing—and more precise keyframing. The Auto Key button you turned on to automatically create keyframes is on by default in LightWave; but as helpful as it is, it can be quite destructive too. There are times when you should use it—for example, when tweaking character animation. Other times, you shouldn't use it—for example, when doing precise mechanical animations. You'll see how this use (or non-use) of Auto Key plays a part in your keyframing actions throughout the book.

NOTE

A quick way to jump to specific keyframes without dragging the timeline slider is to press f, which calls up the Go To Frame requester. Enter a value and press the Enter key, and your timeline slider jumps to the keyframe.

The Dope Track

There's a hidden feature in the Layout timeline that you may or may not have found. If you move your mouse just above the timeline, right in the center, a small arrow will appear. When it does, click the bar that separates the Layout view and the timeline. You'll see an additional timeline pop up, as shown in **Figure 2.9**.

Figure 2.9 Just above the timeline in Layout, you can click to open the Dope Track.

This is the Dope Track, which offers additional control over your keyframes. See, it's all about control—the more you have, the better!

A Dope Track is a short or mini version of a *dope sheet*. What's a dope sheet, you ask? It is a page that outlines all of your keyframes, motions, and timing. LightWave has its own Dope Sheet feature, which we'll get to later in this chapter. For now, the Dope Track is a simplified version of the Dope Sheet that offers you enhanced control over your keyframes. You'll use this during animation tutorials later in this book.

Exercise 2.2 Working with the Dope Track

To get an idea of how the Dope Track works, do the following:

1. Click the top center of the timeline to pop open the Dope Track.
2. You should still have your three-keyframe animation in Layout from the previous exercise, and you can use that. This scene is nothing more than one camera with three keyframes applied at 0, 30, and 60.
3. You'll see what looks like a second timeline appear above the first timeline, as in **Figure 2.10**.

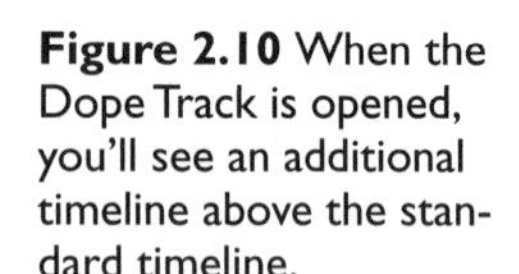

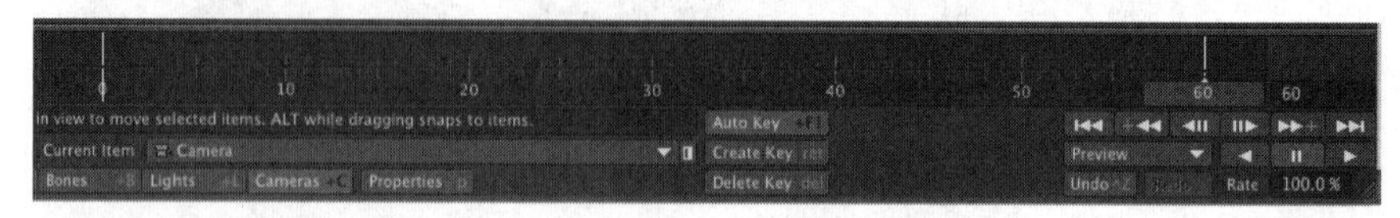

Figure 2.10 When the Dope Track is opened, you'll see an additional timeline above the standard timeline.

4. With just three keyframes applied to the camera, you can see their representations in the Dope Track.
5. If you right-click one of the keyframes in the Dope Track, you get a list of commands available to you, as in **Figure 2.11**.

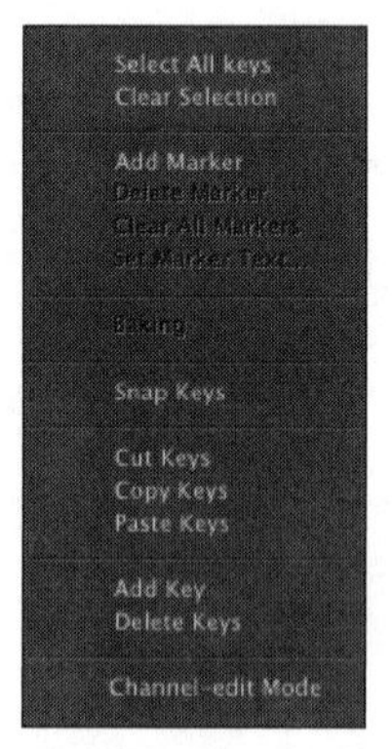

Figure 2.11 Right-click one of the keyframes in the Dope Track, and you are greeted by a list of tools.

Some of these commands are ghosted with such a simple scene. However, as you build more complex animations you'll find these tools very useful. Here are some tips to demonstrate the power of the Dope Track:

- The Dope Track shows keyframes for objects based on their individual X, Y, and Z axes, as opposed to those of the overall scene. If you create a keyframe for an object when its axes are aligned with those of the main scene and then use the Rotation tool to change the object's heading, pitch, or bank, the keyframe you made will still be there but you'll no longer see it in the Dope Track. That's because the object's relative axes will be different from those of the scene.
- The Dope Track enables you to adjust objects' X, Y, and Z positions independently, for any given keyframe.
- In the Dope Track, the left mouse button selects keyframes.
- Hold down the Alt key and click-drag in the Dope Track to select a range of frames called a *local zone.* In this zone, you can *bake* keyframes for Move and Rotate operations. Baking is the process of converting frames interpolated by LightWave into actual keyframes. Holding down both the Alt and Shift keys sets a zone, allowing you to bake a keyframe for all objects in the scene.
- If you hold the Alt key and click-drag to select a range of keyframes in the Dope Track, you can make copies of those keyframes while leaving the originals untouched.

NOTE

Mac users: Remember to Control-click to simulate right-mouse-button functions. Hey, did you go out and get a two-button mouse yet?

- To delete a zone you might have created with the previous step, hold down the Control and Alt keys and drag.
- You can grab the arrows on either end of a zone to make it longer or shorter. Or, grab in the center to move a zone.
- You can snap keyframes in the Dope Track. LightWave's General Options (press o in Layout) allow you to turn on a feature called fractional keyframes. With this feature enabled, you can snap the selected keyframe to the closest whole keyframe, such as 1, 2, or 5. A fractional keyframe is in between a whole keyframe, such as 1.3 or 2.7.
- A really cool feature of the Dope Track is support for copying and pasting keyframes. When you paste copied keyframes in the Dope Track, their placement is determined by the slider in the timeline: The first pasted frame is inserted at the slider position.

NOTE

Don't worry about all of the details of the Dope Track right now. Review the information here, and then when it's time to animate later in the book, you'll see this section in action.

Layout Viewports

Like Modeler, Layout has multiple viewports. Look at **Figure 2.12**. Here you can see the viewport controls at the top of the Layout window, as you did in Modeler. **Figure 2.13** shows the viewing options available for each viewport you're working in, such as Light View or Camera View. **Figure 2.14** shows the viewport render-styles pull-down, which allows you to view objects in Layout as bounding-box or wireframe forms or as solids, even with textures applied.

Figure 2.12 The default Perspective view in Modeler can be changed to any other viewport style from the drop-down menu at the top of the interface.

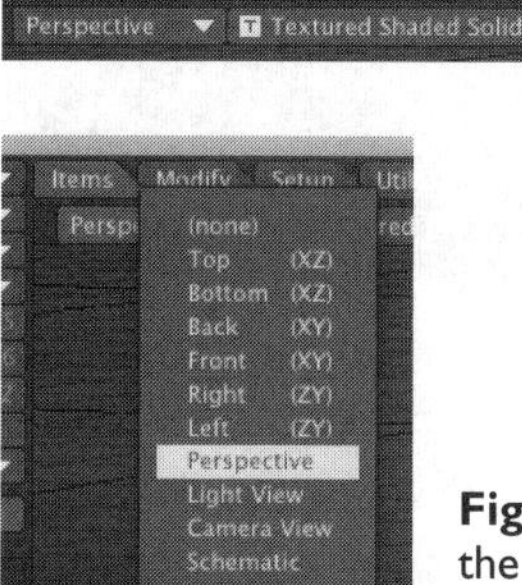

Figure 2.13 Click the list at the top of the Layout viewport to change to a different view.

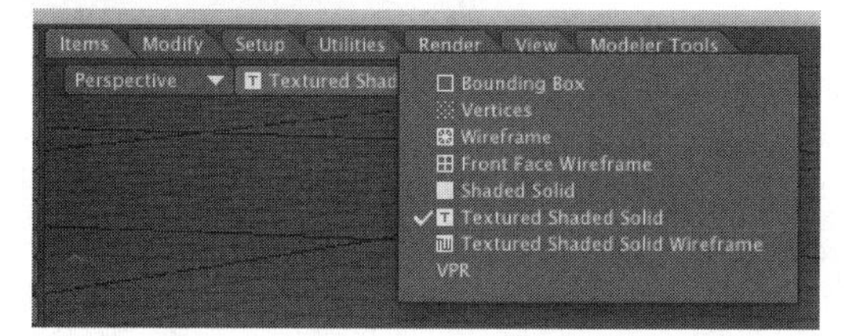

Figure 2.14 You can also choose how the objects in the viewport will be drawn.

VPR

You'll find yourself changing these views often, depending on the project at hand. Just to the right of the viewport styles drop-down at the top of the frame are additional view options such as Bone X-Ray mode. This mode enables you to see any bones applied to an object, even if the object is solid—hence the X-Ray title. There is a great new feature in LightWave 10 called VPR, or virtual preview render. Choose this view from the viewport render-styles drop-down and you'll be instantly presented with a quick preview render of your scene. **Figure 2.15** shows the VPR turned on with a scene, showing the textured airplane, lighting, shadows, and more. This is not a render, and you can work in Layout with this view, which we'll do within the project chapters in this book.

Figure 2.15 Additional view options are available directly to the right of the viewport render-styles drop-down, at the top of LightWave Layout, such as VPR for quick interactive preview renders.

Multiple Viewports

You might be one of the select few who can work in multiple viewports while animating. If you're not sure whether that's your style, press **F3** and you'll see a quad view just like LightWave Modeler (**Figure 2.16** on the next page).

But wait, there's more! Press **F3** again, and again. You cycle through all of LightWave Layout's available viewport arrangements. You can press F4 to go back. Let's say you have a quad view in Layout set, as shown in Figure 2.16. You can set any view to any style you want—for example, you can make two views a Perspective view, one view a Top view, and the other a Camera view. Many animators like to make the Layout viewports match those of Modeler. However, you might find that working in large single views, one at a time, is quite useful.

Figure 2.16 Pressing the F3 key cycles you through LightWave Layout's available viewport arrangements.

NOTE

A great way to work in Layout is to employ your numeric keypad or use the number keys across the top of your keyboard. Press **1** to jump to the Back view looking down the Z-axis; press **2** for the Top view looking down the Y-axis. As you can guess, pressing **3** takes you to the Right view looking down the X-axis. Press **4** to get to a Perspective view, **5** for a Light view, and **6** to switch to a Camera view. Do this as you work, and you'll be flipping back and forth between views without thinking about it.

Viewport Movement Control

To the top right of any Layout viewport are the viewport movement controls, just as you found in Modeler (**Figure 2.17**).

Figure 2.17 At the upper-right side of the Layout interface are the viewport movement controls. Click, hold the mouse button down, and drag the mouse to use them.

It's important to note that you cannot use these controls all the time, in every view. Their availability varies depending on which view you're working in. In Perspective view, the default viewport, these tools are all available. The five buttons are as follows:

- **Center Current Item.** This first button (starting from the left) stays on when clicked. Click it again to turn it off. It keeps the currently selected item—be it a camera, a light, or an object—centered at all times.
- **Move.** The Move button enables you to move your view around in the Perspective, Top, Side, and Back/Front viewports.
- **Rotate.** Click, hold, and drag to rotate your viewport in the Perspective view only.
- **Zoom.** The Zoom viewport tool is useful for all views except Light view and Camera view.

- **Expand.** The Expand view control is great to quickly maximize any viewport. For example, let's say you're using LightWave Layout with a quad viewport style. Click this button in any viewport to maximize it to full screen. Click it again to return to your quad view.

You'll also find two new icons to the right of the Expand icon. When using VPR mode in Layout, you can click the camera icon to take a history snapshot of your view. This enables you to step back to a previously positioned view. The last icon takes you to VPR settings for resolution settings.

Use these viewport controls to take a proper look at your scene. They can help you stay aware of what's going on, and controls like the Center Current Item button can help you quickly find an item you've misplaced in the scene: Click the Center Current Item button, select the missing item from the Selected Item list (see Figure 2.3), and the lost item will instantly jump into view. Zoom out slightly, and you can see where it is in relation to the rest of your scene.

Menus and Tabs

Across the top of the Layout interface are seven tabs. As in Modeler, each tab reveals a menu of tools. When you click one of these tabs (**Figure 2.18**), the toolset on the left side of the interface changes accordingly.

Figure 2.18 The LightWave Layout tab set, across the top of the interface.

It's important to note that the nine buttons at the top left of Layout (starting with the File drop-down) always appear, no matter what tab you've selected. These are key tools and commands you'll use throughout LightWave, in both Modeler and Layout (**Figure 2.19**).

Figure 2.19 The nine buttons at the top left of LightWave Layout always appear, no matter what tab or menu you're working in.

NOTE

Remember that we're using the default LightWave tabs and menus throughout this book. Although you can change the menus to look like anything you want, the default setup keeps these nine tool buttons at the top left of LightWave Layout.

File Menu

Let's talk about the first of these buttons: the File drop-down menu. When we say *drop-down menu* (or just *drop-down*), we're talking about a button that has a small downward-pointing arrow. Click this button and you'll find additional tools (**Figure 2.20**). Note that you do not need to click the arrow to expand the menu; just click anywhere on the button.

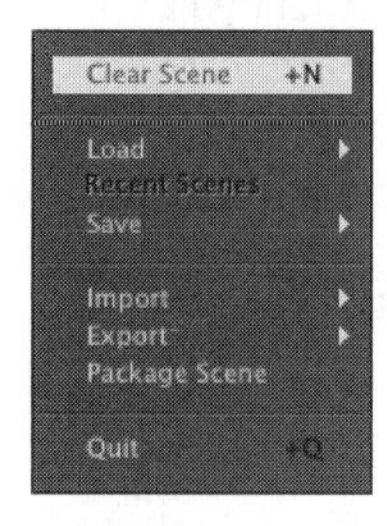

Figure 2.20 The File drop-down menu always appears at the top left of the Layout interface.

The File drop-down menu allows you to load and save scenes and use the new Save Scene Increment feature. Using this feature adds 001, 002, and so on to the end of your scene name each time you save. You can also export scenes through LightWave's Content Manager.

NOTE

Pressing Control+S (Windows or Mac) on your keyboard tells LightWave to Save Scene As, whereas pressing Shift+S automatically saves a scene in increments.

Clear Scene

As the name implies, you can select Clear Scene, or press Shift+N, to clear your scene. After you perform this command, all that is left is a light and a camera. Be warned: You will not have an opportunity to save after you do this, and LightWave does not inform you that data might be lost. It asks you if you're sure you want to clear the scene, but that's it. So, save often!

Additionally, simply loading a new scene overrides your current scene. Therefore, using Clear Scene before you use Load Scene is a wasted step.

Load

The Load submenu in the File drop-down allows you to load scenes, load recent scenes, and load an item from a scene, which is a cool feature. You can also load objects and revert the current scene to its previously saved state.

The Load Items from Scene command in the Load submenu is especially handy for character animation. It allows you to load one scene into your current scene. For example, let's say you create a cool-looking giraffe and set up a workable bone structure for it. Of course, you've saved that scene so that you can work with it later. Then, you build a huge safari scene with textures, landscapes, and lighting. Now all you have to do is use Load Items from Scene and choose the giraffe scene. The giraffe and all of its motions and bones will be imported into your existing scene.

This allows you to set up scenes on their own for both speed and productivity, but use them together for final results.

Import

This submenu provides access to LightWave add-on modules called plug-ins, which can be used to convert models and animations created in other programs. LightWave ships with just one such plug-in, Mocap_BVH_Setup, which lets you apply BioVision motion-capture data to your animations.

Export

Certain third-party applications still work very well with LightWave. However, LightWave's core structure changed with version 6 in the year 2000, and many scenes were no longer compatible with third-party applications. Because of this, NewTek has added the ability to export your scene to LightWave version 5.6 with the Export command, which is also found under the File drop-down menu. And you can export files in VRML (Virtual Reality Markup Language) and Shockwave 3D formats, used for displaying 3D objects on the Web. You can also export a list of your scenes' images, either for later reference or for sharing scene information.

Content Manager

LightWave's Content Manager is extremely handy for backing up your scenes and sending them to coworkers or clients. You see, LightWave's scene file consists of objects or 3D models you create in Modeler. The objects in your scene hold surfacing data, whereas the scene file itself holds motion data. These data files can sometimes be located in various folders around your hard drive. The Content Manager gathers all of the files associated with the current scene and copies them to a directory you specify.

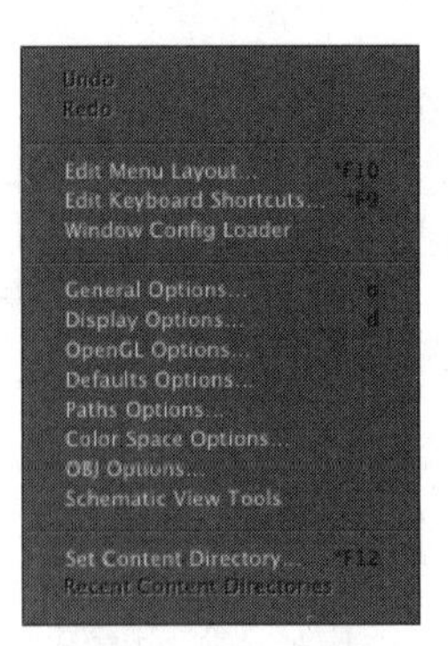

Figure 2.21 The Edit drop-down menu gives you access to key tools like Edit Menu Layout and Edit Keyboard Shortcuts.

Edit Menu

The Edit drop-down menu (**Figure 2.21**) is home to quite a few useful tools that enable you to edit menu and keyboard layouts, change window configurations, and even choose your content directory. The main features you'll use in this drop-down list are the Edit Keyboard Shortcuts and Edit Menu Layout commands.

Undo and Redo

In most circumstances, you'll use Control+Z to undo and the **z** key by itself to redo within LightWave. However, if you want, you can use toolset buttons to do so; they are found in the Edit drop-down list. Remember that you can set unlimited undos in LightWave Layout by pressing **o** for General Options.

There are a few warnings to note about using undo. First, too many undos can kill your system resources! Also, remember that undos don't apply to everything—that is, if you accidentally turn off a texture editor layer on your surface, there's no going back. However, if you create some bad keyframes, undo is an easy way to set them up again.

Edit Keyboard Shortcuts

Everyone likes things customized to their liking, right? LightWave 3D gives you this freedom by allowing you to assign keyboard equivalents to commands throughout the program. This next exercise shows you how to use these Edit features. **Figure 2.22** shows the Edit Keyboard Shortcuts selection.

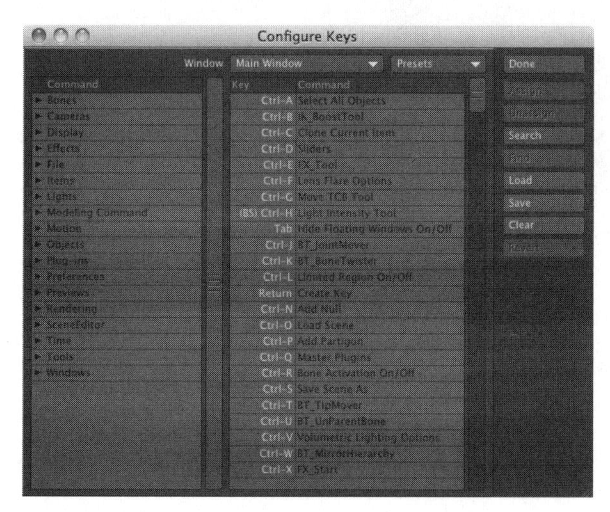

Figure 2.22 The Edit Keyboard Shortcuts panel enables you to rearrange existing keyboard shortcuts as well as create new ones.

NOTE

You can see any existing keyboard shortcut right on the Layout button. Any keyboard shortcut you apply will become visible on the buttons as a helpful reminder.

Exercise 2.3 Editing Keyboard Shortcuts

1. Click the Edit drop-down menu and choose the Edit Keyboard Shortcuts command, or press Alt+F9 (Option+F9 on the Mac).
2. A panel appears where you can choose any of LightWave's tools and apply your own keyboard shortcut (see Figure 2.22).
3. On the left side of the panel are the various commands Layout offers. On the right are keyboard shortcut listings. Scroll down the left side and select the Rendering listing. Click it to expand.
4. Within the Rendering commands, you find Render Globals, LightWave's global control panel. Select it, as shown in **Figure 2.23**.
5. Scroll down the right column to choose a keyboard equivalent to assign the Render Globals command to, perhaps Shift+T.

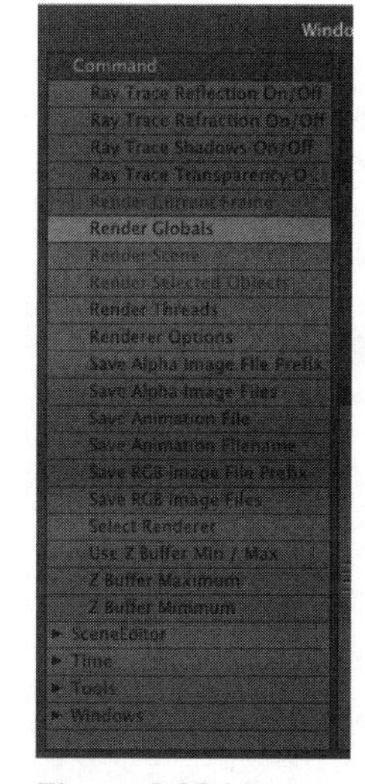

Figure 2.23 It's easy to select various commands from the categories. Here, the Render Globals command is selected.

6. Select the Shift+T keyboard shortcut in the window, and on the right, click the Assign button, as shown in **Figure 2.24**. Click the Save button to keep your changes.

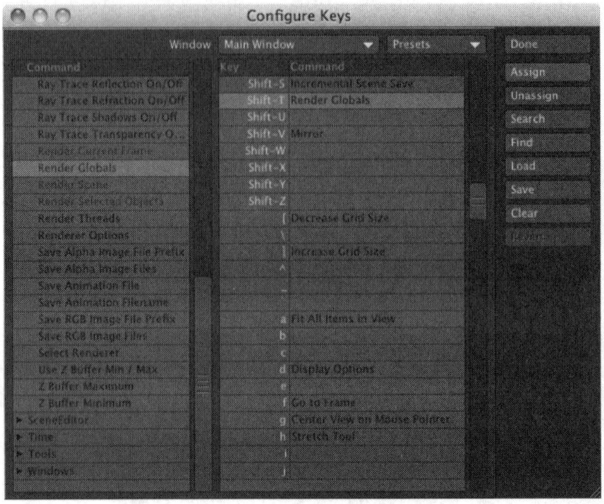

Figure 2.24 Assigning keyboard shortcuts is easy. Just pick a command, pick a key, and click Assign.

7. Assign more keys to your liking, saving each as you go, and click Done.

NOTE

Be sure to use the Save button within the Configure Keys panel to save your keyboard setups. Should you choose to select the default preset, your changes will be gone forever.

You can always go back to LightWave's default keyboard shortcuts by choosing the appropriate preset in the Configure Keys panel. Just click and select from the Presets drop-down at the top right of the panel. You can also set up keyboard shortcuts for the Graph Editor by choosing the option from the Window drop-down.

Another thing to remember is that you can apply these keyboard shortcuts in LightWave's Modeler in the same way. Just select the Edit drop-down in Modeler and repeat the preceding steps.

Edit Menu Layout

Changing keyboard equivalents is great, no question. But if you want to go one step better and really make LightWave your own, try editing the menus!

Exercise 2.4 Editing Menus

1. From the Edit drop-down list, select Edit Menu Layout or press Alt+F10 (Option+F10 on a Mac). You are greeted with a panel that looks very similar to the Configure Keys panel from the previous exercise (**Figure 2.25**).

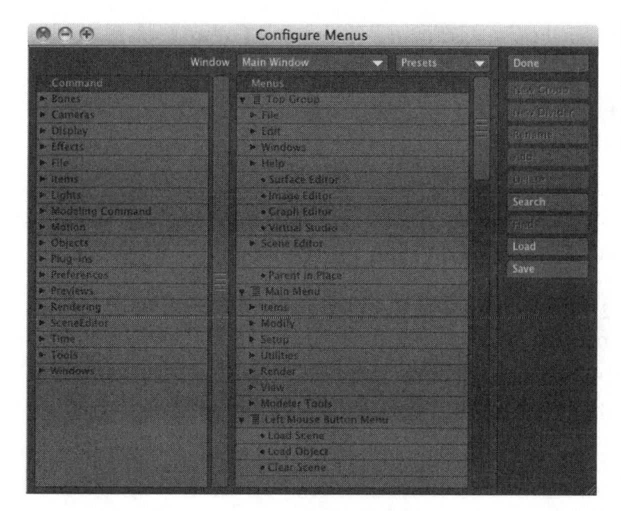

Figure 2.25 The Configure Menus panel, chosen from the Edit drop-down list's Edit Menu Layout command.

2. You'll use the panel the way you did when you edited keyboard shortcuts. Most tools are already out on the interface, but this panel is great for moving buttons, adding new menus, or creating buttons for your third-party plug-ins. Select the Parent in Place listing from the Menus column on the right, as shown in **Figure 2.26**. This determines the location of your new button; it will appear just beneath the Parent in Place button in the Top Group set of toolset buttons.

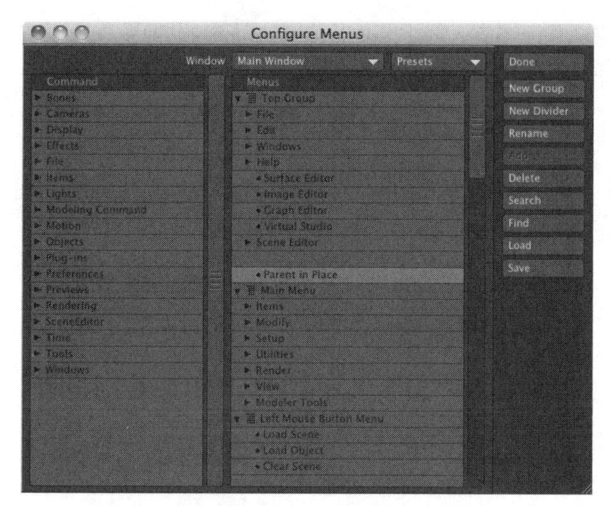

Figure 2.26 You can select and edit any existing menu in the Configure Menus panel.

3. To the left of the panel, select the Rendering category. Expand it, and select Render Current Frame. This option will be dimmed because it's already assigned to the F9 key and has a button, but you can still create another button for it. Once it's selected, click the Add button at the right of the panel and you'll see the command added to the LightWave interface. **Figure 2.27** shows the new Render Frame tool button, just below the Parent in Place tool.

Figure 2.27 Adding a custom interface button is as easy as the click of a button.

By adding the Render Current Frame command to the Top Group toolset, you've assigned it to every tab, so it will always be visible within Layout. If you'd created this button within the Main Menu listings, it would apply only to the selected tab. You can select various tools from the command window on the left and select your new group. Then, click the Add button. You've now added buttons for commands in your own custom group. Feel free to select your new group and choose the Rename button to customize it. You can also drag entries up or down in the Menus column to reorder buttons within toolsets.

You should know a few things about using these configuration panels. When a command is dimmed, that means it's already assigned. However, that does not mean that you can't assign it again. Also, if you ever dislike the menus you've created, you can always choose Default from the Presets drop-down menu in the panel. To follow along with the rest of the book, go ahead and choose the default presets.

Windows Menu

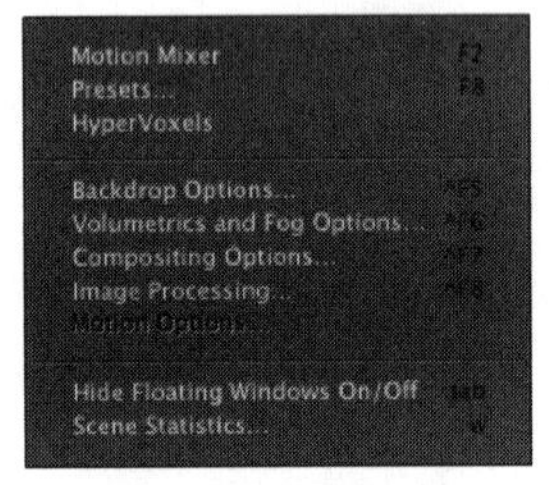

Figure 2.28 The Windows drop-down menu gives you access to many key panels throughout LightWave Layout.

Beneath the Edit menu drop-down list is the Windows menu (**Figure 2.28**). Here, you can access various windows or panels throughout LightWave. These windows are controls for Motion Options, including access to LightWave's nonlinear animation controller; Backdrop Options; Compositing Options; and the Image Processing tab.

You'll be employing all of these windows throughout this book's tutorials. Note the keyboard shortcuts to the right of the listings for quicker access.

Help Menu

LightWave's Help menu (**Figure 2.29**) can be found directly in Layout all the time. This is helpful (pun intended) for accessing LightWave's Web-based help system.

Additionally, you can enter your valid license key in this panel, as well as access LightWave's About section to check your version number, including information about your system's graphics card.

Figure 2.29 The LightWave Help menu gives you quick access to online help and licensing.

Surface Editor

Beneath the Help menu is the Surface Editor. Here, you can apply all of the texturing to your objects. Within the Surface Editor is the Node Editor, new in LightWave v10. We'll explore its powerful network of surface functions later in this book.

Figure 2.30 shows the Surface Editor open without any surfaces. Surfaces will appear once objects are placed into LightWave Layout.

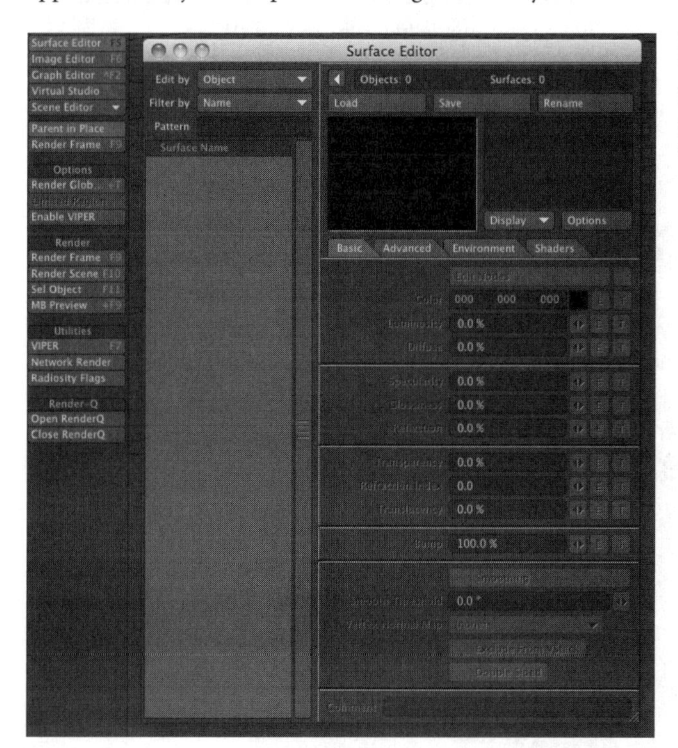

Figure 2.30
The Surface Editor in LightWave is your home for all surfacing.

The Surface Editor is easier to work with than you might think. Again, if you think about the process you can easily navigate through the panel. First, tell the Surface Editor which surface you want to work with. Where did you get that surface? You created it in Modeler with the Change Surface requester, accessed via the Surface button at the bottom of the Modeler interface. After choosing a surface, you work your way down the panel from color to luminosity to transparency and more.

Texturing can be a painstaking aspect of 3D animation and art, but as you'll see in the next chapter, applying basic surfaces and textures is easier than you might think.

NOTE

Throughout the Surface Editor and LightWave, you'll see little E and T buttons. These are important. The E allows you to create an Envelope for the given parameter. What's an envelope? It's a change in value over time. The E button opens the Graph Editor, which lets you animate that change. The T button allows you to apply textures—-spatial variations in value, distributed over a surface. Pressing a T button opens the Texture Editor. If you click an E or a T accidentally, simply hold the Shift key and click the button again to release. Undo does not work for this.

Image Editor

Below the Surface Editor button is the one for the Image Editor (**Figure 2.31**), which is used to load and manage image and movie files within LightWave.

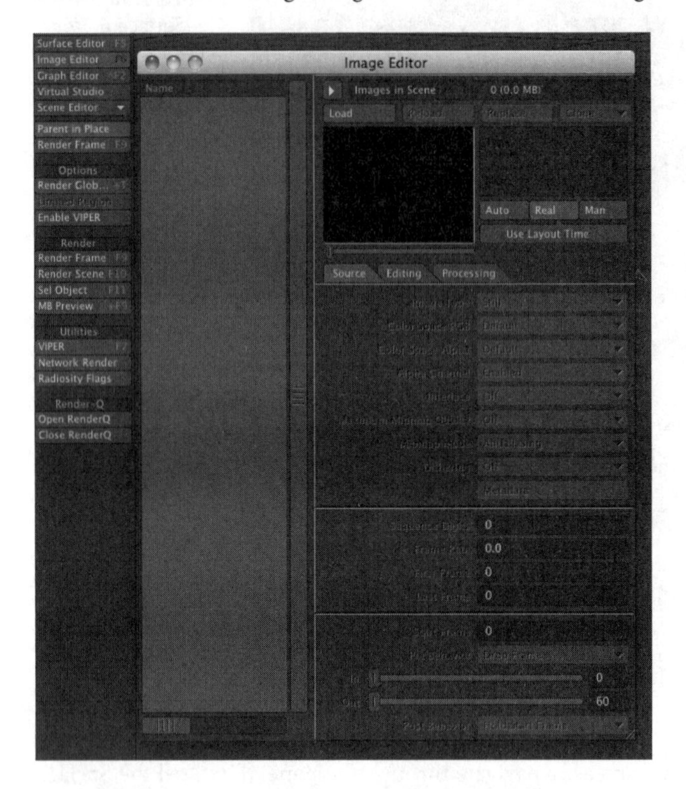

Figure 2.31 The Image Editor in LightWave 10 allows you to load images and movies, as well as edit them and apply effects to them.

You can do more than just load images in the Image Editor; you can edit them! The Processing tab allows you to apply simple enhancements to your images and movies. Additionally, you can apply textures to your images with the T buttons. You'll use the Image Editor in the next chapter to load reflection maps.

Graph Editor

Also part of the eight key menus in Layout is the LightWave Graph Editor (**Figure 2.32**). This panel gives you specific control over the motion channels of your Layout items. Each item, such as a light, camera, bone, or object, has nine motion channels. There is a specific channel of motion for the X, Y, and Z axes for Movement, Scale, and Motion on the H, P, and B (heading, pitch, and bank) for Rotation. You can control all of these channels in the Graph Editor.

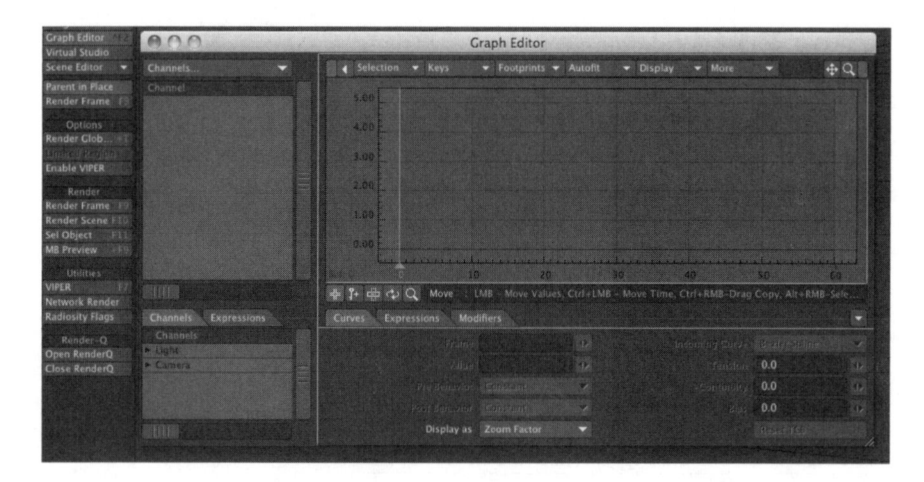

Figure 2.32 The LightWave Graph Editor offers specific control over motion channels for your Layout items.

In the Graph Editor, you can adjust the timing of specific channels. For example, say you've created a spinning top. You have rotated the top over 30 frames, but you need it to continue for 300. Rather than re-keyframing it, you can use the Graph Editor to "repeat" the past behavior of that specific motion channel. But you can do so much more, such as edit keyframes or create them. You can apply various motion plug-ins, such as a texture environment to the Y (up and down) motion channel to simulate an earthquake. As you work through tutorials in this book, you'll use the Graph Editor to perform these functions as well as learn how to navigate the panel.

Virtual Studio

LightWave 10's new Virtual Studio is an amazing addition to this feature-rich program (**Figure 2.33**). The VSE allows you to interactively work through your scenes using a virtual mouse, such as those from 3Dconnexion. You even can hook up a video camera (along with an optional intersperse device) to virtually walk through your 3D scene. Be sure to watch the Virtual Studio video on the book's DVD.

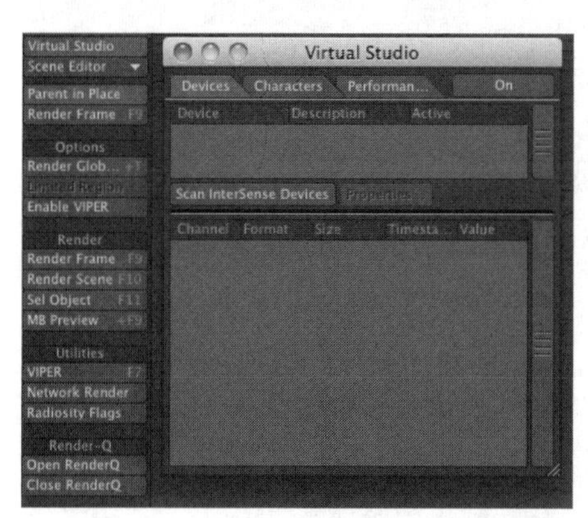

Figure 2.33 The Virtual Studio in LightWave 10 allows you to work interactively within a scene with a third-party device, such as a 3D mouse from 3Dconnexion. You can view a video on the book's DVD showing how the Virtual Studio works (3D_GarageVideos\CH2\CH2_VirtualStudio.mov).

Scene Editor

In the past, you accessed the Scene Editor by clicking a button. LightWave offers a drop-down menu for opening different versions of the Scene Editor—the newer version of the Scene Editor or the classic version you may know and love.

The LightWave Scene Editor is quite powerful, incorporating spreadsheet capabilities, a Dope Sheet, and overall editing of various scene parameters. It does not give you control over every aspect of LightWave, but it can significantly improve workflow by allowing control of multiple items at once. There are five main areas within the Scene Editor: Items, Surfaces, Channels, Property, and Dope Sheet. Exercise 2.5 guides you through a quick overview of the tool.

Exercise 2.5 Working with the Scene Editor

1. From the File drop-down menu, select Clear Scene.
2. From the Scene Editor drop-down menu, select Open. Because of the design of the Scene Editor, you can have multiple instances of the panel open at the same time; to do so, simply select New Instance. Figure 2.34 shows the Scene Editor panel.

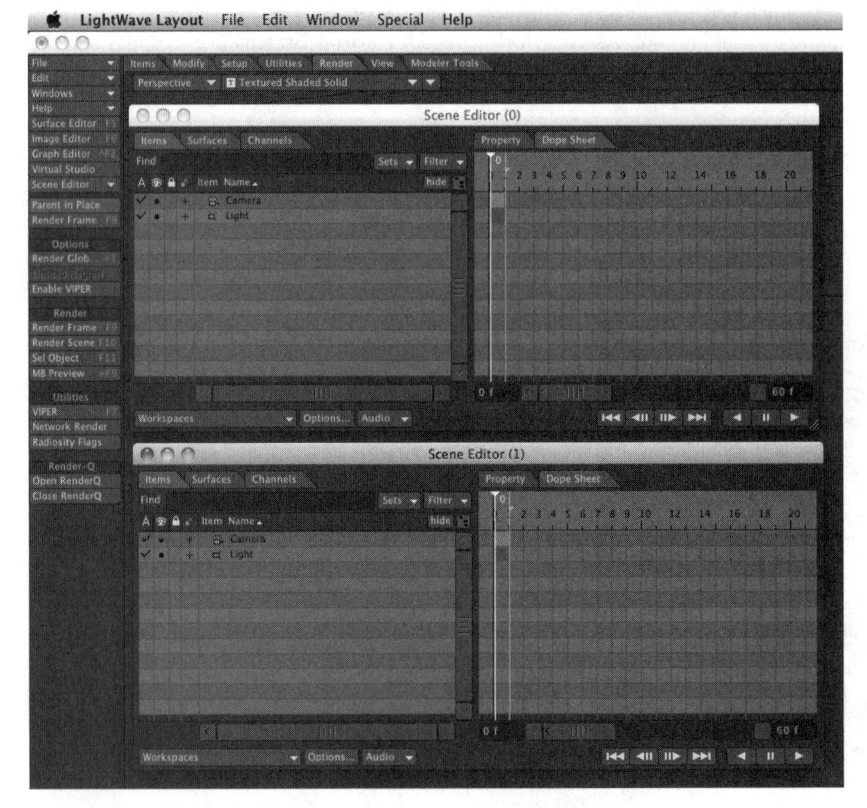

Figure 2.34 A new instance of the LightWave Scene Editor is created, and the panel appears. You can have multiple instances of the Scene Editor open as well.

3. On the left of the panel are the items in your scene, currently just one camera and one light. **Figure 2.35** shows that by clicking the small mark in front of an item, you can expand it to see its channels.

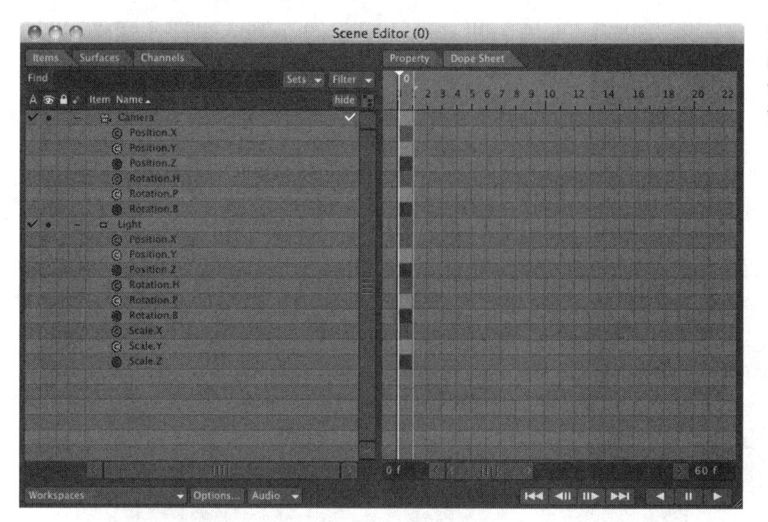

Figure 2.35 The left side of the Scene Editor contains the items you want to control.

4. At the top left of the Scene Editor are three tabs: Items, Surfaces, and Channels. Click the Surfaces tab and the list changes, giving you access to any surfaces in your scene.
5. After you've selected certain surfaces to work with, you can select them on the right and make changes. This is useful for quickly seeing and editing all of your surfaces outside of LightWave Surface Editor. **Figure 2.36** shows a simple scene loaded so you can see the surfaces.

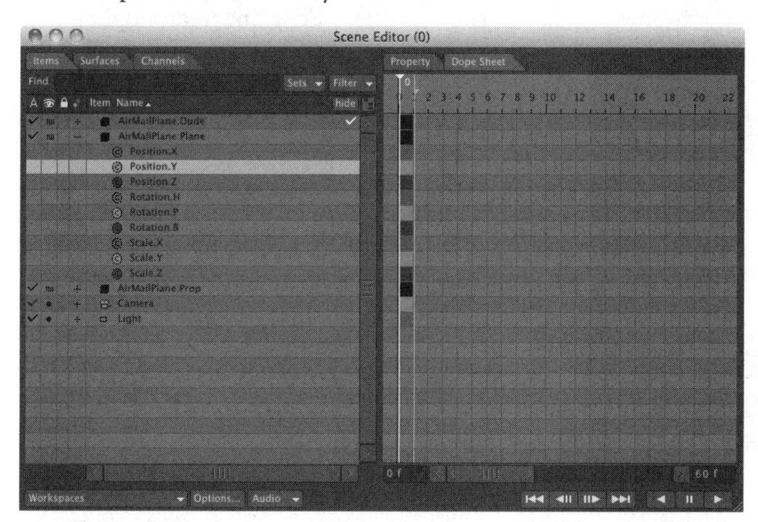

Figure 2.36 With a simple scene loaded, you can quickly see controls for enabling group editing of surfaces.

Dope Sheet

Within the Scene Editor is the Dope Sheet. You can find it in a tab on the right side of the panel. After you set up keyframes and complex motions, especially for characters, the Dope Sheet will be your best friend. The Dope Sheet allows you to see all of your keyframes for multiple items at once. You use it to set the times and numeric offsets, and even to erase keyframes. When you select specific keyframes in the Dope Sheet, you can change their settings values and edit them in the Graph Editor. **Figure 2.37** shows Dope Sheet contents for a character scene loaded from the LightWave content directory.

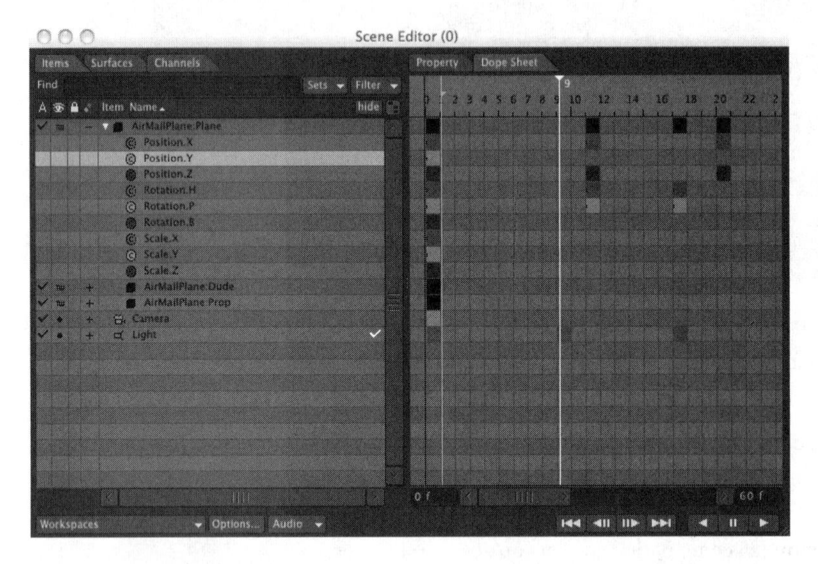

Figure 2.37 When a scene with keyframes is loaded, the Scene Editor's Dope Sheet gives you enhanced control over time, movement, and other parameters.

The Scene Editor is powerful, and to show its uses, we're going to dive right into it in some tutorials later in this book. This chapter's coverage should give you a quick overview of the power behind this cool new addition.

Parent in Place

The Parent in Place button is an on-off switch. When activated, it lets you parent (or unparent) items (objects, lights, etc.) to other items while preserving their keyframed positions and rotations. Parenting and unparenting with this option disabled can cause items to move in unwanted ways.

You'll access and use these key tabs and menus often, which you'll see as you work your way through various tutorials in this book. First, read on to learn about the tool categories of the six main menu tabs in Layout.

Items Tab

Across the top of the Layout interface are six key menu tabs you'll find yourself accessing often. The first is the Items tab (much like Modeler's Create menu tab), which is where you can find the simple item controls, as shown in **Figure 2.38**. Here, you find one-click load tools, which replace, add, and delete functions. In previous versions of LightWave, it took a number of clicks to access these tools, and after a while it became a bit annoying.

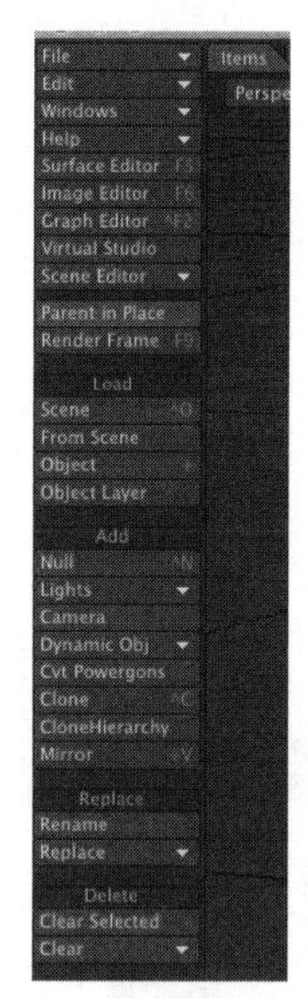

Figure 2.38 Layout's Items menu tab and its toolset, which allows you to load scenes and replace, add, and delete objects.

Load

The first category you see within the Items tab is labeled Load. Tools within this category let you load a scene, which is an entire project containing lights, motions, and objects. You can also load just an object into your scene with the Load Object button. Loading an object is the way to begin creating a scene. Loading new content overwrites whatever you have in Layout, so be sure to save before you load. The category also contains a button for the previously discussed Load Items from Scene command, found under the File drop-down menu, and the Object Layer button. This allows you to load a specific layer of an object. Let's say you create a complex living room, with 12 layers. Layer 5 contains that awesome flat panel plasma television you modeled (because your spouse won't let you buy it!). To load it, select Object Layer, choose the object, and then choose the layer in the requester that appears.

NOTE

When working in Layout, you'll often reload work you've already created. When you apply textures to your objects, you need to be sure to use the Save All Objects command from the File drop-down menu. This saves any textures or surface settings to your objects. Saving the scene alone does not save the surfaces on objects. Saving the scene saves only motion data, light data, and whatever elements you've added to the scene. Colors and textures are saved with objects. Therefore, when you reload your objects, the textures and surfaces you've applied will load as well.

Add

With the Add category of the Items tab, you can easily add items to your scene. These items include null objects—single points that do not show up in the render but help facilitate control throughout your animations—which are useful for parenting, grouping, and effects. Tools in the category also make it easy to add dynamic objects, such as particle emitters, wind, gravity, and collision items. Also within the Items tab's Add category are tools with which you can mirror and clone selected items at the click of a button.

Replace

Replacing objects is easier than ever before with the Replace category under the Items menu. Perhaps you need to replace a simple stand-in object with a high-polygon model for final rendering. Not a problem; just select the item and choose Replace. Also, tools here let you rename any item, including lights, cameras, and other objects.

Delete

The Delete category within the Items tab can be used to quickly clear a selected item or group of items all at once. Use this category for quick-click deletions.

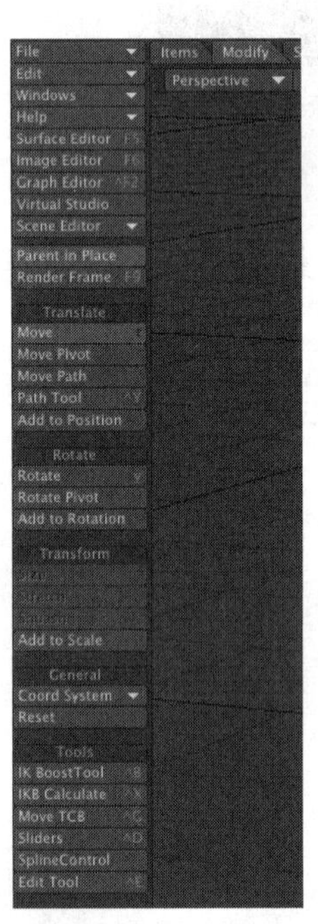

Figure 2.39 The Modify tab contains some of Layout's most frequently used tools.

Modify Tab

You might find that you visit the Modify tab often while working in Layout. Of course, you'll see the same familiar eight menus at the top, starting with the File menu. But if you look farther down as in **Figure 2.39**, you'll see five categories of tools.

Translate

The first category, Translate, houses several Move tools. These are all translate-type functions, as in Modeler. Use them for any item in Layout from bones to objects to lights. It's best to learn their keyboard equivalents too, such as the t key for Move.

Rotate

You'll find the Rotate tools just below the Translate tools. You can rotate any item and specify its pivot point. You'll learn about pivot points during the tutorials in this book.

Transform

Not to be confused with Translate, the Transform category offers various sizing tools, including Squash and Stretch.

General

The next tool category under the Modify tab is quite important to your workflow. Although the category title says General, the options within this category are anything but! They're more global than they are general. You'll find options for the coordinate system, which determines how an item in Layout is controlled in relationship to the 3D world that is Layout. Earlier in the chapter, we characterized LightWave Layout as a big, invisible sphere in which you work. When you change the coordinate system, you tell LightWave to adjust the relationship between the world's coordinates and the items.

Figure 2.40 shows the Coordinate System category selections. You'll also find the Reset button. This is handy for keeping track of your items. Let's say you move your camera around, and then at some point lose track of it. This can happen with any item, even a light. If you first select Rotate (also from the Modify tab) and then click Reset, the rotation resets to the 0,0,0 setting. The same applies for Move. Keep this in mind when you're ready to scrap what you've done and start again without redoing your entire scene.

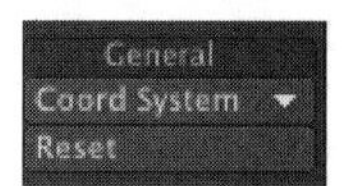

Figure 2.40 The Coordinate System tool category within the Modify tab enables key changes used in animation.

To better understand the coordinate system, look at **Figure 2.41**. This is the default LightWave layout, where the X-axis is left and right, the Y-axis is up and down, and the Z-axis is forward and back. But the coordinate system is set to Local.

Figure 2.41 LightWave Layout, with the coordinate system set to Local.

The object in the scene, the airplane, has default coordinates set to Parent in the Modify tab. That means the object's coordinate axes, represented by the arrow-shaped red, green, and blue *handles* you use to move it along each axis, align with those of the overall layout. The object's green Y-axis handle stands vertically; its red X-axis handle lies down to the side, for left and right; and its blue Z-axis handle points toward the back of the Layout interface. With a local coordinate system, the object will be able to move upon *its own* axis, rather than the world axis within the scene.

Now look at **Figure 2.42** (on the next page). in which the coordinate system is set to World. This makes the object's control handles align with the X, Y, and Z axes of the scene. The airplane object is rotated so that it's leaning upward within the scene; if you use its green Y-handle to move it upward, it will now rise at an angle relative to the overall scene, rather than straight up and down.

Figure 2.42 The object's transform handles are now changed because the coordinate system is set to Local.

You'll use this feature often when working with bones for character animation, as well as mechanical animations. Many times, when setting up hierarchies of parented objects you'll need to change between Parent, World, and Local. Parent and World coordinates are essentially the same thing, except that if your object is parented to another item, it takes on that item's coordinates.

As you work through the tutorials, you'll see how this all comes into play. But remember: As you're setting up your animations, if something does not rotate or move the way you want it to, look to the Coordinate System tool category in the Modify tab.

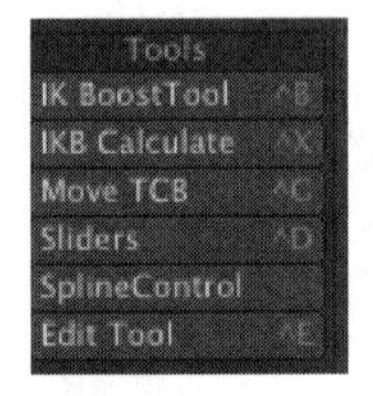

Figure 2.43 The Tools category is home to the IK Boost Tool, as well as Move TCB and others.

Tools

Finally, the Tools category found under the Modify tab is the location of some very powerful tools. As you can see in **Figure 2.43**, these tool names aren't as self-descriptive as the Translate or Rotate tools. These commands are some of LightWave's most important features.

IK Boost Tool

The "IK" in IK Boost Tool stands for inverse kinematics. It is a powerful system primarily used for, but not limited to, character animation. It was originally designed for dynamic simulations with bones and really had nothing to do with character work. However, over the years LightWave users have put it to work any way they can. But part of the IK Boost Tool is Bone Dynamics, which you can learn more about from the video on the book's DVD (3D_GarageVideos\CH2\CH2_BoneDynamics .mov). What is inverse kinematics? In the simplest explanation, it is a system for determining how characters move based on the positions of their limbs and joints, much like a marionette on strings: When you move the string attached to a puppet's hand, its arm follows, moving in a specific way based on the length of the forearm and upper arm and the position of its wrist, elbow, and shoulder joints. That's it! You'll be setting up your own IK in the upcoming character animation chapters.

The IK Boost Tool applies IK to a hierarchy of joined objects or bones and allows you to instantly set parameters, limits, and controls for every aspect of your hierarchy.

IKB Calculate

After you've set up inverse kinematics and bone options with the IK Boost Tool, you can simply click the IKB Calculate button to "capture" movements generated through inverse kinematics in the form of animation keyframes. This is used for bone dynamics especially. You'll see this in full action later in the dynamics chapters of this book.

Move TCB Tool

The Move TCB command is sort of a new incarnation of an old feature. When you create a motion path with an object, LightWave creates a curve. Tension, Continuity, and Bias (TCB) are settings you can adjust for each keyframe on a motion curve. A common application is to set a positive tension for the keyframe at the end of a motion, to make the moving object "ease into" place. If this has always been possible in LightWave, then what's the big deal about the Move TCB button? Up until now, you had to open the Graph Editor, select the specific channel(s) to edit, and apply the appropriate T, C, or B settings. Now, you can use the Move TCB tool directly in Layout. You can see your settings down at the bottom left of the Layout interface in the Info area. All you need to do is press Control+G for the selected item to activate, click and drag in the Layout to set Tension, hold Control and drag to set Continuity, and then right-click for Bias.

Sliders

The Sliders tool lets you attach slider controls to items in your scene for specific control over their behaviors. This is helpful during character animation or precise movements where you want an item to move between two specific ranges. A slider allows you to set minimum and maximum values for a specific action or behavior. Then as you work out the details of your animation, you can simply drag the slider to adjust the attribute within that range. This works on move, rotate, size, and so on.

Spline Control

Spline Control is a tool that, when active, allows you to see a visible and controllable motion path for a specific item. Select the item and turn on Spline Control, and you can click and drag the control handles that appear in Layout to change the shape of the object's motion path.

Edit Tool

Click this little bugger and you'll find that it seems to disable any movements in Layout. But wait! It is actually a very cool little tool. Let's say you added a particle emitter to Layout. Click the Edit Tool, and your particles will be identified numerically. You can then select any one of those particles and move it or delete it. This is great for those annoying particles that won't behave or that just don't belong. Get rid of them.

Setup Tab

The Setup tab in Layout is your pit stop for all things skeletal—that is, this is where you find controls for bones. **Figure 2.44** shows the menu with its tools.

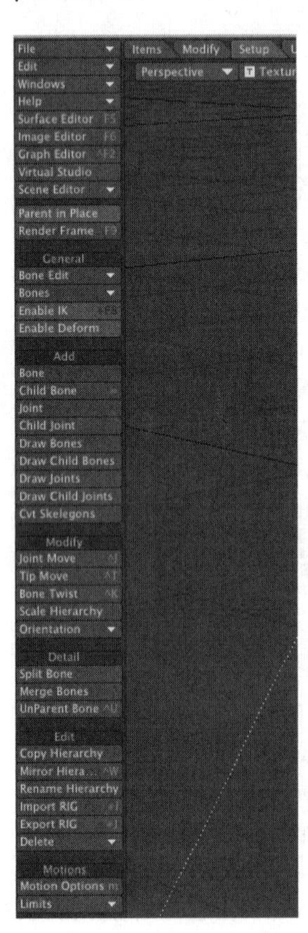

Figure 2.44 The Setup tab in Layout is where you find all the tools needed to work with bones (LightWave's deformation tools) and the Layout equivalent of Skelegons.

General

Yes, there is another General category—this time it's under the Setup tab, and we're talking about deformation tools. The General category offers Bone Edit functions and global settings for activating (or deactivating) bones and inverse kinematics.

Add

The Add category in the Items tab was all about objects, but in the Setup tab, the Add tools concern all things bones. Tools in this category can be used to add a bone, add a child bone, draw bones in Layout, and draw child bones. But another important tool is labeled Cvt Skelegons. This is the Convert Skelegons command that you'll use to change Skelegons (created in Modeler) into bones for use in Layout. Without this, Skelegons in Modeler are useless.

NOTE

Bones are deformation tools, meaning they deform your objects—not only animated characters but also such items as a curtain blowing in the wind, or the pages of a book curling. Throughout the character animation chapter, you'll find yourself guided to these tools for adding and editing bones, splitting them, and much more. In Chapter 1, "LightWave Modeler," we introduced Skelegons. When you create Skelegons in Modeler for an object, they are converted to bones in Layout. You control, edit, and adjust those bones in the Setup tab.

Modify

Once you've added bones to your scene, at some point you'll need to modify them. The Modify tool category provides all that's necessary to adjust your bones. These powerful tools let you move bones' joints and tips, and twist and scale bones. They are handy for properly setting up a perfect character rig.

Detail

Modifications are great, but sometimes when working with bones you need to control more specific details. The Detail tab offers tools to split bones, and not just once. You can take one bone and cut it into four without destroying the hierarchy of your setup. This is useful when you've put a bone into a foot, for example, and then realize you need another one so the foot can bend! You'll also find Bone Fuse, which allows you to put two split bones back together, just in case you didn't want to split them after all. And you can use the UnParent Bone tool here to remove a bone from its hierarchy.

Edit

Again, all of the tools within the Setup tab relate to bones. Use tools in the Edit category to copy hierarchies, rename them, save them, and load them.

Motions

One small category within the Setup tab relates to bones but also, potentially, to every other item in your scene. You can use the Motion Options tool in the Motions category to access a variety of motion tools and plug-ins. This can be for bones, lights, cameras, objects, or any effect item in your scene. Additionally, you can record minimum and maximum joint angles with the Limits drop-down selection.

Utilities Tab

Whenever you need to add plug-ins, edit them, or work with LightWave's LScript scripting language, you can click over to the Utilities tab. **Figure 2.45** (on the next page) shows the menu tab and its tools.

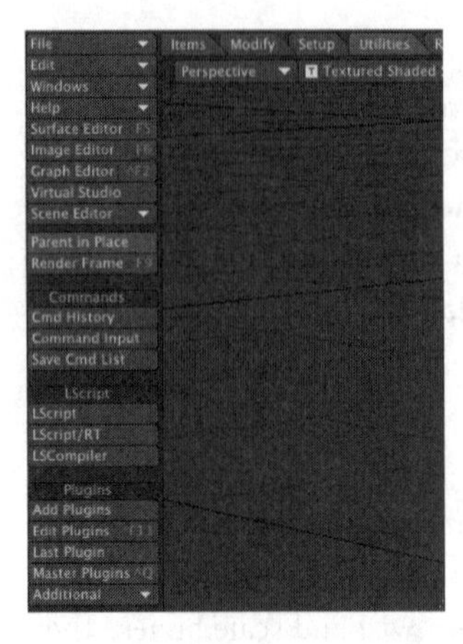

Figure 2.45 The Utilities tab is home to command tools, LScript programming tools, and plug-in tools.

Commands

The Commands category offers controls for looking up your command history or entering specific commands for LightWave to follow. Additionally, if you want to keep track of commands you've used, use the Save Cmd List option. Refer to this for similar projects.

LScript

The LScript category is home to LightWave's custom programming language. Here, you can load preexisting LScripts, use the LScript compiler to build your own, and use LScript/RT to preview how they'll run. Note that the LightWave v10 documentation incorrectly describes a fourth tool in this category, LScript Commander. This powerful tool is actually found in the Additional drop-down of the Plugins category (described below), under the name LS Commander. It lets you create your own plug-in that loads an object, saves it, and then saves the scene, all in one button!

Plugins

The Plugins category is where you find the tools to add individual plug-ins, load multiple plug-ins with the Edit Plugins tool, and quickly find the last-used plug-in. Within this category is the Master Plugins panel, which is where you can load Master class plug-ins, such as LScript Commander. You also see the Additional list, where you can find additional plug-ins and any third-party plug-ins you might have added.

Render Tab

Rendering is the process by which LightWave generates the final output of a scene, using all of the lighting, surfaces, textures, animations, and environmental effects (wind, gravity, and so on) that you create in Layout. If a scene is animated, of course, the process can yield anywhere from hundreds to millions of rendered frames.

In earlier versions of LightWave, rendering tools were sort of hidden—kind of unusual for something so critical to the 3D animation process. If you are a veteran user of LightWave, you'll love the Render menu tab (**Figure 2.46**). When it's time to render, LightWave v10 puts the tools you need right in front of you.

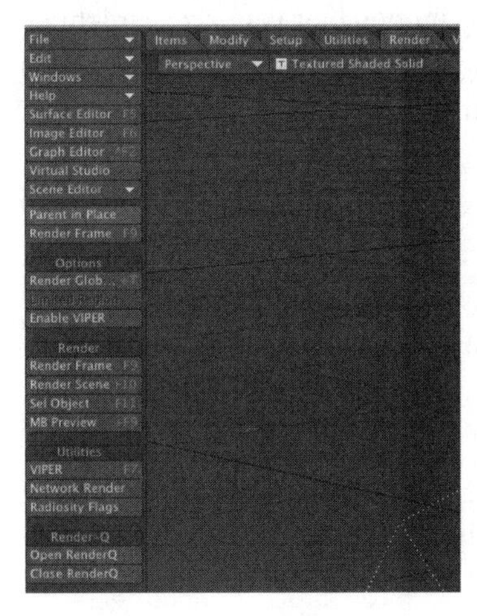

Figure 2.46 The Render tab encompasses all of your necessary render tools. Without these, no final outputs!

Options

The Options tool category houses the Render Globals menu button, where you'll find tools for setting up all of your animation characteristics. Use this panel to set camera resolution for single-frame renders, arbitrary renders, and full-frame animations. You can also set filtering methods, global illumination, and more, all from this one panel (**Figure 2.47**). You'll work through this panel and see how to render locally and over a network in Chapter 12, "Rendering Animations." This category also is where you'll find the Enable VIPER button. This is sort of an on/off switch for VIPER, LightWave's virtual preview render system, which we'll discuss shortly.

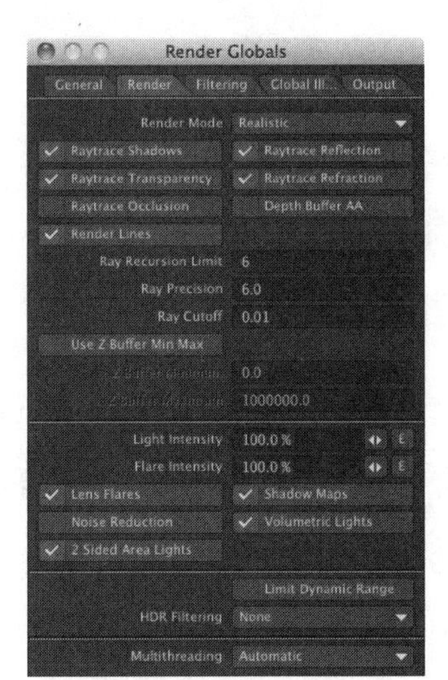

Figure 2.47 The Render Globals panel, accessible from the Render tab's Options tools.

Render

The presence of a Render tool category within the Render tab might seem confusing—or at least redundant—but it all makes sense: The Render tools let you click a button to render a single frame, scene, or selected object, or to preview a motion blur right in Layout. Click MB Preview to see any motion blur your scene might be using. You can also see that there is a Render Frame button. This is why the tool was dimmed earlier in the chapter when you edited menus.

Utilities

NOTE

It should be noted that VIPER is different from VPR. While the new VPR allows full-scene previews directly in Layout, VIPER is quite helpful for previewing Hypervoxels for particle dust, explosions, and other surfacing properties.

The Utilities category of the Render tab is where you find the tools for additional render options. First is VIPER, short for Virtual Interactive Preview Renderer. You can use VIPER to instantly see changes to surfaces, particles, and volumetrics, without performing a formal render. This saves time! You'll use VIPER in the next chapter's tutorials. Another Utilities tool, Network Render, enables you to tie other computers on your network into your rendering. This is especially valuable because it doesn't require copies of LightWave to be installed on the other computers that help yours with rendering.

View Tab

The next menu tab across the top of Layout is the View tab. Here, you can find the necessary tools to control your Layout viewports (**Figure 2.48**).

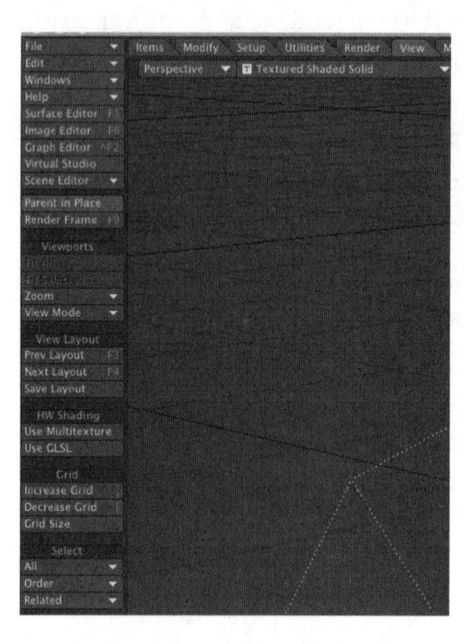

Figure 2.48 The View tab and its associated tools manage Layout's viewports.

Viewports

The sets of tools available in this menu give you additional control when working in Layout. Earlier in this chapter, we discussed the viewports, and you saw how to set up multiple viewports. The Viewports category in the View tab gives access to buttons that control those views. You can also use the Fit All and Fit Selected commands to quickly bring your items to view. Note, however, that these tools only work in certain viewports, such as the Top or Side views.

View Layout

The View Layout tools let you jump between preset layout views, such as single, quad, and so on. If you set up your own view and perhaps click and drag the center of the windows to adjust, you can save that particular layout with the Save Layout button.

HW Shading

The HW Shading, or hardware shading, option enables computers with certain video cards to display multiple textures within Layout. It also enables supported cards to use a high-level shading option known as GLSL, or Open GL Shading Language. Not all video cards support these options, so check the specifications for your particular video card before applying these.

Grid

Also within the View menu is the Grid Size control in the Grid category. If you recognize that LightWave is a big 3D universe that you work within, it should be easy to understand that the Grid Size is the default unit of measurement you work with. In Layout (and Modeler, too), Grid Size is always displayed in the lower-left corner of the LightWave workspace. By default, this measurement is 1 meter in size, as you can see in **Figure 2.49**.

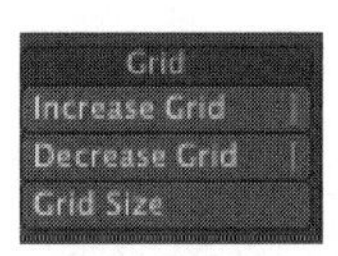

Figure 2.49 LightWave Layout's default unit of measurement, Grid Size, is 1 meter. The Grid Size can be increased or decreased as needed

This means that every grid square you see in Layout, from any view, is 1 meter in size. Count three squares, and that's 3 meters, and so on. The reason you can increase and decrease the Grid Size in the View menu is because not all objects are scaled equally. For example, if you load in a Mars rover spacecraft, your unit of measurement automatically adjusts to the fit the size of the craft. You should be able to move and rotate the object just fine. If you load in the planet Mars, and it is built to scale, the Layout Grid Size might jump to 5 kilometers and your rover will essentially disappear! This is because LightWave's grid adjusts itself to fit this large object. If you find your rover and move it, it will shoot off the screen with the slightest mouse movement. If this happens, you need to decrease the grid size.

NOTE

Adjusting the grid appears to change the size of the camera and lights, but it really doesn't. It only changes the relationship of those items to LightWave's world.

Select

The last category in the View tab contains the Select tools. Here, you can choose from various ways to select objects, lights, and cameras. You can choose to select by name or search by name. You can also select related parent or child items here, in addition to selecting in order, from one item to the next. A quicker way to select, however, is to click the item in Layout and then press the up or down arrow key on your keyboard to select the previous or next item, respectively.

Modeler Tools Tab

The last tab at the top of LightWave v10 Layout is Modeler Tools (**Figure 2.50**). This provides some basic modeling tools within Layout. Nowhere near as powerful as the tools in Modeler, these are mostly useful for setting up simple objects as placeholders. You might not use this area very much, but it can come in handy on occasion when you need a quick primitive object for a scene.

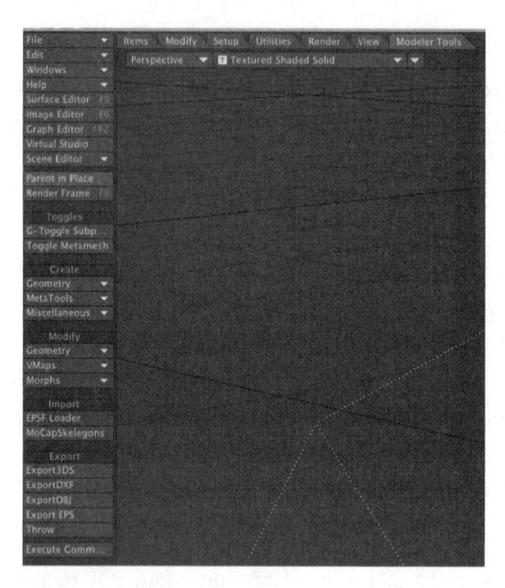

Figure 2.50 The Modeler Tools tab makes basic modeling possible within Layout.

Toggles

Tools in the Toggles category are really switches that turn on and turn off useful functions that were available only in Modeler in previous versions of LightWave. G-Toggle Subpatch globally activates and deactivates subpatch objects you create in Modeler. You might turn subpatches on in Layout when fine-tuning surface attributes, and then turn them off to speed up animation previews. Metamesh Toggle works the same way on objects built using Modeler's Metamesh tool; you can turn this feature on and off here as well, allowing you to work with simpler objects.

Create

In this category, you can create simple geometric shapes, including wedges, toroids (doughnuts), and other primitives. But in order to do so, you need to first create a null object. Do this from the Items tab, under the Add category.

Modify

In this area, you can modify the geometry you've created, with tools such as Squash and Stretch. You can also work with VMaps (vertex maps) that you might have set up in Modeler, or use the Apply, Rotate, and Scale Morph commands.

Import

In this section you have tools that allow you to import EPS and motion capture files.

Export

Animators often work with more than one program, and LightWave has set up tools that allow you to save 3DSs, OBJs, and other popular formats for use in other applications.

Preferences

LightWave, like many programs, has its own set of preferences. However, because LightWave is not native to particular operating systems and utilizes its own custom interface, accessing these options is not as easy as finding an Edit button at top of your computer screen. Instead, press **d** or **o**. The d key calls up Display Options, as shown in **Figure 2.51**.

NOTE

The updated Preferences panel is quite robust. To learn more about this updated LightWave v10 panel, be sure to view the Preferences movie on the book's DVD (3D_GarageVideos\CH2\CH2_Preferences.mov).

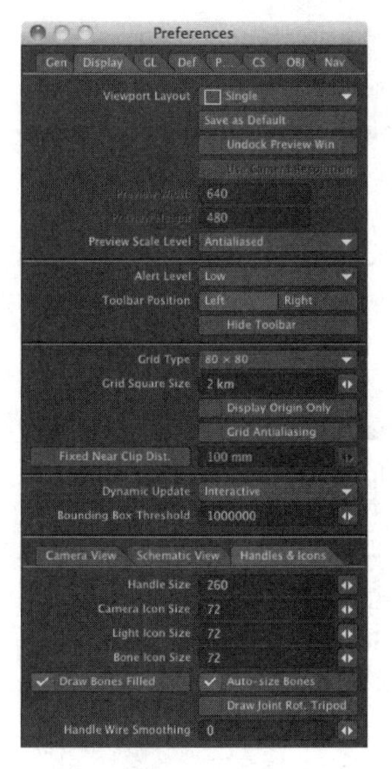

Figure 2.51 Open LightWave's Preferences panel by pressing the d or o key. Here, you can see the Display Options tab, which opens when you press d.

If you had pressed **o**, the General Options tab would have appeared, but both panels are embedded in the Preferences panel. Within the Display Options tab, you have specific control over settings that pertain to what you see in Layout. These are options concerning grid size, overlay colors, and many OpenGL options. The OpenGL, or Graphics Library, is the color shaded and textured views you see in Layout. Your video card determines how many OpenGL options you can support, but these days even the simplest gaming cards work tremendously with LightWave. You can tell LightWave to turn on many OpenGL options concerning lens flares, textures, reflections, and even transparency. The new Preferences panel in LightWave v10 is extensive, but there are a few key areas you can read about here. For the rest, check out the video on the book's DVD.

Bounding Box Threshold

An important value in the Display Options tab is Bounding Box Threshold. You might have installed LightWave and hopped right into Modeler. The model you created ended up being made up of 5000 points and 5200 polygons. When you send your object to Layout for animating, you see the object, but as soon as you move it, it turns into a wireframe box. What's going on? This is LightWave's way of saving system resources. If your object is made up of too many points and polygons, it can significantly slow down your system when you try to move or rotate it. This is because LightWave needs to redraw the object in real time on every frame. If it can't keep up, it stalls.

The Bounding Box Threshold option allows you to set a limit on when LightWave has enough, so to speak. A basic 64 MB video card can have a bounding box threshold set to about 40,000. In other words, if your object is 35,000 polygons, it stays drawn all the time. If it's more than 40,000 polygons, it turns into a bounding box upon any movement. Set this one time, and you can leave it. Note that this does not affect rendering in any way.

General Options

If you press **o** for General Options, you'll jump to a tab with variables that are very important to your working environment, as they help you select color picker style, dialog menu types, control for auto key creation and more (**Figure 2.52**). You can use these settings to change LightWave's Input Device from a mouse to a tablet, and to set how your frame slider is viewed. By default, the LightWave timeline shows frames, but you can change this to show SMPTE (Society of Motion Picture and Television Engineers) timecode units, film timecode, or time in seconds. The most common setting is frames, as in frames per second.

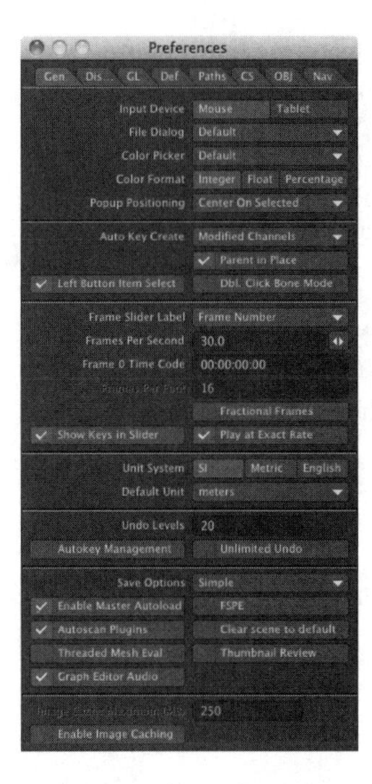

Figure 2.52 The General Options tab within the Preferences panel contains key settings for LightWave Layout.

LightWave also offers its own custom color picker, which you can turn on in this panel. When picking colors for backgrounds or surfaces, for example, this causes LightWave to calls up its own custom color picker rather than the one built into your Windows or Mac system software.

Finally, as mentioned previously, Layout offers multiple undo levels, which can be accessed in this category. Be careful with this. You can't undo everything; primarily, this command is useful for undoing keyframe motions. Let's say you add a few keyframes to your animation and decide you don't like them. Press Control+Z a few times to undo. Again, if you accidentally click Remove Texture in the Surface Editor rather than Use Texture, there is no undo for that! So be cautious.

The Next Step

This chapter has taken you on a brief overview of Layout and how it's organized. You have seen how the menus are arranged and how they work, and you took a tour of the tools available to you.

There is more to learn, and it's about to get more exciting. Soon, you'll be working completely on tutorials, learning firsthand the tools and how they work. What's more, you'll learn why you're instructed to do what you're doing. Subsequent chapters guide you through the basics of lighting, textures, and motions. Then, you'll take this knowledge into longer, full-blown projects.

Too often, books just click you through, leaving the figuring out up to you. *Inside LightWave v10*'s tutorials are designed to ramp you up from beginner to intermediate to advanced tutorials, offering clear explanations along the way.

We have a big journey ahead of us, so take a break, get some caffeine, and get ready to rumble and learn all about creating textures in Chapter 3.

Chapter 3

Texture Creation

In the beginning, somewhere back in the 1980s, a rotating 3D cube was an amazing thing to see. Today, the realism of 3D animation can be very eye-catching, but a good part of this realism comes from two key factors: lighting and surfacing. Gone are the days of rendering objects with simple colors. Today you need to add images, textures, grunge, dirt, shine, reflection, and more to your 3D models to make them look the best they can. In your 3D career, professional or otherwise, you'll find that achieving this realism is a never-ending battle. Note, however, that this struggle is a blessing in disguise. Your mission, should you choose to accept it, is to continually better your work. Once you create a fantastic piece of 3D art, it's time to make a better one! Without forgetting that lighting setups play a big role in determining the realism of your scenes (we'll get to that in Chapter 4), this chapter will introduce you to LightWave's texturing capabilities. This chapter helps you take the next step with LightWave by introducing you to the powerful Texture Editor and teaching you how to navigate and use its interface. You'll learn about these topics:

- Using the Surface Editor
- Organizing surfaces
- Setting up surfaces
- Understanding the Node Editor

NOTE

The word *surface* is used three different but related ways in this chapter: to denote a specific group of polygons on the skin of a 3D object; to describe a collection of attributes (color, reflectivity, bumpiness, and so on) applied to a region to determine its appearance and behavior in a 3D scene; and as a verb ("to surface"), meaning the process of applying those attributes to polygon regions.

Perhaps one of the best things about LightWave's Surface Editor is that it puts everything you need to set up simple-to-complex surfaces in one location. The Surface Editor gives you control over everything you need to create a blue ball, an old man, or a modern city. If you're familiar with the Surface Editor in previous versions of LightWave, you'll find the updated Surface Editor works in much the same way but is definitely improved. Most notably, LightWave v10 brings excellent texturing to the table with both the Surface Editor and the Node Editor. **Figure 3.1** shows the Surface Editor interface at startup, with the Node Editor open.

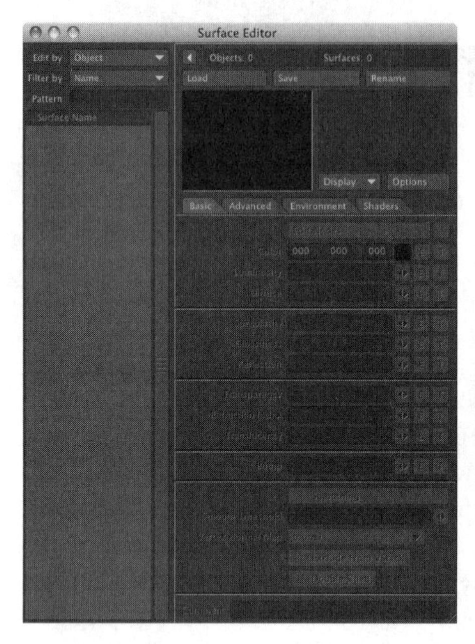

Figure 3.1 LightWave's Surface Editor at startup.

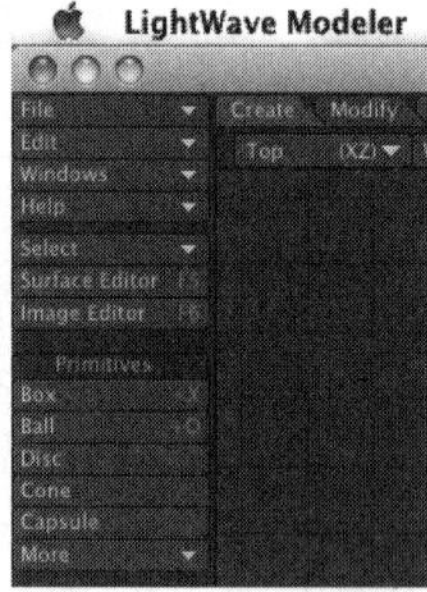

Figure 3.2 LightWave's Surface Editor can always be accessed at the top left in Modeler.

NOTE

Remember that LightWave enables you to completely customize the user interfaces of both Modeler and Layout. However, you should be working with the LightWave default Configure Keys (Alt+F9) and Menu Layout (Alt+F10) settings throughout this book.

You'll get a brief introduction to the Node Editor in this chapter. It's important to understand how basic texturing works, and the Surface Editor is the place to start. In early versions of LightWave, the process of setting up a model's surfaces began during construction, in Modeler. However, you could make only basic surface changes in Modeler—essentially, you could select a group of polygons and name them as a surface. Defining and applying surface attributes such as color and shininess, or adding more complex textures, required moving over to Layout. In LightWave v10, the Surface Editor is accessible in both Modeler and Layout, so you can set up surfaces in either part of the program. This chapter applies to both Modeler and Layout, except for the section on the Node Editor, which is available only within Layout. And while you can access and apply node-based surfacing in Modeler, you can't render, so you won't have much of an idea of what your surface will look like. The Surface Editor button is sixth from the top in Modeler (**Figure 3.2**) and fifth from the top in Layout (**Figure 3.3**). The F5 key also opens the Surface Editor in both Modeler and Layout.

NOTE

Using the Surface Editor in Modeler does not give you access to LightWave's VIPER or to the new VPR discussed in detail later in this chapter. For major surfacing projects, you'll use the Surface Editor in Layout and take advantage of VIPER and/or VPR. VIPER requires rendered data to work, and you can only render in Layout. VPR uses information stored in LightWave's internal buffers for instant feedback. VPR is magic. You'll see.

Figure 3.3 LightWave's Surface Editor is the same in Layout, and it's always accessed at the top left of the interface.

Using the Surface Editor

As mentioned earlier, all of your surfacing needs can be accomplished within the Surface Editor, so you should be familiar with its features. This section guides you through its uses and helps you make sense of the panel. It's much easier than you might think! As with any task, you start by getting organized.

Organizing Surfaces

Good management of your 3D work, from models to keyframes to surfaces, will help you become a better artist. The Surface Editor makes it easy for you to manage your surfaces. **Figure 3.4** shows the Surface Editor as it appears when an object with multiple surfaces is loaded into Layout.

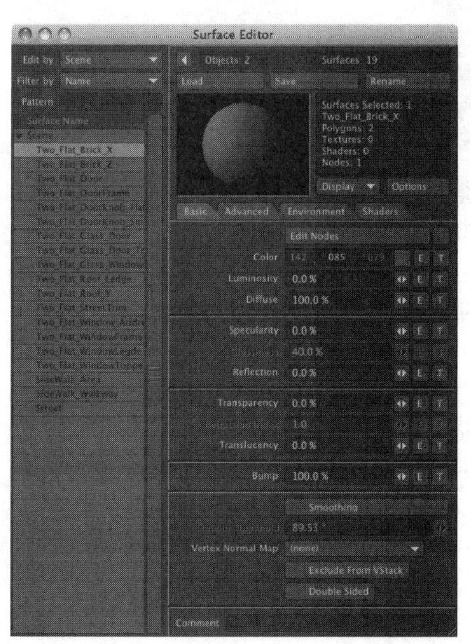

Figure 3.4 The Surface Editor enables you to manage your surfaces easily on an object or scene basis. You also can use filters to organize your surfaces by name.

When you open the Surface Editor after a scene has been loaded, the scene's surfaces are listed in the Surface Name list, as you can see in Figure 3.4. The Surface Name list contains information on every surface in the scene; by default it groups surfaces by object. Clicking the small triangle next to an object's name reveals a list of all the surfaces associated with that object. Note that by default, if an object is selected in Layout when you open the Surface Editor, its first surface will be opened in the Surface Editor. **Figure 3.5** shows the same scene as Figure 3.4, but with a surface of the first object selected. Note that this setup is using the Edit By Object selection from the top left of the Surface Editor, which lists the surfaces with their appropriate objects.

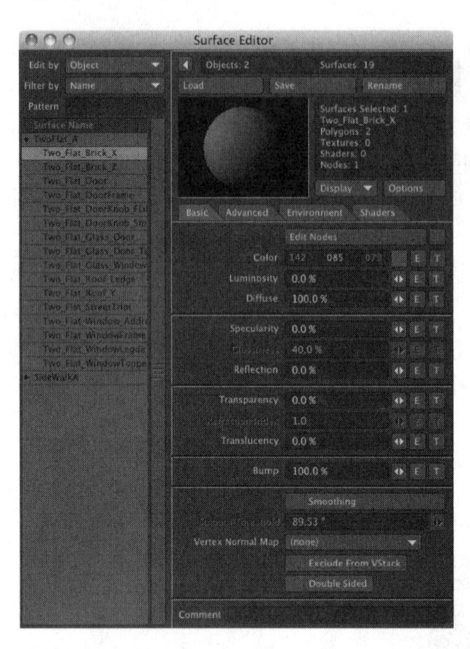

Figure 3.5 Surfaces are grouped with their respective objects if Edit By Object is selected.

When you click the small white triangle next to a surface name in the surface list, your surface settings, such as color, diffusion, or texture maps, won't be available until you click a surface name. You must select one of the surfaces in the list before you can begin to work with it. When you select a surface, you see the surface properties change. Working with a hierarchy like this is extremely productive and enables you to quickly access any surface in your scene.

To save screen space, LightWave's Surface Editor allows you to collapse the Surface Name list by clicking the button marked with a right-pointing triangle above the Load button at the top of the panel. **Figure 3.6** shows the Surface Editor with the collapsed Surface Name list. Click the button again (it now points left) to expand the list, or choose a surface using the Scene drop-down under Surface Name at the top of the panel, as in **Figure 3.7**.

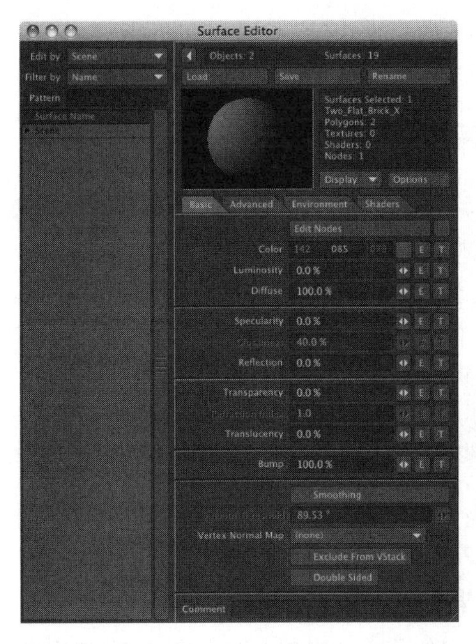

Figure 3.6 You click the small triangle at the top of the Surface Editor panel to collapse the Surface Name list.

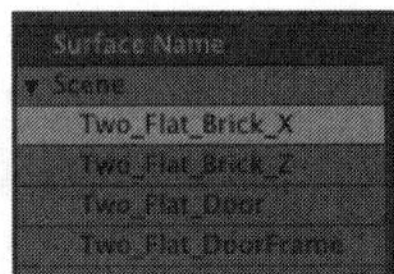

Figure 3.7 You select surface names in a collapsed view by using the Scene drop-down list under Surface Name.

Selecting Existing Surfaces

Take control of your surfaces, and you'll have a better time navigating through the Surface Editor panel. You have three modes to assist you in quickly selecting the surface or surfaces you want:

- Edit By
- Filter By
- Pattern

The Edit By drop-down, found at the top-left corner of the Surface Editor panel, has two options: Object and Scene. Here, you tell the Surface Editor to control your surfaces within just that, an object or the scene. For example, let's say you have 20 buildings in a fantastic-looking skyscraper scene, and eight of those buildings have the same surface on their faces. Using Edit By Object, adjusting that surface's characteristics would mean applying surface settings eight times; with Edit By Scene, changes to surface settings apply globally to all objects that contain that surface.

You should always be aware of the Edit By mode when you're tweaking surfaces. (LightWave remembers the Edit By setting when it saves models and scenes, so check each time you start the program to make sure you're in the mode you think you're in.) Applying and saving scene-wide changes when you mean to change only one object can have grim consequences. To avoid this, always make each surface name unique, and name your surfaces accordingly when building objects. For example, let's say you created a slick interior for an architectural render. In it, there are lots of white marble surfaces. (Why? Who knows, but that's what the client wanted.) To properly isolate and organize those surfaces, you should name the different surfaces so they are unique to the geometry but familiar to you. You could choose something like "interior_marble_stairs," then "interior_marble_columns," and so on. This way, there is no confusion when using the Surface Editor. In addition, creating and naming surfaces properly in Modeler makes surfacing easier, and you end up using the Edit By feature as an organizational tool, not as a search engine.

NOTE

As a reminder, any surface settings you apply to objects are saved with those objects. Remember to select Save All Objects as well as Save Scene. Even though Layout will ask you to save all objects when you quit, it's a good idea to do it on your own. Objects retain surfaces, image maps, color, and so on. Scenes retain motion, items, lighting, and so on. Both objects and scenes should always be saved before you render. This is a good habit to get into!

At the top-left corner of the Surface Editor panel, you'll see a Filter By listing. Here, you can choose to sort your surface list by Name, Texture, Shader, or Preview. Most often, you'll select your surfaces by using the Name filter. However, say you have 100 surfaces, and out of those 100, only two have texture maps. Instead of sifting through a long list of surfaces, you can quickly select Filter By and choose Texture from the drop-down list. This displays only the surfaces that have textures applied. You can select and display surfaces that use a Shader, or you can use Preview. Preview is useful when working with VIPER or VPR mode because it lists only the surfaces visible in the render buffer image.

Just beneath the Filter By setting, you have a field available for typing in a pattern name. The Pattern field enables you to limit your surface list by a specific name, and it works in conjunction with Filter By. Think of this as an "include" filter. Only surface names that "include" the pattern will show up in the Surface Name list. For example, suppose you created a scene with 200 different surfaces, and six of their names include "carpet." Type **carp** into the Pattern field and your list will narrow to surfaces whose names contain that letter sequence—the six carpet surfaces, and possibly others related to carports, escarpments, carp (the fish), and so on. Continue typing the full word **carpet** and your list will probably narrow to just the six surfaces you seek. Handy feature, isn't it? Just remember that if you don't see your surface names, check to see whether you've left a word or phrase in the filter area.

NOTE

You won't have access to the Edit By, Filter By, and Pattern sorting commands with a collapsed Surface Name list. Expand the list to access these controls.

Working with Surfaces

After you decide which surface to work with and select it from the Surface Name list, LightWave provides you with four commands at the top of the Surface Editor panel that are fairly common to software programs: Load, Save, Rename, and Display.

The first command, Load, does what its name implies. It loads surfaces. You can use it to load a premade surface for modification or application to a new surface.

The second command, Save, tells the Surface Editor to save a file with all the settings you've specified. This includes all color settings, texture maps, image maps, and so on. The ability to save surfaces lets you build an archive of useful surfaces you can use again and again.

NOTE

Storing surfaces in LightWave's Preset Shelf, which organizes samples in a visual browser, is often more useful than using the Surface Editor Save command. We discuss the Preset Shelf in detail later in this chapter.

With the third command, Rename, you can rename any of your surfaces—a habit you should get into from the start in your work with 3D surfaces. If you apply preset surface settings called "rusty_steel" to part of a Jeep model, for instance, you might rename that surface "jeep_rusty_steel" to keep things orderly. With a few objects, surface names that really don't mean anything are fine. You could name a rusty surface "Lobesha" and you'd still be able to work without skipping a beat. But as your scenes grow, so do your objects and surfaces. This is why properly identifying surfaces is a good habit to practice right from the start. If you find that a surface name created in Modeler is not exact, you can use the Rename option to clarify or to give a more specific name to a surface.

The fourth command, Display, and its companion Options button determine what you see in the Display window at the top of the Surface Editor panel (the one that contains the sphere in **Figure 3.8**). As you assign and adjust surface attributes in the Surface Editor, you'll see them applied to that sphere, so you can gauge your progress without having to render your scene or model.

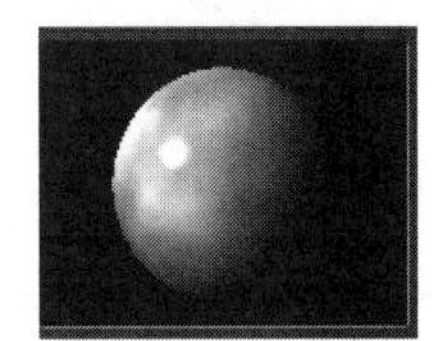

Figure 3.8 Use the Display window within the Surface Editor to preview the results of your surface-attribute settings.

By default, the preview window (**Figure 3.9**) shows how your surface will look with all your surface settings applied collectively. You can use the Display drop-down to switch from this mode (which is called Render Output) to preview the effects of each attribute setting in isolation.

When you need to focus only on color, for instance, choose Color Channel from the Display drop-down (**Figure 3.10**) and you'll see only the color component of the surface, rather than a complex surface with specularity, bumps, and more.

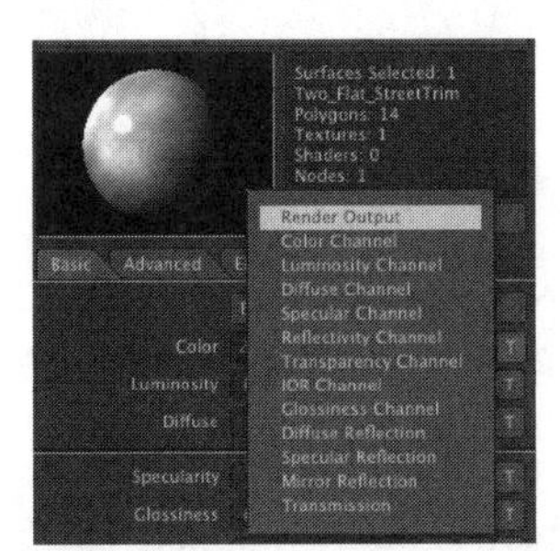

Figure 3.9 The Display drop-down list's default option, Render Output, shows the collective results of all surface-attribute settings in the preview window.

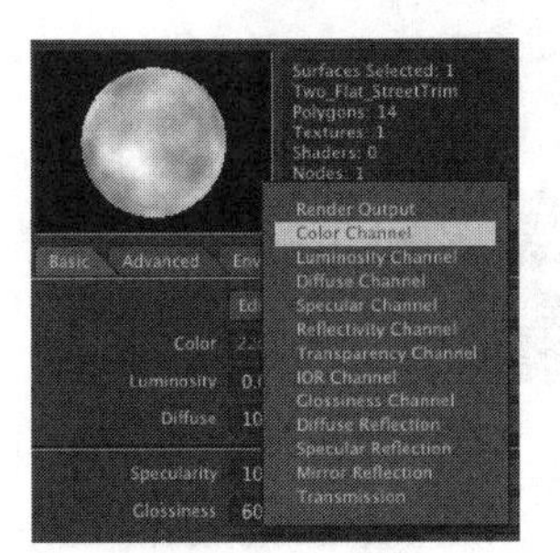

Figure 3.10 The same surface in the Display window with Color Channel selected. Notice that the bump texture and specularity do not display as in Figure 3.9.

You can change this display to any surface aspect you want to concentrate on, such as transparency, glossiness, or reflection. If you are using a procedural texture for luminosity, for example, you might want to display just Luminosity Channel. The choice is up to you. Most commonly, this value can stay at Render Output, but you have the control if you need it.

NOTE

Except for Render Output and Color, all the channels are grayscale, with pure white representing 100 percent of that surface attribute and black being 0 percent.

Click the Options button to the right of the Display drop-down to display a panel that lets you use a cube instead of a sphere as the preview object. The Options button also allows you to change the preview window's background and lighting effects.

The Preset Shelf

Building surfaces is fun, no doubt, but seeing results right away can be even better. The Preset Shelf, a visual browser for surfaces, comes loaded with hundreds of prebuilt surfaces you can apply instantly to your models. (It also holds other types of preset attributes, such as camera handlers and environment handlers.)

To sample the prebuilt surfaces in the Preset Shelf, make sure the Surface Editor panel is open and choose Presets from the Windows drop-down, or just press **F8**. In the Surface Preset window that appears (**Figure 3.11**), click the Library drop-down (labeled WorkSpace, the default name for a new empty library) and choose the Rock surface library. These presets were installed when you installed LightWave 10.

Figure 3.11 The Surface Preset panel is home to hundreds of readymade surfaces, as well as any you decide to add.

To copy a surface setting from the Surface Preset panel to another selected surface, first select the new surface name in the Surface Editor panel and then double-click in the preset surface in the Surface Preset panel. Also, double-click in the preview window to use the Save Surface Preset function. Be sure to have the Preset window open to see the saved surface. Double-click that surface preset to load it to a new surface. Similarly, you can right-click in the preview window for additional options, such as Save Surface Preset. To save a surface to the Preset Shelf, double-click the Display window in the Surface Editor, and the currently selected surface will be added to the library.

NOTE

If you open the Preset Shelf and don't see anything, make sure the Surface Editor panel is open. If it is, you may have moved LightWave's Presets folder, which belongs inside a folder named Programs, in your main LightWave application folder.

If you right-click in the Surface Preset panel, you can create new libraries for organizing your surface settings. You also can copy, move, and change the parameters.

Setting Up Surfaces

The main functions you use to set up and apply surfaces in the Surface Editor occupy four tabs: Basic, Advanced, Environment, and Shaders (**Figure 3.12**). Each controls specific aspects of a selected surface. This chapter introduces you to the most commonly used tabs, Basic and Environment.

Figure 3.12 Surface Editor controls are organized in four tabs.

NOTE

At this point, it's a good idea to assign LightWave's content directory to this book's DVD if you haven't already. Insert this book's disc into your computer. In order to work from the DVD, either install the project files or click the Cancel button if the DVD auto-starts. Press **o** in Layout to access the General Options tab of the Preferences panel. At the top, click Content Directory and set it to the 3D_Content folder on the DVD. Now, LightWave knows where to look for this book's tutorial files.

Basic Tab

Aptly named, the Basic tab is home to all your basic surfacing needs. It's here that you start most surfacing projects (**Figure 3.13**).

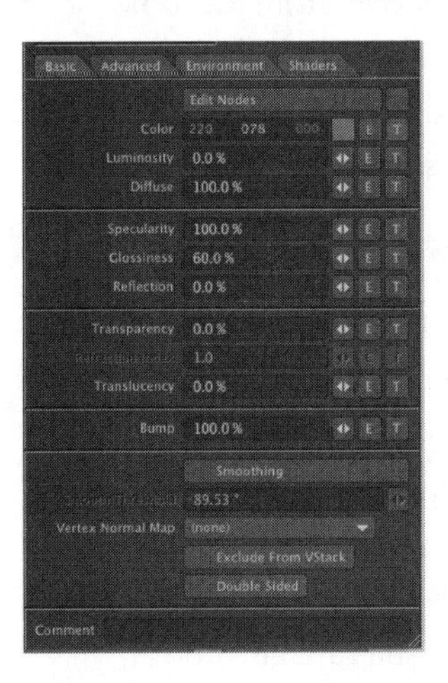

Figure 3.13 The Basic tab in the Surface Editor is home to the most commonly used surface settings.

Within the Basic tab, you'll find the following controls arranged from top to bottom:

- **Edit Nodes**. This feature allows you to control surfaces in an entirely new way. You would click this button and use it instead of the basic Surface Editor. This feature will be introduced shortly.
- **Color**. Here, you can set the color of the selected surface by entering values from 0 to 255 for each of three RGB (red-green-blue) or HSV (hue-saturation-value) color channels. Right-click in the number field to toggle RGB and HSV modes. Click and hold your mouse button on

a channel's numerical setting and slide the mouse right to increase the value or left to reduce it. Or just click the swatch to the right of the numerical field to open the standard color picker for your operating system.

To the right of the Color control, as well as the remaining controls in the Basic tab, you'll find buttons marked E and T. Recall that E stands for Envelope—a function that enables a given surface-attribute value to vary over time. T stands for Texture, a function that lets you vary an attribute's setting spatially, over the area of the surface. We'll cover envelopes and textures later in the chapter.

The rest of the controls in the Basic tab work the same way. Each contains a number field you can click and type into in order to enter a setting. To the right of each number field is a LightWave adjuster called a mini-slider. To use one, click it and, holding down the mouse button, move your mouse left or right to change the setting value. The range of each mini-slider generally covers the observed values for that attribute in natural materials. Many controls let you type in values outside those naturally occurring ranges to achieve special effects.

- **Luminosity**. This controls the brightness, or self-illumination, of a surface.
- **Diffuse**. This is the amount of light the surface receives from the scene. You'll learn more about this shortly.
- **Specularity**. This value specifies the amount of shine on a surface. High Specularity settings are appropriate for surfaces such as glass, water, and polished metal.
- **Glossiness**. Often confused with specularity, glossiness determines how shine spreads on a surface. A surface with high glossiness exhibits tight highlights or "hot spots"; this option is dimmed if specularity is 0.
- **Reflection**. If you want a surface to reflect light, you specify how much with this control; a mirror would have a high Reflection setting. When you want to control what's reflected in a reflective surface, you'll use the Environment tab.
- **Transparency**. This controls the degree to which you can see through a surface.
- **Refraction Index**. This value controls the amount that light bends as it passes through a transparent surface. Material with an index of 1 doesn't bend light at all; the index for glass is about 1.5, and for water about 1.3. This control is dimmed on surfaces with zero transparency.

- **Translucency**. This value specifies the degree to which light can pass through a surface from behind, as it might a thin leaf or piece of paper.
- **Bump**. This controls a function that makes surfaces look irregular. It gives an illusion of surface bumpiness but doesn't actually cause any elevation or depression of the surface geometry. The default setting is 100%.
- **Smoothing**. This shading routine, which is activated by default, makes surfaces consisting of polygons appear smooth. Deselect the check box to turn it off.
- **Smooth Threshold**. When smoothing is turned on, this specifies the sharpest angle between polygons that LightWave should try to smooth out. Generally, the default of 89.5° is too high. A typical beveled surface on a logo should have a threshold of about 30°.
- **Double Sided**. Check the box next to this option if you want selected polygons to exhibit surface attributes on both their front and back sides. Ideally, you don't want to use this unless you have to. All models created in LightWave Modeler have their surfaces facing in one direction. This option fakes it and forces the surface to face the opposite way as well.
- **Comment**. Use this field to enter notes about your surface as reminders or to include more detailed descriptions. This is a great feature when you're sending objects to colleagues and clients.

Environment Tab

Reflect for a moment on reflection. (Wow, that was lame!) If you look at an object and see a reflection, its contents aren't determined by the object itself but by its surroundings, right?

In a 3D setting, surface reflections often include other models within a scene, and those reflections typically are created via a process called *ray tracing*, which generates reflections and shadows based on the location of objects and light sources within a scene. Reflections can also include images of objects that don't exist as models in a scene; reflections of "offstage" objects or backdrops are created as 2D images, which you then overlay onto the reflective surface, a technique known as *reflection mapping*.

The Reflection attribute in the Basic tab controls how reflective a given surface will be; settings in the Environment tab (**Figure 3.14** on the next page) control what appears in reflections generated by the surface. When you're dealing with a transparent surface, the tab provides comparable control over how the surface refracts objects placed behind it in a scene.

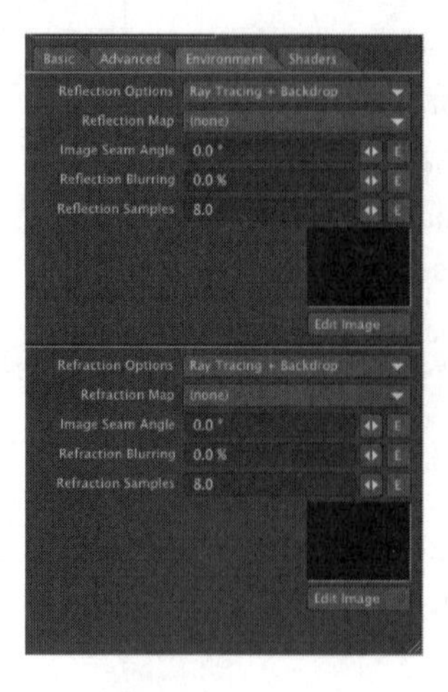

Figure 3.14 The Environment tab gives you access to reflection and refraction controls.

On the Environment tab, you can assign the following:

- **Reflection Options**: the type of reflection applied to a surface: spherical, ray trace, or backdrop
- **Reflection Map**: what image will be reflected
- **Image Seam Angle**: where the seam of a reflected image will appear
- **Refraction Options**: the type of refraction applied to a surface, either spherical or ray trace
- **Refraction Map**: the image file used (if any) for refraction
- **Image Seam Angle**: where the seam of a reflected image will appear
- **Reflection Blurring**: the amount of blur your reflections will have
- **Refraction Blurring**: the amount of blur your refractions will have

The best way for you to get a feel for using the Surface Editor and the Basic and Environment tabs is to try them out for yourself. An excellent way to observe the effect of the settings you choose is to use LightWave's new VPR feature.

Working with VIPER

NOTE

VIPER's ability to preview surface attributes and other effects extends only to changes made using LightWave's built-in editor panels. VIPER cannot display effects or changes made using third-party plug-ins, such as FPrime from Worley Labs (www.worley.com).

VIPER stands for Versatile Interactive Preview Render, and it gives you a preview of certain types of adjustments you can make to your scene in Layout, such as volumetric settings and surface settings. It's important to point out that because VIPER does not do a full-scene evaluation, some aspects of your surfacing are not calculated, such as UV mapping and shadows. This means that VIPER is limited in what it can show. However, it is very useful for most of your surfacing needs, such as specifying color and texture. As you adjust your surfaces, VIPER shows you what's happening and how the surface will look in your scene, without the need to re-render the whole scene. VIPER is available in Layout only.

Exercise 3.1 Working with VIPER and VPR

To get an idea of how useful VIPER is, try this quick tutorial.

1. Start Layout, or if it's already running, save any work you've completed so far and choose Clear Scene from the File drop-down menu (keyboard equivalent: Shift+N).
2. Choose Load Scene from the Load drop-down and open female_head.lws (located in the CH3 folder, inside the 3D_Content folder provided on this book's DVD). You'll see a 3D human female head.
3. Press **F5** to open the Surface Editor panel.

   You'll use VIPER to preview changes made in the Surface Editor, which must be open for VIPER to render and display the surfaces you set.
4. Click Layout's Render tab, and then click the VIPER button in the Utilities tool category. When you do, the VIPER preview window opens and the Enable VIPER button (in the Render tab's Options tool category) is activated automatically (**Figure 3.15**). Press **F7** in any Layout tab to accomplish the same thing.

   When you click VIPER in the Render tab or press **F7** to open the VIPER window, VIPER is enabled automatically. Repeating either of those operations closes the window but leaves VIPER active until you toggle it off using the Enable VIPER button—something you may want to do before running full frame or scene renders.

NOTE

You don't always need to clear the scene before loading a scene. Simply loading a scene overrides your current scene. This two-step process familiarizes you with the available tools and Layout's workflow.

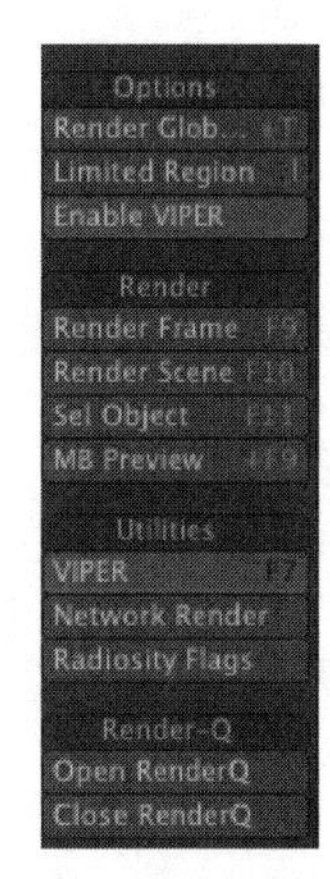

Figure 3.15 The VIPER command is found in Layout only, in the Render tab.

NOTE

Here's the lowdown on the two VIPER-related buttons in Layout's Render tab: The Enable VIPER button makes VIPER pay attention to the rendering buffer, which allows it to preview surface changes in its Display window. The VIPER button opens and closes the VIPER window. Disabling VIPER with the toggle button allows you to leave the VIPER preview window open but frees up system resources to speed frame and scene renders.

5. With the VIPER window now open, click the Render button at the bottom of the VIPER panel. An error message appears stating that VIPER has no surface data to render.

   This is normal. For VIPER to work, it needs you to render a frame so that it can store information from a buffer. Otherwise, VIPER has no idea what's in your scene.
6. Click OK to close the error window, and then press **F9** to render the current frame.

   This renders the current frame and stores the information in LightWave's internal buffer and lets you see surface-setting changes through VIPER.

NOTE

It doesn't matter with a simple "scene" like this, but for more complicated scenes, you might want to disable VIPER while rendering the frame, then turn it back on before continuing.

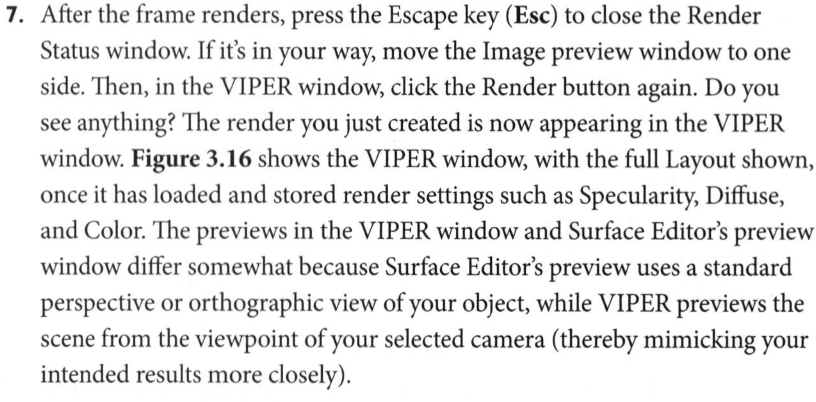

7. After the frame renders, press the Escape key (**Esc**) to close the Render Status window. If it's in your way, move the Image preview window to one side. Then, in the VIPER window, click the Render button again. Do you see anything? The render you just created is now appearing in the VIPER window. **Figure 3.16** shows the VIPER window, with the full Layout shown, once it has loaded and stored render settings such as Specularity, Diffuse, and Color. The previews in the VIPER window and Surface Editor's preview window differ somewhat because Surface Editor's preview uses a standard perspective or orthographic view of your object, while VIPER previews the scene from the viewpoint of your selected camera (thereby mimicking your intended results more closely).

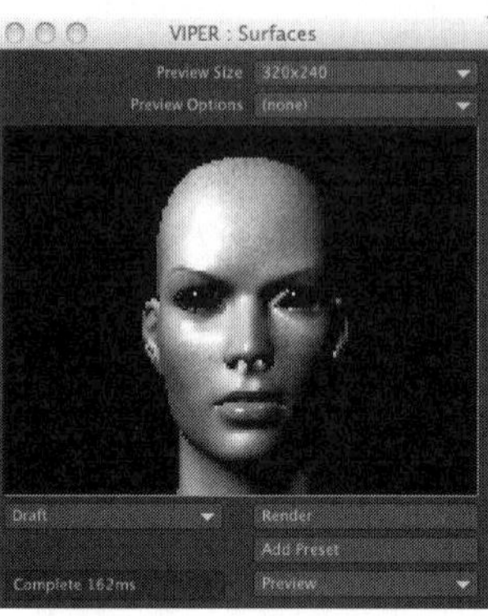

Figure 3.16 Pressing F9 on the keyboard renders the current frame and lets you preview surface changes through VIPER.

8. In Surface Editor, choose "skin lips" from the Surface Name list. To see the surface name, you may need to click the white triangle to the left of the object's name.
9. To quickly see VIPER's interactivity, click the mini-slider to the right of Diffuse in the Surface Editor's Basic tab. Hold down the mouse button and slide your mouse to the left to take the value down to 0, and then release the mouse button. You'll see the VIPER window update, to make the lip area appear black. What you did was tell the surface not to receive any light from the scene, essentially turning off the lights for that surface. A Diffuse value of 0% means light is not diffused, or transferred to the surface.
10. Now, restore the Diffuse value to 100% and continue.

    You'll see various surface settings appear throughout the commands on the right, on the Basic tab.
11. Click the T button to the right of the Color control to open the Texture panel for the skin lips surface (**Figure 3.17**).

NOTE

You may think to yourself, "But Dan, I didn't set up any lights for this scene, so how can the object receive or not receive light?" Remember, Grasshopper: Every default LightWave scene has one camera and one light. Aha!

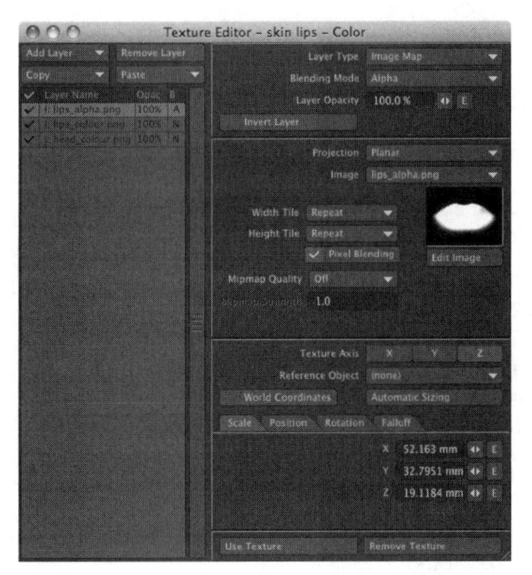

Figure 3.17 Clicking any of the T buttons throughout LightWave, including the Surface Editor, opens the Texture Editor.

NOTE

If the T button to the right of the Color control is dimmed, deselect the Edit Nodes check box located immediately above it.

You'll see that the Layer Type drop-down at the top of the commands is set to Image Map—a setting that lets you apply images to a surface and much more, as we'll see later in the book. For now, select Add Layer and choose Procedural, as in **Figure 3.18**. Deselect the three image map layers.

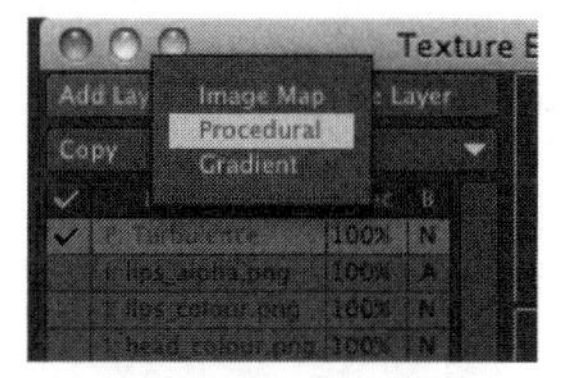

Figure 3.18 The default Texture Editor layer type is Image Map. Change this to Procedural instead.

Procedural textures have no seams, and are often just what the doctor ordered for organic-looking surfaces. Their surface attributes vary via mathematical *procedures*; each *procedural type* yields a different effect. By changing procedure settings within the Texture Editor and combining procedural textures in various ways, you can create a limitless range of organic surfaces. However, with a selected range of polygons, such as the lip area, a procedural texture shows the seam of material area. The benefit is, VIPER shows you the good and bad of adding and editing surfaces, helping your workflow.

The Procedural Type is set to Turbulence, a variation of fractal noise that has been used by LightWave animators for years. Adding Turbulence as the Procedural Type to the current surface color of the lips, which is a pale color, adds variances to the surface, especially if the procedural color is offset to a color like blue.

The Blending Mode is set to Normal, which tells LightWave to add this procedural texture to the selected surface. (Other Blending Mode settings are used when you apply multiple textures to a surface; they determine how textures combine with each other.)

The Layer Opacity is set to 100%, telling LightWave to use this procedural texture to the fullest extent.

12. Make sure the VIPER window is open and visible to the side of the Texture Editor.

    If VIPER is not open, click the VIPER button (not Enable VIPER) in Layout's Render tab. You rendered the scene in step 5, and LightWave remembers that by storing the data in its internal buffers.

13. With the Texture Editor and VIPER open, you can make changes to surface settings and see your changes in real time. **Figure 3.19** shows the VIPER panel.

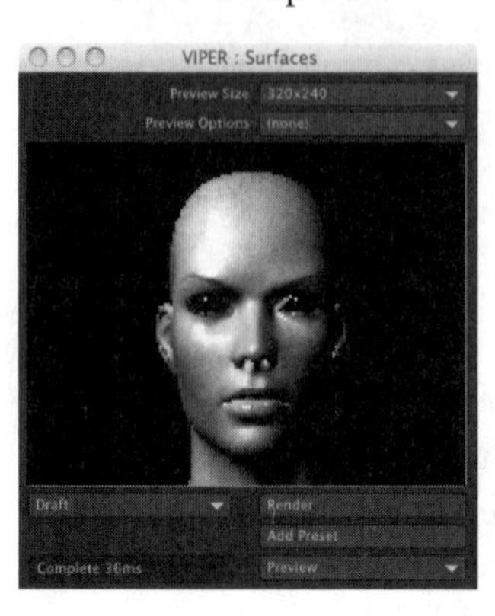

Figure 3.19 Once you've made a render of a frame (by pressing F9), VIPER can now display the render, and you can make surface changes in the Texture Editor (among other places) and see them in real time.

NOTE

The VIPER preview window has default size of 320 × 240 pixels. You can expand it to 480 × 360 or 640 × 480 pixels using the Preview Size drop-down. Adjust the preview window to suit your screen size. When you do so, there's no need to re-render your image. However, if you change scene lighting or object position, or add or remove objects in the scene, you need to re-render by pressing **F9**.

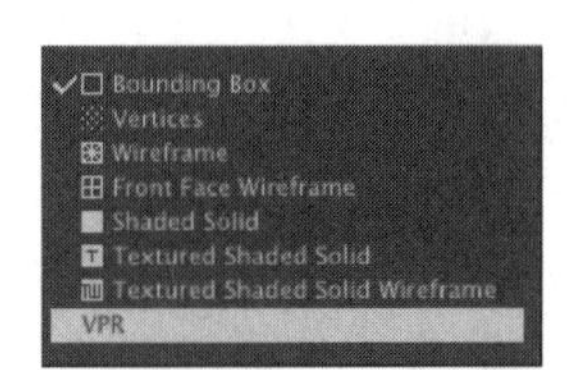

Figure 3.20 To activate VPR mode, just select it as a viewport option.

14. Make certain that the Texture Editor is still open (you get to the Texture Editor by clicking the T button next to Color in the Surface Editor). Next, close the VIPER window. Then in Layout, click the drop-down menu at the top of the interface and change from Texture Shaded Solid view to VPR, as shown in **Figure 3.20**.

15. Back in the Surface Editor, make sure the Texture Editor panel is open. Now, because the procedural turbulent noise texture was a little too heavy, go ahead and delete it by first selecting it in the Layer Name list and then clicking Remove Layer at the top of the Texture Editor.

16. Next, turn the three layers back on by clicking the check marks to the left of the layers. Take a look in the main Layout window. How does that look? Amazing, right? A real-time render directly in your interface. **Figure 3.21** shows the interface with VPR active. Cool, right?

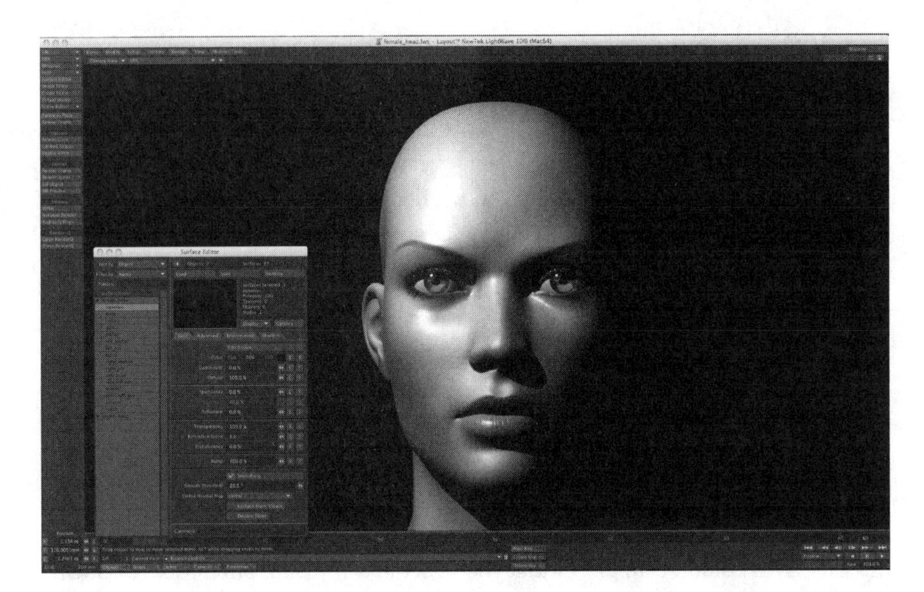

Figure 3.21 Changes to texture-property values such as Color, Scale, and Contrast are easy to see with the VIPER window open.

VIPER and VPR will quickly become your best friends when you're working with LightWave Layout because they save you time. Not only that, many of you may not be mathematical wizards and do not care to calculate every value within the surface settings. Using VIPER can answer many of your questions when it comes to surfacing, especially when using Hypervoxels for particles (discussed in Chapter 10), because you can instantly see the results from changed values. VPR is terrific for interactively working "in" your scene. Using these tools will guarantee that during your 3D work, you'll make a change to a value or setting and utter a loud "Oh, *that's* what that does!" from time to time.

VIPER and VPR Tips

Here are a few more VIPER and VPR tips before you move on:

- Never trust VIPER as your final render. If something looks odd, always make a true render (by pressing **F9** or **F10**) to check final surfacing.
- You can use VIPER to see animated textures by selecting Make Preview from the Preview drop-down list in the VIPER window.
- Press the Escape key (**Esc**) to abort a VIPER preview in progress.
- Click Draft Mode in the VIPER window to reduce redraw time (and render quality).
- Clicking a particular surface in the VIPER window instantly selects it in the Surface Editor's Surface Name list. This is a great feature and can save you a lot of time on complex textured scenes.
- VIPER is available only in Layout, not Modeler.

- VPR works quite well on most computers. Understandably, the more processing power you have, and the bigger your video card, the better your performance will be.
- VPR has many options that can help you work faster and more efficiently. Be sure to watch the VPR video on the book's DVD to see all the features in action.

Common Surface Settings

To take you even further into the LightWave Surface Editor, try applying a reflection in Exercise 3.2.

Exercise 3.2 Applying a Reflection to a Surface

You may sometimes have a project that requires you to use a building, vehicle, machine, toilet, or something completely different from what you're used to working with. This could be an object that you've created yourself, purchased, or downloaded from public archives on the Internet. Follow these steps to apply a simple reflection to a surface:

1. Be sure to save any work you've completed thus far. Start Layout, or if it's already running, choose File > Clear Scene.
2. From the DVD that accompanies this book, load the BigTractor scene from the Chapter 3 projects folder in \3D_Content\Scenes\CH3\. To load the scene, go to the Items tab, and then on the left side of the interface, click the Scene button under the Load category, as in **Figure 3.22**.

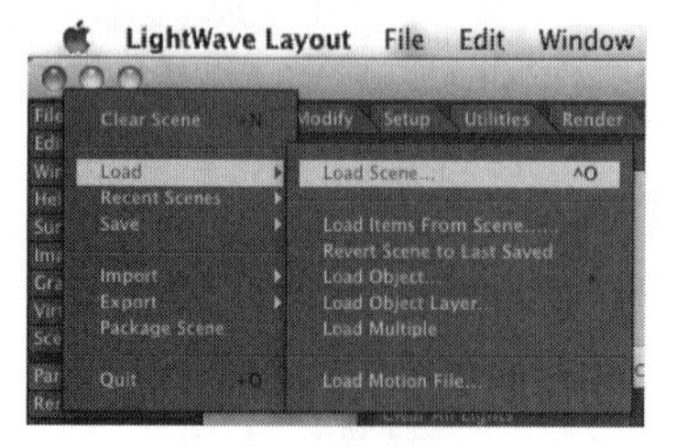

Figure 3.22 Load the BigTractor scene into LightWave to set up some surfaces.

Here's a very handy tip: You can hide all the toolbars and menus in Layout and work with just the keyboard and mouse. Press **d** on the keyboard to access the Display Options tab of the Preferences panel. Select Hide Toolbar (**Figure 3.23**). Now, when in Layout, you can access the Surface Editor (or any other panel) by Control-Shift-clicking in the Layout window (using either the left or right mouse button). This pops up the list of commands and menus you've just hidden away (**Figure 3.24**)! Press **d** again to access the Display Options panel to unhide the toolbar. Now that you know where things are located, just use Alt+F2 to hide and unhide the toolbar. You can also open the Surface Editor quickly by pressing **F5**.

NOTE

Remember that you should be using LightWave's default interface configuration for all tutorials in this book. To make sure you are, press Alt+F10 on the keyboard to call up the Configure Menus panel. Click the Default button from the Presets drop-down list at the upper-right side of the panel's interface. If it is dimmed, you already have the default interface set. Click Done to close the panel.

Figure 3.23 The Display Options tab of the Preferences panel.

Figure 3.24 The list of commands and menus you hid by selecting Hide Toolbar.

3. After the scene has been loaded, click the Surface Editor button on the left side of the interface to open the Surface Editor panel. You should still be in VPR mode.

   You can see that by default, the object name appears in the Surface Name list.

4. If you don't see all the surfaces, just click the small triangle to the left of the BigTractor filename and it will open the Surface Name list for that particular object.

   All the surfaces associated with the BigTractor object appear, as shown in **Figure 3.25**.

NOTE

If you have more surfaces than you do space in the Surface Name list, a scroll bar appears. Simply drag the scroll bar to view the entire surface list.

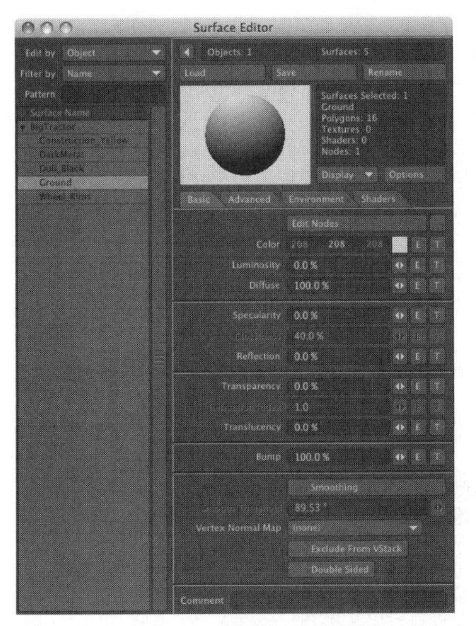

Figure 3.25 When an object is selected in Layout and the Surface Editor is opened, the selected object's surfaces are listed.

NOTE

Naming your surfaces is half the battle when building 3D models. If you name your surfaces carefully, you'll save oodles of time when you have many surface settings to apply. Organization is key! You name your surfaces in Modeler, as explained in previous chapters.

5. LightWave enables you to resize the Surface Editor panel simply by dragging the edge of the panel. Drag the bottom edge to stretch out the panel. You can collapse the panel by clicking the small triangle centered at the top of the interface, and you can simply select your surfaces from the Surface drop-down list.

6. In Layout, make sure you're in Camera view. You should be already, because the scene was saved this way before you loaded it. If not, switch to Camera view by selecting it from the drop-down list at the upper-left side of the viewport title bar. Then, select the Ground surface from the list within the Surface Editor.

   When a surface is selected, the name appears in the information window to the right of the surface preview. The number of polygons associated with that surface also appears. In this case, the selected surface, Ground, has 16 polygons, as shown in **Figure 3.26**. You'll also see a display at the very top of the surface panel that indicates the number of objects and surfaces in the scene.

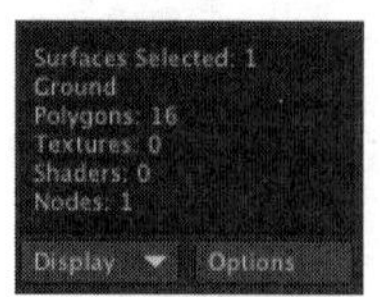

Figure 3.26 Summary information on the selected surface is displayed at the top right of the Surface Editor panel.

7. Because you simply can't have a dull floor, you need to shine it up a bit. You know, make it look pretty. You can even make the ground look like glass or brass! First, you can change the color of the Ground but for now, leave it set to the default white. It's set to the same color as the background so there's a seamless transition.

   Here are a few tips for working with color values:

   - Clicking the small color square next to the RGB values makes the standard system color palette appear. Here, you can choose your color in RGB (red, green, blue), in HSV (hue, saturation, value), or from custom colors you may have set up previously.
   - Right-clicking and dragging the small color square next to the RGB values in the Surface Editor changes all three values at once. This is great for increasing or decreasing the color brightness.
   - Clicking the red, green, or blue numeric value and dragging left or right decreases or increases, respectively, the color value. You will instantly see the small color square next to the RGB values change. You'll also see the sample display update.
   - If you're not keen on setting RGB values and prefer HSV values instead, rest easy. Right-clicking once on the RGB values changes the selection to HSV (**Figure 3.27**).

NOTE

HSV represents hue, saturation, and value. It describes colors directly by their overall color, unlike RGB values, which are three discrete subcolors. HSV is another way to change color values. However, you might have more flexibility using RGB values.

Figure 3.27 Right-clicking any RGB value in the Surface Editor's Basic tab changes the color-selection tool to HSV mode, and vice versa.

- Make sure you're using the display preview options as you like them. Right-click in the surface preview window to show more controls and options (**Figure 3.28**).

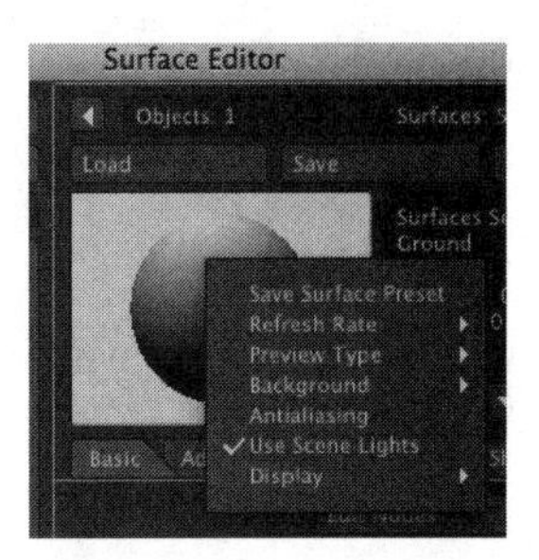

Figure 3.28 Right-clicking in the surface preview window in the Surface Editor offers more control over how the surface is displayed. Here, you can set a checkerboard background, which is great for transparent surfaces.

With the Ground surface set to the soft white color, you still need to see the tractor reflected! You'll need to make the Ground surface shiny. This next tutorial discusses surfacing the glass while introducing you to the rest of the Surface Editor. Remember that you will create many more surfaces throughout the chapters in this book, and that this is a brief introduction to just some of the features.

Exercise 3.3 Surfacing for Reflections

1. Make sure VIPER is opened and set off to the side of the Surface Editor so you can see your changes in real time. You can press **F7** to open it. Or, keep VPR on! The choice is yours based on the speed of your system.

   With the Ground surface still selected as the current surface in the Surface Editor, go down the list of options and set each one accordingly.

2. Make sure that the value of Luminosity (the option just underneath Surface Color) is 0.

   Luminosity is great for objects that are self-illuminating, such as a lightbulb, candle flame, or laser beam. Note though that this does not make your surface cast light unless radiosity is applied, under the Global Illumination tab. This is in the Render Globals panel on the Render tab.

3. Set the value of Diffuse to roughly 60% to tell the glass surface to accept 60% of the light in the scene.

   The Diffuse value tells your surface what amount of light to pick up from the scene. For example, if you set this value to 0, your surface would be completely black. Although you want the glass to be black, you also want it to have some sheen and reflections. A 0 Diffuse value renders a black hole—nothing appears at all.

4. Set the value of Specularity to 40%.

   Specularity, in simple terms, is a shiny reflection of the light source. A value of 0% is not shiny at all, whereas 100% is completely shiny.

   When you set specularity, you almost always adjust the glossiness as well. Glossiness, which becomes available only when the Specularity setting is above 0%, is the value that sets the amount of the "hot spot" on your shiny (or not-so-shiny) surface. Think of glossiness as how much of a spread the hot spot has. The lower the value, the wider the spread. For example, **Figure 3.29** (on the next page) shows two spheres, one with a low Specularity setting of 5% and Glossiness set to 15%. The result resembles a dull surface, like plastic.

Figure 3.29 The sphere on the right has low Specularity and Glossiness settings, which results in a surface that looks dull. The sphere on the left, with high Specularity and Glossiness settings, looks more like glass.

On the other hand, the sphere to the right has a Specularity setting of 75% and Glossiness of 40%. The result looks closer to a shiny glass surface with reflections turned on. A higher Glossiness setting gives the impression of polished metal, or glass in this case. There will be a lot of surfacing ahead in this book for you, such as glass, metal, human skin, and more.

5. Now, back to surfacing the Ground in the BigTractor scene. Set the value of the Glossiness for the surface to 30%.

   This gives you a good, working shiny surface for now. Note, this is also a good formula for glass.

6. Set the value of Reflection for the Ground surface to 40%.

   Most glass and clear plastic surfaces reflect their surroundings. In this case, the BigTractor is placed on a simple ground plane composed of just a few polygons. Just one basic Distant light illuminates the scene, along with one fill light.

7. You should now see the reflection showing up directly in your viewport. Because the Ground surface is flat, the Smoothing option is not necessary. If it were more round, you would want to turn Smoothing on. With objects that are more round, this option will take away any visible facets in the geometry.

NOTE

It's a good idea when setting reflections to make the Reflection value and the Diffuse value add up to roughly 100%. The current surface has Diffuse at 60% and Reflection at 30% for a total of 90%. This is not law, but just a guideline. If your Diffuse setting is 100% and you add a reflection of 40% or more, you'll end up with an unnaturally bright surface.

NOTE

A shader is an algorithm that affects the surface properties of an object. It can change color, reflection, smoothing, reflectivity, and more. Shaders also can add special effects like procedural brick textures or fractal noise. The Smoothing setting employs a *Phong shader*. Developed by Bui Tuong-Phong in 1975, this shader works well on surfaces that emulate plastics, metals, and glass. Later when we get to the Node Editor, you'll learn about LightWave 10's other cool shaders.

8. Click the Environment tab within the Surface Editor panel (**Figure 3.30**).

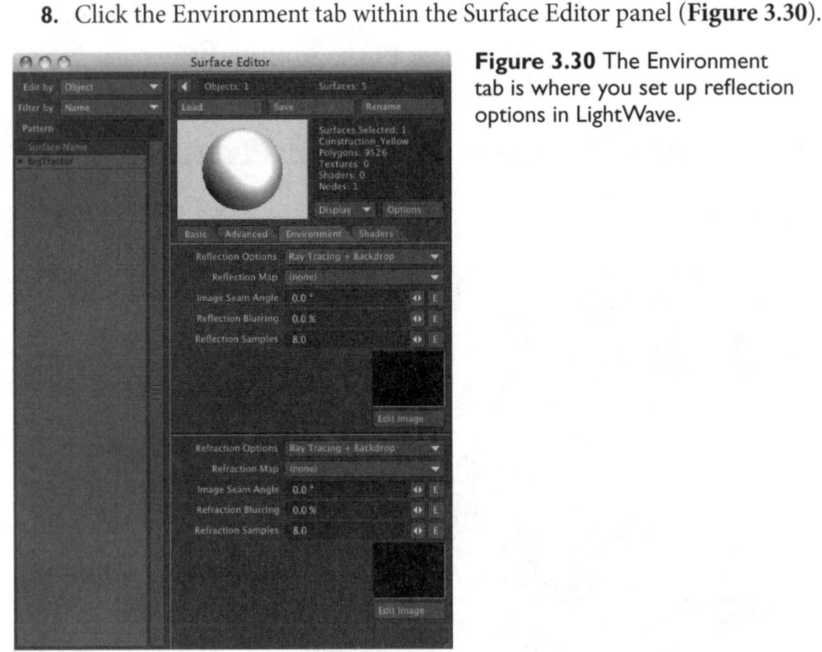

Figure 3.30 The Environment tab is where you set up reflection options in LightWave.

NOTE

Flatter surfaces are sometimes simply "too" smooth, and create odd renders. Reducing their smoothing thresholds can fix that.

9. Make sure Reflection Options is set to Ray Tracing + Backdrop, if it's not already.

   This tells the surface to reflect what's around it (in this case, an essentially bare set). If other objects were in the scene, they would be reflected too.

   Because LightWave can calculate reflections, setting a reflecting image can often help create a more realistic surface. You'd do this for the tractor surfaces, to help them look like metal. Glass-like surfaces, on the other hand, should reflect their surroundings, so ray tracing is used.

10. For ray-traced reflections to work, you need to tell the render engine to calculate this feature. If you don't see a reflection currently, and VPR is on, click the Render tab at the top of the screen and then open the Render Globals panel. Make sure under the Render tab (within the Render Globals panel) that the Raytrace Reflection option is on, as well as Raytrace Shadows. This will tell the render engine to calculate reflection and shadow rays, as in **Figure 3.31**.

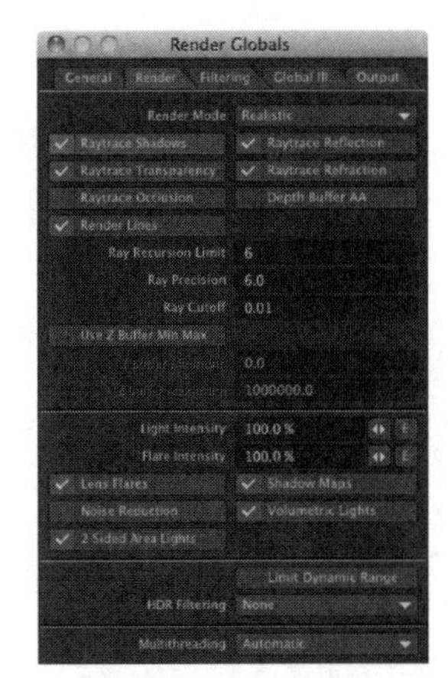

Figure 3.31 For ray-traced reflections to work for a surface, you must tell LightWave's renderer to calculate them.

11. Press **F9** for a single frame render. While you're in the Render Options panel, make sure Render Display is set to Image Viewer (in the General tab) to see a pop-up of your rendered image. **Figure 3.32** shows the render.

Figure 3.32 The Ground surface is very reflective, but the F9 render looks like the VPR in Layout.

What's that? VPR is so powerful that you can see your full render right in Layout, so often the typical F9 preview render is not necessary.

12. Choose Save All Objects from the Save submenu in the File drop-down. This saves the surfaces you've just set. Then, choose Save Scene from the same Save submenu to save the lighting, ray trace settings, and so forth. Now it's time for the metal!

Creating Metallic Surfaces

You might think it would be difficult to match the real-world properties of metal on any objects you create, even a few balls. Believe it or not, this is easy to do within LightWave 10. The right amount of color, specularity, glossiness, and reflection helps create the visual effect. You've created the transparent glass surface, so how about something completely different? In this particular instance, a metal surface could work very well. This same metal can be applied to almost any metallic surfaces you create—from logos, to machines, to fasteners—with only minor variations. This section takes you through the steps required to create a metal surface.

Exercise 3.4 Creating a Metallic Surface

1. In the Surface Editor, select the Construction_Yellow surface. Set the color to a soft gray to simulate a silver metallic surface. Try setting all three RGB values to 180.
2. Set Diffuse to 70%, Specularity to 50%, and Glossiness to 40%.
3. A reflection is needed, so set Reflection to 25%.

   At this point, the surface doesn't look much different than when you loaded it, other than a color change. Remember that other factors, such as surroundings and lighting, play a role in surfacing, but you still need to apply the reflection environment. **Figure 3.33** shows the surface settings.
4. With the Construction_Yellow surface still selected, click the Environment tab (to the right of the Basic tab).
5. Set Reflection Options to Ray Tracing + Spherical Map, as in **Figure 3.34**. This tells the surface to reflect not only what's around it but an image as well.
6. For the Reflection Map option, click the drop-down and select Load Image, as in **Figure 3.35**. Load the image named Tinfoil.tga from this book's DVD.

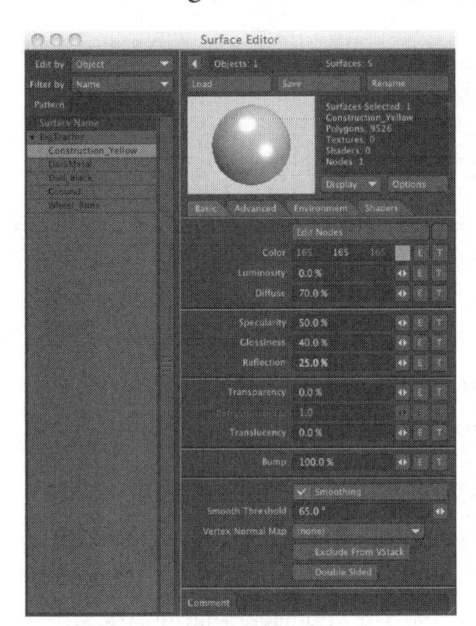

Figure 3.33 Metal surfaces begin with basic color properties and a low Glossiness setting.

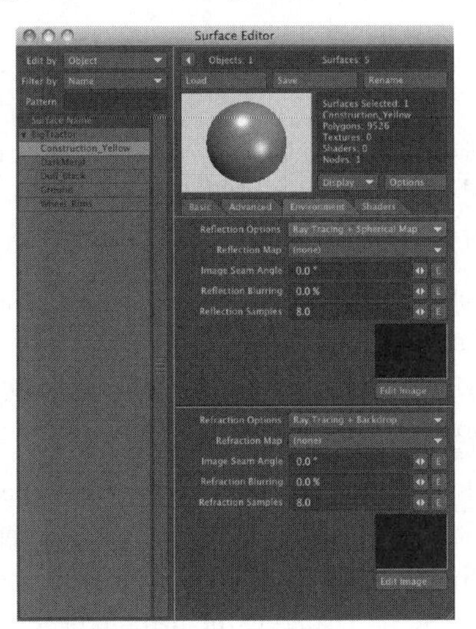

Figure 3.34 The Ray Tracing + Spherical Map setting is a great way to make realistic metallic surfaces.

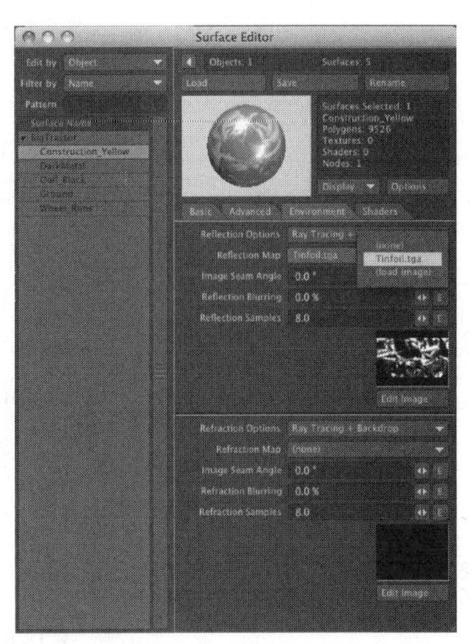

Figure 3.35 You can load an image directly from the Reflection Map drop-down in the Environment tab.

7. Guess what? That's about it for this surface! No need to press **F9** to render a frame and see how it looks. Just check out the scene directly in Layout. **Figure 3.36** (on the next page) shows the new surface applied to the tractor.

Figure 3.36 Adding ray-traced reflections and a reflection image to a gray surface helps sell a metallic look for the area under the glass.

It's subtle, but effective. Experiment a little and see how more reflection looks, a little less, and even add a little Reflection Blur from the Environment tab to change it up.

NOTE

While holding the Shift key on your keyboard, you can select the first surface in the Surface Name list and then select the last surface in the list, and you'll select all of the surfaces. You can then change surface properties for all of them at the same time.

From this point, you can work with any other object surfaces you like, and apply similar metals, glass, or your own combination of both. You can even select all but the glass surface and change the basic gray color to a yellow-orange, and you've now made gold. All the other surface settings still apply.

A few final thoughts on surfacing with reflections: Many factors come into play, such as the glancing angle of the camera, light, and shadows. The angle of the camera in the previous steps could have been moved to reveal more of the reflection. You can also try changing the metal reflections to just a spherical map in the Environment tab, rather than using the Ray Tracing + Spherical Map setting. This tells the surface to reflect only the image.

NOTE

Remember that simply saving a LightWave scene file does not save your surfaces. You must save your object in addition to saving your scene if you want to keep the surfaces applied.

You'll often come across situations where you need to use the same surface settings on multiple surfaces, such as in the previous exercise. With so many variables being set within the Surface Editor, keeping track of identical surfaces could be a problem. Not to mention, you might want a quick reference to the changes you've made to the current surface. This is where the Preset Shelf comes in, to save a surface.

Exercise 3.5 Saving a Surface

If you set up a surface you'd like to keep, you can simply save it in the Preset Shelf. To do this, follow these steps:

1. Make sure the Preset Shelf is open by clicking the Windows drop-down menu and choosing Presets. Then in the Surface Editor, select the Construction_Yellow surface (which you've now changed to gray). Double-click the display preview at the top of the Surface Editor.

   You'll see that surface sample appear, with its settings now saved, in the Preset Shelf (**Figure 3.37**).

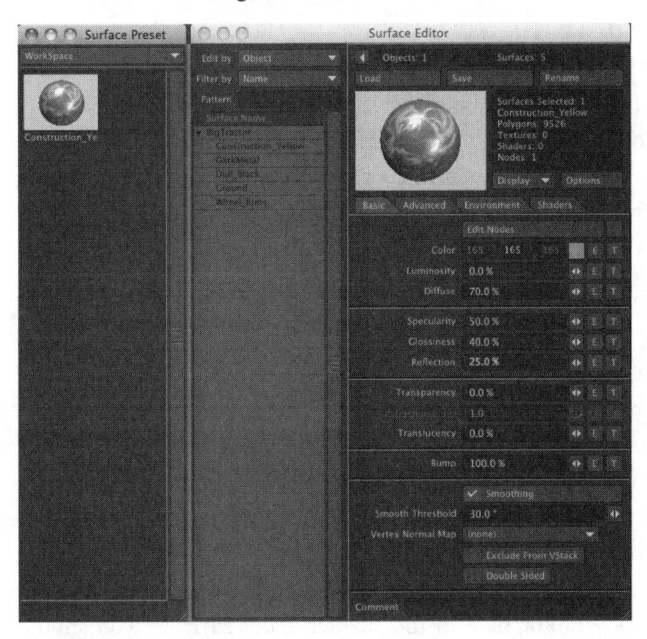

Figure 3.37 Double-clicking the display sample in the Surface Editor, shown on the right, instantly adds those surface settings to the Preset Shelf, shown on the left.

2. Select the second surface you need to apply surfacing to, such as the Ground surface, in the Surface Name list.
3. Go back to the Preset Shelf and double-click the sample you recently added.

   A small window appears, asking you to load the current settings. This is asking if you want the settings from the Preset Shelf sample to be applied to the currently selected surface in the Surface Editor. In this case, you do.
4. Click Yes, and all the surface settings are applied from the preset to the selected Ground surface. For any small changes, adjust as needed in the Surface Editor.

By using a preset to copy and paste a surface, you'll find it's much easier to change one simple parameter, such as reflection, than it is to reset all the surface and reflection properties again.

NOTE

Although double-clicking the sample display is one way to add a surface to the Preset Shelf, you can also right-click the preview window and select Save Surface Preset. You can also just press the **s** key while in the Surface Editor. Finally, you can click Add Preset in the VIPER window.

As you can see from the previous examples, it's not too hard to create simple, good-looking surfaces. The next step is to continue surfacing on your own, using the few simple parameters outlined in the previous pages. Color, diffuse, specularity, glossiness, and reflection form the base for nearly all the surfaces you create. After you have a handle on setting up the basics, read on to learn about the Node Editor. Now, there's a lot more to learn about surfacing, such as texture mapping, bump mapping, and using procedurals for computer-generated textures. You'll do this more throughout the projects in this book, but the information here should have you up and running with the basics of the Surface Editor.

Introducing the Node Editor

Finally, we come to the Node Editor. You could, if you chose, use the Node Editor in place of the Surface Editor 100 percent of the time. That said, the Node Editor isn't really meant to completely replace the Surface Editor. There are times when setting up a quick surface with the Surface Editor, as you've done with the exercises in this chapter, is simpler and more practical than firing up the Node Editor. But the Node Editor can help you take your textures and surfaces to the next level.

LightWave's surfacing has been a layer-based system up until now. This system is still in place, but with the Node Editor, the rules have changed. Node-based texturing is found in many high-end 3D applications, because it allows you to create custom shaders, mix and match various surface properties, and much more. Unlike a layer-based system, the node-based system is like a network. Everything can connect and interact, from a simple surface to advanced materials. This next section will get you up and running with the Node Editor. Later in the book, you'll create more advanced node-based surfaces. One last thing before the project: Although we're discussing the Node Editor here in the chapter about surfaces, you should know that the Node Editor also exists for volumetric lighting and deformations. Of course, you'll use these within the project chapters as well.

NOTE

While the Surface Editor and Node Editor are available in LightWave Modeler, you won't see the effects of the Node Editor except for a sample surface sphere. For full preview of the Node Editor, use it in Layout—even more reason to perform all surfacing in Layout, not in Modeler.

1. In Layout, save any work you've done. Reload the original BigTractor scene. Press **F5** to open the Surface Editor. Select the Construction_Yellow surface listed in the Surface Name list. Then click the Edit Nodes button, as shown in **Figure 3.38**.

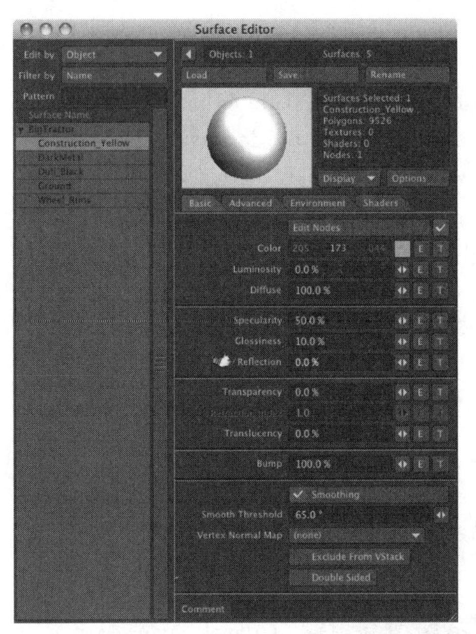

Figure 3.38 Select the surface you want to change, and click Edit Nodes to open the Node Editor.

NOTE

To apply nodes to a specific surface, always select the surface in the Surface Name list. Be aware of this, as you might click the Edit Nodes button without thinking and apply node surfacing to the wrong surface.

2. When the Node Editor opens, position it as you like, and feel free to expand the size of the window by clicking and dragging the lower-right corner. **Figure 3.39** shows the panel.

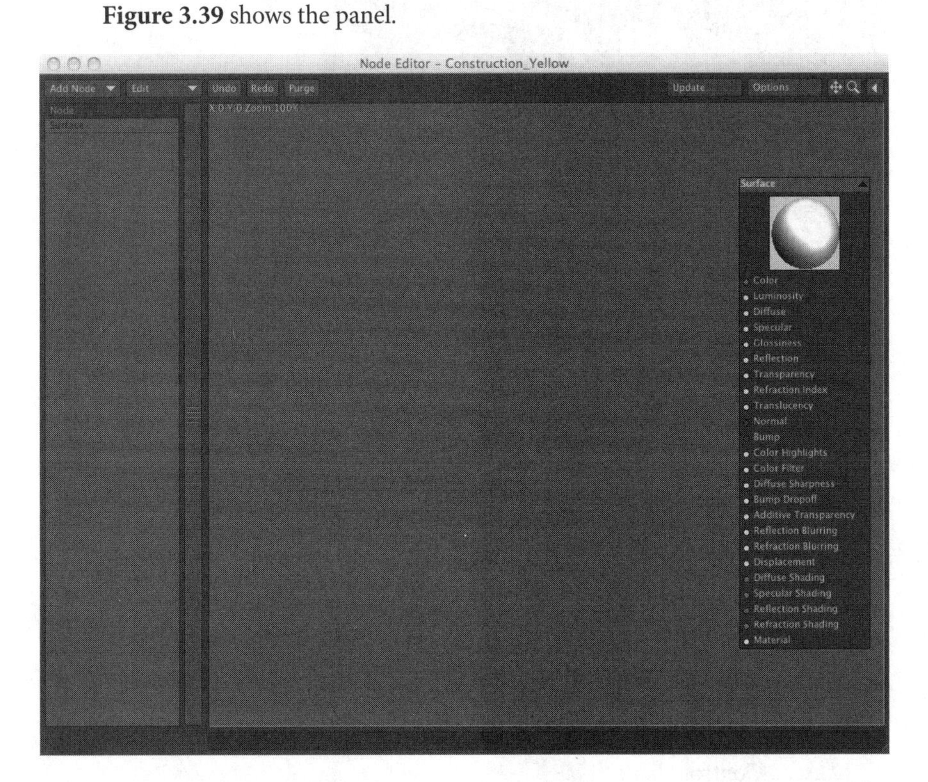

Figure 3.39 The Node Editor open and positioned.

NOTE

If you can't seem to pull any connections off a node, there's a good chance you've sized down the view too much. In the upper-right corner of the Node Editor are move and zoom controls just like in Layout or Modeler. Click, hold, and drag these two icons to adjust the view.

NOTE

A destination node is what drives your render. In a sense, it's the node, or part of the network, that outputs your other nodes.

3. The first lesson to learn is that there will always be a destination node. That's the tall column you see in Figure 3.39. This node looks slightly different in the shading and texturing node (as you see here) than in the lighting or displacement node. Regardless, there will always be the destination node. Click and move it around to fit it to view. You can quickly do this by pressing the **f** key on your keyboard (*f* for fit—get it?).

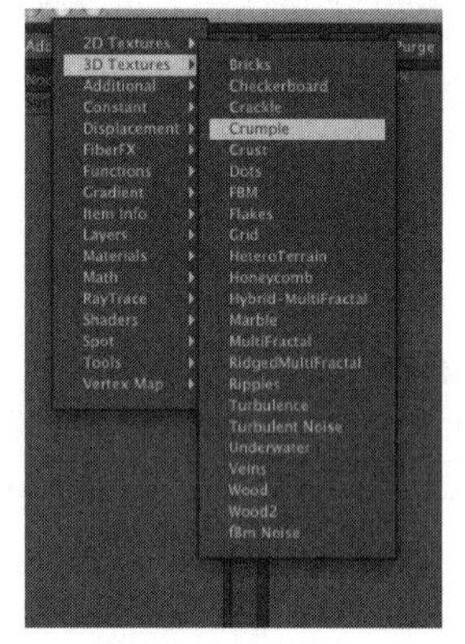

Figure 3.40 Adding a node is easy: simply select one from the Add Node menu. Here, a procedural Crumple node is selected.

4. At the top left of the Node Editor is the Add Node menu. Select this and you'll see a plethora of available nodes, from 2D and 3D textures, to gradients and cool shaders. For now, select 3D Textures, and then select Crumple, as in **Figure 3.40**.

5. It might be hard to wrap your brain around this way of texturing—that's for sure. But don't worry, you'll get it. Just think of these nodes as ingredients that you can mix any way you want to create your final dish. Now, once the Crumple node has been added, it appears in the workspace area, as shown in **Figure 3.41**.

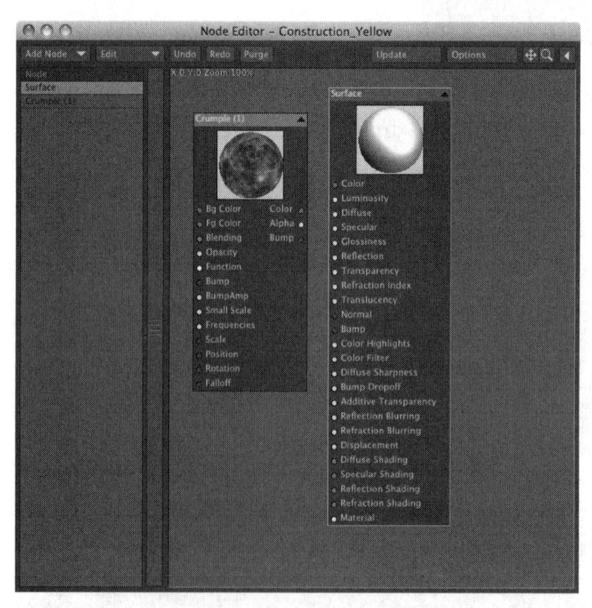

Figure 3.41 The Crumple node added to the workspace area in the Node Editor.

6. Taking a look at the preview thumbnail image at the top of the destination node (which reads Surface), it looks as if nothing has changed. This is correct. Nothing has changed. This is because even though you've added the node, you need to mix it in—that is, place it into the network. To begin getting organized, you can rename the default surface to something more specific. This is a good idea if you're creating larger scenes. Right-click the surface name in the Node list and choose Rename, as in **Figure 3.42**. You'll see that you can also access many other commands with a right-click (Mac users, Control-click).

7. After renaming your surface, you'll see that the destination node now shows the same name. The Crumple node needs to be connected to the destination node in some way. There are multiple ways to do this, and this is really the beauty of the Node Editor. For now, however, just click and drag the red dot for Color from the Crumple node, to the red dot for Color in the destination node. **Figure 3.43** shows the result.

   Guess what? You just used the Node Editor. It's that easy! Of course, you simply added a single procedural texture, but the process is the same no matter what you're creating. You add nodes and make the connections. Easy enough, isn't it? So what's the tough part? The tough part is understanding what connections to make and what all of the different nodes do. While we can't cover every single node in this book, we can show you how to use and, more importantly, understand these different node connections so you can experiment on your own. On the book's DVD is a video for you called "Node-Based Texturing" that will give you a good idea what the node editor is all about. And, you'll perform more complex projects.

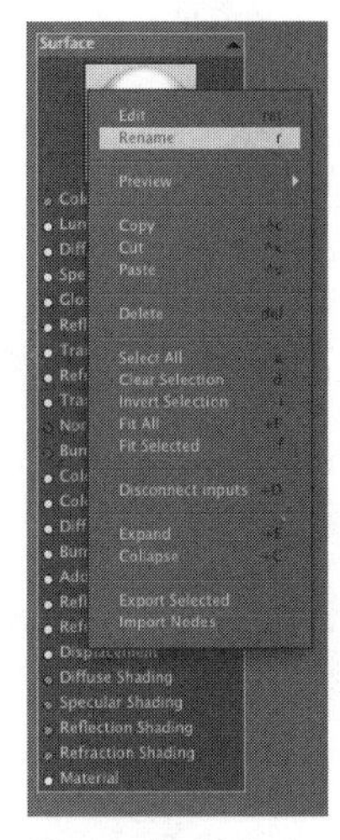

Figure 3.42 Right-click the surface name in the Node list to rename it.

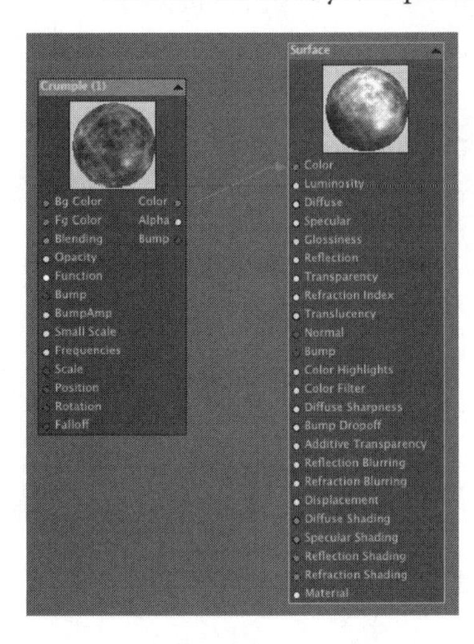

Figure 3.43 To connect a node, click and drag from one node to the next.

Take a look at Figure 3.43, and you'll see that the destination node preview shows the crumple surface applied. If you press **F9** to render a current frame or simply look at the interface with VPR active, the crumple surface is on the tractor. The red arrow you dragged from the Crumple node to the destination node is a connection. There are five types of connections in the Node Editor. To identify each type of connection, NewTek has color-coded them. The red connection you just used is a color connector, and it has inputs and outputs, as you've seen. In most cases, you'll connect color to color as you've done here, even though the Crumple node is mostly gray.

Here is a list of the connection types:

- **Color.** Receives input and outputs RGB color information. These connection types are designated by red dots on the nodes.
- **Scalar.** Designated by a green dot, a scalar connection is a value. You can have inputs or outputs based on single values.
- **Integer.** Great for blending, it is designated by purple dots. In most cases, integers connect to other integers.
- **Vector.** Designated by blue dots, vector connections allow you to control different channels, such as position or rotation.
- **Function.** This is a two-way connection, designated by a yellow dot. Function connections allow you to transform values of the nodes in which they are connected. You should connect functions to functions.

Before you move on to the next chapter to learn about LightWave 10 lighting, let's go a bit further in the Node Editor.

NOTE

You can keep the info panel open for all selected nodes (rather than double-clicking one) by clicking the left-facing triangle in the upper-right corner of the Node Editor panel. This will open a numeric information panel that shows the info and preferences for any node when selected. Often, however, you don't always need specific control for various nodes, so it's closed by default. Certain node controls for things like a gradient can be opened by double-clicking the node itself.

8. Back in the Node Editor, the crumple looks kind of dumpy applied with just a color connection. From the Add Node menu, select a Gradient node, as in **Figure 3.44**.

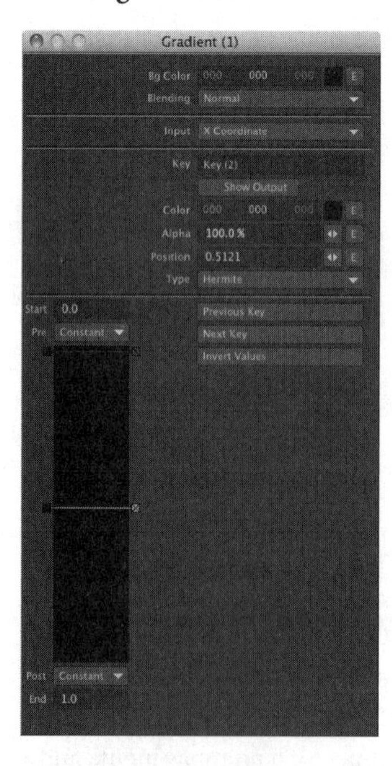

Figure 3.44 A Gradient node will help add color and interest to the Crumple node.

9. A small node is added to the workspace. Now you need to connect this to the existing nodes. You need to build it into your network. Double-click the Gradient node in the workspace. A panel opens showing you specific controls for the node.

10. In the Gradient node panel that opened, you'll see a tall black bar. A gradient allows you to vary settings based on different values. Click in the black bar, and a key is added. You'll see a small line, as in **Figure 3.45**.

11. If you look carefully, you'll see that this key you've added is actually now selected, and it is highlighted with a soft green. The default key is gray. With this new key still selected, change the color to red by clicking and dragging the value where it says Color in the panel. **Figure 3.46** shows the area. Also, if you look at the Key listing in the panel, you can see that Key (2) is selected.

12. Now add another key. Click in the gradient bar to add the key, and then change the color to green by dragging the green value to the right. Remember, to change the RGB values, you can simply click and drag the numeric value. Or you can click the color swatch to open a color palette. **Figure 3.47** shows the new key.

13. Go ahead and create two more keys, making one blue and one white. **Figure 3.48** shows the final gradient. Note that you can click and drag on the keys to slide them closer together or farther apart to change how the gradient looks. Be careful, though; if you click off the key, most likely you'll end up creating an additional key. To remove keys, click the right side of the key itself—there's a small x. This will delete the key. You can add as many keys as you like.

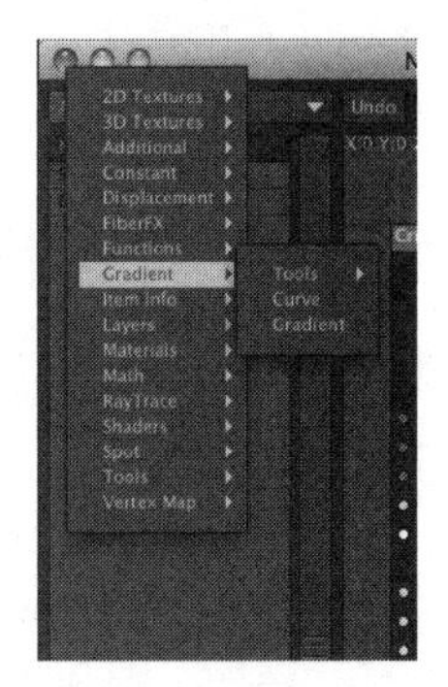

Figure 3.45 The gradient controls allow you to vary different values, such as color. It begins by clicking in the gradient bar.

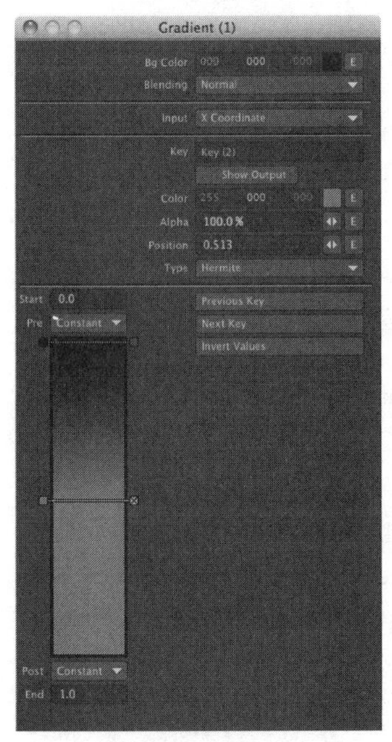

Figure 3.46 Drag the red value to the right to set a red color to the added gradient key.

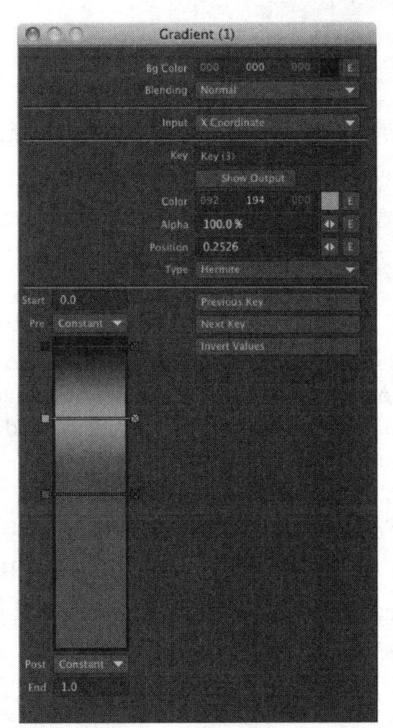

Figure 3.47 Add another key to the gradient bar, and make this one green.

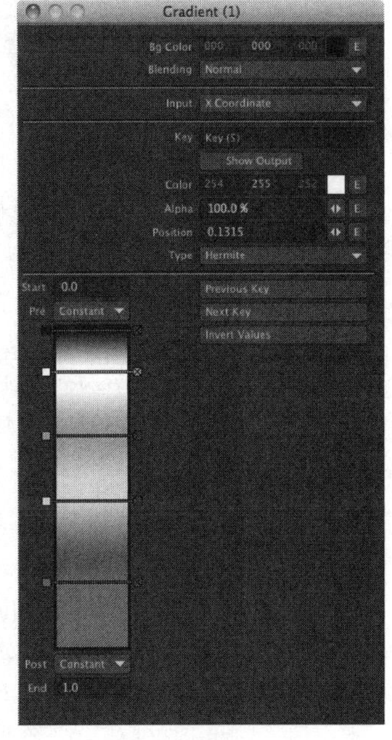

Figure 3.48 Add two more keys, one blue and one white.

14. Close the gradient panel. Back in the Node Editor workspace, you can see that your applied gradient shows in the node itself. Now all you need to do is connect it to the Crumple node. If you drag the Color channel from the Gradient node to the Luminosity input of the destination node, look what happens—the luminous values are changed for the destination surface. These are driven by the luminous output of the gradient. The green is brighter (has more luminance) than the red, and the destination node is updated accordingly, as in **Figure 3.49**.

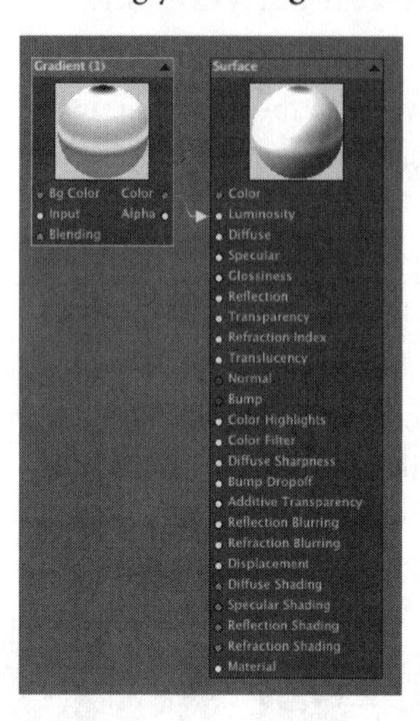

Figure 3.49 Taking the Color output from the Gradient node to the Luminosity input of the destination surface changes the values.

15. Try something different now. First, to "unhook" a connection, just click the arrow to remove it. Take the Color output of the gradient and connect it to the Opacity input of the Crumple node. Just click and drag the red dot, and then drop it on the Opacity input.

NOTE

You don't have to move the nodes around in order to connect them. The system will pull the arrows to wherever you want, but it's not a bad idea to arrange the nodes in left-to-right fashion to help stay organized. Just click and drag the nodes around as you like, remembering to press the **f** key to fit them to view.

16. Take the Color output from the Crumple node, and connect it to the Luminosity input of the destination node. The result is the crumple texture applied and then falling off based on the color values of the gradient. **Figure 3.50** shows the result.

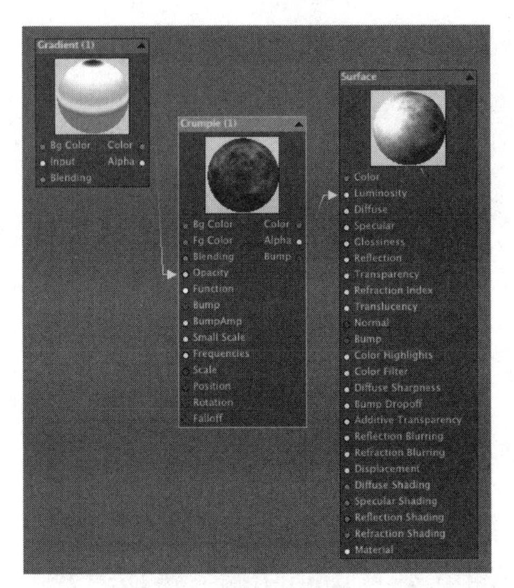

Figure 3.50 With the gradient's color connected to the crumple's opacity, and the opacity's color connected to the luminosity of the destination node, the surface is created.

17. Go back into the gradient controls. If you've closed the panel, double-click the Gradient node to open it again. Then, change the Input setting to Slope. By default, this value was set to X Coordinate, which is why the crumple was applied to the right side of the ball. **Figure 3.51** now shows the Gradient node applied based on the slope of the object. Note that this change fed through the network you've set up. Cool, eh?

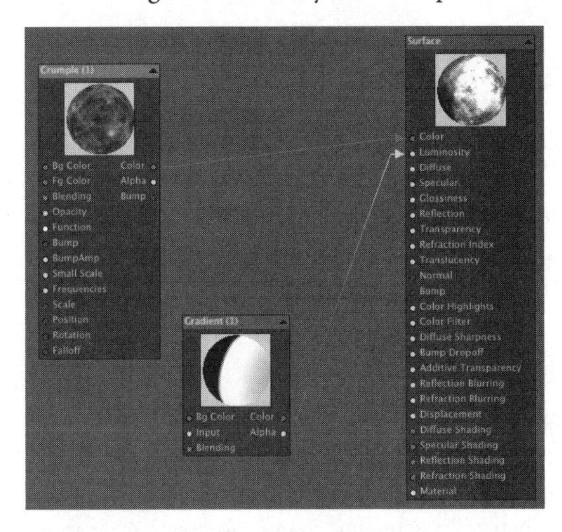

Figure 3.51 Changing the gradient's input setting to Slope also changes how the Crumple node is applied.

18. Here's one more thing to try before you move on: Pull the Color output of the gradient to the Fg Color input of the Crumple node. This puts the gradient RGB values into the foreground color of the crumple texture.

19. Next, take the crumple's Color output and connect it to the Color input of the destination node. **Figure 3.52** (on the next page) shows the result: a gradient blended with the crumple.

Figure 3.52 With the gradient Color output driving the foreground color of the Crumple node, the result is a blended surface.

Clearly, this is just the tip of the iceberg when it comes to using the Node Editor. As you experiment and progress in learning LightWave, you'll use the Node Editor for more complex surface techniques, including lighting and deformations. And speaking of lighting, you'll learn all about that in the next chapter!

The Next Step

From this point on, you can experiment on your own. Add more layers, play with gradients, and adjust procedurals. As a matter of fact, make as many additions and adjustments as you like. Your only limitations are time and system memory! Try adding some of the other procedural surfaces, such as Smokey, Turbulence, or Crust. Keep adding these to your rusty metal surface to see what you can come up with. Try selecting Copy All Layers from the Color Texture menu and applying them as Bump and Specularity textures. The results are endless. In addition, try applying LightWave's powerful surface shaders.

This chapter gave you a broad overview of the main features within LightWave's Surface Editor, including the Texture Editor. There are countless surfaces in the world around us, and it's up to you to create them digitally. As the book progresses, you will use the information and instructions in this chapter to create even more complex and original surfaces, such as glass, skin, metal, and more. The next chapter takes you deeper into the power of LightWave—read on to discover the lighting and cinematic tools available to you.

Chapter 4
Lighting

Working in 3D animation requires you to wear many hats. You're a draftsman, a 3D modeler, a producer, a painter, and even a gaffer—the person on a film set who takes care of the lighting. As a 3D animator, unless you're working in a big animation studio, you do your own lighting. And like many, you might consider lighting to be one of the less important aspects of your 3D animations, or simply an area that's outside your comfort zone. But lighting is crucial to your success as an animator, and fortunately it's not that hard to set up once you learn a few basic rules.

Lighting can be used for so much more than simply brightening a scene. Lighting can completely change the look of a shot. It can convey a mood, a feeling, or even a reaction. Lighting is vital in film, photography, and of course, 3D animation. Basic lighting can make your renders *hot* or *cold*; in other words, the color of the light you choose, where the lights are placed, and other aspects of lighting play a role in the final image. Lighting can improve your animations. But you need to be aware of some basic real-world principles before you can put it all together.

Lighting has an evil twin: texturing. OK, maybe it's not evil, but it can be challenging, and understanding texturing and how it's affected by lighting is one of your main goals as a 3D artist. This is probably one of the areas animators struggle with the most, and an area that can often make or break your project. However, don't worry; LightWave makes it easy to apply complex surfaces and get instant feedback. The look of a texture can change significantly based on the lighting associated with it. So, the two go hand in hand.

The previous chapter introduced you to LightWave 10's surfacing capabilities, including the Node Editor. Take that knowledge and move through this chapter to learn how to light your models and scenes.

This chapter instructs you on the following:

- Understanding basic lighting principles
- Using different light sources
- Enabling radiosity
- Lighting with gobos
- Creating soft shadows
- Interacting with materials

Working with Lights

Eight light types are available in LightWave Layout. Each has a specific purpose, but none is limited to that purpose. One thing to note is that each light has variances in settings. The area light, for example, can be scaled, but the spotlight can't. Distant lights use only rotation for their effect, whereas point lights use only position. Check out the Lighting Basics video on the book's DVD to see them in action.

NOTE

While you're working in LightWave's Modeler, you will not see a light source illuminating your shaded model in a Perspective viewport. Do not let that fool you, because it has nothing to do with your final lighting setup. Lights are available only in Layout.

- **Area lights.** The best choice for creating true shadows, area lights create a brighter, more diffuse light than distant lights and therefore result in greater realism. They do, however, take longer to render than spotlights, distant lights, or point lights.
- **Distant lights.** You can use a distant light for simulating bright sunlight, moonlight, or general lighting from a nonspecific source. Shadows from this light are hard. A distant light's position does not matter to your scene; only its rotation matters.
- **Dome lights.** Used for creating a pseudo-environmental lighting environment, the dome light encompasses the entire scene.
- **Linear lights.** You can use linear lights as elongated light sources, such as fluorescent bulbs and neon tubes. Linear lights can have realistic shadows but consume additional rendering time.
- **Photometric lights.** Photometric lights have become more common in 3D applications over the last few years. This type of light uses a predetermined file called an IES file. You can find more about these file types at www.CGArena.com.
- **Point lights.** You can use a point light to create sources of light that emit in all directions, such as a candle, lightbulb, or spark. Unlike a distant light,

a point light's rotation does not matter in your scene; only its position matters. It, too, yields hard-edged shadows.

- **Spherical lights.** Simliar to a point light, a spherical light might prove a better source of light for bulbs or special effects. Light is more concentrated to a sphere and less streaked than, say, a point light. The size of the light is important too; it affects the sharpness of the shadow. Smaller lights, sharper shadows. Larger lights, softer shadows.
- **Spotlights.** The most commonly used lighting type, spotlights can be used for directional lighting, such as canister lighting, headlights on cars, studio simulation lighting, volumetric lighting, and more. Spotlight rotation and position play roles in your scene. A spotlight's shadows can be either hard or soft with shadow mapping.

The environment in which your animation lives is crucial to the animation itself, which is why we dedicate a chapter to lighting and textures. You should consider color, intensity, and ambient light each time you set up a scene. Too often, tutorials overlook the power of light, but you know better! Using lights, along with shadows, as elements in your animation can be as important as the models and motions you create. As you work through setting up lights in your 3D scenes, you should get used to setting one variable in particular: light intensity, also called brightness.

NOTE

Although we could dedicate this entire chapter and more to theory, design, and usage, we thought it better to demonstrate by doing. This chapter focuses specifically on using LightWave's lighting system so you can achieve results immediately. For an excellent lighting reference book, check out *Digital Lighting & Rendering, second edition*, by Jeremy Birn (New Riders, 2006).

As you work through lighting setups in this chapter and throughout this book, check out the types of lights LightWave has to offer. At the bottom of the LightWave Layout interface, you'll see the familiar item selection buttons—Objects, Bones, Lights, and Cameras. Click the Lights button, and then click the Properties button to the right. Alternatively, you can always press **p** to open any item's properties. You'll see the LightWave Light Properties panel (**Figure 4.1**).

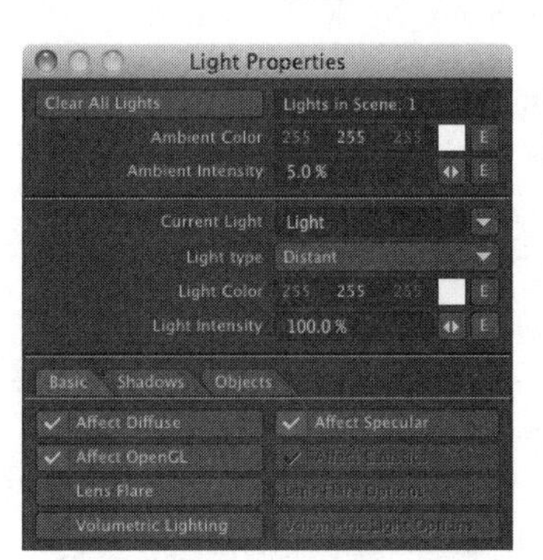

Figure 4.1 The Light Properties panel, as shown with a single default light.

Looking closely at Figure 4.1, you can work your way down the panel, using the following explanations as your guide. At the very top of the panel, you can quickly clear all lights by clicking the Clear All Lights button. Be careful with this, as it clears *all* the lights in your scene, except for the default distant light. If you've changed the default light, clicking this option resets it. Next to the Clear All Lights button, you'll see an information display called Lights in Scene.

NOTE

The Current Light drop-down list near the top of the Light Properties panel contains the name of each light in your scene. The default single distant light is named, simply, Light. Select this entry in the list and you can quickly rename it. You can do this for any light you add. Lighting in 3D animation is an art all its own.

Another interesting part of LightWave when it comes to lighting is the Global Illumination option. This is an important area of your 3D lighting setup. However, you won't find Global Illumination settings in the Lights panel but in the Render Globals panel. We'll cover these settings just after the basic lighting information, later in this chapter.

Light Color

The color of the light you use is important and useful in your images and animations because it can help set tone, mood, and feeling. No light is ever purely white, and it's up to you to change LightWave's default pure-white light color. The color selector works the same as the other color selectors in LightWave. You can also animate the RGB values with the Graph Editor. In LightWave, you can even animate colored lights. Clicking the E button takes you to the Graph Editor, allowing you to vary the light color over time. Very cool! You'll use this for all kinds of things, such as animating a rock concert where you need to have fast-moving lights shining on the stage. By animating the light color, you can change the colors over time at any speed you want.

Light Intensity

When you start LightWave Layout or choose Clear Scene, by default there is always one light in your LightWave scene. It has a light intensity of 100% and is a distant light. Although you can use this one light and its preset intensity as your main source of light for images and animations, it's best to adjust the light intensity to more appropriately match the light and the scene at hand.

Did you know that light intensities can range from values in the negative to values in the thousands? You can set a light intensity to 9000% (or higher) if you want, just by typing in the value. The results might not be that desirable and may even be unstable, but you never know what your scene might call for. In general, if you want to create a bright, sunny day, you can use a point light, which emits light in all directions, with a light intensity of 150% or so for bright light everywhere. On the other hand, if you want to light an evening scene, perhaps on a city street, you can use spotlights with light intensities set to around 60%. As you build scenes throughout this book, you'll be asked to set up different light types, with varying intensities. This will also help you get a feel for setting the right intensity.

NOTE

The mini-slider (the left and right arrows) next to the Light Intensity setting in the Light Properties panel allows you to click and drag values ranging from 0 to 100. However, by manually entering values, you can set higher or even negative values!

Negative lights, or "dark lights," can also be handy depending on the scene you're working on. Whereas lights with a positive light intensity can brighten a scene, negative lights can darken a scene. You might be asking why you would darken a scene with a negative light instead of just turning the lights down. For example, you might have to add a lot of light to make areas appear properly lit. Depending on the surfaces you've set, the extra light might make one area look perfect while making other areas too bright. This is where negative lights come into play. Adding a negative light (any light with a negative light intensity value) takes away light from a specific area.

Adding Lights

In most cases, you're going to use more than a single distant light in your 3D scenes. This section shows you how to add lights. Follow these simple steps to add lights to LightWave Layout to get a feel for how they work. And remember, unless you're working with Auto Key enabled, you'll need to create a keyframe to lock your lights into position after they're moved, just like objects.

Exercise 4.1 Adding Lights to Layout

1. Jump into Layout, and load the UnlitTractor scene from the book's DVD. This is similar to the scene file from Chapter 3, but with one default distant light.
2. Make sure you are in Perspective view so that you have a full view of Layout. You can press **4** to quickly jump to the view. On the Items tab, under the Add category, select Lights, and then select Spotlight to add a spotlight to the scene. **Figure 4.2** shows the menus.

   You can choose to add any type of light you want.
3. Before the light is added to Layout, a Light Name panel appears (**Figure 4.3**).

Figure 4.3 After you add a light, the Light Name panel appears, enabling you to set a specific name for your light.

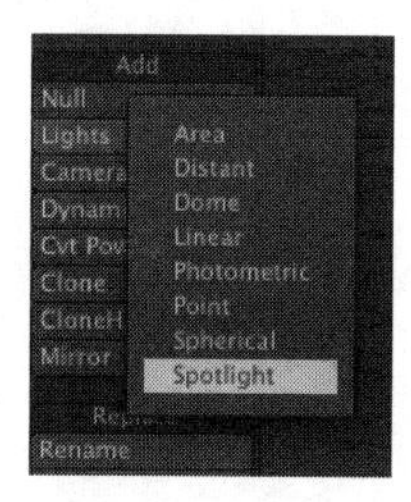

Figure 4.2 You can add lights directly in Layout under the Items tab.

4. Type the word **Fill** to name the new spotlight.

NOTE

You don't have to change the name of a new light. Instead, you can accept LightWave's default light name by clicking OK when the Light Name panel appears. By default, LightWave names new lights Light (1), Light (2), Light (3), and so on.

   Layout places the new light at your scene's origin point (the 0 coordinate shared by the X, Y, and Z axes).

5. Move this new spotlight off and to the side of the tractor. Then rotate it so it points to the tractor, as in **Figure 4.4** (on the next page).

Figure 4.4 Move the light off and to the side of the tractor to cast light onto the darker areas of the tractor.

Adding lights is as simple as that. Certainly there's more to it, such as cloning and mirroring, so read on.

Clone Lights

Besides adding lights, you can clone lights. Cloning a light creates an exact duplicate of a selected light. This includes the light's color, intensity, position, rotation, and so on. Any parameter you've set will be cloned. Cloning lights is just as easy as adding lights, but it's often good to do after you're sure of your existing light's settings. You don't want to clone a light 20 times, only to realize that you forgot to change the color! You'd need to make changes to 20 lights. However, should you have to make changes to many lights at once, you can quickly select the lights to change in the Scene Editor. **Figure 4.5** shows two lights in the Scene Editor selected at once.

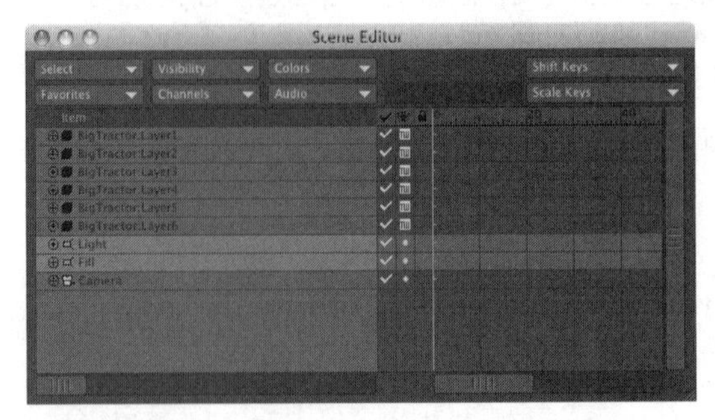

Figure 4.5 If you have one light, two, or twenty, you can use the Scene Editor to edit variables for those lights all at once.

To clone a light, first select the light to be cloned in Layout, and then select the Clone button under the Items tab in the Add category. Enter the number of clones (copies) of the light you want in the pop-up panel, and click OK or press Enter. Shazaam! The selected light is cloned. You know what else? This operation works the same for cloning objects or cameras. **Figure 4.6** shows the command.

NOTE

You can multiselect lights directly in Layout. Just hold down the Shift key and select them. Then rotate, move, and so on.

Figure 4.6 You can clone lights (or any other item) directly in Layout from the Items tab.

Mirror Lights

You know what's cool? Mirroring your light! Let's say you move the light to a specific position. Use the Mirror button in the Add category on the Items tab. Select a light (or other item in Layout) and click the Mirror button in the Item tab's Add tool category. Choose the axis to mirror across, and go! **Figure 4.7** shows the operation. You can also choose to mirror around an object's keyframes or at frame 0. Mirroring at frame 0 is important for more complex setups such as bone rigs for characters.

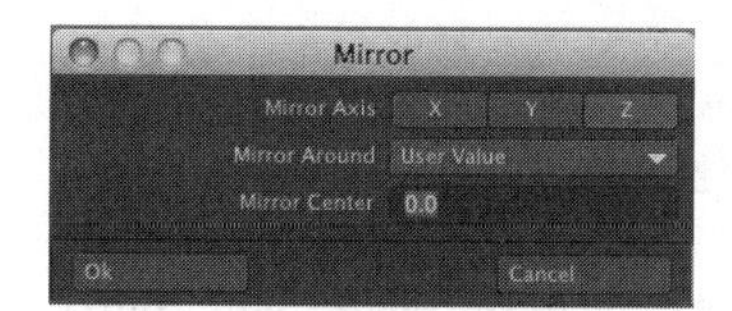

Figure 4.7 In addition to cloning lights, you can mirror them.

Ambient Light and Ambient Color

Did you know that the light around you is either direct or ambient? Direct light comes predominantly from a light source. Ambient light has no specific source or direction, such as the light underneath your desk or behind a door.

Back in the Light Properties panel, you can set the intensity of your ambient light. To open it, click the Lights button at the bottom of the interface and then press **p** or click the Properties button. The Ambient Controls are at the top of the panel. A typical Ambient Light setting is around 5%, which is LightWave's default value. In some cases, it is better to lower the value, sometimes to 0%, and use additional lights for more control over your scenes. Don't rely on ambient light to brighten your scene. Instead, use more lights to make areas brighter. This will create a more dramatic look, with more depth in the final render.

You also can set the color of your ambient light so that the areas not hit by light still have some color to them. Let's say you have a single blue light shining on an actor on a stage. Only the portions of the actor upon which the light falls directly will be lit. If you want to reveal more of the actor, or just lessen the severity of the boundary between light and shadow, you can apply an Ambient Intensity setting. Set the Ambient Color values to the same shade of blue as the light, and your shot will look accurate. Remember, ambient light hits all surfaces, not just those that are unlit by actual lights, which is why knowing about ambient intensity is important.

Lens Flares

The lens flare, often overused but needed, was introduced in LightWave v3. Lens flares are a popular addition to animated scenes, because too often when you add a light (such as a candlestick) to a scene, the light source emits but no generating source is visible. By adding a lens flare, you can create a small haze or glow around the candlelight. You can also add lens flares to lights on a stage, sunlight, flashlights, and headlights on a car. Any time you have a light that is in view in a scene, you should add a lens flare so the viewer understands that the light has a source. Lens flares in LightWave can be viewed directly in Layout before rendering. You'll be setting up lens flares later in this chapter.

Volumetric Lights

You need to be aware of one more area when it comes to LightWave lighting before you start working through exercises. Volumetric lighting is a powerful and quickly rendered effect that can create beams of light. Have you ever seen how a light streaks when it shines through a window? The beam of light that emits from the light source can be replicated in LightWave with *volumetrics*. Volumetric settings add volume to a light source. Additionally, you can add textures to a volumetric light to create all sorts of interesting light beams.

Global Illumination Options

Have you ever stopped to look around you? Take your face out of this book or away from the computer for a moment, and just look around. Whether you're at your desk, in your living room, or outside, everything has global lighting properties. You can control these global properties—global light intensity, global lens flare intensity, ambient intensity, ambient color, radiosity, and caustics—on the Global Illumination tab of the Render Globals panel. To open it, click the Render tab at the top of the Layout interface, and then click the Render Globals tool button. The Global Illumination settings are found in the Global Illum tab, among the five settings tabs at the top of the panel (**Figure 4.8**).

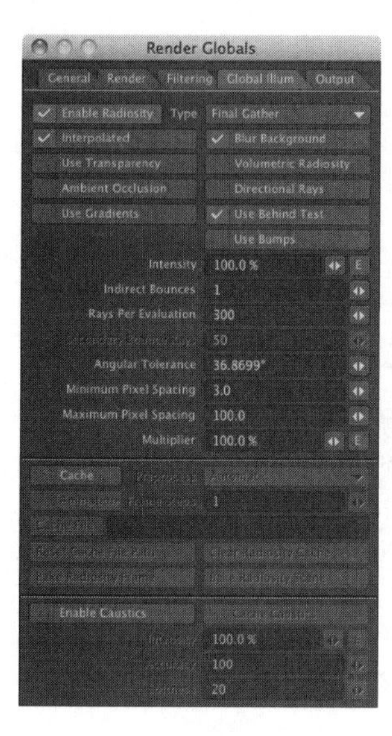

Figure 4.8 The Global Illumination control tab, found in the Render Globals panel, governs such properties as global light intensity, global lens flare intensity, radiosity, and caustics.

Global Light and Lens Flare Intensity

In the Global Illumination panel, click the Render tab at the bottom of the panel. At the bottom of the panel is a (light) Intensity value, currently set at 100%. Because it's in the Render Globals panel, it globally changes the intensity on all lights in your scene. This can be useful for scenes that have multiple lights that need to become brighter or dimmer over time.

Let's say you're animating a stage play or musical concert, for example. You have 29 spotlights shining on the stage, the players, and the actors. All their intensities are randomly and quickly changing to the beat of the music, and perhaps focusing on key performers. At the end of the song, you want all the lights to fade out equally. Instead of setting the light intensity 29 times for each light, which you could do through the Scene Editor, it is better to ramp down the Global Light Intensity setting. Similarly, if you have lens flares applied to these lights, you can globally change the Flare Intensity setting for lights, just below the Intensity setting.

Radiosity and Caustics

Also within the Global Illumination panel (within the Render Globals panel) are the Enable Radiosity and Enable Caustics settings. These two features in LightWave enable you to take your 3D creations even further by adding more real-world lighting properties.

NOTE

The radiosity and caustics features are not active by default. You need to activate them to see their effects on a scene, but be warned—rendering times will increase.

Radiosity is a rendering solution that calculates the diffused reflections of lights in a scene. It is the rate at which light energy leaves a surface. This also includes the color within all surfaces. In simpler terms, radiosity is bounced light. A single light coming through a window, for example, can light up an entire room. The light hits the surfaces of the objects and bounces, lighting up the rest of the room, in turn creating a realistic image. Ambient light is often considered a poor man's radiosity. You can use ambient light to brighten areas not directly lit by lights.

You'll use radiosity and learn more about its settings in Chapter 8, "3D Product Shots."

Caustics are created when light is reflected off a surface or through a refracted surface. A good example is the random pattern often seen at the bottom of a swimming pool when bright sunlight shines through the water. Another example is the dapples of light that appear on floors or ceilings when light glints off a crystal vase or a gold-plated statue.

Applying Lights in LightWave

You will encounter many types of lighting situations when creating your animation masterpiece. This next section steps you through a common lighting situation that you can use for character animation tests, product shots, or logo scenes.

Simulating Studio Lighting

One of the cool things about LightWave is that you don't have to be a numbers person to make things happen. You can see what's happening throughout the creation process from object construction to surfacing to lighting. Exercise 4.2 introduces you to basic three-point lighting often used in everyday video production. You can apply this lighting style to LightWave and create a photographer's backdrop (or *cyc*, short for *cyclorama*) to act as a set for your objects. Creating a set in LightWave is a good idea so that even simple render tests are not over a black background. By rendering objects on a set, you add more depth to your animation.

The goal of this project is to introduce you to a common lighting setup that can be useful in just about any type of render situation when simulating studio lighting. You'll use a premade scene from this book's DVD.

Exercise 4.2 Simulating Studio Lighting

1. In Layout, load the unlit_female_head.lws scene from this chapter's folder on the accompanying DVD (in the "3D_Content\Scenes\Ch4\" directory).

   This loads the multilayered object, which includes eight layers—all the parts of the model, from teeth to skin. The light box is a flat polygon that will be used to help light the subject. **Figure 4.9** shows the loaded scene in Wireframe mode.

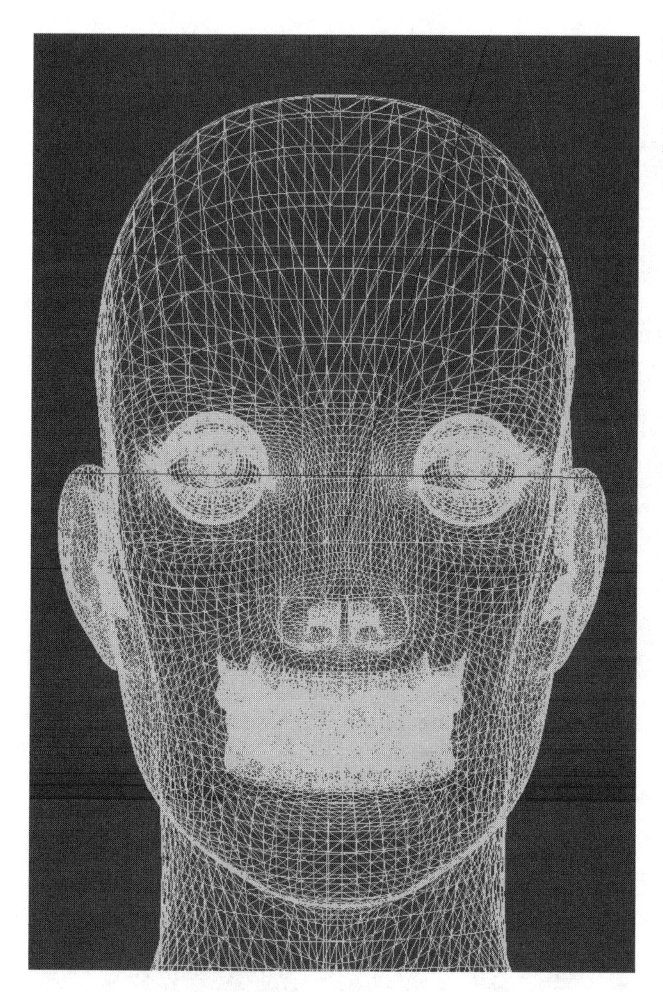

Figure 4.9 A pre-existing scene with one multilayered object, perfect for testing some lighting configurations.

2. Click the Lights button at the bottom of the Layout interface (or press Shift+L) to select the only light currently in the scene, which is generically named Light. (If the scene contained more than one light, you'd also need to select the one you want to work with from the Item drop-down.) This is a distant light and is not the most effective lighting. To see how it lights the scene, press **F9** to render the current frame (**Figure 4.10** on the next page).

   To see the render when you press F9, be sure that you have Image Viewer selected for Render Display with a chosen resolution, or choose Render Frame from the Render drop-down.

3. The render looks flat and ordinary, and you need some definition from the background. Add a spotlight from the Add category in Layout, under the Items tab.

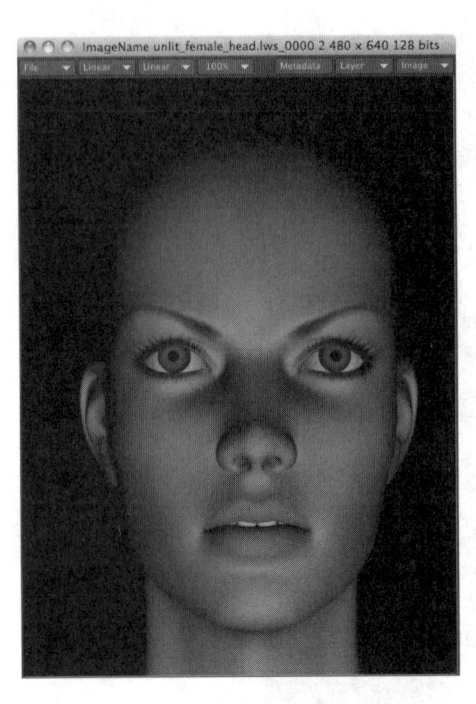

Figure 4.10 Pressing F9 lets you preview a render of the current frame. By default, the render isn't any different from what you see in Layout.

4. Name the light **backlight**, and position it up and behind the female head object. In the Light Properties panel, set the Light Intensity to 140%. You can select Lights at the bottom of the interface, and then press the **p** key to open the panel. **Figure 4.11** shows the render, with the Light Properties settings. You can turn Shadows to Shadow Map within the Light Properties panel as well.

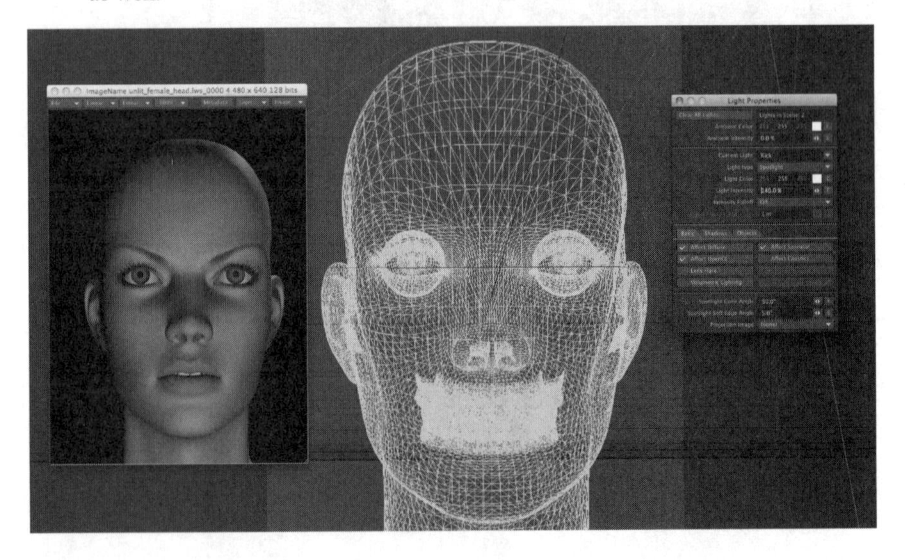

Figure 4.11 Adding a kick light to the back of the model helps separate her from the black background.

NOTE

If you want to convert the Shadow Map Size to actual megabytes, square the size value, multiply by 4, and divide by 1,000. So, (2000 × 2000 × 4) ÷ 1000 = 16MB. That means a Shadow Map Size of 2000 will take an extra 16MB of memory for calculation.

NOTE

Three-point lighting is a common lighting setup used in many studios. It consists of a key light, which is the primary source of brightness; a fill light, which is less bright than the key and used opposite the key; and a backlight, sometimes referred to as a hair light, which is used to separate the subject from the background. You'll find a similarly set scene called studio_lit_female_head.lws on the book's DVD.

The trick to this simple setup is using bounce cards. In a real photography studio (such as www.AblanGallery.com) large softboxes are used for photographing people. In the 3D world, directional lights like spotlights can be harsh. But with a colored board, set to white or off-white, you can bounce light and softly diffuse the surface of the model.

If you view the scene from a Perspective view, you'll see two bounce cards. One is white and off to the right of the model. Its surface is bright white and has a Luminosity value. The other board is off-white and is used to bounce light underneath the model. But when you rendered before you didn't see the effect of these. That's because on their own, objects can't cast light. With Global Illumination turned on, they can.

5. In the Render tab, open Render Globals. In the Render Globals panel, click into the Global Illum tab and click Enable Radiosity. Press F9 again. Your model now looks completely different, and actually too lit! **Figure 4.12** shows the render along with the Global Illumination settings.

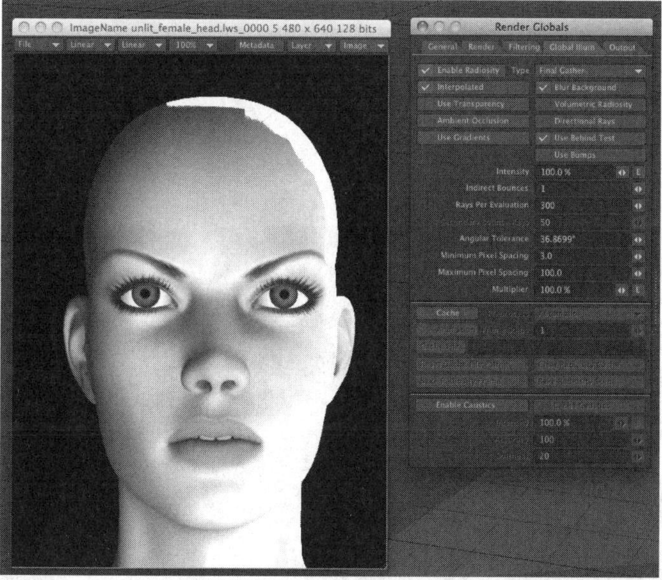

Figure 4.12 Turning on Enable Radiosity allows the bounce cards to cast a soft, diffuse light on the scene, but the scene is too bright with the existing spotlights.

6. Jump back to the Light Properties panel and bring the Light Intensity to 0% for both lights. Alternatively, you can deselect Affect Diffuse for each light and they won't affect the surface. However, other properties will still be affected, such as specularity.

NOTE

You can use shadow maps only with spotlights.

7. Press F9 to render again, and you'll see a much softer look to the model, but with a slight darkness on the left side. **Figure 4.13** shows the render.

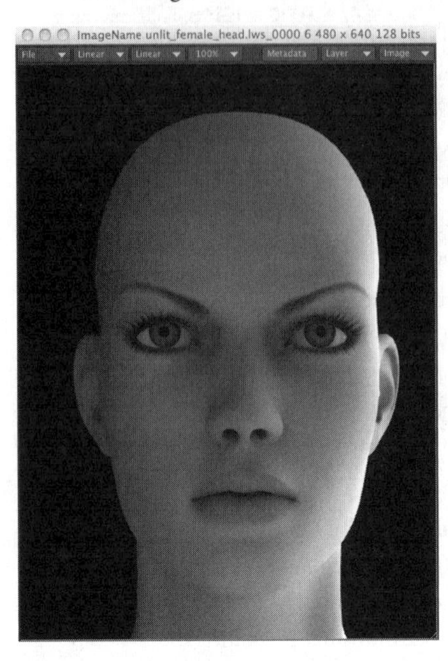

Figure 4.13 Turning down the intensity of the existing light sources will help even out the values with radiosity applied.

NOTE

You can quickly choose different lights in the Light Properties panel by clicking the small arrow to the right of the Current Light drop-down list.

8. Select the back spotlight you created earlier. Clone it one time by pressing Control+C. Move this clone to the top front left of the female model. Set the Light Intensity value to 45% and press F9 to render. Ah! Now there are catchlights in the model's eyes, but a nice soft diffuse from the bounce card on the right. **Figure 4.14** shows the render, along with the Perspective view to see the lighting setup.

Figure 4.14 Adding a spotlight to fill the darker area of the model's face works well to enhance her surfacing, while the Enable Radiosity setting allows the bounce cards to fill in other areas.

Enhanced Lighting with HDR

Now that you have some basic lighting set up and can see how useful radiosity can be, it's easy to take your lighting a step further. HDR (High Dynamic Range) is a technique that allows you to use an image as a light source. However, HDR images hold more data within them than meets the eye. But LightWave can see what's there, so let's see how it works.

Exercise 4.3 Enhanced Lighting Setups

1. Continue from the previous scene, making sure Enable Radiosity is still selected in the Global Illum (Illumination) tab in the Render Globals panel.
2. From the Windows drop-down menu, choose Backdrop Options. This will open the Effects panel, with the Backdrop tab selected.
3. From the Add Environment drop down menu, select Image World. When the plug-in loads, double-click it to see the settings, as shown in **Figure 4.15**.
4. From the DVD included with this book, load the road.hdr image from the Light Probe Image selection. **Figure 4.16** shows the image. Set the Heading Offset to 90. And then bring Brightness for the HDR image down to about 80%.

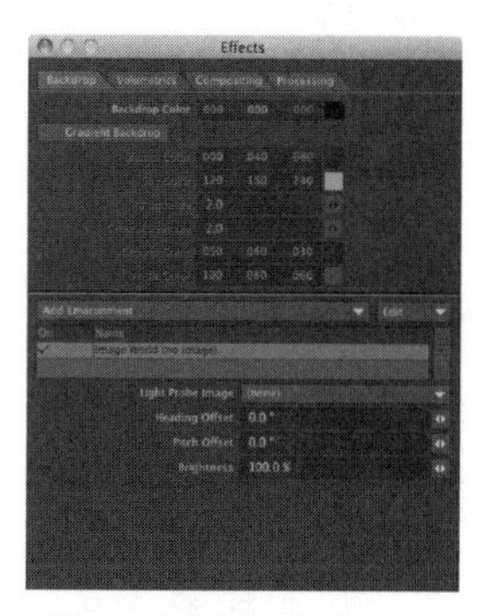

Figure 4.15 Add the Image World plug-in from the Add Environment menu in the Backdrop tab of the Effects panel.

Figure 4.16 An HDR image used for environmental lighting.

5. With the HDR image loaded, you don't need the other light sources. Go ahead and delete the extra spotlights, and make sure the main light has Affect Diffuse deselected in the Light Properties panel.
6. Next, delete the bounce card objects. **Figure 4.17** shows Layout from a Perspective view with the changes.

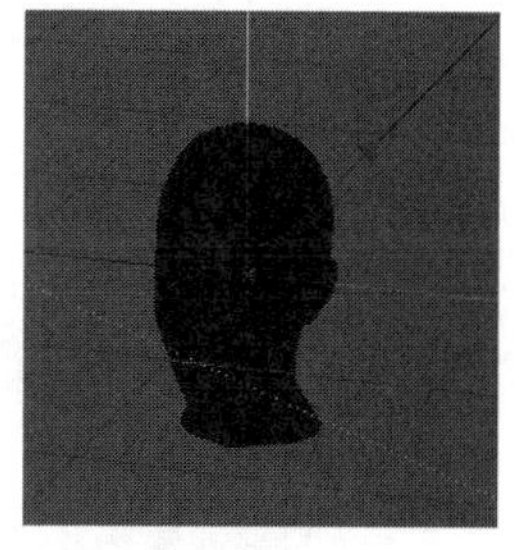

Figure 4.17 Layout in Perspective view with the bounce card objects deleted.

7. That's it! Instead of pressing F9 to render, turn on VPR from the top of the Layout interface, rather than Shaded Solid. **Figure 4.18** shows the interface with VPR active and with the Image World settings.

Figure 4.18 With an HDR image set in place through the Image World plug-in, the color values within the image light the scene entirely.

HDR images are a remarkable way to light your scene, not only for ease of use, but more for blending your 3D object into a real world. The world around us has light of different temperatures bouncing and diffusing all over the place, and by using an HDR image in LightWave, you can mimic the real world.

Using Projection Images on Lights

LightWave's Projection Image feature is a useful lighting tool that mimics real-world lighting situations in which cookies or gobos are used to throw light onto a set. A *gobo*, also referred to as a *cucoloris* or *cookie*, is a cutout shape that is placed in front of a light, sort of like a cookie cutter. Certain areas of the gobo hold back light, whereas other areas let light through. In Exercise 4.4, you use a gobo that creates the look of light coming through trees.

Although the previous exercise was basic in design, it is the core lighting situation for many of your LightWave scenes. Perhaps with a slight variation, this basic three-point lighting scheme can be used for product shots, animated plays, logos, and much more. Things like simple stage sets, equipment, figures, generic objects, or any element can benefit from this type of lighting design. Of course, you are not limited to using just three lights for these types of situations. You can start with the basic three, and then add or remove lights to highlight certain areas, brighten dark areas, or use additional lights as projection lights.

The gobo image is nothing more than a Photoshop file of a black-and-white windowpane. Using a simple image-editing program, it was converted to grayscale mode, its contrast was boosted, and the image was blurred. When this image is applied to a spotlight, the white areas allow light to shine through, whereas the black areas do not. The blurring helps create a soft, less harsh look where the light falls off.

TIP

Gobo images can be created with a paint package such as Adobe Photoshop. Image dimensions should match your render resolution, and 24-bit color depth generally works best for most applications. However, if it's a smaller image that's not viewed close-up in your 3D scene, you can save memory and use 8-bit images. Perhaps you just need to project a small logo onto a wall? A smaller image would serve your needs well. Video-resolution gobo images should have pixel dimensions of 720 × 486.

Exercise 4.4 Creating Gobo Lights

1. Continuing from the last project, use the same scene. Select the single spotlight left in the scene and name it **Gobo Light** or something similar. You can rename lights from the Light Properties panel. The idea is that you stay organized by identifying the lights properly as you set them up. Select the new spotlight and press **5** on the keyboard to switch to Light view.
2. At the bottom of the Light Properties panel, load the SixWindowCookie.tif image from the book's DVD.
3. Press **5** on the keyboard to jump to the Light view. There, you'll see the projection of the image through the light. The white areas will let light pass

through, and the dark areas will hold it back. Blurring the image helps blend the transition. **Figure 4.19** shows the shot.

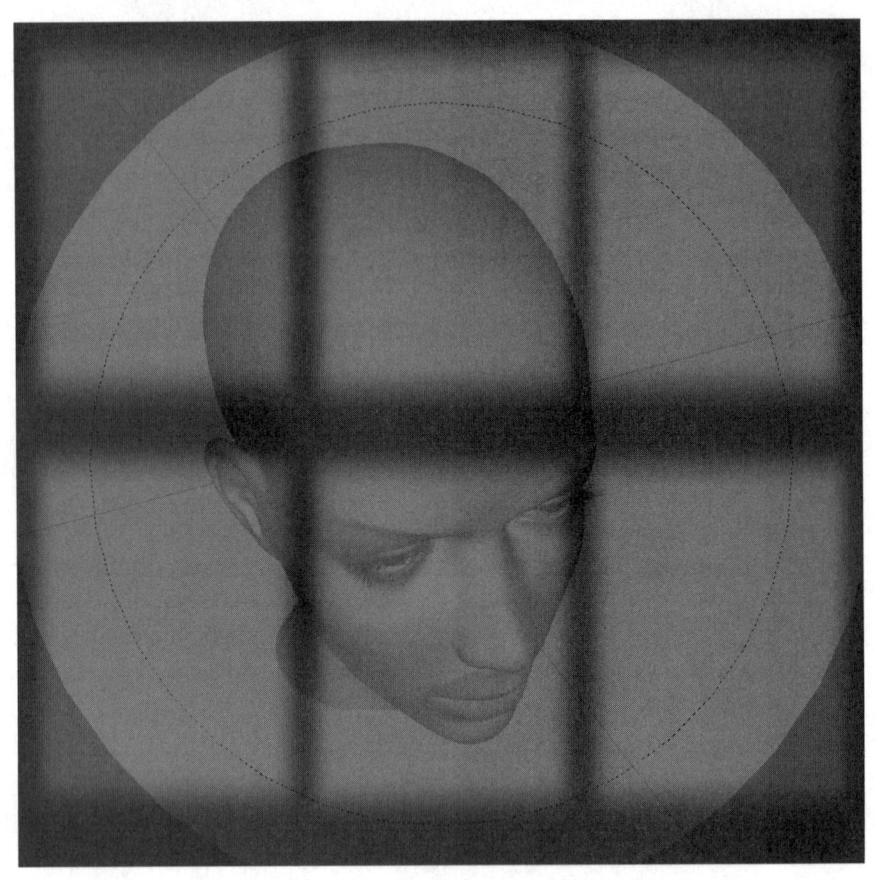

Figure 4.19 The SixWindowCookie.tif image in Light view.

4. Move the gobo light up and to the upper-right or upper-left side of the scene. Height doesn't matter too much; just be sure your projection will be able to hit the set. Point the light onto the floor, and be sure to create a keyframe for it at frame 0 to lock it in place.

   Remember, everything should have a keyframe at the first frame of your animation even if it is not moving. In this case, the first frame is 0.

5. Make the new gobo light slightly off-white in color and set Light Intensity to anywhere from 40% to 60%.

6. After the image has been loaded, press **F9** to render. You'll see what appears to be light through a window, across the face of the object. The light is now projected through the grayscale image, which you can see from Light view (see **Figure 4.20**). You can take a closer look at the gobo image in the Image Editor. Note that your image might appear slightly different due to variances in light placements.

NOTE

While you can't tell LightWave to create off-white lights by default, you can change multiple lights to off-white (or any other color) at the same time. Select all of the lights you want to adjust, and change the color settings in the Light Properties panel to affect all of the lights at once. In the same way, you can modify other light properties for all selected lights.

Figure 4.20 With the gobo image in place, you now see the shadows of a windowpane across the subject's face.

You can load this final scene into Layout from this book's DVD and check the final settings if you want. The scene is called studio_lit_female_head_enhanced.lws (in the "3D_Content\Scenes\Ch4\" directory). Take a look at it and modify it for your own scenes if you like.

Adding gobos is easy. But it's probably a more powerful feature than you realize. Creating a simple pattern on a set is nice, but you can accomplish much more with gobos:

- Use a grayscale image of tree branches to simulate shadows from a tree.
- Use color images for added dimension. Darker areas will hold back more light, and lighter areas will shine more light. For example, you can create the effects of light through a stained-glass window.
- Use softer, blurry images for added effects.
- Use animation sequences as projection images.
- Use imported movie files! Create real projected movies in your animation by projecting an AVI or QuickTime movie onto a movie screen in 3D.
- Create custom shapes and project them onto your set to create the look of light coming through a stage light projection system.

Using Area Lights

Distant lights and point lights produce hard-edged, ray-traced shadows. Ray-traced shadows take more time to calculate, which of course means more time to render. Spotlights also can produce ray-traced shadows, but with spotlights you have the option to use shadow maps, which take less time to render than ray-traced shadows. Softer than ray-traced shadows, shadow maps use more memory to render than ray-traced shadows. Ray-traced shadows use more processing power.

Area lights also can produce realistic ray-traced shadows, but to do so they require more rendering time. For example, say a person is standing outside in bright sunlight. The shadow that the person casts has sharp edges around the area by the subject's foot, where the shadow begins. As the shadow falls off and away from the subject, it becomes softer. Ray-traced shadows from distant lights, point lights, and spotlights cannot produce this effect—neither can shadow maps. Only area lights can produce these true shadows and create a softer overall appearance to animations.

Spotlights are the most common lights, and they are the most useful for your everyday animation needs. But on occasion, the added rendering time generated from area lights is worthwhile. An area light is represented in Layout by a flat square and emits light equally from all directions except at the edges, producing very realistic shadows.

Exercise 4.5 Working with Area Lights

1. From the book's DVD, load the AreaLightTractor.lws scene. Select the single default light, and then press **p** to open the Light Properties panel. Change Light Type from Distant to Area Light.
2. Change the Light Intensity setting to 75%. Keeping the default 100% Light Intensity setting could be too bright, and the image would appear washed out. Area lights are often "hotter" than spotlights and also give you more control.
3. Move the Light Properties panel aside and return to Layout. Rotate the light and place it above the tractor.
4. If the new area light is not selected, select it and change your Layout view to Perspective to get an overall view of the scene. **Figure 4.21** shows the Perspective view and the light newly positioned above the tractor object. The area light appears as a box outline. This light is positioned in front of the tractor, closer to the ground. Not ideal. All you've done now is change the type of light you're using. Everything else, such as position and rotation, has remained the same.

Figure 4.21 The Perspective view with a distant light converted to an area light.

5. In Layout's Render tab, click Render Globals. Then, on the Render Globals panel's Render tab, select Raytrace Shadows to have LightWave calculate shadows for the area light, as shown in **Figure 4.22**.

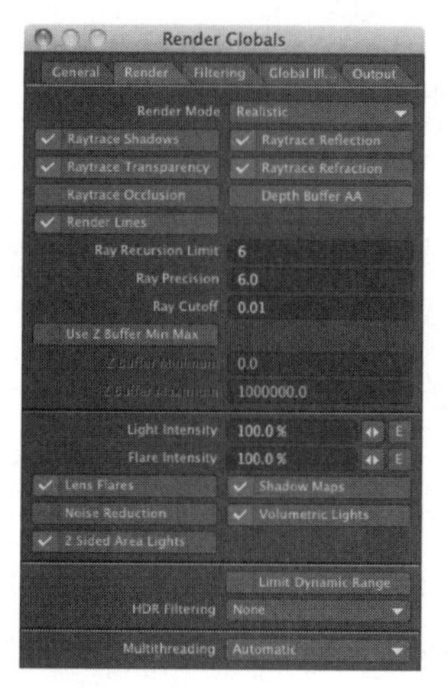

Figure 4.22 Make sure you tell the render to calculate for shadows and other options.

NOTE

To help set up lights in Layout, change the Maximum Render Level setting to Textured Shaded Solid. You can find this setting by clicking the drop-down arrow to the right of the viewport style buttons at the top of Layout. Make sure Max OpenGL Lights is set to at least 1 or above from the Display Options panel (press d). Also, always make sure that the Affect OpenGL option for the light in the Light Properties panel is turned on. This makes the light source's effect visible in Layout and helps you line up the direction of the light source.

NOTE

While you're in the Render Options panel, make sure you choose a Preview setting, such as 320 × 240. This enables you to see the render as it's being drawn. Also make sure that Render Display is set to Image Viewer to see a full-sized version of your render when it's complete. The full-sized version will be 640 × 480, as this is its resolution setting by default. You can also change this setting in the Render Globals panel. You'll learn more about different resolutions (and not of the New Year's kind) in Chapter 5, "3D Cameras."

6. With the light selected, go to Layout's Modify tab and choose Size. Click and drag the area light so that it's about 4 times its original size, then turn on VPR in Layout to see the light and how it affects the objects. You'll see that the shadow has a soft edge, as shown in **Figure 4.23**.

Figure 4.23 Setting the area light above the model and increasing the size creates a much softer shadow, which often gives your scene a more realistic look.

NOTE

The cool thing about area lights is that you can size them. Because the area light here was originally a spotlight, its size has remained. If, however, you created a new area light, you would need to increase the size to soften the shadows. By increasing their size, you soften their shadows. Don't forget to keyframe any size changes. You can use the Size tool on the Modify tab. Try it out!

Sizing a light might seem odd, but it helps spread the amount of light and thereby the shadow as well. Area lights take a long time to render, but they produce the best results.

Here are a few more things to remember when using area lights:

- Quality settings can be adjusted. The default Area Light Quality setting of 4 results in 16 samples per area light. Values of 2 and 3 result in 4 and 9 samples per area light, respectively.
- Linear lights perform like area lights but emit light from a two-point polygonal shape, similar to a fluorescent tube.
- You can mix spotlights, distant lights, point lights, and linear lights with area lights for added effects.

Earlier in the chapter we mentioned that textures play a key role in how your lighting affects your objects. This couldn't be more true for a scene such as the one you've been working on here.

Glass, copper, and metallic surfaces work well because they reflect their environment. The Environment setting is currently black, which you can change by going to the Windows drop-down menu and choosing Background Options. But what happens with the highly reflective surface is that it reflects a black backdrop, which blends with the color of the surface. The reflection also picks up the cup and ground nearby, as well as the light box (the large flat polygon off camera). These added elements create the illusion of a metallic surface. Nice, isn't it? In the past, many artists would simply have the metallic surface reflect an image, but reflecting the environment is a bit more convincing.

NOTE

If you increase the size of the area light, the shadow softens. However, it might appear grainy or jagged. If so, simply increase the Area Light Quality setting in the Light Properties panel. The default is 4—good for most renderings. Often, setting a value of 5 works slightly better but takes more render time. Isn't that always the case? Note that 5 is your maximum value.

From here, you can tweak the scene and perhaps add colored lighting as you like. Experiment with the information provided in this chapter and see what variations you can come up with. One dramatic thing you can do is to bring the intensity of the key light down, and then increase the Fill and Radiosity settings. Have the key light only as an accent, so that the scene is primarily lit from behind.

The Next Step

The information in this chapter can be applied to any type of scene you create in LightWave, from outdoor scenes, to sets, and even to fantasy-type renders. It can be applied to any of the exercises and projects in this book. These basic lighting setups and core functions apply to all of your LightWave work in one way or another, either in simple or complex form. Use the information here to branch out on your own and create different lighting environments. Use lights to your advantage—remember, there are no wires or electricity bills to worry about when creating virtual lighting situations. You don't need to worry about lightbulbs burning out either!

Experiment by adding more lights to your everyday scene or perhaps taking some away. Use negative lights, colored lights, dim lights, overly bright lights, and whatever else you can think of to make your models and animations look as good as they can. But what will make them stand out from the rest of the pack is your own creative input. Don't worry about rules too much. Learn the basics, understand how the tools work, and try it out! If you think you'd like more light on a particular area of the scene, add it. Don't ask people on Internet forums—just try it!

What adds even more interest to your scenes is the camera. LightWave 10's camera tools are quite powerful, so turn the page to understand this updated feature set.

Chapter 5

3D Cameras

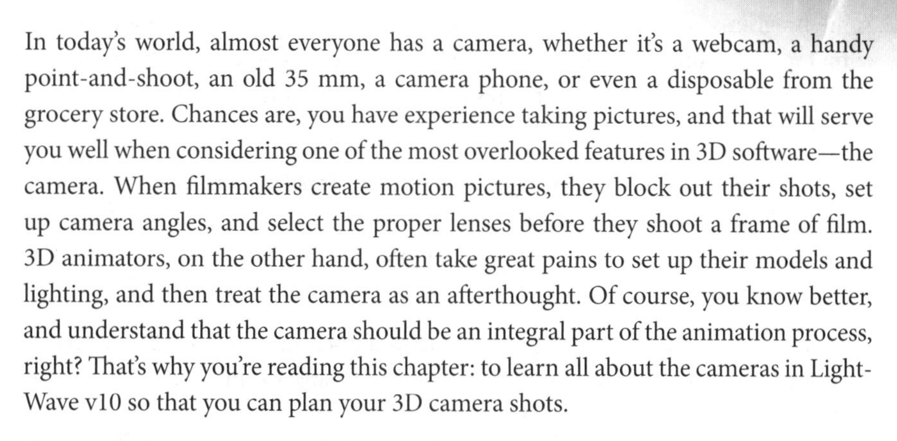

In today's world, almost everyone has a camera, whether it's a webcam, a handy point-and-shoot, an old 35 mm, a camera phone, or even a disposable from the grocery store. Chances are, you have experience taking pictures, and that will serve you well when considering one of the most overlooked features in 3D software—the camera. When filmmakers create motion pictures, they block out their shots, set up camera angles, and select the proper lenses before they shoot a frame of film. 3D animators, on the other hand, often take great pains to set up their models and lighting, and then treat the camera as an afterthought. Of course, you know better, and understand that the camera should be an integral part of the animation process, right? That's why you're reading this chapter: to learn all about the cameras in LightWave v10 so that you can plan your 3D camera shots.

The art of 3D animation involves more than creating models, applying textures, and setting keyframes. 3D animation is an art form all its own, and it's still in its infancy. Part of learning about this new and fascinating art form is understanding the digital camera. I don't mean the kind of digital camera you pick up at the local electronics store, but the kind inside the computer software—it's your digital eye.

This chapter introduces you to everyday camera techniques that you can apply to your LightWave animations. The camera and its settings, placement, and angle play a significant role in every LightWave animation you create. And just as in a television studio or on a movie set, with LightWave you can set up more than one camera in your scenes. Cameras also can be animated, a topic we'll begin exploring in Chapter 6, "3D Animation."

If you have any experience in photography or videography, the transition to "shooting" in LightWave will be smooth and you'll find that LightWave takes the camera to new levels you never thought possible. This chapter covers:

- Working with the 3D camera
- Exploring real-world camera settings
- Applying 3D cameras
- Adding and using alternative cameras

Focus on Cameras

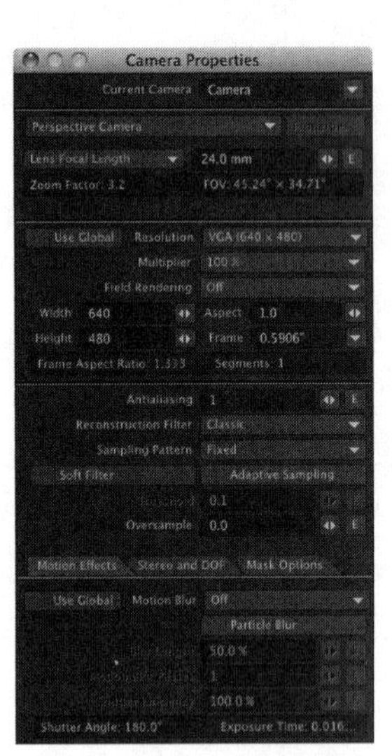

Figure 5.1 The LightWave Camera Properties panel.

At this point, you're probably familiar with LightWave's workflow. You should know that cameras are available in LightWave Layout, not in Modeler. As you work with Layout, you'll become familiar with the various Properties panels associated with objects and lights. The Camera Properties panel controls all the necessary camera settings, such as resolution, focal length, depth of field, masking, and more. However, you won't find render options in this panel. Those are located in the Render Globals panel, which you'll find by clicking Render Globals in Layout's Render tab. Some programs, such as Adobe After Effects, contain all camera, resolution, and output information in the same panel. LightWave uses the Render Globals panel as a single location for setting project resolutions, output options, render properties, and more.

By now, having used several of Layout's Properties panels in earlier chapters, you can probably guess how to open the Camera Properties panel (**Figure 5.1**): Click the Cameras button at the bottom of the Layout interface, and then click the Properties button (or press **p**).

Near the top of the Camera Properties panel, you'll see an item labeled Resolution. **Figure 5.2** shows one of the range of resolutions available to you. You'll learn about using these a bit later in this chapter.

Figure 5.2 LightWave offers a wide range of camera resolutions and different types of cameras.

Setting Up a Camera

Advanced Camera
Classic Camera
Orthographic Camera
Perspective Camera
Real Lens Camera
Shift Camera
Surface Baking Camera

Figure 5.3 LightWave 10 has many different types of cameras, which you'll see in action throughout the book.

LightWave 10 has introduced a whole bunch of cameras (by the way, as most 3D animators know, "bunch" is a technical term). That's right, *cameras*, as in more than one, offering you even more options. This chapter introduces you to LightWave cameras and provides the groundwork for using them in different projects throughout the rest of the book. **Figure 5.3** shows the available cameras in LightWave. The different camera names sound confusing, but soon you'll see how they all come together. You'll learn what each camera is for and when to use it.

LightWave 10's cameras are not only easy to use, but easy to set up as well. Creative camerawork can be useful for any type of scene, moving or still, and we've set up a number of projects along these lines for you to learn from. More specifically, you can use multiple cameras when you have a large scene that has action that needs to be covered from various angles, such as a stage play, a virtual walkthrough, or an accident re-creation. Multiple cameras can help you save time setting up animations that need to be viewed from different angles. Using the Camera Selector plug-in from the Master Plugins panel, you can switch between specific cameras during rendering. Also, you can render passes from any camera in the scene. In Exercise 5.1, you'll begin exploring the creative use of cameras in LightWave 10.

Exercise 5.1 Working with Cameras

1. After saving any work you've done prior to this exercise, go to the File menu in Layout at the upper left of the interface and select Clear Scene. If you're just starting LightWave, there's no need to clear the scene. LightWave remembers what you worked on last, but it does not load that project automatically.
2. Select the Items menu; under the Add category, click Camera. Now you have two cameras in the scene: the default camera that's always in a blank scene and the camera you just added.

   When you click Add Camera, a small panel appears, asking you for a name. You can give the camera a new name or just click OK to use the catchy default name "Camera," which appears with a number next to it, "Camera (2)," because the default camera is named Camera as well—and is now denoted as Camera (1). A third camera would be Camera (3), and so on.

   If the default names get confusing, you can always rename any camera later.
3. Click OK to add a second camera to Layout.

   You'll set up each camera separately, so the first thing you must do is select the specific camera you want to work with. Adding, selecting, or deleting cameras is the same as selecting any other scene items, such as objects or lights.
4. Click the Cameras button at the bottom of the interface.
5. From the Current Item drop-down, choose which camera you want to use.
6. To rename a camera, select the Rename command from the Replace category under the Items tab.

   It really doesn't matter if you are working with one camera, two cameras, or ten—the settings are the same. Simply point and shoot!

   To get the most out of multiple cameras, set them up in a way that will be most beneficial to your animation. For example, suppose that you need to re-create a traffic accident and the client wants to see the accident from a bystander's viewpoint, an aerial viewpoint, and the driver's viewpoint. By adding three cameras to your scene and setting them in the desired positions, you can render the animation from any view. What's even cooler in LightWave 10 is that each camera can be of a different type. For example, you can set up a Classic camera (as you've done here) to render the majority of your animation. Then, you can set up a second camera as an Orthographic camera to render just a side view of your scene. Set up your third camera as a Real Lens camera, allowing you to specify a particular lens, such as a Canon 24–70 f/2.8L attached to a Canon 5D. Very specific, and very cool.

Setting Camera Resolution

After you've chosen the camera you want to work with, Resolution is typically the first setting you apply in the Camera Properties panel. This setting determines the width and height at which images shot through the camera will be rendered. LightWave also will set the appropriate pixel aspect of your rendered images when a resolution is specified.

NOTE

Rendering is a generic term for creating or drawing an image. This is done in LightWave by pressing **F9** for single frames (Render Current Frame) and **F10** for multiple frames (Render Scene). Press **F11** to render the currently selected object only.

NOTE

You might find it confusing that you can set up camera resolution in two places in LightWave 10. You're not alone! It is confusing. The goal in this section is to have you understand resolutions and settings. Where you set them is not as important right now. But you can get into the habit of setting up everything globally. Click the Use Global option in the Camera Properties panel, and then just use the Render Globals panel to set everything else.

The resolution you choose in the Camera Properties panel determines the final output size of your images and animations. It's important to understand that you can set the output resolution in two locations in LightWave 10. You can set it in the Camera Properties panel, as you've seen here. But you can also enable the Use Global option in the Camera Properties panel, and your resolution can then be set in the Render Globals panel, found on the Render tab. For now, we'll use the standard Camera Properties panel for our examples.

The default resolution is VGA mode, which is 640 pixels wide by 480 pixels tall. This resolution is of a medium size, which is common for most computer work. You also can choose SVGA, which is 800 by 600 pixels, or XVGA, which is 1024 by 768 pixels. These are good resolutions to work with if your images or animations are being used in a computer environment, such as in QuickTime or AVI formats. You also have resolutions such as SWXGA, which is 1366 × 768, a popular resolution for many HD monitors. You'll find that LightWave 10 offers film-resolution presets as well, all found within the Resolution drop-down. The reason you'd use some of these higher resolutions is to match video or film, either imported or composited, or perhaps because it's a resolution you're rendering to for later use.

Most likely you're creating animations that will never leave the digital world. That is, they'll be rendered to an image file or movie file, edited in a digital editing program, and either presented online via outlets such as YouTube or burned to a disc. This new digital world makes creating 3D outputs less confusing and simply a matter of worrying about the right resolution for your project. At the same time, you don't have to adhere to broadcast standards if you're not broadcasting or displaying in a specific setting. You can render animations with a square shape, a tall rectangle shape, or any combination of width and height.

NOTE

QuickTime is Apple's basic multimedia application and format, now common on both Macintosh and Windows computers. Rendering an animation to a QuickTime movie creates a playable computer file. AVI (Audio Video Interleaved), developed by Microsoft, is another type of compressed audio/video format. Each has varying levels of compression, so check your particular computer system for your ideal setting.

NOTE

In 1953, the National Television Standards Committee (NTSC) developed the North American television broadcast standard. The NTSC standard is 60 half-frames, or fields, per second, with 525 lines of resolution. PAL stands for Phase Alternate Line. The PAL standard, which most of Western Europe uses, is 625 lines of resolution at 50 fields per second.

Setting the Resolution Multiplier

A great time-saving feature in LightWave is the Resolution Multiplier (**Figure 5.4**). It lets you output an accurate version of the final render at a different size (usually smaller than the final version, to save time) without changing the actual pixel dimensions of the project. This is perfect for cranking out scaled-down versions of a render for testing or client-approval purposes, and it does a super job with enlargements as well. Multiplier values are limited to 25%, 50%, 100%, 200%, and 400%.

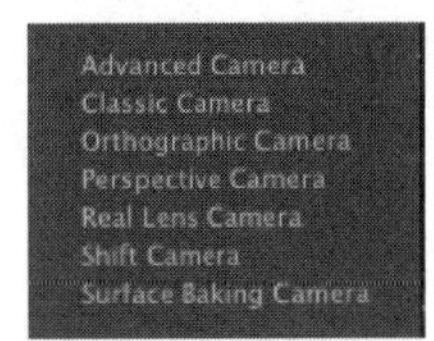

Figure 5.4 The Resolution Multiplier gives you an accurate view of your render at smaller or larger sizes.

Understanding the Pixel Aspect Ratio

You probably know that the images on your computer screen consist of tiny dots called *pixels*. You may even know that *pixel* is short for *picture element*, and that all pixels are rectangular. What you may not realize, however, is that all pixels are not created equal. What sets them apart is their shapes, which are described in terms of *aspect ratio*—the proportion of their width to their height. Images created for display on computer screens have square pixels, with an aspect ratio of 1.0. Images prepared for display on TV screens are another matter. Images generated for high-definition TV would be set to 1920 × 1080 resolution. The common "720p" resolution is 1280 × 720. Both, however, would be rendered to square (1.0) pixels.

In the course of most animations, LightWave sets appropriate camera and output pixel resolutions automatically, so you don't have to memorize all this. But it's wise to familiarize yourself with the effects of pixel aspect ratio settings so you'll recognize what's happening in case problems arise.

For example, suppose you have a perfect square in your image. If you use an Aspect setting of 1.0, LightWave renders the square using the same number of pixels for its width and height. This looks good on your PC monitor, but if you show the image on an NTSC TV, it looks tall and goofy. This is because televisions have tall pixels and, although the same number of pixels make up the square's height and width, because they are "tall" they make the box tall. If you use an Aspect setting of .9, LightWave compensates and the image looks correct. An NTSC television pixel aspect ratio might not always be exactly .9, but it won't be 1.0. All that being said, even rendering to HD video, a common standard, can still give you an odd look if the pixel aspect is off. So be careful with this setting and check it, as well as your target resolution, before you render.

Field Rendering

Beneath the Resolution and Multiplier options in the Camera Properties panel you'll see the Field Rendering option. Like the Aspect setting, this setting is used when preparing animation for output to analog videotape. Activating field rendering tells LightWave to mimic the process analog video devices use to "draw" images on television screens: Each frame of video is divided into two *fields*, one consisting of the even-numbered horizontal rows of pixels and the other consisting of the odd-numbered rows. First, one field is drawn and then the other, completing the frame via a process called *interlacing*. (NTSC video draws screen images at a frequency of 30 frames per second, or 60 fields per second.) Standard 3D renderings are not interlaced, which generally means higher quality, but playing them back on interlaced devices can make motion look choppy, especially when objects are moving swiftly and close to the camera. Field rendering lets your animations synchronize better with an interlaced display, so motion looks crisp and clean. You can set LightWave to render the even or odd fields first.

Exercise 5.2 Working with Aspect Ratios

To give you an idea of how the different aspect ratios work, open LightWave Layout and perform the following steps:

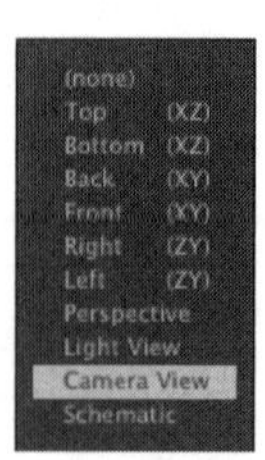

Figure 5.5 Resolution and the results of setting the pixel aspect ratios can be seen only through the Camera view in Layout.

1. Clear the scene from the File drop-down menu. Then, select Camera View in the selection drop-down at the top of the Layout window (**Figure 5.5**).

   Remember that, although resolution settings can be seen directly in Layout, you won't see the stretching due to an incorrect aspect in Layout. Rather, Layout merely shows you what portions of the scene will be in the rendered image. It is the projection of this image on the display device that causes the stretching, if any.

2. To make sure that Show Safe Areas is selected, press the **d** key to enter the Display Options tab within the Preferences panel.

3. Select Show Safe Areas under the Camera View tab at the bottom of the interface, as shown in **Figure 5.6**.

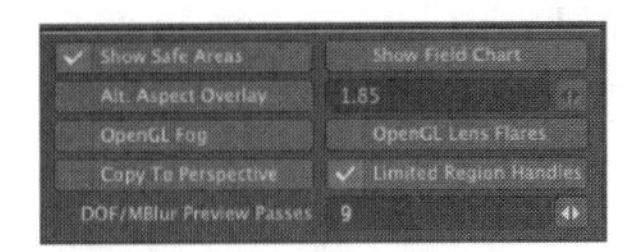

Figure 5.6 Selecting Show Safe Areas on the Display Options tab turns on a visible outline through the Camera view in Layout.

NOTE

Safe areas are important to use as shot references. The outer line represents the video-safe area—any animation elements outside this area will not be visible on a standard 4:3 ratio television monitor. The inner line represents the title-safe area; no text in your animations should travel beyond this bounding region. Video has something called overscan, and the area you're not seeing is within this region. Broadcast monitors allow you to view overscan, but standard 4:3 televisions do not. Keeping within these guidelines will help your relationship with video professionals as well.

4. Close the Display Options panel by pressing **d** again or **p** (for properties).

   Figure 5.7 shows the Camera view with the safe areas enabled and with a scene loaded. This safe area represents the title-safe and video-safe areas of your view. You should set up animations with this feature enabled to ensure that you know how your animation will appear when it is recorded onto videotape.

Figure 5.7 When Show Safe Areas is enabled, you'll see a television-style shape around your field of view through the camera.

NOTE

You can change the color of the safe area outlines by changing the overlay color selection on the Display Options tab (press **d**) of the Preferences panel. Doing this also changes the color of any overlays seen in the Camera view, such as field chart.

5. Select Camera from the bottom of Layout (or press Shift+C), and then choose the Properties panel (or press **p**). Move the Camera Properties panel over to the far right of the screen, revealing more of your Layout window.
6. Go to the Resolution drop-down list and select D1 (NTSC Widescreen), as shown in **Figure 5.8**.

   This resolution changes the width to 720 and the height to 486, with a pixel aspect ratio of 1.2.
7. Press **p** to close the Camera Properties panel if it's cluttering your workspace. Otherwise, feel free to leave it open.

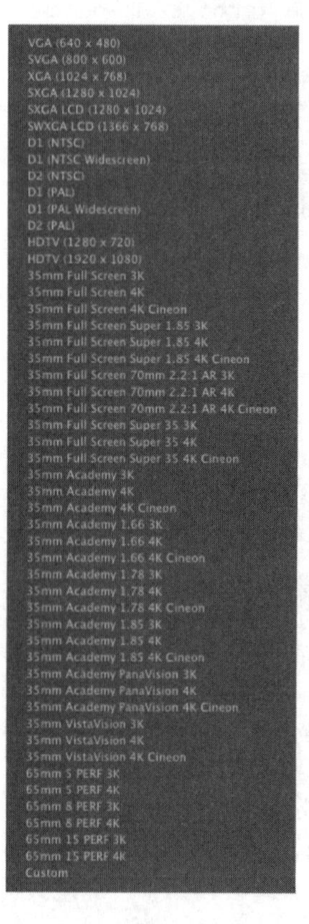

Figure 5.8 You have a number of choices when it comes to resolution, such as LightWave's widescreen settings. Setting a resolution to D1 (NTSC Widescreen) changes the pixel aspect ratio to 1.2, making the safe area viewed through the Camera panel appear stretched.

The safe areas now appear stretched with the widescreen resolution option. The darkened areas on the left and right of the interface (through the Camera view) are minimal, compared to the first 640 × 480 resolution. These areas represent the scene that is outside of the frame, based on the resolution you've set.

Figure 5.9 You can interactively control the pixel aspect ratio by clicking and dragging the small slider buttons.

8. Press **p** again to open the Camera Properties panel. Grab the mini-slider button next to the Aspect field and drag it back and forth. **Figure 5.9** shows the slider button. You should see the safe area field of view changing in Layout.

As an animator, keep in mind that the pixel aspect ratio affects your renderings. Changing the resolution changes the size of the image, whereas changing the pixel aspect ratio changes the target pixel shape, which also can distort your final output if it is not set properly. Always remember what the target display device is, and set your resolution and aspect ratio accordingly. For example, if you're rendering an animation for computer video and you accidentally set Resolution to D1 (standard for NTSC Widescreen broadcast video), your final animation will appear stretched when imported into an animation recorder or nonlinear editing suite. The computer will take the full image and squeeze it to fit the television-size frame your nonlinear editor or animation recorder uses. This happens because widescreen is the incorrect resolution for the standard video recorder. Resolution also determines the pixel aspect ratio, and D1 (NTSC Widescreen) applies the incorrect setting for converting widescreen to video.

NOTE

A quick way to hide any open panels is to press the Tab key. To unhide, press Tab again.

Setting Limited Region

Every now and then, there might be a situation in which the resolution settings are not the exact size you need for rendering. You sometimes might need to render just an area of an animation, saving valuable rendering time. For example, if you have an animation that has many objects, textures, reflections, and more, test-rendering the full image might take up too much of your time—especially if you want to see how one small area of the scene looks in the final render. Using the Limited Region setting helps you accomplish this. Activate it by choosing Render Globals in the Render tab and selecting the option at the bottom of the General tab, as shown in **Figure 5.10**.

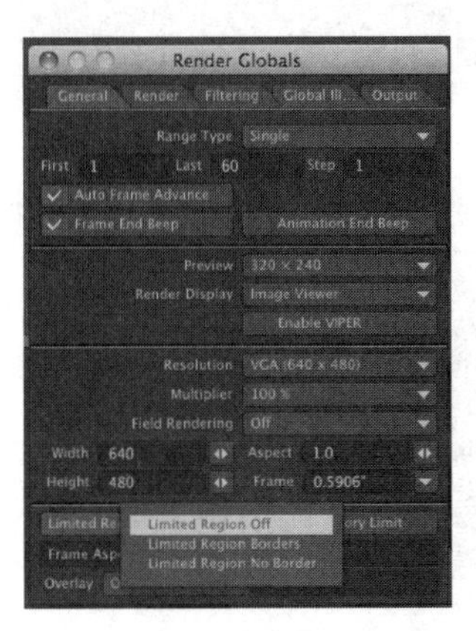

Figure 5.10 Limited Region lets you control the area of the screen to be rendered.

You can have a limited region with or without borders. The borders setting may not have the effect you expect. For example, let's say your camera resolution is set to 1024 × 768, and you set a limited-region render to just a small portion of the frame. With borders on, you'll see the full 1024 × 768 rendered frame, but only the limited region will display your 3D elements. LightWave will render only what's in that limited region, while presenting it full frame. With no borders, LightWave renders just your limited region.

You can easily turn on a limited region directly in Layout by pressing **l** (lowercase L). Also, you can simply select the option on the left side of the screen from within the Render tab. You see, we told you that there are many ways to do one thing in LightWave! Now, with Limited Region active, a yellow dotted line appears, encompassing the entire Layout area. From here, you can click the edge of the region and resize it to any desired shape. **Figure 5.11** shows a limited region for a small area of a scene. **Figure 5.12** shows how the image renders would look in the Render Display window with this Limited Region setting.

Figure 5.11 You can resize the limited region directly in Layout to render a selected area of the animation.

Figure 5.12 The limited region's rendered image is just the area assigned in Layout.

Limited Region settings are also useful for creating images for Web sites using LightWave. Perhaps you want to animate a small spinning globe or a rotating 3D head. Rendering in a standard resolution draws unwanted areas, creating images that are not only the correct size but also larger. Setting up a limited region can decrease file size and create renders in the exact size you need, such as a perfect square. Limited Region essentially renders a portion of what normally would be a larger image. Try using a Web GIF animation program and render out a series of small GIF files, set up with a limited region. The GIF animation program imports the sequence of images to create one playable file. Limited Region works differently from a custom resolution. You can specify a limited region as any size and for any area on the screen, whereas setting a custom resolution sets only the specific size for the center of the screen. Also, Limited Region enables you to render limited regions of very high-resolution images. A custom resolution would not work this way. To turn off Limited Region, just press **l** (lowercase L) while in Layout or turn off the button from within the Render tab.

NOTE

If you render an image or animation with the Limited Region Borders setting, the image will appear with a border that represents the rest of the unrendered frame. Rendering with Limited Region No Border displays only the limited region.

Segment Memory Limit

Head back over to the Render Globals panel (on Layout's Render tab) and, to the right of Limited Region, you'll see the setting Segment Memory Limit. Too often, you'll run out of RAM while you are creating animations. RAM, or the memory in your computer, is used up quickly by many images, large objects, and hefty render settings. The Segment Memory Limit feature lets you tell Layout the maximum amount of memory to use for rendering. Lower values allow you to render a frame in segments, which means the frames might take a bit longer to load and execute. The trade-off is that you don't need as much memory.

For faster renders, you can increase the segment memory. Setting the segment memory to 60 MB (that is, 60 MB of RAM) often enables you to render higher resolutions in one segment. LightWave's Segment Memory setting is a maximum setting. This means you can set this value to be the same as the amount of RAM in your system, and LightWave will use only what it needs, often eliminating the need for your system to use virtual memory or a scratch disk. However, setting this value to your full system memory is probably not a smart idea, as the Segment Memory Limit default setting is already 256 MB, usually more than you need for most projects.

NOTE

Remember that higher resolution settings require more system memory, so be careful when setting very high resolutions and high segment memory limits.

When you click the Segment Memory Limit button, a small panel pops up, asking you to enter a value. You can enter a value as large as you want, provided you have the memory in your system. When you click OK, LightWave asks whether you want to make this value the default. Click Yes, and you won't have to change this value when you start creating another animation scene. **Figure 5.13** shows the Segment Memory Limit selection in the General tab of the Render Globals panel.

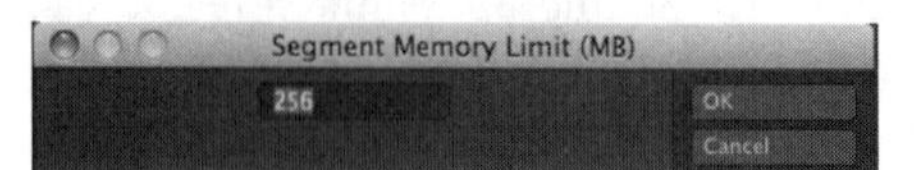

Figure 5.13 Setting a segment memory limit tells LightWave how much memory is available for rendering. Setting a higher value allows LightWave to render animation frames in one pass.

Rename and Select Current Camera

Figure 5.14 All of your scene's cameras can be selected within the Camera Properties panel, from the Current Camera selection list.

Because LightWave allows you to add more than one camera to your scene, you need a way to select them to adjust each item's properties. The Current Camera selection list is at the top of the Camera Properties panel. If you have not added any cameras to your scene, you will see only the item "Camera." Just as in the Light Properties panel, you can select and rename this camera (or any you've added) directly in the Camera Properties panel. If you have added multiple cameras, they will be listed here (**Figure 5.14**). All cameras are available for selection in the Current Item selection list at the bottom of the Layout interface as well. No matter what type of camera you've chosen—a Classic camera, an Advanced camera, or otherwise—they can all be selected here.

Lens Focal Length and Zoom Factor

Two interrelated settings, Zoom Factor and Lens Focal Length, are often misunderstood, and therefore overlooked, when it comes to working with cameras in LightWave. These attributes are different ways of expressing the same thing; change either one, and the other changes accordingly. Essentially, they define the range between the widest focus and tightest focus available through your camera's lens. Have you ever used a camera that allows you to switch from a standard lens to telephoto (for shooting at long distances) or macro (for magnifying small subjects)? Changing focal length or zoom factor in LightWave does much the same thing, only in a virtual way that gives you a practically infinite choice of lenses. By animating changes to these settings, you can even "morph" one lens into another to vary your scenes.

The default focal length is 24 mm, as shown in **Figure 5.15**.

Figure 5.15 LightWave's default zoom factor is 3.2, or the equivalent of a 24 mm focal length.

The default, which is equivalent to a standard medium-wide video camera lens, is a good starting point for most animations, but to make something come alive in 3D, you'll want to "change lenses" in the course of your animation. **Figure 5.16** shows a scene with the default Zoom Factor setting. The image looks good, but the scene lacks depth. But take a look at **Figure 5.17**, in which the same shot has a zoom factor of 1.5, or a Lens Focal Length setting of 32 mm. This creates a nice wide-angle view. Notice how wide the shot looks and how much depth is in the image. The camera is pushed in close to the subject—notice how the image looks more three-dimensional. This setting is only an example, and you should try different zoom factors on your own to see what works best for you.

Figure 5.16 A scene set up with the default Zoom Factor setting of 3.2, or a Lens Focal Length setting of 24 mm, looks fine but lacks depth.

Figure 5.17 The same scene with a Zoom Factor setting of 1.5 gives the shot a lot more dimensionality and makes it much more interesting.

NOTE

Each camera you add to Layout can have a different zoom factor. For example, in the Camera Properties panel, you can select one camera and set the zoom factor so that it renders like a telephoto lens. Then, you can select another camera in the Camera Properties panel and make it render like a wide-angle lens. Each camera in LightWave can be set differently.

The cameras in LightWave are just as important as your objects. Don't overlook the possibilities of changing the zoom factor over time. Using LightWave's Graph Editor, you can animate the zoom factor with stunning results.

The focal length itself is measured in millimeters. The larger the focal length value, the longer the lens, and the tighter the focus on (or the closer you'll be to) the subject. For example, a telephoto lens might be 180 mm, and a wide-angle lens might be 12 mm. Because focal lengths represent everyday camera settings, just as with your 35 mm camera, you may be more comfortable working with lens focal lengths instead of zoom factors. You can do this by selecting the desired option from the Focal Length drop-down list. Once chosen, your setting will appear in the Camera Properties panel. However, if you do have specific camera lenses you wish to match, you can use the Real Lens camera, which we'll explore shortly.

Field of View (FOV)

In addition to zoom factor and lens focal length, you can set up a camera's field of view (FOV) using the horizontal or vertical FOV settings. **Figure 5.18** shows the additional options in the Camera Properties panel.

Figure 5.18 You have the option to choose horizontal and vertical Field of View (FOV).

Changing the values for zoom factor automatically adjusts the lens focal length, the horizontal FOV, and the vertical FOV. The horizontal and vertical fields of view give you precise control over the lens in LightWave. The two values listed next to FOV are the horizontal and vertical fields (horizontal is the first value). Working with FOV is useful in real-world situations where you need to match camera focal lengths, especially when compositing.

Don't let all these settings confuse you. The Zoom Factor, Lens Focal Length, and horizontal and vertical FOV settings all enable you to set the same thing. Simply use the one you're most familiar or most comfortable with—or choose whatever is called for to match a real-world camera. There is no inherent benefit in using one over another.

Antialiasing

When you render an animation, it needs to look good, right? Certainly your model needs to be built correctly, but there are render settings you can apply to enhance the final output. The edges need to be clean and smooth, and no matter how much quality you put into your models, surfaces, lighting, and camera technique, you won't have a perfect render until you set the antialiasing. Antialiasing cures the jagged edges between foreground and background elements. It is a smoothing process that creates cleaner-looking animations. **Figure 5.19** shows a rendered image without antialiasing; **Figure 5.20** shows the same image with a low Antialiasing setting applied.

Figure 5.19 Without antialiasing, the rendered image can look jagged and unprofessional, especially when animated. Notice the edges of the model are jagged, or stair-stepped. This is not the result of a bad model but rather an un-antialiased render.

Figure 5.20 After antialiasing is applied, even at a low setting, the image looks cleaner and more polished. You'll see that the edges of the model are smooth, as is the shadow.

Antialiasing can really make a difference in your final renders. **Figure 5.21** shows the available Antialiasing settings, including different variations of PLD (Pixel Lattice Deformation). PLD can save you time, depending on the render. It uses data from the edges of your models and realigns them for the final image. The higher you set the PLD, the more calculations will be done. You'll use different Antialiasing settings throughout the projects in this book to see how they differ.

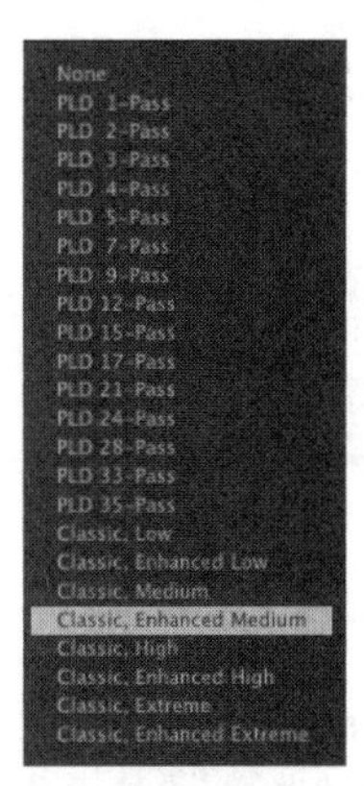

Figure 5.21 You can choose from a range of Antialiasing settings, from none at all to Enhanced Extreme.

The higher the Antialiasing setting, the more LightWave will clean and smooth your polygon edges. Of course, higher values mean added rendering time. Any of the Enhanced antialiasing settings will smooth your image at the subpixel level, which takes a bit more time to render but produces better results. In most cases, Medium to Enhanced Medium antialiasing yields great results. The Reconstruction Filter setting is one more way that LightWave can produce top-notch renders, by using sophisticated calculations to reconstruct the data for the final image.

Adaptive Sampling

Although you can set up an antialiasing routine for your renders, you still have to tell LightWave how it should be applied. Adaptive sampling is a flexible threshold that LightWave employs to evaluate the edges in your scene. Lower values evaluate more, enabling a more accurate antialiasing routine. Higher values evaluate less. A default setting of 0.1 is an average Threshold value. Changing this to 0.01, for example, adds to your render times but helps to produce a cleaner render. A good way to work with adaptive sampling is to set a higher Antialiasing setting, with a not-so-low Threshold. For example, Enhanced Medium antialiasing, with a Threshold setting of 0.1, renders reasonably well (depending on your scene) and produces nice-looking images. For more details on adaptive sampling, refer to your LightWave manual.

Soft Filter

As an additional help to eliminate sharp, unwanted edges in a scene, you can turn on the Soft Filter option in the Camera Properties panel. As an alternative to setting higher antialiasing routines, you can choose a lower Antialiasing setting with Soft Filter applied. Soft Filter adds a small blur to your render, creating a "soft-focus" look that can make some renders appear too blurry. Its setting is either on or off. Sorry, no variable amounts!

Motion Effects

At the bottom of the Camera Properties panel are three tabs. Each tab offers even more control over your camera's settings. The first one, Motion Effects, is home to some common, everyday functions like motion blurs.

Motion Blur

Figure 5.22 Motion blur is applied to a fast-moving object in a scene. Motion blur helps add the feeling of movement because in real-world cameras, the shutter speed is not fast enough to freeze the action.

When antialiasing is applied (at a setting of at least Low), the Motion Blur option becomes available. From time to time, you may need to create motions that mimic real-world properties, such as a speeding car or a fast-moving camera. To give things a more realistic look, you can apply motion blur to your scene. Motion blur in LightWave combines several semi-dissolved images on each frame to give the effect of blurred motion. Motion blur mimics real-world actions. Remember that the multiple rendering passes used with antialiasing are needed to compute the dissolved images, which is why antialiasing needs to be set to Low or higher. But you can quickly see what your motion blur will look like right in Layout (**Figure 5.22**) by clicking MB Preview on the Render tab or by pressing **Shift+F9**.

Apply the motion blur effect any time you have something fast-moving in your scene. Even if it's only a slight motion blur, the added effect will help "sell" the look. If your animation is perfectly clean, perfectly smooth, and always in focus, it won't look realistic. It will look better with some inconsistencies, such as motion blur.

NOTE

You'll also see a check box for Use Global on the Motion Effects tab in the Camera Properties panel. Enabling this option turns off the controls here and makes them accessible in the Render Globals panel.

Motion blur also is important to actions like the flapping of a bee's wings, the spinning of an airplane's propellers, and so on. Many animated objects moving at high speed will require you to set the Motion Blur option. If you look at spinning propellers in the real world, all you see is a blur. To re-create that look in LightWave, turn on Motion Blur in the Camera Properties panel.

One last thing: LightWave's VPR mode also allows you to view Motion Blur in real time, directly in Layout. Simply turn on the option from the drop-down menu at the top of the interface.

Classic Motion Blur

To activate LightWave's Classic motion blur, antialiasing must be active. If it's not, LightWave will turn it on automatically when you activate antialiasing. Antialiasing redraws the edges of the geometry in the scene and blurs them accordingly.

Photoreal

Another type of Motion Blur setting is Photoreal. Basically, this motion blur can be more accurate, allowing you to specify the number of motion blur samples. More samples means cleaner blurs. But here's the cool part: With Photoreal, you don't need to set antialiasing. Not that you'd want to render a scene without antialiasing, but when you need to perform a render test to see your blurs in action, Photoreal comes in handy.

Blur Length

Blur Length is the amount of motion blur you want to use. The default setting for this option is 50%, which produces nice results. Depending on the animation, you may want to set this value slightly higher—for example, to 60% or 65%—for more blurring. When you apply the Blur Length setting, corresponding Shutter Angle and Exposure Time values appear beneath the Blur Length window. Most of your motion-blurred animations should have a 50% Blur Length. This is because the blur length relates to the amount of time the theoretical film is actually exposed. Because of the physical mechanism, a film camera can't expose a frame for 1/24 of a second, even though film normally plays back at 24 frames per second. It turns out that this rotating shutter mechanism exposes the film for only 50% of the per-second rate; thus, a setting of 50% for Blur Length is perfect.

Particle Blur

The Particle Blur setting applies a special type of motion blur to particle systems—groups of similar small objects that behave in some ways like a single entity. Use it to blur animations of explosions, receding starfields, snow, rain, and the like. A Blur Length setting of 50% works well for Particle Blur.

Stereo and Depth of Field (DOF)

The second tab area at the bottom of the Camera Properties panel is named Stereo and DOF (**Figure 5.23**).

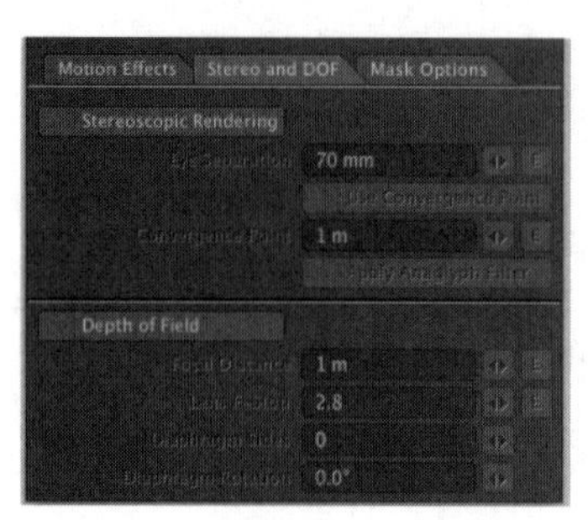

Figure 5.23 The Stereo and DOF tab offers stereoscopic rendering and depth of field functions to your cameras.

Stereoscopic Rendering

On the Stereo and DOF tab in the Camera Properties panel, you can turn on the Stereoscopic Rendering option, which lets you create 3D movies (for viewing with special glasses), ViewMaster-style stereoscopic still images, and even *lintography*, the specialized printing process (used to produce 3D trading cards, for example) in which plastic is overlaid on a processed 2D image to give an illusion of depth. When this option is turned on, Layout renders left and right stereoscopic images for each frame in your project. To output red-and blue-tinted versions for viewing with classic 3D glasses, choose Windows > Image Processing and select Anaglyph Stereo: Compose from the Add Image Filter drop-down list. To output images for video-based virtual-reality glasses and headsets, instead choose Field Render from the same drop-down list and make sure the Field Rendering option is turned on in the Camera Properties panel. The Eye Separation value tells LightWave how far apart to render the left and right stereo images; the default mimics the average separation of adult human eyes.

Working in real-time for stereoscopic rendering is huge in terms of workflow and productivity. For a demonstration and better explanation of this feature, visit the book's DVD and watch the "Stereoscopic" video.

Depth of Field

Checking the Depth of Field option enables your LightWave camera to mimic an optical effect you've experienced yourself if you've ever looked through a camera lens. When you focus your camera on a subject, you'll notice that objects that are nearer or farther away than the subject appear less sharply focused than your subject. The range of distance in front of and behind the subject in which other objects stay in focus is called *depth of field* (DOF). High depth of field keeps objects in focus in front of and behind the subject and creates a sense of spaciousness; shallow depth of field "flattens" the scene, so that only the subject is in sharp focus.

NOTE

One of the benefits of depth of field, beyond adding depth to your animations, is to direct the viewer's attention. By changing the focus from say, an animated element to a static element, you effectively are telling the viewer where to look.

You can only activate Depth of Field if the camera has Antialiasing set to a medium or better level (PLD 7-pass or higher, or Classic-Medium or better). Checking the Depth of Field box then activates the Focal Distance and Lens F-Stop controls that you'll use to manage camera focus and adjust its depth of field. This is adjustable directly in Layout's OpenGL view.

Adjusting the depth of field is a fantastic way to add real depth to your animations. Without DOF, everything is in focus, as in **Figure 5.24**.

Figure 5.25 shows the same image with DOF applied. Notice how the top of the building becomes out of focus farther away from the camera.

Figure 5.24 Without Depth of Field applied, everything in your scene is in focus.

Figure 5.25 With Depth of Field applied, the image is out of focus farther away from the set focal distance.

Focal Distance

When you apply DOF, you must also tell the camera where to focus by setting a *focal distance*. The default setting is 1 meter (1 m), and you can type any value into the Focal Distance field. Objects at the focal distance are in sharp focus in your frame, and those nearer or farther away will be out of focus to some degree, depending on how you use *f*-stop settings to control DOF (as discussed in the next section).

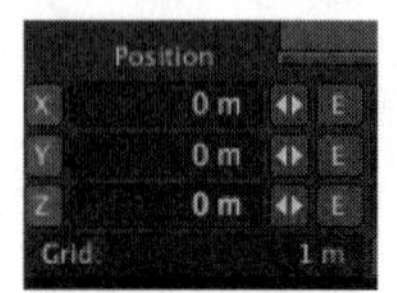

Figure 5.26 LightWave's default grid setting is 1 m, but you'll want to adjust the grid size to match your project.

Using LightWave's grid, which is the measurement system in Layout, you can easily determine the correct focal distance for a camera by counting the number of grid squares between the camera and the object you want in focus. Check the bottom of Layout's information window (**Figure 5.26**) to determine the grid size for the current view and multiply that by the number of squares to calculate the distance. (The default grid setting is 1 m, but in larger scenes such as the one in Figures 5.25 and 5.26, LightWave may automatically scale the grid size up to 5 m or higher.)

At a grid size of 5 m, a focal distance of 15 m would be appropriate for an object 3 grid squares away from the camera. Objects nearer to and farther away from the camera will be out of focus.

F-Stop

Just as you would with a real-world camera, you adjust depth of field in a LightWave camera by adjusting its *f*-stop setting.

The human eye automatically adjusts to brighter or darker lighting situations. Under low light, an eye's iris and pupil open to allow in the maximum amount of light. Bright sunlight, on the other hand, makes the human eye close to protect the eye.

By the same token, cameras also have an iris that allows in more or less light. Although the human eye smoothly opens and closes to control incoming light, cameras need to have this control set. This is done through *f*-stops.

F-stops are numerical values that represent the amount of varying degrees of light transmission. A smaller *f*-stop allows more light into the camera and reduces the depth of field, whereas higher values allow less light into the camera but increase the depth of field. Here are the common *f*-stop numbers used in the real world:

- ***f*1.4**—Softest focus; allows a lot of light into the camera
- ***f*2.0**
- ***f*2.8**
- ***f*4.0**
- ***f*5.6**
- ***f*8**
- ***f*11**
- ***f*16**
- ***f*22**—Sharpest focus; allows little light into the camera

Range Finder for DOF

Counting grid squares as I've described is adequate for setting camera focal distances, but it can get tiresome. Here's a trick for creating an automatic range finder using a *null object*, a special type of object you can place in LightWave scenes for your own reference or guidance but that are never included in scene renders.

1. Click Null on the Items tab to create a new null object; rename it in the panel that appears (or just use the default name, **Null**), and click OK.
2. New objects are always selected by default, so press **p** to open this item's Object Properties and choose Range Finder from the Add Custom Object drop-down list (**Figure 5.27**).
3. Double-click Range to Camera in the Custom Object Name list, and in the numeric Range Finder pop-up that appears, leave Camera as the Item setting and check the Draw Link box (**Figure 5.28**).

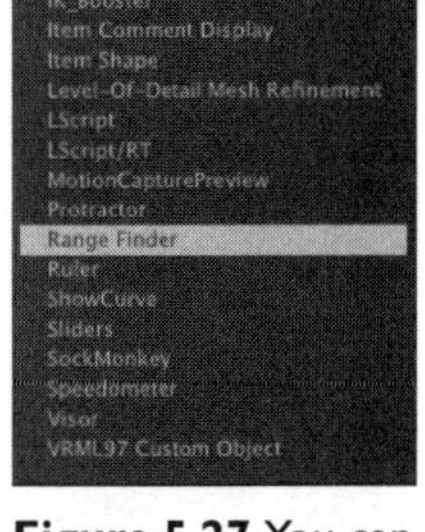

Figure 5.27 You can add a custom object to quickly measure distances in Layout from any item, such as the camera, for setting DOF measurements.

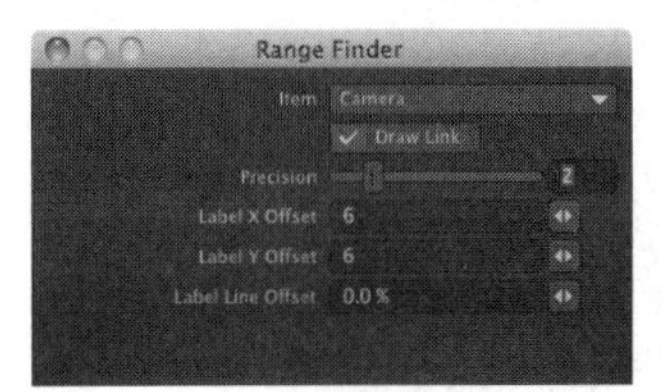

Figure 5.28 The Range Finder pop-up allows you to set the Camera as a link.

To use your range finder, select Null in the Current Object drop-down list. You'll see a small set of control handles and a value appear around the null object. With Auto Key enabled at the bottom of the interface, press **t** to select the Move tool and drag Null slightly. You'll see a line between the camera's pivot point and the Range Finder null. Make sure that Auto Key is enabled, and move the null. Remember, everything in your scene needs a keyframe to stay in place, even if it's not animated. You'll see the measurement values change, as shown in **Figure 5.29**. This value is your distance from the camera that you can easily use to set the depth of field. If you're specifically trying to set the focus on an object, simply put the Range Finder null on the object and take the measurement. This is a good way to calculate rack focuses for animating depth of field, as well. You can easily do this in LightWave by animating the focus values in the Graph Editor.

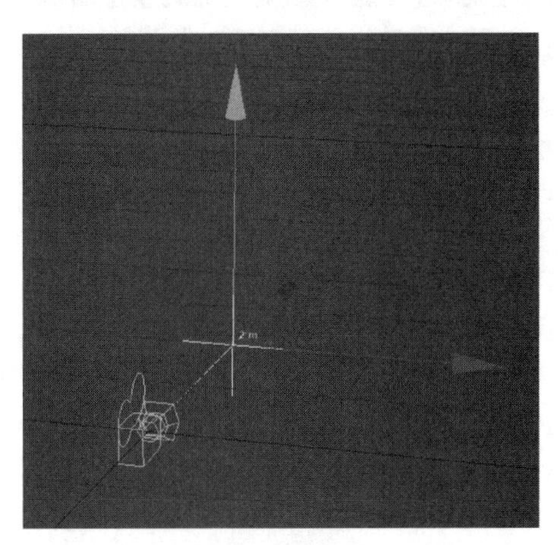

Figure 5.29 With the Range Finder custom object added, and with Auto Key on, you'll see a target line between the selected item (Camera) and the Range Finder. Couldn't be easier!

Mask Options

The final tab available in the Camera Properties panel that allows you to enhance the LightWave camera is named Mask Options (**Figure 5.30**). Here, you can tell the camera to render certain areas while excluding others. Areas that are excluded from the render, or *masked*, are denoted by a color. This option is great for setting up pseudo-widescreen renders or a letterbox effect. You can set values for Left, Top, Width, and Height, as well as Mask Color. **Figure 5.31** shows a rendered image with mask options applied. You can use these options to create letterboxed images, simulating a 16:9 or widescreen look on a 4:3 television.

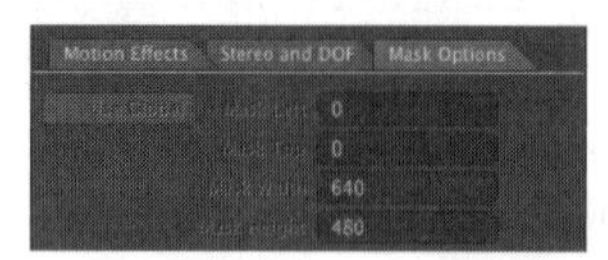

Figure 5.30 The Mask Options tab in the Camera Properties panel enables you to mask areas of your Camera view for rendering.

Figure 5.31 Mask options are great for rendering only portions of animations while setting a color for the unmasked area.

NOTE

Remember that masking covers up your rendered image based on the parameters you set. It does not resize your image.

You can see that the control available to you for LightWave's cameras can be a significant element in the animations you create. Too often, the camera is ignored and left in place. This is a crime—remember the camera when you animate! Animate it as well as your objects.

Camera Concepts

Do you want to incorporate the camera more into your animations but not know where to begin? You may find yourself in situations where you don't know how to frame a shot or how to decide where to place the camera. This next section provides you with some basic instruction that you can use throughout any of your animations.

View in Thirds

To many animators, looking through a camera lens is like looking at a blank canvas. Where should you begin? How should you view a particular shot? Your first step in answering these questions is to get a book on basic photography and cinematography. References such as these can be invaluable to animators as well as a great source of ideas.

One of the first lessons such a book will teach you, and which you can apply when looking through your LightWave camera, is that images with subjects smack in the center are dull. Unbalanced compositions have a certain tension that makes them more engaging than those that are symmetrical.

So to make your shots, or compositions, more interesting, mentally slice the image in thirds, either vertically or horizontally. If there's a single subject to your composition, align it along one of the imaginary dividing lines, rather than in the center of the frame. If there are two subjects in the frame, let one dominate the larger two-thirds of the frame and place the other in the smaller portion, rather than giving them equal prominence. (If you're shooting two subjects of similar size, doing so may require you to get creative with your camera angle by placing one subject in the distance and the other in the foreground.) **Figure 5.32** shows a photograph of a room. It's a shot you can mimic in LightWave.

NOTE

Using Composition Overlay, found in the Display Tab of the Preferences panel, you can have a rule of thirds overlay placed right on your screen. Additionally you can set up Golden Sections, Golden Spiral, and others.

A shot framed in thirds takes into account not only the main focus but also the surrounding areas of the frame. If you visualize the image in thirds, as in **Figure 5.33**, you can see that areas of the scene fit into place. Try to visualize three vertical and three horizontal areas when viewing your shots.

Figure 5.32 A photograph of a room might serve as a good reference for building 3D scenes as well as for framing shots.

Figure 5.33 When you visualize your shot in thirds, elements within the photo fall into place. Apply the same principle to cameras in LightWave.

By framing your shot in thirds in the vertical and horizontal views through the camera, you have areas to fill with action. Remember, you need to visualize this grid when setting up camera shots in LightWave. There is not an option for doing this. By visualizing, you can begin to think more about your shot and how to frame it.

When thinking of thirds while setting up a shot, don't be too literal. Your objects don't need to line up exactly into each third area. Visualizing your camera shot in thirds is a way to help frame the entire field of view. Don't be afraid to try different camera angles and different perspectives. **Figure 5.34** shows the rule of thirds applied to a 3D scene in LightWave.

Figure 5.34 Visualizing a shot with the rule of thirds in LightWave can help you place objects and position your camera.

Camera Angles

After you get the hang of framing a scene, the next thing you should think about is the camera angle. Consider what you are trying to portray in the render. Do you want the subject to look small, or should it be ominous and looming? What you do with the camera in LightWave helps sell the mood of your animations to the viewer. As good as your models and textures might be, your shot needs to work as part of the equation as well. **Figure 5.35** shows a 3D building from a typical point of view. Shots like this are good for general views, fire safety, environment concerns, and so on.

Figure 5.35 Setting your camera to a bird's-eye point of view makes the shot unthreatening.

What if your goal is more than purely informational? Say you're preparing a "virtual unveiling" of a proposed building design, and you want to convey a sense of grandeur. **Figure 5.36** shows how a different camera angle changes the feel of a shot.

Figure 5.36 A wider camera angle, set low in front of the building, gives a grander look and feel to the shot.

Taking this a step further, you can also employ "dutch" camera angles, a cinematic technique that conveys a feeling of uneasiness or a creepy mood. You might shoot your building this way if you wanted to hint to your audience that trouble is brewing inside. **Figure 5.37** (on the next page) shows a shot similar to Figure 5.36 but with the camera rotated on its bank, or *dutched*.

Figure 5.37 Rotating the camera on its bank sets up a dutch angle that conveys the feeling of something being wrong, creepy, or uneasy.

Additional Camera Types

You'll use the techniques presented in this chapter throughout your LightWave career. However, LightWave v10 introduces some powerful cameras, allowing you to do things like make an object a camera or create a camera based on the exact real-world camera and lens you specify. The next section introduces you to the different camera types, and you'll use variations of them throughout projects in this book.

Classic Camera

You can use the Classic camera if you want to render older LightWave scenes. **Figure 5.38** shows a shot rendered with a default Classic camera.

Figure 5.38 A 3D shot rendered with a Classic camera and default settings, such as a Zoom Factor setting of 3.2.

Advanced Camera

The Advanced camera, new in LightWave v10, allows you to re-create lenses and real cameras not normally found in 3D applications.

For instance, the Advanced Camera option lets you define objects (mesh items) as cameras so you can obtain an entirely different look and gain more control than you could with a normal camera. For example, you can't really distort a camera, but with an object set up as a camera, that object can be bent, distorted, warped, and so forth, thereby distorting what your camera sees. Quite cool!

The Advanced Camera option also lets you create spherical cameras. This allows you to render an entire scene in a spherical shape, sort of like a severe fish-eye lens. The advantage becomes clear when you're creating HDR (high dynamic range) images. An HDR image is one that holds more data than a normal image. A normal image would be one that contains intensities up to 255 RGB. While an HDR image might look the same, the computer will understand that it is higher intensity and can use it for lighting a scene.

Later in the book you'll see the Advanced camera in action, and you'll learn how the various settings work.

Orthographic Camera

The Orthographic camera is a little tricky to understand. When you render a scene, LightWave shoots out *rays*—these rays are used to calculate all sorts of things, such as shadows and reflections. You have more control over these rays in LightWave v10 than at any time before, and the Orthographic camera is just one way to work with different rays. With the Orthographic camera, rather than rays bouncing all over the scene, their direction is the same.

So what does that really mean? It means that you can create a camera with a *forced perspective*. A forced perspective in computer graphics is more an optical illusion than anything else. In a sense, it's almost the opposite effect of a fish-eye lens, which widely distorts the image. The forced perspective flattens out the image, even when viewing 3D objects. A forced perspective makes your image appear flatter and closer than with a typical camera. **Figure 5.39** (on the next page) shows the same shot as Figure 5.38 but rendered using the Orthographic Camera option to set up a render without any perspective.

Figure 5.39 The Orthographic camera is a multipurpose camera that allows you to render without perspective—great for architectural or illustrative 3D work.

Perhaps you're a designer working in Autodesk AutoCAD or PTC Creo Elements/Pro. You could use an Orthographic camera for engineering or architectural renders, or for shots in which you need to see more of the model than can normally be seen in a single render from a standard camera. When a perspective created from a wider camera might take away from the object or scene you're rendering, an Orthographic camera might do the trick. Before this camera was implemented in LightWave v10, artists would often pull the camera far away from the scene and then zoom in to create a similar look.

Perspective Camera

The Perspective camera renders like the Classic camera, but with a few differences. The Perspective camera renders the scene from top to bottom. In many cases, more-complex scenes render faster this way. The Perspective camera will render points and lines, which are used to generate smoke, fog, and other *particle effects*, in which a system of tiny individual objects behaves like a single entity. This is the default camera.

Real Lens Camera

The Real Lens Camera option is great for real-world photographers and lets LightWave cameras mimic many popular still cameras. Emulations include pro-caliber SLR (single-lens reflex) camera-and-lens combinations, and even point-and-shoot models from Nikon, Canon, and Olympus.

Tilt Shift Camera

A super cool addition to the LightWave camera system is the addition of the Tilt Shift camera. Mimicking a real-world tilt-shift lens, this camera allows you to create selective focus to your scenes. Selective focus means that you can have one area sharp and one area out of focus. The result can give you a miniature look.

Surface Baking Camera

The Surface Baking camera will come in very handy for game designers, architectural animators, and anyone who wants to speed up lengthy animations. The Surface Baking camera allows you to "bake" your textures into one large image map. Say, for example, you have a complex scene with many image-mapped textures, procedural textures, ray-traced shadows, radiosity for global illumination, and so on. That would all take a long time to render, especially if your scene is 30 seconds, 1 minute, or longer. By using the Surface Baking camera, you render once, and all the calculations LightWave needs to perform are saved to an image map you specify. Then, you reload that image and apply it to your entire scene. One image map contains all of the other image maps, procedurals, reflections, shadows, and so on. With that, you can turn off advanced ray-tracing features, complex lighting, and so forth, and LightWave can then crank through the frames for final render output in no time. The Surface Baking camera looks at each pixel in your render as a UV coordinate. (You'll learn more about UVs a bit later in the book.) The UV will allow you to conveniently map a large image around complex shapes. The process can be time-consuming, but the camera is optimized to take full advantage of computers with two or more processors.

The Next Step

The cameras in LightWave are compelling storytelling tools— whether your story is a flying logo, a simulation of a car accident, or an animated epic. When you model, you create shapes and animate them. When you animate, your motions create a mood, and without the proper camera angles your work will not be as powerful.

To understand this better, it may help to think about some of your favorite movie directors and the way they use camera placement to aid their storytelling. Quentin Tarantino movies, for instance, often include a shot framed with the camera looking out from the inside of a car trunk. Imagine how different one of those scenes would feel if it were shot from a long side view instead, or from overhead, or from the perspective of another character. Or think of the famous opening scene of *Citizen Kane*, and how the intimacy of the dying word "Rosebud" might have changed if it were delivered in a wide shot of Kane's bedroom instead of in a close-up on his whispering lips.

That said, don't worry about becoming the next Welles or Hitchcock. Experiment! Practice setting up different types of shots. Load some of the scenes from your LightWave directory that installed when you loaded the program. Study the camera angles used there and try creating your own. Use reference books from real-world situations, mimic the cinematography in movies, and most importantly, experiment. This chapter should get you thinking about the cameras in LightWave and the shots you can create and animate.

A large portion of what goes into a shot involves lighting and environments. Be sure to use a generous combination of lighting, textures, motions, and, of course, cameras in your projects. Before you do that, you need to create some models! And hey, didn't you hear that LightWave was an animation program? Turn to the next chapter to learn how to keyframe and put items in motion. Then, you'll get into simple modeling and animation, branching out to more complex models and working your way up to dynamics and more.

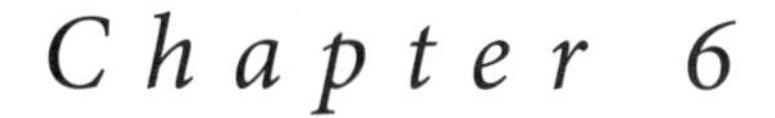

3D Animation

Here's how the American Heritage Dictionary defines *animation*: "The act, process, or result of imparting life, interest, spirit, motion, or activity." Motion. Activity. When you think about animation, you think about movement. Movement in animation is created with keyframes, and you might think that this should have been the first topic discussed in this book, given that LightWave is an animation program. However, knowing how to create an effect and understanding where to make the right adjustments saves you not only time but aggravation as well. Understanding timing is a constant in an animator's career, and it's also the focus of this chapter. As you know, 3D image creation isn't always about movement, and regardless of whether you're dealing with still or moving images, understanding the environment in which you are working is key to your success as an animator and 3D artist. There are so many facets to 3D animation—from modeling to texturing, lighting, and even scripting—that it's sometimes a real headache trying to figure out where to start.

LightWave 10 is uncluttered yet very functional. Many programs fill up the screen with useless icons; thankfully, LightWave names buttons clearly. This enables you to focus on your creative goals instead of having to figure out what a particular icon means. Going one step further, LightWave's powerful Graph Editor offers you complete control over a specific item's motion and timing. This item can be a camera, an object, a light, or any other type of parameter that can be enveloped or changed over time. As I mentioned in Chapter 2, "LightWave Layout," you'll find those little E buttons throughout the LightWave interface. This chapter discusses what to do with those Es when you click them.

NOTE

You'll find the E buttons next to the controls for attributes, such as Surface Color, that can be changed over time in the Graph Editor. Why E? A long time ago, in a galaxy far, far away (Topeka), LightWave was born with a tool called Envelope. (Technically, animating a motion channel is "enveloping" its values.) Envelope evolved into the Graph Editor but retained its ancestral initial. Here, you can animate just about any value or channel in LightWave. If you feel that the next version of LightWave should have "A" for animate rather than "E" for a nonexistent Envelope panel, email our friends at NewTek.

NOTE

An *expression* is a LightWave function that lets you set specific operations based on mathematical statements. For example, you can select an animated wheel object and create an expression that tells Layout, "When the wheel rotates a full 360 degrees, turn on a light and rotate another object." Expressions are very powerful and one of LightWave's most advanced features.

The Graph Editor that opens when you click an E button also gives you control over every channel of an item, such as the X position, heading rotation, dissolves, light color, and so on, all over a set duration. Each channel can be controlled through the use of expressions, modifiers, or even keyframes, all from within the Graph Editor. The Graph Editor is used to edit any type of parameter that can be enveloped or, as the nontechnical folk like to say, animated. In this chapter, you will learn about the following:

- Creating motion with keyframes
- Using motion splines
- Adjusting motions
- Working with the Graph Editor

Creating Motion with Keyframes

You might think that the title of this section is redundant. Creating motion with keyframes? Duh! How else would you do it? Well, actually there are many ways in LightWave 10 to create motion without keyframes: procedural motions, expressions, and, of course, dynamics. Dynamics enable you to move one item and have it affect another item. Or, you can just add gravity to an object and watch it move.

So why even use keyframes? Timing. To create an animation that's really "in the pocket," you need to master the art of timing. It is an art, and you've either got it or you don't. Timing is everything—in life, in comedy, and in animation. In 3D animation, you control timing with keyframes. The more often you work with keyframes, the more quickly you'll get a feel for animation timing.

Keyframing is the act of setting or marking an animatable attribute in time. For example, when you want a ball to move from point A to point B over two seconds, you need to set a keyframe at point A to tell LightWave to "start here" at point A in time. Then you add another keyframe, two seconds later in the timeline at point B, to say "end here at point B." The way it moves from that point is up to you, but each stop, detour, or change in orientation it makes along the way will be controlled by additional keyframes. Wobbles? Keyframes. Bounces? Keyframes. Get the idea?

Keyframing goes beyond just animating position and rotation. In LightWave, "animatable attributes" encompasses properties such as light intensity, color, and a host of surface characteristics. Essentially, if a Layout characteristic has a numeric value, you can animate changes to that value over time. And the way you control those changes is with—say it with me—keyframes. As you'll see later in the chapter, animating surface attributes also often combines keyframes with another powerful Layout tool, the Graph Editor.

Because the Layout interface was covered in previous chapters—as was navigating the timeline—this chapter focuses on putting you to work. You'll start by setting up some basic keyframes. From there, you'll use multiple objects and then learn how to set targets and parents and adjust the motions in a variety of ways.

Automatic Keyframing

The Auto Key button at the bottom of the Layout interface is turned on by default. We discussed this briefly in Chapter 2, but the following is a hands-on tutorial to further explain when and why to use this feature. Auto Key does multiple things: It adjusts the values of existing keyframes automatically; it automatically creates keyframes where none are present; and it creates keys on all channels, or only on modified channels. For the Auto Key feature to automatically create keys, you need to make sure the Auto Key Create option is enabled in the General Options tab (press **o**). Set this to Modified Channels so that any commands, such as Move, Rotate, Size, or Stretch, are remembered for selected items at the current frame. Exercise 6.1 explains this feature further.

Exercise 6.1 Using the Auto Key Feature

For this exercise, you won't even need to load a scene or any objects. The Auto Key feature in LightWave makes creating animations pretty easy. Almost everything in LightWave can be animated! For that reason, this quick project will have you animate the two default items in Layout, the camera and the light.

1. Open LightWave, and if you're already working on something, save it. Then from the File drop-down menu, select Clear Scene. You'll see a Perspective view with the default camera and light visible, as in **Figure 6.1** (on the next page).
2. Select the camera in one of two ways: by clicking directly on it, or by choosing the Cameras button at the bottom of the interface.

Figure 6.1 A simple scene with two default items, a camera and a light, ready to be put in motion.

3. When selected, the camera will be highlighted in yellow and you'll see a dotted projection extend out from the camera, as shown in **Figure 6.2**. This area is what the camera sees.

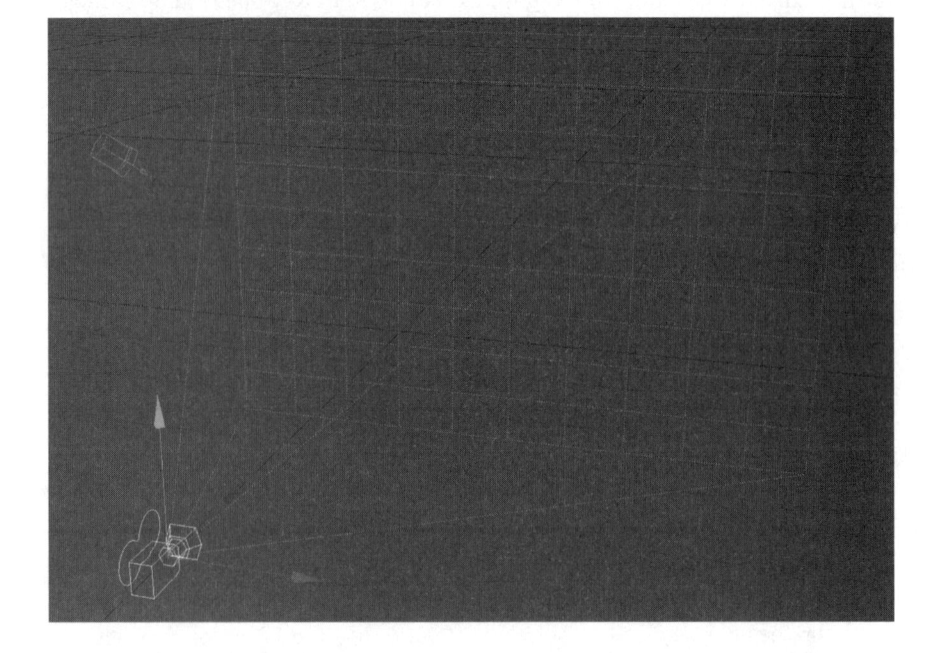

Figure 6.2 When you select a camera, Layout highlights it in yellow and extends a dotted line from its "lens" to indicate its field of view.

NOTE

The virtual cameras shown in Layout scenes are merely representational. Their focal points are at their pivot points—where their positioning handles appear when they're selected—not at their drawn "lenses."

4. Make sure your timeline is set to frame 0, which will be the start of your simple animation.

   To understand how Auto Key works, you'll compare creation of a simple camera animation with Auto Key on and off.

5. If it's activated, click the Auto Key button at the bottom center of the Layout interface to turn it off. (The button is white when Auto Key is on and blue when it's off.)
6. Press **t** to activate the Move tool. This tool is also found on the Modify tab.
7. With the Move tool active, click and drag the green handle that appears for the selected camera. Drag it up slightly from its current position, about 2 m or so, as shown in **Figure 6.3**.

NOTE

In the Layout window, you'll notice that there is always a key at frame 0 by default. Thus, an object is locked in place even without Auto Key. Auto Key merely lets you make an adjustment at frame 0 (or any other existing keyframe) without having to re-create the key.

Figure 6.3 Using the Move tool, drag the camera up a bit on the Y-axis.

8. Click and drag the timeline slider forward to another frame.

   The camera seems to jump back to its original position. Move the slider back to frame 0, and the camera returns to its original keyframed position. Unless you set a keyframe (or reset an existing one) after you change an object's position, orientation, or other attributes, the adjustments aren't captured and LightWave "forgets" them.

9. Click the Auto Key button to activate it (the button will turn white) and repeat steps 6 and 7.
10. Drag the slider to frame 60, the last frame of your animation. (LightWave's default length for new animations is 60 frames.)

NOTE

If you can't see the object to grab it, you can switch to the Back view by pressing the number 1 on the keyboard. Single-button-mouse Mac users, remember to use Control-click for right-mouse-button commands. Also, you can use your right mouse button (or equivalent) to quickly control up and down (Y-axis) movements.

This time, the camera stays where you put it. Auto Key automatically reset the keyframe in frame 0 to capture your camera move.

11. With the timeline slider at frame 60, click and drag the blue handle for the camera and move it to the back of Layout, as shown in **Figure 6.4**. Auto Key automatically creates a new keyframe this time, capturing the new position information.

Figure 6.4 With the timeline slider at frame 60, the camera is moved to a new position.

So now your animation has two keyframes: one at frame 0, indicating the camera's starting position, and another at frame 60, reflecting its end position. Let's see how the camera gets from the first keyframed position to the other.

12. Drag the timeline slider back and forth and you'll see the camera move through the scene. LightWave automatically fills in (also commonly known as "in-betweening") the motions needed to move objects between keyframes. Congratulations, you just made an animation!

    This is a very basic example, but the principles are the same for even the most complex objects. Pick a point in time, position the item, and you're building an animation.

13. Now, press **y** to select the Rotate tool. At frame 60, click and drag the red ring to rotate the camera 180 degrees so that it's facing in toward your current view (**Figure 6.5**).

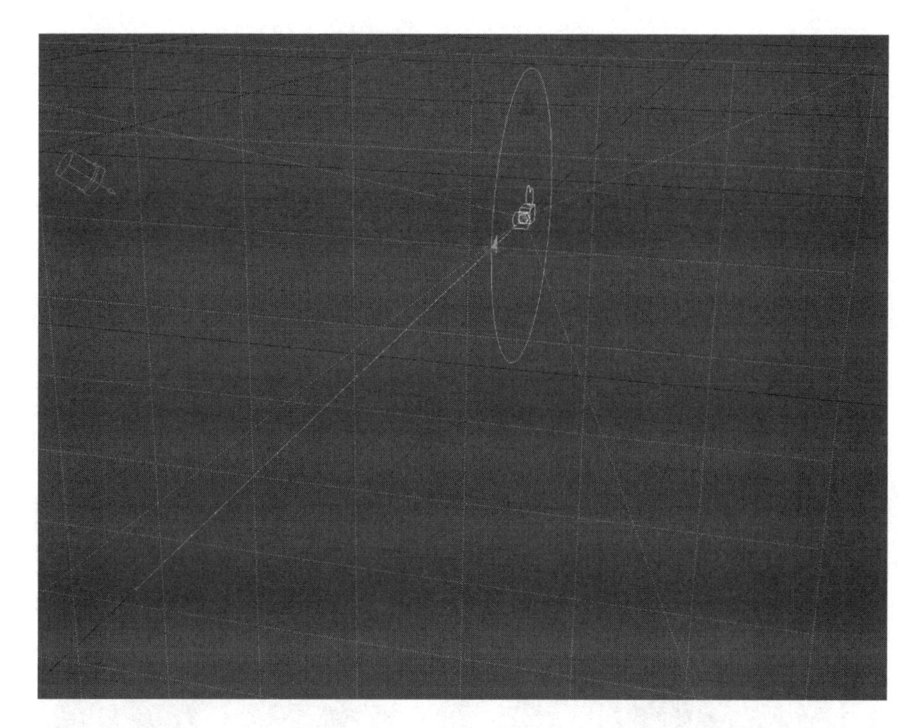

Figure 6.5 With the timeline slider at frame 60, rotate the camera so it faces the scene.

14. Click the Rewind button, at the bottom right of the interface, and then the Play button (the right-facing triangle). The camera will now move from frame 0 to frame 60, across the scene down the Z-axis, rotating as it goes.

To recap, at frame 0, Auto Key captured the camera's position along the X, Y, and Z axes and its H, P, and B (Heading, Pitch, and Bank) rotation coordinates. At frame 60, the position and rotation changes you made were also recorded in a new keyframe, and LightWave interpolated the movements in between the two keyframes. Welcome to animation!

15. To help you visualize movement within your project as you work in individual frames, LightWave can display a motion path that shows the route an object will take between keyframes. To see your camera's motion path, press **o** to open the LightWave Preferences panel and check Show Motion Paths on its OpenGL tab.

16. Drag the timeline to about frame 30, deactivate the Auto Key button at the bottom of the interface, and then move the camera to a new position.

17. Once the camera is in a new position, click the Rewind button and then the Play button to see the animation. Notice a change? Of course not. With the Auto Key feature off, the position change for the camera was not recorded. You'll also see that its motion path didn't change.

18. Slide the timeline back to frame 30. Turn Auto Key back on. Now move the camera again to a new position, and this time rotate it a little as well. Feel free to change the camera position on the Y-axis too.
19. You'll see that the motion path has now changed (**Figure 6.6**). Click the Rewind and Play buttons to watch the motion along the new path. Now the camera moves among three keyframes: 0, 30, and 60. Each keyframe stores object position and rotation information in time. The keyframes tell the camera to "be here" or "stay here" at a specific point in time.

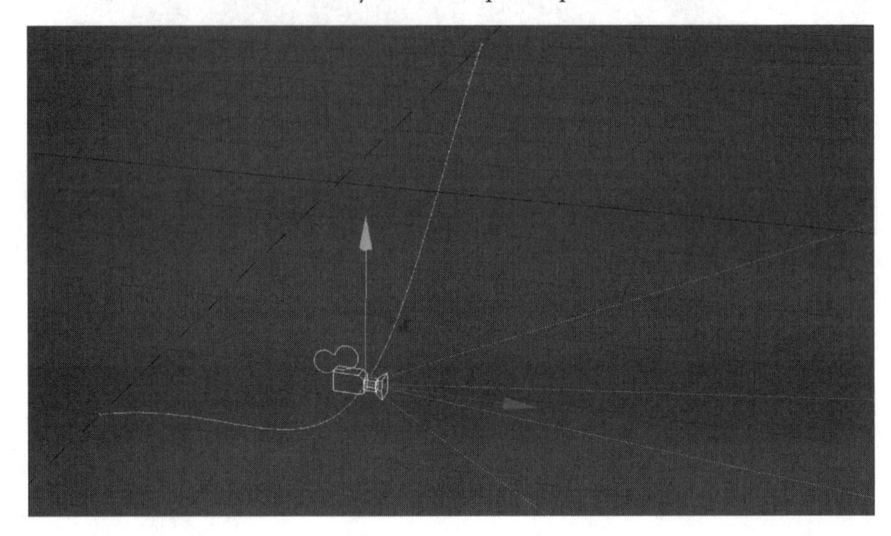

Figure 6.6 When Auto Key is active and Show Motion Paths is turned on, manual adjustments to camera position are reflected in its motion path.

NOTE

Using the Auto Key feature also requires that the Auto Key Create option be set to Modified Channels. You can find this by pressing **o** to open Layout's Preferences panel, in the General tab.

A word of caution about Auto Key: It can be quite helpful in setting up animations, but it can also be hazardous when you're working on crowded scenes that require precise object placement. Accidentally nudge the wrong object with Auto Key on, and you can lose hours of painstaking adjustments. For those situations, you'll want to become adept at manual keyframing.

Manual Keyframing

Auto Key appeals to our natural sense of the world. When you move something, it should stay where you put it. But there are times when Auto Key doesn't provide enough control. In many ways, it's like using a point-and-shoot camera. Everything is automatic and easy, but sometimes the automatic methods, which work more than 90 percent of the time, won't let you do what you need to do. Just as a great photograph may demand manual camera control, LightWave setups with nuanced model motion and interaction require manual keyframing. Manual keyframing is vital to superb timing in your animations, and while you can't develop that overnight, a few practice animations can get you started.

A good way to work is to turn off the Auto Key Create option in the General Options tab (press **o**) and work only with Auto Key enabled. While it's not necessary to do, the Auto Key adjusts existing keyframes without the need to create them again after any changes are made. If there are no keyframes already created, either manually or with the Auto Key Create option previously enabled, LightWave will not create any keyframes automatically. If you accidentally move the timeline, you won't create unwanted keyframes, destroying a precisely placed item.

So, here's how you can think of it: If there are already keyframes for a Layout item, working with Auto Key on at the bottom of Layout will automatically record and keep any changes made to that item at that frame. If Auto Key Create is off in the Options panel, any changes you make to an item that does not yet have a keyframe will not be recorded.

Exercise 6.2 Manual Keyframing with Auto Key

Before you begin, there are a few things you should know: When there's a blank scene and you load a single object into it, that object should automatically be selected. If you click to select the item and it's not selecting, be sure you have Left Button Item Select turned on in the General tab of the Preferences panel (press **o**), as in **Figure 6.7**. If the control handles do not appear in the center of the object, make sure that the Show Handles option is turned on in the OpenGL tab within the Display Options tab (press **d**).

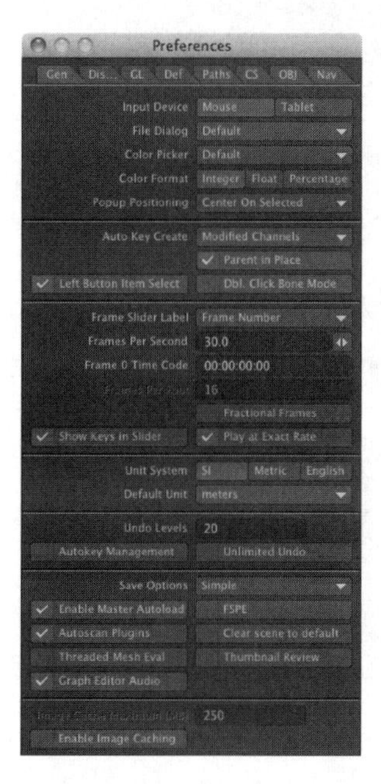

Figure 6.7 The Left Button Item Select feature is found on the General tab of the Preferences panel. Press o to open the panel.

By default, Layout assigns new scenes a duration of 60 frames, or 2 seconds. If your animation runs longer than that (most do), just increase the last frame number in the timeline. Be sure to add extra frames after your last keyframe, to give viewers time to register the actions that occur at that last keyframe. You can change the default animation length in the Preferences panel (press **o**) by changing the default frame number on the Defaults tab (listed as Def). You'll need to quit and restart Layout to keep these settings.

Keyframing manually is more deliberate than using Auto Key alone. But what confuses many new animators is deciding when to use Auto Key and when to use manual keyframing in their animations. But you don't have to worry about that! This exercise will instruct you on deliberately setting keyframes while still keeping the Auto Key feature active.

1. A scene has been created for you to begin keyframing. Here, the cup will fall, bounce slightly, and land on the saucer. Load the scene by going to the File drop-down list and selecting File, then Load Scene. Choose the Cup_o_Tea_Static.lws scene from the book's DVD in the CH6 folder of the 3D_Content directory. Alternatively, you can load a scene by clicking the Scene button under the Load category of the Items tab. **Figure 6.8** shows the scene loaded into Layout.

Figure 6.8 A simple scene, ready to be put in motion.

2. With the teacup scene loaded, be sure the frame slider at the bottom of the Layout interface is at 0, be sure Auto Key is enabled, and activate Auto Key Create on the General Options tab within the Preferences panel (press **o**) to have keyframes created automatically.

3. Select Modified Channels from the selection area of the Auto Key Create command, as in **Figure 6.9**. In Modified Channels mode, new keyframes are created only for those channels that have been changed, whereas setting Auto Key Create to All Motion Channels creates a new keyframe for everything in your scene anytime you make a change to your selected item. This feature is not something you'll use often, but at times you might need it. Suppose you're creating an animation of characters dancing on a stage and each item's motion channels (position and rotation) need to follow specific timing; creating keyframes with All Motion Channels enabled will save you time.

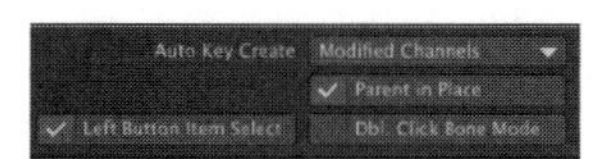

Figure 6.9 Be sure to set the Auto Key Create option to Modified Channels in the General Options tab.

It's often convenient when animating to assemble all the objects or characters in a scene exactly as you want them to end up, then work backward to specify how they got there. Let's do that with our teacup and saucer. We want them to be arranged as they are in the current scene at the end of our animation, so we'll place the current scene in the final frame and then keyframe backward.

4. Make sure you're in a Shaded Solid view, from the top of Layout. Click the Objects button at the bottom of Layout, and then choose the CupAndSaucer: Cup listing from the Item drop-down list to select the teacup object. It will be highlighted with a yellow bounding box—that is, a wireframe box will appear as a representation of the object's 3D space. This animation is 200 frames long, so create a keyframe for the teacup at frame 200, the last frame. Since it's already in its "final" position, you can simply lock it in place now. Click the Create Key button beneath the timeline. It will have a 0 for the Create Key At entry because your timeline is at frame 0. Enter **200** in the requester, and make sure that Selected Items is chosen and that all of the channels are clicked, as in **Figure 6.10**.

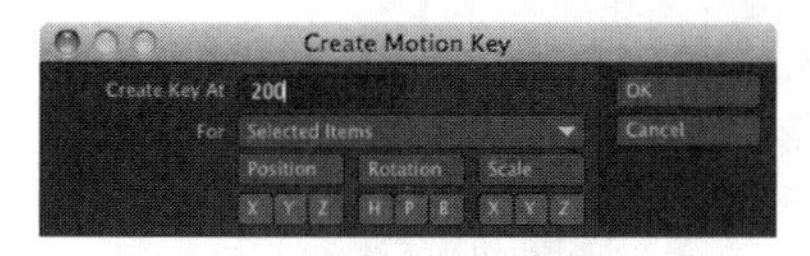

Figure 6.10 Create a keyframe at 200 for the cup.

5. Click OK to close the Create Motion Key panel. With the timeline at 0, and with the cup selected, press **t** to select the Move tool (or click the Move tool on the Modify tab). Move the cup up in the scene, about 1.5 m, by clicking and dragging its green (Y-axis) handle, or use your right mouse and drag for Y-axis movement. You can see the amount of movement in the numeric display at the lower-left corner of Layout (**Figure 6.11**).

Figure 6.11 Move the teacup up and away from the saucer.

6. Now you should see a small white line tracing from the saucer to the cup. This is a motion path. Because you created a keyframe at frame 200, and you

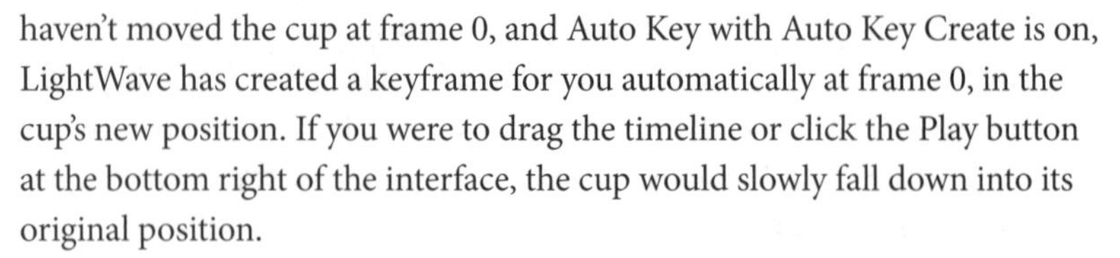

haven't moved the cup at frame 0, and Auto Key with Auto Key Create is on, LightWave has created a keyframe for you automatically at frame 0, in the cup's new position. If you were to drag the timeline or click the Play button at the bottom right of the interface, the cup would slowly fall down into its original position.

NOTE

If you don't see a motion path, you need to make it visible. Press **o** to open the Preferences panel and check Show Motion Paths on its OpenGL tab.

7. Click and drag the timeline slider forward to frame 200. The cup should be resting on the saucer at this point, in its original position. This is also where you want the cup to land when it first falls down. You can copy the current keyframe value by clicking the Create Key button (or pressing Enter) and then enter **10** in the Create Key At field (it will read 200 because this is the current frame your timeline slider is on). After you enter 10, click OK. You've now copied a keyframe. **Figure 6.12** shows the keyframe.

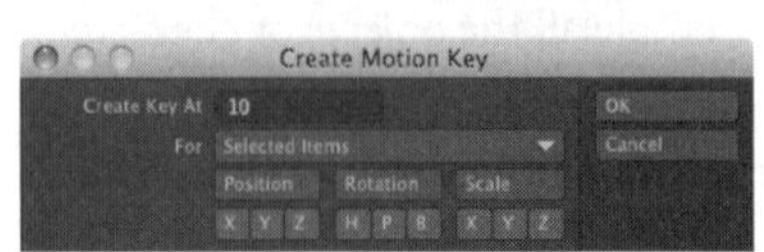

Figure 6.12 Make a keyframe at frame 10, with the cup in the same position as in frame 200.

8. With the teacup still selected, make sure your timeline is on frame 10. Then, press **y** to activate the Rotate tool (also on the Modify tab). When the tool is active, you'll see rings around the selected object. Click and drag the blue ring to rotate the cup on the Bank channel about 30 degrees. You'll see the degree of the rotation in the lower-left corner of the interface. Then move the cup up slightly so it's not going through the saucer. **Figure 6.13** shows the example.

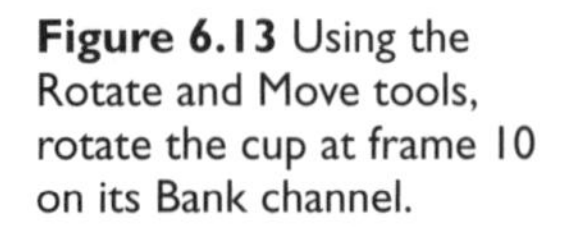

Figure 6.13 Using the Rotate and Move tools, rotate the cup at frame 10 on its Bank channel.

NOTE

A quick way to jump to any frame in Layout is to press **f** to call up the Go To Frame command. When it appears, just enter the desired frame number and press Enter (or Return on a Mac). Note that you do not need to highlight and delete the value in the Go To Frame requester. The old value will be highlighted when the requester appears, so you can just type the new frame number to replace it.

9. Drag the timeline slider to frame 20. Now use the Move tool by selecting it from the Modify tab (or by pressing **t**), move the object up a bit, and give it different rotation. Remember that you can press **y** to jump to the Rotate tool. **Figure 6.14** shows the change.

Figure 6.14 Using the Move and Rotate tools, reposition the cup at frame 20.

NOTE

Because the Move and Rotate commands are used so often, Layout provides many ways to get to them. In addition to clicking their tool buttons on the Modify tab or pressing **t** for Move and **y** for rotate, you can press the spacebar to cycle through the Move, Rotate, Size, and Stretch tools. Additionally, if your computer mouse has a scroll wheel, you can use it to toggle between Move, Rotate, and Stretch.

10. Click the Rewind button, at the bottom right of the interface, just above the Preview menu. Then click the Play button, which is the right-facing arrow, also at the bottom right of the interface.

    When you play the animation, you'll see your cup fall and quickly bounce. It's sort of OK, but it drifts through the saucer. What's up with that? Didn't you keyframe it at frame 10 to land on the saucer? You did, but because LightWave's motions are actually spline curves, there's a fluidity between keyframes. This interpolation is your friend in most animations, but often you need to control it. We'll set up a few more keyframes first, to finish the animation, and then you'll see how to control the "drifting" you see before and after set keyframes.

11. Press **f** to call up the Go To Frame command. Enter **200** to jump to the cup's final resting position, and then copy its keyframe information to frame 30, using the method described in step 7.

NOTE

You don't need to move the timeline slider to set keyframes throughout an animation if you're manually setting keyframes. However, moving it helps keep you organized and aware of the current animation frame.

Click the Play button. You should see the teacup move and rotate between keyframes 0 and 30. You can shuttle through the animation by grabbing the timeline slider and dragging.

Pretty good start, but there are still a few problems with the motion, right? The cup doesn't really bounce or land realistically; it sort of floats and drifts a bit before it comes to a rest. Because LightWave creates motion curves between keyframes, you need to control the curves for each keyframe. You can do this with the Graph Editor. However, there is a quicker way to change this motion right in Layout. We'll use that option first and then use the Graph Editor, so you can see both methods.

Before you tweak the teacup animation further, note that you can delete keyframes as easily as you create them. Press the Delete Key with the frame slider on a keyframe, and the Delete Motion Key dialog will open, with the current frame already selected (**Figure 6.15**).

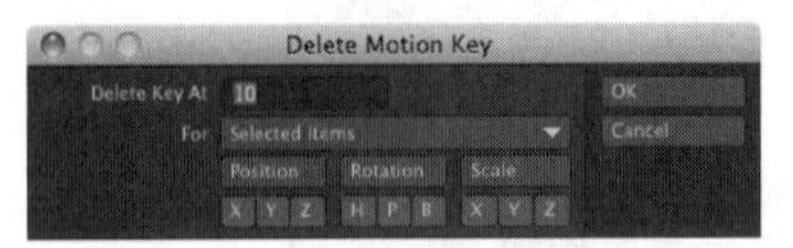

Figure 6.15 Deleting keyframes works the same as creating them. Select an item to adjust, go to a specific point in time, and click the Delete Key button at the bottom of Layout.

As with creating keyframes, the timeline slider does not need to be on the specific keyframe to delete a key. Enter the number of the key you want to delete when the Delete Motion Key dialog opens. Again, use your numeric keypad to save time! And remember, just as you can create keyframes for specific channels, you can delete them as well.

The tutorials in this motion chapter are really basic, and probably the simplest things to do in this book, but it's important for you to get the hang of keyframing. You told the cup to be at a certain position at frame 0, the beginning of the animation. Then you moved the object to its resting position at the end of the animation at frame 200. Then you told LightWave to copy that position of the cup at frame 10, and again at frame 30. You also changed its position and rotation at frame 20. It will then sit there until frame 200, unless you make another keyframe change. LightWave interpolates the frames between 0 and 200, even if there is no movement from 30 to 200. Sort of like magic, you made an animation. Automagically, the motion curve that the computer created is the in-betweening that traditional animators would have to draw by hand. (*Automagically* is a technical term.)

Control Curves with the Move TCB Tool

Now you'll move on to correcting the "drift" in the teacup animation. You'll start by using Layout's Move TCB tool, and later in this chapter you'll explore an alternate approach that uses the Graph Editor. The Move TCB tool, found on Layout's Modify tab, is perfect for quickly controlling the motion curve created from multiple keyframes.

Exercise 6.3 Working with the Move TCB Tool

1. If you don't have your teacup scene still in Layout with the multiple keyframes you created, load the Cup_o_Tea_Motion.lws scene from this book's DVD.

   Click the Play button again to review the animation. The teacup droops down too low, into the saucer object, on frame 10. Due to the motion curve, the teacup slides between the curves. Not desirable, but fixable.

2. Press **f** to call up the Go To Frame window and type **0** (zero), or drag the slider to the beginning of the timeline.

3. On the Modify tab, select the Move TCB tool, shown in **Figure 6.16**. Alternatively, you can press Control+G to activate the tool.

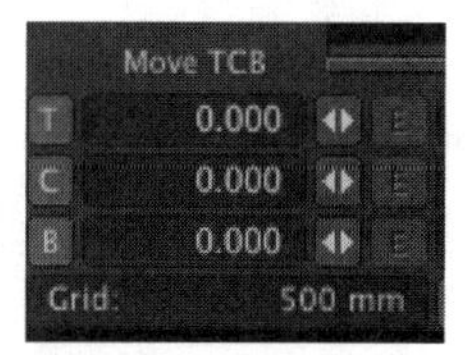

Figure 6.16 The Move TCB tool, which can be found on the Modify tab in Layout.

4. Note the info area on the bottom left of the Layout screen. You'll see that this area now lists values for T, C, and B—shorthand for Tension, Continuity, and Bias. Clicking and dragging in the current frame will increase or decrease the tension for the current frame, which is 0.

5. Click and drag to the right until the tension reads 1.0, as in **Figure 6.17**.

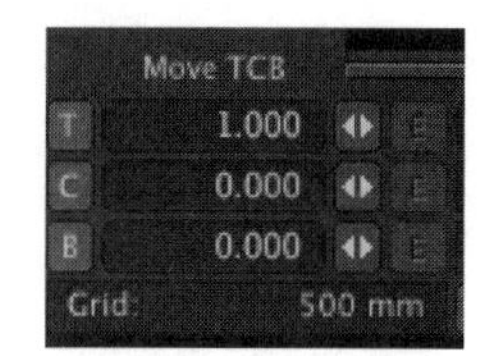

Figure 6.17 A Tension value of 1, as reflected in the Move TCB tool's info area.

6. Go to frame 10 and this time, set a tension of –1.0 by clicking in the Layout window and dragging to the left.

7. Now set a 1.0 tension for frames 30 and 200. This will help control the motion at these keyframes. Leave frame 20 alone. You want the cup to come up to this keyframe and drop back down. Setting a tension value here would make it pause in mid-air.

   Play back the animation, and you'll see that the teacup starts out slower and hits the saucer with more force. It bounces up at frame 20, comes to rest at frame 30, and then holds firm through frame 200. The ease in and ease out at frames 0 and 30, respectively, are set with a positive tension value. The negative tension value helps to force the motion for the teacup at frame 10. But notice that frame 10 still slopes down into the saucer. While the motion of the fall and bounce are better, the motion still needs a bit of adjustment. The reason is that settings for each keyframe in a motion curve affect all the other keyframes. You set keyframes before and after frame 10, and the motion settings before and after the frame affect frame 10's settings. Fortunately, this is easy to adjust.

8. Go to frame 10, and select the teacup. Simply move it up on the Y-axis enough so that it rests on the saucer, as in **Figure 6.18**.

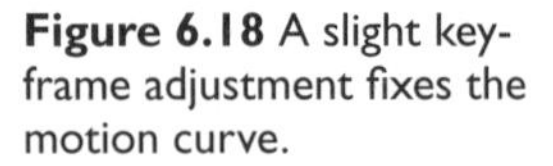

Figure 6.18 A slight keyframe adjustment fixes the motion curve.

You can add frames to a resting position by simply creating another keyframe. For example, if you wanted the teacup to stay in place only until frame 150, you would create an additional keyframe in the same position. Just think about your timeline process and what you're trying to accomplish. Be specific in what you want your object to do, and you'll have an easier time creating motions.

There are a few things you need to know about TCB and how to set the values:

- T, C, and B values can range from –1.0 to 1.0.
- Tension is used to ease in or ease out of a keyframe. You would set a tension of –1.0 to make an item slow down as it reaches its keyframed position. On the flipside, you'd use a tension of 1.0 to make an object speed up as it reaches its specified position—perhaps for things like a ball bouncing. As you've seen, to set tension using the Move TCB tool, just click and drag in an item's desired keyframe.
- Continuity is used to smooth or punctuate changes in motion. A positive continuity setting tells an object to "glide" smoothly as it passes through a

keyframe. A negative continuity setting briefly "freezes" an item in its keyframed position before its motion continues, and is useful for exaggerated or robotic character movements. To set continuity using the Move TCB tool, hold the Control key and click and drag in an item's desired keyframe.

- Bias is used for setting up anticipation. You can set a positive bias to create slack after a keyframe. Let's say your fire truck is speeding around a corner. Add bias to that keyframe, and it will slide around that corner. A negative bias creates slack before a keyframe. You could use this for, say, a racecar before it goes into a sharp turn. To set bias using the Move TCB tool, right-click and drag with the right mouse button in Layout for an item's desired keyframe to change Bias.

Keyframe Rules for Thought

There are a few more things you should know about keyframing in LightWave 10. A common misunderstanding with keyframes is that the more of them you have, the more control you will have in a scene. Not so! When you create keyframes in LightWave, you're creating curves. If you've worked in an illustration program like Adobe Illustrator, you'll know that you can build a smooth curve with as few as three points. But if you were to add more points—or, in this case, more keyframes—it would be that much harder to control timing and fluidity in your motions.

A good rule of thumb to use when setting keyframes is to start by setting your object's first and last keyframes, and then set any that fall in between. For example, say you want an object to move down a path and around an obstacle. The movement needs to be smooth, and trying to guess the timing might be tough to do. Set the beginning keyframe and then the ending keyframe to create the initial motion path. If you drag the timeline slider, the object moves between the two keyframes. If you move the timeline slider to the point where the object would move around the obstacle, you'll have the exact frame to set your next key. By creating the keyframe at this point, you've adjusted the motion path evenly.

In later chapters, you'll have many more opportunities to work with advanced keyframe techniques.

Navigating the Graph Editor

You've now worked through a series of basic keyframing steps. The process of creating keyframes for our simple exercise is the same as the one used for large-scale animation projects. The only difference is that big projects have a lot more keyframes. Overall, the increase in complexity results from the fact that there simply are more items to control in larger scenes. To help manage scenes that contain multiple keyframes, LightWave provides the Graph Editor.

You can access the Graph Editor by clicking the Graph Editor button at the top left of the screen in any Layout tab, or you can press Control+F2 to call up the panel (**Figure 6.19**).

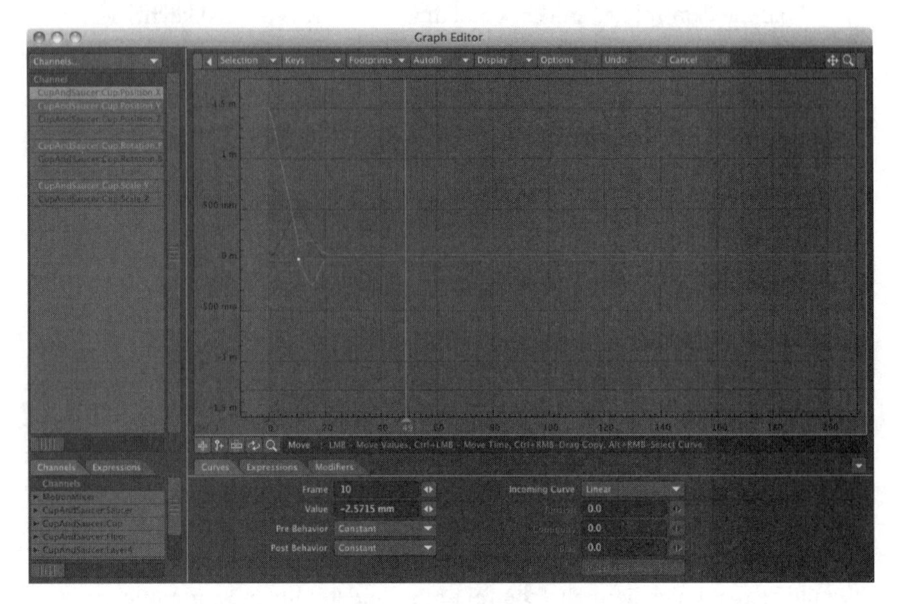

Figure 6.19 Opening the Graph Editor from the top left of the Layout interface gives you specific controls over your item's motions.

When you open the Graph Editor, you'll notice four general areas:

- The Curve Bin is the upper-left quadrant (**Figure 6.20**) of the panel (you won't see the name "Curve Bin"). This is the area of the Graph Editor where you place and select the specific channels (the curves) you want to edit.
- The Curve Window zone is in the largest area, the upper-right quadrant (**Figure 6.21**). This is the area where you edit curves. Here, you can adjust attribute values, edit keyframes, and more.

Figure 6.20 The Curve Bin zone of the Graph Editor is the area where you put channels you want to edit.

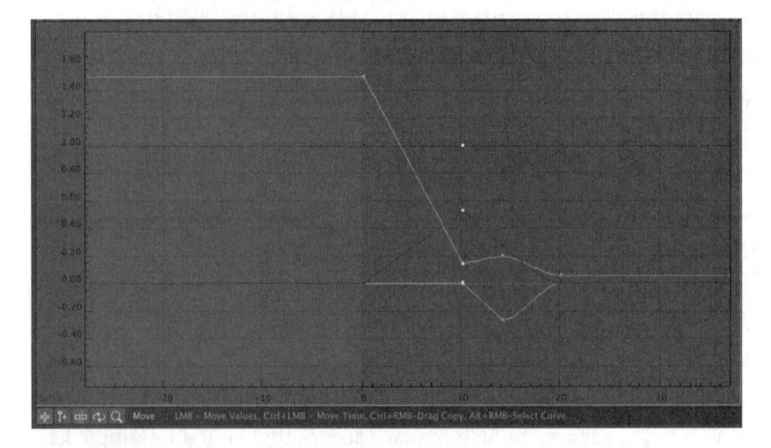

Figure 6.21 The Curve Window is the large main area of the Graph Editor, where all curve editing takes place.

- The Curve Controls zone is in the lower-right quadrant (**Figure 6.22**). Here you can set frames, values, behaviors for keys, and modifiers, apply expression plug-ins and spline controls, and so on.

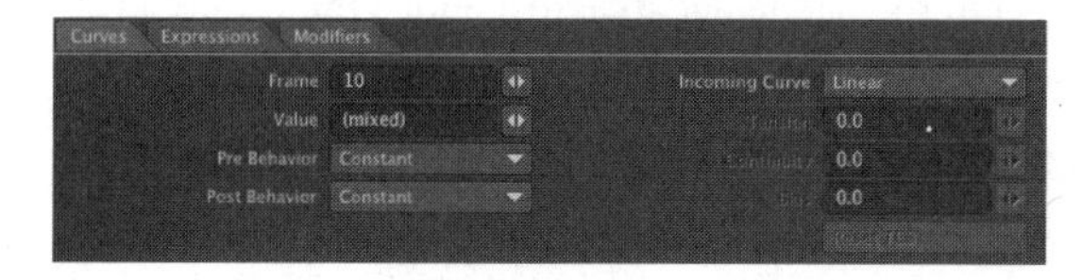

Figure 6.22 The Curve Controls zone, in the lower-right quadrant of the Graph Editor, is where you set specific controls, such as expressions, modifiers, spline controls, and more.

- The Scene zone is in the lower-left quadrant and shows the elements of your current scene (**Figure 6.23**). Lights, cameras, and objects are listed here, and you can select any or all of their channels and drag them into the Curve Bin to begin editing. This area also shows you any expressions that might be applied.

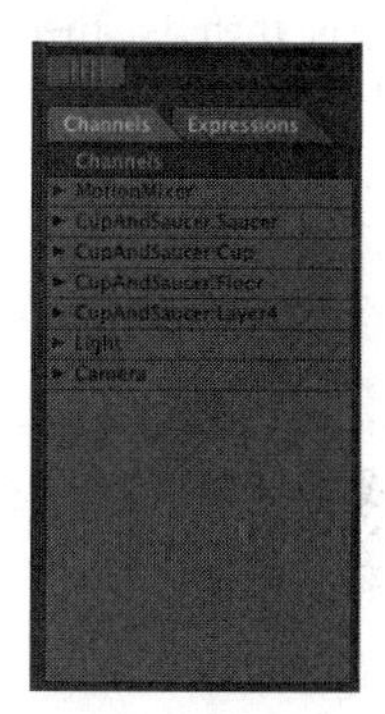

Figure 6.23 The Scene zone, in the lower-left corner of the Graph Editor, shows a list of items in your currently loaded scene.

You will work with each zone to adjust, modify, or create various motions, timing, and values for LightWave elements. Here you can control all Layout items, from the camera to lights to objects—including color, light intensities, morph envelopes, and more. You may be asking yourself where you should begin with the Graph Editor and wondering what it really does. Good questions! The Graph Editor is a complex part of Layout, one that is best explained through examples.

The exercise in the following section illustrates how to navigate through the Graph Editor interface.

Working with Channels

When you begin creating an animation, you will often need specific control over one keyframe or a group of keyframes. The Graph Editor gives you this control, but you first must understand how to set up the channels with which you want to work. This exercise introduces you to working with the Position and Rotation channels for a light and a camera.

Exercise 6.4 The Position and Rotation Channels

1. In Layout, save any work you've been doing and select Clear Scene from the File drop-down menu. Then, select the default camera.
2. Click the Graph Editor button on the toolbar (or press Control+F2) to enter the Graph Editor.

   You don't need to load anything into Layout as you follow along here.

   Look at **Figure 6.24**, and you'll see that the attributes in the Scene list (lower-left quadrant) relate to the items in Layout, such as the camera. In the upper-left quadrant, you'll see all of the camera's channels already loaded. If you've got an item selected when you open Graph Editor, all that item's channels

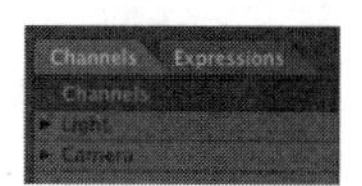

Figure 6.24 The Scene list in the lower left of the Graph Editor shows the items in your scene. Clicking the small white triangle next to an item expands it to show all its channels. The selected camera in Layout has all of its motion channels loaded in the Curve Bin.

NOTE

You can maximize the Graph Editor window by clicking the standard system maximize button next to the X in the top corner of the panel window. You can also reorder items in the Curve Bin by clicking and dragging them. Neither action affects your scene.

will automatically load into the panel. Click the small white triangle next to the Camera entry in the Channels tab to expand and display all the appropriate motion channels for the camera.

3. Double-click the Light label in the Scene list area, just above the Camera listing. This is in the lower-left corner of the Graph Editor interface.

   Double-clicking the Camera item adds all its channels to the Curve Bin, overriding any channels already in the bin. Doing this now makes those channels available for editing. If you were to hold the Shift key while double-clicking, you'd add to the current list of channels in the Curve Bin.

   You can also just click and drag a specific motion channel from the Scene list to the Curve Bin. This is great if you just want to add a selected channel or two. If you hold the Shift key, select a channel, and then select another channel, all channels in between will be selected. You can then drag those channels to the Curve Bin. And, as in many areas within LightWave, such as the Surface Editor, holding the Control key while selecting enables you to select noncontiguous channels.

4. Go back to the Scene list area at the bottom left of the Graph Editor and expand the Camera item's channels, if you haven't already, by clicking the small white arrow to the left of the Camera label. **Figure 6.25** shows the expansion.

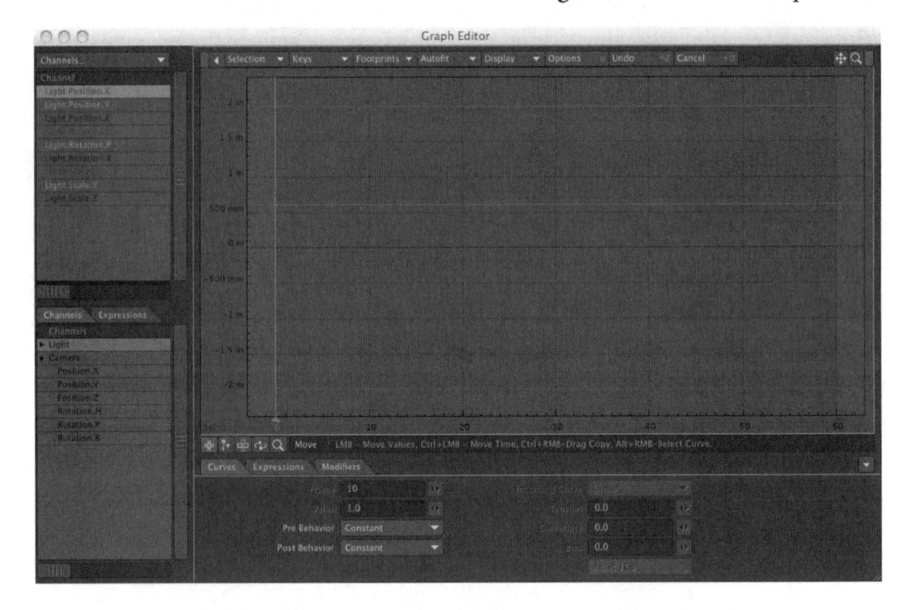

Figure 6.25 When you expand an item's channels, you can use the scrollbar on the right of the Scene Display quadrant to access them; you can also resize the display area.

5. Double-click any of the Camera's channels in the lower-left zone.

   The channel is now added to the Curve Bin and replaces any other channels stored there. (You can add more channels to the Curve Bin without replacing the active channels by holding Shift when you double-click a channel.)

NOTE

You can resize the individual quadrants in the Graph Editor by placing your mouse cursor on the borders between areas and then clicking and dragging them.

6. To add the Position.X and Rotation.H channels to the Curve Bin, hold down the Control key and click their name listings. Then drag them up to the Curve Bin. This is another way of adding channels without replacing them.

Now that you know how channels are added to the Curve Bin, you can modify or edit them in many different ways.

NOTE

If you have noncontiguous channels (channels not in order) to select, use the Control key rather than the Shift key to make your selections in the Scene list.

Working with the Graph Editor

Editing curves is one of the primary functions of the Graph Editor. To help understand the flow of editing curves, think of your workflow as progressing from bottom left, to top left, to top right, to bottom right.

Editing Curves

Layout generates editable curves anytime you specify a change in a setting's value over time, a change to control object position and rotation, or a change to any animatable property of a light, object, camera, or surface. No matter what the property or attribute is, you work your way through the Graph Editor the same way, and the Curve Window is where you control its curves.

Figure 6.26 shows the Graph Editor in full frame with the same teacup scene from earlier in this chapter loaded (Cup_o_Tea_Animated.lws). Use your own version of the scene, or load it from the book's DVD.

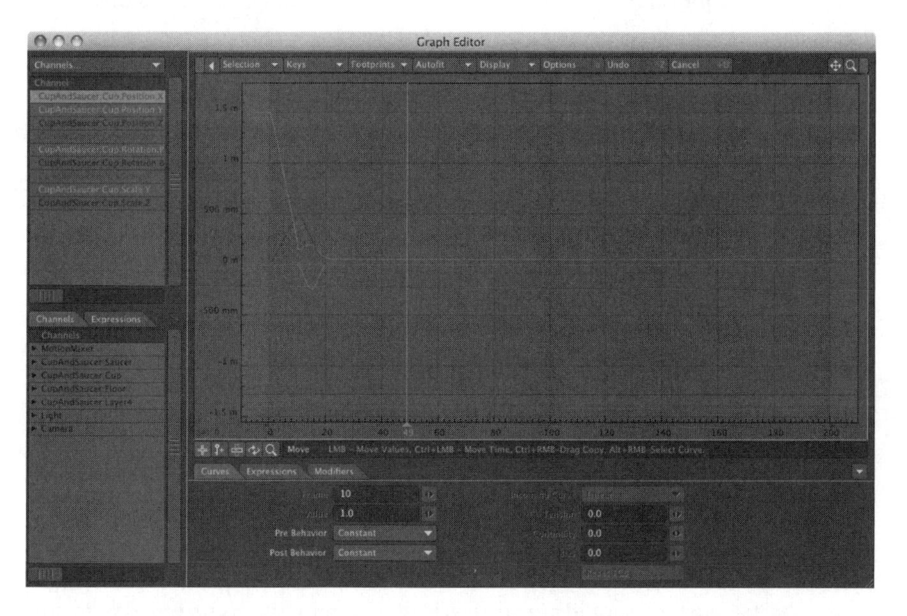

Figure 6.26 With a scene loaded into Layout and the tea cup object selected, opening the Graph Editor reveals all motion channels already in place in the Curve Bin for the selected teacup object.

In Figure 6.26, the first channel (Position.X) in the Curve Bin is selected by default. In the Curve Window, the channel that represents the object's X position is highlighted. On your computer, you'll notice that each position channel has a specific

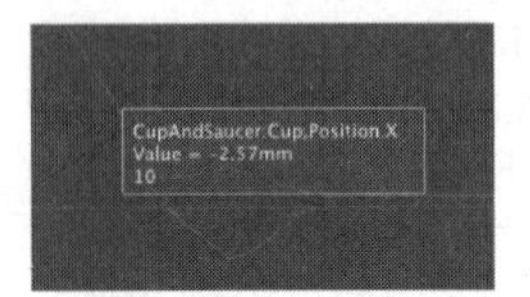

Figure 6.27 Moving the mouse pointer over a keyframe instantly displays the keyframe number, the value, and which channel (such as Position.X) you're working with.

color in the Curve Bin: X is red, Y is green, and Z is blue. You can change these default colors in the Preferences panel. The same color represents the corresponding curve in the main Curve Window. If you move the mouse pointer over one of the small colored dots (which represent keyframes) on an active curve (in this case, the item's motion path), numeric information appears (**Figure 6.27**).

If you like, and have the screen real estate, feel free to resize the Layout window and the Graph Editor to keep both panels fully visible all the time. To resize the Graph Editor, you can do the following:

1. Drag the lower-right corner of the Graph Editor window. Make sure that the window is not maximized.
2. Click and drag the Layout window from the top of the panel, and move it to the upper-left portion of your screen.
3. Open the Graph Editor and resize it as well. Move it beneath the Layout window.

Additionally, you can keep the Surface Editor and Preset Shelf (found under the Window drop-down) open while you're working in Layout if you like, perhaps also using the Dope Track. This is beneficial because you can make a change, see the result in Layout, and continue working. You do not have to continually open and close panels—simply leave them open. Either a large monitor or a dual-monitor setup is helpful for screen real estate when setting up configurations like this.

Adjusting Timing in the Graph Editor

The Graph Editor enables you to do many things, such as create, delete, or adjust keyframes for specific channels. You can also modify various entities within LightWave, such as surface color and light intensities. One of the more common uses for the Graph Editor is adjusting the timing of elements in your LightWave scenes. The Graph Editor has many uses, which you will inevitably take advantage of at some time during your career as an animator.

Exercise 6.5 Working with the Graph Editor

NOTE

As you work through scenes with the Graph Editor open, the channels will not automatically update in the Curve Bin. You can choose Get Layout Selected from the Selection drop-down (Shift+G) to update the Graph Editor.

1. Load the Train scene into Layout from the 3D Content directory on this book's DVD.

   This loads a simple scene with the train pulling into frame, stopping, backing up, and turning. It has a rotation and position change throughout the animation.

2. The Train object should already be chosen because the scene was saved with it selected. Open the Graph Editor.

   You'll see that all the object's channels are automatically loaded into the Curve Bin. However, in this tutorial, you're adjusting only the object's timing on the Z-axis; therefore, the remaining channels are not needed. For safety, so you don't accidentally change a curve you don't want to, isolate the specific curve to edit in the Curve Bin.

3. In the Scene window, expand the Train:Engine listing and double-click the Rotation.H channel. All existing channels in the Curve Bin will be replaced by the Rotation.H channel (**Figure 6.28**).

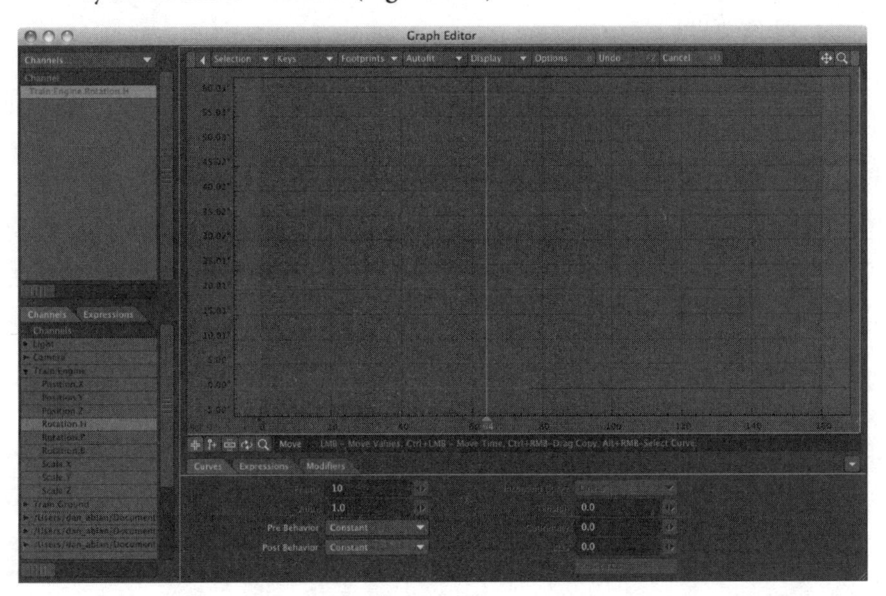

Figure 6.28 Double-clicking the Rotation.H channel in the Scene Bin adds the motion channel to the Curve Bin.

The Rotation.H channel already existed in the Curve Bin before you double-clicked to add it by itself. You can, however, select all of the channels you're not interested in using and remove them. You can right-click the selections and choose Remove from Bin (**Figure 6.29**). You also can choose Remove Channel from Bin (**Figure 6.30**) or Clear Unselected Channels (**Figure 6.31**) from the Selection drop-down at the top of the Graph Editor panel.

NOTE

If you take a close look at the functions available in the Selection drop-down, you'll see that you can do much more than simply remove channels. You can clear the Channel Bin, reverse selections, select all curves, and more. Experiment with these options to get a feel for their uses.

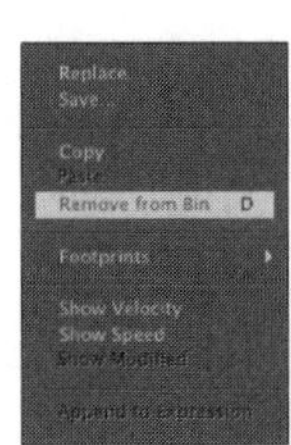

Figure 6.29 To remove selected channels, you can right-click the selections and choose Remove from Bin.

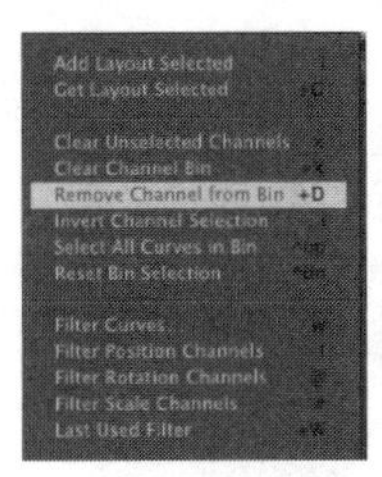

Figure 6.30 Choosing Remove Channel from Bin from the Selection drop-down list removes selected channels from the Curve Bin.

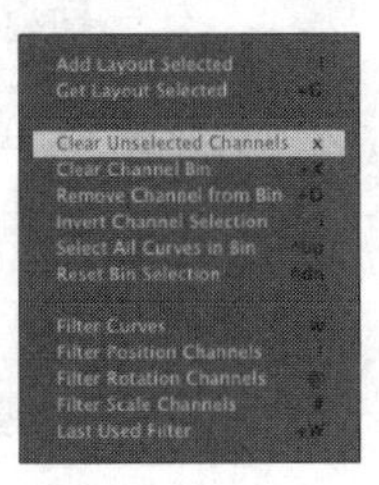

Figure 6.31 The Selection drop-down list at the top of the Graph Editor gives you access to a number of controls, including the ability to clear unselected channels from the Curve Bin.

You don't *have* to remove channels you don't plan to edit from the Channel Bin, but clearing channels you don't need helps keep the Channel Bin uncluttered and organized. It also prevents you from accidentally editing the wrong curve.

4. Back in the Curve Bin, select the single Rotation.H channel (if it's not already selected, since it's the only channel there). You'll see it highlighted in the Curve Window.

   This represents the motion of the H (Heading) channel for the object. The tall vertical line is the current frame.

5. Move your mouse over the first small dot (the first keyframe) on the curve for Rotation.H to see the information for that keyframe (**Figure 6.32**).

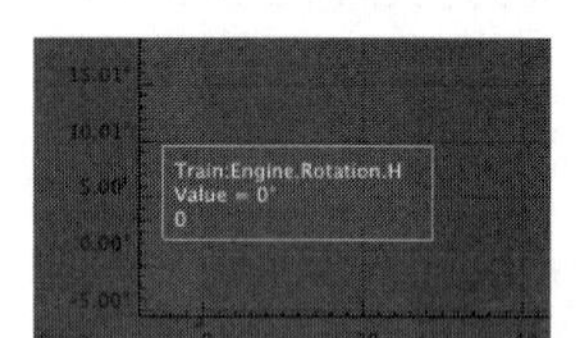

Figure 6.32 Move your mouse pointer over the first dot, which represents the first keyframe for the Pitch (P) rotation motion channel.

   The information tells you what curve it is; in this case, it is Rotation.H for the Train:Engine object. It also tells you the frame number of the keyframe and the value of the relevant setting at that frame. In this case, the setting value is the object's rotation at frame 0, which reads –0 degrees. This means the object is not rotated at frame 0. As the object rotates in successive frames, its rotation value is reflected in the Curve Window.

   It can be hard to identify that first keyframe in the curve. To simplify this, you can use the Graph Editor's Custom Point Color function.

6. While still in the Graph Editor, press **d** to call up the Graph Editor Options panel with its Display tab open. Click Custom Point Color at the bottom of the list, and the color selector will become active, as in **Figure 6.33**. The default color, white, is fine, so simply click OK to close the panel. Your keyframes in the Curve Window will now be easier to identify.

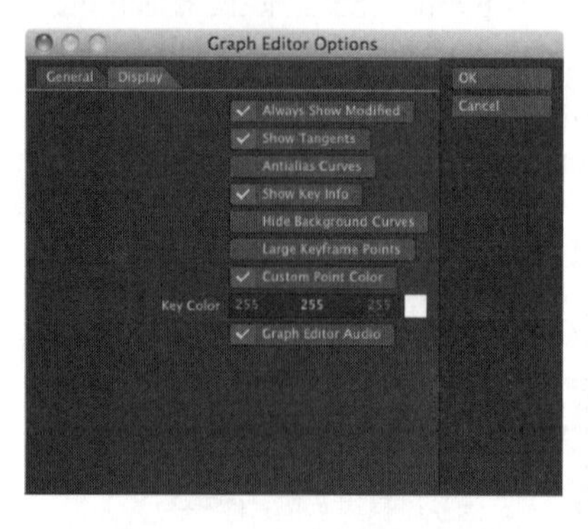

Figure 6.33 Setting the Custom Point Color option in the Graph Editor Options panel helps make a curve's keyframes more visible.

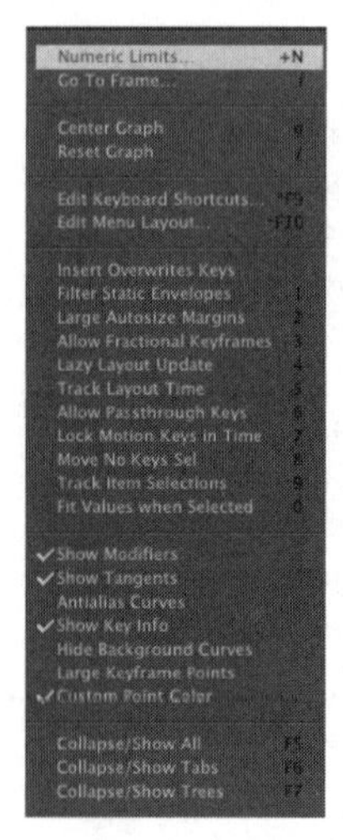

Figure 6.34 The Display drop-down list at the top of the Graph Editor interface gives you controls for working in the Graph Editor Options panel.

A number of other commands within the Graph Editor Options panel can help you when working with the Graph Editor. You can also access these commands and others easily by clicking the Display drop-down list from the top of the Graph Editor interface. **Figure 6.34** shows the list of commands for Display.

7. In the Curve Window, click the first keyframe to select it. Be sure that the Move edit mode button is selected. It is the first button located above the Curves tab, beneath the Curve Window, as shown in **Figure 6.35**. You can directly click the key to select it, or use the right mouse button to draw a region of selection. This second method is good for selecting multiple keyframes.

   With Custom Point Color active, you'll see the keyframe highlight slightly, and the values throughout the Curves tab will appear at the bottom of the screen, as shown in **Figure 6.36**.

Figure 6.35 The Move edit button in the Graph Editor resides just below the Curve Window, along with Add, Stretch, Roll, and Zoom. Selecting a specific tool displays the appropriate keyboard legend. Here, the Move tool is selected, enabling you to move selected keyframes in the Curve Window.

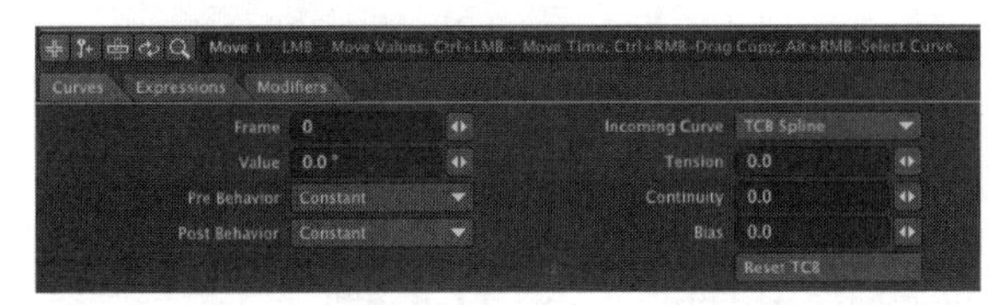

Figure 6.36 When a keyframe is selected, the commands in the Curves tab area become available. Here, a right-click and drag lasso-selects the key.

NOTE

Beware of clicking around too quickly in LightWave. It happens to the best of us! Doing so in the Graph Editor can really screw up your keyframes, because it's easy to click-select a keyframe and then accidentally click-drag slightly to change its value. Instead of clicking in the window to make a selection, right-click to make a lasso selection. Not only will you be sure you're getting the correct keyframe (they are pretty tiny), you also won't accidentally change it, because the lasso tool can't change settings values.

The middle of the Graph Editor interface offers five small tool icons for you to choose from: Move, Add, Stretch, Roll, and Zoom. When you select one, information is displayed to its right, explaining its function and keyboard shortcut.

You can use the Move tool to select and move single or multiple keyframes in the Curve Window.

8. Select the key at frame 75. Next, choose the Move tool and click and drag the keyframe in the Curve Window.

   Notice that you can move only its value (up and down). Doing this changes the position of the object in Layout.

9. Move the keyframe up to set the value around 20 degrees.

   Let's say you do not want the Train:Engine object to rotate until frame 85, rather than starting its motion right at frame 75. This kind of delayed movement is easy to do in the Graph Editor.

10. Make sure that the Move tool is selected. While holding down the Control key, click and move the 75 keyframe to the right. You'll see the frame number appear over the keyframe (**Figure 6.37**).

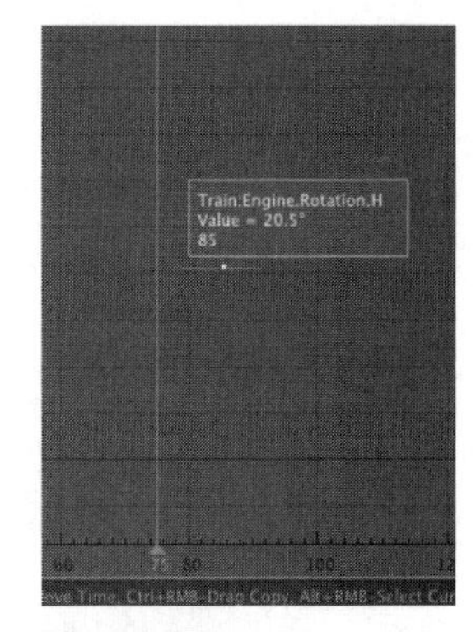

Figure 6.37 Holding the Control key and moving selected keyframes adjusts timing. You didn't realize it was this easy, did you?

NOTE

If you don't care to hold down the Control key and use the mouse, you can type in a keyframe number instead. At the bottom of the screen in the Curves tab, you can enter the selected keyframe by clicking in the Frame field and typing its frame number. You also can set values by typing in the Value field.

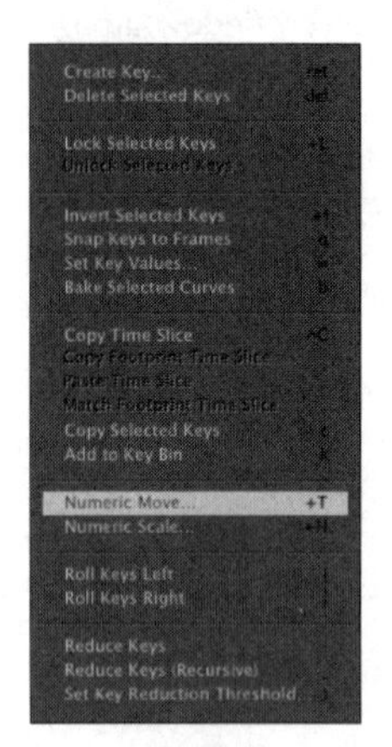

Figure 6.38 The Numeric Move selection enables you to set a specific numeric value to move a key.

11. Adjust the value and keyframes of selected objects and return to Layout to see the effects. You can adjust values by dragging the keyframes in the Curve Window or by entering them numerically in the Curves tab area.

    Additionally, you have a number of key controls available from the Keys drop-down list at the top of the Graph Editor panel. **Figure 6.38** shows the Numeric Move selection, which enables you to numerically set offset values. Soon you'll get the hang of editing in the Graph Editor.

Take a look at your animation. Click the Play button to see how the values you've edited in the Graph Editor have changed the object's motion. Feel free to play around with various movements of keys from different channels in the Graph Editor to see the results.

There's much more to the Graph Editor than this. One really good option to try out is Lock Selected Keys, from the Keys menu. This is really handy if you don't want to accidentally move a perfectly set keyframe. The first part of this chapter guided you through basic navigation and editing of channels and keyframes. Next, you'll learn about moving groups of keyframes, adjusting their curves, and adding modifiers to them.

Copy Time Slice

Going beyond basic keyframing, you can control your animations with the Copy Time Slice command. Let's say you'd like to copy an object's position at a point where there is no keyframe. What do you do? You could do it manually, by writing down the Move and Rotation values for that frame and entering them in a new keyframe. A much easier way, though, is to use Copy Time Slice in the Graph Editor.

Exercise 6.6 Using the Copy Time Slice Feature

1. Select the curve you want to edit, such as the Position.Z channel, using the files from Exercise 6.5. You can double-click this channel in the Scene Bin to quickly add it to the Curve Bin. Drag the timeline bar to the desired frame of motion, such as frame 45 (in the main Curve Window), as shown in **Figure 6.39**. To drag the timeline slider, grab it from the bottom.

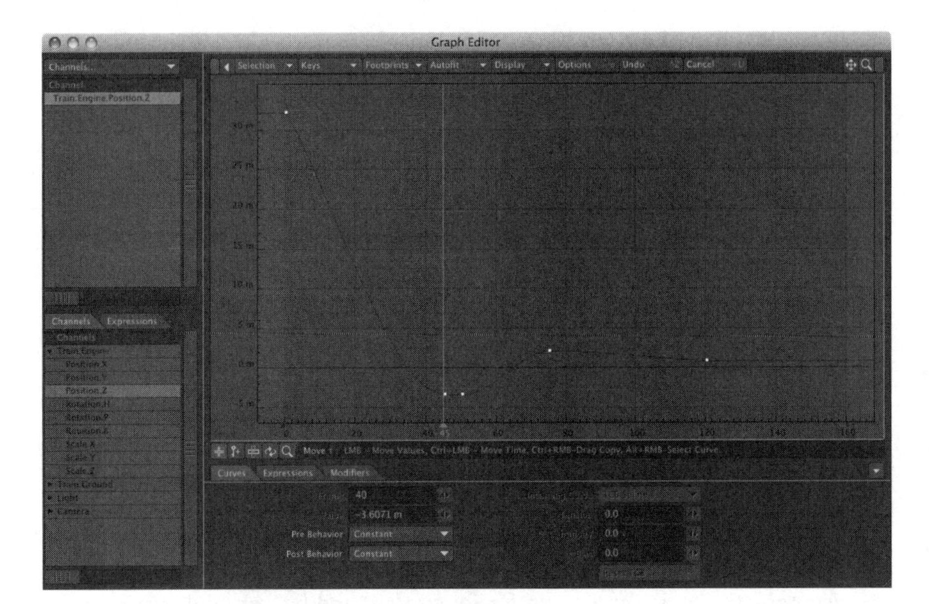

Figure 6.39 Use the timeline slider in the Graph Editor to move through your item's motion.

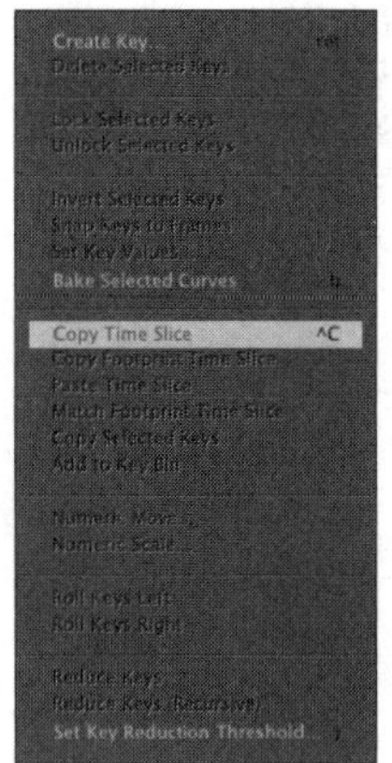

Figure 6.40 The Copy Time Slice command, accessed from the Keys drop-down list, captures the channel values for whichever frame is selected with the timeline slider.

2. From the Keys drop-down list, select Copy Time Slice (**Figure 6.40**).
3. Drag the timeline slider to frame 140, where there is no keyframe.
4. From the Keys drop-down list, select Paste Time Slice. A new keyframe is created with the values from the previous position.

NOTE

You can also use the keyboard shortcuts for Copy Time Slice: Control+C for copy, and Control+V for paste. This is the same for Macintosh and Windows systems.

Copy Time Slice is an extremely handy function of the Graph Editor. If you set two keyframes in Layout for an item—at frames 0 and 90, for example—LightWave will interpret the motion for the frames in between those two keys. Earlier you read about "in-betweening." Using Copy Time Slice enables you to copy the settings LightWave has calculated for any interpolated frame and copy them to any other frame or keyframe on that curve.

Multicurve Editing

But wait! There's more! You can also use multicurve editing when you want to edit multiple curves simultaneously or use curves of different items as references. By selecting the desired curves in the Curve Bin (as demonstrated earlier in this chapter), you can edit them together as one in the Curve Window. You easily can drag and drop curves from the Scene Display window (in the lower-left zone of the Graph Editor) into the Curve Bin. For example, you might combine the Position.X of an object with the Rotation.Y of a light, and add in the Scale.Z of a camera. You can use any channel you want.

NOTE

Here's a really quick way to instantly select all curves in the Curve Bin. Hold the Control key and press the up arrow key. Deselect all by holding the Control key and pressing the down arrow key.

Foreground and Background Curves

When you add selected curves to the Curve Bin, you can see them in the Curve Window and view them as either foreground or background curves. Curves that are selected in the Curve Bin will become editable foreground curves in the Curve Window; curves that are not selected will be non-editable background curves.

Working with foreground and background curves has its benefits. You can interactively cut and paste keyframes from one curve to another. You can also replace an entire curve with another, or lock areas of curves together. By having multiple curves selected when you create keys, the curves can be identical at those selected areas during an animation. Additionally, you have the ability to compare one curve to another, such as a light intensity to the H rotation of a camera. If you remember how Chapter 1, "LightWave Modeler," talked about using layers both for reference and as a tool, the same can be said for foreground and background curves in the Graph Editor. This next exercise demonstrates some of these features.

Exercise 6.7 Working with Foreground and Background Curves

1. Clear Layout (you can press Shift+N) and open the Graph Editor. You might need to click into the Layout window to activate the Shift+N command to Clear Scene. If the Graph Editor was already open, it will automatically be cleared with the Clear Scene command.
2. Move Camera Position.X and Light Position.Y to the Curve Bin. Do this by expanding the item in the Scene Display (bottom left) and then dragging the desired motion channel up into the Curve Bin.
3. When loaded, hold down the Shift key and select both channels in the Curve Bin.

   You'll see both curves highlighted in the Curve Window. Right now there are only straight lines because the channels have no motions applied.
4. Select the Add Keys button beneath the Curve Window (**Figure 6.41**).
5. Click once in the top area of the Curve Window and once near the bottom right, similar to **Figure 6.42**. You'll see the two curves adjust to the keys you just created.

NOTE

Remember that you can click and drag on the bar between the Curve Bin and the Scene Display windows in the Graph Editor to quickly resize the two windows.

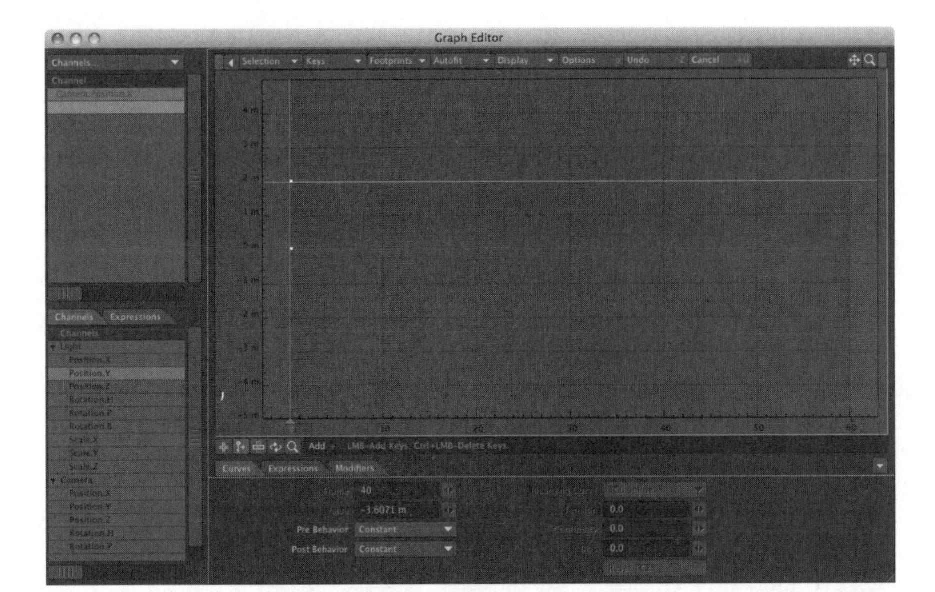

Figure 6.41 You can choose to add a key from the Graph Editor window, and you can also use the Move, Stretch, Roll, and Zoom commands.

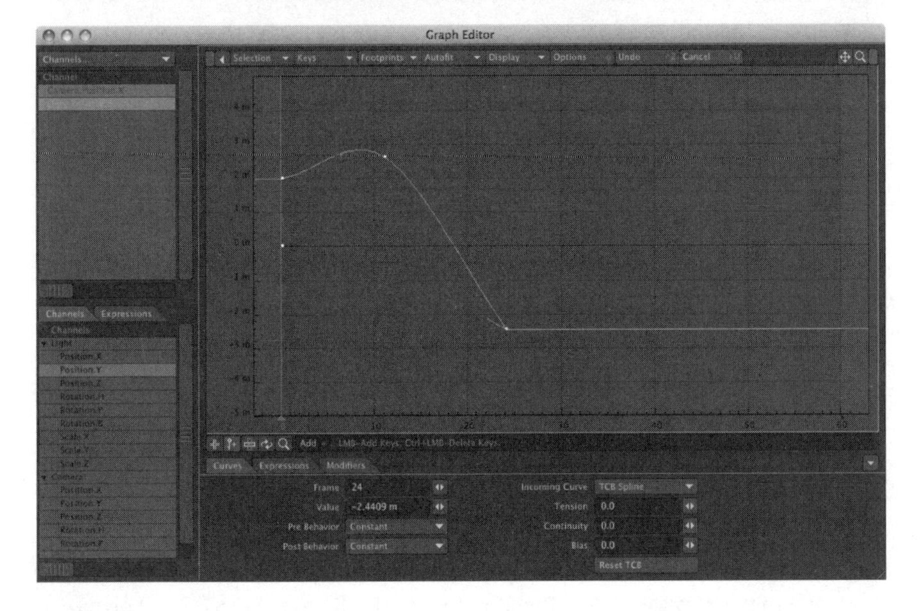

Figure 6.42 You can create keyframes for the selected motion channels directly in the Curve Window.

NOTE

At times, your curve may be out of view in the Curve Window. As in Modeler and certain views in Layout, just press **a** to "fit all."

Navigating the Curve Window

When you select multiple curves, you can edit them together, create keyframes together, and so on. However, you also can adjust one of these curves based on the background curve: Simply select only the curve you want to adjust in the Curve Bin. The remaining curves in the Curve Bin appear slightly darkened in the background of the Curve Window. From there, you can select the Move tool and click and drag a keyframe to change its value. Here are a few quick steps to remember when working in the Graph Editor:

- Select the Move keyframe button (in the center of the Graph Editor) and click and drag to adjust the selected key(s).
- Select the Move keyframe button and click and hold the Control key to adjust the selected key's position in time—for example, to move a keyframe from frame 5 to frame 15.
- Hold the Alt key and click in the Curve Window to adjust the entire Curve Window view.
- Press **.** (period) to zoom in on the Curve Window; press **,** (comma) to zoom out.
- Press **a** to fit all contents of the Curve Window into view. For example, after you're done working in a zoomed view of the Curve Window, press **a** to instantly fit all editable keyframes into the window.
- Press Shift+G to import curves into the Graph Editor. There's no need to close the Graph Editor, select your next item in Layout, and then reopen the Graph Editor to add a particular curve. Instead, just move the Graph Editor aside, select an item in Layout, return to the Graph Editor, and press Shift+G to update with the new selection.
- Choose Numeric Limits from the Display drop-down list at the top of the Graph Editor window (or press Shift+N) to set minimum and maximum frames for the Curve Window (**Figure 6.43**).
- Holding Control+Alt while moving the mouse left and right, or up and down, drags and zooms the Curve Window. You also can set a minimum and maximum value. Alt-drag options are similar to those used in Layout's Perspective viewport.

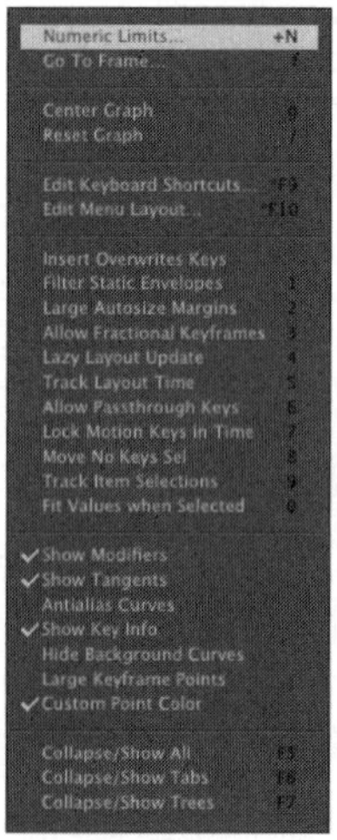

Figure 6.43 Use Numeric Limits to control the frame and value settings in the Curve Window.

Exploring Additional Commands in the Graph Editor

In addition to the commands you'll use most often as you animate your scenes, you should know about the Graph Editor commands that can help you increase the speed of your workflow. As you've learned in other areas of LightWave, right-clicking in certain areas gives you access to additional tools that enable more control. The same goes for the Graph Editor.

Footprints

A handy feature of the Graph Editor is its ability to create *footprints* for a selected channel. To help you keep track of your adjustments to a keyframe or curve, a footprint cues you visually to remind you how the item looked before you began adjusting it. A footprint also lets you retrace your steps, or *backtrack*, if you choose to undo an adjustment. Follow this next tutorial to learn more about footprints.

Exercise 6.8 Creating Footprints

1. Open Layout, clear the scene, and open the Graph Editor.
2. Select the light in the Scene window of the Graph Editor and drag it to the Curve Bin.

   All the motion channels for the light are added to the bin, as shown in **Figure 6.44**.
3. Select the light Rotation.P, which is the Pitch rotation for the light. Of course, any selected channel will do for this exercise.

   When a channel is selected, you'll see it highlighted in the Curve Window.
4. Select the Add Keys command (the second small icon beneath the Curve Window), and then click throughout the Curve Window to create some keyframes for the selected channel. **Figure 6.45** shows the channel with a few keys added.

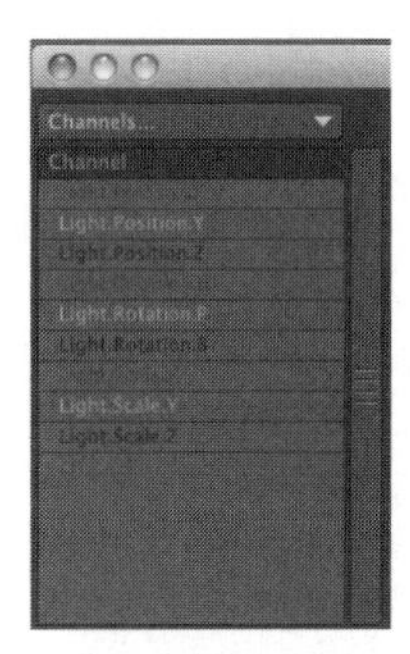

Figure 6.44 Selecting just the light from the Scene Display area and dragging it to the Curve Bin adds all its motion channels.

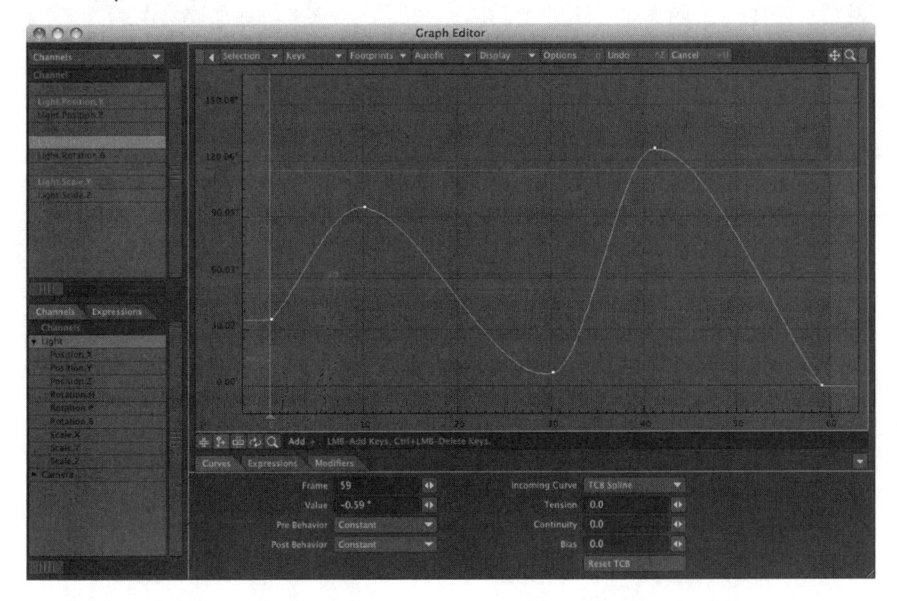

Figure 6.45 A few keyframes are added to the light's Rotation.P channel in the Curve Window.

5. Go back to the Curve Bin, and with the Rotation.P channel still selected, right-click it to open the pop-up menu.
6. Choose the Footprints selection and then select Leave Footprints. You also can do this through the Footprints drop-down list at the top of the Graph Editor, as shown in **Figure 6.46**.

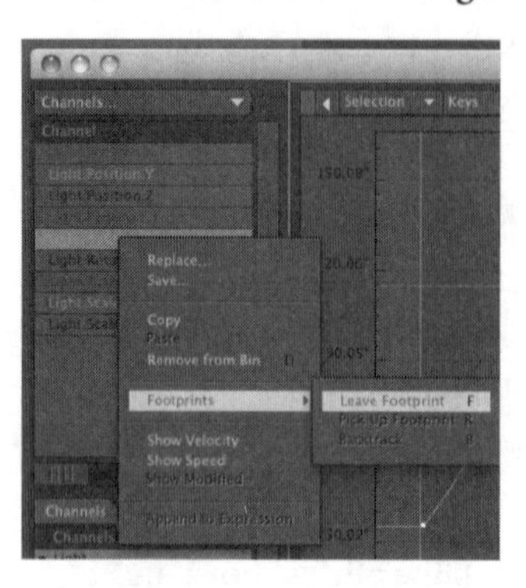

Figure 6.46 Right-click a selected channel to select the Footprints option, or select the Footprints drop-down list at the top of the Graph Editor.

NOTE

You also can hold the Shift key and double-click in the Curve Window to select all keys. Move mode must be selected to do this. Clicking once in the blank area of the Curve Window deselects keyframes.

It won't look like much has happened in the Curve Window, but wait.

7. Right-click and drag to select all your keyframes in the Curve Window.
8. With all the keyframes selected, select the Move tool (by pressing **t**) and click and drag in the Curve Window to move the entire motion curve up, as shown in **Figure 6.47**.

You'll see a faint line above the curve you just moved. This is the footprint that tells you where your curve was.

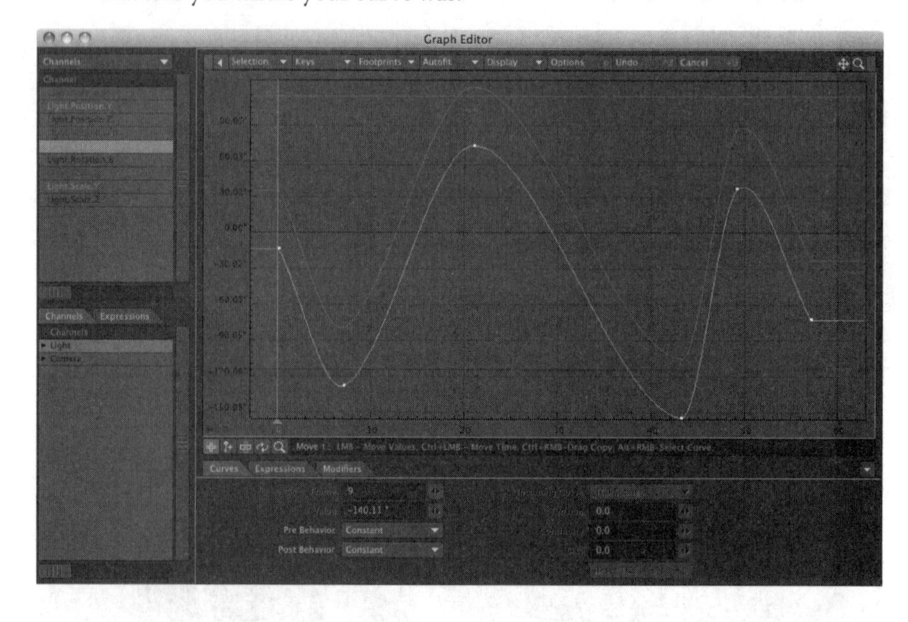

Figure 6.47 When the Footprints option is enabled, moving one or more keyframes reveals the footprint.

9. Go back to the Curve Bin, right-click again on the Rotation.P channel, and choose Pick Up Footprint or Backtrack, or choose one of these commands from the Footprints drop-down list. (Note the keyboard shortcut for each command on its respective button.)

   Picking up the footprint removes it from the Curve Window. Selecting Backtrack resets any channel adjustment to the footprint position.

Footprints provide a simple way for you to keep track of what you're doing and where you've been while working in the Graph Editor. It's easy to make too many changes and lose your place when adjusting various channels. The Footprint option helps you organize your steps by enabling you to retrace your steps if you need to.

Using the Curves Tab

At the bottom of the Graph Editor interface is the Curves tab. (This area is unavailable until a keyframe is selected.) Here, you can set the value of a selected keyframe and adjust its pre- and post-behaviors. For example, suppose that you have created a spinning globe that takes 200 frames to make a full 360-degree revolution. Your total scene length is 600 frames, and the globe needs to rotate throughout the animation. Instead of setting additional keyframes for the globe, you can set the post-behavior to repeat. After the globe completes its 200 frames of motion, the Graph Editor's post-behavior takes over. You can also set pre-behaviors. A pre-behavior is what happens before the first keyframe. You can set either pre- or post-behaviors to the following settings:

- Reset, which reverts the current value to 0.
- Constant, which holds a value equal to the first key's value in a pre-behavior, or the last key's value in a post-behavior.
- Repeat, which replays the motion from the first keyframe to the last for the duration of the scene.
- Oscillate, which repeats a channel behavior from the first keyframe to the last, then reverses it from the last keyframe to the first, for the duration of the scene. For example, if you change a spotlight's heading rotation between frame 0 and frame 30, an Oscillate post-behavior will swing it back to its original position in frames 31–60, then repeat the whole back-and-forth process until your scene ends.
- Offset Repeat, which is similar to Repeat but offsets the difference between the first and last keyframe values.
- Linear, which keeps the curve angle linearly consistent with the starting or ending angle.

The Curves tab also is home to Spline controls. Earlier in the keyframing section of this chapter, we discussed how to use the Move TCB tool in Layout to adjust Tension, Continuity, and Bias (TCB). Remember, LightWave's motion paths (the channels that you're editing in the Graph Editor) are curves. Using TCB is one way to work with these curves, but LightWave offers more control than simple TCB splines.

Spline Controls

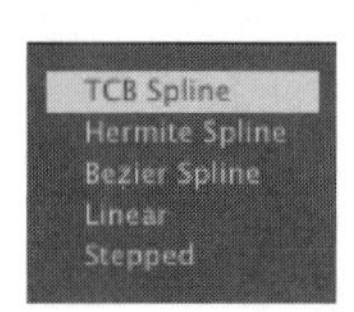

Figure 6.48 LightWave has numerous curve types from which to choose.

When an item or its elements are put into motion in LightWave, it instantly has a curve. The Graph Editor gives you control over the individual channels of an item's motion, as you've seen throughout this chapter. You can adjust the keyframes of the curve that is created with various types of splines. **Figure 6.48** shows the Incoming Curve types. An incoming curve is the type of curve that precedes a keyframe. This is an important setting because not only should you be able to control a curve and motion, but you also should be able to control what happens before and after a curve. Perhaps you want to have an object drift a bit before it goes into full motion, or maybe you want to have an item hold in place before it moves. Setting the Incoming Curve type offers you more flexibility in how an item behaves for a selected key.

TCB Splines

TCB splines are easy to set and are useful for creating realistic motions. As mentioned earlier during the keyframing section, the values for each spline range from 1.0 to –1.0.

A tension value of 1.0 is the most commonly used TCB spline because it enables an item to ease in or out of a keyframe. For example, a 3D-animated car needs to accelerate. Setting it in motion without a custom tension setting (at the default T value of 0) causes the car to jump from sitting still to moving at a constant rate, without having to speed up. Try it if you like; it's very unnatural.

TCB Shortcuts

LightWave enables you to quickly and easily control Tension, Continuity, and Bias controls in the Graph Editor. You don't even need to click! Simply move your mouse over a particular keyframe. Press **F1** and drag the mouse to the left to set a negative Tension, or drag to the right to set a positive Tension. Do the same for Continuity with **F2** and Bias with **F3**. Cool stuff.

TCB splines are not the only spline controls you have when it comes to controlling keyframes. LightWave 10 employs Hermite and Bezier spline curves as well.

Hermite and Bezier Splines

Although TCB splines are often used for common, everyday animated elements, such as flying logos or animated cars, Hermite and Bezier splines offer a wider range of control.

Both Hermite and Bezier splines can help you control your curve. It's up to you to experiment and try both when working with the control of an item's motion. Knowing when to apply curve controls such as these is important. As you work through the tutorials in this book, the necessary controls are used so that you can see the direct effect. Keep an eye out for their use. You might find, however, that the majority of animations you create work best with simple TCB-adjusted curves.

Hermite splines have tangent control handles that allow you to control the shape of a curve. **Figure 6.49** shows a sequence of three keyframes with Hermite splines added to the middle keyframe. Its handles are adjusted.

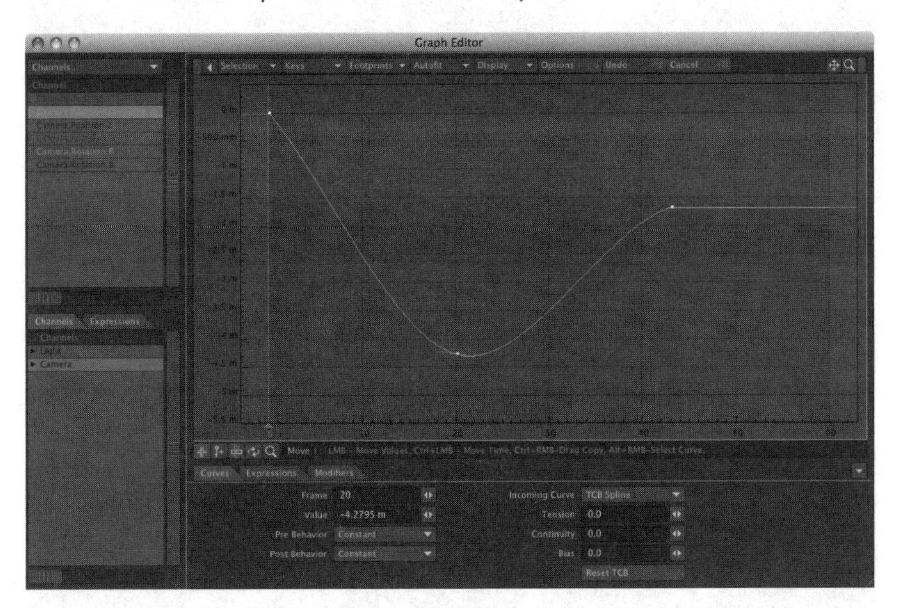

Figure 6.49 Hermite splines are added to the middle keyframe. These splines offer more control than regular TCB splines.

Figure 6.49 shows three keyframes—one high, one low, and one high again—in a sort of bell shape. However, the middle keyframe has a Hermite spline applied and the left handle of it has been pulled down quite a bit. The figure shows how an adjustment to one keyframe can have a drastic effect on the shape of a curve. You can do this by clicking and dragging the small purple handles that appear on a selected keyframe after the spline is added.

If you apply a Bezier curve, you acquire a different type of control than for a Hermite spline. A Bezier spline is a variant of a Hermite spline and also shapes the curve. **Figure 6.50** (on the next page) shows the same bell curve of three keyframes with one handle of the Bezier curve pulled down drastically.

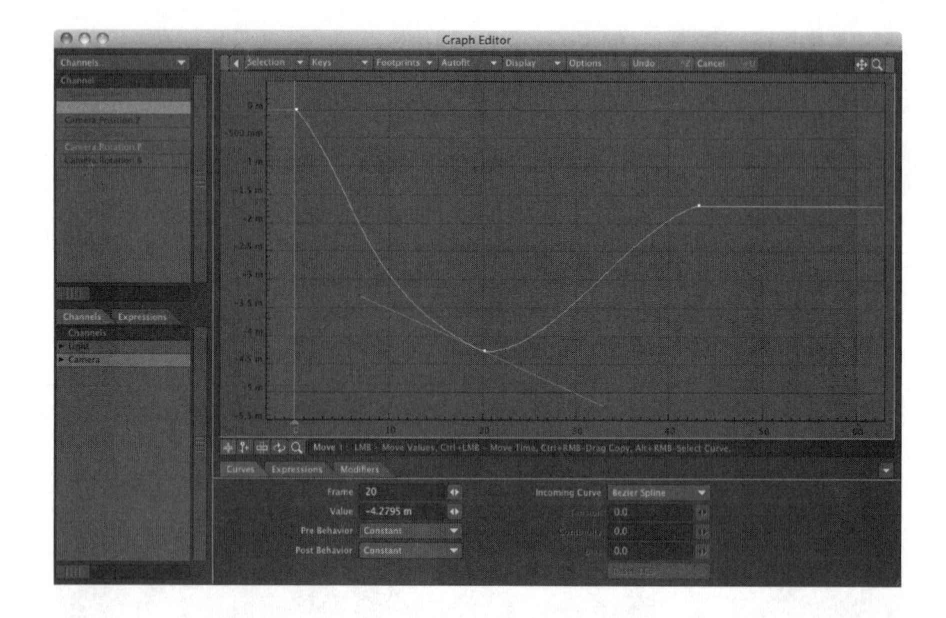

Figure 6.50 Bezier splines, although a variant of Hermite splines, work when the next key is also set to Bezier.

Stepped Transitions

Using a stepped transition for an incoming curve simply keeps a curve's value constant and abruptly jumps to the next keyframe. **Figure 6.51** shows three keyframes similar to those in Figure 6.50, but with a stepped transition applied.

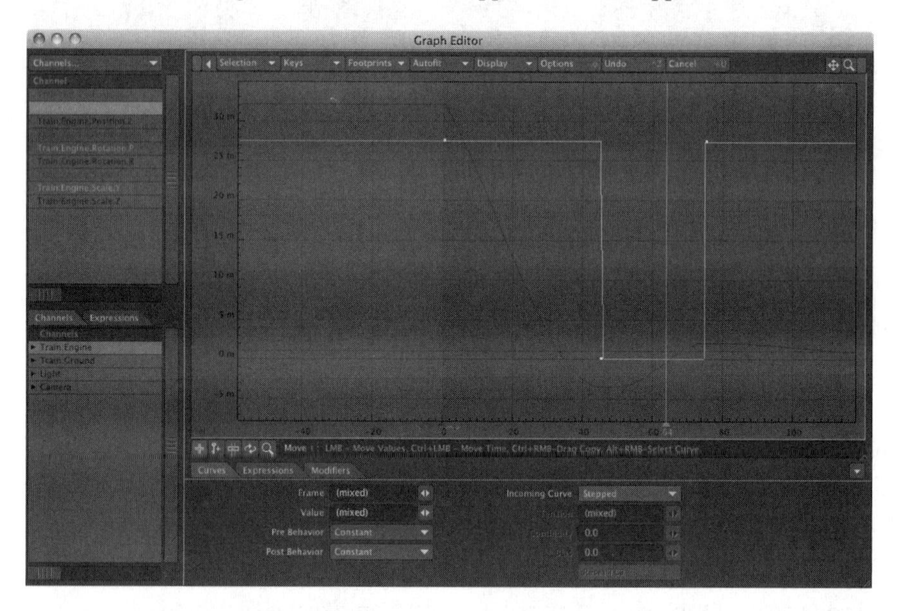

Figure 6.51 Stepped transitions for curves abruptly change your motion from one keyframe to the next.

Stepped curves are usable when you want to make drastic value changes between keyframes for situations such as lightning, interference, or blinking lights. You might also find that applying stepped transitions works well for pose-to-pose character animation at times.

Whether you create motions in the Graph Editor or simply adjust preexisting ones, you should understand the amount of control the Graph Editor gives you. The Graph Editor in LightWave 10 even enables you to mix and match spline types for individual channels. Follow along with this next exercise to make and adjust curves in the Graph Editor. Although you have many options for curve control in LightWave's Graph Editor, using the Tension, Continuity, and Bias (TCB) controls can provide the most natural motion for your animations.

Press **o** in the Graph Editor to open the General Options tab of the Graph Editor Options panel. Here, you can set Default Incoming Curve values as well as other default parameters (**Figure 6.52**).

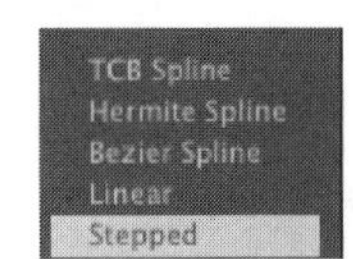

Figure 6.52 You can define the Default Incoming Curve in the General Options tab of the Graph Editor Options panel. Press o to access this panel.

NOTE

By default, the Graph Editor opens with your currently selected Layout item's channels already entered into the Channel Bin. You can leave the Graph Editor open while you work, but if you want to have additional item channels to edit, you need to manually bring them into the Channel Bin. However, if you press Shift+G, the Graph Editor is updated with the currently selected item in Layout. What's more, you can turn on Track Item Selections from the General Options panel of the Graph Editor.

Exercise 6.9 Creating and Adjusting Curves

Start by saving anything you've been working on in Layout and then clear the scene. These next few steps provide the information to create curves and adjust them so that certain areas match perfectly. These techniques can be used with any of your projects.

1. Open the Graph Editor, and in the Scene Display, double-click the Position.Y channel for the camera.

   The Camera's Y position is now added to the Curve Bin, and your Graph Editor interface should look like **Figure 6.53**.

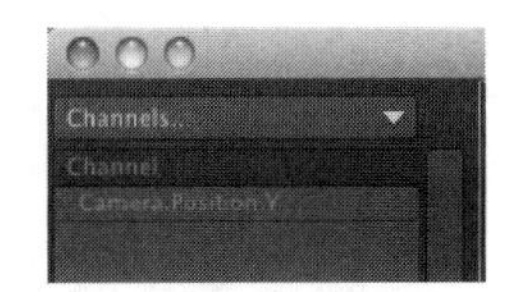

Figure 6.53 Double-clicking the camera's Y position channel adds it to the Curve Bin.

2. Expand the channels for the light in the Scene Display by clicking the small white triangle.
3. Hold down the Shift key and double-click the light's Position.Y channel to add it to the Curve Bin. If you don't hold the Shift key while double-clicking, the new selection overrides anything already added to the Curve Bin.
4. In the Curve Bin, hold down the Shift key and select both the Camera.Position.Y and Light.Position.Y channels. Or, hold Control and press the up arrow on your keyboard.

5. Select Add mode, and in the Curve Window, create three keyframes to the right of the first keyframe at zero. **Figure 6.54** shows the Graph Editor with the additional keyframes.

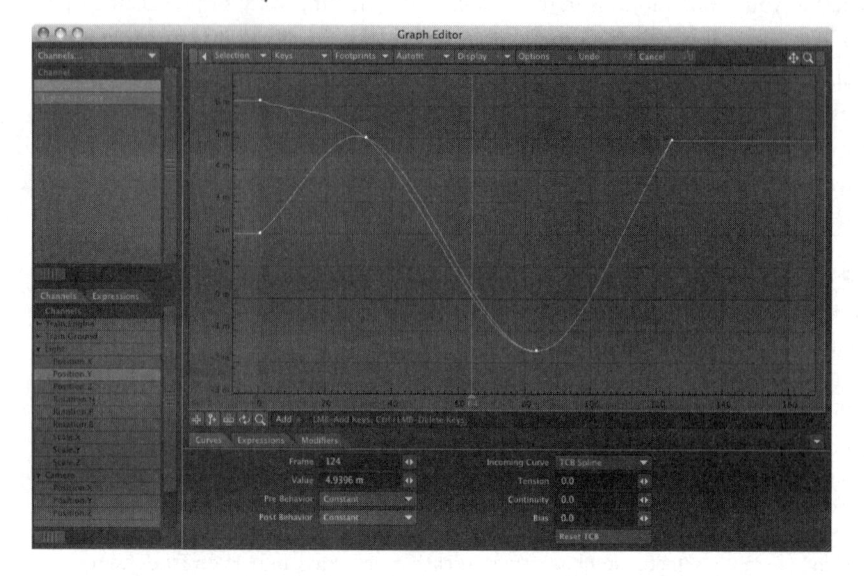

Figure 6.54 With multiple curves selected, you can create identical keyframes for both channels at once.

6. Select just the Camera.Position.Y channel in the Curve Bin. This automatically deselects the Light.Position.Z channel.
7. Select Move mode and move up the last keyframe.

   You'll see the Light.Position.Y channel in the background. You've created similar motions on the Y-axis for both the camera and light, but toward the end of the motion, the value has changed. **Figure 6.55** shows the adjusted channel.

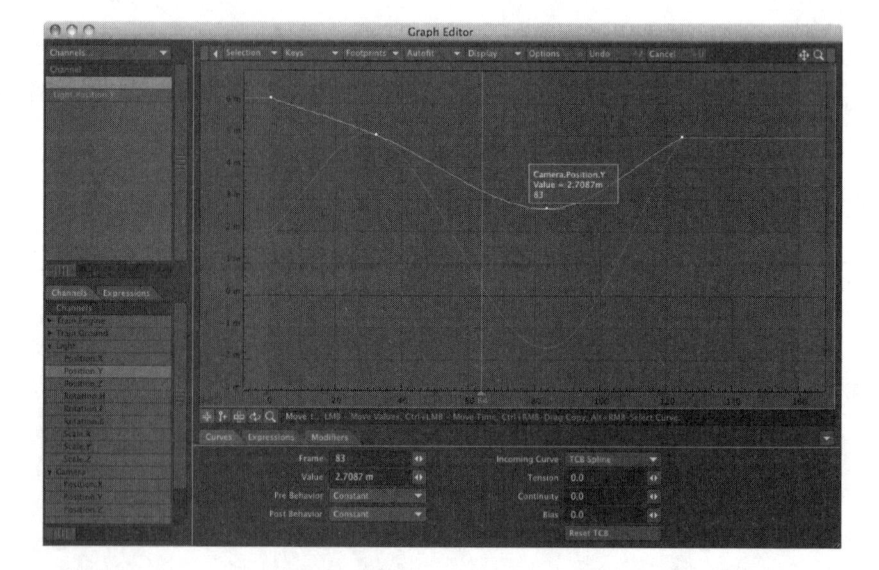

Figure 6.55 One keyframe in a pair of matching channels is adjusted.

NOTE

When modifying identical channels on one keyframe, you need to compensate surrounding keyframes slightly. Because of the spline curves, one keyframe affects another.

A more realistic example of matching curves is a formation of flying jets. Each jet flies in unison, swooping, looping, and twisting in perfect sync. After the formation, one or two jets might need to fly off from the pack. Using the preceding example, you can easily select the appropriate channel and adjust the value at the desired keyframe.

It's easy to see where you would move the jet in Layout, but in the Graph Editor, translating the visual motion to a value might take a little more work. Don't worry; this next exercise helps you adjust values in the Graph Editor.

Editing Color Channels

Everything discussed in this chapter with respect to object position and rotation also applies to settings such as light intensity, object dissolves, and much more. Let's look at LightWave Graph Editor's ability to animate color channels, which is really cool for animating such things as stage lighting or a gradually changing sunset.

Exercise 6.10 Animating Color Channels

1. Close the Graph Editor, clear the LightWave scene, and then select the scene's default light by selecting the Lights button at the bottom of the LightWave Layout interface.
2. Press **p** to enter the light's Properties panel. You can also get to the Properties panel by clicking the Properties button at the bottom of Layout.

   You will see a series of small buttons labeled E. As mentioned earlier, these let you access envelopes, meaning their accompanying values can be animated—changed automatically over time, in the course of an animation. Anywhere you see them throughout LightWave, they will guide you right back to the Graph Editor. However, when you access the Graph Editor in this manner, you have control over only the specific area from which you have selected an envelope, such as Light Color.

   It's important to note that entering the Graph Editor by using the E buttons tells LightWave that you want to perform a specific function. For example, if you click the E button next to Light Color, you're telling LightWave that you want to animate the Light Color, and the Graph Editor opens accordingly. Entering the Graph Editor on its own from the Layout interface would not enable you to animate the Light Color initially. After you've entered the Graph Editor using any E button, the value you enter remains there until you clear it. Therefore, you need to enter the Graph Editor from particular E buttons only once.

3. Click the E button next to Light Color, as shown in **Figure 6.56**.

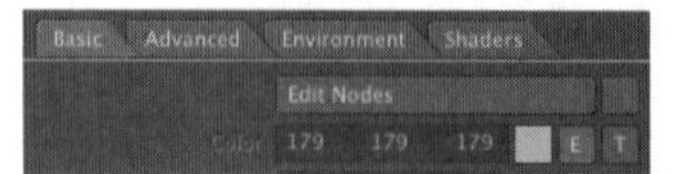

Figure 6.56 The E (Envelope) button guides you to the Graph Editor for specific control over Light Color.

After you've clicked the E button, the Graph Editor panel opens. It looks essentially the same as when you used it earlier this chapter, but now there's a strip of color along its bottom edge. LightWave enables you to use the Graph Editor's capabilities on color channels as well as motion channels. **Figure 6.57** shows the Graph Editor with the color channel.

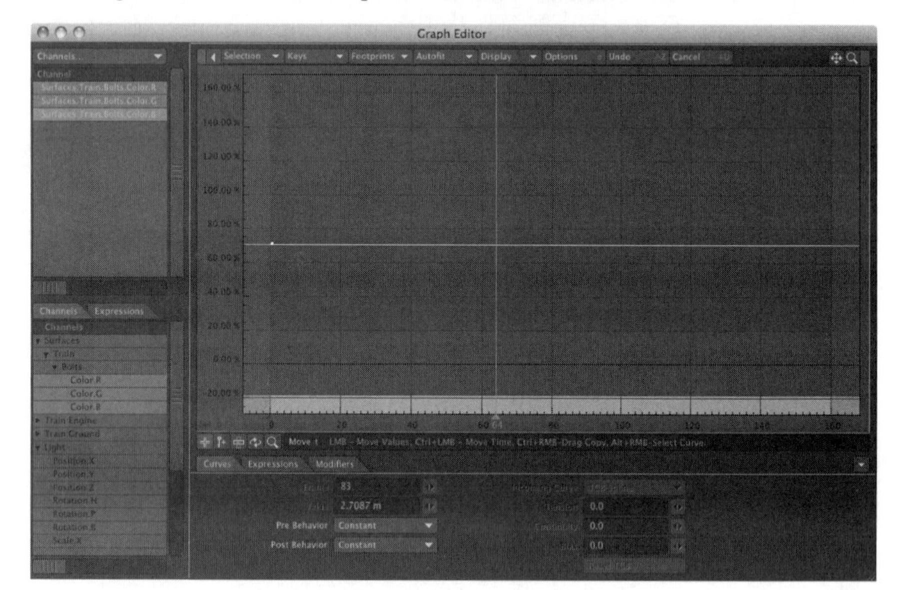

Figure 6.57 By clicking the E button for Light Color, the RGB values are now added to the Curve Bin and available for animation.

In Figure 6.57, the Curve Bin doesn't show position, rotation, or scale channels, but rather color channels.

4. Select a color channel, such as Light.Color.G, for the green color value. You can also select all color channels at once if you like. By default, though, they should all be selected as soon as you click the E button.

5. Create a few keyframes in the Curve Window as you've done previously in this chapter. Then, right-click one of the keyframe points and choose Open Color Picker.

   Use the system's standard color picker to choose a new color for the keyframe. **Figure 6.58** shows what just one color channel looks like after it's been adjusted.

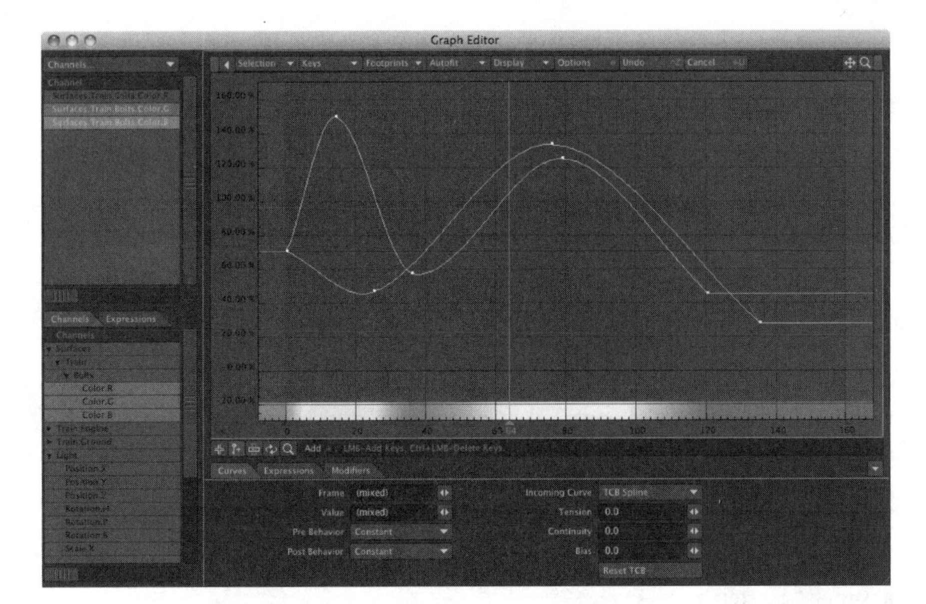

Figure 6.58 Scaling the value for a particular RGB color channel changes the color channel for a set keyframe.

6. You can change the value of a key as well. From the Curves tab at the bottom of the Graph Editor, adjust the value and watch how the curve changes.

   You'll see the color you've selected appear as a gradual change in the Curve Window.

7. Set colors for the other keyframes and adjust their values accordingly to set precise timing. Experiment with these values to see the different types of results you can achieve.

   You can cycle colors like this for lights, backgrounds, textures, just about anything! And all this goes back to one thing—timing! Cycling lights is cool, but if you master the timing and keyframing aspects of animation, you can make your lights *dance*!

The Next Step

So there you have it—keyframing, timing, splines, curves, motions, and the Graph Editor in Layout. While the Graph Editor is a home base for your animations and envelopes, it's not always necessary for putting objects in motion. When you want more control, or need to animate color values, intensities, and more, the Graph Editor is the way to do it.

Before long, you'll be setting up motions without even thinking about it. At times, you'll be able to create full animations without using the Graph Editor; other times, you'll keep it open while you work. Try using the Selection drop-down list above the Curve Window to access more control over your keyframes. LightWave's panels are nonmodal, which means that you don't have to be in a certain "mode" to keep them open. Additionally, you can shrink the size of Layout and configure your computer screen to show Layout, the Graph Editor, and even the Surface Editor all at once. Remember that you can collapse the left side and lower portion of the Graph Editor to reveal just the Curve Window, too.

Don't let motions, keyframing, and the Graph Editor overwhelm you. A good way to work is to use traditional keyframing methods directly in Layout so that you can see what you're doing, and then use the Graph Editor for tweaking and adjustments. As with much of LightWave, you have multiple ways to achieve the same result. Refer to this chapter any time you need to control your keyframes with splines or specific modifiers or when you need specific control over individual channels. You'll find yourself using the Graph Editor for adjusting timing, clearing motions, saving motions, creating object dissolves, or animating color channels more often than you think. Practice creating, cutting, and adjusting keyframes and channels in the Graph Editor. Just remember one thing—save often! Save in increments so you can always take a step back!

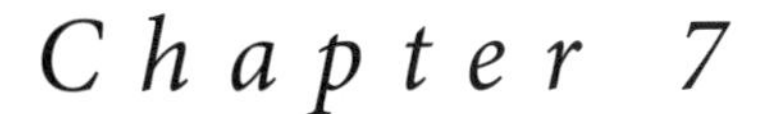

Motion Graphics

Motion graphics is not an old term. In years past, animated elements were simple and to the point. But as technology has evolved, so has what you can do with your digital tool chest. When you hear the term "motion graphics," it can mean anything from animated pictures to swirling flourishes to, of course, title and broadcast animations. For that reason, this chapter will demonstrate a tutorial that gives you the best of both worlds: animated graphic elements that you'll create, as well as animated 3D fonts.

Animated text is the bread and butter of many 3D animators, and it's also a good way to get started creating some of the most basic 3D models there are—animated letterforms. Although this basic 3D creation does not take an enormous amount of modeling skill, it will help you feel more comfortable with LightWave, and it'll provide you with skills you can put to work right away for your clients. (Seeing their name, company slogan, or logo in glorious 3D never fails to impress.)

And not every 3D animation job is for broadcast television; a significant market exists for motion graphics in corporate and industrial video environments, in DVD production, and of course, on the Web. This chapter focuses on modeling text and graphical elements in LightWave Modeler that can be animated into broadcast-style animations. This chapter takes you full speed ahead into a complete broadcast-style animation that goes beyond the typical chrome flying logo of days gone by. LightWave 10's new powerful rendering engine, layout visuals, and excellent texture tools will make your job easier, especially when developing motion graphics. **Figure 7.1** (on the next page) shows a still from the finished animated logo that you will create.

Figure 7.1 The final logo you'll create in this chapter.

This chapter instructs you on techniques you can use for top-quality work. You'll put things in constant motion, not just in one tumbling animated element. This chapter gives you the knowledge to create stunning professional graphics and animations—and it will also get you excited about doing it! You'll learn about the following:

- Working with Modeler's font tools
- Modeling text
- Setting up a text-based scene
- Importing background animations
- Creating smooth, continuous motions
- Creating 3D text from EPS files

Modeling 3D Text

Take a look at any television news or entertainment show and you'll see that they have one thing in common: text graphics and animations. Such graphics and animations are bold, colorful, and downright cool to look at. Creating graphics and animations for video can be fun and lucrative. Networks and TV stations in major markets pay well for animation packages for their news shows and for titles and "bumpers"—those short animations that appear when shows go into and out of commercial breaks. Animation packages must represent the feeling and style the broadcaster is trying to convey for the station—serious and strong, classy and cute, sharp and hip, and so on. Animated titles and logos are also used widely in corporate and industrial videos, professional wedding videos, and even home videos.

LightWave is all you need to create professional broadcast animations. You'll see in this chapter how simple models put together with proper surfacing and lighting can create a cool and unique 3D look. You'll take it a step further using top lighting techniques and slick reflections and glows.

Often, text and logo animation jobs are done in multiple passes and composited in programs like Adobe After Effects, in an editing application like Adobe Premiere Pro, or in a motion graphics application such as Apple's Motion. But because those tools are not always available, this chapter will show you how you can model text, import moving backgrounds, and animate text using nothing but LightWave (and your growing modeling and animation skills).

Working with Backdrops in Modeler

For this project, you'll start by working with text in Modeler. One thing you should remember when working through these tutorials is that text modeling is not just for titles and logos. You can use text to create shapes or various animation elements, such as using a 0 (zero) for a doughnut shape, or the letter I for an I-beam in a construction scene. Text shapes in 3D are just additional three-dimensional shapes. Think in those terms and you'll have an easier time making the most of the toolset. Follow along to begin creating and surfacing text in Modeler.

Exercise 7.1 Setting Up Backdrop Images in Modeler

1. Open Modeler.

   Start by creating the background elements. Your client has a design that was initially created flat for a print piece. You've been hired to make it in 3D, and you'll use LightWave to bring this flat (and fairly dull) design to life.

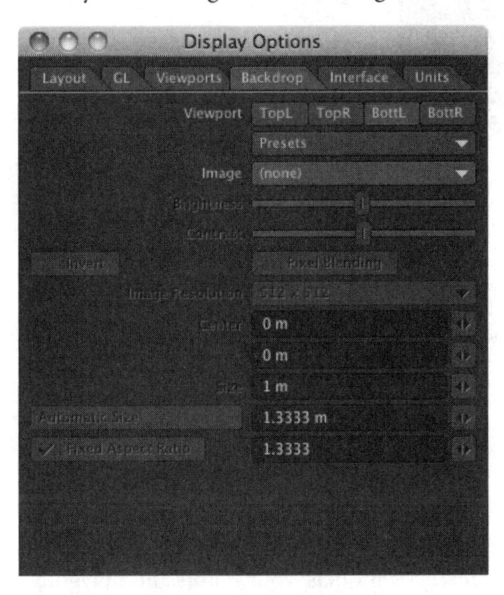

Figure 7.2 Begin creating your titling package by using the Display Options panel to load a background image.

2. Press **d** to open the Display Options panel. Click its Backdrop tab and then click the viewport button labeled BottL, which stands for bottom left (**Figure 7.2**).

3. For the Image selection in the panel, click Load Image and load OffsetCircle.jpg from the Chapter 7 folder on this book's DVD (in the "3D_Content\Images\CH7\" directory).

NOTE

You can load an image in any format that LightWave accepts, which includes common formats such as JPEG, TIFF, TGA, PNG, and even PSD (Adobe Photoshop's native file format). If you can't seem to load an image, there's a chance that your input-output plug-ins are not properly loaded. You can load them by going to the Utilities tab, selecting Edit Plug-ins, and then choosing Scan Directory. Point the scan to your installed LightWave plug-ins folder and click OK.

Here, you can import various images as background references to build from. This image is a circle within a circle that your client uses behind their main title font. They think it's the next thing in brand identification. You just know it as a circle and consequently you'll need to build this letter from the flat image.

After the image is loaded, you'll see it appear in the bottom left viewport, as shown in **Figure 7.3**. Telling LightWave to use BottL for the viewport means that the loaded image is placed in that particular view.

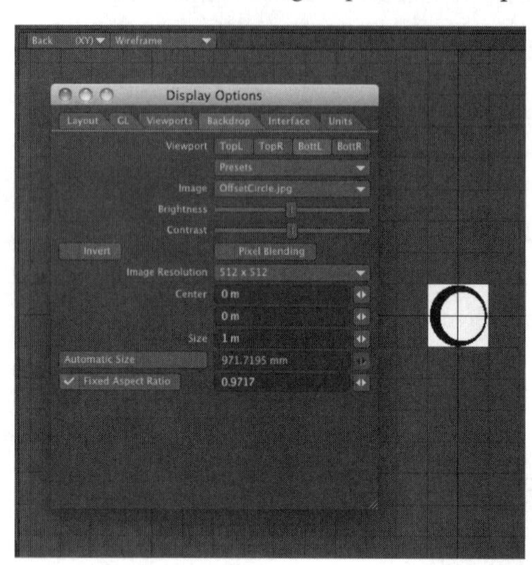

Figure 7.3 Loading the background image instantly shows it in the bottom left viewport.

As you can see, the image is a bit smaller than the viewport. Creating in 3D is relative, and building a tiny logo or a large logo makes no difference when it comes to rendering. However, you'll have an easier time flying a camera through the logo's elements if you make it a bit larger than this default size. You might also notice some serious jagged edges around the image.

4. In the Backdrop tab of the Display Options panel, change the Size to 5 m from the current 1 m.
5. Change the Image Resolution setting to 2048 × 2048. This will allow you to see the image clear and sharp in the background.
6. Bring the Brightness and Contrast settings down so that the backdrop image is not overpowering. When you create 3D models, your points and polygons might be hard (or impossible) to see if the backdrop image is excessively bright. Dim the backdrop until you can just see it as a reference. Click OK and then press **a** to fit the image into view. **Figure 7.4** shows the results of the last three steps.

NOTE

Changing the Image Resolution setting in the Display Options panel has nothing to do with the actual resolution of the image or your 3D model. This is a display option only. LightWave allows display resolutions up to 4096 pixels.

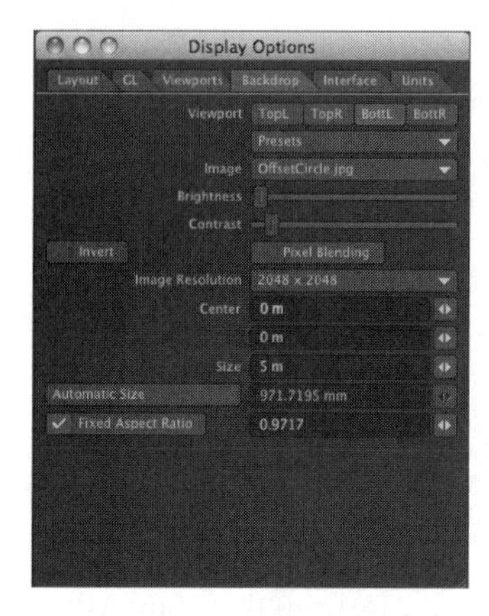

Figure 7.4 Increasing the size and resolution of the background image while decreasing the brightness and contrast gets the background image ready for modeling.

7. Just in case you want to use this backdrop later, go ahead and save it. Click Presets in the Display Options panel's Backdrop tab. Choose Save Current Backdrop (**Figure 7.5**) and give it a name such as **OffsetCircle_bkd**. Then when you want to use this again, just click Presets and Load Backdrop.

Figure 7.5 Save your backdrop to keep your settings for future use.

You're now ready to begin creating the background blocks that your camera will fly through. Read on to create these elements.

Building Over Images

Using 2D images in your 3D modeling process is not only a good idea but also a smart way to create accurate models. The following technique is something you might find yourself using often in Modeler. You can use it for characters, automobiles, and, in this case, a logo. Designers like to create cool print design elements, which often create nightmares for animators to set in motion. However, by placing an image in the background as you've done in the previous steps, it's quick and easy to build 3D elements right over the image.

Figure 7.6 Use the Maximize Viewport button to make the bottom left view full screen.

Exercise 7.2 Using Backdrop Images for Modeling

1. With the same backdrop image (the one you named OffsetCircle_bkd) loaded into the bottom left view, select the Pen tool from the Create tab. Then, click the Maximize Viewport button (**Figure 7.6**) at the upper-right corner of the viewport at bottom left. This expands your view to full screen. You'll click it again later to return to a quad view.
2. Press . (period) a few times to zoom in to the view. Or click, hold, and drag on the Zoom tool at the top right of the viewport.
3. With the Pen tool, click with the left mouse button to create roughly 30 points, evenly spaced. Click the points around the OffsetCircle image, as shown in **Figure 7.7**.

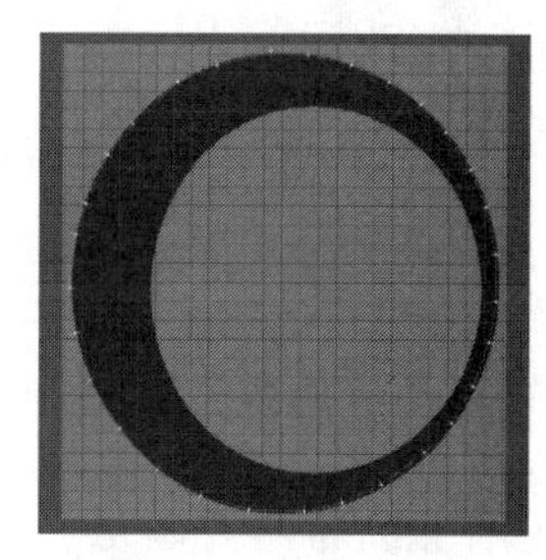

Figure 7.7 Use the Pen tool to click around the outline of the OffsetCircle image; each click creates a point in a polygon.

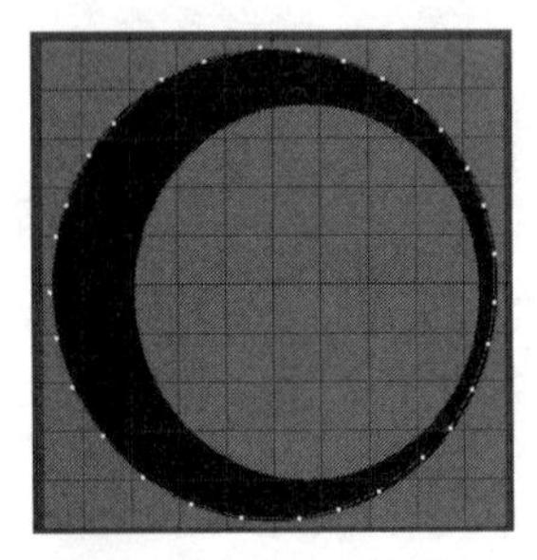

Figure 7.8 Going back to a quad view shows the polygon you've created with the Pen tool.

4. The Pen tool instantly creates polygons by connecting points in succession as you click them. Click the Pen tool button again to deactivate the tool, and then click the button in the upper-right corner of the viewport to return to a quad view. You should see a shape in the Perspective view, similar to **Figure 7.8**.

NOTE

If you don't see your model in Perspective view, its visible, editable surface, or *surface normal*, is probably facing away from you, toward the negative Z-axis. Press **f** to flip the normal forward.

5. You have the first part of the logo built, so save it! Press Control+S to Save As, and save it as **OffsetCircle**. Each version you create from this point will be saved in increments as 001, 002, 003, and so on, using Shift+S.
6. Start working in a new layer. To do this, click an empty layer button in the top right of the interface. How do you know if it's an empty layer? A layer that has geometry in it will have a small black dot. Pick a layer without the dot. In a new layer, also using the Pen tool, create about 22 evenly spaced points around the center space of OffsetCircle, as shown in **Figure 7.9**.
7. Save your work by pressing Shift+S. This will save your object as a new version with an incremental save. At this point you don't need the background image, so press the **d** key, and in the Backdrop tab of the Display Options panel, set Image to None.
8. You may have noticed that the object you created with the Pen tool looks kind of chunky. No worries; we'll make it smooth and clean soon. For now, make sure that the larger circle is in the foreground layer and that the center circle is in a background layer, as shown in **Figure 7.10**. To place a layer in the background, simply click beneath the slash on the layer button.

NOTE

A cool feature in LightWave is the ability to save in increments. After you save an object or scene for the first time, each time you press Shift+S afterward, you'll save an incremental, numbered version of your project. For safety's sake, get in the habit of using Shift+S to make incremental saves. That way, even if you make a mistake in an editing session, you'll have the previous version as a backup.

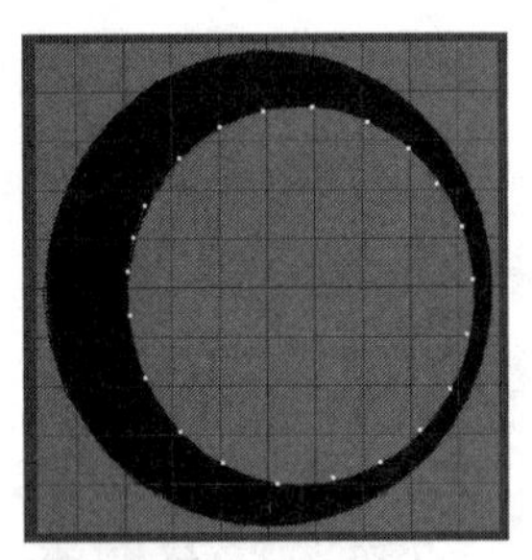

Figure 7.9 In a new layer, use the Pen tool to outline the center space in OffsetCircle.

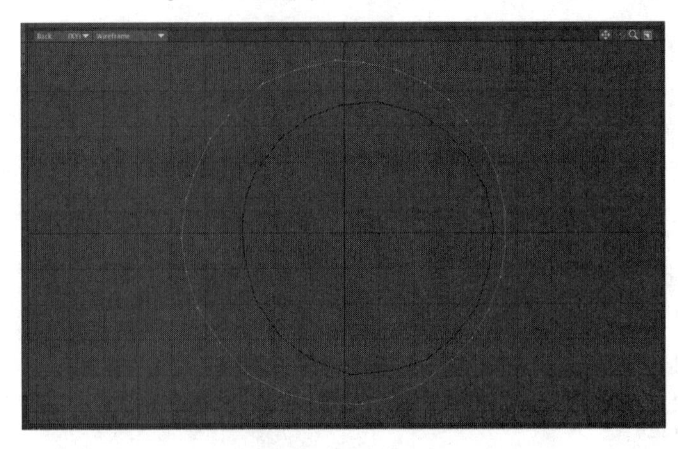

Figure 7.10 Place the larger part of the circle object in a foreground layer and the center of the object in a background layer.

9. In the Construct tab, click the Drill tool (found in the Combine tool category), or press Shift+R to activate the tool and open the Template Drill panel.

   The Drill tool allows you to "drill" a flat (2D) shape in one layer through one or more objects or shapes in different layer(s). (The Solid Drill tool works similarly but uses a 3D object as the "drill.")

10. In the Template Drill panel, click the Operation button marked Tunnel; then click the Axis button labeled Z (**Figure 7.11**). Click OK, and in a moment, you'll see a nice hole in the center of the letter outline (**Figure 7.12**). Save your object!

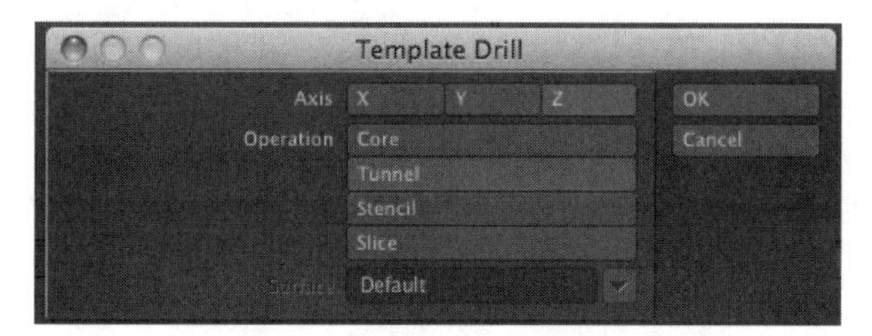

Figure 7.11 Use the Drill tool's Template Drill panel to create a hole in OffsetCircle.

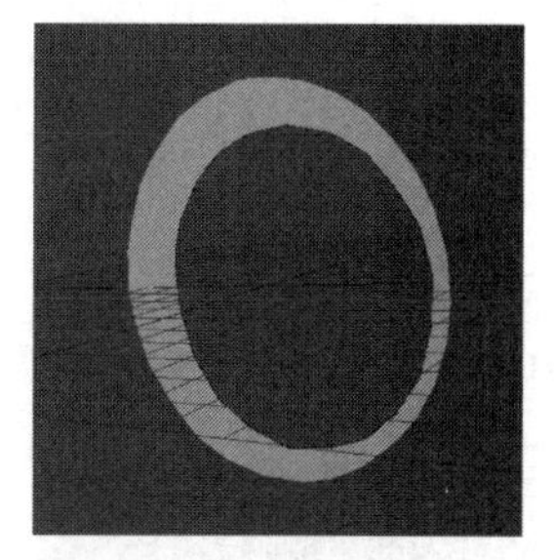

Figure 7.12 Using a Tunnel operation takes the background layer and cuts it through the foreground layer.

You built these objects using the Back view, which faces down the Z-axis; choosing Z aligns the drill operation along that axis. The Tunnel operation works as its name implies, using the background shape to bore a tunnel through the foreground shape. If you choose the Drill function, it performs just like the Template Drill, except that it's used for objects that have more than two sides—that is, objects that have more dimensionality.

11. Now you need to clean up the points and smooth them out a bit. Select two points on the outer edge, in sequence. Then, from the Select drop-down menu at the top left of the interface, choose Select Loop. This will select all the continuing points.

12. Press Control+T to activate the Drag tool, and then click and drag on points to smooth them out, as shown in **Figure 7.13**.

13. After you've positioned the points, save your work. Press the spacebar to deactivate the Drag tool, and then press / (forward slash) to deselect the points.

14. If you've expanded the viewport, collapse the full-frame view by clicking the small icon in the top right of the viewport, returning you to a quad view.

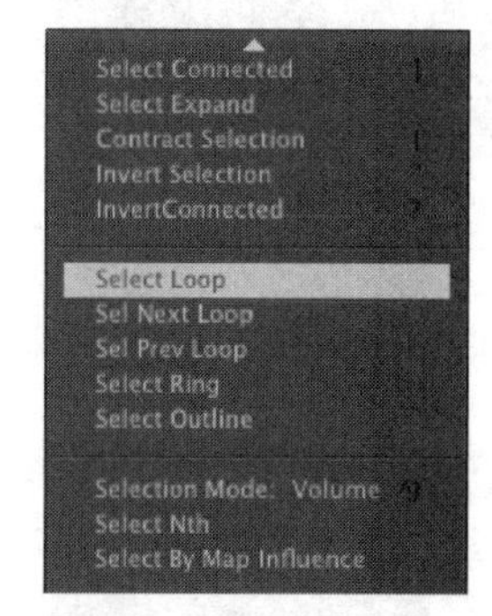

Figure 7.13 Using the Drag tool, you can fine-tune the position of the object's points.

NOTE

You easily turn the backdrop image on and off. Press **d** to open Display Options and on the Backdrop tab of the Display Options panel that opens, click the BottL viewport. Change Image to None to remove the image from the background of the viewports. The image is still loaded in Modeler, but it is not displayed. You may find yourself turning the background image on and off a few times while you are modeling, for visual reference. The backdrop image is not part of the model, but it's still loaded in Modeler whether it's visible or not. You can delete it for good from Modeler through the Image Editor.

NOTE

If you feel like your model needs a few more points in certain areas, you can first select the polygon (in Polygons mode) and then choose Add Points from the Subdivide category on the Multiply tab. Then, click with the Pen tool on the edge where you'd like to add a point.

This model is complete. This OffsetCircle object, looming large and semitransparent, will appear in the background of our final scene. You'll call this object up later in Layout.

NOTE

If you would like to completely remove the image from Modeler, open the Image Editor, found on the top left of the Modeler interface. Select the image in the panel and press Delete on your keyboard.

A few more things to know about using background images:

Pen isn't the only tool you can use to trace background images. Try the Sketch, Bezier, and Spline Draw tools; you can even use a background image as a reference when creating full 3D primitives or other objects. You're using the Pen tool in this project because it creates polygons as soon as the points are laid down. If you'd used the Bezier tool, you'd have been creating curves, which would have required an extra step to "freeze" the curves into polygonal faces. Remember, polygons are necessary to apply a surface and render. The Bezier or Spline Draw options will create a smoother edge and are very useful for more detailed objects. Be sure to watch the video on the book's DVD to learn how to use this tool over backdrop images (3D_GarageVideos\CH1\CH1_SplinesInModeler.mov).

Exercise 7.3 Creating Text in Modeler

When you create text in LightWave Modeler, you don't always have to use a backdrop image.

1. From the File menu, choose Close All Objects. This clears all geometry from LightWave Modeler. Then, press **a** to fit and reset the views.
2. Press **n** to open the numeric panel. Then, on the Create tab, click the Text button (in the Text tool category) or press Shift+W to activate the tool dialog (**Figure 7.14**).

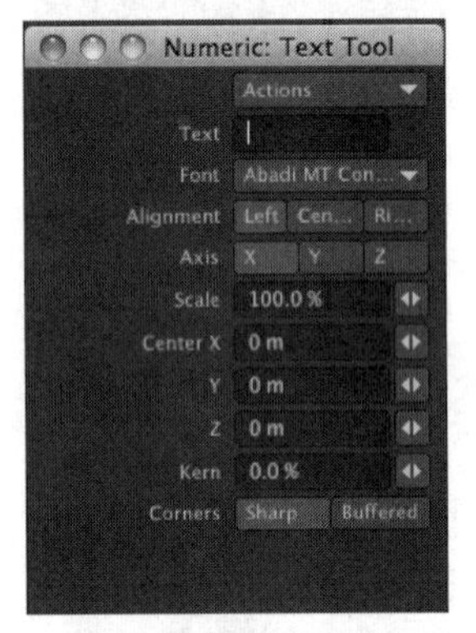

Figure 7.14 The Text tool active with the Numeric panel open, accessible from Modeler's Create tab.

3. Depending on the fonts on your system, the first font listing that appears might look sort of messed up. Certain system fonts won't display properly in Modeler, but the majority of your installed fonts should work in LightWave. Click the Font drop-down list in the Numeric dialog box. You'll see a list of your installed fonts, as shown in **Figure 7.15**.

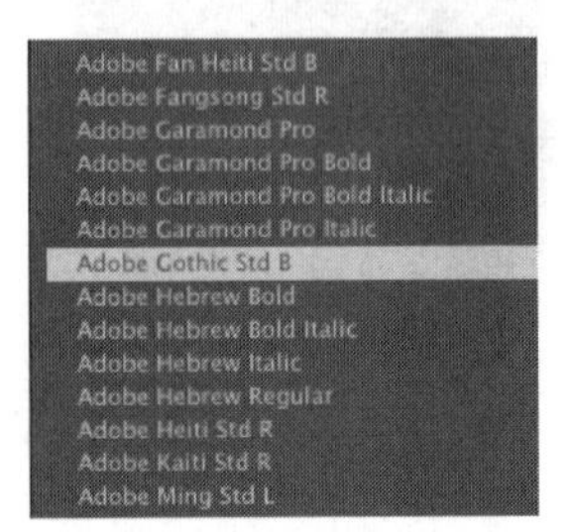

Figure 7.15 The Font drop-down list in the Numeric dialog box lists your installed fonts.

4. Pick an ordinary font, such as Book Antiqua. Any font will do, so if you don't have this font, pick another, such as Arial. After you've chosen a font, click OK.
5. Now, click the Text button, and then click in the Back viewport. You'll see a cursor appear. Your keyboard is now a typewriter, and LightWave will not respond to keyboard equivalents. Type **WDMA**, the call letters for the Ablan Broadcast Network (**Figure 7.16**).

Figure 7.16 With the Text tool, you can add type to Modeler projects.

With the Text tool active, you can interactively adjust your font. You must do this before you deselect the tool, however. When you deselect the tool, the text object will become polygons, just like a box, a ball, or anything else you might create. You can then size, adjust, and change the shape as you like;

however, turning the Text tool back on does not allow you to edit this text but rather creates new text. With the light blue text cursor still active, you can click and drag the top of the cursor to size the fonts. And you can click and drag the bottom vertical slash to adjust spacing between letters. Click and drag the lower-right corner of the cursor to position your text.

6. In the Numeric panel, you can also add your text, rather than typing it out in the Modeler interface. You can also adjust the placement, alignment, and so on, as shown in **Figure 7.17**.
7. If you like, you can change what text you're typing right in the Numeric window as well. For now, set the Center X, Y, and Z values all to 0.

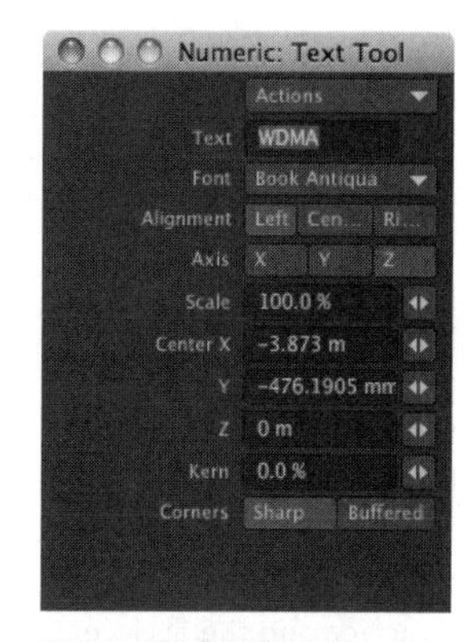

Figure 7.17 The Numeric panel for the Text tool allows you to change your fonts as well as set sizing options.

8. Close the Numeric panel, and then click the Text tool to turn it off. Press **a** to fit the type you just created into the viewport. **Figure 7.18** shows your soon-to-be-3D text.

Figure 7.18 Once your text is sized, close the Text tool and press a to fit your logo to view.

9. Press Control+S to Save As, and save your font as **WDMA_Flat**. It's a good idea to always save a flat version of type-based objects, in case you want to use them as an element in your animation, or perhaps need to rebuild the full logo. Press Control+S again and save the fonts as **WDMA_3D**. Now your flat version is saved and safe. Your newly saved version will be made into a 3D logo with a few more modeling tools.
10. Press **F2** to center the text. This will move it to the 0 coordinate shared by the X, Y, and Z axes. On the Multiply tab, click the Extrude tool under the Extend category.

NOTE

If you're on a Mac and the F2 command doesn't work, you can go to System Preferences and, under the Keyboard & Mouse tab, select the "Use all F1, F2, etc. keys as standard function keys" check box.

11. In the Top view, click and drag to extrude the text about 200 mm on the Z-axis, as shown in **Figure 7.19**.

Figure 7.19 To create depth for your text, use the Extrude tool.

12. Press the spacebar to turn off the Extrude tool. Press **s** to save.

You now have 3D text! Congratulations! OK, it's not that great-looking—but it will be! You need surfaces, and more importantly, bevels!

Exercise 7.4 Surfacing and Beveling Text in Modeler

LightWave Modeler offers you a lot of control. You can build just about anything your brain can conjure. But when it comes to 3D text, you really have no reference. If you build a lamp, or a house, or even a dog, you can use the real thing for comparison, but huge flying letterforms are scarce, so how do you determine what they should look like? As a start, take a look at what major networks are doing with 3D text. You'll see a lot of letters with slick, gleaming surfaces and beveled edges—and that's what you'll be using in the logo you create.

1. The process of applying bevels to type is easy, but there are a few things to do first. To get the most out of your 3D text in the final animation, you'll want to apply separate surfaces to the faces and sides of the text and to the bevel you'll soon create. To begin, press / to deselect all and then press **q** or click the Surface button at the bottom of the interface to open the Change Surface dialog box.

NOTE

The Surface button at the bottom of the Modeler interface and the Surface Editor button at the top left of the interface do very different things. The Surface button at the bottom of the interface creates surfaces for your objects. The Surface Editor button at the top left of the interface changes your surface settings. Be sure to click the right button based on your task.

2. You use the Change Surface dialog box to create surfaces. Enter **WDMA_Sides** in the Name field.

   Despite its name, the Change Surface dialog box is used to *create* surfaces—identify them and assign colors to them. In case that's not confusing enough, if you try to use it to change the color of an existing surface, you'll see an error message that says "Control Is Disabled." The reason for this is that when you create or identify a surface and assign it a color, there's no going back—at least within the Change Surface dialog box. To change the surface's color settings, you must use the Surface Editor. So again, Change Surface is not really about changing surfaces; it's about creating them. However, if you assign a color in the Change Surface dialog box, that color will be attached to the selected geometry and show up in Layout when you render. You can, of course, change this value later in the Surface Editor.

3. After you've entered the name WDMA_Sides, turn off Make Default. Then click OK. Leaving Make Default on would mean that any new geometry you created in Modeler would be named WDMA_Sides. It's good practice to have any nonsurfaced geometry assigned the generic name, "default," so you can easily spot polygon regions that don't have assigned surfaces. Don't worry about setting a color just yet. Click OK to close the panel.

   You just applied a surface name to your entire object. If no specific geometry is selected, actions you take in Modeler, including changing a surface, apply to your entire object. So why did you use "_Sides" in a name applied to all surfaces of every letter? Because it happens to be easier to select and rename the flat faces of the letters than it is to select all their side surfaces separately. If we select and rename the faces, everything left over will be assigned the correct "_Sides" surface name. Clever, huh? (In fact, before we name the letter surfaces, we're going to use the same trick again to add and name a surface bevel.)

4. Click the Polygons selection-mode button at the bottom of Modeler, or press the spacebar a few times to cycle to it. Then, select just the faces of the letters. You can do this quickly in the Perspective view by holding the Shift key and clicking each face (**Figure 7.20**).

Figure 7.20 Select just the faces of the letters.

5. With the three letter-face polygons selected, click the Surface tool again (or press **q**), and type **WDMA_Bevel** in the Name field. Change the color slightly, perhaps to a light blue, to distinguish it from other parts of the object that are assigned surface names. You will change any colors assigned here in Layout; colors assigned in Modeler help you tell named surfaces apart. Click OK to close the Change Surface dialog box.

   You're probably wondering why you named the letter faces "WDMA_Bevel." Good question. The Bevel tool adds new polygons to the current selection, and if a surface name has been assigned to that selection, it applies that name to the new geometry. So we're temporarily naming the surface polygons "_Bevel" to apply that name to the new bevel geometry. When we're done beveling, we'll click those easy-to-select letter-face polygons one more time and finally give them their proper name.

6. With the faces still selected, press **b** to call up the Bevel tool.

7. Click and drag in any viewport to bevel the selection. Click and drag up to set the Shift, and click and drag left or right to change the Inset. You can also press the **n** key to open the Numeric panel. You'll want to bevel your text to about 10 mm for the Shift, and 7 mm for the Inset (**Figure 7.21**). Think of the Shift property as pushing and pulling the selected geometry. Inset, then, is more like increasing or decreasing the size of the selected geometry.

NOTE

Beveling can be awkward unless you pay close attention to your mouse movements. Concentrate first on forward-backward motion, which controls the bevel's *shift*, and then focus on just left-right motion, which controls *inset*. When you randomly click and drag, it's difficult to bevel accurately. Also, be sure not to bevel so much that the polygons cross over each other. You want only a slight bevel for added depth.

Figure 7.21 Bevel the selected faces of the letters.

8. If you look closely at the Perspective view (see Figure 7.21), you'll see that the letter-face polygons are still selected, and the new bevel geometry is

not; so press **q** again to open the Change Surface dialog box and change the surface name for the selection to **WDMA_Face**. Set a varying color to make sure that your surface name takes effect. This is not always necessary, and is merely an organizational step. You don't need to assign a color when you create a surface name. And even if you have two surfaces that will have the same surface and texture later on, such as the sides and bevel of the text, it's still a good idea to give each its own surface name. The reason for this is not only flexibility in surfacing, but also for smoothing. Certain surfaces will be smoother than others, even with the same color and reflections applied. **Figure 7.22** shows the beveled and surfaced text.

Figure 7.22 With the newly beveled selection surfaced, you now have surfaces applied to the face, bevel, and sides of the text.

9. Press the spacebar to turn off the Bevel tool. Then press / to deselect all geometry. Press Shift+S to save your work. Place the text object in a background layer by clicking beneath the slash in its layer button (**Figure 7.23**).

Figure 7.23 The text object is now in a background layer.

Since this element is being animated as one object, you can leave it all on the same layer. However, you might need to adjust the pivot point so that it can be animated properly.

Pivot Points in Modeler

Each layer in Modeler has its own X-Y-Z coordinate system, and when you create (or add) an object to a new layer, the object is centered by default on the layer's origin point (coordinates 0, 0, 0). Modeler also uses that origin point as the object's default *pivot point*, around which it will spin when rotated. This is fine for many things, but for precise animation, it can cause problems. This section shows you how to change objects' pivot points.

Exercise 7.5 Setting New Pivot Points in Modeler

1. Start by selecting the layer with your WDMA logo from the previous exercises. This model's center is probably pretty close to the origin point. It was at this position, the default pivot point, when you pressed **F2** earlier to center it. But since you've extruded and beveled it, the pivot is now at the face of the object. The pivot did not change—the object did.

   The default pivot point for this object will not cause too many issues when animating in Layout; however, it could be a little more precise.

2. Go to the View tab, and then select the Pivot tool under the Layers category, as shown in **Figure 7.24**.

Figure 7.24 Select the Pivot tool in the View tab to adjust pivots for any layer.

3. When you activate the Pivot command, crosshairs appear in the viewports. Because you centered the flat object before you extruded, the WDMA letters look like they have a centered pivot if viewing from the Back view. However, upon closer inspection from the Top view, the pivot is at the face of the object, rather than the center. Move the pivot to the center of the object in the Top view (**Figure 7.25**). Be careful to pay attention to all views and move it on the Z-axis as well as the X-axis and Y-axis.

Figure 7.25 Manually move the pivot for Layer 1's object.

4. Save your work!

You can set the pivots for any of the layers in a project, but you do not have to turn off the Pivot tool to change layers. Just change to the new layer, adjust the new pivot, and away you go.

You've now created all the base animation elements for the logo treatment. The next steps are to build the main logo and create the subtext that you'll animate as individual letters.

Importing EPS Files

LightWave also offers you the ability to import Adobe Illustrator files or EPS files. This is extremely handy for more complicated graphics designed out-of-house; as an animator, you'll often be hired to animate a logo you haven't designed. When you import a logo as an EPS file, Modeler automatically recognizes its outlines as spline curves you can scale, "freeze," and surface. No tracing of a background image is required. This not only saves tons of time, it also allows you to create a more accurate 3D version of the original piece. To better explain how this feature works, there's a cool tutorial video on the book's DVD showing how to use this feature of Modeler.

Animating Text

Now that you have your base objects, it's time to put it all together in Layout (**Figure 7.26**). Once in Layout, you can begin setting up your animation. First, you'll set the placement, and then the lighting. After that's in place, you'll enhance the surfaces and set up camera moves. Are you ready? Good, then head to the book's DVD for a great interactive movie on putting this full animation together. You'll see how helpful LightWave's VPR mode is for real-time previews right in Layout. The movie is called SceneSetup.mov.

Lighting, Motion, and Backgrounds

Until now, you've seen the basic setup before lighting is in place. What you do next is totally up to you. Many people put everything in motion first, then light, then render. Others light first, then animate. Here, we'll do a little of everything!

Lighting is important in any scene, even a relatively simple logo animation. You'll learn how to set up lighting for your scene and how to animate the text you've built—including the pivot points you changed. From there, you'll create a cool moving background that provides an interesting environment for your scene. Included on this book's DVD is a video showing you how to light this motion graphics scene. You'll learn first-hand by seeing the exact setup with a clear explanation and visual results. Go watch the video now! It's called MotionLighting.mov and it's in the CH7 folder of the book's DVD.

Once you have a good working animation and lighting setup, you can use additional lights for added interest. And what will really make this project stand out is the surfacing and background. We have much more to cover with LightWave, and it's time to move on.

The Next Step

This chapter took you through some of the most basic LightWave operations. But the tools used, and the process in which you use them, are always the same no matter how complex your project might be. The next step, after you watch the videos on the book's DVD, is to move on to Chapter 8 and learn about modeling products. As for this logo project, it's up to you to use these steps and procedures to create your own logo for your company, for your client, or just for fun. In this chapter you've learned how to build over background images and use the text-creation tools. The videos for this chapter will extend your learning even further. And remember that as you model and texture, you also have to tweak. Tweak, tweak, tweak! There's always more you can do with a scene, so take some time and do it.

Any little changes you make to your models and scenes are what give your animations that extra something. You'll take your modeling and layout skills a step further in the next chapter.

Chapter 8

Modeling Everyday Things

In its early years, few people would have described digital 3D as art (least of all most of its creators). Modelers and animators did some design work, of course, but they were mainly technicians. The time and money required to create 3D models, and the highly specialized (and limited) tools available to do the job, limited 3D's uses to diagramming, engineering, and occasional Hollywood special effects. Today it's different. Computing power, software advancements, and the ever-growing world of 3D content make truly artistic 3D model creation possible, and open the doors for you to go beyond your job as a 3D expert to create 3D scenes simply for the joy of creating. This chapter explores some of LightWave's potential as an artistic tool.

Modeling Fruit

When you take a drawing or painting class, one of your first subjects is typically a still life—a grouping of objects that usually includes fruit or flowers, plus other items that contrast with them in texture, such as bowls or glassware. This chapter will take you on a journey in creating a still-life scene, but you'll model and surface the objects, instead of painting or drawing them. Along the way, you'll become even more familiar with the tools in LightWave 10.

Here are some of the key areas discussed in this chapter:

- Using LightWave Modeler tools
- Building everyday objects
- Positioning objects in Modeler
- Working with points, edges, and polygons
- Using more advanced modeling tools
- Building a still-life set

Clearly, the number one thing you need to complete any 3D project is patience. You might see some people's work online and wonder just how they create those 3D images. Here's how they do it: They work at it! There is no magic "make art" button in 3D (not even in LightWave). But by knowing the tools, and understanding your goal, you too can create anything you want. This chapter will help you do just that by breaking down the elements and stepping you through them, one piece at a time. If you're ready, get a snack and a drink and start creating.

Begin with Bananas

Talk to anyone who has taken an art class and they will most likely tell you that there's always fruit. Not to eat, but to re-create, through drawing or painting. That's what this chapter is going to have you do, but digitally and in 3D. You'll start with the leader of the fruit pack, the banana.

Exercise 8.1 One Banana, Two Banana, Three Banana, Four

If a catchy little tune popped into your head when you read this project's title, you're definitely showing your age. Yes, we're talking about Fleegle, Bingo, Drooper, and Snorky—the Banana Splits gang from the '70s television show. What does this have to do with modeling a 3D banana? Nothing! But it was a great way to get the exercise going. Now, on to the project:

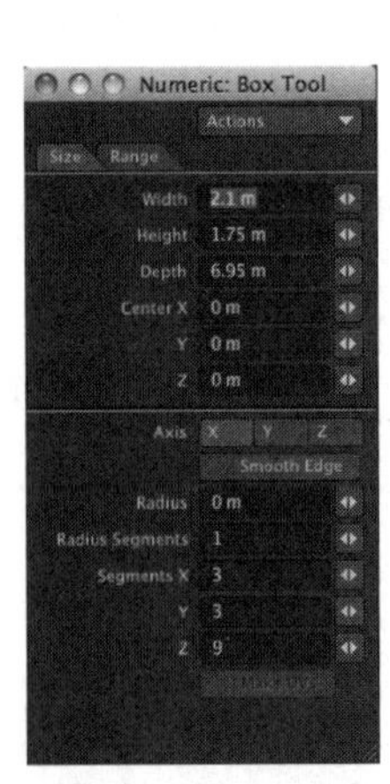

Figure 8.1 Create a box with multiple segments to begin creating a banana.

1. Open LightWave Modeler. This project begins by modeling the fruit that will be placed in your soon-to-be-modeled fruit bowl. You'll start with a banana. Click the Create tab and select the Box tool.
2. Press **n** to open the Numeric panel, select the Size tab if it's not already selected, and create a box by entering the values shown in **Figure 8.1**.
3. Once you've entered the settings, close the Numeric panel or move it aside, and then press the spacebar to quickly turn off the Box tool. Remember, you can turn off tools by pressing the spacebar. Choosing another tool automatically turns off the current tool.
4. Save your work.

5. Press the spacebar again, until the Edges selection-mode button is highlighted at the bottom of the interface.
6. In the Back view, at the bottom left, using your right mouse button (the Control key and mouse on the Mac), lasso-select the upper-right corner of the box. This will select the edge running along the top corner, down the Z-axis, as shown in **Figure 8.2**.
7. Now select the three other edges. To do this, hold the Shift key to add the selection, and then right-click around each corner from the Back view. **Figure 8.3** shows the four selected edges.
8. Now you'll bevel the selected edges. You can't use the usual bevel command when it comes to edges. For this, you'll use the EdgeBevel tool. On the Multiply tab, select EdgeBevel under the Extend category. You can also just press Control+B. As soon as you do, you'll see the edges expand, as in **Figure 8.4**.

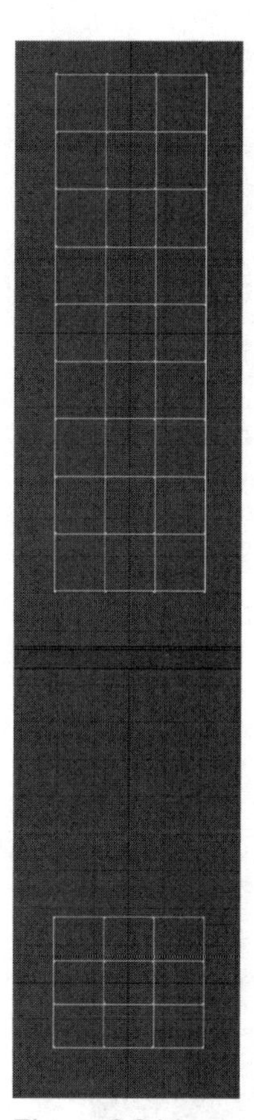

Figure 8.2 Lasso-select the top right edge of the box.

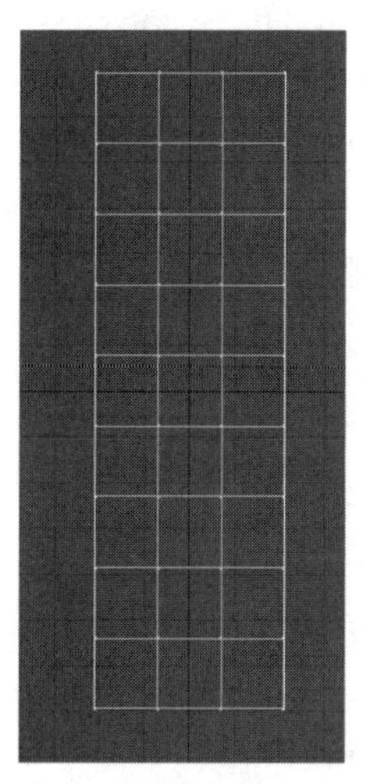

Figure 8.3 Select the remaining three edges. Now, all four edges of the box should be selected.

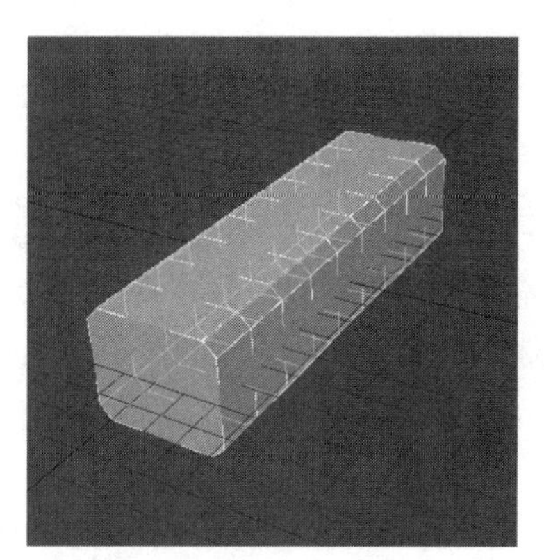

Figure 8.4 As soon as you activate EdgeBevel, your model begins to change.

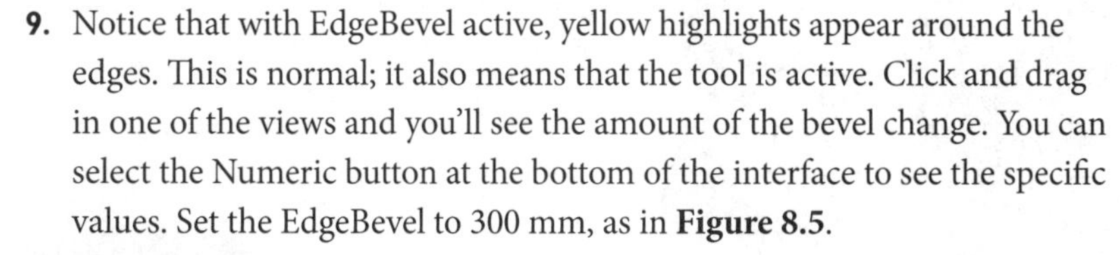

9. Notice that with EdgeBevel active, yellow highlights appear around the edges. This is normal; it also means that the tool is active. Click and drag in one of the views and you'll see the amount of the bevel change. You can select the Numeric button at the bottom of the interface to see the specific values. Set the EdgeBevel to 300 mm, as in **Figure 8.5**.

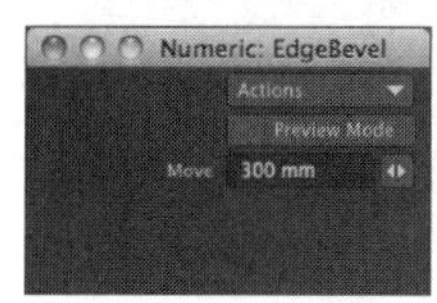

Figure 8.5 Set the EdgeBevel to 300 mm.

NOTE

The requester for Edge-Bevel shows an option to enable Preview Mode. Doing so allows you to preview the EdgeBevel, which is shown with blue outlines in the viewports. The bevel is not actually applied but only previewed.

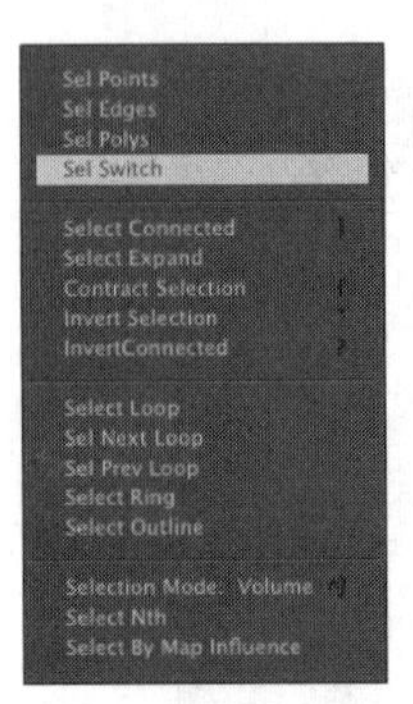

Figure 8.6 You can use Sel Switch to convert from one selection to another.

10. Close the Numeric panel and turn off EdgeBevel. You'll notice that the edges are still selected. That's good, because you can tell Modeler to convert this selection from edges to polygons. From the Select drop-down menu at the top left of the interface, choose Sel Switch, which switches your selection from edges to polygons, as shown in **Figure 8.6**.

NOTE

How does Modeler know to switch the current selection to polygons? Good question! If you had Edges selected, the next option is Polygons. If you had Polygons selected, the next option is Points. If you had Points selected, the next option is Edges. Just as you press the spacebar multiple times to toggle between the three selection models, the Sel Switch tool works in a similar fashion.

11. With the newly created polygons now selected, click the Multishift tool on the Multiply tab under the Extend category. Then, open the Numeric panel from the bottom of the interface. Basically, you want to bevel these polygons running down the corners of the soon-to-be banana. But LightWave's Bevel tool will separate the multiple polygons. Instead, Multishift can be used to bevel groups of polygons.

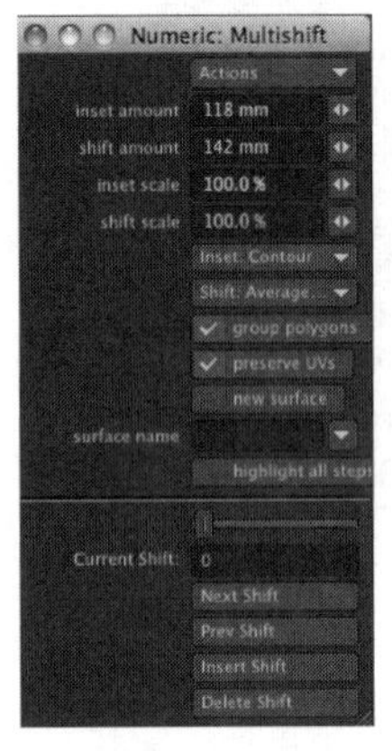

Figure 8.7 Using Multishift, you can bevel large groups of selected polygons.

12. In the requester for Multishift, make sure Group Polygons is checked on. Then, click and drag in a viewport to bevel the selected polygons. Moving the mouse left and right will change the Inset amount, while moving the mouse up and down changes the Shift amount. Set the values to 118 mm for the Inset, and 142 mm for the Shift. **Figure 8.7** shows the values.
13. Turn off the Multishift tool and close the Numeric panel.
14. Save your work. Feel free to save incrementally by pressing Shift+S.
15. In the Back view, select the center row of polygons for each side of the elongated box. You might find that some of the end polygons become selected as well, and that's normal. After you select the desired polygons, hold the Control key and click the polygons you want to deselect. **Figure 8.8** shows the selection.

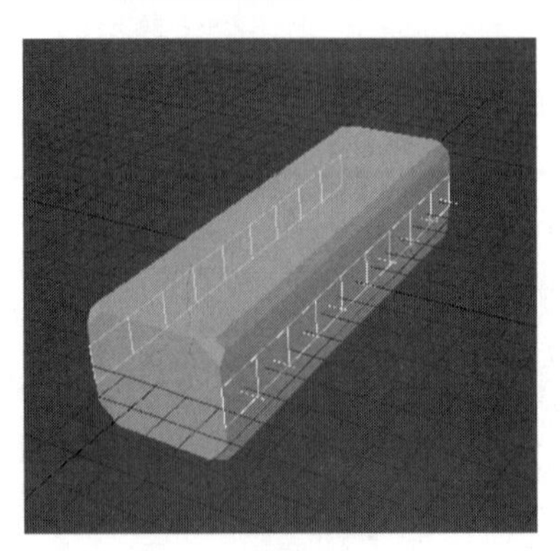

Figure 8.8 Select the center row of polygons for each side of the box.

16. At the bottom of the Modeler interface is the Modes menu. Click this and choose Action Center: Selection. This tells Modeler to apply tools based on the selection, not on the mouse position, as it was by default.
17. Then, press Shift+H to activate the Size tool. Click and drag in the Back view to expand the size of the selection about 15 percent. As you click and drag, pay attention to the lower-left corner of the interface. The Numeric panel will show your Size value as you use the tool. The default is 100%, so you'll want to click and drag to size the selection to 115%. **Figure 8.9** shows the result.

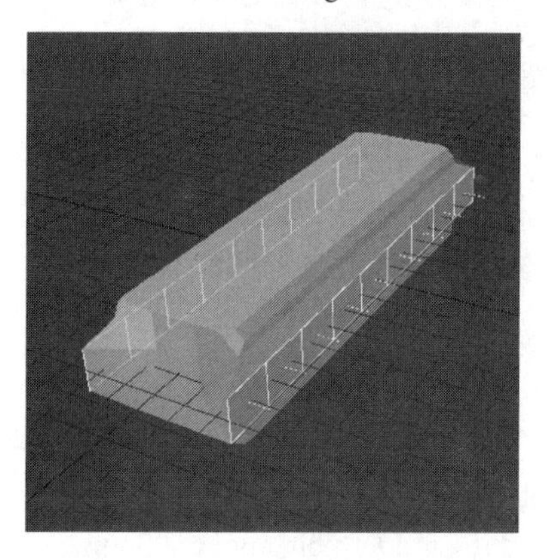

Figure 8.9 Increase the size of the selection by 15 percent.

18. Turn off the Size tool by clicking it or pressing the spacebar. If you look at Figure 8.9, you might notice that the ends of the object are a bit gnarly. Let's fix that. First, deselect the currently selected polygons by pressing the / key on your keyboard. You can also click into a blank portion of the menu in Modeler.
19. Change to Points selection mode at the bottom of the interface to tell Modeler you want to work with points (also known in the 3D industry as vertices).
20. In the Right view, using your right mouse button (Control-click on the Mac), lasso-select the endpoints of the box on the negative Z-axis. You should have 28 points selected, as shown in **Figure 8.10**.

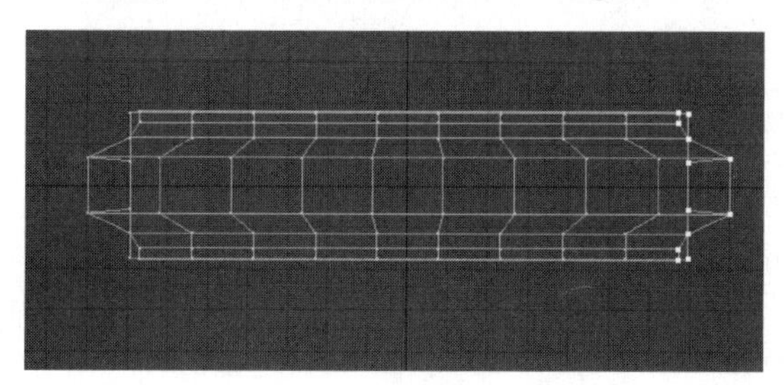

Figure 8.10 Lasso-select the endpoints on the negative Z-axis.

21. Now, position your mouse just to the front of the selection, and take a look at the info area at the lower-left corner of the interface. As you move the mouse, you'll see the numeric position. Note the Z-axis position at about 4.25 m. Then, press **v** to access the Set Value dialog box.
22. Choose Z for the axis, and enter the value you noted from your mouse position, 4.25 m. Click OK and the selected points will jump to that value on that axis, as shown in **Figure 8.11**.

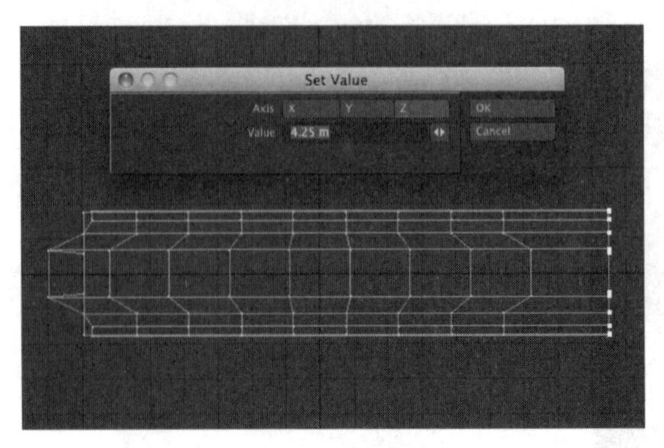

Figure 8.11 Using the Set Value dialog box, you can quickly adjust all points to one position.

23. With the newly positioned points still selected, activate the Move tool (press **t**) and then move them back toward the model a bit, about 500 mm.
24. Now you'll bevel the polygons on this end. You adjusted the points using Set Value to flatten out the polygons. This will make your life easier when trying to bevel. But you want to bevel polygons, not points, so rather than deselecting points and reselecting polygons, use the Sel Switch command as you did earlier. From the Select drop-down menu at the top left of the interface, choose Sel Switch. The selected points now change to selected edges. Run the command again, and the selected edges become selected polygons.
25. Press Shift+A to fit the selection to view.
26. When you bevel polygons, there are times when the geometry crosses over itself, creating unwanted results. So before you bevel, adjust a few points. Press Control+T to activate the Drag tool. Then, click and drag the points that make up the ends of the EdgeBevels you created earlier. Do this in the Back view.

    It's important to understand that first rule of modeling here—if nothing is selected, whatever you do applies to everything. So if you were to drag points in the Back view, the points would change all the way down the elongated box. But since just the polygons are selected from step 24, the point adjustment from the Drag tool in the Back view affects only the selection. The result is that you're editing only the end of the object.

27. Drag the points in to flatten out the EdgeBevels, as shown in **Figure 8.12**.

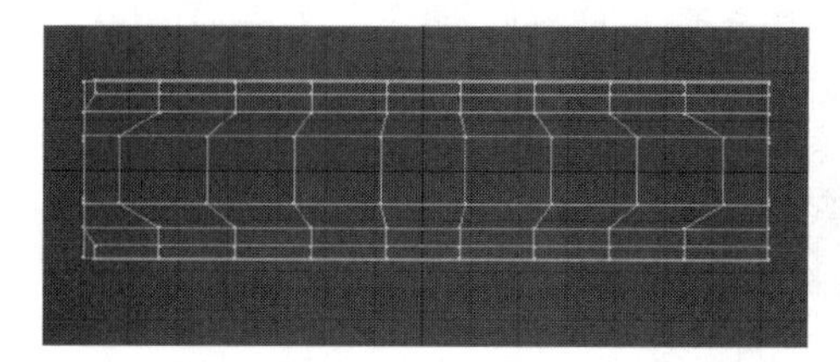

Figure 8.12 Using the Drag tool on selected polygons, you can click and drag the points of the EdgeBevels to flatten them out.

28. Once you've adjusted the EdgeBevels, select the Multishift tool on the Multiply tab. Click and drag the selected polygons to 225 mm for the Inset and 535 mm for the Shift. You can use the Numeric panel as you did earlier for specific value entry. **Figure 8.13** shows the change.

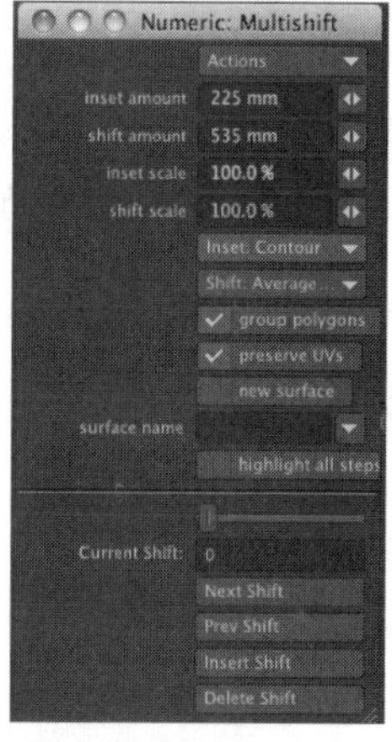

Figure 8.13 Using Multishift, bevel the end polygons to create one end of the banana.

29. Right-click one time to reset the Multishift tool, effectively adding to the existing geometry with a new bevel. Multishift the selection without allowing the corners to cross, about 344 mm for the Inset and 920 mm for the Shift. **Figure 8.14** shows the operation.

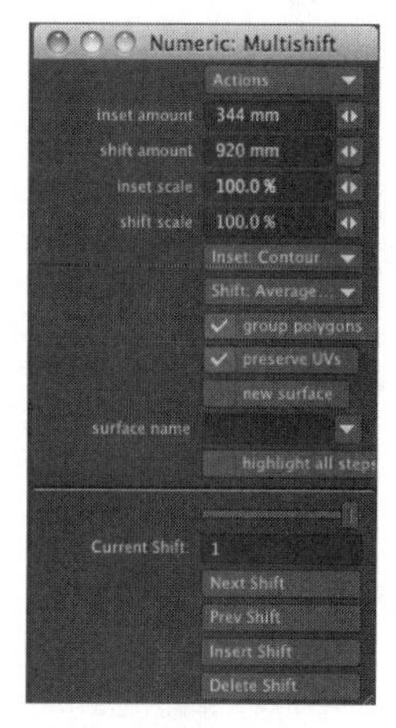

Figure 8.14 Perform one more Multishift to multiply the selection, but be careful not to cross the corners.

30. Press Shift+H to select the Size tool. This will automatically turn off the Multishift tool. Reduce the selection size down to about 80%, as in **Figure 8.15**.

31. Deselect the ends of the edge polygons, leaving just the nine polygons that make up the center, as shown in **Figure 8.16**. If it's easier, deselect all polygons and then select just the center nine polygons.

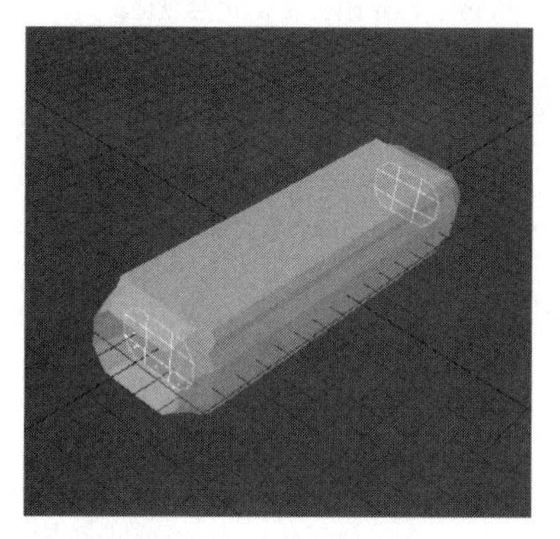

Figure 8.15 Now that you have additional geometry for the end of the object, you can scale it down. This will help avoid edges and points from crossing over each other as they would with the Multishift tool.

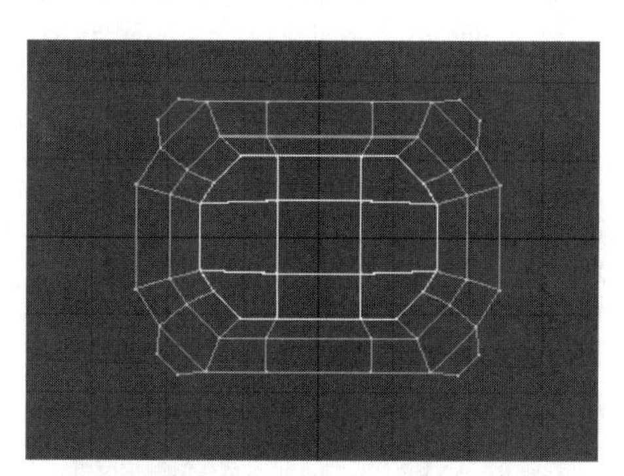

Figure 8.16 Deselect the small edge polygons in the corners, leaving just nine polygons selected.

32. You need to use Multishift again, but if you kept the edge polygons selected, you would start to see some serious errors. So with just the nine polygons selected at the end of the object, turn on Multishift and set the Inset to 240 mm with a 305 mm Shift. **Figure 8.17** (on the next page) shows the result.

33. Turn Multishift off, then turn it on again to extend the selection just one more time. But this time, apply a Shift value of only 240 mm (**Figure 8.18**).

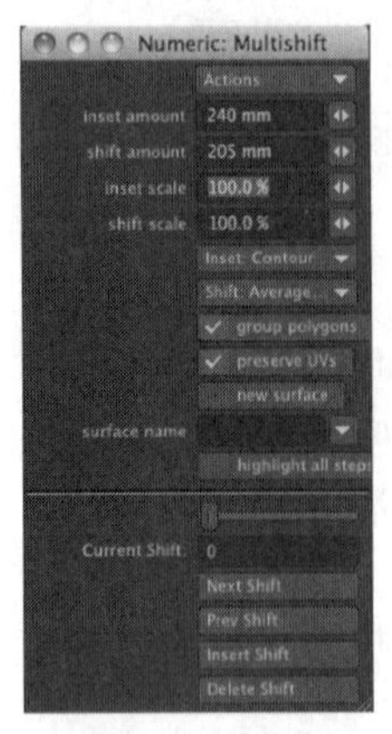

Figure 8.17 Using Multishift, extend the end polygons just a bit farther.

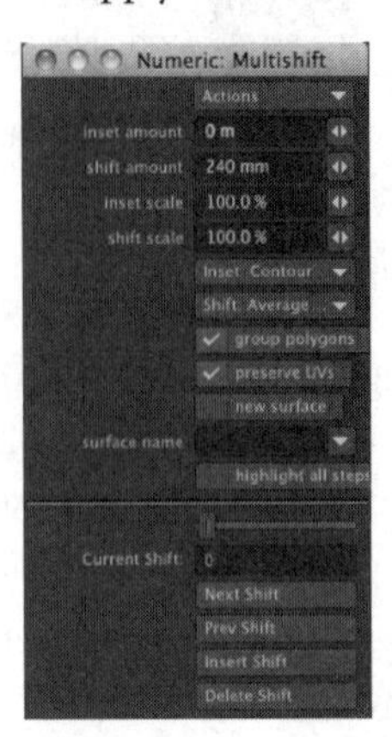

Figure 8.18 Multishift the selection again, but only for a Shift value, not for an Inset value.

34. Close the Numeric panel and turn off the Multishift tool. Then, deselect the polygons.
35. Save your work!
36. Select the four points that make up the very center of the newly created polygons, and size them down, as in **Figure 8.19**. This helps even out the mesh at the end, and will allow you to add additional Multishift operations if you want.

Figure 8.19 Scale down the center points on the end of the geometry.

You're probably wondering at this point how it's all coming together, so before you move on to add more details, how about taking a look at the overall progress?

37. Make sure any points or polygons are deselected. Then, press **a** to fit all objects to view.

38. Press the Tab key. What? You got an error? That's OK—don't worry. Click OK to close the error warning and press Tab again to turn off the attempted subpatch. Close the second error box.

    You see, the beveling of edges earlier in the chapter changed the subpatch mesh so that some of its polygons have more than four sides. Earlier versions of LightWave balked at that, but LightWave 10 can handle larger polygons using Catmull-Clark subdivisions.

39. From the bottom of the interface, you'll see the SubD-Type drop-down menu. Change this to Catmull-Clark.

    Catmull-Clark subdivisions are sometimes referred to as *n-gons*. Essentially, by using this method of subdivision, your objects do not need to conform to just three or four vertices like the old Subpatch method. The original Subpatch method still works well, and modeling with quads (polygons with four vertices) in mind is always the best way to approach a model. However, at times you need to go beyond convention, and this is where Catmull-Clark subdivisions come in handy.

40. With the SubD-Type set to Catmull-Clark, press the Tab key. Ah, no error message! **Figure 8.20** shows the banana starting to take shape.

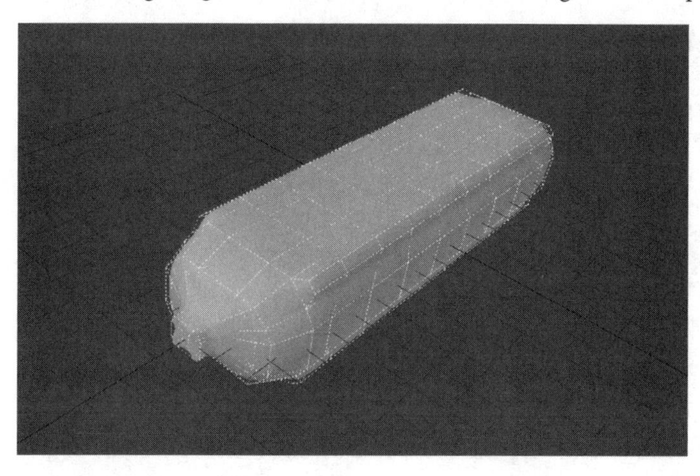

Figure 8.20 Using Catmull-Clark subdivisions, the original box is starting to look like a banana. Sort of.

41. Make a few more detail changes and you're almost there. First, press the Tab key to turn off the SubD mode. It's sometimes better to work with subdivision mode disabled for speed and visual ease. It can be confusing to see the subdivision cage when trying to adjust edges.

42. Make an incremental save by pressing Shift+S.

43. Now, how about tightening up the shape of the end polygon? Make sure Polygons selection mode is set at the bottom of the interface, and Control-click the nine polygons that make up the end of the banana.

44. Press Shift+] (the right bracket key) to expand the selection, as in **Figure 8.21**.

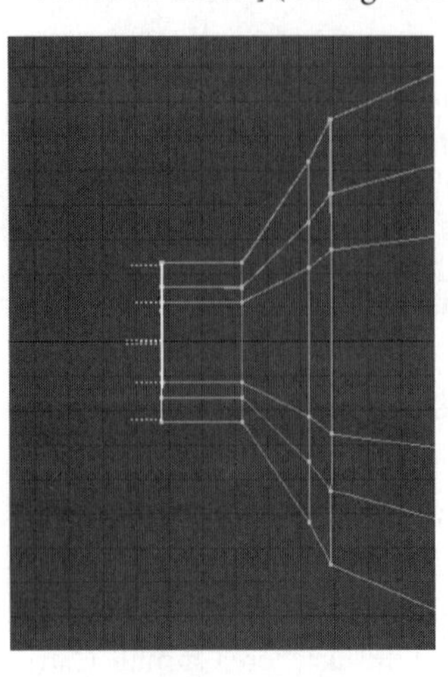

Figure 8.21 Select the end polygons of the banana.

45. Press **h** to select the Stretch tool from the Modify tab.

46. Stretch the selection to about 65% along the X-axis and 93% along the Y-axis, as in **Figure 8.22**.

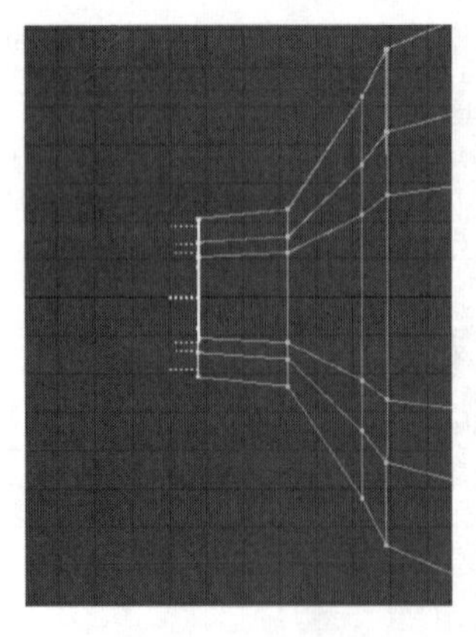

Figure 8.22 Scale the end of the banana so that it's more a square than a rectangle.

47. Turn off the Stretch tool (or press the spacebar), and then deselect the polygons (press /).

48. In the Top view window, click any edge of the banana tip's base. Then, from the Select drop-down menu at the top left of the interface, choose Select Loop. The entire edge loop will be selected (**Figure 8.23**).

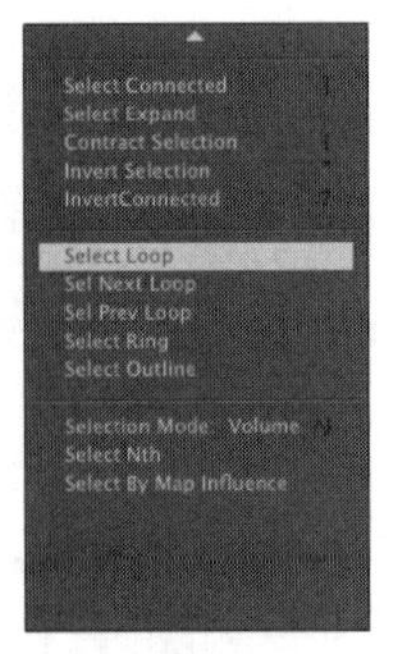

Figure 8.23 The Select Loop option lets you quickly select an entire edge.

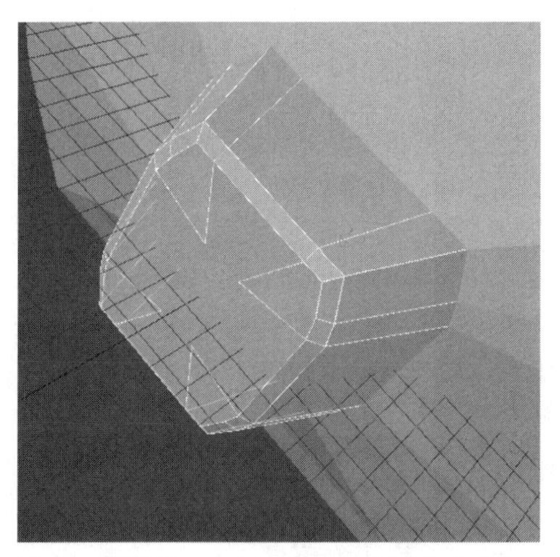

Figure 8.24 Bevel the edge to add detail at the neck of the banana.

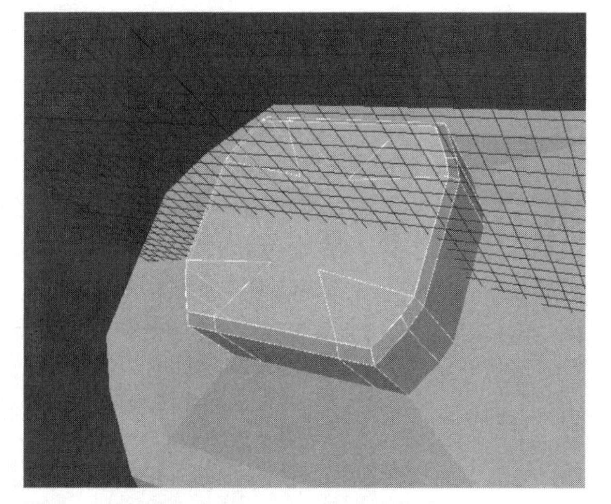

Figure 8.25 Bevel the outer edge of the banana tip.

49. With the edge selected, press Control+B to activate the EdgeBevel tool. Click and drag to bevel the selected edge about 20 mm or so (**Figure 8.24**).
50. Select the outer edge of the banana tip, and bevel it as well (**Figure 8.25**).
51. Using the right mouse button, lasso-select the points of the end of the banana and extend them about 180 mm on the negative Z-axis, as shown in **Figure 8.26**.
52. With the points still selected, change the Action Center setting to Mouse (mentioned earlier in step 16), using the Modes drop-down list at the bottom of the interface. Then, press **y** to select the Rotate tool. Click and drag slightly in the Top view, directly on the edge of the selected points, to rotate the selection in a clockwise direction, about 15 degrees. By setting Action Center to Mouse, you're telling Modeler to make adjustments based on your mouse position. Therefore, a Rotate command will pivot around where you click and drag. **Figure 8.27** shows the rotation.

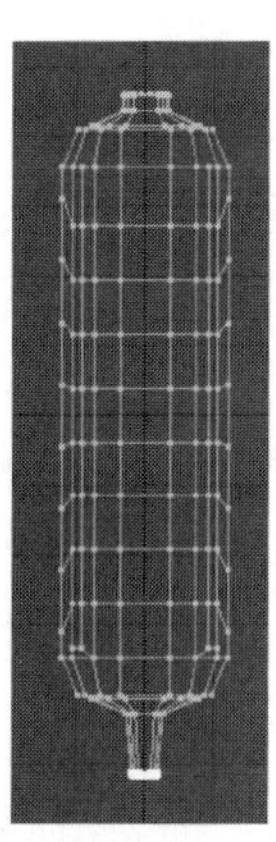

Figure 8.26 Select the points around the end of the banana and move them out on the negative Z-axis.

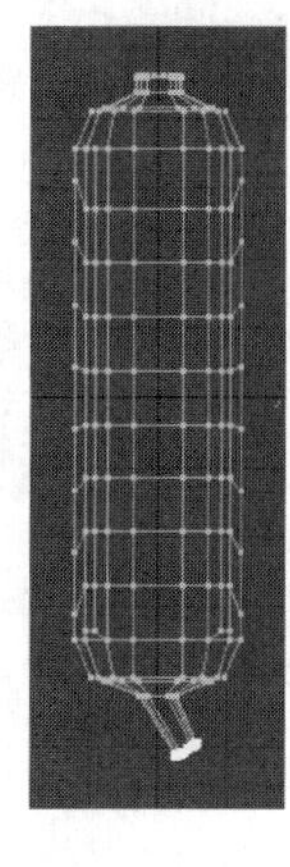

Figure 8.27 Rotate the endpoints about 15 degrees.

53. At this point, you can use all of the tools and procedures we've already covered in this project to adjust the model as you like. Feel free to use the Drag tool to adjust the ends, bevel additional edges, and sort of "mess up" the model a bit so it's not so perfect. On your own, repeat the Multishift, Drag, and Size operations on the other end of the banana. The only difference is that there wouldn't be as much of a stem as there is on the end you've already been working on. **Figure 8.28** shows one way in which bevels and other adjustments can be applied to the opposite end of the banana.

Figure 8.28 Use the Drag, Multishift, and Size tools to create the base of the banana on the opposite end of the model.

54. OK, now all you need to do is bend it. On the Modify tab, select Bend. Then in the Back view, click in the center of the object and drag to the right. Bend the object as you like.

55. One last thing to get you in a banana state of mind: Press **q** and apply a surface name of **Banana** to your model. Also, give it a bit of a yellow color. You can always change this later. Save your banana. **Figure 8.29** shows the result.

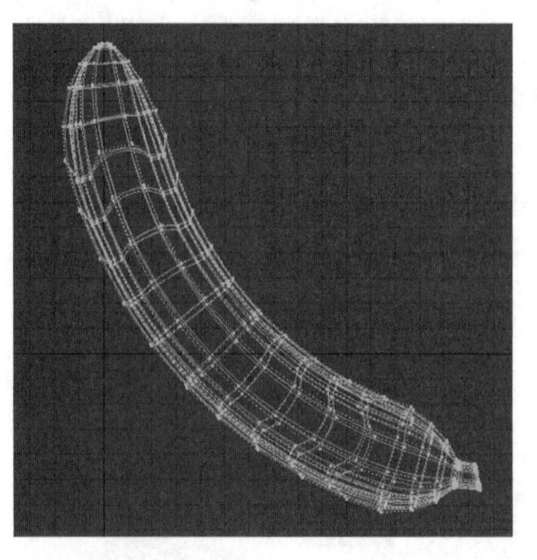

Figure 8.29 Bend the banana as you like and add a surface to it.

At this point, you can adjust the model as you like. Perhaps the banana made here is too fat. No problem. Undo the bend, then using the Size tool in the Back view, adjust the banana. Then, bend again. You can also use the right mouse button to lasso-select any ring of points around the banana, and then size them to add imperfections in the shape, and so on.

This project showed you how a simple box can be made into an organic shape. LightWave's edge tools, multiply tools, and basic modification tools allow you to easily create any shape you like. Add to that Catmull-Clark subdivisions and you can work without having to keep your model to three or four vertices.

This is just the first part of the still-life project, but also the longest. The next projects will have you model some additional fruit such as an orange and grapes. From there, you'll build a bowl and a set for the objects.

Orange You Glad You Got This Book?

Wow, these project titles are lame, but it's just so easy to make stupid jokes. Why should modeling fruit be so serious? This next project will show you how to model an orange. Sure, it's just a ball, but there are a few small details you'll add to help "sell" it.

Exercise 8.2 Model an Orange with the Multishift and Magnet Tools

1. In Modeler, be sure your banana from the previous project is saved. Then, from the File drop-down menu at the top of the interface, select New Object.
2. Creating an orange is easy, and most of its detail will come from surfacing. But there are a few things you'll do now. First, on the Create tab, select the Ball command.
3. Holding the Control key to constrain all axes, click and drag in the Top view to draw out a ball on the Y-axis. This should be about 3 m in size.
4. Still holding the Control key, click and drag in either the Back or Right view. Alternatively, you can draw out at once in the Perspective view.
5. Press the spacebar to commit to the new object. **Figure 8.30** (on the next page) shows the model.
6. Press **F2** to center the object at the origin. Press **a** to bring the model to view.

Figure 8.30 Create a ball with a radius of 3 m on every axis.

7. Taking a look at the top of the ball, you can see how the geometry all comes together. It's not that smooth and useful in many situations, but for an orange, these "poles" at the top of the ball can help create the detail. You want to select five areas of edges at the top of the ball. Starting from the center point, and making sure you're in Edge selection mode, click to select the edges, as shown in **Figure 8.31**.

Figure 8.31 Select two edges from the center point at the top of the ball. Do this five times.

NOTE

When selecting the edges at the top of the ball, be careful not to select the edges at the bottom of the ball. This will happen if you use a Wireframe view to select. Instead, select the edges in a wireframe shaded view, such as the Perspective view. Pressing Shift+A to fit the selection to view will also help you see if you have more selected than you should.

8. The selected edges do not need to be even and, in fact, shouldn't be. These edges will become the area where the stem will be. With the edges selected, press Control+B for EdgeBevel and bevel them about 20 mm, as shown in **Figure 8.32**.

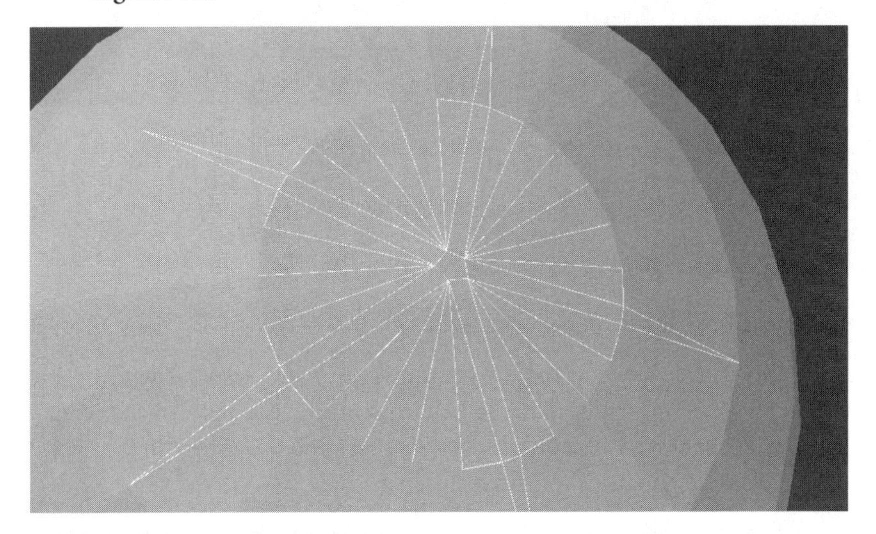

Figure 8.32 Bevel the selected edges.

9. Turn off EdgeBevel, and then choose Sel Switch from the Select drop-down menu. This changes the selected edges to selected polygons. Be sure to deselect any unwanted selections. You might have a few extra outside of the initial edge areas.
10. Using the Multishift tool from the Multiply tab, click and drag to bevel the selected polygons just a bit. Bevel them about 5.8 mm for the Inset, and 4 mm for the Shift. **Figure 8.33** shows the operation.
11. Turn off the Multishift tool. The polygons will still be selected, and you'll adjust them next.
12. Save your orange!
13. Click the Modify tab and select the Magnet tool. This will give you the effect of the Drag tool, but with a falloff.
14. Right-click (Control-click on the Mac) in the Top view and drag. You'll see a blue outline appear (**Figure 8.34** on the next page). This determines the amount of influence the Magnet tool will have.

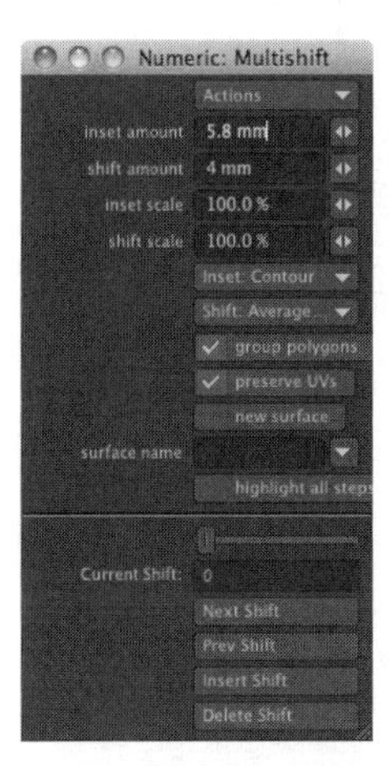

Figure 8.33 Bevel the selected polygons with the Multishift tool.

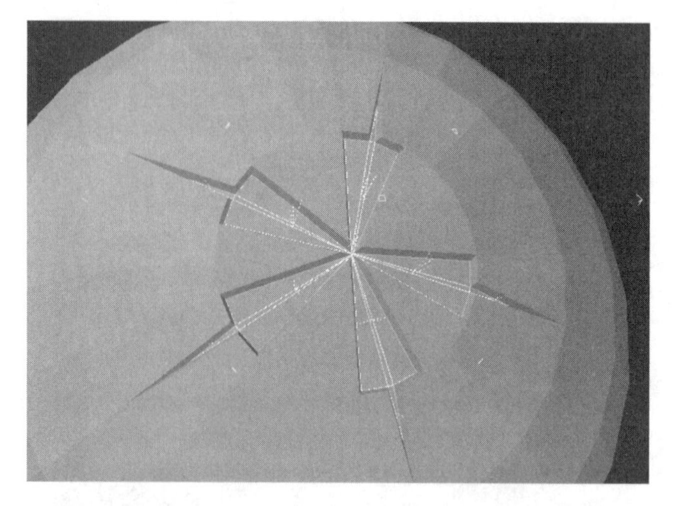

Figure 8.34 Using the right mouse button with the Magnet tool, you tell Modeler how much influence the tool has.

15. Click and drag down on the selected polygons in the Back view. Remember, this is a drag tool with a falloff, so what you'll see is the polygons being moved, but only within the circumference area you specified with the right mouse button. **Figure 8.35** shows the operation.

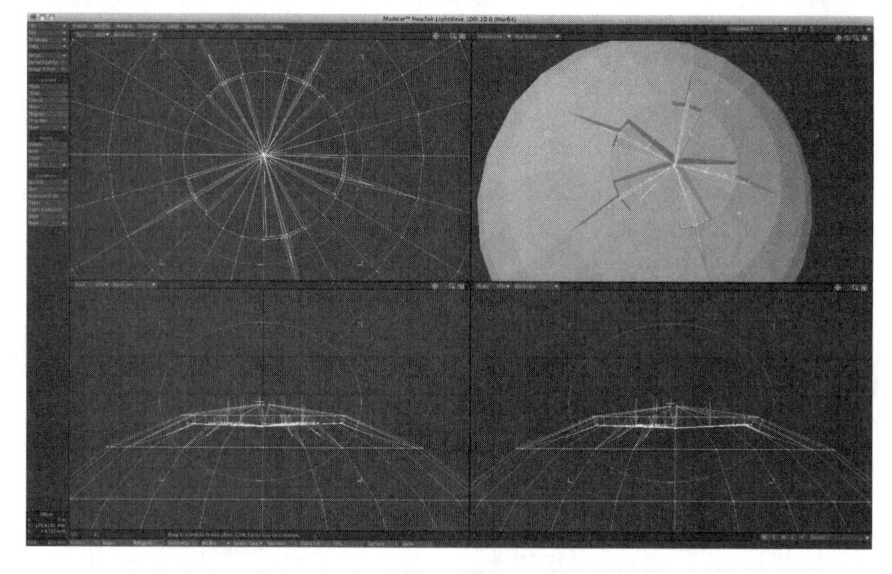

Figure 8.35 Use the Magnet tool to bring just the center of the selected polygons down into the orange.

16. Turn off the Magnet tool (press /) and then deselect the polygons. Save the object. Then, press the Tab key to turn on subdivision surface mode. You should still be using Catmull-Clark subdivisions (**Figure 8.36**).

Figure 8.36 With Catmull-Clark subdivisions applied, the bevels at the top of the orange start to shape up.

17. Press Control+T to turn on the Drag tool. Now, take some time and click and drag the points around the top of the orange to smooth out the beveled areas. Just shape it, and clean it up so that the bevels are more separations in the skin rather than sharp cuts (**Figure 8.37**).

Figure 8.37 Use the Drag tool to adjust the shape of the orange.

18. Save your model when you're done tweaking. Then, note that the rest of the orange is simply too round. You need to shape it slightly. Use the Magnet tool again, but this time, set the range of influence (with the right mouse button) to encompass most of the orange. Then, with the left mouse, click to effectively push parts of the orange to shape it. **Figure 8.38** shows the effect.

Figure 8.38 Use the Magnet tool to shape the orange, or basically deform it a bit, so it's not so perfectly round.

19. Press **q** to call up the Change Surface dialog box. Create a surface name of **Orange** for the object and give it a little color. Save your work.

Much of the orange's surface will really come from texturing, which you'll do later, so be sure to refer to Chapter 3, "Texture Creation." But the initial shape is also important, as you've seen in this project. Now, let's move on to using a few more modeling tools to create grapes.

Create a Cluster of Grapes

This next project will show you how to create a cluster of grapes in LightWave 10 Modeler. Later, you'll call up this object and place it in a large bowl that you'll model, along with the banana and orange.

Exercise 8.3 Bunches of Fun with the Clone and Magic Bevel Tools

1. Save anything you've been working on, and from the File drop-down menu, select New Object.

   You might have noticed that you're not building with layers in these projects. You could if you wanted to—create the banana in one layer, the orange in another, and the grapes in a third layer. But instead, you're building entirely new objects. This is good because these objects can be used to build your 3D library, as they are saved as individual objects. It also helps eliminate any confusion as to what you're working on, and for this project, you'll use multiple layers to help the modeling process. Having multiple objects in different layers might make your life difficult with the upcoming steps.

2. On the Create tab, select the Ball tool. Create a ball the same size as you did in the previous project (when you created the orange). Press **F2** to center the ball. **Figure 8.39** shows the ball.

3. Press **h** to activate the Stretch tool, and then click in the Back view and drag up slightly to elongate the ball. **Figure 8.40** shows the result.

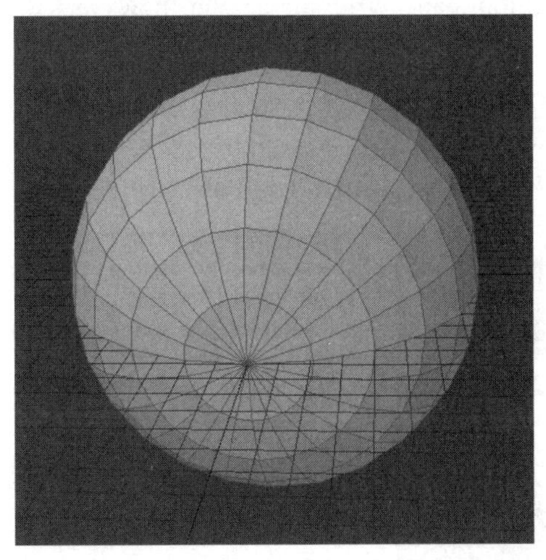

Figure 8.39 Begin creating grapes by making a simple ball.

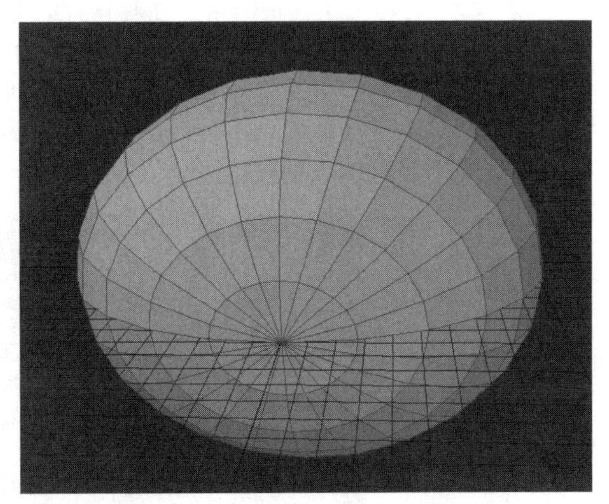

Figure 8.40 Use the Stretch tool to elongate the ball.

4. Click a new layer at the top right of the interface. Place the ball as a background layer by clicking beneath the slash mark in the first layer.

5. On the Create tab, click the Random Points tool in the Points category. In the panel that appears, enter **35** in the Points field and then check on Sphere and Falloff, as shown in **Figure 8.41**.

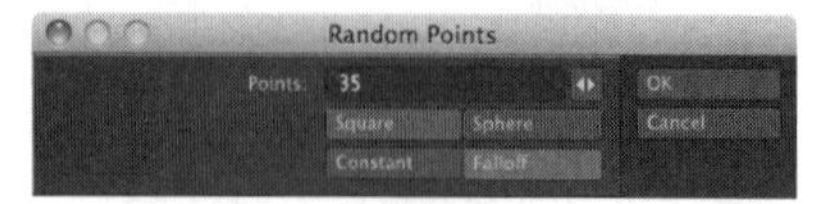

Figure 8.41 Use the Random Points tool to create a clump of points.

6. You'll see a group of points created in the views. The points might be hard to see, but there's a way you can adjust that in Modeler. Press **d** to call up the Display Options panel. Click the Interface tab, and check Simple Wireframe Points. Set the Point Size to 3.5, as shown in **Figure 8.42**.

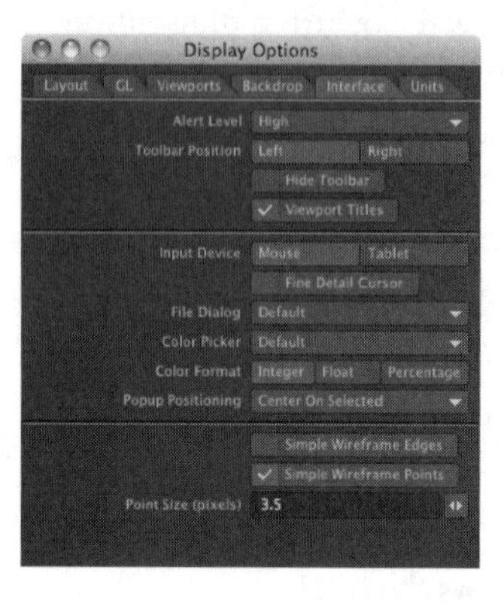

Figure 8.42 Increase the visual appearance of points in the Display Options panel.

7. Click OK to close the Display Options panel. With these points now created, press ' (the apostrophe key) to reverse layers. This puts Layer 1 in the foreground and Layer 2 in the background.

8. On the Multiply tab, click the More drop-down menu in the Duplicate category. Select Point Clone Plus. A large panel appears (**Figure 8.43**).

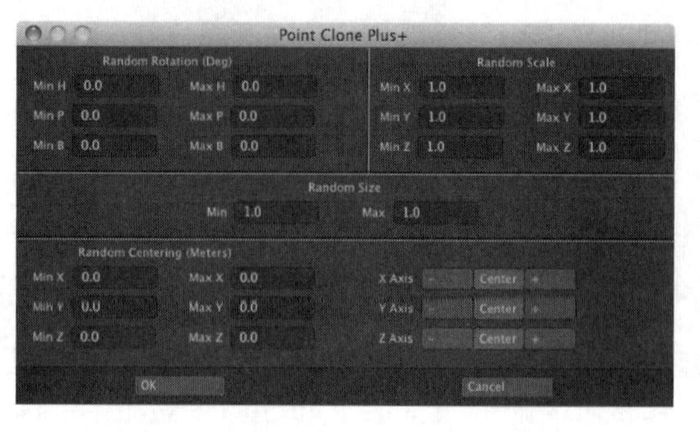

Figure 8.43 Once the Point Clone Plus tool is set up, you'll be able to duplicate your foreground object based on the point positions in the background layer.

9. Enter a few settings:

For Random Rotation:

- Min H: **20**
- Min B: **30**

For Random Size:

- Min: **0.75**
- Max: **1.0**

10. Leave all other settings at their defaults. Basically, the Point Clone Plus tool will generate duplicates of the foreground layer (the ball) based on the position of the points in the background layer. The values you've just set are simply adding some randomness to the duplicated objects. Click OK to close the Point Clone Plus tool and see what happens (**Figure 8.44**).

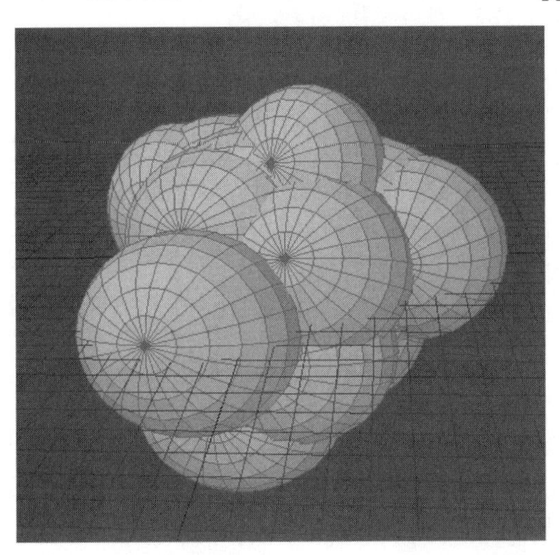

Figure 8.44 The Point Clone Plus tool creates 35 duplicates of the ball (grape), each with randomness throughout.

11. Wow! Those are some fat grapes! Why did this happen? The size of the initial ball was too large based on the position of the points. Click Control+Z (Command+Z on the Mac) to undo the Point Clone Plus operation.
12. Press Shift+H for the Size tool, and size down your grape about 30 percent. Then, rerun the Point Clone Plus tool. The settings you've entered will still be there. Click OK, and you'll see a clump of grapes, as in **Figure 8.45**.

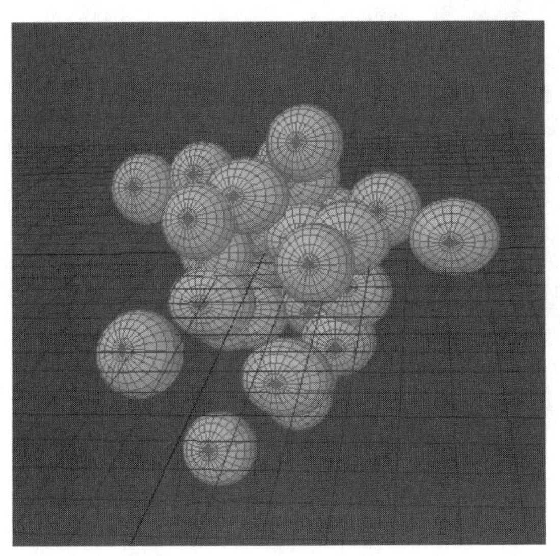

Figure 8.45 Using Point Clone Plus along with a ball has created a clump of grapes.

13. A few grapes might be overlapping other grapes, and some might be floating too far out from the rest. You can easily move these with a few steps. Making sure you're in Polygons selection mode, click once on a grape. Then press the right bracket key, the shortcut for the Select Connected command. Every polygon connected to that selection (the rest of the individual grape) is now selected. Press **t** and move the grape.
14. Feel free to resize, rotate, and adjust the grapes as needed. You don't need to be too precise because these grapes will end up in a bowl, but if you plan to use them later for something more close-up, try to align them more accurately so that none are overlapping. If you feel you need an additional grape or two, select one, press Control+C to copy, move the selected grape, and then press Control+V to paste.
15. To deselect, press the / (forward slash) key.
16. Continue adjusting the grape positions as you like, and remember to save your work.
17. Press **q** to open the Change Surface dialog box. Create a surface named **Grapes**, and give it a bit of color. Perhaps you prefer red grapes over green seedless? Click OK to close the panel and save your object.
18. To create a stem for added impact, go to a new layer, leaving the grapes in a background layer. This process can get tedious to make a branch extend from each grape. However, it's easy to create the initial look, starting with a box.
19. Create a small box just above the clump of grapes in the new layer, as shown in **Figure 8.46**.

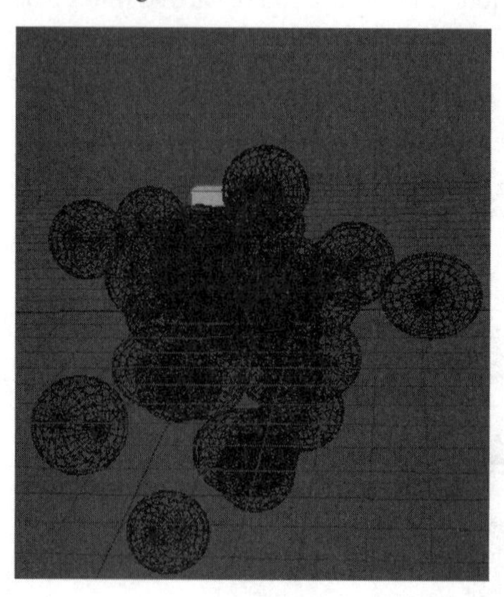

Figure 8.46 To begin creating the stem for the grapes, build a small box above the grapes in a new layer.

20. Select just the bottom polygon of the box, as shown in **Figure 8.47**.

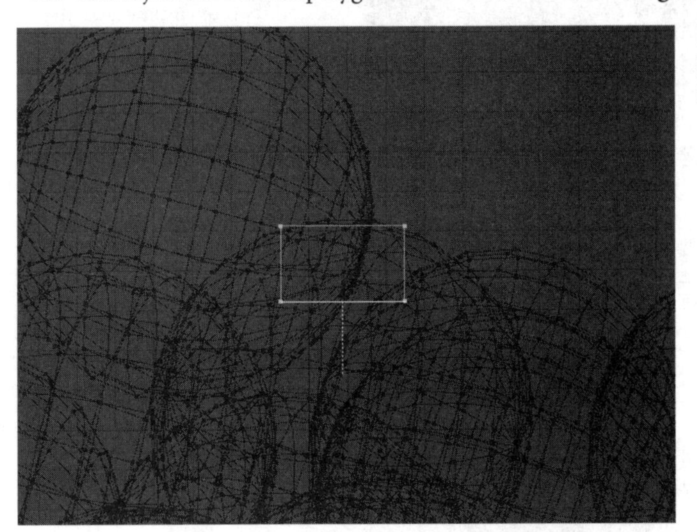

Figure 8.47 Select just the bottom single polygon of the box.

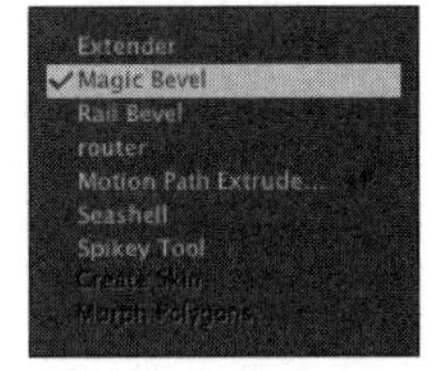

Figure 8.48 Choose the Magic Bevel tool from the Multiply tab's Extend category.

21. Click the Multiply tab, then click the More drop-down menu in the Extend category and select Magic Bevel, as shown in **Figure 8.48**.
22. When you turn on the Magic Bevel tool, you'll see small circles appear around the box (**Figure 8.49**).
23. Click and drag the circle at the bottom of the box, and drag downward into the grapes. You can do this in the Back or Right view. Feel free to move the mouse slightly to create a curvature. **Figure 8.50** shows the result.

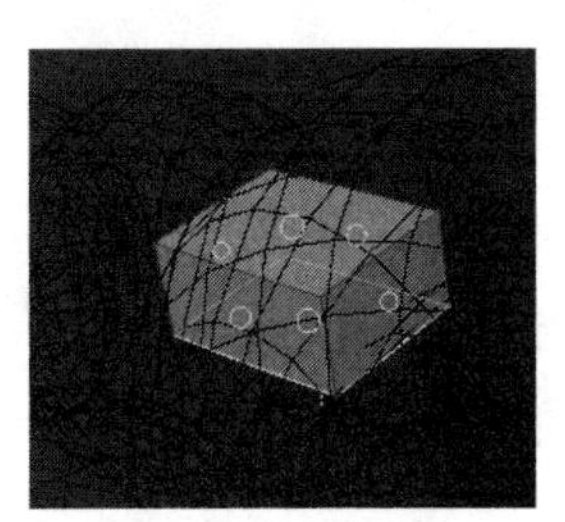

Figure 8.49 Magic Bevel begins with small circles on each polygon.

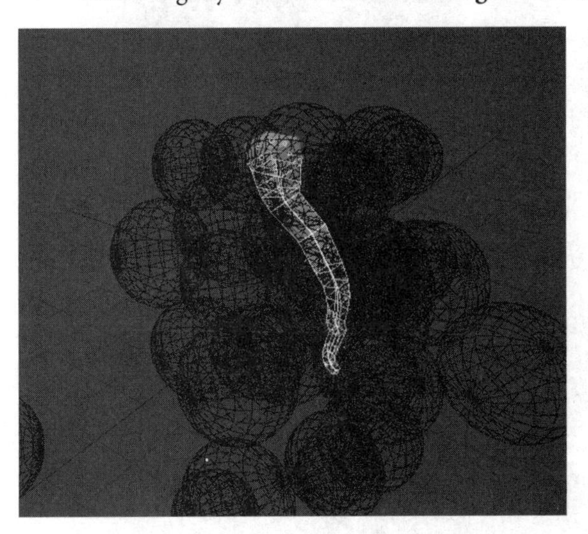

Figure 8.50 Click and drag the bottom circle to instantly create a multiple-beveled object.

24. Press the spacebar to turn off the Magic Bevel tool. Then, click its button to turn it on again. You'll now see circles for the Magic Bevel on each of the newly created polygons (**Figure 8.51** on the next page).

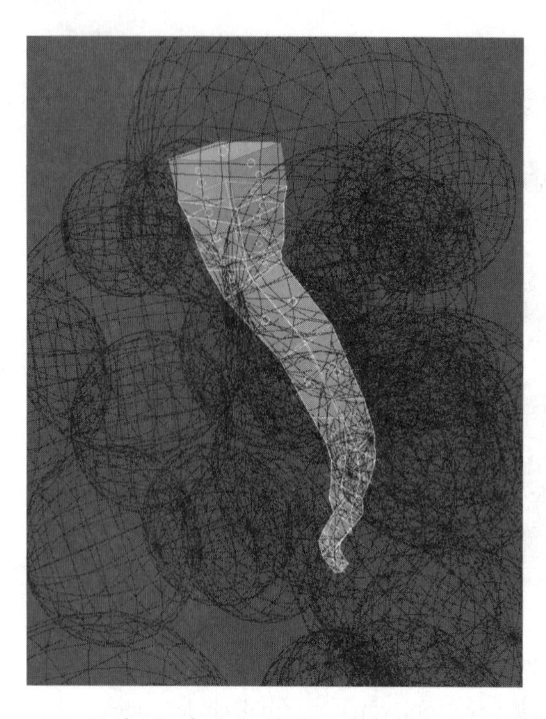

Figure 8.51 Turning Magic Bevel off and then on again resets the tool so you can apply it to newly created geometry.

25. In the Back view, click and drag downward from the middle of the stem, creating another branch, like the one shown in **Figure 8.52**.

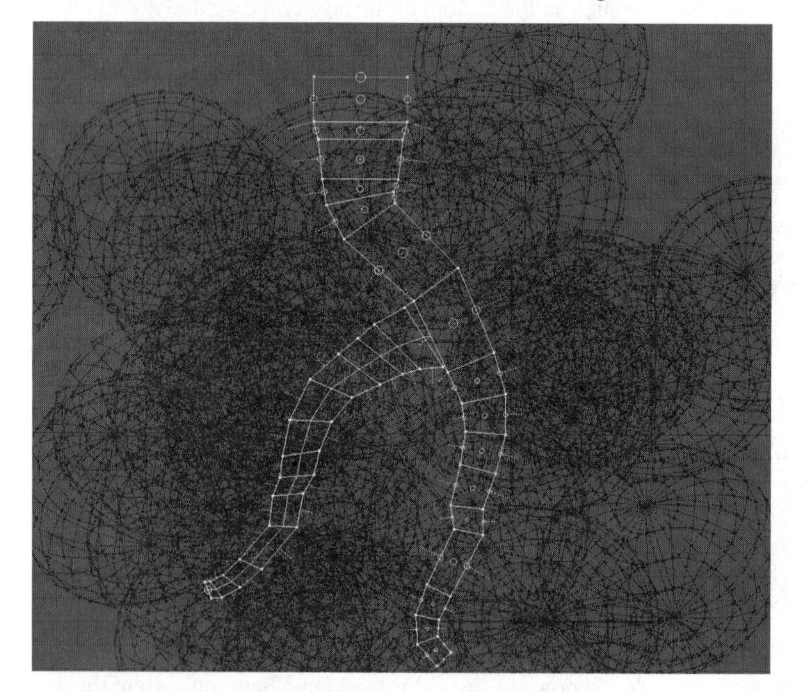

Figure 8.52 Create another branch from the middle of the original stem.

26. In the Right view, create another stem.

27. From here, you can apply new Magic Bevels to the stems you've created. If you open the Numeric panel, you can adjust their scale. Changing the value to 100% prevents the bevel from tapering as it extends when you click and drag. You can also choose to spin the bevels as they are created.

28. After you've created a few branches, press the spacebar to turn off the Magic Bevel tool. Then, press / to deselect.

29. Make sure Subpatch is selected in the SubD-Type drop-down list at the bottom of the Modeler interface, and then press the Tab key. You'll see the beveled box become smooth (**Figure 8.53**). Subpatch is the LightWave native subdivision surface setting and it likes polygons made up of three or four points. However, there are times when polygons within models are made for more than three or four points, and for those, you would choose the Catmull-Clark subdivision option.

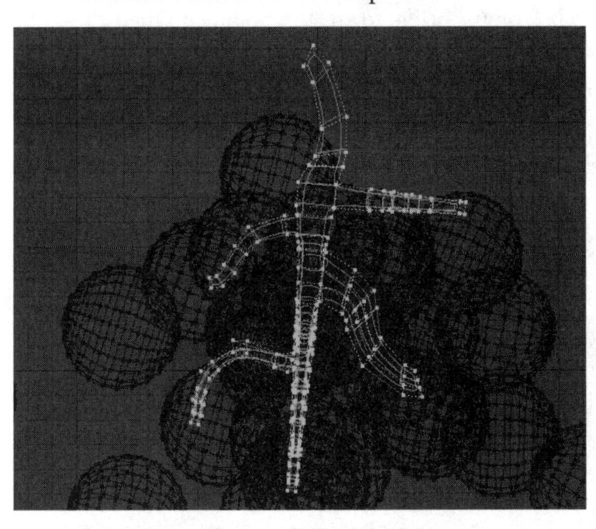

Figure 8.53 Apply subdivision surfaces to the stem by pressing the Tab key.

30. You can adjust points as you like, and even bevel a single polygon on the stem before you apply a Magic Bevel, to help determine the shape. When you've finished shaping the stem, assign it a surface using the Change Surface dialog box (press **q**).

31. Press Control+X (Command+X on the Mac) to cut the stem from the current layer. Switch to the grape layer, then press Control+V (Command+V on the Mac) to paste it. Save your object.

NOTE

You can also apply subdivision surfaces to the grapes to smooth them out.

The stem is not attached to the grapes, but you can connect it up if you like. Use the Magic Bevel tool to drag a stem bevel right to each grape, or move the grapes around to touch the stem, but keep in mind that the stem is not going to be seen too closely in the final shot, since the grapes will be sitting in a bowl. And hey, speaking of bowls, let's make one!

Building a Fruit Bowl

Building a fruit bowl doesn't sound very exciting, does it? This next project, while not glamorous or too complex, is nevertheless important for your still-life scene. Furthermore, you can use the lathing technique it demonstrates to build plates, glasses, and other similar vessels.

Exercise 8.4 Sculpting with Splines and the Lathe Tool

1. From the File menu in Modeler, select New Object.
2. Press the comma key three times to zoom the Modeler view. This changes the overall grid to 2 m. You can see the grid size in the lower-left corner of the interface.
3. On the Create tab, select the Spline Draw tool in the Curves tools category.
4. In the Back viewport, click on the origin to create a point, and then click a few grids to the right along the X-axis, then again slightly above that, and so on, until you have an arc of nine or ten points that provides a cross-section of the bowl's outer profile, from its center on the Y-axis to its outer rim on the right (**Figure 8.54**).
5. Click a little to the left of your last point to create a lip for your bowl, then click a new series of points, more or less parallel to the first set, to shape the bowl's inner-surface profile, ending back at the Y-axis (**Figure 8.55**).

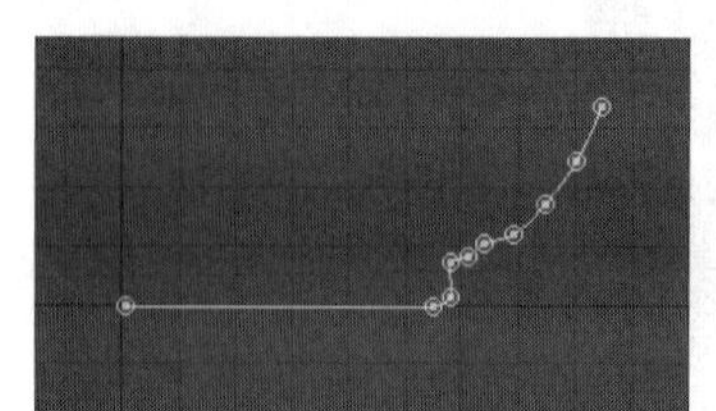

Figure 8.54 Using the Spline Draw tool, you can begin creating a curve to model a bowl.

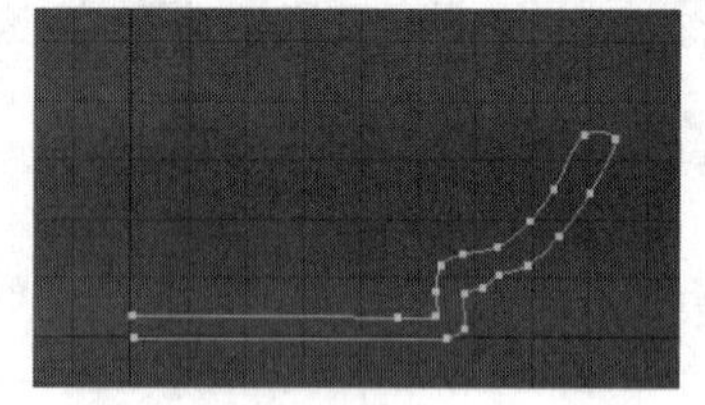

Figure 8.55 Continue creating points to finish building the cross-section of the bowl.

NOTE

If you find that it's difficult to create a point close to another point, just click a bit farther away, and then drag the point in closer to the desired position.

6. Before you commit to this curve, you can click and drag any point you've created to adjust it. Be careful to precisely click on any point you want to adjust. Clicking *near* a point will add a new one and continue your curve.
7. When you've got the points along the curve positioned as you like, press the spacebar to turn off the Spline Draw tool.
8. Switch to Points selection mode, and select the two endpoints on the Y-axis.
9. Press **v** to open the Set Value dialog box. Choose X for the Axis, and set the value to 0 m. Click OK, and the selected points will be positioned exactly at the origin. This is important for the upcoming steps.
10. Deselect the two points.

11. From the Multiply tab, select the Lathe tool from the Extend category.
12. Press **n** to open the Numeric panel, and you'll quickly see the tool activate. The default axis for the lathe is the Y-axis, so that's good! You'll also see that End Angle is set to 360 degrees; that's also good, because we want to apply the lathed shape through a full circular sweep. (If you'd wanted to make a "half-bowl" [or Hollywood Bowl] shape instead of a fruit bowl, you could have set End Angle to 180 degrees.) The only default setting you need to change is Sides, from 24 to about 48. This will help smooth out the object, as shown in **Figure 8.56**.

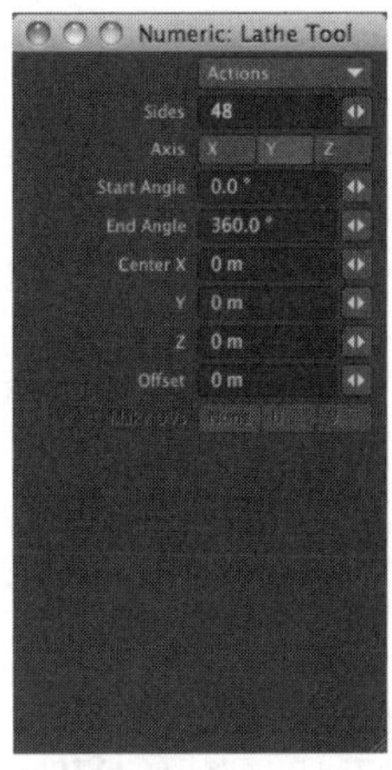

Figure 8.56 Changing the Sides value to 48 adds more detail to the lathed curve.

13. Press the spacebar to turn off the Lathe tool. Use the Change Surfaces panel (press **q**) to give it the surface name **Bowl** (how original!), and then save the object. **Figure 8.57** shows the final bowl.

Figure 8.57 The final fruit bowl, before it's filled up with tasty treats.

14. Save your bowl (press **s**).

    Now that you've seen how the Lathe tool works, can you see why it was important to use the Set Value dialog box to set those two endpoints? We lathed around the Y-axis, and setting the X-values of the endpoints to 0 ensured that they'd lie on that axis, at the bowl's exact center. Positive X-values for the endpoints would have created a hole in the bowl, and negative X-values would have caused the center of the bowl to overlap itself, complicating the model needlessly. Neither error would really be noticeable once fruit is placed in the bowl, but you should learn to build items like this the right way.

Perhaps you want to make a bottle or a glass? Use this exact process for a clean, smooth model. You can also use a Spline Curve with the Lathe tool to create very tight but smooth corners—sort of the same effect as beveling an edge, but with less work.

Now, let's fill up the bowl.

Exercise 8.5 Filling a Fruit Bowl

You could use Modeler to arrange your still life by loading each piece of fruit and the bowl and pasting them each into separate object layers, but you'll have more flexibility if you simply load each object into a scene in Layout and position them there.

1. Open LightWave Layout and click the Items tab. From the Load category, select Object. When the Load Object dialog box appears, you can select all of the objects you created in this chapter: the banana, the orange, the grapes, and the bowl. Click OK to load them. **Figure 8.58** shows the objects loaded from the Perspective view.

Figure 8.58 The four objects you created in this chapter are loaded into LightWave Layout.

2. The objects aren't quite in the bowl, are they? That's OK—you can easily position them now. First, select the Orange object. Press Shift+H to size the object. Scale it up to about 1.8. You can click and drag to size it, and watch the values in the lower-left corner of the interface.
3. Note that your Auto Key should be on and the timeline slider at frame 0. Once the orange is up to size, press **t** to select the Move tool. Move the orange up on the Y-axis until it rests on the bottom of the bowl. You can then move it off to one side of the bowl.
4. With the orange still selected, press Control+C to activate the Clone tool. When the Clone dialog box appears, enter **5** to make five copies of the orange.
5. You can use the up arrow on your keyboard to select each orange copy. Then, move each one to fill the bowl, as in **Figure 8.59**. Don't be afraid to rotate them for a more random look, and place one on top of another.

Figure 8.59 Clone the orange and position the copies in the bowl using the Move and Rotate tools.

6. Save your scene by pressing Shift+S. Name the scene **FruitBowlSetup** or something similar.
7. Now take your banana and position it on top of the orange. Remember that when you select the Move and Rotate tools, you can use the handles to specifically control position on a desired axis. **Figure 8.60** shows the banana in place.

Figure 8.60 The banana you modeled is positioned on top of the oranges.

NOTE

When using the Move tool, dragging with the right mouse button constrains movements to the Y-axis. With the Rotate tool, dragging with the right mouse button constrains to the Bank channel.

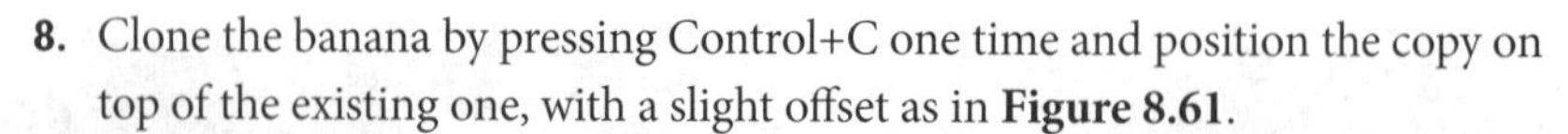

8. Clone the banana by pressing Control+C one time and position the copy on top of the existing one, with a slight offset as in **Figure 8.61**.

Figure 8.61 A second banana suddenly becomes top banana.

9. Finally, select the grapes and position them with the other fruit, resting on the oranges and the side of the bowl. Feel free to resize, rotate, and reposition the grapes until you like the way they look. **Figure 8.62** shows the bowl of fruit.

Figure 8.62 The bowl is now full of fruit in Light-Wave Layout.

10. Save your scene and hop back into LightWave Modeler. You can press **F12** to get there.

You can see that working in Layout to position, size, and clone the objects is a bit easier than doing so in Modeler. You can quickly clone, position, and rotate in real time. Perhaps more to the point, Layout is where you'll render the final scene. Now there's one more thing to do: Create a set for the fruit bowl.

Building a Set for the Still Life

When creating a still-life scene, you need more than just a bowl of fruit. You can't just have a bowl of fruit floating in 3D space. Instead, you can use a cloth. Yes, LightWave can create cloth, and in this exercise, you'll model it. In this project, you're not animating the cloth, but it'll be fun to model it.

Exercise 8.6 Modeling a Tablecloth

1. In LightWave Modeler, create a new object.
2. Create a box in the Back viewport, specifying **5 m** for the width and **8 m** for the height. For the segments, enter **8** for the X, **11** for the Y, and **1** for the Z, as shown in **Figure 8.63**.
3. Turn off the Box tool. If you can't see your object in the Perspective view, make sure the polygons are facing toward the negative Z-axis. You can press **f** to flip them.
4. Press the Tab key to activate subdivision surfaces for the object.
5. Make sure you're in Polygons selection mode, and using the right mouse button, lasso-select around the top two-thirds of the polygons, as shown in **Figure 8.64**.

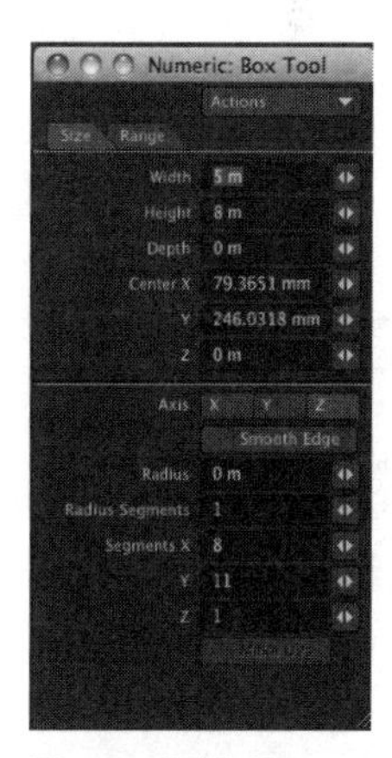

Figure 8.63 Create a tall, flat box with multiple segments to begin making your cloth.

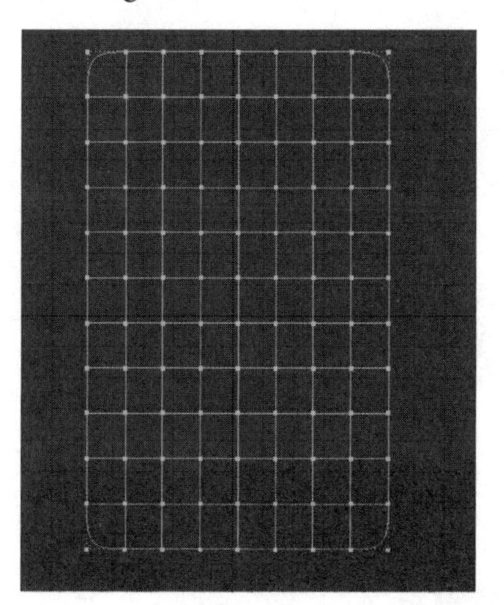

Figure 8.64 Lasso-select the top two-thirds of the box.

6. On the Modify tab, select the Rotate tool. Make sure your Action Center is set to Mouse from the Modes drop-down menu at the bottom of the interface. Then, in the Right view, click and drag at the very bottom of the selection, and bend the selected polygons back on the Z-axis. **Figure 8.65** shows the example.

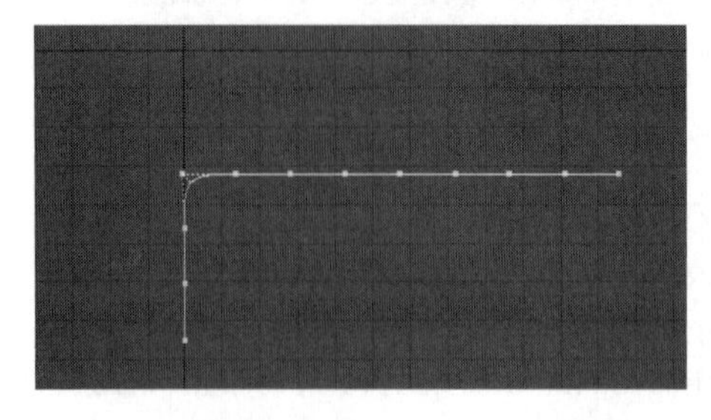

Figure 8.65 Using the Rotate tool, the tall box is bent backward to create a smooth fold.

7. The reason you're rotating the selection rather than bending is that you want to create a tabletop look. The Rotate tool, in combination with the subdivisional surface, makes a tight, smooth edge. Now, turn off the Rotate tool, and then deselect the middle third set of polygons, so that only the top third remains selected.
8. Activate the Rotate tool again (press **y**) and then click on the base of the selection to rotate the selection upward. Don't rotate a full 90 degrees; give it just a bit of a pitch (**Figure 8.66**).

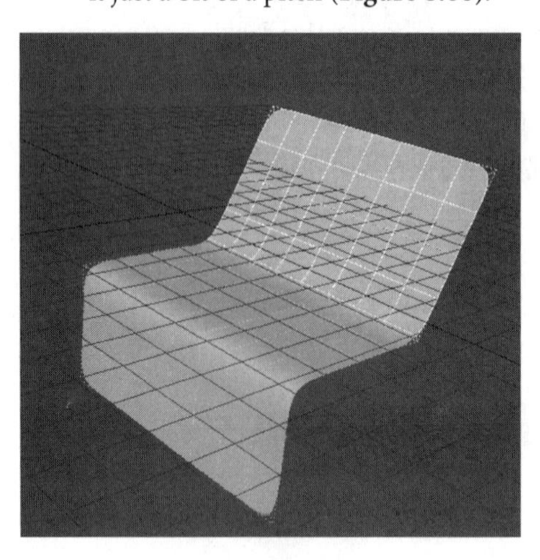

Figure 8.66 Rotate the top third of the object upward to create the back of the tabletop set.

9. Deselect the polygons, apply a surface name to the object using the Change Surfaces dialog box (press **q**), and then save it as **ClothSet** or something similar.

10. Select the second row of polygons from the top, as shown in **Figure 8.67**.

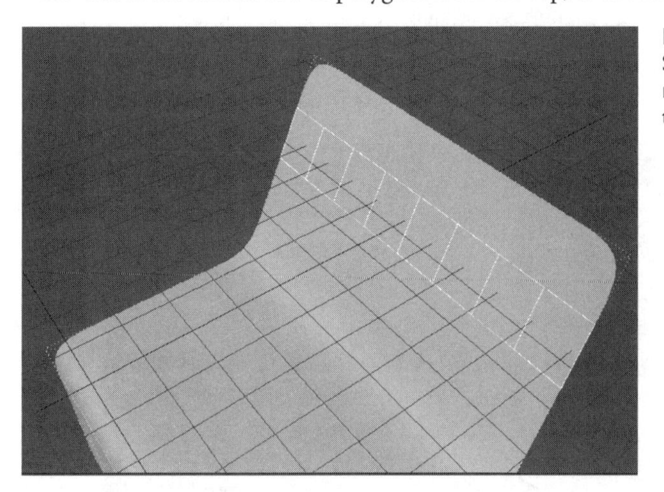

Figure 8.67
Select the second row of polygons from the top of the set.

11. On the Multiply tab, select QuickCut 1 from the More drop-down list under the Subdivide category. The selected polygon will be split in two, and the new points will automatically be selected.
12. With the points selected, press **t** to activate the Move tool, and then move the selected points forward along the Z-axis just a bit, to create a bump in the cloth.
13. Press **y** and, in the Back view window, rotate the selection slightly (**Figure 8.68**).

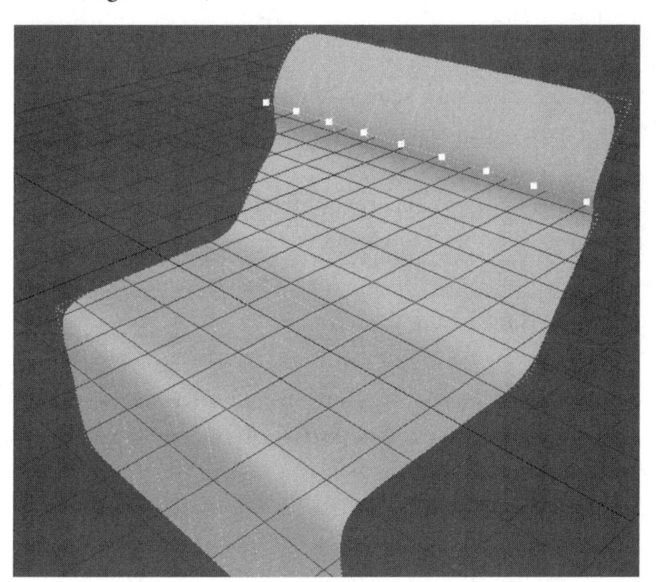

Figure 8.68
Move and rotate the split row of points to create a bump in the cloth.

14. Click the Polygons selection-mode button and Control-click each polygon in the row beneath the row of points you just adjusted to select the entire row.
15. Run the QuickCut 1 command again, and move the newly created points back toward the first bump, creating another ripple (**Figure 8.69**).

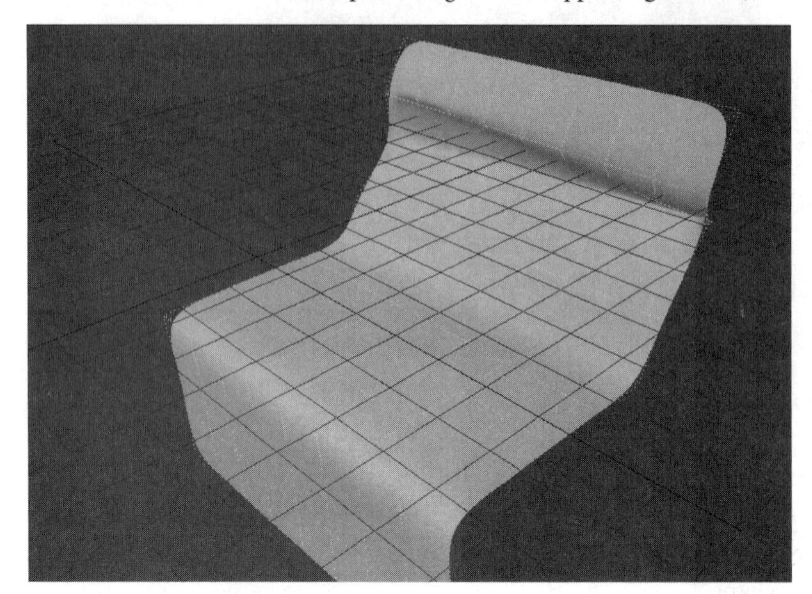

Figure 8.69 After another QuickCut operation, move the second row of points to help fold the cloth a bit more.

16. Save your model.

    From here, you can continue bending, quick cutting, and adjusting points to create folds in the cloth. You can use the Drag tool (Control+T) to click and drag any points for added adjustments. What makes this work is that you're adjusting the points of the model in a subdivision surface mode. That helps smooth out all the geometry, thus making a smooth cloth. When you've finished, save the object and send it to Layout. You can send it to Layout by using the command in the upper-right corner of the Modeler interface (click that small triangle to access the Send to Layout command). You can also just load it in Layout as you did with the fruit.

17. In Layout, position the set underneath the bowl of fruit. If you need to size the set, make sure Auto Key is enabled so that your changes are captured.
18. Be sure to check your cloth set position not only from the Perspective view, but from a Right or Left view as well. **Figure 8.70** shows the setup from the Perspective view.

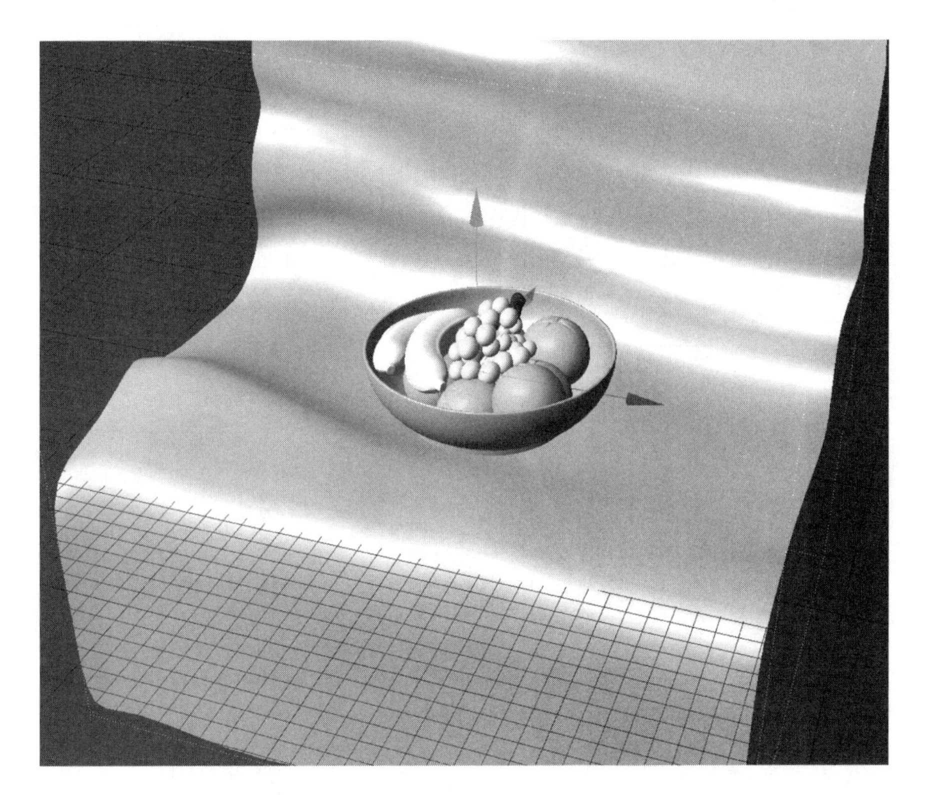

Figure 8.70 The modeled cloth is positioned and sized to fit under the bowl of fruit, in Layout.

19. Save your scene.

There you have it! Still life! Well, it's not complete yet. LightWave offers you control to model just about anything you want. There are many ways to build objects, and this chapter gave you a very good overview of the toolset and how it can be used to create smooth organic shapes. You can take the exercises here even further by modeling more fruit, such as a pear or an apple. How about taking the lesson of the bowl and creating a wine bottle to add to the scene?

The Next Step

What's really going to make this shot stand out is the texturing, lighting, and rendering. You'll be doing all of this soon, but before you move on to these key Layout features, stay in modeling mode and learn how to create more detailed objects in the next chapter.

Chapter 9

Particle Animation

Particle animation, collisions, dynamics. What are these terms, so often thrown around in the 3D world? They are your tools for creating cool special effects in LightWave layout. People often equate the term *particle* with 3D animations involving small dots, such as fireworks. Although you can create sparklers and animated dust using particles in LightWave, that's only the beginning. Particles are also used to generate wisps of smoke, fire, snow flurries, and even swarming bees. For many 3D-animation pros, the enhanced particle tools, and the new dynamics capabilities introduced in LightWave 10 (and discussed in detail in this and the next chapter, "Dynamics in Motion"), are enough by themselves to justify the cost of the software. You might hear the term *dynamics* often in computer graphics. Without getting too technical, the concept of dynamics in LightWave refers to the ability of animated objects to influence one another's motion and interact naturally. But more than their value, these tools give you control and flexibility over the types of images and animations you can create. That, my friends, is what makes LightWave great!

This chapter takes you into the world of LightWave particle animation. We'll start with the basics so you can familiarize yourself with how the particle tools function in Layout. From there, we'll apply surfacing to particles using HyperVoxels to create smoke, fire, and water effects. Then we'll explore how you can apply dynamics, such as wind and collisions, to the particles. In this chapter, you'll learn about the following:

- Working with particles in LightWave 10
- Creating surfaces for particles using HyperVoxels
- Using dynamics to change particle motions

NOTE

To be clear, particles are not objects, points, splines, or curves. However, if you create an emitter as a "Partigon" you will generate single-point polygons.

Particles In LightWave

Many 3D pros think you need to run out and buy the expensive stand-alone particle creation tools to get decent particle animation. Although dedicated tools have their benefits, you'll see from the following project that you can achieve exceptional particle animation using nothing but Layout. For most everyday animation projects, the robust, easy-to-use particle engine in LightWave is all you need.

NOTE

The LightWave HyperVoxels tool lets you add smoke-like surfaces to particles, as well as more solid forms for things like water, rocks, and gaseous liquids. HyperVoxels apply to points of an object or to particles.

Creating a Basic Particle-Motion Scene

In this project, you don't create anything with the particles; you merely apply them to a scene to see how you can interactively adjust parameters for instant feedback.

Using Emitters

The first thing you should know is that for particles to "live" in a scene, they need an *emitter*. You can think of the emitter as a faucet where your particles spill out. The various settings within the particle control panel enable you to adjust how the particles come out, how many, how quickly, and so on. Standard LightWave particle emitters are nonrendering objects you place in your scene, but you can also designate any object as an emitter. A ghostly figure drifting through the air, for instance, might emit a smoke trail consisting of particles with HyperVoxels applied. There aren't any strict rules about when to use an object as an emitter and when to use a standard emitter; the task at hand usually determines your choice.

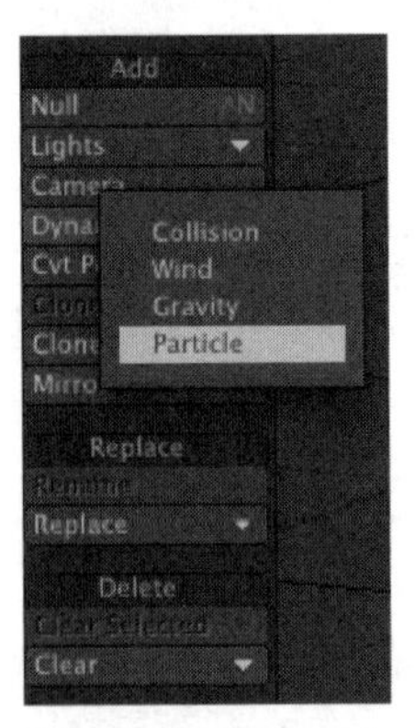

Figure 9.1 You add a particle emitter from the Add category of the Items tab, just as you would with an object, light, or camera.

Exercise 9.1 Create a Particle Emitter

1. Open LightWave Layout.
2. On the Items tab under the Add category, click the Dynamic Obj button and choose Particle, as in **Figure 9.1**. When the Add Particle Emitter panel appears, you could type a new name, but for now simply leave the default name, "Emitter" (**Figure 9.2**).

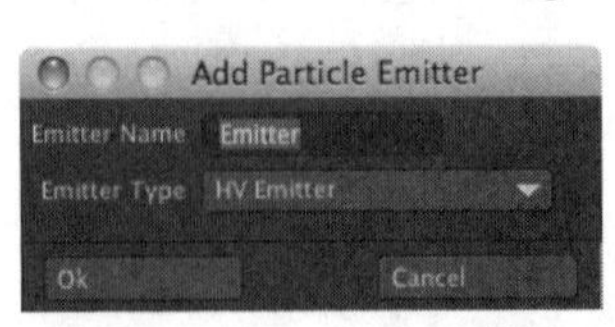

Figure 9.2 After an emitter is added, you can apply a name to it and tell LightWave to make it an HV emitter or a Partigon emitter.

3. Change the Emitter Type selection in the Add Particle Emitter panel from the default, HV Emitter, to Partigon.

   What's the significance of this change? An HV emitter generates points, which aren't rendered unless HyperVoxels are applied to them (hence the "HV" in the emitter name). HyperVoxels are a type of *volumetric effect*, which simulate fluid, diffuse materials within a defined physical volume, such as the cone of light generated by a streetlamp, or the confines of a room. HyperVoxels and other volumetric effects are used for rendering phenomena such as smoke and fog, which absorb and diffuse light without reflecting it directly—effects that cannot be approximated easily using traditional polygon-based modeling.

   A Partigon emitter, on the other hand, generates *single-point polygons*, particles that render without HyperVoxels. Partigons can cast and reflect light directly, and you can apply surface characteristics to them. Use Partigons to produce particle systems made up of discrete, tiny objects, such as snow, confetti, or the spray of a sparkler.

4. After the emitter is added, you'll see an outlined box in the Layout view, and the FX_Emitter panel will pop up (**Figure 9.3**). In the timeline at the lower right of the interface, set the last frame of the animation to **200**.

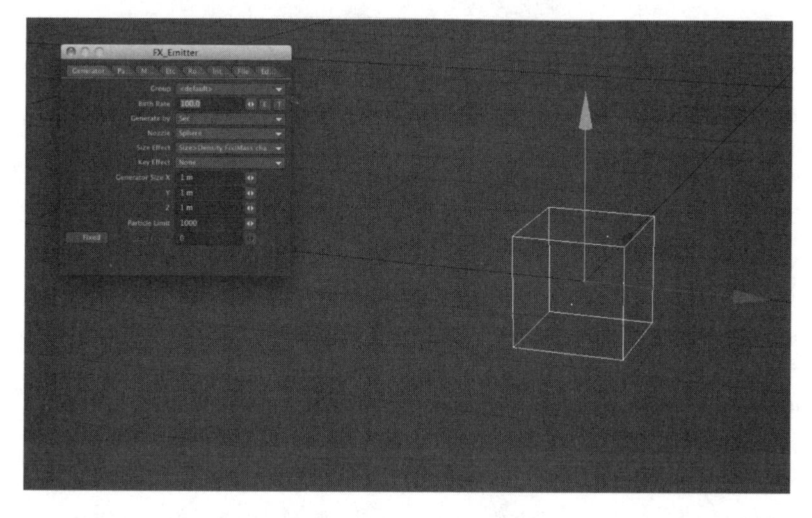

Figure 9.3 After a particle emitter is added to Layout, it's represented by a bounding box, and the FX_Emitter panel appears.

5. Make sure Auto Key is enabled; click the Auto Key button beneath the timeline if it's not.

   Before you move on, press **o** to open the General Options tab within the Preferences panel. Make sure that Modified Channels is selected in the Auto Key Create drop-down. This means that when Auto Key is turned on, it will automatically generate keyframes as you make positional or rotational changes at different points in time in Layout.

6. Back in Layout, make sure the emitter is selected and then press **t** to activate the Move tool.

7. Press the Play button and drag the emitter around in Layout. Look at that—instant particles (**Figure 9.4**)!

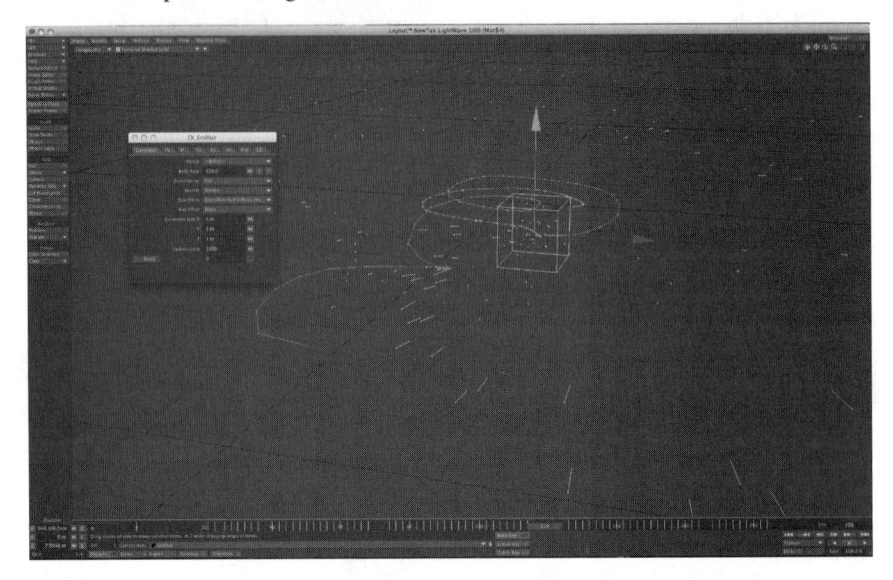

Figure 9.4 By using Auto Key with Auto Key Create set to Modified Channels, you ensure that your motions are recorded in real time in Layout. Moving the particle emitter around shows the spray of particles.

This effect is great for spraying particles in all directions, as you'd see in a sparkler or in water shaken from a just-bathed dog, but it lacks control. The particles fall out of the emitter without any rhyme or reason. For most other particle systems, such as a stream of smoke or a running faucet, you'll want your particles to flow in a more controlled fashion. You'll learn how to make that happen in the next exercise.

Controlling Particles

It isn't necessary to always move the particle emitter to see moving particles. The particles can move on their own in a variety of ways. This next section shows you how to create a particle stream to simulate smoke, and with minor modifications it is also good for water fountains, molten lava, gooey chocolate, and more.

Exercise 9.2 Controlling Particle Flow

1. Select Clear Scene from Layout's File drop-down. Make sure Auto Key is active, and then add a new particle emitter as you did in Exercise 9.1. Name it **Smoke** when the Add Particle Emitter dialog box appears.

2. For the Emitter Type setting in the Add Particle Emitter dialog box, choose HV Emitter.

   You'll notice that the particle emitter (named "Smoke") is a set size. You can scale it down to fit objects in your scene (**Figure 9.5**). With smoke, such as you'll be creating here, the emitter is often a small, concentrated point of origin, such as a pipe or cigar.

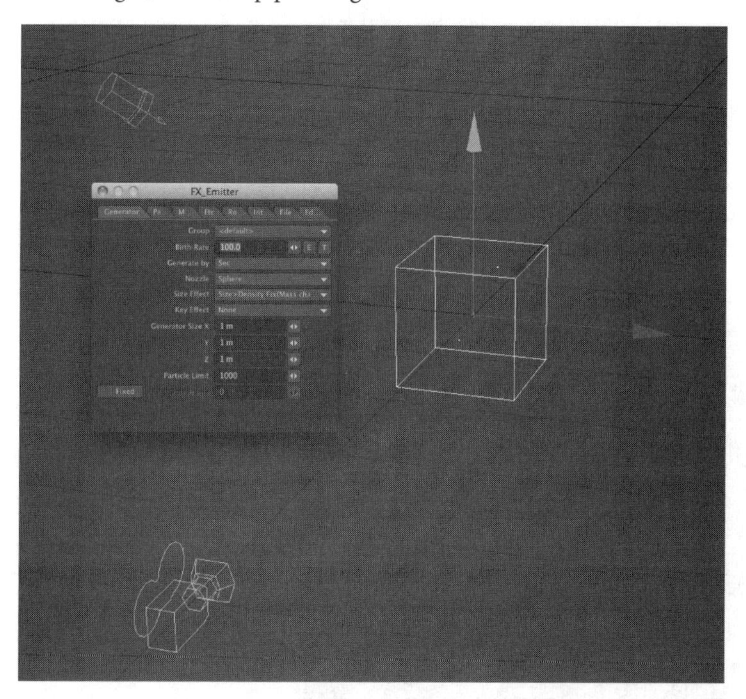

Figure 9.5 Adding a particle emitter to the scene gets you started, but first you'll need to scale it down.

3. When the FX_Emitter panel appears, move it aside as needed, so you can see the emitter in the scene. Set the last frame of the animation to **300** and move the timeline slider to frame 0.
4. In the Generator tab of the FX_Emitter panel, change the X, Y, and Z size values to 35 mm, as shown in **Figure 9.6**.

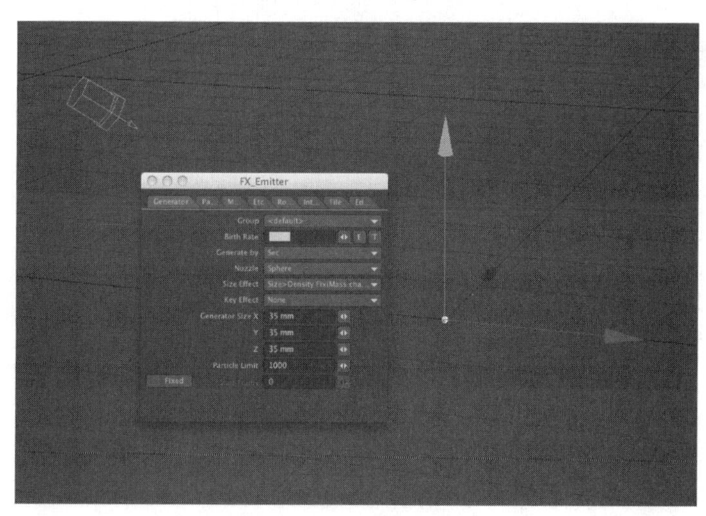

Figure 9.6 Scale the emitter's generator to a tiny 35 mm cube to begin creating smoke.

NOTE

Should you accidentally close the FX_Emitter panel, don't worry! Select the emitter item in Layout and press **p** to open the Object Properties panel. Click its Dynamics tab, and then click the item name that begins "FX_Emitter" in the list on that tab. You'll see all the controls, as in **Figure 9.7**. You can also find the FX_Emitter panel in the Additional list of plug-ins, on the Utilities tab.

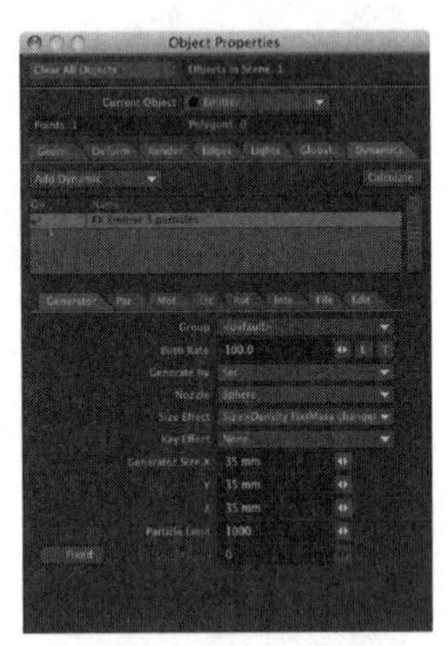

Figure 9.7 In case you accidentally (or intentionally) close the FX_Emitter control panel, you can find the panel again under the Dynamics tab within the Object Properties panel.

Changing the Generator Size in the FX_Emitter panel tells the emitter to be larger or smaller at the point where particles emerge. Changing the actual size of the emitter in Layout scales the emitter itself, not the area of particle generation.

5. In the FX_Emitter panel, click the Motion tab and bring the Velocity Y value to 400 mm, as in **Figure 9.8**. Press the Play button, in the lower-right corner of Layout, and you'll see the particles start to stream upward. Note that a negative velocity value on the Y-axis would send the particle stream downward.

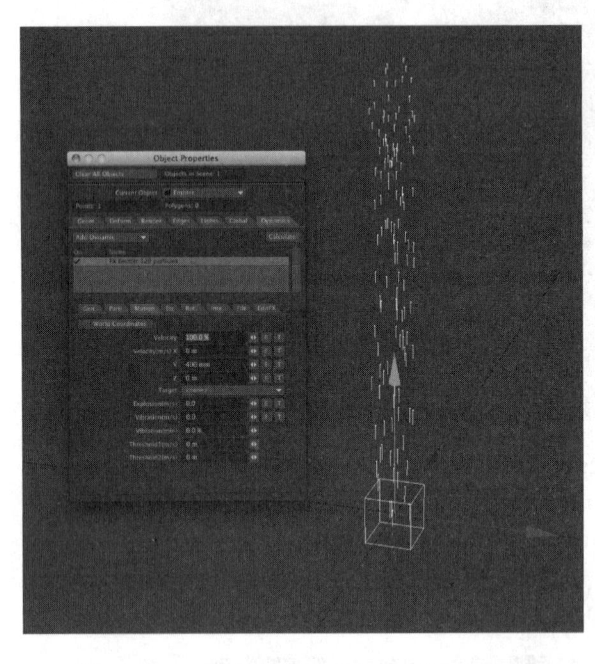

Figure 9.8 Increasing the Velocity value for the Y-axis shoots the particles upward.

You can see that the particle preview updates in real time as you adjust FX_Emitter settings. You can click and drag the arrow buttons to the right of a value for true interactivity. Play around with the Velocity values for X and Z to see how the particles are affected, and then revert to a Y velocity of 400 mm and X and Z velocities of 0.

6. Now that the particles are being generated in the right direction, move the camera around for a better view of the particle stream. Right now, we have an upward spray of points—not exactly wispy smoke.
7. Set the Birth Rate value to 60. This tells LightWave to emit, or "give birth" to, 60 particles per *x*, in which *x* represents the unit (second, frame, collision event, wind event) specified in the Generate By drop-down. For now, leave the Generate By unit set to Sec, so that 60 particles are generated every second.

8. Click the Motion tab and bring the Explosion value to 0.105, and you'll see the particles spray outward, as in **Figure 9.9**. Now try adding a little vibration. Set the Vibration (m/s) value to 0.195 and the particles have a bit of randomness—sort of a scattering effect.

NOTE

Remember that you can play the animation and make value changes to your particles at the same time. This is the best way to set up particle animations, because you can see exactly what your changes are affecting.

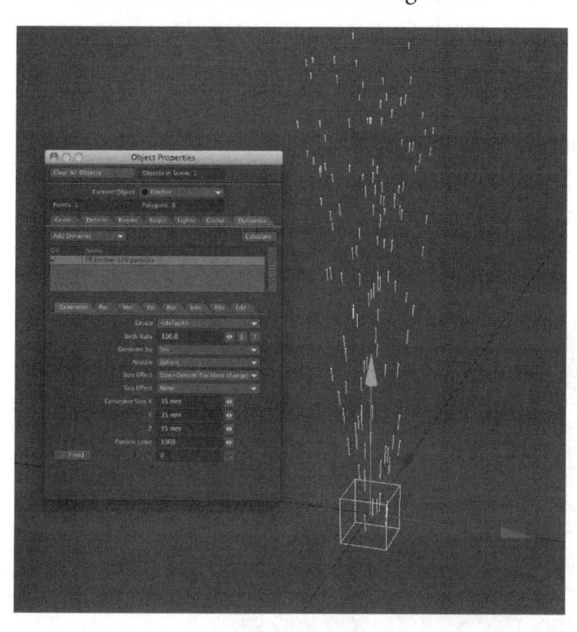

Figure 9.9 Changing the Explosion value makes your particles spray outward, while the Vibration setting adds randomness.

9. The second Vibration setting is a minimum percentage that you can apply as well. For now, leave this at 0%. If the first Vibration setting applies the value, or the amount, this second setting determines how much of that amount is used.

10. The particles are moving too fast for smoke. So, up at the top of the Motion tab, set the Velocity value to 20%. This causes the particles to move a little more slowly, more like rising smoke. **Figure 9.10** shows the settings.

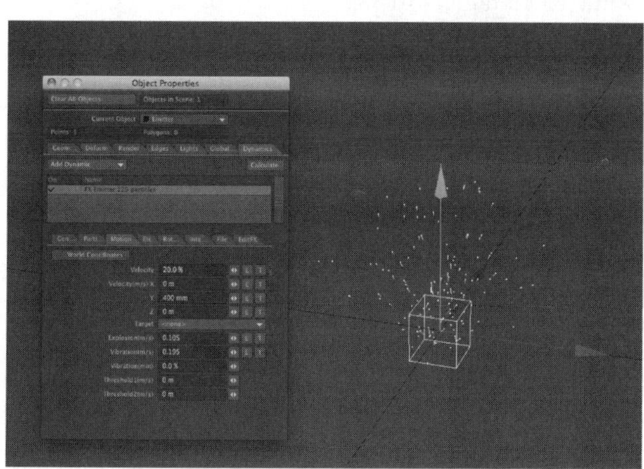

Figure 9.10 Changing the Velocity setting can speed up or slow down your particle stream.

If you watch the particles flow, they seem to be moving evenly at first, but by setting a Velocity value only on the Y-axis, you're sort of pushing the particles. You want them to appear as if they drift upward. Right now, they come out and just hang in midair. You'll also notice that with the Velocity value changed, the particle stream is much shorter.

11. Click the Particle tab, and set the Particle Weight value to 3.85 or so (**Figure 9.11**). This boosts the particles' momentum so they'll flow a bit farther. Then, on the same tab, set the Life Time value to 120. This tells the particles to "live" for 120 frames and then go away. While you're at it, set the + – setting to 10. This is a plus or minus randomization for the Life Time setting. It's good to use so that the particles don't all die off at the same time but with a variation of up to 10 frames.

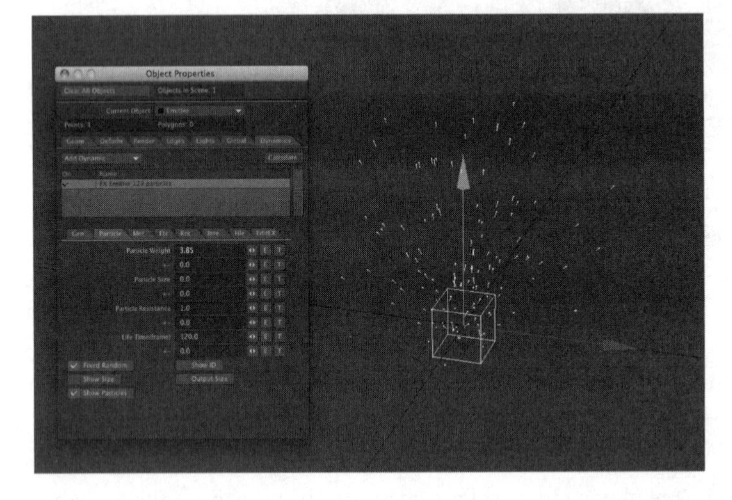

Figure 9.11 Adjusting the Particle Weight and Life Time settings help the particles flow and die a bit more naturally.

NOTE

If you set the Life Time value to 0, you're telling the particles to flow infinitely. If you leave the value at 60, the particles would only last 60 frames (2 seconds).

12. You might notice now with these changes that the particle stream fans out a bit too much. So, jump back to the Motion tab and decrease the value for Explosion to .0655 and for Vibration to .0385.
13. Finally, save your scene.

Your LightWave 3D manual gives a good description of the numerous settings and values available to you in the Particle FX_Emitter panel. You should reference this as you work with the tools. These first two exercises have introduced you to particle emitters and the controls available to them. But you can do much more with this system, and you can change how this smoke floats through the air.

Working with Particle Wind

Have you ever been visiting a friend and, later that night, found yourself craving a hamburger? So you find the only place open, one of those all-American pub restaurants, and you grab the first available table. You place your order and sure enough, the old lady with long, dirty, gray hair in the booth next to you lights up a cigarette. What happens? The smoke drifts right over to you as you're trying to eat. While we can't offer a solution for *that* situation in this chapter, it is possible to control the direction of smoke in LightWave. Read on to learn how easy it is to determine where your wind blows.

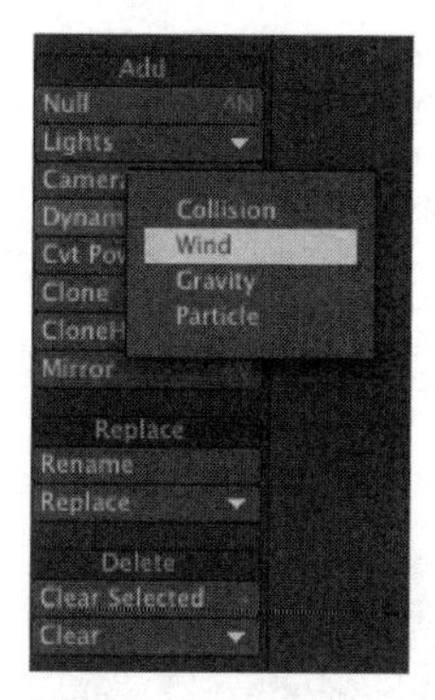

Figure 9.12 Add a wind effector to the scene, in the same way that you added a particle emitter earlier.

Exercise 9.3 Adding Wind to Particles

1. Continuing from the previous project, make sure your scene is saved. Then, using the Items tab, add a wind effector to the scene by choosing Wind from the Dynamic Obj drop-down menu (**Figure 9.12**).
2. If your FX panel was already open from working with the particle emitter, it will automatically change over to the FX_Wind properties. If the panel does not appear, select the wind effector and then press **p** to open its Properties panel. Click the Dynamics tab and select the FX Wind listing.
3. Because you scaled down the size of the particle emitter in Exercise 9.2, your wind effector is much too large for it. So, in the FX_Wind properties panel, set Radius to something like 60 mm (**Figure 9.13**).

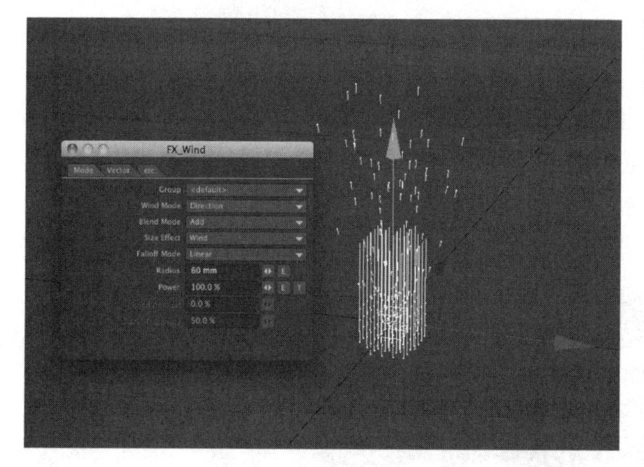

Figure 9.13 Change the radius of the wind to fit the scene.

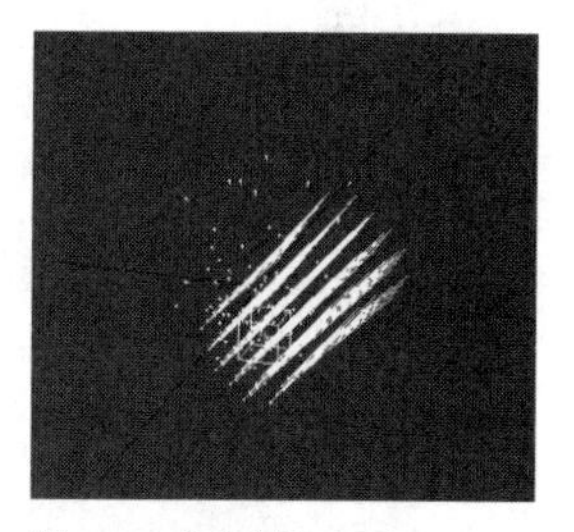

Figure 9.14 Rotating the wind effector has a direct effect on the particle stream.

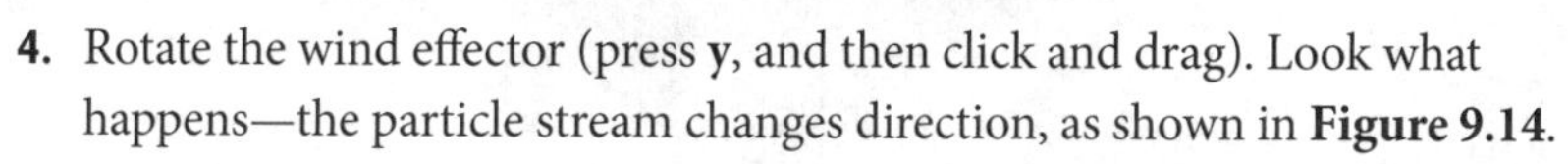

4. Rotate the wind effector (press **y**, and then click and drag). Look what happens—the particle stream changes direction, as shown in **Figure 9.14**.

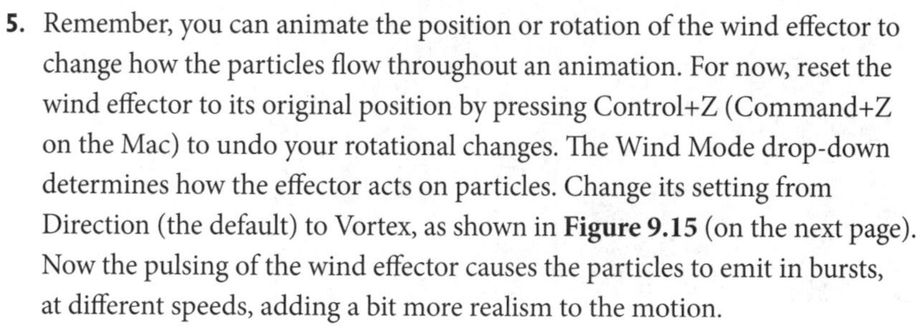

5. Remember, you can animate the position or rotation of the wind effector to change how the particles flow throughout an animation. For now, reset the wind effector to its original position by pressing Control+Z (Command+Z on the Mac) to undo your rotational changes. The Wind Mode drop-down determines how the effector acts on particles. Change its setting from Direction (the default) to Vortex, as shown in **Figure 9.15** (on the next page). Now the pulsing of the wind effector causes the particles to emit in bursts, at different speeds, adding a bit more realism to the motion.

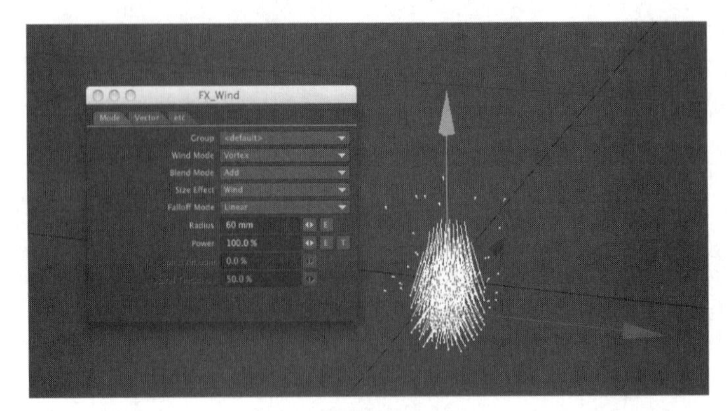

Figure 9.15 Change the Wind Mode setting to Vortex for random emitter control.

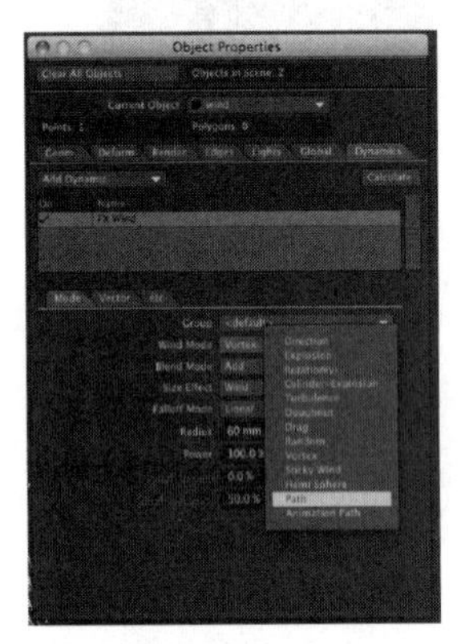

Figure 9.16 A second wind effector is added to the scene, and its wind mode is set to Path.

Experiment with the various wind modes to see how they affect the particles. If you find a motion value you like, use it. Remember, you can leave the layout animation playback going to see the particles moving while you make changes to the wind.

6. Your scene can contain more than one wind effector, which is pretty cool. So, add another wind effector from the Dynamic Obj drop-down menu on the Items tab.
7. For the second wind effector, set its radius to about 120 mm. Then, set Wind Mode to Path, as shown in **Figure 9.16**. The wind will help "steer" the particles to create a stream of smoke.
8. Move the timeline slider to frame 0, and then select the second wind effector. Activate the Move tool (press **t**) and drag the effector down, close to the base of the particle emitter, as shown in **Figure 9.17**.

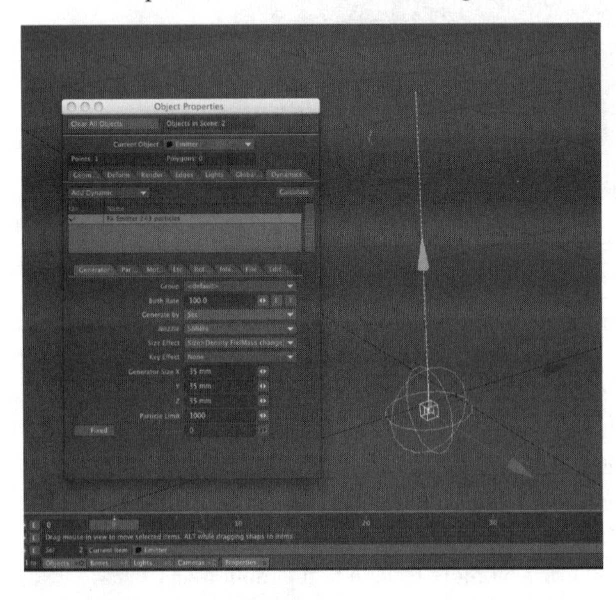

Figure 9.17 Move the second wind effector down toward the base of the particle emitter.

9. Move the timeline slider to frame 80, and then move the wind effector up about 1 m along the Y-axis, and slightly to the right along the X-axis (**Figure 9.18**).

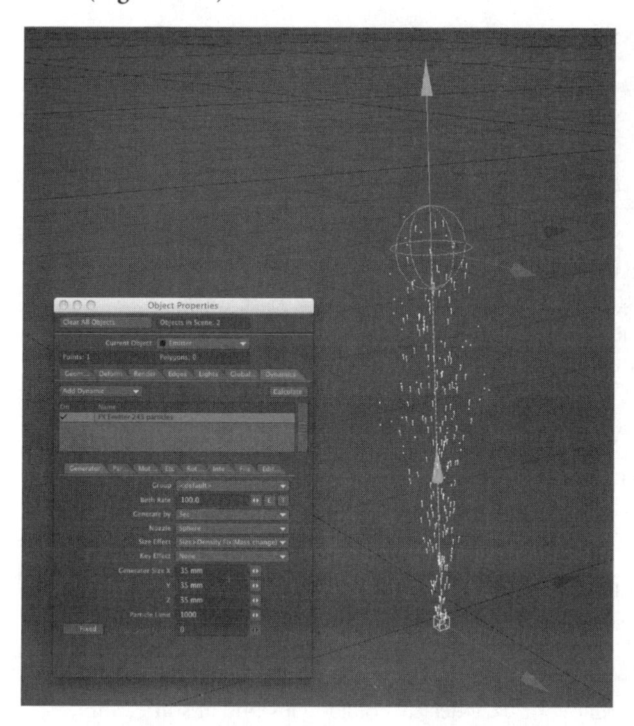

Figure 9.18 Create a second position for the wind effector.

10. Go to frame 160 and move the wind effector again, about 1 m over to the right along the X-axis. **Figure 9.19** shows the position.

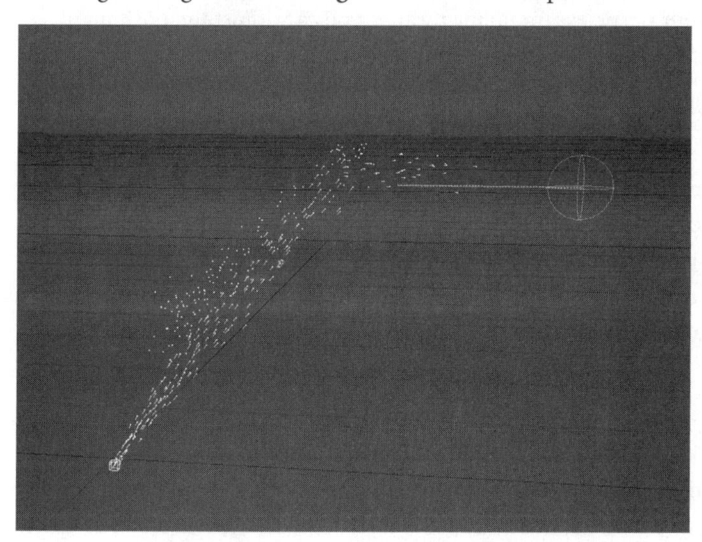

Figure 9.19 At frame 160, move the wind effector to the right along the X-axis.

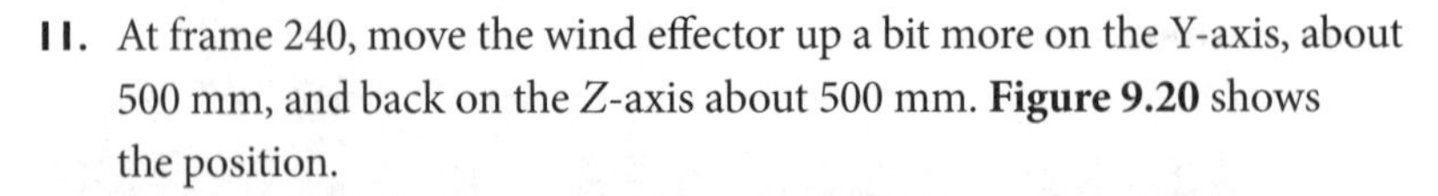

11. At frame 240, move the wind effector up a bit more on the Y-axis, about 500 mm, and back on the Z-axis about 500 mm. **Figure 9.20** shows the position.

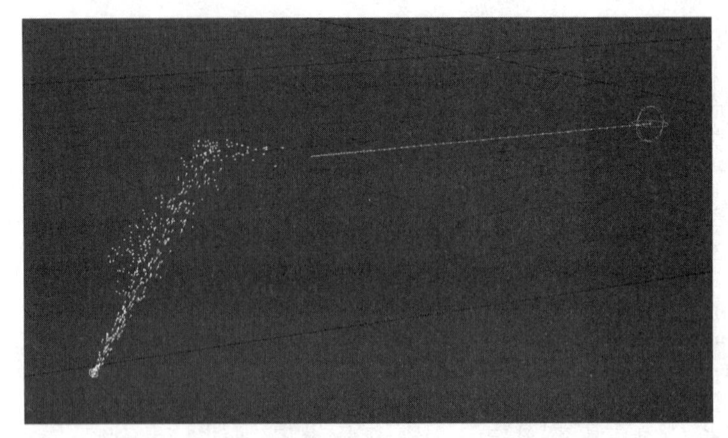

Figure 9.20 Move the wind effector up on the Y-axis for frame 240, and back on the Z-axis.

12. Click the smoke effector to select it, and then change its Life Time setting to 300. Because the path wind is now dragging the particles, you'll want them to live a bit longer.

    You see, the point here is that you can work through your particle animation and make changes to key factors such as lifetime, velocity, and others at any point. Your settings are always adjustable.

13. Finally, if you find that your particles sort of hang around at some point, there's a chance that the path wind is not large enough to carry them all. So, all you need to do is select the second wind effector and enlarge its radius. If your particles jam up in any area, you can adjust the position of the wind effector.

14. Tweak, adjust, and experiment, and then save your scene.

The path wind feature is very powerful. This exercise introduced you to it, but you can go further by rotating the wind at certain keyframes. What would that do, you ask? How about twisting smoke for things like jet exhaust or tornados? Cool stuff. There's a video called VisualParticle.mov, available as a free download from www.3dgarage.com, that corresponds to this chapter, showing you more about the different particle settings. Be sure to check it out. For now, let's move on to learn about collisions.

Introducing Particle Collisions

This next section will show you how to apply collision behavior to your particles. The goal is to make particle systems behave realistically when they encounter obstacles in their paths. Think of smoke hitting a ceiling before it dissipates, or water splashing as it hits the bottom of a sink. The next exercise takes the basic emitter example discussed in the previous exercises and expands it by changing its particle flow with collisions.

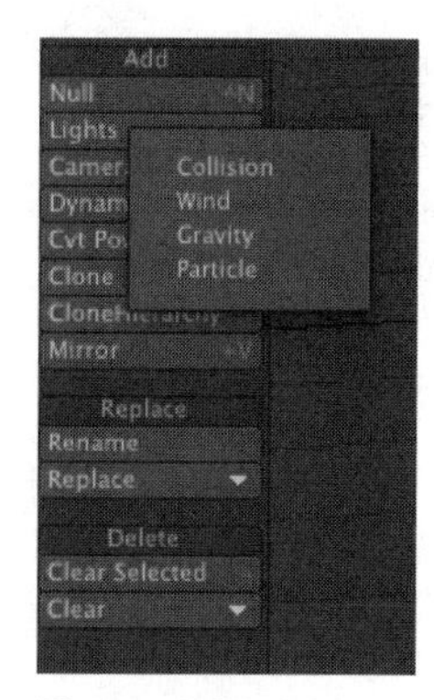

Figure 9.21 Add a collision effector to the scene.

Exercise 9.4 Interactive Particles

1. Use the scene you created in Exercise 9.3 or load the ParticleSmoke scene from the Chapter 9 folder on this book's DVD. Resave the scene as **ParticleCollision**.
2. Choose Collision from the Items tab's Dynamic Obj drop-down (**Figure 9.21**). You can add dynamics to any scene this way.
3. Take a look at the FX_Collision Properties panel that popped up after you added the collision effector. If you don't see it, in the Object Properties panel select the Collision dynamic on the Dynamics tab and the appropriate controls appear within the panel. Then, check the layout, and note that your particles have sort of exploded all over your scene. It appears that they are already colliding with the collision effector, as you can see in **Figure 9.22**.

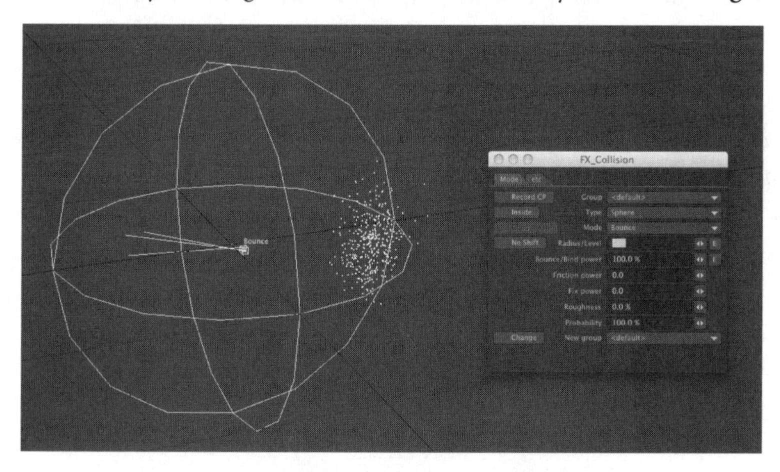

Figure 9.22 Once a collision effector is added to a scene, it immediately goes to work affecting the particles.

4. The default shape of the collision effector, which can be embedded in any object in your scene, is a sphere. We want a flat surface instead for this scene, so in the Properties panel for the collision object, choose Plane from the Type drop-down. Take a look at **Figure 9.23** (on the next page) and you'll see that this creates a collision plane floating above the Y-axis. This is because its Radius/Level setting is 1 m. Changing the Radius/Level setting is similar to changing the radius of the particle emitter, as you did earlier in the chapter. Set this option to 500 mm.

   Setting the Type drop-down to Plane is good for particles hitting a floor or wall, and so on, rather than a box or sphere. If you had, say, a building or a car, you could set Type to Object.

NOTE

You might have noticed that on the Dynamics tab within the Object Properties panel, you can also add effectors, such as collision. The difference is that adding an effector here will attach it to an object. Since there are no objects in this particular scene, you've added a collision from the Items tab instead.

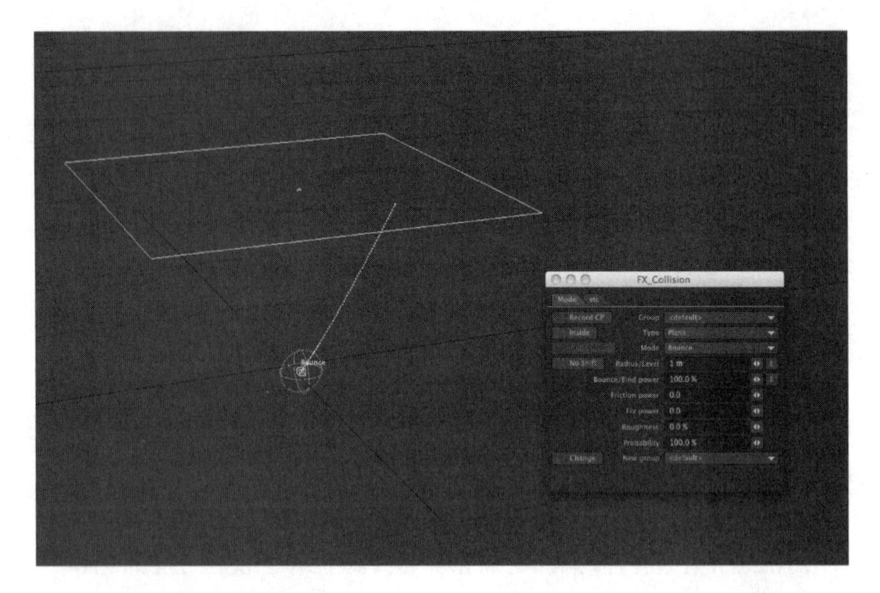

Figure 9.23 New collision planes have a default Radius/Level setting of 1 m.

Remember, this is as basic as it gets, but collisions work the same no matter what particle scene you're setting up. The difference here is that you're working only with effectors and emitters. You can make any object a collision, and place your particle emitter into any object. Be sure to view the VisualParticle.mov movie file (again, available as a free download from www.3dgarage.com) to see this in action.

5. Press **t** to activate the Move tool and move the plane up about 1 m along the Y-axis; then create a keyframe at frame 0 to lock it in place.

   Mode is set to Bounce, telling the collision plane to, well, bounce particles that strike it. Alternate settings cause particles to stick to the surface, sink into it, and so on. You'll see that the Bounce/Bind Power option is set to 100% in the Properties panel. This essentially determines the strength of the collision. For now, this value is fine.

6. Save your scene with your changes.
7. Drag your timeline slider or click the Play button in the lower-right corner of the interface to see the particles flow. You'll see them stream up and flow along with the pull of the wind you set up in Exercise 9.3, but now they'll stop and spread out when they hit the collision plane.
8. Click the Inside button in the FX_Collision panel. This tells the particles colliding to be affected in the interior of the collision object, and not just at its surface. Since this object is a flat plane, and it has no interior, this has the effect of stopping the particles from passing through the collision object, so they stay beneath it (**Figure 9.24**).

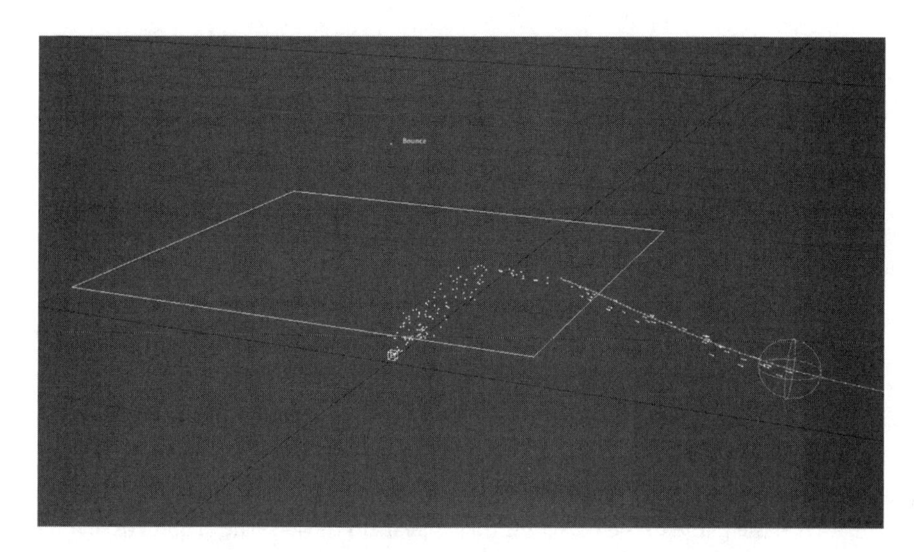

Figure 9.24 Inserting a collision plane in the particle stream does not stop the wind effector that's pulling the particles, but it deflects the particles' motion.

NOTE

Particles can be hard to see in Layout. So when previewing a particle animation, it may be helpful to select the scene's particle emitter(s) first to highlight them and make them easier to see. While shaping the flow of your particle stream, you may also want to set the emitter's Life Time value to 0 on the FX_Emitter panel's Particle tab, to make the emitter generate particles indefinitely, without "timing out."

As you've seen in these few exercises, making particles interact and applying dynamics is not difficult. You've easily added an emitter, added wind effectors, and included an animation path. You then made those particles interact with an object by adding a collision dynamic. But there's one other thing that might be really helpful: surfacing the particles.

Surfacing Particles

It's possible to exert a ton of control over your particles using things like gravity and collision dynamics, and if you watch the videos for this chapter (available as free downloads from www.3dgarage.com), you'll see more examples. But you can take even the simple particles created here a step further by setting up a cool surface for them. And once the surfaces are set, you can still go back and make changes to the particle emitter and interactively change the parameters with more vibration, less wind, or faster velocity for cooler effects. For now, these particles are cool, but what good are they? If you render a frame, you'll see nothing. If there were objects loaded in the scene, you'd see only those render, and you still wouldn't see the particles. That's because you created an HV emitter earlier in the chapter, meaning you must apply HyperVoxels to them to make them visible.

Another type of emitter you could add is a Partigon emitter. It works similarly to an HV emitter, except that it generates single-point polygons that will show during a render. These are great for tiny sparks, water sprays, or even stars.

Three surfacing options are available for HyperVoxels: Surface mode, for solid blobby objects; Volume mode, for 3D clouds and smoke; and Sprite mode. Sprites are like 2D surface maps that emulate the effect of a HyperVoxel when it's applied to a 3D volume. They render much more quickly than true 3D HyperVoxels. These settings have no effect on the particles' motion in Layout, but only on their appearance. They are fast, great for smoke effects, easy to set up, and always visible in Layout!

Exercise 9.5 Surfacing Particles for Smoke

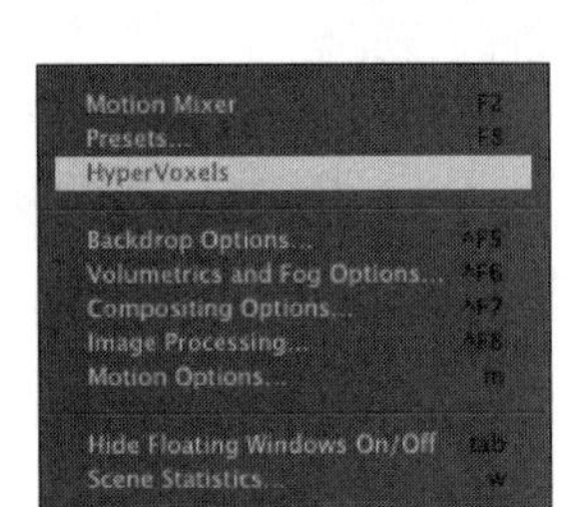

Figure 9.25 Press Control+F6 to open the Volumetrics tab of the Effects panel, home of the HyperVoxels volumetric control.

1. Load the scene you completed in Exercise 9.4, or load the ParticleCollision scene from the CH9 folder of this book's DVD. Then press Control+F6, or select Volumetrics and Fog Options from the Window drop-down menu at the top left of the Layout interface. You can also choose HyperVoxels from the Window drop-down menu, but you should understand that HyperVoxels is an effects plug-in. The Effects panel will appear with its Volumetrics tab active (**Figure 9.25**).
2. Select HyperVoxels from the Add Volumetric drop-down, and then double-click the name in the object list that appears in the tab. The HyperVoxels panel will open.

   You'll see the name of the HV_Emitter ("Smoke") grayed out in the Object Name list (**Figure 9.26**).

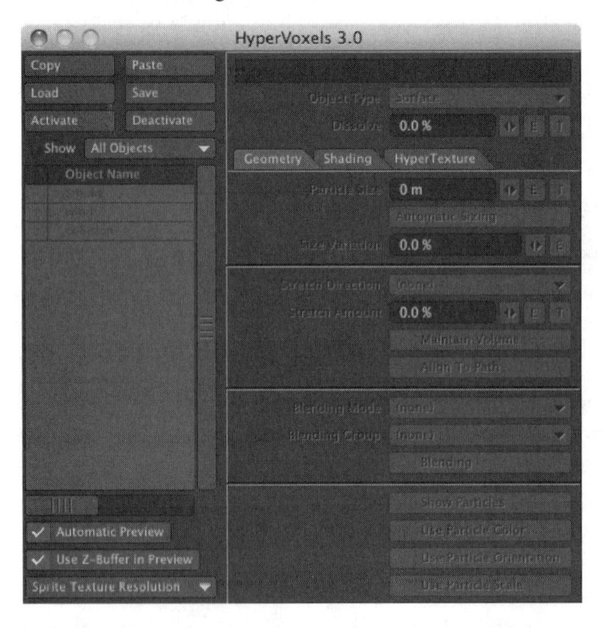

Figure 9.26 As soon as you load up HyperVoxels, your particle emitter is visible but inactive in the Object Name list.

3. To activate HyperVoxels for the particle emitter, either double-click the Smoke entry in the Object Name list, or select it once and click the Activate button just above the upper-left corner of the Object Name list window.

   The grayed-out controls in the panel's Geometry tab will become active, and you'll see that the Particle Size setting has been set for you automatically.

4. Move the timeline slider to a frame in which some particles have been emitted. You'll be previewing your particle-surface settings directly in Layout with VPR, so we need to work in a frame in which some particles appear.
5. Now, the best way to begin setting up smoke for these particles is to use VPR. Choose this view option from the top of the Layout window.
6. VPR can show the particles in any view, but remember that they'll render only from the selected camera. If need be, position the camera in such a way that you can see the particle stream. A quick way to do this is to press the Tab key to hide any open settings panels; select the camera in Layout; switch the view mode to Camera; press **t** to activate the Move tool; and click and drag in the scene window to move the camera in closer to the particles. When set, create a keyframe at frame 0 to lock the camera in place, and then press Tab to unhide the HyperVoxels panel.
7. In the VPR layout window, you'll see some white blobs. By default, HyperVoxels uses Surface as the Object Type. This is great for lava, blood, shaving cream, and things of that nature. It's also great for water, and you'd just need to add transparency and reflections for the effect. But if you change the Object Type to Sprite, you can make great-looking smoke. Go ahead and change the Object Type setting in the HyperVoxels panel to Sprite.
8. Click and drag the Particle Size mini-slider and change the setting to 40 mm.
9. Set Size Variation to 180% to randomize the size of the Sprite particles a bit. Note that although the mini-slider for Size Variation maxes out at 500%, you can manually enter a value much higher than that for added control.
10. Set Stretch Direction to None, so that the particles don't stretch based on their movement. You would use a stretch direction if you were creating fast-moving particles, or perhaps pooling water. Make sure Align to Path is checked.
11. Click the Shading tab and then set the particle color to a grayish blue, using settings of (or close to) R: 172, G: 175, B: 200.

    Just as you set up textures throughout the book using LightWave's Surface Editor, you can do the same here in the HyperVoxels panel. You can apply a texture to the HyperVoxel particles just as you would for an object's surface.
12. Set Luminosity to 70% for a softer look. Set Opacity to about 90%. Making this value lower would add more brightness, almost a glow, to the particles.
13. Set Density to 55% to break up the smoke a bit.
14. Set Number of Slices to 7, the maximum. LightWave defaults to 1 slice. As stated, a sprite is a slice of a HyperVoxel. The more slices, the more detail, but of course, the more rendering time. In some cases, a setting of 1 is all

NOTE

If you want to see how this setting looks, go ahead and make a preview of your particle animation directly in the VIPER window. From the Preview drop-down menu, click Make Preview. After the preview is generated, play buttons will appear. You can stop the preview generation at any time by pressing the Esc key on your keyboard.

you need, but in this case, 7 gives you the cleanest render. **Figure 9.27** shows the settings.

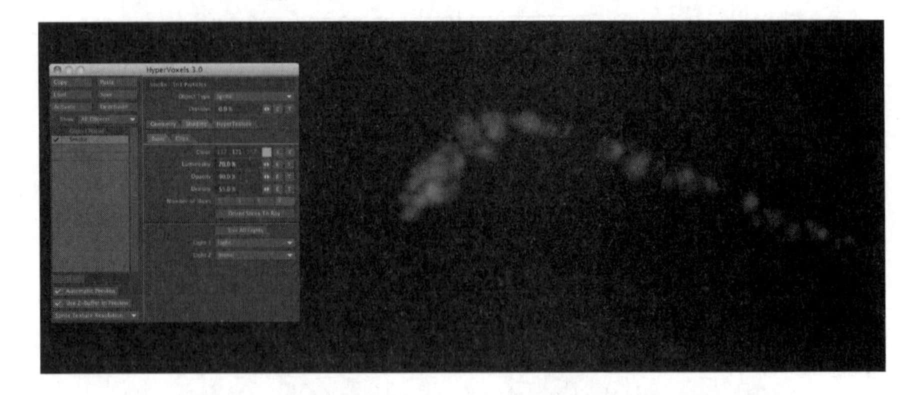

Figure 9.27 Tweak just a few sprite-surface settings and the particles start looking like smoke.

NOTE

The Orient Slices To Ray setting is designed to keep the slices pointing towards the camera. This helps cut down on render time, allowing the system to calculate for only what the camera sees.

15. Click the HyperTexture tab and choose Turbulence from the Texture drop-down. This applies more variation to the HyperVoxel surfaces. You can experiment with other settings if you like. Set Texture Effect to Billowing and leave the other values at their defaults. Essentially, you're applying an animated texture, characterized by billowing turbulent noise, to the particle surfaces. The results are easier to see than to describe.
16. Slowly drag the timeline slider and watch your particles move, with HyperVoxels applied.
17. Save your scene, and then experiment. Note that what you see in the VPR window is what you'll see when you render your particles. If you're using just VIPER, the preview is not as accurate. They look much better if you press **F9** for a full frame render.

What you've done here (**Figure 9.28**) is basic, but for many types of particle animations, nothing more complex is necessary. With the power of LightWave's particles, in combination with HyperVoxel surfaces, added textures, and even gradients, the possibilities are endless. Endless how? Read on for another variation on these particles.

NOTE

You can speed up render times slightly by turning off the Volumetric Antialiasing option in the Volumetrics area of the Effects panel (press Control+F6). If you're using volume-based HyperVoxels, antialiasing will help create a cleaner final render. But for sprites, you can get away with having this setting turned off.

Figure 9.28 As you adjust particle-surface settings, remember that VPR will allow you to see instant changes to backdrops as well as particle surfaces.

Using Images on Particles

Yes, you read that heading correctly—images on particles. Although it sounds odd, it's actually a very handy feature for all sorts of animations—falling snow, falling leaves, bubbles—whatever!

Check this out.

Exercise 9.6 Using Images on Particles

1. With the same scene loaded from the previous exercise, open the Image Editor. Load the MapleLeaf.png image from the CH9 folder of this book's DVD, as shown in **Figure 9.29**.

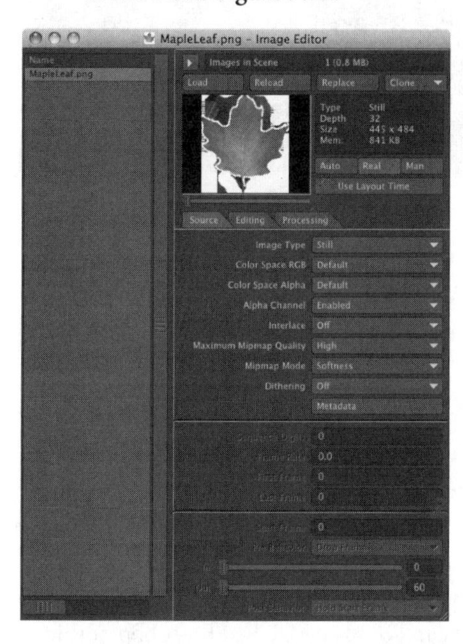

Figure 9.29 Loading a 32-bit image from the Image Editor can make your particle systems flow with pictures!

2. Back in the HyperVoxels panel, make sure you're still using Sprite for Object Type.
3. Next, click the panel's Shading tab, and then select the Clips tab that appears there.
4. Select the MapleLeaf image from the Add Clip drop-down. Watch what happens in Layout—you'll see the leaf image applied to the particles. They grossly overlap each other and probably are showing a white outline, but that's OK.
5. Change the Alpha setting to Embedded. Then, go back to the Geometry tab and set Particle Size to about 15 mm and Size Variation to 50%; Stretch Direction should still be set to None. **Figure 9.30** (on the next page) shows Layout with the MapleLeaf image in place.

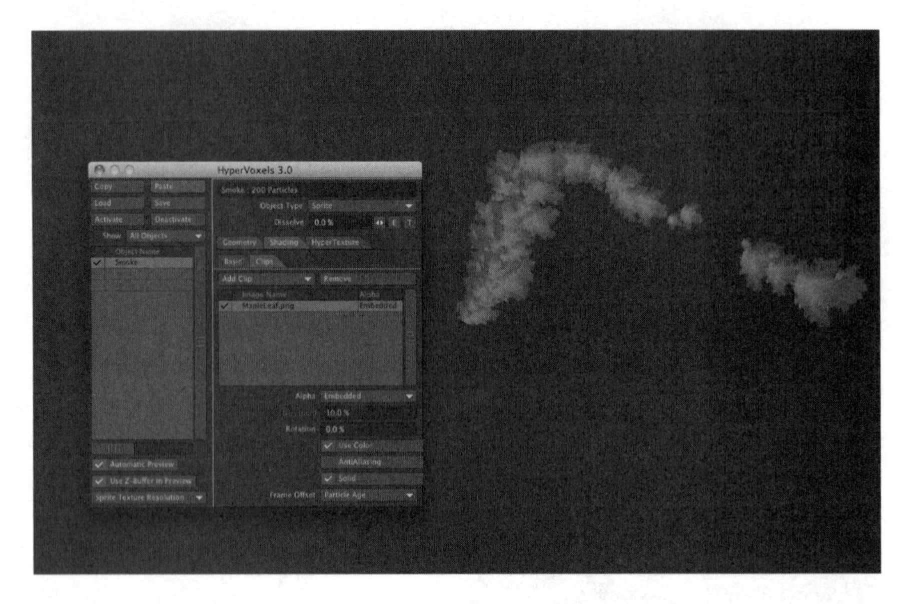

Figure 9.30 A small image is replicated and applied to every particle in the emitter using a HyperVoxel sprite and clips.

That's it! You now have a stream of floating leaves. HyperVoxel sprites with clips are quite useful. As we just saw, one of the reasons they're so useful is that you can take tiny images and animate them quickly using particles. You can see them directly in Layout, so you know what's happening with their size and color, and they always face the camera.

Of course, you can adjust the motion of the particles, perhaps by adding another wind effector at the top of the path to make the particles spread out as they reach their end. You can also change the emitter to a large, long, flat shape to emit sprite clips such as coins, bubbles, puffs of smoke, and so on. Or how about multiple streams, each with an image of a letter? The examples here should get you started with your own particle animations. All you need to do is create a 32-bit image so that the Alpha channel is embedded. You can do this in Adobe Photoshop. Just load up the image you want, place it on a transparent background, and save.

Editing Particles

You can do a lot to particles within LightWave. As you've seen, you can push them, pull them, make them collide with other objects, and so on. They can look like foam, smoke, or leaves. But what happens when you have everything looking just as you like, and then some pesky particle, following the semi-random rules of particle motion, goes astray and gets in the way of your animation? You don't have to live with it; you can edit your particles. Read on to learn how.

Exercise 9.7 Editing Particles

1. Load the Particle Image scene from the CH9 Scenes folder on this book's DVD.
2. Go to a Perspective view and arrange the viewport so that you can see the majority of the particles.
3. Select the particle emitter named "Smoke" and press **p** to open the Properties panel.
4. Click the Dynamics tab in the Properties panel and select the FX_Emitter listing. Click the Calculate button in the middle of the panel.
5. After the calculation is complete, drag the timeline slider, and you'll see the particles moving. There are one or two that are sort of hanging out of the stream, so let's remove them.
6. To fix these crazy particles, click the EditFX tab in the FX_Emitter properties.
7. Click the Edit tool, and then select one of the wayward particles directly in Layout, as shown in **Figure 9.31**. When the particle is selected, you'll see a line appear—that's its motion path, also shown in Figure 9.31. The number you see is its ID.

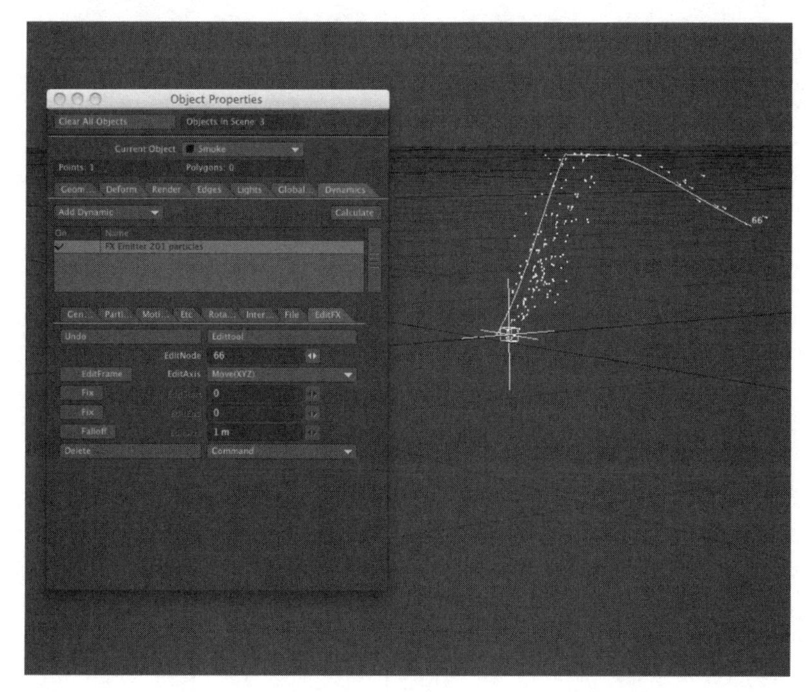

Figure 9.31 With the Edit tool in the FX_Emitter properties, you can isolate any particle.

8. When the particle is selected, click the Delete button in the FX_Emitter properties and the selected particle will be deleted. You can also just reposition the particle using the Move tool (press **t**).
9. Repeat steps 7 and 8 as needed to remove (or move) any other stray particles in the stream.

Cloning a particle, copying its motion path, and rotating its path are just some of the other things you can do on the EditFX tab.

The Next Step

This chapter introduced you to some of the coolest features in LightWave's arsenal. The information in these exercises can easily be applied to projects of your own and ones for your client. You'll find that particles are so fun to use, you'll be looking for projects to use them in. Be careful, though—don't let your client know how easy it is! For now, turn the page and learn about more dynamic effects you can create in LightWave beyond particles.

Chapter 10
Dynamics in Motion

3D animation can be fun and rewarding, especially when you get into the cooler effects that can really bring a scene to life. In the previous chapter, you were introduced to LightWave 10's particles. This chapter will take you even further by showing how to create various dynamic effects for creative animations. These dynamic effects let you make animations in which objects collide realistically and influence each other's motion in a way that obeys natural laws such as gravity, momentum, and shock absorption. Tools like these will help take your animations to the next level. You will work through various projects so that you can quickly and easily learn how to apply these powerful tools to just about any animation. In this chapter, you'll learn about the following:

- Dynamics-related panels and tools
- Hard-body dynamics, governing solid, rigid objects
- Soft-body dynamics, governing objects that are yielding but resilient
- How to make objects collide and react

Dynamics in LightWave

The word *dynamic* is an adjective that relates to energy or to objects in motion. What puts these objects in motion in LightWave are clever commands that you control. To use any of the dynamics in LightWave, you just need to think about what you want an object to do.

Let's say you have created a fun character with a big, uh, animator's belly. As your character walks, you want his girth to shake a bit. Although you could use bones with a weight map and apply bone dynamics, a simpler and more effective method is to apply a "soft" dynamic to the jelly belly. Or perhaps you're an avid bowler (or aspire to be). Instead of wearing those silly shoes to go bowling, just create some 3D bowling balls and pins and use hard dynamics and collisions to send the pins flying—without having to manually keyframe the ball's contact with each pin in its path or each struck pin's contact with other pins around it, and so on. LightWave motion dynamics features let you place objects in your scene, tell them how to move and interact with other objects, and then turn them loose to interact with each other—without manually keyframing all of their collisions and encounters. Once you've learned all the necessary buttons and processes, LightWave dynamics can make your scenes come to life. Now, take a quick tour of the dynamics-related panels to familiarize yourself with them.

Understanding Dynamic Controls

Dynamics in LightWave are easy to set up after you understand how the panels work and what the controls mean. **Figure 10.1** shows the SoftFX dynamics panel. This panel is accessed through the Dynamics tab within the Object Properties panel, just as particle effect controls were in the previous chapter. You can see from the image that there are six tabbed areas within the dynamic controls.

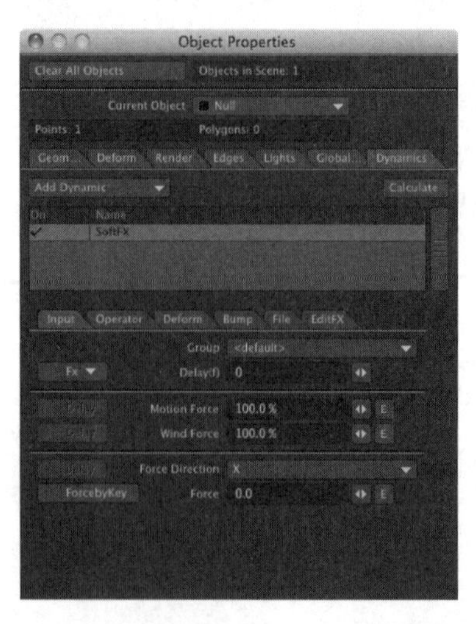

Figure 10.1 When a dynamic is applied, the controls are found within the Object Properties panel.

The number of tabbed areas varies depending on which dynamic you apply. As the tutorials progress in this chapter, you'll see how the different areas are used.

The types of dynamics you can apply to objects are as follows:

- Cloth
- Soft
- Hard
- Emitter (for particles)
- Wind
- Collision
- Gravity

Each of these dynamic types has a similar set of commands and controls. When you apply a dynamic to an object, you need to think about your process, just as you do when modeling or animating. Think about where you are going with the animation and what you want to do with it. Once you understand that, you can choose the appropriate dynamic for your object and know what tabbed area to access within the controls.

Hard-Body Dynamics

Hard-body dynamics have been around for a while, but few ordinary mortals have been able to take advantage of them. Complex scripting requirements and heavy calculations often made this top-notch feature available only to a few. Now, thanks to some clever programmers at NewTek, this feature is available interactively in LightWave 10.

Hard-body dynamics applies to objects that behave as rigid solids. When hard bodies collide, they retain their shapes without compressing or yielding. Think of marbles, billiard balls, or anvils. Hard-body dynamics control how these objects behave when they run into each other, based on properties such as gravity, weight, and density.

Exercise 10.1 Creating Hard-Body Dynamics

This tutorial will take a few basic objects and show you how to make them interact. From there, you'll change variables to see the how the dynamic toolsets work.

1. Open LightWave Layout.
2. Load the Solids model from the Chapter 10 folder of this book's DVD (**Figure 10.2** on the next page). This model has just one layer, containing a few geometric shapes set up as an "obstacle course." Also, load the Ball model from the DVD's Chapter 10 folder. You'll use dynamics to animate the Ball object as it rolls around, and interacts with, the Solids model's shapes.

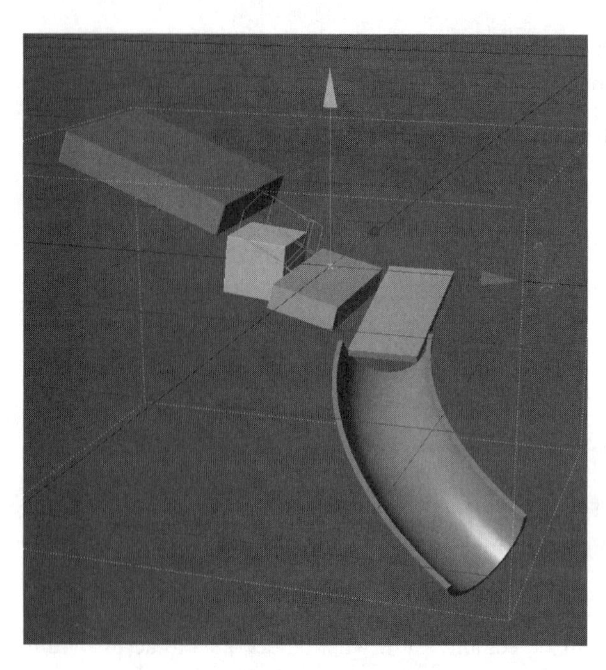

Figure 10.2 The Solids model loaded, ready for some dynamic action. Exciting, isn't it?

NOTE

If either the light or camera icon gets in the way of working, simply move it out of view. This project is a lesson in dynamics, and you won't be lighting or rendering.

3. Select the ball and move it up on the Y-axis so that it's positioned above the top of the highest box. Create a keyframe at 0 to lock it in place, as in **Figure 10.3**.

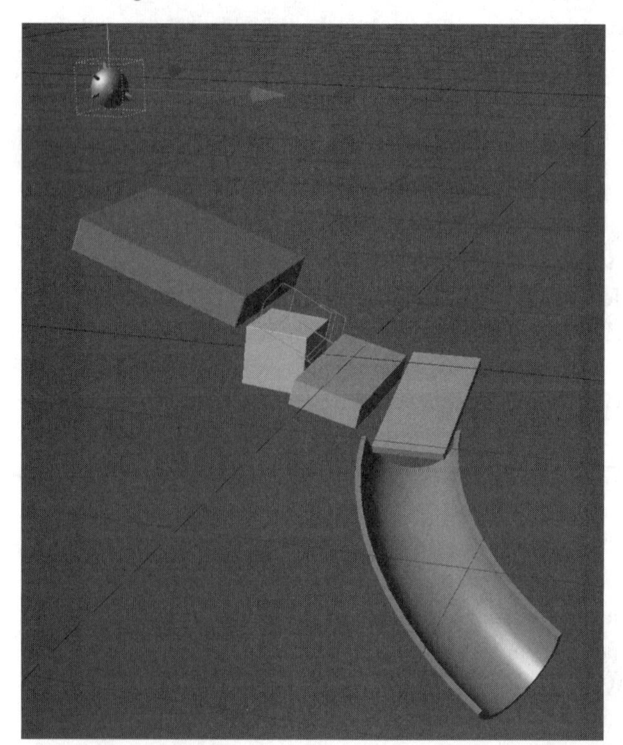

Figure 10.3 Position the ball at the top of the slide.

4. With the ball selected, press **p** to open the Object Properties panel. Although this tutorial is simple, you'll see how cool the dynamic effects can be.
5. Click the panel's Dynamics tab, and select Hard from the Add Dynamic drop-down to apply a HardFX dynamic to the Ball object (**Figure 10.4**). Position your view so you can see the slide, ball, and Properties panel. Select the HardFX listing to see its controls.

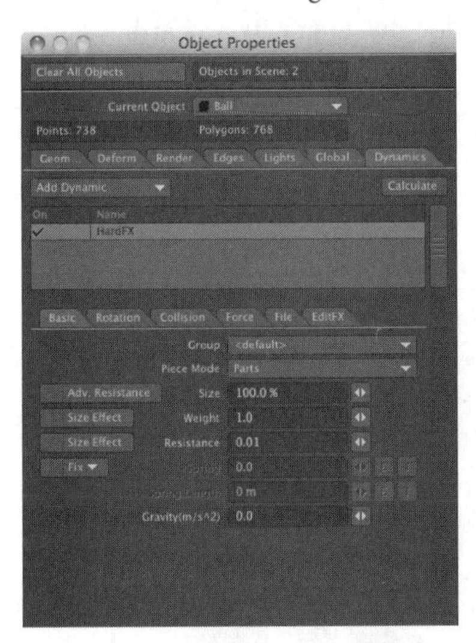

Figure 10.4 Add a hard dynamic to the ball.

6. Now that you've come this far, it's a good idea to save the scene. Save this scene as **SolidsSetup** and then save it again as **SolidsWorking**, or something similar. The idea behind this is that at any point, you can call up the setup scene and start again.

NOTE

Don't forget that you can also press Shift+S to save incremental versions of your scenes.

7. In the Object Properties panel, choose the Solids object and add a collision dynamic to it from the drop-down list, as in **Figure 10.5**.

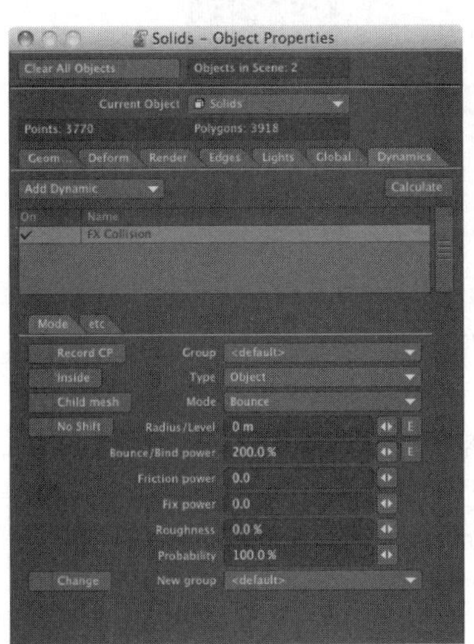

Figure 10.5 Use the Object Properties panel to add a collision dynamic to the slide object.

8. If you click the Calculate button on the Dynamics tab, nothing happens. You've not yet given the dynamics any properties. So, go back to the Ball object and select the HardFX listing to access its controls. You need to click it only once for the controls to appear on the Dynamics tab.
9. The first thing you want to do is give the ball some gravity. In the Basic tab of the HardFX controls, set Gravity to –9.8. It's the last setting in the drop-down, and it corresponds to the acceleration due to gravity on Earth, 9.8 meters/second^2. (The negative value reflects the fact that gravity pulls downward, along the negative Y-axis.)
10. Set the last frame of the animation to 400.
11. Click the Calculate button on the Object Properties panel's Dynamics tab. Whoa! The ball falls and bounces down the solid object (**Figure 10.6**)!

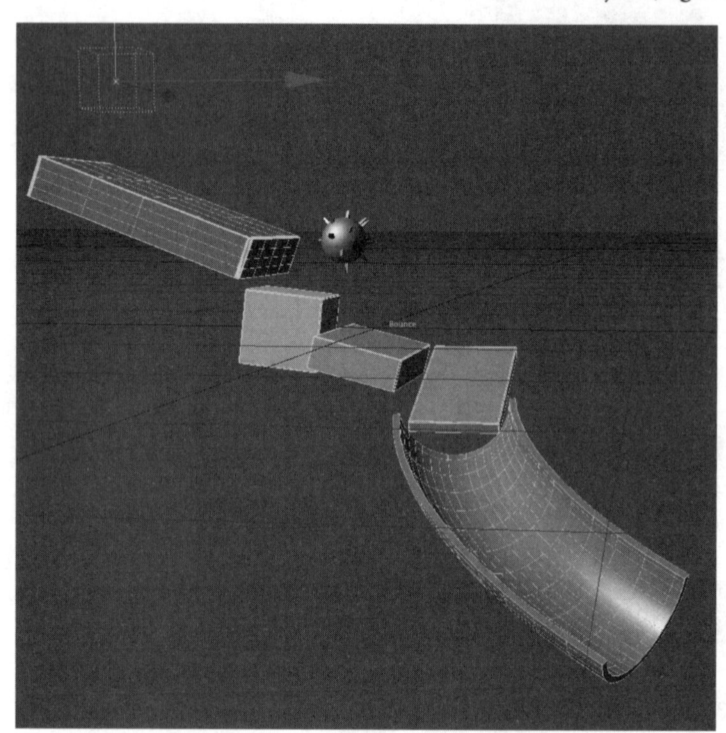

Figure 10.6 With two dynamics applied, your animation starts to have interaction.

Believe it or not, that's all there is to it! You've just created hard-body dynamics. However, there are many more controls to play with, so save the scene and move on to experiment a little.

You might have noticed that the ball doesn't quite fall down through all of the obstacles. A few more adjustments are in order.

12. Back in the Object Properties panel, select the FX Collision listing for the Solids object. Then, set the Bounce/Bind Power to 40% (**Figure 10.7**).

The default 200% is way too "bouncy," which is why this ball fell, and then bounced off into the air.

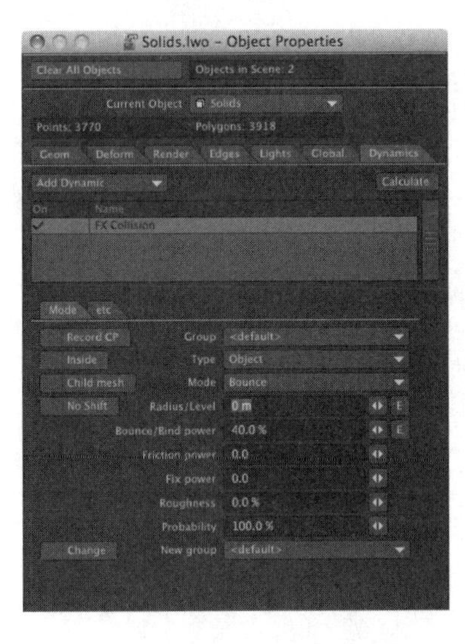

Figure 10.7 Reduce the Ball object's Bounce/Bind Power setting to 40% from the default 200% to stop it from careening out of the scene.

13. Click the Calculate button again, and the ball now slides down the objects better. But it's still not quite right, is it?

14. Select the Ball object in the Object Properties panel, and then select the HardFX listing.

15. Increase the value of the Weight setting to 0.2. This will make the ball heavier. If you calculate again, the ball slides much better. But it *slides*. It should roll, shouldn't it? You can change this too.

16. On the Rotation tab, change the Impact Effect from Force to Roll (**Figure 10.8**).

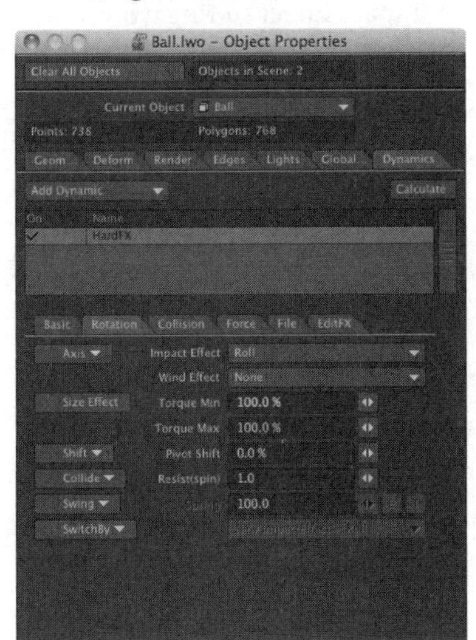

Figure 10.8 Adding weight to the ball and changing the Impact Effect to Roll will change how the ball behaves.

17. Click the Collision tab and change the Collision By option from Node to Sphere (**Figure 10.9**).

    The Node setting tells LightWave to use every point within the object to calculate collision dynamics. That can be significant for complex models and interactions, but in a simple scene like this, containing simple geometric objects, the Node setting simply slows down your animation with excess calculation. Once you've set the Collision By option to Sphere, click the Calculate button.

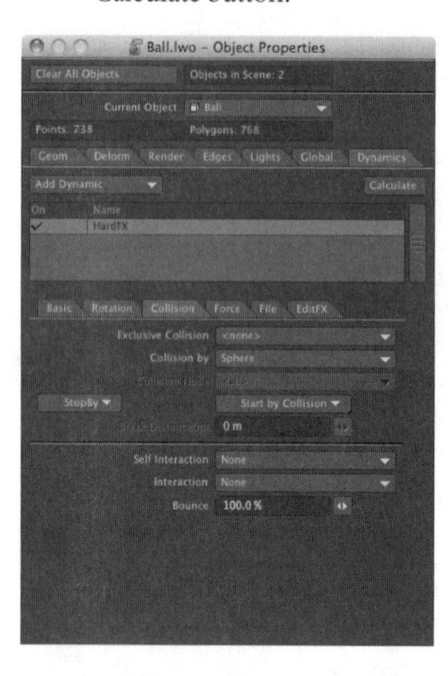

Figure 10.9 Adjusting the Collision By option lets your ball roll down the obstacles.

18. Once the calculation is finished, click the Play button at the bottom of the interface and you'll see the ball roll smoothly down the solid objects.

19. Click the Rotation tab, and to the left of the Impact Effect setting, you can tell the ball to roll on a specific axis only. Click the Axis drop-down list. It's set to Free, but you can change this to the Y-axis (which might apply to a spinning top), the X-axis (for a wheel or yo-yo), and other variations. The Free setting is best for a rolling ball, so you don't need to change anything here, but it's a good idea to familiarize yourself with this important control.

20. You can also change some of the other values, such as Wind Effect and Torque. If you increase the Torque Max value to 300%, for example, the ball will roll faster than it is currently moving. A good example of this is a children's ball thrown into water, which has a lot of torque coming out of the child's hand. It spins faster than it is moving (or sliding) on the water. Another example is a bowling ball thrown down an alley. Additionally, you can give the ball a Resist (Spin) setting to have it hold back on its spin amount.

Adjusting Other Collision Effects Controls

With just a few changes to these settings, you can make objects interact with each other. However, you might have noticed that there are more controls for collision effects than you've used here. **Figure 10.10** shows these controls, which appear on the Dynamics tab of the Object Properties panel.

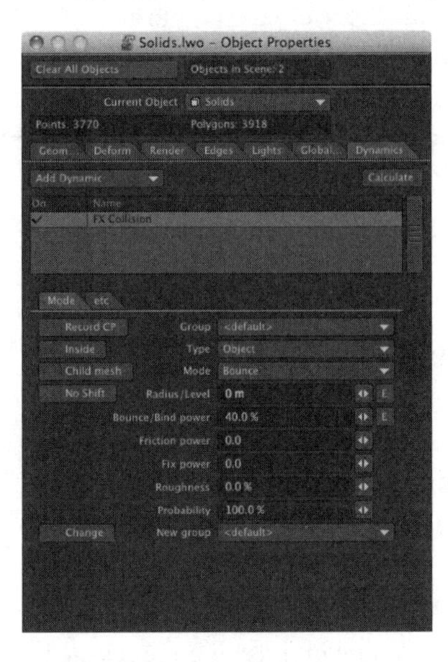

Figure 10.10 The collision controls are located mainly on the Mode tab, part of the Dynamics tab of the Object Properties panel.

The following list provides a rundown of its controls and settings:

- Setting a group through the Group drop-down is useful for times when you're working with larger scenes and multiple objects. For instance, let's say you have three slides going in this scene. You could create a group so that the collision and hard-dynamic objects are tied together and don't react to other objects with dynamics applied. It's a way of separating and isolating dynamics, while maintaining control.
- The Type drop-down specifies the surface shape that the selected object "shows" to objects that collide with it, and that is used to calculate the results of that collision, such as the angle at which a given object will ricochet away from its surface. The Object setting uses all the points on an object's surface to calculate collision results; it provides the most realistic dynamics but requires a lot of processing power and rendering time. The Sphere, Box, and Plane settings calculate collisions as if the selected object, no matter how complex in shape, were one of those simpler objects. These options result in collisions that are not as precise, but they suffice in many instances, often appear no different, and can save a lot of rendering time. The Object-Subdiv setting lets you apply different collision properties to surface subpatches within a single object.

- The Mode drop-down determines how objects will react to the selected object when they collide with it. The default Bounce setting causes objects that strike the selected object to, well, bounce off it. Other options include Stick, Erase, Event, Scatter, and Attract. Stick and Attract have the effects you'd expect on colliding objects. Erase causes objects that strike the selected object to disappear from the scene. The Event setting causes the selected object to act as if it has been struck by another object when noncollision dynamic events occur, such as the activation of a wind effector. The Scatter option causes colliding objects to bounce off the selected object in a random fashion.
- The Radius/Level setting can change the collision position. For example, if you change this value from 0 m to 400 mm and then click the Calculate button again, the ball won't fall and drop down the slide like it did before. Instead, it will "collide" with the slide before it actually touches it, because you've made the ball's collision radius larger than its actual physical radius. Keep this setting at 0 for this project.
- The Bounce/Bind Power selector controls the strength of the collision behavior specified in the Mode drop-down: how bouncy a Bounce Mode setting is, how sticky a Stick setting is, and so on. Use the mini-slider or type in a percentage value to adjust these settings.

NOTE

When setting Radius/Level or Bounce/Bind Power, you can click the E buttons to the right of the values to change these settings over time. Make your ball bounce hard, and then suddenly stick.

- The Friction Power control, also adjusted via the mini-slider or by typing a number into its requester, determines the amount of resistance the selected object's surface exerts on other objects as they roll or drag across it. Increasing Friction Power for the slide to 20.0 rather than 0, for instance, causes the ball to move down the slide at a slower rate because of the extra friction. You can play with this value to see how the dynamics react, but for this project keep the setting at 0.
- You can increase the Fix Power and Roughness to change how the collision reacts throughout the animation. Let's say you increase Fix Power to 20. The ball will not bounce as much on the collision. It will not slow down, but rather stay attached to the collision object more throughout the calculation. Roughness, on the other hand, will make the ball bounce around, sort of like rough terrain. Set the value to, for example, 40%, and you'll see the ball bounce down the slide. Change these values to add variations to see how the ball movement changes as it moves down the slide.
- Finally, you can set the Probability, telling LightWave the percentage of probability that the collision should happen. Right now, it's set to 100%, meaning there's a 100% probability of a collision. Lower this value, calculate again, and see the difference.

Within the HardFX controls, which are located on the Dynamics tab found in the Object Properties panel, click the Collision tab and then click the Start By Collision drop-down selector. Choose Collision in the Start By drop-down, and the ball's dynamic effects will remain turned off until the ball collides with another object. Triggering the effect using this collision-detection method saves processing time. You can set a Stop By collision event in the same way. Simply click the Stop By drop-down selector and choose Stop By Event. The event would be the collision. In the previous exercise, turning on the Start By Collision option would yield a ball that just sits in the air, that doesn't fall, and that doesn't roll. If something were to hit it, like a 3D hand or baseball bat, this collision would start the effects.

As you can see, setting up hard-body dynamics is not too complicated if you slow down and think about the process. Think about what you're going for, and it'll come together. In the previous exercise, you had a ball, which you told LightWave was a "hard" object. If you calculated after applying this setting, you might have seen an error. That's because LightWave doesn't have anything to work with, and you need to set something for this object to interact with. So, you told the ball to collide with the Solids object. The Solids object had a "collision" applied.

So how about going a step further? The next exercise will show you how to shatter glass in 3D.

Exercise 10.2 Modeling for Dynamics

This exercise will show you how you can blow apart a window. The technique can be used for anything, from a creature crashing through a brick wall to a bowling ball knocking down a set of pins. The project you'll do here will show you a quick technique for creating a window in Modeler, and then show you how to use dynamics in Layout to crash an object through it, essentially shattering the window—another hard-body dynamic effect.

1. Open Modeler and select the Box tool from the Create tab. Create a box in the bottom left (Back) view, about 10 m by 5 m, with multiple segments. You can do this by pressing **n** to open the Numeric panel and then setting the number of segments. Create about 24 segments or so for the X and 10 for the Y. This doesn't have to be exactly like it is here; just make sure your box has many segments so that it can be broken apart. **Figure 10.11** (on the next page) shows the model.
2. If you've created your flat box and can't see it in the Perspective view, press **f** to flip its polygons.
3. Press Shift+J to activate the Jitter tool (also found on the Modify tab).

Figure 10.11 Create a box in Modeler that has multiple segments along its X and Y axes.

4. In the Jitter panel that appears (**Figure 10.12**), enter 400 mm for both the X and Y values. Leave the Z-axis setting at 1 m.

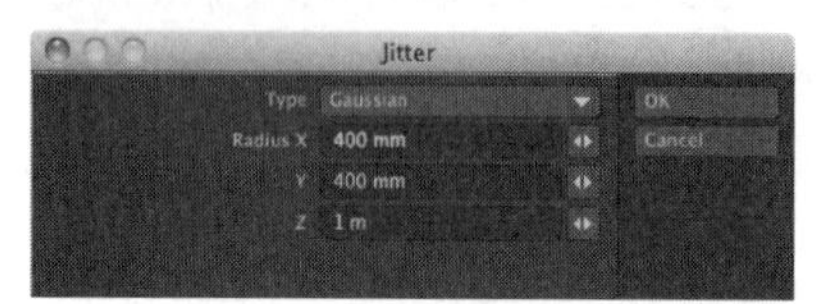

Figure 10.12 Use the Jitter tool to shake up the shape of the polygons.

5. Switch to Points selection mode at the bottom of the interface.
6. Now, carefully select the very bottom-left point of the box, and holding the Shift key, select the point immediately above it, as shown in **Figure 10.13**.

   You're selecting two points sequentially to tell Modeler which way you want your selection to go, for the next step.

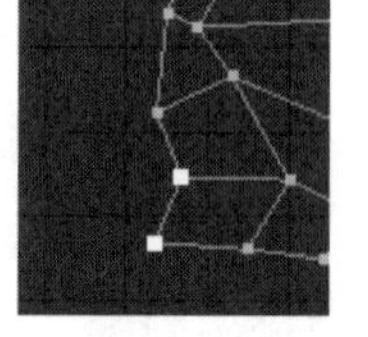

Figure 10.13 Select, in order, the bottom-left corner point and the point just above it.

7. So, from the Select drop-down at the top left of the interface, choose Select Loop, as shown in **Figure 10.14**.

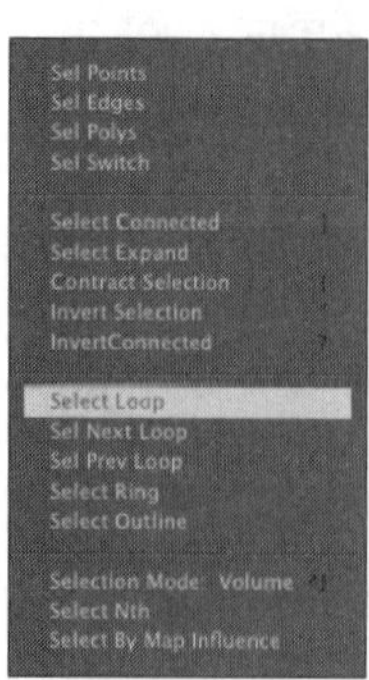

Figure 10.14 Choose Select Loop to automatically continue the selection of points.

8. Once you choose Select Loop, LightWave Modeler continues selecting points for you around the entire box, as shown in **Figure 10.15**.

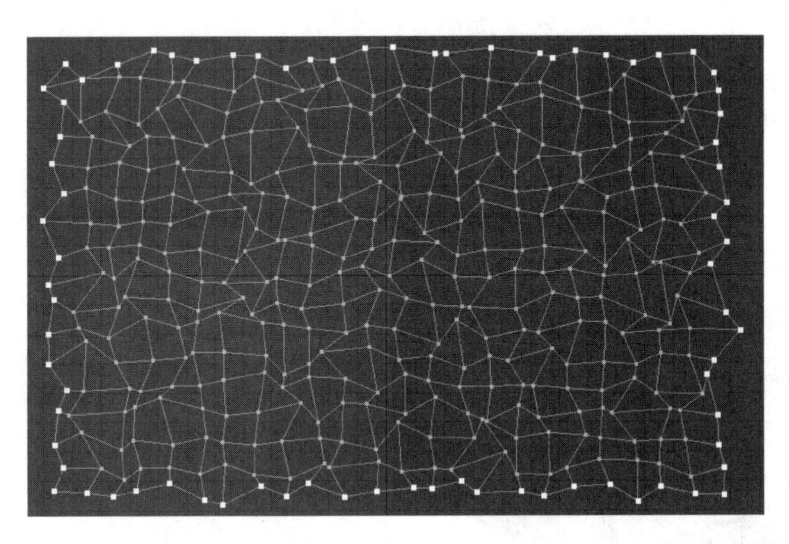

Figure 10.15 Using Select Loop is an easy way to select the points around the entire box.

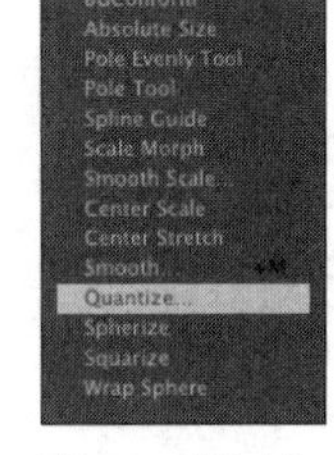

Figure 10.16 Select Quantize on the Modify tab.

9. With the entire outer edge of points selected, click the Modify tab, and at the bottom left under the Transform category, click the More drop-down button and then choose Quantize, as shown in **Figure 10.16**.

10. In the Quantize dialog box, leave all axis settings at 500 mm, as shown in **Figure 10.17**. You can simply enter **.5** and press the Tab key to get a 500 mm setting.

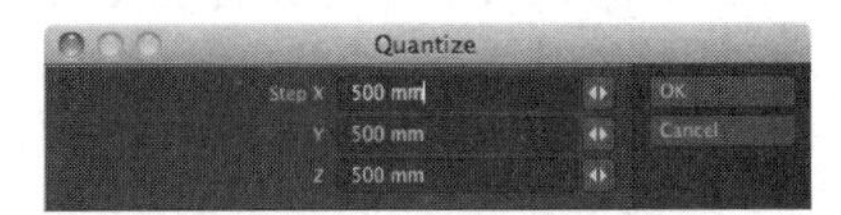

Figure 10.17 Set the Quantize value to 500 mm.

11. Click OK to apply the Quantize values, and as you can see from **Figure 10.18**, the selected points even out, except for a few.

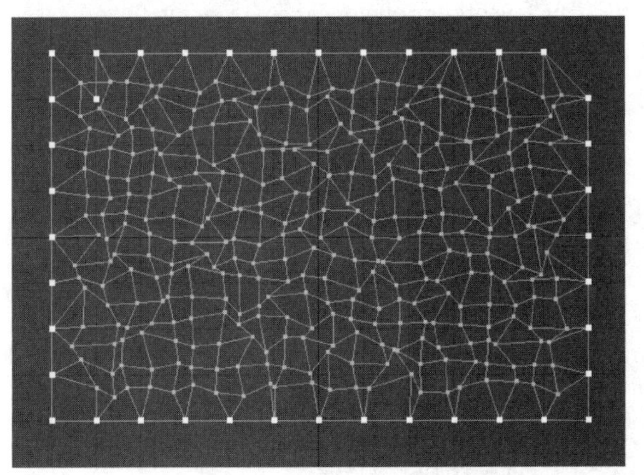

Figure 10.18 Using the Quantize tool, you can even out the selected points.

12. Press Control+T to activate the Drag tool, and then drag the few points that are sticking out of the perimeter back into line with the other points.

NOTE

There's another way you could have created this model to this point. After you created the segmented box, you could have selected all of the polygons of the model except for those that make up the outer edge, and then applied the Jitter tool. Only those selected polygons would have Jitter applied, leaving the outer edge nice and even. The reason this exercise showed you another method was simply to have you work with a few more of Modeler's tools. So, now you know. The choice is yours for future projects.

13. Save your model as **GlassWindow** or something similar. You're not quite finished.

14. Switch to Polygons selection mode, and then press **w** to open the Statistics panel (**Figure 10.19**). Look to the 4 Vertices listing. Click the plus (+) sign to its left, and all the polygons with more than four vertices will become highlighted.

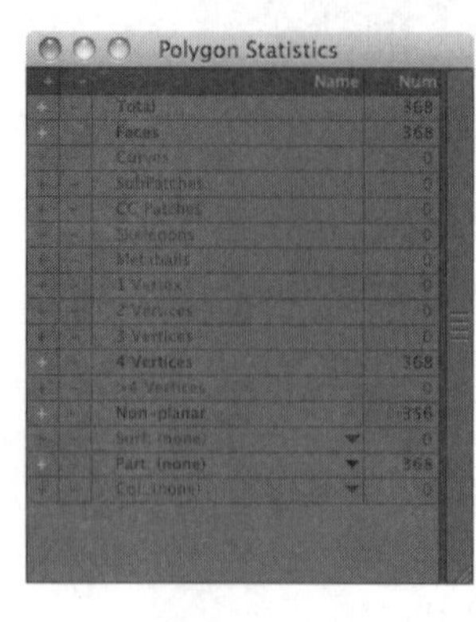

Figure 10.19 Use the Statistics panel to select polygons with more than four vertices.

15. Taking a look at your selection, it pretty much seems that all the polygons have more than four vertices. That's fine, and while you're not going to subpatch these polys, go ahead and press Shift+T to *triple* them—which is LightWave-speak for converting a selected group of polygons into triangles. These triangles will become "shards" of glass in the shattered-window animation.

16. After you've tripled the polygons, click the Align button on the Detail tab. You might get a message saying that 20 polygons have been flipped. The Align tool looks at all the polygons, sees that the majority of them are facing in one direction, and flips the few other polygons that are facing the other direction (**Figure 10.20**).

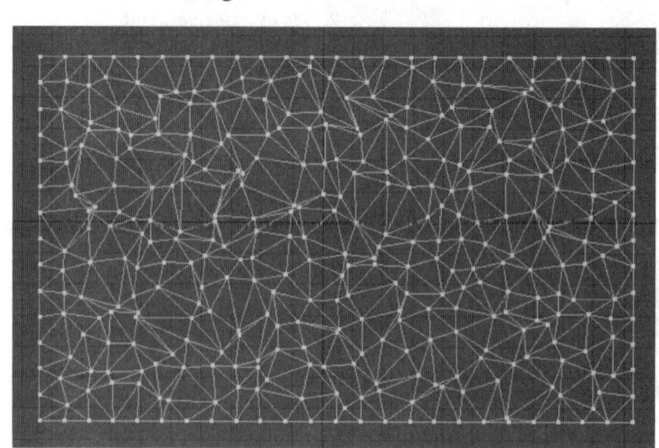

Figure 10.20 Triple the polygons to break them up more, and use the Align tool to make them all face the same direction.

17. We have one last thing to do, and this is probably the most important step. On the Detail tab, select Unweld. The reason this step is important is because in order to have another object break apart this glass window, the multiple polygons you just created can't be attached to each other. **Figure 10.21** shows the tool.

Figure 10.21 Use the Unweld command to disconnect all the polygons.

The adjacent polygons of your model share common points and side segments; in LightWave lingo, these polygons are *welded* together. The Unweld command converts each selected polygon into a discrete, self-contained object with sides and vertices all its own. Applying the Unweld command to the window surface will allow the dynamics engine to shatter the window by animating each triangular segment as an independent "shard." If you did not unweld the points, the dynamics engine could only move or push the entire window object, even though it consisted of multiple segments.

NOTE

Even though unwelding separates each segment, the window is still one solid object. And, without using dynamics to break up the object, moving the object in Layout will still move the entire object, not the segments.

18. After you've unwelded the points, save the object. That's it! Your window is created.

If you want, select various polygons and apply different surface names to them. Select a few polygons, for example, press **q**, and then give those panes of glass a specific name and color. Deselect, then select some other panes, surface, color, and so on. The GlassWindow file in the Chapter 10 folder of this book's DVD has this already done for you.

Exercise 10.3 Shattering Glass

This next exercise will shatter the glass window object built in the previous exercise. It's similar to the earlier hard-body exercise, but with a few differences in settings.

1. Load the GlassWindow_Setup scene from this book's DVD. This is a glass window, much like the one created in Exercise 10.2, with its surface polygons unwelded. The main difference between this model and the window created in the previous exercise is that it contains a white-to-blue background, which won't appear until you render your scene.

   The dynamic collisions that will shatter the window object in this exercise require the window object's polygons to be unwelded—converted to discrete, self-contained polygons that share no points or segments. Recall that we used the Unweld command in Exercise 10.2 to separate the window's surface polygons into "shards" that can be animated independently.

2. Set the scene's final frame number to 200, using the number field at the bottom right of the timeline, and then select Collision from the Dynamic Obj drop-down on Layout's Item tab (**Figure 10.22** on the next page).

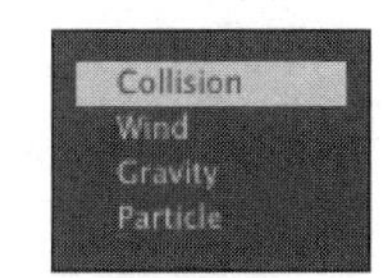

Figure 10.22 Add a dynamic object straight into Layout from the Items tab.

   How is this different from the collision you added in Exercise 10.1? In that exercise, you added an object (named Solids) and told LightWave to make it a collision object. In this exercise, you're creating a collision effector, which we'll use to blow apart the GlassWindow object. Instead of building another object, you can just apply a dynamic effect directly. You can then even add a HyperVoxel explosion of particles to the effector to enhance the effect.

3. When you add the collision effector, a panel will appear, inviting you to name the collision. This will be the only collision in the scene, so just click OK to keep the default name, Bounce. (This name is applied because the default collision mode option is Bounce.) The FX_Collision panel will appear, and you'll see a wireframe sphere appear in the scene, representing the collision effector (**Figure 10.23**).

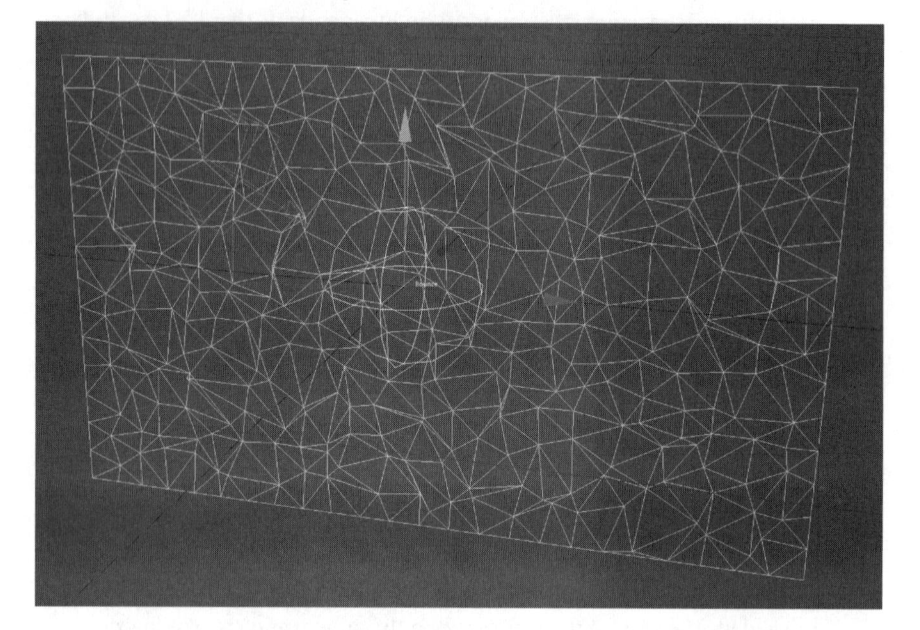

Figure 10.23 A dynamic collision effector in Layout, as represented by a wireframe ball.

Take a look at the FX_Collision control panel, and you'll notice the same controls that appeared on the Object Properties panel's Dynamics tab throughout Exercise 10.1. LightWave often provides multiple locations for its controls.

4. In the FX_Collision panel, increase the Radius/Level value to 2 m, as in **Figure 10.24**.

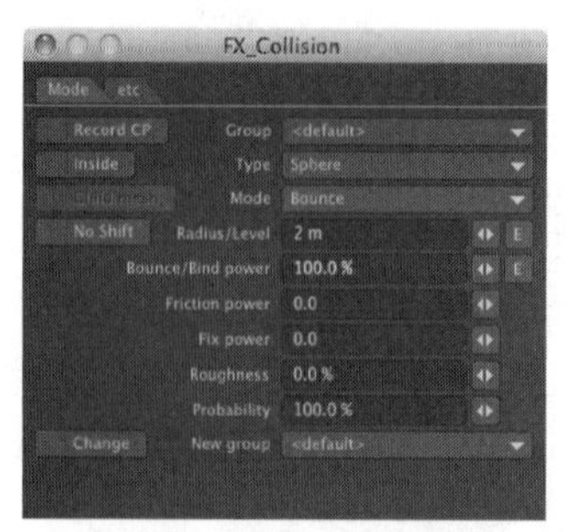

Figure 10.24 Increase the collision dynamic from the FX_Collision control panel.

5. Click the Layout window and press **t** to activate the Move tool. Drag the collision object along the negative Z-axis until its entire volume is behind the GlassWindow object, and then create a keyframe at frame 0 to lock it in place.
6. Move the frame slider to frame 60, and then reposition the collision object along the positive Z-axis, until it is entirely in front of the GlassWindow object, and create a keyframe to lock it in place. **Figure 10.25** shows frame 60 and the motion path the collision object follows between frames 0 and 60.

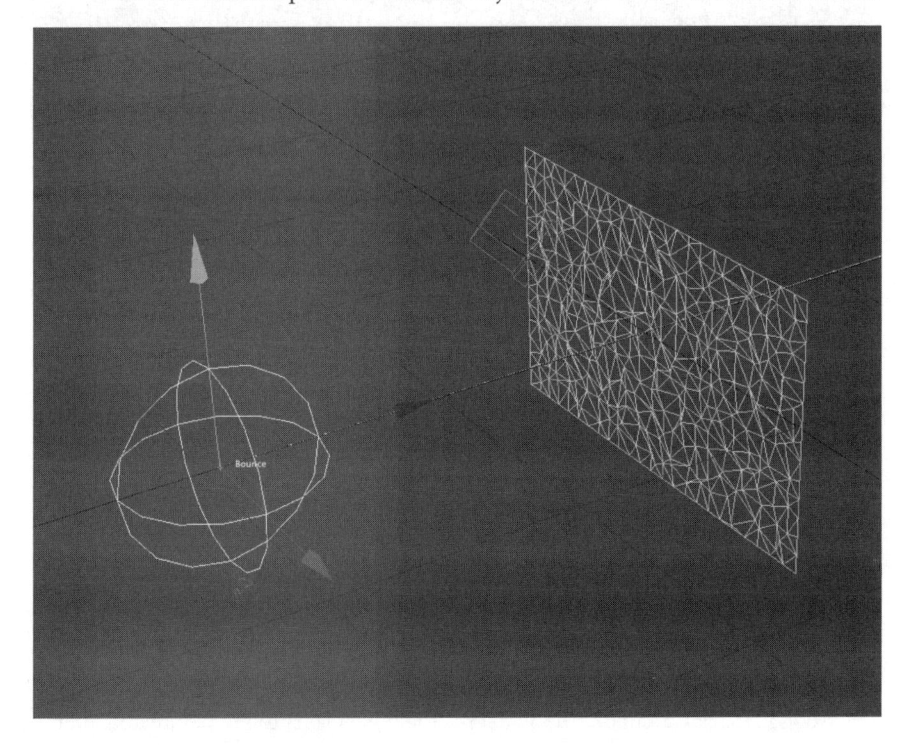

Figure 10.25 A small animation is created with the collision dynamic.

7. Keep the collision object selected and press **p** to open the Object Properties panel. Click the Calculate button on its Dynamics tab.

   Nothing will happen because you do not have anything to calculate. For the GlassWindow object to break apart, you must apply a hard dynamic to it.
8. Click the GlassWindow object to select it (if it isn't selected already), and then select Hard from the Add Dynamic drop-down on the Object Properties panel's Dynamics tab (**Figure 10.26**).

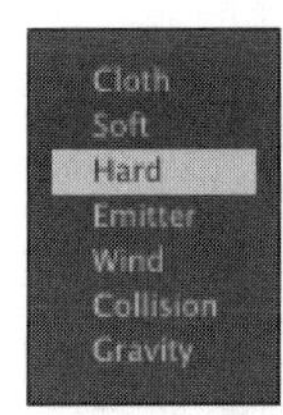

Figure 10.26 Add a hard dynamic to the collision effector.

9. Select the HardFX listing to access the controls, and you'll see that Parts is selected in the Piece Mode drop-down. Change this to 1Piece and click the Calculate button. The collision dynamic in Layout hits the object and pushes the entire object away. This control is important to how your object breaks apart.

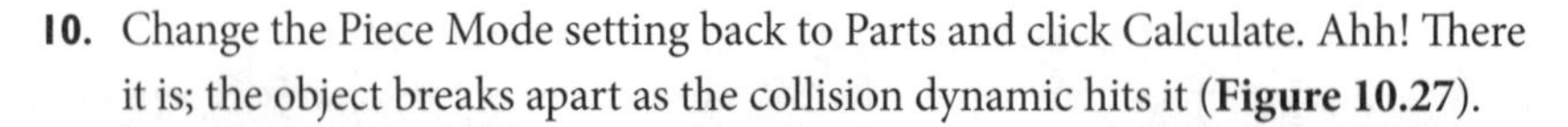

10. Change the Piece Mode setting back to Parts and click Calculate. Ahh! There it is; the object breaks apart as the collision dynamic hits it (**Figure 10.27**).

Figure 10.27 Setting the Piece Mode to Parts allows the pane of glass to be shattered.

11. You're probably noticing that the pieces of GlassWindow break apart, but sort of drift off and do not really have any weight or motion of their own. In the HardFX controls for GlassWindow, choose –9.8 from the Gravity drop-down. Click Calculate, and you'll see the object start to fall before and after the collision. That's better, but you don't want LightWave to apply the gravity until the collision happens.
12. Click the Collision tab of the HardFX controls and check Start By Collision, as shown in **Figure 10.28**. Then click Calculate again. GlassWindow sits still until the collision effector strikes it, and then its pieces expand and begin to drop.

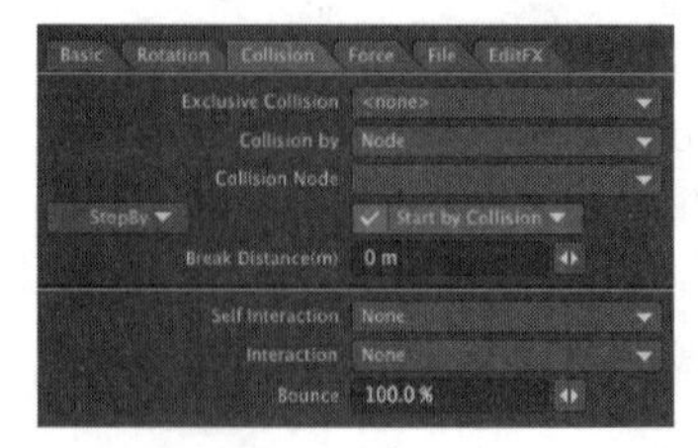

Figure 10.28 Check the collision effector's Start By Collision box to make the GlassWindow object sit still until it breaks apart.

From this point on, it's a matter of tweaking the settings and observing the results until the animation looks the way you want it to look. None of the remaining steps in this exercise are essential or strictly "correct." Try them all to acquaint yourself with the effects of the controls they describe, and decide for yourself if you want to keep the suggested settings, apply higher or lower values, or discard the adjustments altogether.

NOTE

If you want to make sure the exploding pieces do not collide with one another, you can choose Box from the Self Interaction drop-down on the Collision tab of the Object Properties panel's Dynamics tab. Be careful, though, because this will greatly increase calculation times. You can always cancel a calculation by pressing the Control key.

13. Click the Basic tab of the HardFX controls and increase the Weight setting to 35.0. This increases the weight of the pieces when they break up, resulting in heavier parts, which have more inertia and hit the ground faster. If you were animating something like paper, this weight value would be less, about 5 or 10.
14. Click into Layout and select the dynamic collision object. Use the Dope Track to cut the keyframe at frame 60 and paste it at frame 20, and then click Calculate again. This increases the collision effector's rate of acceleration as it collides with GlassWindow, and just like in the real world, that increases the force of the impact. By the same token, pasting the keyframe at, say, frame 120 will reduce the rate of acceleration and lower the force of impact.
15. Set the Impact Effect to Roll in the HardFX panel's Rotation tab (**Figure 10.29**). This will make the shards of glass spin as they spread away from the collision. Try playing with the Min and Max torque values to add more variety.

Figure 10.29 Set the Impact Effect to Roll to make the shards spin as they shatter and fall.

16. Add one more thing to this animation and then get ready to learn about soft-body dynamics. Choose Collision from the Dynamic Obj drop-down on the Items tab to add another collision object to the scene, and type **Ground** when prompted to give it a name.
17. When the FX_Collision panel opens for the Ground object, choose Plane from the Type drop-down. This makes a flat collision plane.
18. Change the Radius/Level value for the Ground object to –7 m. This tells the collision to happen beneath the GlassWindow object, at –7 m on the Y-axis. Click the Calculate button and you'll see the exploding parts now fall and hit a ground surface (granted, there is no visible surface).
19. The shards bounce a little too much when they hit the ground, don't you think? So, reduce the Bounce/Bind Power value to 80% in the FX_Collision panel for the ground plane. Click Calculate again, and you'll see the pieces fall and bounce randomly, as in **Figure 10.30** (on the next page).

Figure 10.30 A Plane-type collision object makes the parts fall and bounce on the ground.

20. Finally, you can use the Camera view to set up a cool moving camera as the glass breaks and flies toward you. **Figure 10.31** shows a render with VPR. Save your scene!

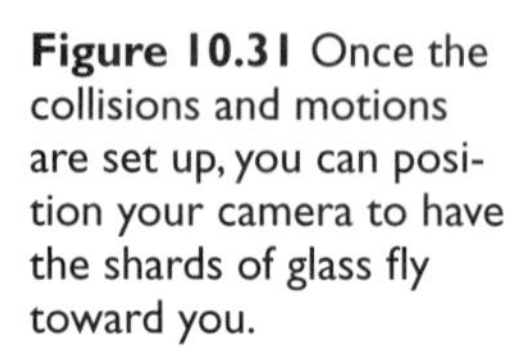

Figure 10.31 Once the collisions and motions are set up, you can position your camera to have the shards of glass fly toward you.

You can use the techniques from the preceding examples to set up just about any collision in which rigid objects crash together and break apart or scatter. Here are a few more tips you can try when working with hard-body dynamics:

- On the Rotation tab in the HardFX panel, change Wind Effect to Roll. When your parts are exploded after the collision, they'll roll, as if blown by the force of a shockwave in the air, radiating from the impact point. This adds a nice touch to exploding objects.
- On the Rotation tab of the HardFX panel, change the Torque Min and Torque Max values to balance the amount of initial and ending spin and motion on the exploding parts.
- Try changing the Pivot Shift value so that the exploding pieces rotate differently. At 0%, each part rotates around its own center point. Change this value to 100%, and the parts rotate as a group around a much larger radius, as if you'd moved all of their pivot points individually. You can also set this to just an X Shift, Y Shift, or Z Shift from the drop-down control to the left of the value requester.
- Increase the Resistance setting on the HardFX panel's Basic tab, to slow down the exploding parts.
- If your exploding parts hop like little bugs after they land, try lowering the Ground object's Bounce/Bind Power setting.
- Use the EditFX panel (as you did in Chapter 9, "Particle Animation") to select and remove or reposition any individual shards as they scatter from the collision.
- Experiment with one setting at a time. Have fun!

What about soft things, like blankets or pillows? How do soft-body dynamics differ from cloth dynamics? When should you use one over the other? Read on to learn about more cool features of the dynamics in LightWave 10.

Soft-Body Dynamics

What is a soft-body dynamic? Is it just for making plump characters move naturally? That's one thing it can do. But soft-body dynamics can do much more. A soft-body dynamic applies to any object that is… well, soft! More specifically, it's anything that is soft and resilient; its surface yields when something hits it, but it reverts to its original shape after the collision. Think of a water balloon, a sofa cushion, or perhaps even the pants on a walking character.

Exercise 10.4 Working with Soft-Body Dynamics

1. In LightWave Layout, save any work you've done and clear the scene.

2. Load the Pillow object from the Chapter 10 folder of this book's DVD. Set up the view to a comfortable Perspective view and open the Object Properties panel for the object. **Figure 10.32** shows the scene.

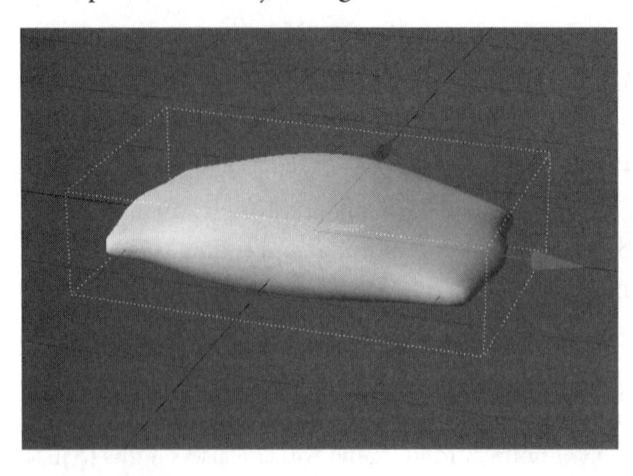

Figure 10.32 Load the Pillow object into Layout and view the scene from a Perspective view.

3. On the Dynamics tab in the Object Properties panel, add a soft dynamic from the drop-down list for the Pillow object.
4. Click the Layout window, and choose Collision from the Dynamic Obj drop-down on the Items tab. When prompted, type **Ground** to name the new object, which will provide a ground collision.
5. For this collision dynamic, set Type to Plane and set Radius/Level to 0 m.
6. Select the Pillow object and create a keyframe for its current position at frame 15.
7. Use the Move tool (press **t**) to raise the Pillow object up about 20 m along the Y-axis (**Figure 10.33**). Create a keyframe at frame 0 to lock it in place.

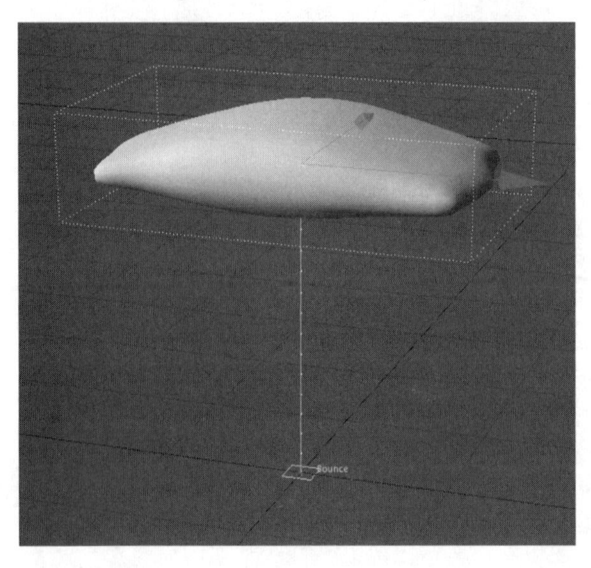

Figure 10.33 Two keyframes are set for the Pillow object.

8. Click the Calculate button in the Dynamics tab and watch the pillow fall. It bounces sort of like gelatin when it strikes the collision object.

   Not very effective for a pillow…

9. Click the Deform tab within the SoftFX controls. Make sure Collision Detect is set to All. Exclusive Collision should be set to None. Increase the Collision Size value to about 6 m, as in **Figure 10.34**.

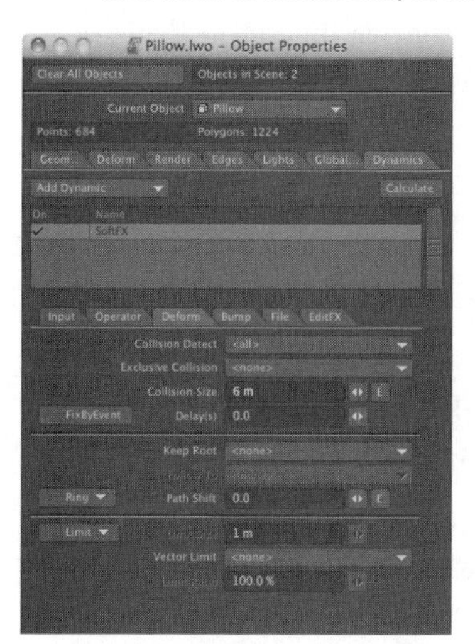

Figure 10.34 Changing the values on the Deform tab tells the pillow how to react to the collision.

10. Click the Calculate button. The pillow drops and looks better. It still bounces a bit too much, though.

11. On the Operator tab for the pillow's SoftFX, set the WaveCycle option for the Operator1 Map to 2.0. Then, set the WaveSize value to 0.2, as shown in **Figure 10.35**. Click Calculate again and your pillow looks more natural dropping into the scene.

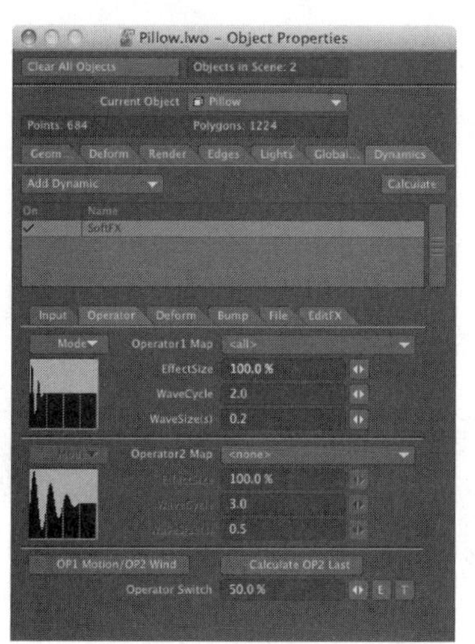

Figure 10.35 Changing the pillow's WaveSize and WaveCycle settings balances the amount the pillow bounces when it hits the ground.

> Changing the WaveSize value for the pillow tells LightWave how to calculate the motions after the dynamic is applied. You can even see a small thumbnail window of the wave's motion, starting off more intense on the left and fading off over time to the right.

As you can see from this exercise, setting up objects with soft-body dynamics is easy. What other things can you think of to create with soft-body dynamics? Aside from things like tires hitting the ground or animating gelatin, soft-body dynamics can also be used for characters. You can define a *point set* in Modeler by selecting a group of points and then clicking New for Selection Set (the S button) at the bottom right of the Modeler interface. Then in Layout, use that selection set and the deformer for soft-body dynamics to make a character's body parts jiggle. Fun stuff!

The Next Step

This chapter introduced you to hard- and soft-body dynamics. Even though the tutorials were simple, their methods and results are the same whether you're building New York City in 3D or just a ball and box.

I can't emphasize this enough: Practice! Experiment! Change a value; see the results. Work with one value at a time, and as always, consult your LightWave 3D manual for any specific technical questions. Now, turn the page and learn about LightWave 10's bones tools for deforming objects.

Chapter 11

Bones and Rigging

The focus of this chapter is bones, Skelegons, and proper character setup for animation. As with the previous *Inside LightWave* books, we won't bore you with technical babble about theory and muscle structures; rather, this chapter discusses the following:

- Understanding bones
- Working with Skelegons for character rigs in Modeler
- Weighting characters for precise control
- Rigging characters directly in LightWave Layout

Understanding Bones

Bones are deformation tools; they *deform* your models so they can bend, twist, stretch, and contract realistically, without requiring all of their limbs and other body parts to be modeled and animated as separate objects. Without bones, creation of figures that move naturally in their skin (or in clothing, fur, feathers, and so on) would be virtually impossible, and animated figures would all resemble robots or marionettes. Bones let you model characters as "solid" objects, and then give them movement and life. Given all that, keep the idea in the back of your mind that bones can also be used for other purposes, such as animating billowing curtains or a beating heart. **Figure 11.1** shows a bone in Layout.

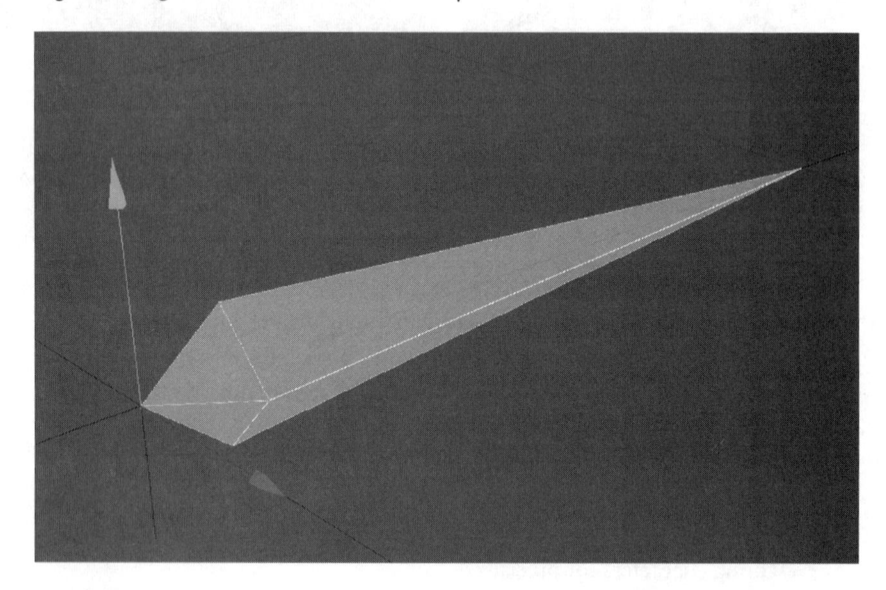

Figure 11.1 A bone in Layout looks like a necktie. It does not render, but it exerts powerful control over its associated object.

There are two types of bones in LightWave, the Z-axis bone and the Joint bone. Each type deforms your object, but a Joint bone can help you create some very cool squash and stretch actions in your animations. To better understand the comparisons of the two bone types, look at the video called CH11_BoneType.mov on the book's DVD.

Bones aren't difficult to use, but you must follow some rules to make them work properly. First, and most importantly, every bone must be associated with an object. The purpose of a bone is to deform an object, so a bone without an object has no purpose in and of itself. So you must attach every bone to an object, even if it's just a null object. Exercise 11.1 provides the steps to do just that.

Exercise 11.1 Creating Bones in Layout

1. Start Layout, or if it's already running, choose Clear Layout from the File drop-down menu at the top left of the interface. Then click the Setup tab. This is where all of Layout's bone controls are located. If you look to the

Add category on the left, you'll see that all the commands are grayed out. You have no objects loaded, so LightWave won't let you add any bones to the scene. Select the Items tab at the top of Layout and select Null from the Add category.

This null object is your base, or root, object. Even though bones need to be associated with an object, the object can be just a null object.

2. Rename the null object if you like, but the default name, Null, is fine. With the null object selected (as the only object in the scene, it's selected by default), click the Setup tab. Then, from the Add category, select Bone and then Add Bone. LightWave asks you to rename the bone. Just click OK for now.

You'll see a 1 m bone, like the one in Figure 11.1, extending along the Z-axis from the null object's position at the origin point (**Figure 11.2**).

TIP

Instead of clicking away from the Setup tab to the Items tab to add a null object, you can always just press Control+N on your keyboard to quickly add a null object.

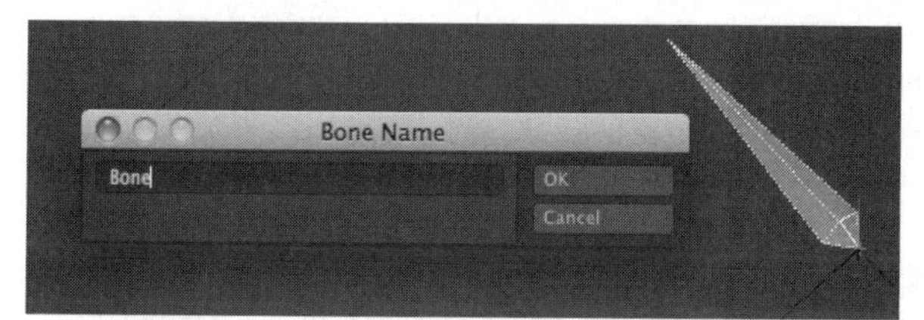

Figure 11.2 Adding a bone to a null object creates a 1 m bone extended along the Z-axis.

Next, you'll set up a chain of bones by adding "child" bones to the one you just made. Just as child objects depend on and move with their parent objects, "child" bones are controlled by parents and can be used to set up subtle or complex object deformations.

3. With the first bone selected, click the Child Bone button. Click OK because you don't need to set a name when the requester asks you to.

You'll see a bone attached to the end of the previous bone (**Figure 11.3**).

Figure 11.3 You can add child bones to create a hierarchical structure.

TIP

Using the Scene Editor, you can recolor bones for easier visibility and better organization in Layout. The color change does not affect the bone's function, only its visibility.

4. Add one more child bone as you did in step 3. A quick way to add child bones is to press = (the equal sign key). After it is added, select the first bone and rotate it. Press the up arrow key twice to change the selected bone.

   When the parent bone rotates, you'll see the child bone rotate as well. If you select and rotate the second bone, its child bone rotates, too.

   This hierarchical structure is explained in detail in the section "Creating Hierarchies." For now, you can think of this structure as similar to your own arm. The shoulder is connected to the upper arm, which is connected to the forearm, which is connected to the hand, and so on. If you move the shoulder, the other parts of your arm move as well.

   This quick-and-dirty example showed you how to create bones in Layout. The base object that you assigned bones to does not have to be null—it can be anything you want, from a character to a snake to a piece of paper. Anything you want to deform can have bones added to it. Granted, this wasn't very exciting, was it? Read on, and we'll see bones in action.

Figure 11.4 The Penguin object is loaded into an empty layout, ready for some bones!

NOTE

Bones deform objects and their surfaces by repositioning the points that make up their surface polygons. In order for an object to be deformed correctly using bones, its surfaces must consist of multiple polygons. A cube with just eight vertices, or points, will not deform well with bones, but if its faces are subpatched or subdivided into multiple squares, the same cube becomes more malleable and can be deformed by bones.

Exercise 11.2 Adding Bones to Objects

This exercise takes you a step further than the previous one by showing how to put bones into an object. From there, you'll see how bones can be used to manipulate the shape of an inanimate object.

1. First, check the bottom of the Layout interface to make sure that Auto Key is enabled. When working with bones, it's good to use this feature because you can concentrate on motions, and LightWave will record the changes. Select Clear Scene from the File drop-down list in Layout. Load the Penguin object from the 3D_Content\Objects\CH11\Penguin.lwo folder on this book's DVD. We'll add bones to the character to control its movement. **Figure 11.4** shows the penguin model, as seen in Layout's Perspective view with VPR active.
2. Press **3** on your keyboard or numeric keypad to switch to the side view (Right).
3. With VPR active, make sure both OpenGL Overlay and Bone X-Ray mode are on from the top of the layout interface (it's the tiny drop-down arrow to the right of the viewport style button). This will help you see the placement of bones (**Figure 11.5**).

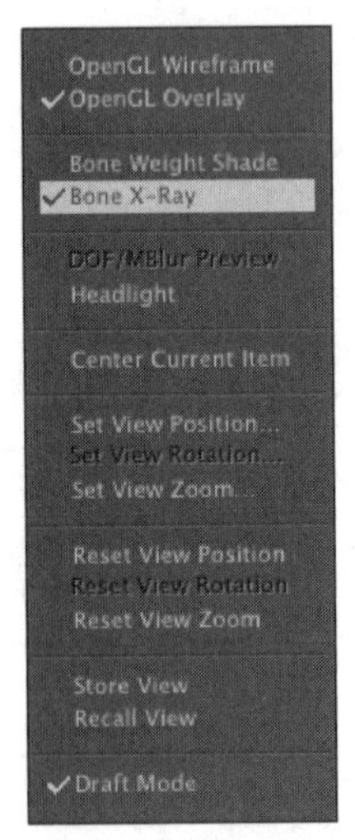

Figure 11.5 Change your view to look at the Right side and switch to a Front Face Wireframe style.

4. With the penguin model selected, click the Setup tab and then click Bone in the Add category. Enter the name **Body** for this bone in the panel that appears and click OK. You'll see a bone added to the object at the base of the foot (**Figure 11.6**).

   The bone might be a bit hard to see because its outline is dotted to indicate that the bone is not yet active. Also, despite appearances, the bone is not actually added to the bottom of the foot; it's associated with the entire penguin model, aligned along the Z-axis.

5. The bone position now needs to be set so that it can properly control the object. Select Move from the Modify tab (or press **t**) and move the bone up to the middle of the body.

6. Click the Rotate tool on the Modify tab (or press **y**) and rotate the bone so that the pointy edge is facing up, with a 90-degree Pitch value, as displayed in the info window at the lower-left corner of the Layout interface (**Figure 11.7**).

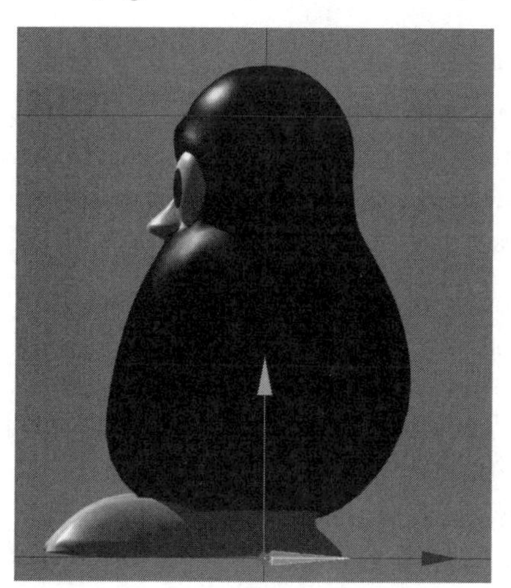

Figure 11.6 After a bone is added, it needs to be put into place.

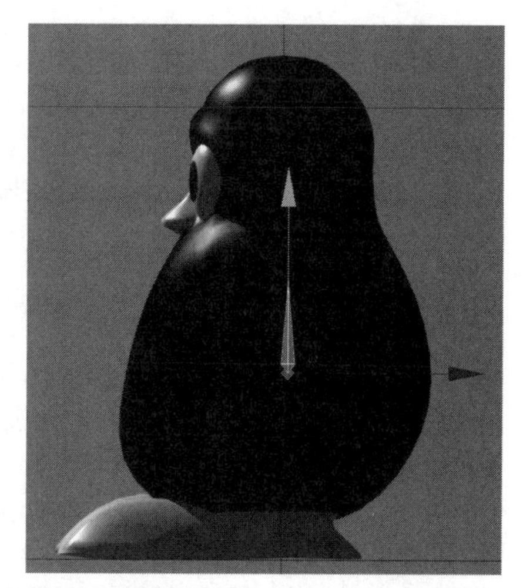

Figure 11.7 Move and rotate the bone so that it rests in position pointing up and in the middle of the penguin.

7. With the single bone selected, press **p** on your keyboard to open the bone's Properties panel. In the middle of the panel, change the Rest Length setting to about 1.5 m, as shown in **Figure 11.8** (on the next page). This measurement represents your Layout Grid Square Size. Changing Rest Length tells LightWave to give this bone a larger range of influence—that is, the area or range that the bone is affecting.

   When scaling a bone to match the length of a model's limb, spine, or what have you, you must adjust its rest length, not its size. This can't be stressed

NOTE

Front Face Wireframe is a good viewing option for bones because LightWave shows only the wireframes visible to your view. This simplifies what you see, making placement of bones much easier. A normal wireframe view will show not only what's in view of the camera, but the other side of the object as well, sometimes making it a bit confusing to determine the shape, size, angle, or position of the object.

NOTE

When adjusting sub-patched objects such as the penguin model, it's sometimes easier to hide surface subdivisions. To do so, set the Display SubPatch Level to 0 in the Object Properties panel. (Select the object and press **p**.)

NOTE

The object's Render SubPatch Level does not affect the way you see it in Layout. It can be set higher than the Display SubPatch level, perhaps to 6. When the object is rendered, it will be smooth and subdivided.

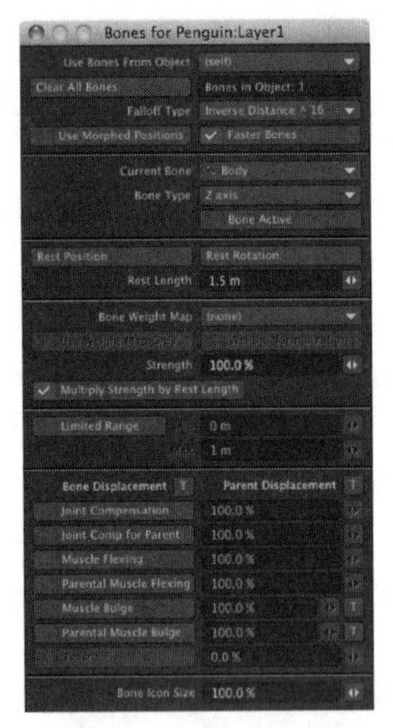

Figure 11.8 Change the Rest Length setting of the bone so that it will deform a larger area. Do this from the bone's Properties panel.

enough. The Rest Length setting is the final length of the bone before it is made active—in other words, its resting position. The number one mistake LightWave animators make with bones is to use the Size tool and change the actual size of the bone instead of its rest length.

Once a bone's rest length is set and the bone is activated, resizing the bone will cause a comparable size change in the portion(s) of the model influenced by the bone. A simple application of this would enable an object to "breathe" by expanding and contracting slightly; more advanced applications could allow objects to inflate, characters to shrink, and so on.

What you've done here is create a spine for the Penguin object. These bone techniques can be used for any type of character or object to build arms and legs, tentacles, wings, and so on.

8. Save your scene by selecting File, Save, and then Save Scene. You can also just press **s**.

Creating Hierarchies

What exactly is a *hierarchy*? Your fingers are attached to your hand, your hand is attached to your wrist, and your wrist is attached to your forearm, and so on. Move the shoulder, and the attached bones move with it. That's a hierarchy! You can create hierarchies of bones and objects in LightWave that work the same way.

Hierarchies of bones and objects in LightWave work according to two distinct but related sets of rules, known as *forward kinematics* and *inverse kinematics*, both of which are essential to realistic movement. Forward kinematics is the process we've just described, whereby moving an object also causes movement of objects below it in a hierarchy: Move a thigh bone, and you also move the shin, ankle, and toes. Inverse kinematics is the reverse effect, in which an object moves those above it in a hierarchy: If something (a bicycle pedal, for example) lifts a model's toes, the attached ankle and knee should rise and bend accordingly. This section demonstrates how to build bones into hierarchical structures that enable both forms of kinematics.

Setting Child Bones

Adding a child bone to an existing bone starts out much like duplicating the parent bone: The new child bone inherits its parent's size, position, and rest length. Setting up that first bone is the hardest part. Once it is in place, you can set child bones. And because they will be "children" of the base bone, their scale will match the penguin better when added, unlike the first bone.

Exercise 11.3 Creating Child Bones

1. This first bone you created in the previous exercise will begin the hierarchy of the penguin body, meaning that it is the parent bone. Each bone that extends from this one is a child bone. If the parent bone moves, its child bones move with it. Make sure the Body bone is selected, and on the Setup menu tab in Layout, click Child Bone in the Add category. Note that you can also use the = key. Name this new bone **Neck**.
2. You can see that an exact duplicate of the Body bone is attached right above it. Change this new bone's Rest Length setting to about 600 mm so that its tip meets the base of the head area, as in **Figure 11.9**. Now if you rotate the Body bone, the new child bone moves with it.
3. Now add another child bone, naming it **Head**. Change the Rest Length setting to about 1.6 m.
4. Add another child bone, which you can also name **Head**. In Layout, you'll now have Head (1) and Head (2) bones. Rotate this bone on its pitch to point down to the nose, about 148 m. You can do this by first pressing **y** on the keyboard and then grabbing the green handle and dragging. Or you can click in the Numeric panel at the bottom left of the Layout interface and directly enter the value. Change this bone's Rest Length setting to 1.85 m so that it encompasses the face. **Figure 11.10** shows the setup.

NOTE

If you forget to name a bone when you create it, don't worry. Just select the bone, and on the Items tab, select Rename from the Replace category.

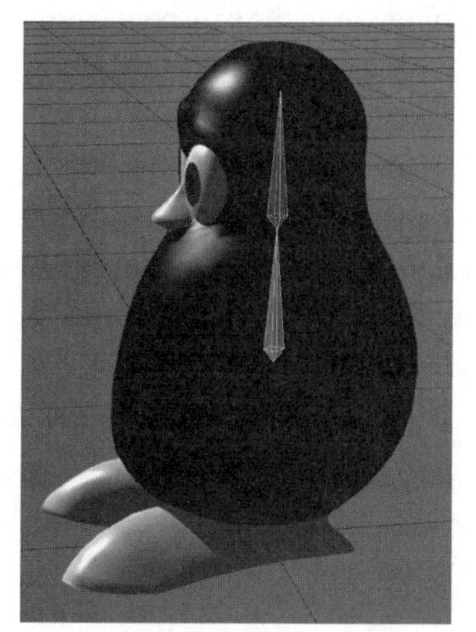

Figure 11.9 A child bone is added to the Body bone, creating a hierarchical duplicate.

Figure 11.10 A second head bone is added and rotated to fit the face of the penguin.

The reason you created this "face" bone—that is, a second head bone—was to help keep the structure intact as it's deformed. Because the character's head is large, the single head bone deforming it might distort the face. But

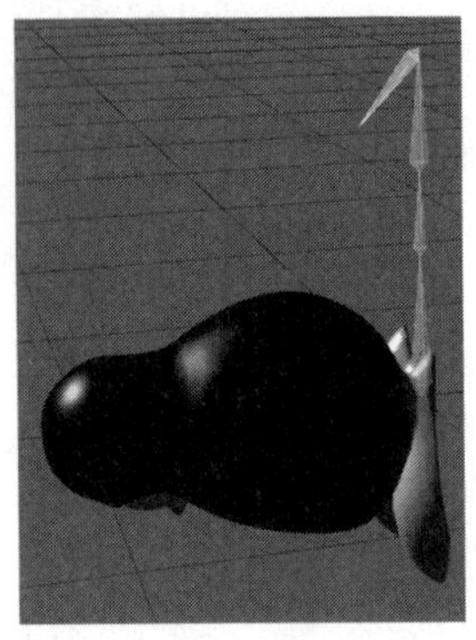

Figure 11.11 Activating a bone by selecting it and pressing **r** tells the bone to influence the model. When only one bone is influencing the model, the model responds accordingly.

the added head bone helps hold the face as the Neck bone moves it. You'll see how this works shortly.

The bones are now in place, but they are not yet influencing the model. This is because they are not active. If you rotate say, the Neck bone, the two head bones should follow, but the head of the character won't move. Now you need to activate the bones. Activating tells LightWave where you want the bones to rest and begin working. But here's the thing—people often set their bones to rest, and suddenly, their object disappears or becomes grossly deformed. Try it out and see.

5. First, make sure all of the bones are in their original positions if you've moved them. Select the second head bone and press **r**, the shortcut for Activate Bone. Your object changes positions, essentially falling over, as in **Figure 11.11**.

   Do you see what happened? The object seems to be messed up, and many animators will stop here and freak out, usually e-mailing the author of this book! But wait! Read on. You did nothing wrong.

   What's happening at this point is that the bone you've set into position is now active and influencing the model. However, it is the only bone influencing it, so the model is deforming based on the position of *only* this bone. When you activate the other bones, the model returns to its proper shape and position. Start activating the bones, beginning from the base bone, and your object will not distort this way.

NOTE

Pressing Control+R deactivates a bone. Press **r** to activate it again.

6. Use the up arrow to select the next bone, press **r**, and repeat the bone activation by pressing **r** for each bone.

   When you activate all the bones, the model returns to its original shape. This is because all bones are now active and properly influencing the deformation of the model. When only one bone was active, such as the last bone for the object, the entire penguin was being influenced by only one bone.

Figure 11.12 When the bones are in place and active, rotating deforms the object.

NOTE

LightWave provides visual cues for differentiating between active and inactive bones. Active bones have solid outlines and inactive bones have dashed outlines. And remember, you can change the color of these lines to make bones easier to see by using the Scene Editor's Visibility commands.

7. Go back to the Perspective view and change the Maximum Render Level setting in the scene to Shaded Solid. Select the Body bone and press the **y** key to rotate the bone. You'll see the object deform, as in **Figure 11.12**.

8. Feel free to change the Bone Icon Size setting, at the bottom of the Bone Properties panel, as in **Figure 11.13**. You can make a bone's visible shape smaller or larger, but this has no bearing on the bone's effect on the object. It's just to give you control over visibility.

Figure 11.13 Set Bone Icon Size to 100%.

9. Press Control+Z to undo the Body bone rotation so the character is in its original position. Select the Neck bone and rotate it. You'll see the head bend along with the neck. But it's not quite right because the body deforms along with the motion, as in **Figure 11.14**.

Figure 11.14 Rotating the Neck bone deforms the entire object.

When the Body bone rotates, the entire penguin body rotates, but you'll notice that the penguin's eyes don't deform along with it. That's because they are separate objects. You created the penguin eyes in separate layers. The bones that influence the body object do not affect other objects, even those within the same model.

In the next exercise, you'll learn how adding hierarchies to the model will let you deform the eyes and ensure that they move along with the penguin's head. You'll also use additional hierarchies to make the motion of the penguin's lower body independent from that of its upper body and to control the movement of its feet.

Creating Multiple Hierarchies

The body and head bones you've added work very nicely to bend and animate the upper part of this object, but you're not quite seeing the results you want just yet. You might think that because you've already created a hierarchy of bones, you don't need to build onto this existing chain. However, you can create an entirely different hierarchy elsewhere within the object. You created the first hierarchy starting with the Body bone. You rotated it upward so that the rotational pivot point of the bone was at the middle of the body, similar to a hip. Now you'll create a similar hierarchy pointing downward into the base and feet of the penguin.

Exercise 11.4 Setting Up Multiple Hierarchies

1. Select the Penguin object. Then, on the Setup tab, click Bone in the Add category. Name it **Base**. Note that this does not create a child to the Body bone but rather a new individual bone. Move and rotate the Base bone so it rests just below the Body bone, essentially mirroring it, as in **Figure 11.15**.
2. With your new Base bone still selected, choose Child Bone from the Setup tab's Add category and enter **RightFoot** as the name for the child bone.
3. Press **1** to switch to a front view. Press **y** to activate the Rotate tool and rotate the child bone (the RightFoot bone) until its heading is 90 degrees. You can do so by dragging the red rotation handle, or by pressing **n** to enter the value numerically at the lower-left corner of the interface.

Figure 11.15 Add a bone to the Penguin object, move it up, and rotate it so that it points down into the character.

4. With the RightFoot bone selected, press **p** to open the Bone Properties panel and set the Rest Length value to about 655 mm, so that the tip of the bone is at the center of the right foot (**Figure 11.16**).
5. With the RightFoot bone selected, add another child bone (or press =, the shortcut for Add Child Bone). Leave the default name, RightFoot (2), unchanged.
6. Rotate this bone, which is the anklebone. Set the bone's Heading value to 90 degrees, so that it's pointed down into the foot. Then, change its Rest Length setting to about 485 mm so that the tip of the bone ends in the middle of the foot (**Figure 11.17**). You can check the bone's position by pressing **3** for a side view and then **1** to go back to a front view.

Figure 11.16 Rotate the RightFoot bone 90 degrees and set the Rest Length value so that its tip ends at the center of the right foot.

Figure 11.17 Begin creating the bones that will control the foot by adding a bone that acts as an ankle.

The reason you're creating a child bone from the RightFoot bone in this hierarchy is to create a human-like structure. The RightFoot (2) bone will serve as the penguin's anklebone.

7. With RightBone (2) still selected, add another child bone by pressing =. Leave the default name, RightBone (3).
8. Set this bone's Pitch value to 90 degrees, so it points down into the foot. Then, set Rest Length to 1 m, as in **Figure 11.18**.
9. Add one more child bone and set the Rest Length to about 1.3 m, slightly larger than the previous bone, so that it extends to the front of the foot, as in **Figure 11.19**.

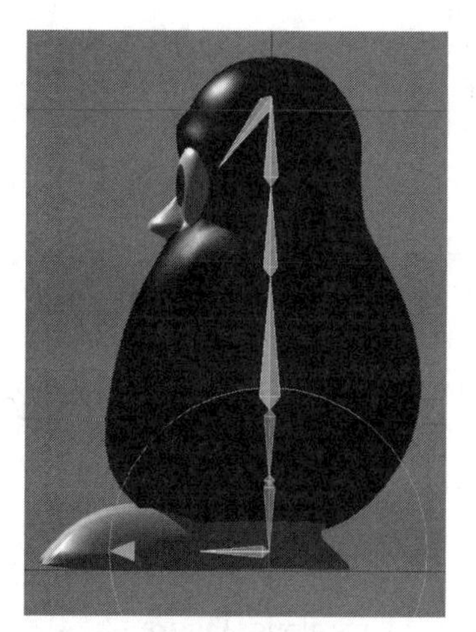

Figure 11.18 Another child bone is added and positioned for the right foot.

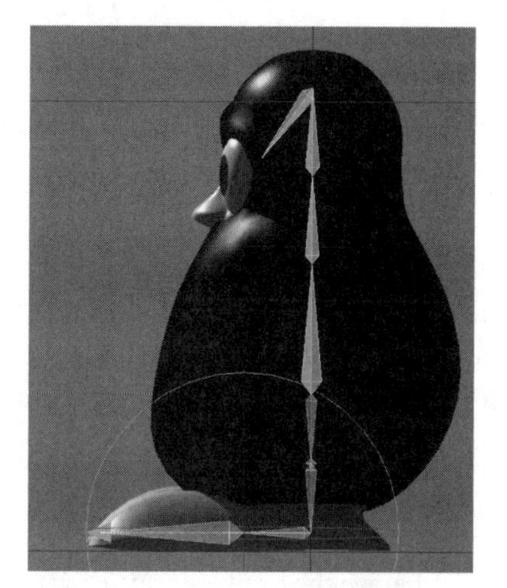

Figure 11.19 One more child bone is added for the front of the foot.

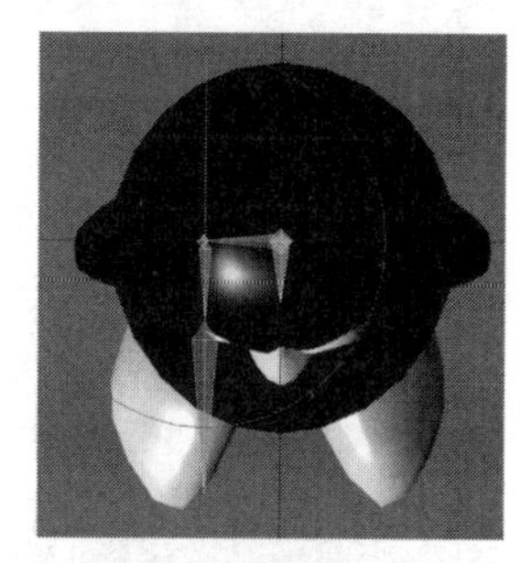

Figure 11.20 While the bones seem to fit the foot in the Side view, the Top view shows that their heading is off.

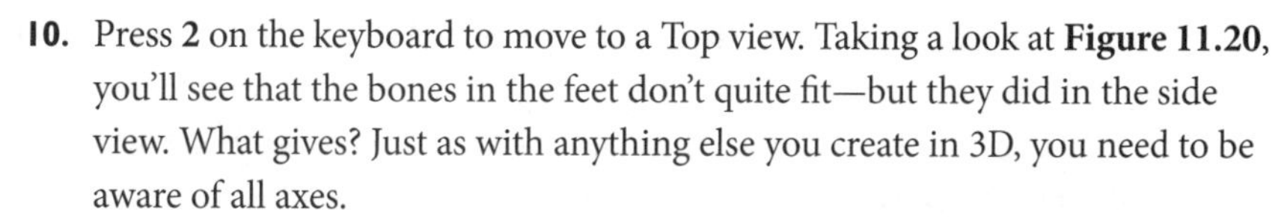

10. Press **2** on the keyboard to move to a Top view. Taking a look at **Figure 11.20**, you'll see that the bones in the feet don't quite fit—but they did in the side view. What gives? Just as with anything else you create in 3D, you need to be aware of all axes.
11. Click RightFoot (3) to select it, and then press **y** to activate the Rotate tool. Rotate the bone until its Heading value is about 76 degrees. **Figure 11.21** shows the change.
12. Save your scene.
13. Now, activate all the bones by selecting each bone and then pressing **r**.
14. After the bones have been activated, select the Neck bone. Press **y** to turn on the Rotate tool, and then use it to rotate the neck. You'll see the head move around, and the body stays in place. Also, there's a nice, smooth flow between the head and the body (**Figure 11.22**).

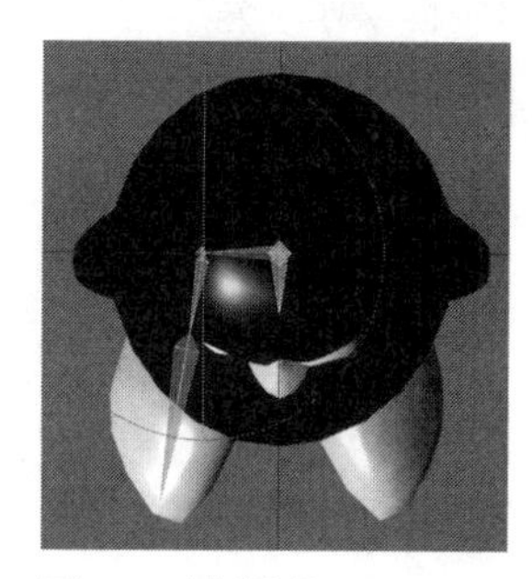

Figure 11.21 By rotating the first bone in the base of the foot, you also rotate its child, easily aligning the foot bones.

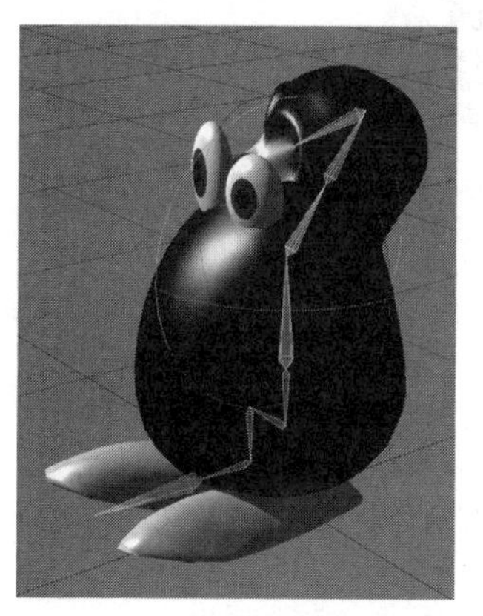

Figure 11.22 Once bones are added to the base of the model, the head can be moved and the body stays put.

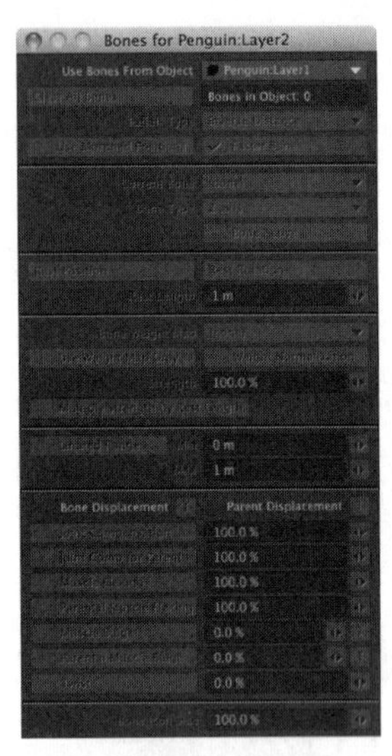

Figure 11.23 Tell the eye object layer to use the bones from the body of the penguin, Layer 1.

15. You still need to fix those floating eyes! Select the first eye in Layer 2. Do this by first choosing the Objects button at the bottom of the LightWave interface, telling LightWave that you want to work with Objects. Then, select Layer 2 from the Item drop-down list, also at the bottom of the interface.
16. Click the Bones button at the bottom of the interface. Then, press **p** to open the Bone Properties panel. Since no bones are associated with the selected object (the eye), the panel will show that there are no bones. Click the Use Bones From Object drop-down list at the top of the Properties panel (it says "self" by default) and choose Layer 1, which contains the Penguin-body object (**Figure 11.23**). This tells the eye object to use the bones from the body object.
17. Now select the second eye, and repeat the previous step. Select the Neck bone and move the head around. The eyes now follow along (**Figure 11.24**).
18. Save your scene.
19. Move down to the feet and select RightFoot (2), the small bone that serves as an anklebone. Press **y** to activate the Rotate tool and twist the bone. What happens? The feet move (**Figure 11.25**). Yes, *both* feet. You want to move just the one foot. Even though the feet are attached to each other, you should still be able to move each one independently. So, you need to create another hierarchy for the left foot.

Figure 11.24 When the eye objects use the bones from the penguin-body layer, they follow when the penguin body is deformed.

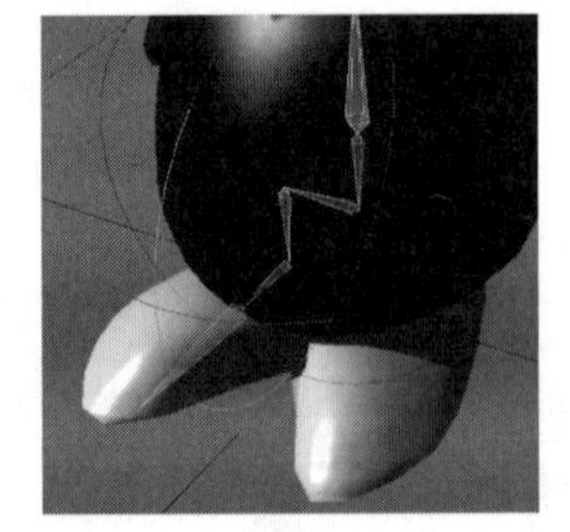

Figure 11.25 Rotating just the right anklebone deforms both feet.

Bones On
Bones Off

Figure 11.26 Turn the bones off before you edit them.

20. Before you edit any bones, it's a good idea to deactivate them. You can do this quickly by going to the Setup tab and selecting Bones Off from the Bones menu, under the General category, as shown in **Figure 11.26**. You can also press Control+R to deactivate a selected bone.

21. With the bones turned off, click RightFoot (1) to select it (**Figure 11.27**).

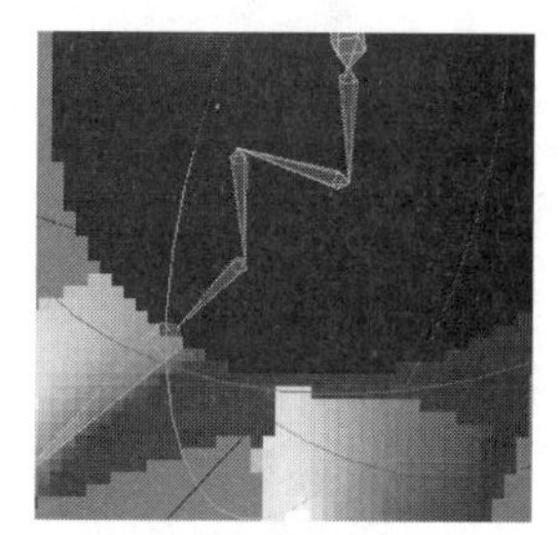

Figure 11.27 Select the first RightFoot bone, which is the second bone in the bottom hierarchy.

22. In the Setup tab's Edit tool category, click Mirror Hierarchy. This opens the Bone Setup: MirrorHierarchy panel. You'll see that the selected bone, RightFoot (1), is chosen in the Root of Hierarchy drop-down at the top of the panel (**Figure 11.28**).

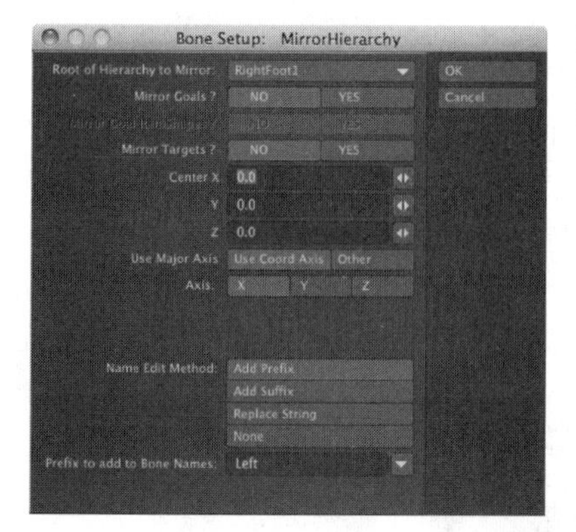

Figure 11.28 The Bone Setup: MirrorHierarchy panel is simple and powerful.

23. Most of the Bone Setup: MirrorHierarchy panel settings can be left at their default values. In the Axis drop-down list, choose X. You want to mirror this hierarchy of bones across the X-axis.

24. For the Name Edit Method option, choose Replace String. For the Replace This String setting, enter **Right**. For the With This String setting, enter the word **Left**. This tells the Mirror Hierarchy tool to give the new mirrored bones the same names as those in the selected hierarchy, but with "Left" substituted for "Right" in their names.

Figure 11.29 It's easy to set up the bones for the left leg with the Mirror Hierarchy tool.

25. Click OK and the entire bone hierarchy will be mirrored. **Figure 11.29** shows the result.

26. On Layout's Setup tab, click Bones and then click Bones On to reactivate the bones in the model. Select the Base bone, which is the parent bone to both sets of legs. Press **y** and rotate this bone. You'll see both sets of legs deform (**Figure 11.30**). OK, they're really just feet—but you get the idea!

27. Save your work!

Figure 11.30 Rotating the Base bone, which is the parent to the bone hierarchies for both legs, causes realistic deformation of the penguin feet.

Even though you've added bones to the upper and lower body, moving the feet causes a bit of unwanted deformation in the body. The foot bones aren't deforming the rest of the penguin too much to be annoying to look at, but you can add even more control by using the Bone Weight tool.

Bone Weights

In LightWave, the relative "heft," or resistance to motion, of objects (or portions of objects) is controlled by a special type of UV surface map called a *weight map*, which assigns weight values to points on a model's surface. LightWave provides several methods of generating weight maps, but one of the quickest is Modeler's Bone Weights tool.

You activate the Make Bone Weight Map panel (**Figure 11.31**) by selecting a bone or an object associated with a bone and clicking Bone Weight on Modeler's Map tab. The panel lets you use the selected bones to generate weight-map settings for the associated objects, without having to select individual points or polygons on those objects. This tool can be a real time-saver, and often provides a great first step for creating maps that you can fine-tune later by tweaking the settings for individual points. The Bone Weights tool can also be used to make global changes to weight maps you've built the "old-fashioned" way—by specifying weight values for individual points and polygons.

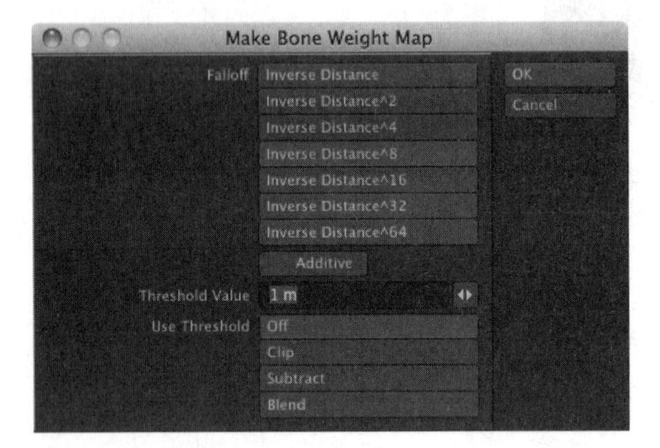

Figure 11.31 The Make Bone Weight Map panel in Modeler.

To use the Bone Weights tool, you must first set up Skelegons, which we'll be discussing shortly.

The Make Bone Weight Map Panel

The first step in understanding the use of bone weights is to explore LightWave's weighting features in Modeler. Weight maps enable you to scale the falloff of various tools in LightWave. With a weight map, a bone affects points according to the weight you set. The result is a controlled influence that eliminates the problem you saw in the previous exercise, when the base bone movement deformed some of the body of the Penguin object. The next few sections will help explain some base bone weighting functions so that you better understand how to use them.

Falloff

The Falloff setting in the Bone Weights panel determines the degree to which an applied weight setting is "concentrated" within a bone and how evenly it is distributed over the surface of the associated object. The setting works mathematically and is expressed as one of several preset exponential Inverse Distance values. The default value, Inverse Distance (with an implied exponent of 1), causes weight concentration to fade in direct proportion to any affected points' distance from the bone. Higher exponential settings, ranging from 2 to 118, cause the influence to fade far more rapidly and concentrate the applied weight proportionately closer to the bone itself.

Additive

If you turn on the Additive option, the Bone Weights settings are automatically applied to all bones with the same name—a big time-saver for every bone named "spine" in a sea urchin model, or even both "shin" bones in a human figure.

Threshold Value

The Threshold Value setting defines a capsule-shaped "border," a fixed distance from a bone, at which the bone's weight settings cease or change. Its setting value is a distance, the radius of influence, expressed in meters (or millimeters).

Use Threshold

The four options for this setting determine how a bone's influence on an object's weight map changes at the edge of the "capsule" defined by its Threshold Value setting. The Off setting means the Threshold Value setting is ignored. The Clip setting sets weight values for all points outside the threshold to 0. The Subtract option causes weight values to fade to 0 at the threshold distance, then continues decreasing weight values (by assigning them negative values) at distances greater than the Threshold Value setting. The Blend option, which is often the most useful, causes weight values to fade steadily to 0 within the "capsule" (like the Subtract setting), but sets all values beyond the threshold distance to 0 (like the Clip setting).

Applying Weight Maps

Exercise 11.5 instructs you on the method of weighting. This process is done in Modeler and enables you to tell a bone to control a specific area rather than the entire object. For example, with weighting, moving the lower leg would not affect the upper area of the penguin.

Bone weights enable you to specify regions of influence. Much of the time when creating character animation you'll be building your model from the ground up, and you can assign weight maps as you go. However, you can also use existing models from a previous project, from another artist, or perhaps from this book's DVD.

Exercise 11.5 Creating Weights

1. Open Modeler and load the Penguin_toWeight object from this book's DVD (3D_Content\Objects\CH11\Penguin_toWeight.lwo). **Figure 11.32** shows the model loaded. Press **a** to fit the model to the view, to match the figure.

Figure 11.32 An existing model is loaded into Modeler and is ready to have weights assigned to it.

In Exercise 11.4, you created two four-bone hierarchies, each consisting of a top legbone, an anklebone, and two foot bones. Now you only need to set up some weight maps for these hierarchies, and your model will deform properly in Layout.

2. Choose Polygons Selection mode by clicking the Polygons button at the bottom of the Modeler interface. Next, press the Tab key to turn off SubPatch mode to make the model easier to work with. You'll turn it back on again when you've finished.
3. Press **w** to open the Statistics panel (**Figure 11.33**). Toward the bottom of the panel, click the Surface listing. This will show you all of the penguin's surfaces that you created when you built the character in Modeler. Select the Feet surface.

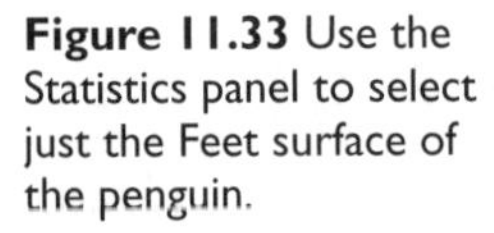

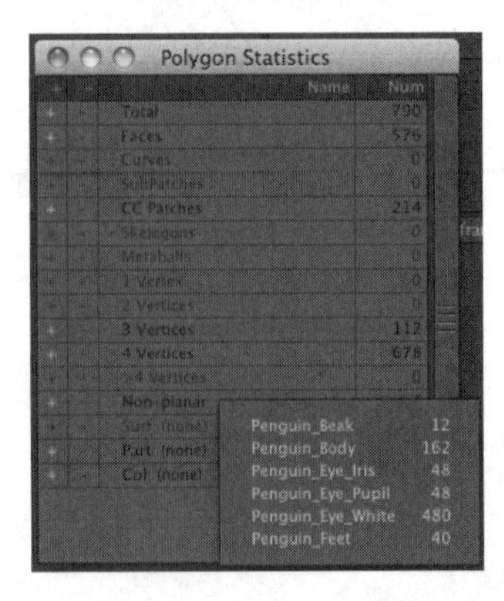

Figure 11.33 Use the Statistics panel to select just the Feet surface of the penguin.

4. You want to weight each foot separately, so right-click (Control-click on the Mac) and drag to lasso the polygons in the character's left foot and deselect them. **Figure 11.34** shows the selection performed in the Side view.

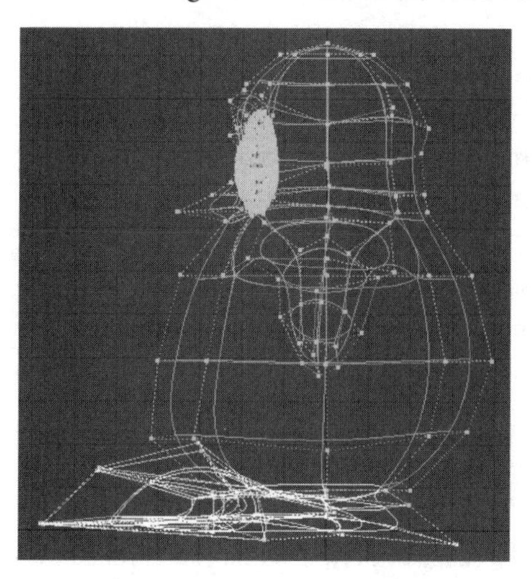

Figure 11.34 Lasso one of the penguin's feet to deselect its polygons.

5. With the polygons of the right foot selected, click the W button at the bottom of the Modeler interface (next to the T, M, C, and S buttons) to choose Weight mode. In the drop-down list next to these buttons—which reads (none)—select (new), as shown in **Figure 11.35**.

   The Create Weight Map panel appears. You'll use it to assign a weight map to the selected polygons.

Figure 11.35 Choose Weight mode from the bottom of the Modeler screen, and then choose (new) to create a new weight map.

6. In the Name box, type **Penguin_RightFoot**. Keep the Initial Value option checked and leave its value at 100%, as shown in **Figure 11.36**.

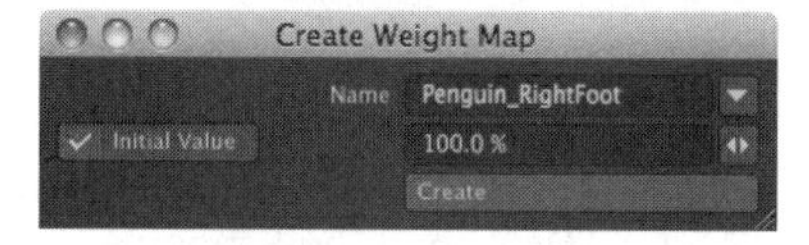

Figure 11.36 Type the name of the new weight map.

You've now created a weight map for the right foot of the Penguin object, but if you remember, there are four bones in the entire leg—well, at least if you can call it a leg. Are you wondering why bones are mentioned here? Good question! Although weight maps can be used for many things in LightWave, such as controlling textures, you can also use them to control bone influences. By setting up a weight map in Modeler and giving it the same name as a bone, you tell Layout that the specified bone should deform only the portion of the model defined by that weighted map. For example, a weight map named RightFoot will automatically be associated with the bone named RightFoot. LightWave will automatically apply the weight map in Layout.

This is a good time to change your Perspective view (or any view) to Weight Shade render view mode. When you view your model in Weight Shade mode (selected from the top of each viewport), you can see the weight applied as bright red.

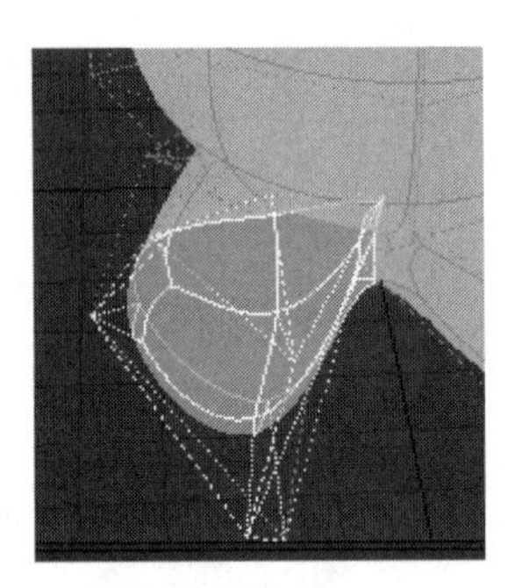

Figure 11.37 Another weight map is added to the right foot of the Penguin object.

7. Deselect the right foot polygons, and select the left foot polygons. Select (new) again from the drop-down next to the S button to create a weight map for this selection. Enter the name **Penguin_RightFoot**, as shown in **Figure 11.37**.

   You can assign weight maps to selected polygons or points, but if you apply a weight map to selected polygons, you are really applying the weight to the points of the selected polygons. Selecting polygons over points (or vice versa) for setting weight maps is your choice. However, polygons are sometimes a better choice for weight map selection because it is much easier to see what is and (more importantly) what is not selected.

8. Save your model by pressing Control+S (PC) or Command+S (Mac). Saving the object saves the weights you've applied.

That's all there is to it! You've identified a range of polygons that is controlled by a bone in Layout. Remember, you use Modeler to create weight maps. You can adjust them in both Modeler and Layout, but creation is always done in Modeler.

As your models become more complex, you can select points or polygons and weight them as you like. Weights are not always needed, but it's important to understand how they work. Often, you don't even need weight maps, and proper bone placement will be more than enough to animate your character.

This next exercise instructs you on the method of assigning a particular bone of your model to the weights you've just created in Layout. As a result, the bone will influence only the weighted area.

Exercise 11.6 Assigning Weights

1. Hop on into LightWave Layout. From this book's DVD, load the Penguin_Bone_Weight scene. You'll find it in the 3D Content\Scenes\CH11 folder of the 3D_Content directory.

2. In the top left of Layout, make sure Bone X-Ray mode is on. This allows you to see the bones in the object. This feature is often hard to find, but you access it by clicking the tiny drop-down arrow to the right of the viewport render style button. Then select the RightFoot (3) bone of the Penguin object and press **p**.

3. In the Bone Properties panel, select Penguin_RightFoot as the weight map for the Bone Weight Map option, as shown in **Figure 11.38**.

Figure 11.38 Assign a weight map to the RightFoot (3) bone of the object from the Bone Properties panel.

4. Press the down arrow key to select the next bone, RightFoot (4), and then also assign the Penguin_RightFoot weight map to it.
5. Close the Bone Properties panel and select the RightFoot (3) bone. Press **y** to rotate the bone around. You'll see, as in **Figure 11.39**, that only the foot reacts. The upper portion of the penguin is not affected at all.

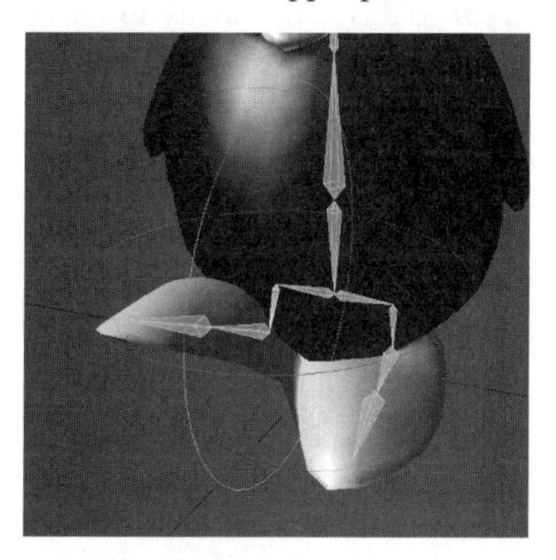

Figure 11.39 Assigning weight maps to bones alleviates any problems of bone movements influencing areas of the model they shouldn't.

6. Go ahead and repeat the steps for the LeftFoot bones, assigning the appropriate weight map.
7. Save your scene!

The subtlety of using weight maps with bones is that they confine the influence of bones to the surface regions you want to deform. For a model like our little penguin, using a weight map for the feet is ideal because the model's parts are so close together, unlike a tall, skinny alien or a four-legged animal. If their influence wasn't constrained by weight maps, moving any of those short, tightly packed leg bones could cause unwanted deformations across most or all of the penguin's surface. But a simple weight map corrects this problem.

Note that the penguin does not need a weight map for its body or head, because we want that part of its body (unlike its feet and torso) to deform as a single seamless surface, rather than as a set of discrete parts. It would hinder the overall look of the character if its head were clearly articulated from its chest, for instance. When a character like this turns its head, you want its chest and belly to twist as well.

NOTE

When working with the Auto Key feature, remember that movements, rotations, and the like are recorded. If you happen to rotate a bone and deform the object when you didn't intend to, you can always undo. LightWave 10 has multiple undos in Layout for actions such as moving or rotating a bone. Just press Control+Z (Command+Z on the Mac), and you're all set. (Just pressing **z** is the shortcut for redo.) You can set the undo levels in the General Options panel by pressing **o**.

NOTE

There's a little trick in LightWave you can try when setting up additional bones and weights. If you give a weight map created in Modeler exactly the same name as a bone (capitalization included), Layout will apply the map to that bone automatically when you load the model into a scene.

Skelegons

As you worked through the setup of just a few bones for the penguin earlier in this chapter, you probably realized that applying bones can be a tedious process. And it can! Skelegons often speed the setup of bone structures, because you build Skelegons along with your model as you work in Modeler.

Skelegons are polygons that resemble bones, and eventually they become bones in Layout. You create and modify Skelegons in Modeler as if they were polygons and then convert them to bones in Layout. The benefit of this is the ability to set up bones for a character in a Perspective view, using modeling tools such as Drag and Rotate. What's more, any Skelegon-based skeletal structure you create for a character is saved with the model. This means you can set up full bone structures for individual characters and load them into a single scene later.

When you create a character with Skelegons, you can adjust its skeletal structure at any time. In addition, you can create one base skeletal structure and use it over and over again for future characters. The next exercise gets you right into it by setting up Skelegons for a full figure.

NOTE

If you intend to reuse a model's Skelegon-based structure, be sure to save a copy of the model and its Skelegons in Modeler before you move your model into Layout. Once you convert Skelegons to bones in Layout, they can't be changed back to Skelegons.

Creating Skelegons in Modeler

There are a couple of ways to create Skelegons in Modeler. You can build them point by point or use the Draw Skelegons feature. In the point-by-point approach, you apply single-line polygons (pairs of points connected by either a line polygon or a curve) to Skelegons. The Draw Skelegons feature is a fast, easy way to create a skeletal structure, and it is the focus of the next exercise.

Exercise 11.7 Creating Skelegons

This exercise uses an existing model to demonstrate how quick and easy it is to set up a full hierarchy for a human character. Using the bone weight information from the previous exercises and the Skelegons information provided here, you'll be moving a fully articulated character in no time. However, you're going to use a feature in LightWave that will automatically apply weights to the character. The trick is keeping the Skelegons in the same layer as the geometry. However, for the purpose of providing visual examples, this tutorial shows you the Skelegons in a separate layer.

1. In Modeler, save any work you might have been doing and create a new object by pressing Shift+N.
2. From this book's DVD, load the BlueGirl object (3D_Content\Objects\CH11\bluegirl.lwo). This is a killer model that is easy to rig, thanks to William "Proton" Vaughan. Thanks, William!

3. Select a new layer, making BlueGirl a background layer. Bring the bottom right viewport to a full screen and, on the Setup menu tab, click Skelegons (**Figure 11.40**).

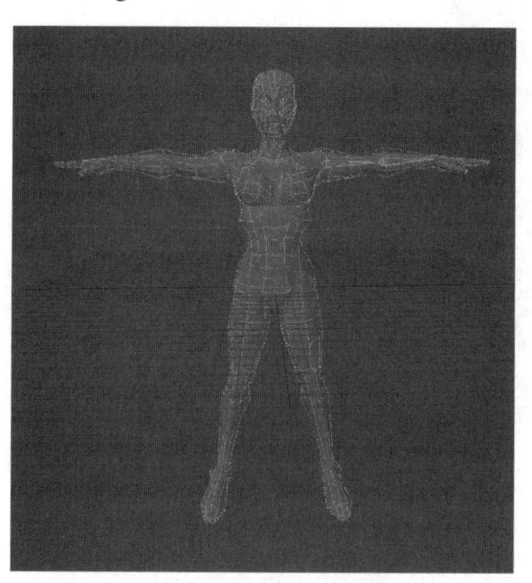

Figure 11.40 To create Skelegons, start with a blank layer but put your model in a background layer for alignment.

4. You start building the skeletal structure for BlueGirl's upper body first. Click and drag from the waist of BlueGirl, up to about her chest, as shown in **Figure 11.41**.

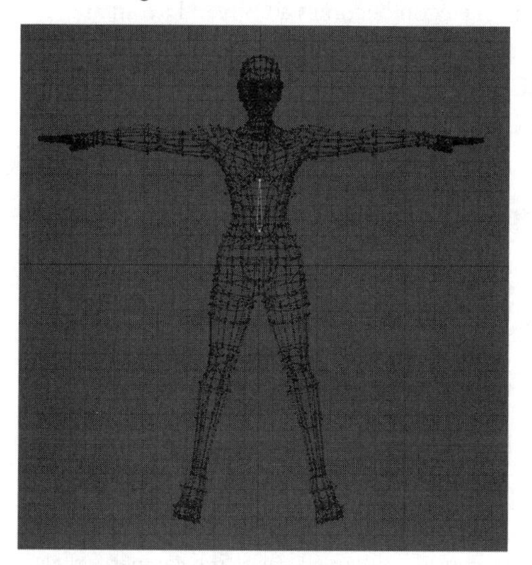

Figure 11.41 Create the first Skelegon, which will be the parent bone of the upper-body hierarchy.

NOTE

Be careful to click and drag just once. It's very common for people to click, let go of the mouse, and then click and drag again. Although you can't see it, doing that creates a tiny little bone that will haunt you later in Layout.

5. With the initial Skelegon still selected, click above it to create an additional Skelegon reaching to the base of the neck. This Skelegon will become a child bone later in Layout (**Figure 11.42** on the next page).

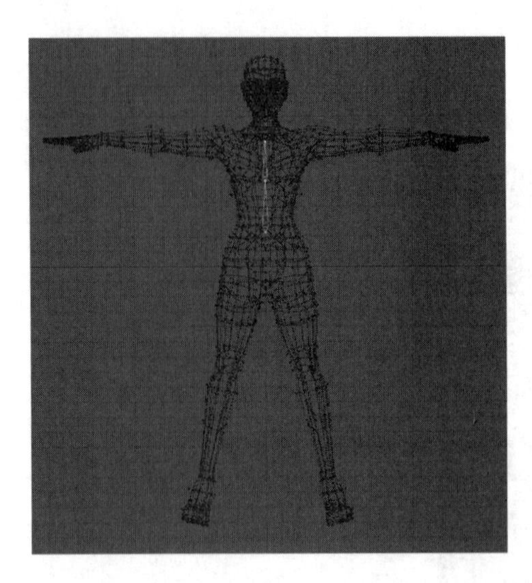

Figure 11.42 Create a second Skelegon that leads to the base of the neck.

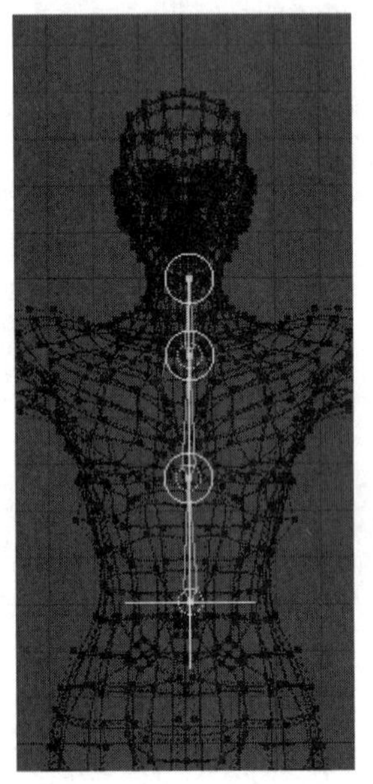

Figure 11.43 Create a Skelegon for the neck.

6. Now click again, further up the neck, to create yet another Skelegon (**Figure 11.43**).
7. Click once more, at the top of the head, to create one more Skelegon and finish the hierarchy.

   Each Skelegon should start and end at a joint within the character. For example, the Skelegon for the head should begin at the base of the head and end at the crown. When the Skelegon becomes a bone in Layout and is activated, it will rotate from that base, which will then rotate the head. If you were to place it too high, in the middle of the head, rotating it would deform the head in an uncomfortable way, to say the least. Placed too low, it would cause the character to wring her own neck.

   The small circles around the ends of the Skelegons are their control handles. If you are in Draw Skelegons mode (which you activate by clicking the Create Skelegons button), clicking outside one of those circles draws a Skelegon between the clicked location and the last handle you made to the one before it. You can adjust a Skelegon in Draw Skelegon mode by clicking within its handle.

NOTE

With the Numeric panel open (press **n** to open it), you can set a name for the Skelegon and create a weight map assignment all at once using the auto weight map feature. In order to do this, you must draw your Skelegons in the same layer as the geometry that the Skelegon-based bones will control. The Digits selection in the Numeric panel for Skelegons tells Modeler to sequentially name the Skelegons as you create them. Sometimes, you might not set a name for each Skelegon, so Modeler names them Bone01, Bone02, Bone03, and so on. In addition, these settings (in the Numeric panel) determine how the weight map is applied to the geometry based on the Skelegon you've created (in the same layer as your geometry). This is a real-time implementation of the Bone Weights function.

Now if you screw up while creating Skelegons—accidentally creating too many, for example—don't worry! It's a common mistake. Just press the spacebar to deactivate the Create Skelegons (or Draw Skelegons) tool, and then press the Delete key to get rid of the accidental creation. Select Skelegons and create them again, remembering to name them and set the weights in the Numeric panel if you want. You can also select one Skelegon as you would a polygon and delete it individually. Then select the last polygon in the chain, choose Draw Skelegons, and continue. The next Skelegon you create will be properly added into the hierarchy.

NOTE

For a full-body character with full weight maps, it's always good to take advantage of the automatic weight map. The reason is that you'll save time selecting and assigning individual bones in Layout for the full character. With the auto weight map feature, once your Skelegons are active, your weight maps will already be applied.

8. Press the spacebar to turn off the Create Skelegons command. Then select the second Skelegon in the middle of the chest and click the Create Skelegons tool again. Doing this tells Modeler to begin creating child Skelegons from the selected Skelegon.
9. Now create four Skelegons for the character's left arm, as shown in **Figure 11.44**.

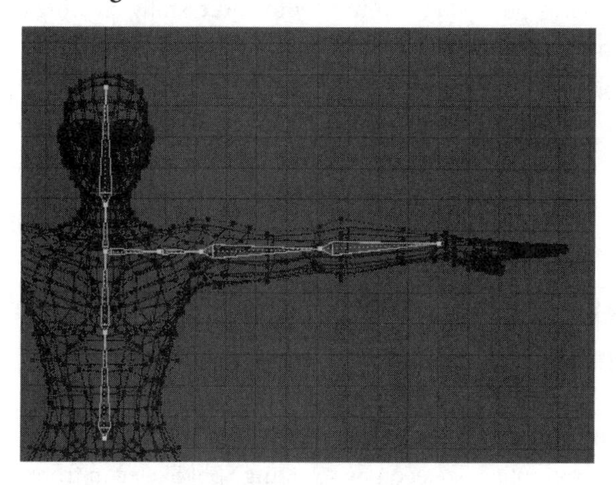

Figure 11.44 Create four more Skelegons for the character's arm.

10. On the Setup menu tab, select Skelegon Tree. When the panel comes up, drag its corner to expand it, if necessary, to see all its contents.

    You'll see a hierarchy of Skelegons named Bone01 (the first Skelegon you drew), Bone02, and so on (**Figure 11.45**).

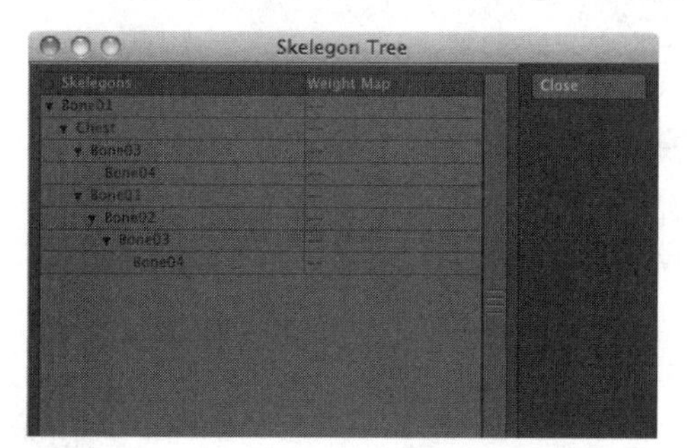

Figure 11.45 The Skelegon Tree panel helps you manage your Skelegon structures.

NOTE

Because no name was applied for the first Skelegon, it reads simply Bone01. Every Skelegon thereafter uses the same name. Remember that you can name each Skelegon as you create it in the Numeric panel. After you name a Skelegon, each one you create from that point takes on that name as well.

11. Double-click the second bone listing under the Skelegons heading. Double-clicking calls up the Rename Skelegon command. Type **Chest**, as it was created in the chest area of the object.

    Continue renaming Skelegons in this panel. Note that the panel can't stay open while you work, so finish your business and then close it to move on.

12. Save your object. Saving the object also saves the bone structure.

    From here, you can create the Skelegons for the legs. However, you need to build these Skelegons from the original mid-section Skelegon—building Skelegon hierarchies in the opposite direction of those you created for the arms.

NOTE

If you name the Skelegon and the weight map identically, the weight maps are automatically applied in Layout when the Skelegons are converted to bones. Note that Skelegon and weight-map naming are case-sensitive.

Creating Skelegons for the legs can be slightly tricky because you need to build the Skelegons in another layer.

Completing the Skelegon Rig

The process you've just completed puts you on your way to successfully creating a bone structure for bipedal characters. You still would need to build the leg structure of the character for both legs. The advantage of Skelegons is that you can quickly and easily mirror the structure for the opposite side of the object. You don't have to draw Skelegons again because Skelegons are a polygon type. You can apply Modeler tools to them and adjust their position, size, and so on.

Here are a few additional tips about Skelegons:

- You can use them like polygons, adjusting the points and varying the size.
- You can load Skelegon structures back into Modeler and adjust or add on to them at any time.
- If you have created a full structure for a creature but realize later that you need more control, you can split a Skelegon by selecting Split Skelegon from the Construct tab. Also, you can select multiple Skelegons and split them at once. The split will always just slice a selected bone into two equal-sized smaller Skelegons.
- You can define a weight map for a Skelegon, just as you can for a bone, using tools on the Detail tab.
- If you need to separate Skelegons in a hierarchy, you can use the Unweld command, found on Layout's Detail tab.
- You can instantly create Skelegons from points of an existing object by selecting the points and clicking Convert Skelegon. The command button

is tucked in the More drop-down menu within the Skelegons tool category, on Modeler's Setup tab.

Using Skelegons in Layout

Skelegons are Modeler tools that do their most important work in Layout, where you convert them to bones that control your model and assign weight maps created for each Skelegon.

When you're constructing Skelegons in Modeler, it's often convenient to build them on separate layers from the objects they'll control, so you can arrange the Skelegons without disturbing the associated objects. Before you load a Skelegon-containing model into Layout, however, you should cut and paste each finished Skelegon into the layer that contains the associated objects. This ensures that when each Skelegon is converted to a bone in Layout, it will be associated with the correct object.

If you assign a weight map you create in Modeler the same name as a Skelegon, you automatically apply the map to that Skelegon (and to the bone it will become upon conversion in Layout).

After your model is loaded into Layout with Skelegons, you can simply select the Cvt Skelegons command from the Setup Menu tab. A pop-up window will tell you how many Skelegons were converted to bones. From there, your bones will be visible and usable in Layout.

Beyond this exercise, you can select portions of the model to assign weight maps, just as you did with the Penguin object earlier in this chapter, and then apply the bones in Layout. You can go further and select the regions of points on the full BlueGirl object, assign a weight map, and apply the bone weights. If you remember, applying weights to the feet of the Penguin object enabled you to control the influence of bones—you can do the same throughout the body, for the head, the arms, the legs, and so on. Remember that the Skelegon Tree panel in Modeler shows the name of the weight map that will be used if you've created one. If you've assigned weights in the Numeric panel along with a bone name, your weights should automatically be assigned to the appropriate bone in Layout.

The exercises here are basic and straightforward. However, much of your character work does not need to be more complex than this. It's simply a matter of putting in the time to create bones and Skelegons for your entire model. You can go further by adding Skelegons for BlueGirl's fingers and even her toes. At any time, LightWave enables you to bring this model back to Modeler, make adjustments, and add more Skelegons or weight maps.

NOTE

LightWave's bone tools are too powerful and versatile to cover in just one chapter, so be sure to check out all the cool video tutorials for this chapter (and others) from 3dgarage.com available on this book's DVD. Learn about new bone tools for LightWave 10 and the new IK Boost tool.

NOTE

If Layout has Expert mode set from the General Options tab in the Preferences panel, you don't see a Skelegons to Bones conversion message. Instead, it is highlighted in the status bar underneath the timeline at the bottom of the interface.

The Next Step

To see the most complete coverage of bones, open up the 3dgarage.com video content on this book's DVD and you'll find additional video tutorials to accompany this chapter. You'll find a video (CH11_IKBoost.mov) showing how to use LightWave 10's IK Boost tool, a fast, easy way to create inverse kinematics. You'll find a tutorial video called CH11_LayoutBones.mov which takes you through more of LightWave's bone features, including exporting hierarchies, mirroring, and working with the new Bone Displacements tool in CH11_BoneDisplace.mov. Because bones are not just for characters, I've also included a video called CH11_NonBones.mov that covers nontraditional bone use.

This chapter introduced you to bones and Skelegons and how to create both. You saw how to set bone weights to control the influences of bones. The weighting applies to many areas of LightWave, especially character animation.

With the basic knowledge presented here, you can practice setting up full characters, whether they're full humans, simple characters, or even inanimate objects, such as a chrome toaster. Regardless of the type of character, the bone and Skelegon information here still applies. Position bones using the Drag tool and use the Mirror tool to copy the Skelegons. See what other kinds of uses you can apply these tools to, such as creating animals, aliens, or your own fascinating creatures.

Skelegons and bones are powerful animation tools in LightWave. Of course, one chapter can't present all possible uses of these tools. With the right project and a little time, however, you'll be setting up skeletal structures faster than you could have imagined.

Chapter 12

The LightWave Render Engine

LightWave provides you with a variety of rendering methods that are easy to set up and use. You've seen throughout the book that right from the starting gate you can use VPR, the viewport preview render function, to instantly see your rendered scene as you work. But for final animations, you'll also want to use the full set of rendering tools LightWave is famous for.

In this chapter, you'll learn about the following:

- Applying global settings the Render Globals panel
- Setting up renders for animations
- Saving renders
- Changing render color space
- Using the RenderQ control

Working in the Render Globals Panel

Figure 12.1 shows the LightWave Render Globals panel in Layout. You can find this panel by first going to the Render menu tab at the top of Layout and then clicking the Render Globals command on the left side of the interface.

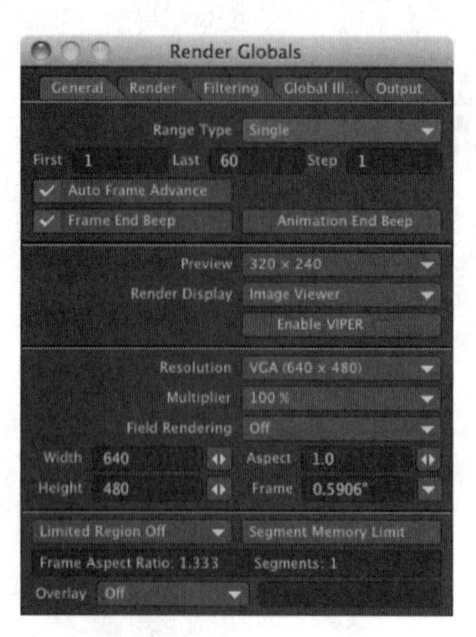

Figure 12.1 The LightWave Render Globals panel is one location where you can set up your camera and rendering options.

You'll find that the LightWave render engine is one of the best in its class. It's fast, efficient, and—most importantly—good at what it does. As you can see from the images throughout this book and on NewTek's Web site, LightWave produces the highest-quality renders in its class. Through the software's radiosity rendering, area lighting, and shadow options, the LightWave rendering engine can deliver beautifully rendered images and animations. But before you get to that level of rendering, it's good to know the process of setting up an animation to render.

The Render Globals panel might seem confusing at first. It's a part of LightWave that houses your camera properties, render options, and saving properties. You can work with the Camera Properties panel as you have throughout this book and in the past, but you can also work in just the Render Globals panel tool. On a simple level, you can set up properties, including resolution, for your camera for rendering. Then, use the Render Globals panel to save your animation.

You can also tell the Camera Properties panel to "Use Global" and then set your resolution, output settings, and more, all within the Render Globals panel. If you do that, what happens to the Camera Properties panel, you ask? You can still use this panel for various camera controls. All other render-related settings will be done in Render Globals. The Use Global option is found in a check box right in the middle of the Camera Properties panel (**Figure 12.2**). By selecting the Cameras listing at the bottom of the Layout interface and then pressing **p**, you'll find this panel. In the middle of the panel, you'll see that the Use Global option is checked. The resolution settings are now ghosted. When you set the resolution in the Render Globals panel, those values will be applied. This alleviates the problem of jumping back and forth between the Camera Properties panel and the Render panel to set up an animation. Additionally, the Render Globals panel is useful for dealing with multiple cameras in a scene, and for having only one place to make sure that all cameras are rendering the same resolution/size, and so on.

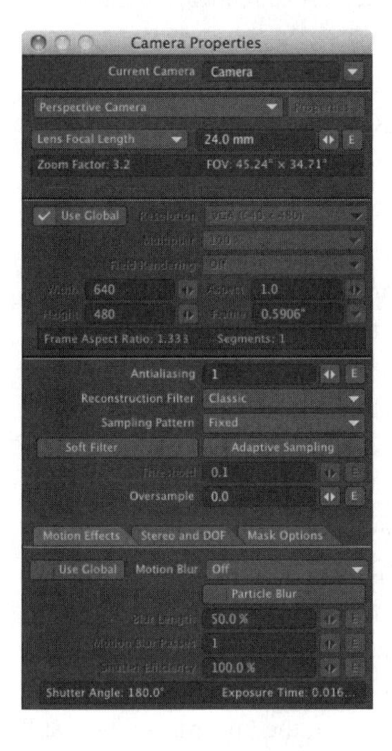

Figure 12.2 To use the Render Globals panel fully, make sure Use Global is checked within the Camera Properties panel.

Setting Up an Animation to Render

Before you can render an animation (on one machine or across a network), you need to set up the animation properly. There are a few details you need to run through first to properly set up an animation for rendering, all of which will be done in the Render Globals panel.

Using the Render Globals panel, you can check your settings for rendering. For proper camera placement, these values should be set up before you begin animating, and it's always a good idea to double-check them before you render. In addition, you can set up any motion blur, field rendering, or antialiasing here.

Range-Type Rendering

Normally you wouldn't find too much information in this chapter about single-frame rendering, because it's a very old process not often used anymore. This process involved a special cable connected to a broadcast-quality tape recorder. From there, using a single-frame command setting, LightWave would render a frame, and then record it directly to tape. Today, animators render to digital movie formats, such as AVI or QuickTime, and also image sequences. Press **F9**, and you've rendered a single current frame. But there's more to this feature in LightWave 10. At the top of the Render Globals panel, you'll see a selection named Range Type. Here, you have three options for rendering:

- **Single:** Setting Range Type to Single tells LightWave to render one frame at a time. Pretty easy, huh?
- **Arbitrary:** This cool setting enables you to render a range of frames. Let's say you wanted to render frames 1 through 10, as well as 12, 13, and 20. Set these frames in the panel, and away you go! LightWave renders the specific frames.
- **Keyframe:** Here, you pick one object for the keyframes on which to render. Say you wanted to render the penguin from Chapter 11, "Bones & Rigging," on just the Z-axis. Set those values next to Range Type and render your animation. The Keyframe option renders the frames that have keyframes on an object's channel. For example, if you had a keyframe on the Z channel for a light at 0, 12, 30, 45, and 60, those frames would be rendered with this setting.

General-Purpose Rendering

After you've chosen the Range Type setting you'll use, you need to set up the rest of the render options. Most often, to render a full animation, you'll choose Single as the Range Type. This exercise guides you through the kind of rendering most commonly used by LightWave animators: rendering that generates animations for video or computer work. If, however, you are using LightWave for rendering anything other than video or computer work, such as film or print, the information here still applies, and the differences are noted.

Exercise 12.1 Creating a Basic Render

1. In Layout, load the RenderMe scene from this book's DVD.

   This scene is from Chapter 7, "Motion Graphics," with surfaces, animation, and camera settings applied. **Figure 12.3** shows the scene when loaded.

   Generally, you would have set up your camera when you set up the animation in Layout. You'd do this because a different camera setting can change how your Layout setup looks. The first thing to do when you're ready to render is display the Camera Properties panel. You are ready to render when you have all your lighting, textures, and motions in place. This scene has all these in place.

Figure 12.3 A premade scene loaded, for you to test out some rendering.

2. Make sure your scene is set up in the Camera view. You can press **6** on your keyboard for a quick change. Select the camera (if it's not already selected) and press **p** to enter the Camera Properties panel. When the panel opens, click the Use Global option. Also make sure that Use Global is checked on under the Motion Effects tab.

   The Current Camera setting at the top of the panel should read Camera, because there is only one camera in the current scene.

3. From the Render tab at the top of Layout, click the Render Globals option on the left of the interface.

4. Set the Resolution to HDTV (1280 x 720). Make sure that the Resolution Multiplier is set to 100% for actual-size output. You'll see the Width and Height values change when you do so.

5. You won't need to change the Segment Memory Limit setting because LightWave defaults to 256 MB. A value this high means that a rendered frame will be drawn in one pass. If you're short on system memory, you can use a RAM setting lower than 256 for rendering. In that case, the Segments value can be greater than 1—say, 64 or 32 (the pre-LightWave 10 default value). Your project won't render as quickly, but your scene will still look great.

   LightWave now has more memory with which to work and will render your frames in single segments.

6. Click over to the Filtering tab at the top of the panel. Set Antialiasing to PLD 9-Pass, with a Classic Reconstruction Filter. Then, click Adaptive Sampling.

NOTE

While you're working, it's not necessary to have antialiasing on, but you definitely want it on for your final renders. Although you have the choice of Low to Extreme settings, I recommend that you render all your animations for video in at least Enhanced Low Antialiasing. Medium or Enhanced Medium Antialiasing can provide you with a cleaner render. High Antialiasing is overkill and a waste of render time for video. It might actually make your images look blurry.

A lower PLD pass will render faster but have less filtering accuracy. A higher PLD pass will take longer to render but result in a very accurate render. PLD 9-Pass is a good midpoint value for most render jobs.

Activating this setting tells LightWave to look for the edges to antialias in your scene. The Threshold value compares two neighboring pixels, and a value of 0 sees the entire scene. A good working value is .1. You can set the value higher, which lowers rendering time but performs a less accurate antialiasing.

7. Set Motion Blur to Photoreal. With future renders, you can experiment with setting this value higher for more blur, or lower for less. There are no particles in this scene so you don't need to check Particle Blur.
8. Shutter Efficiency should remain at 100%. This is another option in LightWave to help simulate a real-world camera and the shutters it uses. **Figure 12.4** shows the panel.

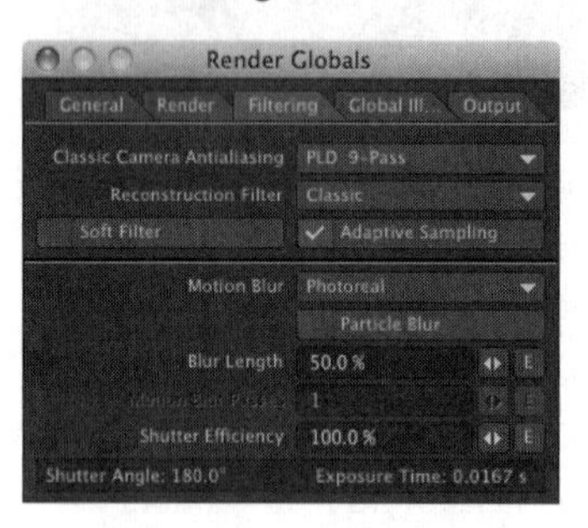

Figure 12.4 Make sure properties are set in the Filtering tab to keep your renders clean.

9. Save your scene, and all of your settings are saved along with it.

You should visit the Render Globals panel at least twice during an animation, if not more—once to set up the camera and zoom factors before beginning animation setup, and once before you are ready to render to set up antialiasing, motion blur, field rendering, and proper resolution size. From here, you can set up the other options in the Render Globals panel.

Exercise 12.2 Creating a Render with LightWave

1. With the RenderMe scene from this book's DVD still loaded, open the Render Globals panel.

Figure 12.1 shows the Render Globals panel. You can see First (indicating first frame of render) and Last (last frame of render) values at the top of the panel. If your LightWave animation in Layout has a first frame of –30 and a last frame of 300 (or any start or end frames different from the customizable default values of 1 and 60), it will not render those frames unless they are entered here.

The frame numbers you assign to your timeline in Layout do not automatically apply in the Render Globals panel.

Leave First set to 1, and set Last to 300 (10 seconds). LightWave defaults to a last frame of 60; however, you can change this default in the General Options panel (press **o**).

2. Set the Step value to 1 to render every frame. A render-frame Step value of 2 would render every two frames, for example.
3. Click Auto Frame Advance. A crucial setting!

   This tells LightWave to advance to the next frame and continue rendering, which is very important for full animations!
4. Turn off the Render Display by setting it to None.

NOTE

Frame End Beep is useful for monitoring the completion of your rendered frames, but is not necessary. It's kind of annoying after a while. However, LightWave lets you change the default frame end beep to a specific sound file. This can be even more fun with the new Render End Beep to tell you your scene is finished rendering.

NOTE

The Image Viewer and Image Viewer FP render display remembers your rendered frames. Turn this on while performing test renders on individual frames (press **F9**) and leave it open. You can select any of your previously rendered images from its Layer list. You also can view the Alpha channel in this viewer and save an image.

5. Click the Render tab at the top of the Render Globals panel.
6. Make sure Ray Trace Shadows is on, but not Ray Trace Reflection or Ray Trace Refraction. These options are not needed in this particular case.
   No refraction is used in this scene, so keeping this option on would only increase render times. If you wanted your object to reflect what's around it, such as other objects, the set, or props, you'd first set a reflection value in the Surface Editor (or Node Editor) and then turn on Ray Trace Reflection. The same applies to Ray Trace Refraction, for instance, if you wanted a transparent object such as a glass to refract light traveling through it.

   You also can add Ray Trace Transparency for objects that need to have a transparent surface reflect a certain way, such as a car window. For now, this can be left off.
7. Render Mode is usually set to Realistic and is not often changed. However, you do have the option to render wireframe or quickshade versions of your animations here.
8. Click Extra Ray Trace Optimization. Set the Ray Recursion Limit value to 6. The higher the value, the longer LightWave takes to render, but the more accurate your Ray Tracing is.

   The Ray Recursion Limit setting, which doesn't often change, determines the number of times LightWave calculates the bounced rays in your scene. In the real world, this is infinite, but in LightWave, you can set a Ray Recursion Limit value up to 24. Changing this setting increases render times. A good

NOTE

Setting a Ray Recursion Limit value too low for scenes that have transparent surfaces may result in a black, opaque surface instead of a see-through surface! If this happens, just up the Ray Recursion Limit value a bit.

working value is 12. However, setting a lower value of 6 or 8 can be a real time-saver when using the Ray Trace Reflection option. For best results, try not to set this value lower than 6. If you find render errors, such as black dots, bring this value back up to 12 or so.

NOTE

This book was written for LightWave 10.0, which now supports multithreading up to 64 processors!

9. If your computer has more than one processor, select 2, 4, 8, 16, or even 64 for Multithreading. If you have only one processor, set Multiprocessing to 1. Better yet, leave this set to Auto and LightWave will set it for you.

   Some plug-ins might not be compatible with multithreading, so remember to check this setting if you find errors in your render.

10. Back in the General tab, you can set Overlay to display the Frame Number, SMPTE Time Code, Film Key Code, or Time in Seconds in the lower-right corner of your animation.

    This is good for reference test renders. In addition, when one of these values is set, you can add a note in the Label area. This feature comes in handy when you're doing test renders for clients who have a history of not paying and/or of stealing your work. You can put a copyright notice in the upper corner, for example.

NOTE

Saving regularly before any render (even a single-frame render) is a good habit to get into.

11. After you've set all the render options, be sure to save your scene.

    Those are the main parameters you must set up to render an animation. However, you still need to tell LightWave where to save the files and what type of files to save. The next section discusses the various file formats and procedures for saving your animations.

Saving Renders

Within the Render Globals panel is another tabbed area, titled Output. This area is where you tell LightWave what type of file you want to save, where to save it, and in which format it should be saved. **Figure 12.5** shows the Output tab within the Render Globals panel.

The first area within the Output tab is the Save Animation selection. This confuses many people. You're creating an animation in LightWave, right? Save Animation! It makes sense—but it means something a little different. Clicking Save Animation enables you to save your rendered frames as one animation file, in a format such as AVI, QuickTime, or RTV (Video Toaster). It saves one complete file, as opposed to a series of individual rendered frames. You select different types of animations to save by using the Type selection option. Note that you'll need a Video Toaster board from NewTek for the RTV option.

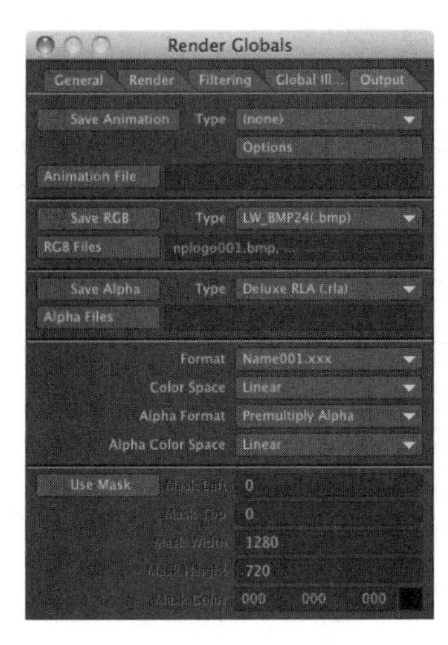

Figure 12.5 A render is no good if you don't tell the system where to save it. You do that here in the Output tab.

Using Save Animation is great for previewing QuickTime movies or for using Aura and Video Toaster, but you also can save individual frames—and do so at the same time. If you select the Save RGB button, you're telling LightWave to save the individual frames as they're rendered. Similarly, with Save Animation, you select from a variety of RGB formats in which to save your animations by selecting the one you want from the Type drop-down list, as pictured in **Figure 12.6**.

COLOR SPACE

This is a great new addition to LightWave, and it allows you to change the color space of your renders. Why would you do this? Often, an animation output is mixed with a video edit later in postproduction, and sometimes the color values don't quite match. Additionally, the color space in LightWave 10 offers you greater control over how your scene lighting appears. To make things clearer, there's a video on the book's DVD all about color space.

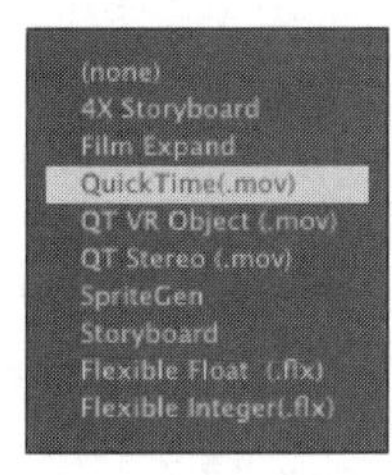

Figure 12.6 You can save directly to an animation file simply by choosing the appropriate type.

Finally, in the Output tab, you also can save the Alpha channels of individual frames. This is great for later compositing in a postproduction environment. Remember that all these file types can be saved with one rendering. You can save a QuickTime or AVI file, plus the RGB and alpha files, all at once. Depending on what's in your scene, you can save a sequence of 32-bit files, such as TIFF or PNG, and the Alpha channel will be embedded in the RGB frames. Simply load that sequence into your compositing program and you'll instantly be able to blend it into other projects.

When all this is set—the camera resolutions, the rendering information, and the output file information—you're finally ready to render your animation. Press the **F10** key to render your animation. Congratulations!

NOTE

You might have a high-resolution frame that needs to render over a long period of time. You can tell LightWave to automatically save this frame by setting up the render options as though you were rendering a full-length animation. Set the RGB format, output filename, and location for saving, and then click Auto Frame Advance. Make the First frame and the Last frame the same frame you want to render—say, frame 10. LightWave renders that frame and saves the RGB, and because it's also the Last frame, rendering then stops.

Render Selected Objects

If you click the Render tab in Layout, you'll see the Sel Object option under the Render category on the left of the interface. Because LightWave enables you to select multiple objects, you can save significant amounts of rendering time with this option. In the Scene Editor or in Layout, you can select all objects at once by holding the Shift key and clicking the objects. Rendering selected objects has two useful functions:

- It saves render time by rendering only the objects you're interested in at the moment.
- It enables you to render multiple passes of the same animation with or without certain objects. This is great for special effects or compositing, or even for rendering before-and-after sorts of animations.

RenderQ

A terrific feature that you might find exceedingly useful on long weekends is the RenderQ control. From the Render tab in Layout, you'll find RenderQ on the left side of the interface. Clicking this button brings up a panel that lets you create batch renders very simply. Figure 12.7 shows the RenderQ window with multiple scenes loaded. You can set up as many as you like and let the rendering begin. When one animation finishes, LightWave loads the next and automatically starts rendering. However, there's one huge thing you need to do to get this to work. You must make sure that your scene is saved with all the information properly set up from within the Render Globals panel, such as what to save, where to save it, how much to render, and so on. Basically, if you've set everything up as described in this chapter, just save the scene with the render setup, and load 'er up in the RenderQ.

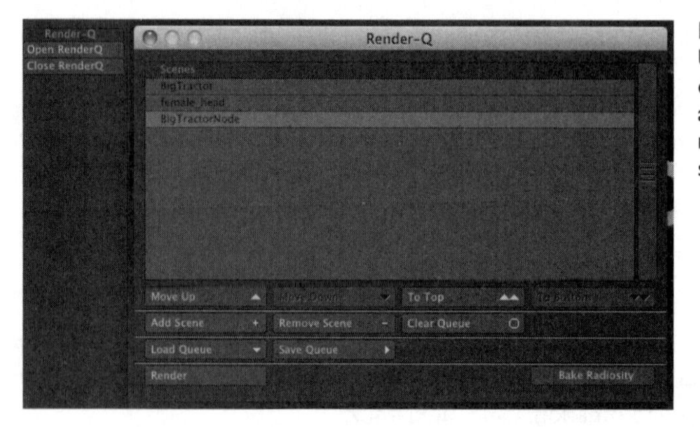

Figure 12.7
Use the RenderQ command to set up a batch render of multiple LightWave scenes.

Thoughts on Rendering

You can refer to this section of the book often when it's time to render your animations and images. But then you have to answer the question that arises: "What's next?" When your animations are complete, the next step is to bring them into a digital animation recorder and lay them off to tape or edit your final animations with audio and effects in a nonlinear editor.

No matter what you create in LightWave, unless you export your scene or model to another artist, you must render your scene. Someday, you might not need to render, as processors and video cards become increasingly powerful. For now, though, LightWave still has to render, just like any other 3D application. But you'll find that the rendering engine inside LightWave is one of the best around. It's strong and stable, and most importantly, it produces beautifully rendered images.

NewTek has added many OpenGL enhancements. These speed up your workflow and give the poor **F9** (Render Current Frame) key a break. Work through the exercises in this book and make your own animations anytime you can. You can't be in front of your computer 24 hours a day—well, maybe you can, but you shouldn't. If you need to be in front of a screen, try going out to a movie! When you get ready to take a break, set up a render. Don't just wait until the animation is "perfect." Render often and see how your animation looks. You might find new ways to enhance it and make it even better. Or you might just find that it's perfect the way it is. Now, if they only had a way to do LightWave while driving to work…

The Next Step

As you've seen, LightWave has plenty of rendering power. These examples can help you maximize your use of your computer, as well as your time. There's not much more to it, other than using moving images rather than stills. Use programs like Apple Final Cut Pro, Adobe After Effects, or even Apple's Motion for compositing final rendered images, and make your work really stand out!

Appendix

Plug-ins and Additional Resources

So we've come to the end of our story... wait, not that type of book. But just the same, we're at the end of the book, and I hope you've not only learned a lot about what LightWave can do, but also been inspired to create your own 3D masterpiece.

There are just a few more things you should read up on before moving forward into the great wide world of 3D. This appendix will cover the following:

- Backing up your scenes
- Exporting scenes and objects for use in other programs
- Finding and using plug-ins and third-party resources
- Using the additional (non-project) material on the DVD

Exporting Scenes and Objects

Every once in a while, you might find you need to use another 3D application. Ah! The horror! But yes, it's true. A carpenter always has more than one tool in his tool chest, and a serious 3D artist (or just self-proclaimed software junkie) shouldn't be any different. LightWave 10 offers new ways to export your model into different formats.

Figure 13.1 shows the Export panel found within the File drop-down menu in Layout. Here, you can see that you're able to export an object as Collada, an ever-growing format used in many 3D programs, such as Google's Sketch Up. You'll also find FBX, or Filmbox, another popular format.

Figure 13.1 Every once in a while, you need to export an object in a different format.

Within the list, you'll see that you can also export your LightWave scene to older formats. Why would you do this? Often, you might need to work with an older plug-in that hasn't been upgraded, or you have another machine with an older version of LightWave on it. Perhaps you're working with other artists who aren't as current as you. Whichever the case, you can handle it.

Package Scenes

The LightWave 3D content directory has baffled users for years, but at the same time, it has helped keep your content organized. Not having the content directory set properly could result in an incomplete scene loading, with missing files and rogue objects. Even worse would be trying to export that scene for use on another system, or sending it to a coworker, or simply backing it up. Well, fret no more, friends: Using the Package Scene option (shown in **Figure 13.2**) allows you to easily export your scene in all its glory. The Package Scene option will find all parts of your scene, including objects and images, and then export them in a single location. At the same time, you can specify targeted directories and paths while consolidating your scene.

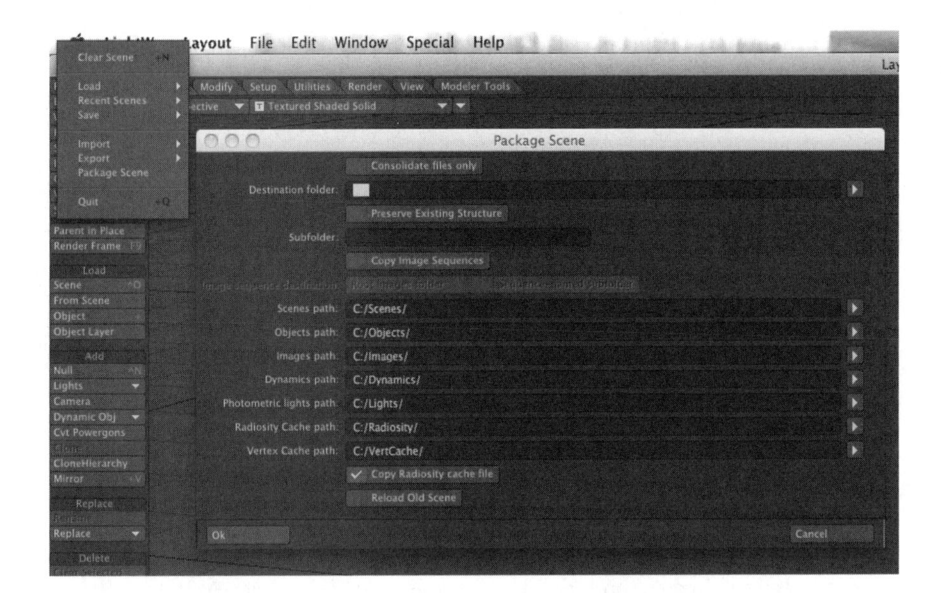

Figure 13.2 The Package Scene panel found in the File drop-down menu in Layout. Consolidate away!

Working with Plug-ins

LightWave's architecture is built around plug-ins. It would be cool if there were a book covering just the plug-ins, because there are so many of them. Add to that the crazy amount of third-party plug-ins available to you—some for purchase, many for free—and you can find yourself in plug-in heaven. You've used LightWave plug-ins throughout the book already. Many of the tools and commands used in Modeler and in Layout are plug-ins! This section will give you a better understanding of where the plug-ins are located and how to work with them.

You'll find plug-ins throughout LightWave Modeler and Layout. These plug-ins are necessary and have various purposes. They are divided into the following categories:

- **Animation I/O:** Plug-ins used for input and output.
- **Animation UV:** Plug-ins used for animated UV maps.
- **Channel Filter:** Plug-ins that perform direct control over channels, such as expressions and Motion Mixer.
- **Custom Object:** Plug-ins that are used for object control, such as particle effects.
- **Displacement:** Plug-ins that can shape and deform objects, be they points or polygons.
- **Environment:** Plug-ins that add functionality to Layout environment variables, such as SkyTracer2.

- **Frame Buffer:** Plug-ins used for certain types of render display, such as the new DV View, found within the render options.
- **Global:** Plug-ins that look at an entire scene, such as Spreadsheet Scene Manager.
- **Image I/O:** Plug-ins for loading and saving images. Generally, you won't access these plug-ins directly, but you'll use their functions when loading or saving in both Layout and Modeler.
- **Image Processing:** Plug-ins that control the various image-related functions, such as pixel calculations for SasLite for fur and Image Filters for things like Bloom and Corona.
- **Layout Command:** Plug-ins used in Layout to control the interaction of other plug-ins that use representation in Layout.
- **Layout Tool:** Plug-ins used for specific Layout tools, such as Bone Twist, Bone Scale Hierarchy, IK Boost Tool, Sliders, and more.
- **Modeling:** Plug-ins and tools used throughout LightWave Modeler.
- **Motion:** Plug-ins for various motion operations, such as Jolt! or Gravity.
- **Object Importer:** Plug-ins for importing object formats other than just LightWave.
- **Object Replacement:** Plug-ins used to replace objects during the course of an animation.
- **Rendering:** Plug-ins used for textures and shaders.
- **Scene Master:** Plug-ins for various scene-related functions, such as Proxy Pic for item selection.
- **Volumetric Effect:** Plug-ins used for effects like ground fog.

Where to Find LightWave's Plug-ins

In Layout, finding the various plug-ins that ship with LightWave is easier than it is in Modeler. Modeler's plug-ins are accessible usually via a button added within the interface, or a selection in a list. In Layout, most plug-ins can be accessed from various areas throughout the program. Those areas are as follows:

- The Object Properties panel, for Custom Object plug-ins and Displacement Map plug-ins.
- The Motion Options panel, for a selected item's motion plug-ins.
- The Effects panel, home to the plug-ins for the Environment (Backdrop tab), Volumetrics (Volumetrics tab), and the Pixel Filter and Image Filter plug-ins (Processing tab).
- The Graph Editor, found under the Modifiers tab, including plug-ins such as Oscillator.

- The Master Plugins list, found under the Utilities tab.
- The Additional drop-down list, found within the Utilities tab. These plug-ins range from basic system tools to key functions to third-party plug-ins.

Loading Plug-ins

When you install LightWave, your plug-ins are already loaded for you. However, there may come a time when you want to reload certain plug-ins or add third-party plug-ins. You can do this through Layout or Modeler, regardless of the plug-in. The information within the plug-in file is read by LightWave, and the plug-in is installed in the proper place in one of the areas in the preceding list.

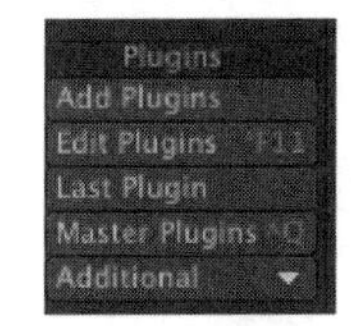

Figure 13.3 Plug-in options and controls in Layout are accessible from within the Utilities tab.

Loading plug-ins is very easy, and you should need to do it only one time. LightWave writes the information to a configuration file when you close the programs. In Layout, you can click to the Utilities tab, and you'll find a Plugins category. There, you can access various plug-in commands, such as Add Plugins, Edit Plugins, Last Plugin, Master Plugins, or select from the Additional list. **Figure 13.3** shows the Plugins category within the Utilities tab in Layout. **Figure 13.4** shows the Plugins category within the Utilities tab in Modeler.

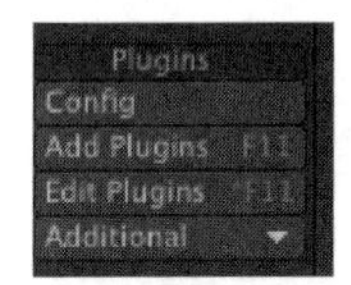

Figure 13.4 Plug-in options and controls in Modeler are also accessible from within the Utilities tab.

The easiest way to add plug-ins in LightWave is to use the Edit Plug-ins panel and select Scan Directory. Click this, and point your system to the Plug-Ins folder. Select OK, and in a moment, a small dialog box appears telling you how many plug-ins were added. **Figure 13.5** shows the Edit Plug-ins panel.

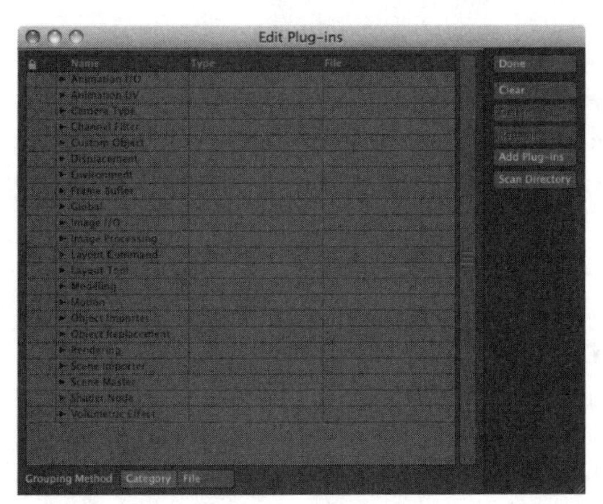

Figure 13.5 The Edit Plug-ins panel allows you to load all plug-ins in one click for both Layout and Modeler.

To add more than one plug-in, you can use the Scan Directory option. To add just a single plug-in file, click Add Plug-ins, point your system to the plug-in, and click OK. You can also delete or rename plug-ins in the Edit Plug-in panel. Image filters are available in the Effects panel as well as the Image Editor, and so on. Other plug-ins, however, such as Pixel Filter, or Modeler plug-ins, are only available in specific locations. You'll also notice that plug-ins vary in name, based on their usage, such as a modifier, tool, command, or generic plug-in.

LScripts

LScripts, custom "mini-programs" written in LightWave's custom scripting language, are also loaded as plug-ins, although they are slightly different. If you have an LScript you've written or one that was compiled from a third-party source, you can load it the same way you do a regular plug-in. Select Add Plug-in, and then select the LScript. Certain plug-ins, such as LScripts, are available in more than one location.

Learn Your Tools

LightWave's Layout and Modeler are extremely powerful creation tools. The tools within LightWave require a lot of time and experimentation. I hope the information in this book has given you a good indication of what can be accomplished using LightWave. There's nothing better than knowing the tools that are available to you. To expand even further on the powerful plug-ins throughout LightWave, here are a few more references you might find helpful when creating surfaces and rendering.

More References You Can Use

The tables listed in this appendix are tremendous assets for creating the various surfaces and resolutions available to you in LightWave.

Now, I'd like to say that this book is the be-all, end-all to LightWave learning, but that wouldn't be fair. Not fair to you, that is! There are so many resources out there, it'll make your head spin. Because of that, I've included a comprehensive list of other LightWave learning resources, as well as books and videos related to the art of 3D modeling and animation.

Reading References

Some might say that books are becoming a thing of the past, because of the Internet and various learning videos on the market. Not so! In fact, book production is greater than it ever has been! So here are some great books that you can use to help learn the art of 3D. There are so many out there, so search online, at your library, and at your local bookstore.

- Ablan, Dan. *Digital Cinematography & Directing*. New Riders, 2003.
- Ablan, Dan. *Digital Photography for 3D Imaging and Animation*. Wiley Publishing, 2007.
- Birn, Jeremy. *Digital Lighting & Rendering*. 2nd ed. New Riders, 2006.

- Culhane, Shamus. *Animation: From Script to Screen*. St. Martin's Press, 1990.
- Kerlow, Isaac V. *The Art of 3D: Computer Animation and Imaging*. 2nd ed. John Wiley and Sons, 2000.
- Lord, Peter. *Creating 3D Animation*. Harry N. Abrams, 1998.
- Maestri, George. *Digital Character Animation 3*. New Riders, 2006.
- Thomas, Frank, and Johnston, Ollie. *The Illusion of Life: Disney Animation*. Disney Editions, 1995.
- White, Tony. *The Animator's Workbook*. Watson-Guptill Publications, 1988.

These are just a few books of interest, and there are more emerging every day. Browse online, read reviews, and check around to see who's used a book you're interested in. Get feedback and see if it's right for you. Often, one simple tip or idea alone is worth the price of a book, especially when you're in the middle of a project! Head on down to your local bookseller and browse the shelves yourself. Getting your hands on a book before you buy it gives you the opportunity to review it and see if the info you need is in there.

Audiovisual References

Like most people, you enjoy a good, thick LightWave book. You can read it on the train, in bed, even while in the bathroom! But sometimes, you want to see something being done. You want to hear the click of the mouse. If that's the case, there are plenty of visual reference materials out there to help you learn LightWave as well as many other applications. Below is a list of great learning resources:

- **3D Garage** (`www.3dgarage.com`): 3dgarage.com has been in the forefront of high-quality video training for LightWave as well as Photoshop and other key software packages. This site offers downloadable HD video training.
- **Lynda** (`www.lynda.com`): lynda.com now offers LightWave 10 video training, hosted by the book's author, Dan Ablan.
- **Class On Demand** (`www.classondemand.net`): Class On Demand sells not only LightWave training videos and DVDs, but also tutorials for Video Toaster, Speed Razor, and many other applications. If you're not looking for a course but rather an inexpensive spot tutorial, you've come to the right place. Visit the site to check out the full list of topics, and check with your local reseller for pricing.
- **Desktop Images** (`www.desktopimages.com`): Desktop Images has been around for years, teaching cool LightWave techniques to students around the globe. Visit the site for updates and information on products.
- **Kurv Studios** (`www.kurvstudios.com`): Kurv sells LightWave training DVDs with specific topics of interest.

Web Resources

Often the best place for information is right on your computer! The Internet is a terrific place where you'll find not only information on the latest version of LightWave but tutorials as well. While many tutorials require a little figuring out on your part, there are a ton of freebies that can help you pick up a quick tip or technique. Here is a list of just a few LightWave-related Web sites you can check out:

- **NewTek, Inc.** (`www.newtek.com`): The home of the makers of LightWave, this is a great place to begin learning with many online tutorials, free of charge.
- **LightWave Tutorials on the Web** (`http://members.shaw.ca/lightwavetutorials/Main_Menu.htm`): You'll find plenty of LightWave resources here.
- **3D Links** (`www.3dlinks.com/tutorials_lightwave.cfm`): This is another user-based site that is a great resource.
- **3D Palace** (`www.3d-palace.com`): This site includes information for LightWave and other 3D applications.
- **MD Arts** (`www.md-arts.com`): This is simply a great LightWave tutorial page.
- **Creative COW** (`www.creativecow.net`): The COW has forums where you can discuss LightWave and many other related applications. Find links to more information there.
- **Foundation3D** (`www.foundation3d.com`): The LightWave Group is a cool site for forums, links, and tutorials.
- **Simply LightWave** (`www.simplylightwave.com`). What more can you say? Simply LightWave! Check it out for some great tutorials.
- **Dan Ablan** (`www.danablan.com`). The author's site has more links to LightWave information and training.

These are just a few sites, but searches on Google.com, Lycos.com, and Yahoo.com yield a plethora of wonderful resources. Some may or may not be helpful in your situation or project, but it doesn't hurt to check them out. You never know what you can pick up!

Be sure to cruise the forums as well. They're great places to view, discuss, and critique 3D work. Try these:

- **NewTek Forums** (`www.newtek.com`)
- **CGTalk** (`http://forums.cgsociety.org`)
- **3D World** (`www.3dworldmag.com`)
- **SpinQuad Forums** (`www.spinquad.com`)

And there's much more out there. Search, and you shall find. Happy learning!

What's on the DVD

The DVD that accompanies this book is full of resources. In addition to containing all the files that you installed at the beginning of the book to help you work through the exercises and to help you with LightWave 10, it also contains additional video material. The following sections contain descriptions of the DVD's contents and of how to use the content included for the tutorials in this book. In addition, exclusive video tutorials have been included just for this book, direct from 3D Garage (www.3dgarage.com). These quick-start tutorials help you get up to speed quickly and easily with LightWave.

For specific information about the use of this DVD, please review the installation information in the Introduction to this book and the ReadMe.txt file in the DVD's root directory. This file includes important disclaimer information as well as information about installation, system requirements, troubleshooting, and technical support.

Technical Support Issues

If you have any difficulties with this DVD, please check out our tech support website at www.peachpit.com. Go to Contact Us, then select Digital Products Help from the Please select Your Query pull-down.

DVD Contents

We've literally packed the DVD with hours of video to enhance your learning experience. On the DVD, you'll find:

- Hours of additional video tutorials to complement the chapters, exclusively from 3D Garage
- High-quality color JPEGs of the book's screen shots
- All the scene files for the book's projects and tutorials
- Royalty-free textures and backgrounds from Dan Ablan's very own portrait studio, `www.AblanGallery.com`

Using the Video Files

In order to play the 3D Garage video tutorials supplied on the book's DVD, you'll need only QuickTime. They were recorded with the H.264 codec and work on both PC and Mac. The video tutorials are supplements to the chapters, some of which coincide with the tutorials in the book and some that stand on their own. Be sure to check out all of them for additional tips and tricks. Be sure to view the ReadMe file on the disc to see a rundown of the videos included. Be careful, there's a lot of video tutorials! These videos won't be found anywhere else. They were created exclusively for this book.

For more video training and LightWave courseware, visit `www.3dgarage.com`.

NOTE

This DVD uses long and mixed-case filenames, requiring the use of a protected mode CD-ROM driver.

System Requirements

This DVD was configured for use on systems running Windows NT Workstation, Windows 98, Windows 2000, Windows XP, and Macintosh OS X or OS 9. It should work without issue in Windows 7, Windows Vista, and Mac OS X 10.5 and above.

Loading the DVD Files

To load the files from the DVD, insert the disc into your DVD/CD-ROM drive. If AutoPlay is enabled on your machine, the DVD setup program starts automatically the first time you insert the disc. You can copy the files to your hard drive or use them right off the disc.

Index

Symbols and numbers

' (apostrophe key), 250
= (equal sign key), 316, 322
] (right bracket key), 240
/ (slash key), 33, 35
3D Animation Basics video, 3
    See also animation
3D cameras. *See* cameras
3D Garage resources, 357
3D Links Web site, 358
3D modeling basics, 3
    See also modeling
3D Palace Web site, 358
3D World Web forum, 358
8-bit vs. 24-bit images, 135

A

Ablan, Dan, 356, 357, 358
AblanGallery.com, 360
about this book, xvii–xviii
Action Center, 36
    Mouse mode, 36, 241
    Selection mode, 36, 235
activating bones, 320, 323, 325
adaptive sampling, 158, 343
Add category
    Items tab, 67
    Setup tab, 73
Add Dynamic drop-down, 293
Add Keys button, 200
Add Node menu, 112
Add Particle Emitter panel, 268–269, 270
Add Plug-ins option, 355
Add Points option, 221
Additive option, 327
Adobe Photoshop, 135
Advanced camera, 169
Affect OpenGL option, 139
Align to Path option, 283
Align tool, 302
Alpha channels
    embedded, 285, 286
    saving, 347
ambient light, 125–126
angles, camera, 166–168
Animation: From Script to Screen (Culhane), 357
animation
    color channel, 211–213
    defined, 173
    dynamic effects, 289–312
        collisions, 293–299, 303–309
        hard-body, 291–309
        modeling for, 299–303
        soft-body, 309–312
        types of, 290
    particle, 267–288
        collisions, 278–281
        control options, 270–274
        editing options, 286–288
        emitters, 268–270
        images, 285–286
        surfaces, 281–284
        wind and, 274–278
    rendering, 339–349
        batch, 348
        general-purpose, 342–346
        range-type, 341–342
        saving renders, 346–347
        selected objects, 348
        setup for, 341–342

animation, rendering *(continued)*
single-frame, 342
speeding up, 284
text and logo, 215–229
backdrop images, 217–222
beveling text, 225–226
creating text, 222–223
importing EPS files, 228
lighting, 228
pivot points, 227–228
setting up in Layout, 228
surfacing text, 224–225
animation I/O plug-ins, 353
animation UV plug-ins, 353
Animator's Workbook, The (White), 357
antialiasing, 156–157, 284, 343–344
apostrophe key ('), 250
arbitrary rendering, 342
area lights, 120, 138–141
quality settings, 140, 141
ray-traced shadows and, 138
sizing/resizing, 140, 141
working with, 138–140
Art of 3D: Computer Animation and Imaging, The (Kerlow), 357
aspect ratios. *See* pixel aspect ratios
Attract setting, 298
audiovisual resources, 357, 359–360
Auto Frame Advance option, 345, 348
Auto Key Create option, 175, 180, 183
Auto Key feature, 175–180
caution about, 180
creating keyframes with, 47–49
exercise on using, 175–180
manual keyframing with, 181–187
recording of motion by, 331
auto weight map feature, 335
AVI file format, 147, 347
Axis drop-down list, 296

B

Back view, 5, 177
backdrop images, 217–222
building elements over, 219–222
deleting from Modeler, 222
hiding/displaying, 221
saving, 219
setting up, 217–219
Backdrop tab, 217
background curves, 200–201
background layers, 13–14
backlight, 130, 131
backtracking, 203, 205
baking process, 50
Ball tool, 243, 249
bananas, modeling, 232–243
Basic tab, Surface Editor, 91–93
batch rendering, 348
Bend tool, 242
Bevel tool, 225–226
beveling text, 225–226
Bezier splines, 207–208
Bezier tool, 222
bias, 189
Billowing effect, 284
Birn, Jeremy, 121, 356
Birth Rate setting, 272
Blend option, 327
Blending Mode settings, 97
blur effects
Motion Blur option, 158–159
Particle Blur option, 160
reflection and refraction, 94
Blur Length setting, 159
Bone Icon Size setting, 321
Bone Properties panel, 317, 318, 322, 324, 330–331
Bone Setup: MirrorHierarchy panel, 325
Bone Weights tool, 326
Bone X-Ray mode, 52, 316, 330
bones, 313–338
activating, 320, 323, 325
adding to objects, 316–318
controls for, 72
creating, 314–316
deactivating, 320, 324
editing, 325
explained, 314
hierarchies of, 318–325
adding child bones, 318–321

setting up multiple, 321–325
naming/renaming, 315, 319
positioning, 317, 322
recoloring, 316, 320
rest length of, 317–318
rotating, 320–321, 322, 323
Skelegons, 332–337
creating, 332–336
tips about, 336–337
using in Layout, 336
video tutorials, 314, 333, 337, 338
weights, 325–331
assigning, 330–331
creating, 328–330
settings for, 326–327
book resources, 356–357
Boolean functions, 21
borders, limited region, 151–152, 153
bounce cards, 131
Bounce setting
hard-body collisions, 298, 309
particle collisions, 280
Bounce/Bind Power option
hard-body collisions, 294–295, 298, 307
particle collisions, 280
Bounding Box Threshold option, 80
bowls
filling with fruit, 258–261
steps for modeling, 256–257
Box setting, 297
Box tool
glass windows and, 299, 300
still-life objects and, 232, 261
brightness
background image, 218, 219
setting for lights, 121
Bump option, 93

C

C button, 40
Calculate button, 287, 294, 295, 305–306
Camera Properties panel, 144
Current Camera selection list, 154
Field Rendering option, 148, 160
Mask Options tab, 164
Motion Effects tab, 158
Render Globals panel and, 144, 146, 340–341
Resolution option, 144, 146
Soft Filter option, 158
Stereo and DOF tab, 160
Use Global option, 146, 159, 340, 343
Camera Selector plug-in, 145
Camera view, 148–149, 308, 343
cameras, 143–172
adaptive sampling settings, 158
angle settings, 166–168
antialiasing settings, 156–157
depth of field settings, 161–163
field of view settings, 156
field rendering option, 148
focal distance setting, 161–162
f-stop settings, 162
lens focal length, 154–156
limited region settings, 151–153
mask options, 164
motion effects, 158–160
multiple, 47, 145
naming/renaming, 145, 154
overview of, 143–144
pixel aspect ratios, 147–148
range finder for, 162–163
resolution settings, 146–147
rule of thirds and, 165–166
segment memory settings, 153–154
selecting, 154
setting up, 144–146
Soft Filter option, 158
stereoscopic rendering option, 160
types of, 144, 168–171
Advanced camera, 169
Classic camera, 168
Orthographic camera, 169–170
Perspective camera, 170
Real Lens camera, 170
Surface Baking camera, 171
Tilt Shift camera, 171
virtual, 176
zoom factors, 154–156

Caps Lock key, xviii, 11
Catmull, Edwin, 36
Catmull-Clark subdivisions, 36, 239, 246–247, 255
caustics, 128
Center Current Item button, 53
CG Talk Web forums, 358
Change Surface dialog box, 38
  still-life modeling and, 248, 252, 255, 262
  text creation and, 224, 226
Channel Bin, 195–196, 209
channel filter plug-ins, 353
channels
  Alpha, 285, 286, 347
  animating color, 211–213
  displaying color, 89
  footprints used for, 203–205
  removing from Curve Bin, 195
  selecting noncontiguous, 193
  setting up in Graph Editor, 191–193
character modeling
  bones for, 313–338
    adding, 316–318
    child, 318–321
    creating, 314–316
    hierarchies of, 318–325
    weights of, 325–331
  Skelegons for, 332–337
    creating, 332–336
    tips about, 336–337
    using in Layout, 336
Child Bone button, 315
child bones, 315
  activating, 320
  creating, 315–316, 319–321
child layers, 12
Clark, Jim, 36
Class on Demand, 357
Classic camera, 168
Classic motion blur, 159
Clear All Lights button, 121–122
Clear Scene command, 55
Clip setting, 327
clips, 285, 286
Clips tab, 285
Clone button, 125
Clone tool, 258, 260
cloning
  lights, 124–125
  objects, 258, 260
  particles, 288
Close All Objects command, 222
cloth
  animating, 312
  modeling, 261–265
Collada file format, 352
Collision By option, 296
Collision Detect setting, 311
collision dynamics
  controls for, 297–299
  hard-body, 293–296, 303–309
  particle, 278–281
  soft-body, 310–312
collision effectors
  hard-body collisions, 304–307
  particle collisions, 279
Collision option, 279
collision plane, 279, 280–281
Collision Size value, 311
color
  bone, 316, 320
  cycling, 213
  light, 122, 125–126, 136
  safe area outline, 149
  surface, 91–92, 102–103
Color category, 25
Color Channel option, 89
color channels
  animating, 211–213
  displaying, 89
color connections, 114
Color control settings, 91–92
color picker, 81
color space, 347
color vertex maps, 40
Combine tools, 21
Commands category
  Layout, 74
  Modeler, 28

Comment field, 93
composition issues
    camera angles, 166–168
    rule of thirds, 165–166
Composition Overlay, 165
Configure Keys panel, 58
Configure Menus panel, 58–60, 100
connections in Node Editor
    connection types, 113–114
    making node connections, 113, 116
    unhooking node connections, 116
Constant setting, 205
Construct tab, 20
content directory, xx–xxi, 2, 10, 41, 91
Content Manager, 56
continuity, 188–189
contrast, background image, 218, 219
Convert Skelegon command, 337
Convert tools, 22
cookies, 135
coordinate system, 69–70
Copy Time Slice feature, 198–199
copying/pasting
    keyframes, 51
    surfaces, 109
CORE application, xiv, xvi
Create category, 78
Create Key button, 183, 184
Create Motion Key panel, 183
Create Skelegons tool, 335
Create tab, 16–18
Create Vertex Color Map option, 40
Create Weight Map panel, 329
Creating 3D Animation (Lord), 357
Creative COW Web site, 358
Crumple node, 112
cucoloris, 135
Culhane, Shamus, 357
Current Camera selection list, 154
Current Item selector, 46
Current Light drop-down list, 122
Curve Bin, 190
    adding channels to, 192–193
    removing channels from, 195
    reordering items in, 192
    selecting all curves in, 200
Curve Controls zone, 191
Curve Window, 190
    creating keys in, 200–201
    editing curves in, 193–194
    moving keyframes in, 197
    navigation of, 202
    Numeric Limits option, 202
    selecting all keyframes in, 204
curves, 23
    adjusting values for, 210–211
    controlling with Move TCB tool, 187–189
    creating in Graph Editor, 209–211
    editing in Graph Editor, 193–194, 199–200
    foreground and background, 200–201
    importing into Graph Editor, 202
    multicurve editing, 199–200
    selecting in Curve Bin, 200
    spline controls, 206–208
    stepped transitions, 208–209
Curves category
    Create tab, 17–18
    Detail tab, 23
Curves tab, Graph Editor, 205–211
custom object plug-ins, 353
customizing Modeler viewports, 7–8
Cvt Skelegons command, 337
cycling lights, 213
cyclorama, 128

D

dark lights, 122–123
deactivating bones, 320, 324
Deform tab, 311
deformation tools, 314
Delete category, 68
Delete Motion Key dialog box, 186
deleting
    images, 222
    keyframes, 186
    particles, 288
    plug-ins, 355

deleting *(continued)*
Skelegons, 335
See also removing
Density setting, 283
depth of field (DOF), 161–163
focal distance and, 161–162
f-stop settings and, 162
range finder for, 162–163
DeRose, Tony, 36
deselecting selections, 33, 35
Desktop Images Web site, 357
destination nodes, 112
Detail tools
Layout, 73
Modeler, 22–24
Diffuse setting, 92, 103, 104
Digital Character Animation 3 (Maestri), 356
Digital Cinematography & Directing (Alban), 357
Digital Lighting & Rendering (Birn), 121, 356
Digital Photography for 3D Imaging and Animation (Alban), 356
direct light, 125
Direction setting, 275
displacement plug-ins, 353
Display command, 89
Display Options panel
Backdrop tab, 217
Bounding Box Threshold option, 80
Hide Toolbar option, 100
Image Resolution setting, 218
Interface tab, 250
Layout, 79–80
Modeler, 40–41
Show Safe Areas option, 149
Display SubPatch Level setting, 317
displaying
backdrop images, 221
color channels, 89
menus, 100
panels, 151
surface subdivisions, 317
toolbars, 100
See also viewing options
distant lights, 120
dome lights, 120
Dope Sheet, 49, 66
Dope Track, 49–51, 307
Double Sided option, 93
Drag tool
backdrop images and, 221
glass window modeling and, 301
positioning bones using, 338
still-life modeling and, 236, 242, 247, 264
Draw Skelegons mode, 334
Drill tool, 221
drop-down menus, 55
Duplicate tools, 20
dutch camera angle, 167–168
DVD included with book, xx–xxi, 359–360
contents of, xx, 360
loading files from, 360
playing videos on, 360
setting content directory for, xx–xxi, 91
system requirements for, 360
tech support website, 359
Dynamic Obj button, 268
Dynamic Obj drop-down menu, 275, 279, 303, 307
dynamics, 267, 289–312
collision, 293–299, 303–309, 310–312
controls for, 290–291, 297–299
explained, 290
hard-body, 291–309
collision controls, 297–299
creating, 291–296
modeling for, 299–303
shattering glass, 303–309
tips for working with, 309
soft-body, 309–312
types of, 290
Dynamics tab, 272, 279, 290, 293, 297, 299

E

E buttons, 61, 173–174, 211–212, 298
EdgeBevel tool, 233–234, 241, 245

Edges category
  Detail tab, 23
  Selection tab, 30
Edges selection mode, 233, 244
Edit By modes, 87–88
Edit category, 73
Edit Keyboard Shortcuts panel, 57–58
Edit menu, 56–60
Edit Nodes button, 91, 111
Edit Plug-ins panel, 355
Edit Tool, 72, 287
EditFX panel, 287, 309
editing
  bones, 325
  curves, 193–194, 199–200
  keyboard shortcuts, 57–58
  lights, 124
  menus, 58–60
  particles, 286–288
editors
  Graph Editor, 62–63, 189–213
  Image Editor, 62, 285
  Node Editor, 84, 110–118
  Scene Editor, 64–66
  Surface Editor, 60–61, 83–110
  Texture Editor, 61, 97–98
  Virtual Studio, 63
  See also menus
effectors
  collision, 279, 304–307
  smoke, 278
  wind, 275–278
Effects panel
  plug-ins accessed from, 354
  Volumetrics tab, 282, 284
Embedded Alpha setting, 285
emitters, particle, 268–274
  control options, 270–274
  creating, 268–270
  explained, 268
Enable Radiosity setting, 131, 132, 133
Enable VIPER button, 75, 95
Envelope tool, 174
envelopes, 61, 174
environment plug-ins, 353
Environment tab, 93–94, 105
EPS files, 228
equal sign key (=), 316, 322
Erase setting, 298
Event setting, 298
Expand button, 54
Expert mode, 337
Explosion setting, 273
Export category, 79
Export submenu, File menu, 56, 352
exporting scenes/objects, 352
expressions, 174
Extend category, 19–20
Extra Ray Trace Optimization setting, 345
Extrude tool, 223
eye objects, 324

F

Falloff setting, 326–327
FBX file format, 352
FiberFX category, 27
field of view (FOV), 156
Field Rendering option, 148, 160
File drop-down menu, 9
file formats, 218
File menu, 55–56
fill light, 131
Filter By modes, 88
Filtering tab, 343–344
filters
  Reconstruction Filter, 157
  Soft Filter, 158
Fix Power option, 298
focal distance, 161–162
focal length, 154–156
fonts, 222–223
footprints, 203–205
Force option, 295
forced perspective, 169
foreground curves, 200–201
foreground layers, 13–14
forums, Web-based, 358
forward kinematics, 318
Foundation3D Web site, 358

fractional keyframes, 51
frame buffer plug-ins, 354
Frame End Beep option, 345
frames
  jumping to, 49, 185
  rendering, 146
  See also keyframes
Free setting, 296
Friction Power control, 298
Front Face Wireframe style, 316, 317
fruit bowl
  filling, 258–261
  modeling, 256–257
fruit modeling, 231–255
  bananas, 232–243
  grapes, 249–255
  oranges, 243–248
f-stop settings, 162
function connections, 114
function keys, 10, 223
FX_Collision Properties panel
  hard-body dynamics, 304
  particle collisions, 279–280
FX_Emitter panel, 269, 271–272, 287
FX_Wind properties panel, 275

G

General Options panel
  Layout, 80–81
  Modeler, 41
General tool category
  Layout
    Modify tab, 68–70
    Setup tab, 72
  Modeler Map tab, 25
Generator Size options, 272
Geometry tab, 282, 285
glass surfaces, 103–106
glass windows
  modeling for dynamics, 299–303
  shattering, 303–309
Global Illumination panel, 127–128
  Enable Radiosity option, 131, 133
Global Illumination tab, 103, 126–127
global plug-ins, 354
Glossiness control, 92, 103–104
GLSL shading option, 77
Go To Frame requester, 49, 185
gobos, 135–137
  creating, 135–137
  explained, 135
  tips for using, 137
Gradient nodes, 114–116, 117
grapes, modeling, 249–255
Graph Editor, 62–63, 189–213
  accessing, 190
  adjusting values in, 210–211
  animating color channels in, 211–213
  channels setup in, 191–193
  controls used in, 173–174
  Copy Time Slice feature, 198–199
  curves in
    background curves, 200–201
    creating/adjusting, 209–211
    editing, 193–194, 199–200
    foreground curves, 200–201
    selecting all, 200
  Curves tab, 205–206
  footprint creation, 203–205
  light color and, 122
  maximizing the window for, 192
  moving keyframes in, 197–198
  multicurve editing, 199–200
  opening with E buttons, 61, 174, 211–212
  Options panel, 196, 209
  overview of zones in, 190–191
  plug-ins accessed from, 354
  quadrant size, 192
  resizing, 194
  right-clicking in, 202–203
  spline controls, 206–208
    Bezier splines, 207–208
    Hermite splines, 207
    TCB splines, 206
  stepped transitions, 208–209
  summary points on using, 213–214
  timing adjustments, 194–198
  tips for working in, 197, 202

tool icons, 197
updating, 194
zoom factor and, 156
graphics. *See* motion graphics; text and logo animation
Gravity setting, 294, 306
grid
focal distance determined using, 162
size control options for, 77
Grid category, 77
Grid Size control, 77
ground collisions
hard-body dynamics, 307–308
soft-body dynamics, 310–312
Group drop-down list, 297
G-Toggle Subpatch, 78

H

handles, 69–70
hard-body dynamics, 291–309
collision controls, 297–299
creating, 291–296
modeling for, 299–303
shattering glass, 303–309
tips for working with, 309
HardFX controls, 294, 299, 305–306, 309
HDR images, 133–134, 169
Help menu, 60
Hermite splines, 207
Hide Toolbar option, 100
hiding/showing
backdrop images, 221
menus, 100
panels, 151
surface subdivisions, 317
toolbars, 100
hierarchies of bones, 318–325
child bones, 318–321
explained, 318
multiple, 321–325
Hierarchy view option, 14
horizontal FOV setting, 156
HSV color values, 102
HV emitters, 269, 270, 281
HW Shading option, 77
HyperTexture tab, 284
HyperVoxels, 268, 269, 281–284
HyperVoxels panel, 282–284, 285

I

IK Boost Tool, 70–71, 337, 338
IKB Calculate button, 71
Illusion of Life: Disney Animation, The (Thomas and Johnston), 357
Image Editor, 62, 285
image I/O plug-ins, 354
Image Map setting, 97
image processing plug-ins, 354
Image Seam Angle control, 94
Image Viewer, 106, 129, 139, 345
Image Viewer FP, 345
Image World plug-in, 133
images
backdrop, 217–222
building over, 219–222
deleting from Modeler, 222
HDR, 133–134, 169
particle, 285–286
projection, 135–137
Impact Effect setting, 295, 296, 307
Import category, 79
Import submenu, File menu, 56
importing
curves, 202
EPS files, 228
in-betweening process, 178, 199
incremental save, 220
info area, 35
Info panel
Modeler, 38
Node Editor, 114
Initial Value option, 329
Inside button, 280
installing LightWave 3D, xix–xx
integer connections, 114
intensity, light, 121, 122–123, 127
interactive particles, 278–281

interfaces
  Layout, 44–54
  Modeler, 4–15
interlacing, 148
Inverse Distance values, 327
inverse kinematics, 70–71, 318
item selection buttons, 46
Items tab, 67–68

J

Jitter tool, 300, 302
Johnston, Ollie, 357
Joint bones, 314

K

Kerlow, Isaac V., 357
key light, 131
keyboard shortcuts
  assigning, 58
  editing, 57–58
  saving, 58
keyframes, 45, 47–51
  adjusting values of, 211
  Auto Key feature, 47–49, 175–180
  controlling curves for, 187–189
  creating, 47–49, 175–187
  deleting, 186
  displaying info about, 194
  Dope Track, 49–51
  fractional, 51
  frame number for, 198
  jumping to specific, 49, 185
  keeping track of, 48
  lasso selection of, 197
  manually setting, 180–187
  motions created with, 174–189
  Move TCB tool and, 187–189
  moving in Graph Editor, 197–198
  rendering, 342
  rule of thumb for, 189
  selecting all, 204
  TCB values, 188–189
Kurv Studios, 357

L

Lasso select mode, 33–34
Lasso tool, 197
Lathe tool, 257
Layer Opacity option, 97
layers, 9–15
  background, 13–14
  explained, 9–10
  foreground, 13–14
  naming, 12
  parent and child, 12
  reversing, 250
  viewing, 14
Layers category, 31
Layers panel
  opening, 10
  selecting layers in, 13, 14
  viewing layers in, 14
Layout, 43–82
  bones, 314–318
    adding to objects, 316–318
    creating, 314–316
  Dope Track, 49–51
  editors
    Graph Editor, 62–63
    Image Editor, 62
    Node Editor, 110–118
    Scene Editor, 64–66
    Surface Editor, 60–61, 83–110
    Virtual Studio, 63
  Expert mode, 337
  hiding toolbars/menus in, 100
  interface overview, 44–54
  item selection buttons, 46
  keyframes, 45, 47–51
    Auto Key feature, 47–49
    creating, 47–49
    Dope Track, 49–51
  menus, 54–60
    Edit menu, 56–60
    File menu, 55–56
    Help menu, 60
    Windows menu, 60
  Parent in Place button, 66

positioning objects in, 258–261, 264–265
Preferences panel, 79–81
Display Options, 79–80
General Options, 80–81
Skelegons in, 337
tabs, 67–79
Items tab, 67–68
Modeler Tools tab, 78–79
Modify tab, 68–72
Render tab, 74–76
Setup tab, 72–73
Utilities tab, 73–74
View tab, 76–78
timeline, 45–46
viewports, 51–54
movement controls, 53–54
multiple viewports, 52–53
VPR feature, 52
workspace, 44
layout command plug-ins, 354
layout tool plug-ins, 354
Layout tools, Modeler, 27
Left Button Item Select feature, 181
lens flares, 126, 127
lens focal length, 154–156
Life Time setting, 274, 278, 281
Light Name panel, 123
Light Properties panel, 121–122
Light view, 135
lights, 119–141
adding, 123–124
ambient, 125–126
area, 138–141
caustics, 128
cloning, 124–125
color of, 122, 125–126, 136
cycling, 213
global illumination options, 126–128
HDR images used as, 133–134
intensity of, 121, 122–123, 127
lens flares, 126, 127
mirroring, 125
naming/renaming, 123, 135
overview of, 119–120
projection images on, 135–137
radiosity, 127–128, 131, 132
rotating, 123–124
selecting, 125
studio, 128–132
text and logo, 228
textures and, 119, 141
types of, 120–121
volumetric, 126
Lights button, 121
Lights in Scene display, 122
LightWave 3D
CORE technology, xiv
installing, xix–xx
NewTek manual, xv–xvi
plug-ins, 353–356
reference materials, 356–360
supported file formats, 218
Lightwave Tutorials on the Web, 358
Limited Region settings, 151–153
linear lights, 120, 140
Linear setting, 205
lintography, 160
List view option, 14
Load button, 86, 88
Load category, 67
Load Items from Scene command, 55–56, 67
Load Object button, 67
Load Object dialog box, 258
Load Scene command, 182
Load submenu, File menu, 55
loading
objects, xxi, 11–12, 67
plug-ins, 355–356
scenes, 55–56, 67, 182
local zone, 50
Lock Selected Keys option, 198
logo animation. *See* text and logo animation
Lord, Peter, 357
LScript category
Layout, 74
Modeler, 28
LScript Commander, 74

LScripts, 28, 74, 356
Luminosity setting
  HyperVoxels panel, 283
  Surface Editor, 92, 103
Luxigons, 26
LWO files, 9
Lynda.com, 357

M

M button, 40
Macintosh computers
  function keys, 10, 223
  right mouse button, xv, 34
Maestri, George, 356
Magic Bevel tool, 253–255
Magnet tool, 245–246, 248
Make Bone Weight Map panel, 326
Make button, 39
manual keyframing, 180–187
Map tab, 24–26
mapping, reflection, 93
Maps category, 30
Mask options, 164
Master Plugins panel, 74, 355
Max OpenGL Lights option, 139
Maximize viewport button, 6, 7, 219
Maximum Render Level setting, 139, 320
MD Arts Web site, 358
Measure category, 24
memory
  segment, 153–154, 343
  system, xviii–xix
  video, xix
menus
  editing, 58–60
  hiding, 100
  Layout, 54–60
    Edit menu, 56–60
    File menu, 55–56
    Help menu, 60
    Windows menu, 60
  Modeler, 15
  See also editors
metallic surfaces, 106–108
Metamesh Toggle, 78
Mirror button, 125
Mirror Hierarchy tool, 325
Mirror tool, 338
mirroring lights, 125
Mode drop-down, 298
Modeler, 1–42
  Action Center, 36
  backdrop images, 217–222
    building elements over, 219–222
    hiding/displaying, 221
    saving, 219
    setting up, 217–219
  Change Surface panel, 38
  deleting images from, 222
  Display Options panel, 40–41
  General Options panel, 41
  importing EPS files into, 228
  Info panel, 38
  interface, 4–15
  layers, 9–15
    explained, 9–10
    foreground/background, 13–14
    naming, 12
    parent/child, 12
    viewing, 14
  Make button, 39
  menus, 15
  Numeric panel, 37
  objects, 9–12
    explained, 9
    loading, 11–12
  overview of, 2–3
  pivot points, 227–228
  selection modes, 32–35
  Skelegons in, 332–337
    creating, 332–336
    tips about, 336–337
  Statistics panel, 37
  SubD-Type options, 36–37
  Surface Editor, 84, 85
  tabs, 15–32
    Construct tab, 20–22
    Create tab, 16–18
    Detail tab, 22–24

Map tab, 24–26
Modify tab, 18–19
Multiply tab, 19–20
Selection tab, 29–30
Setup tab, 26–27
Utilities tab, 28
View tab, 30–31
text development in, 222–226
creating text, 222–223
surfacing/beveling text, 223–226
toolset, 15
vertex map tools, 39–40
viewports, 4–8
customizing, 7–8
position controls, 6
styles, 7–8
views, 5, 7
Modeler Tools tab, 78–79
modeling
cloth, 261–265
fruit, 231–255
bananas, 232–243
grapes, 249–255
oranges, 243–248
plug-ins for, 354
still-life objects, 231–265
bowl, 256–261
fruit, 231–255
positioning and, 258–261, 264–265
tablecloth, 261–265
windows for dynamics, 299–303
Modes category, 29
Modes menu, 235
Modified Channels mode, 183, 269, 270
Modify category
Modeler Tools tab, 79
Setup tab, 73
Modify Selection category, 29
Modify tab
Layout, 68–72
Modeler, 18–19
Morph feature, 40
Morph tools, 26
Motion Blur setting
Camera Properties panel, 158–159
Render Globals panel, 344
motion effects, 158–160
motion graphics, 215–229
overview of, 215–216
video on lighting, 228
See also text and logo animation
Motion Lighting video, 228
Motion Options panel, 354
motion paths, 179–180, 183–184, 288
motion plug-ins, 354
Motion tab, 273
motions
automatic keyframing, 175–180
controlling curves, 187–189
manual keyframing, 180–187
Motions category, 73
mouse buttons, xv, 34
Mouse mode, 36, 241
Move button, 53
Move edit button, 197
Move TCB tool, 71, 187–189
Move tool
Auto Key feature and, 177
bone positioning and, 317
collision dynamics and, 305, 310
Graph Editor and, 197–198
manual keyframing and, 185
particle animation and, 270, 280, 288
right mouse button and, 259
still-life modeling and, 236, 259, 263
wind effectors and, 276–278
multicurve editing, 199–200
Multiply tab, 19–20
Multiprocessing option, 346
Multishift tool, 234, 237–238, 245
Multithreading option, 346

N

naming/renaming
bones, 315, 319
cameras, 145, 154
layers, 12
lights, 123, 135
plug-ins, 355

naming/renaming *(continued)*
- Skelegons, 335, 336
- surfaces, 102, 112
- weight maps, 331

negative lights, 122–123
Network Render tool, 76
NewTek resources, 358
n-gons, 239
Node Editor, 84, 110–118
- Add Node menu, 112
- connection types, 113–114
- gradient controls, 114–117
- info panel, 114
- move and zoom controls, 111
- opening with Edit Nodes, 111
- Surface Editor and, 110

nodes
- collision dynamics and, 296
- connecting, 113–114, 116
- destination, 112
- gradient, 114–117
- surfacing using, 110–118
- unhooking, 116

NTSC video standard, 45, 147
null objects, 163, 315
numeric keypads, 7
Numeric Limits option, 202
Numeric Move selection, 198
Numeric panel, 37
- Bevel tool, 225
- Box tool, 232, 299
- EdgeBevel tool, 234
- Lathe tool, 257
- Multishift tool, 234
- Size tool, 235
- Skelegons, 334
- Text tool, 222–223

O

object importer plug-ins, 354
Object Properties panel
- Dynamics tab, 272, 279, 290, 293, 297, 299
- plug-ins accessed from, 354

object replacement plug-ins, 354
objects, 9–12
- adding bones to, 316–318
- cloning, 258, 260
- explained, 9
- exporting, 352
- loading, xxi, 11–12, 67
- null, 163, 315
- positioning, 258–261, 264–265
- rendering selected, 348
- saving, 67, 108

Object-Subdiv setting, 297
Offset Repeat setting, 205
off-white lights, 136
Opacity setting
- HyperVoxels panel, 283
- Layer Opacity option, 97

OpenGL options, 80, 316, 349
Operator tab, 311
Options category, 75
oranges, modeling, 243–248
Orthographic camera, 169–170
Oscillate setting, 205
Output tab, 346–347
overlay color options, 149
Overlay settings, 346

P

Package Scene option, 352–353
PAL video standard, 147
panels
- hiding/showing, 151
- nonmodal nature of, 213–214
- *See also specific panels*

parent bones, 316
Parent in Place button, 66
parent layers, 12
Particle Blur setting, 160
Particle Size setting, 283
Particle Weight setting, 274
particles, 267–288
- colliding, 278–281
- controlling, 270–274
- deleting, 288

editing, 286–288
emitters for, 268–270
images on, 285–286
interactive, 278–281
Life Time value, 274, 278, 281
overview of, 267–268
Perspective camera and, 170
previewing, 281, 283, 284
repositioning, 288
sizing/resizing, 283, 285
surfacing, 281–284
wind and, 274–278
Partigons, 268, 269, 281
Parts category, 24
Parts option, 305–306
pasting. *See* copying/pasting
Patches category, 22
Path Wind Mode, 276
Pattern field, 88
Pen tool, 219–220, 222
penguin modeling exercise
adding bones to objects, 316–318
hierarchies of bones, 318–325
weights of bones, 325–331
Perspective camera, 170
Perspective view, 5, 44, 51, 220
Phong shader, 104
photometric lights, 120
Photoreal setting, 159, 344
Photoshop application, 135
Piece Mode setting, 305–306
pillow collision dynamics, 310–312
pivot points, 227–228
Pivot Shift value, 309
Pivot tool, 227
pixel aspect ratios, 147–151
explained, 147–148
resolution and, 150, 151
working with, 148–151
Pixel Lattice Deformation (PLD), 157
Plane option
hard-body collisions, 297, 307, 308
particle collisions, 279
soft-body collisions, 310
Play button, 179, 185
PLD setting, 157, 343–344
plug-ins, 353–356
categories of, 353–354
deleting, 355
finding, 354–355
loading, 355–356
LScript, 356
renaming, 355
scanning for, 355
Plugins category
Layout, 74, 355
Modeler, 28, 355
Point Clone Plus tool, 250–251
point lights, 120–121
point sets, 312
points
adding, 221
pivot, 227–228
Points category
Create tab, 17
Detail tab, 23
Selection tab, 29
Points selection mode, 32–33, 235
polygons
beveling, 236–237
selecting, 302
single-point, 268, 269
Polygons category
Create tab, 17
Detail tab, 23
Selection tab, 30
Polygons selection mode, 33, 261, 264, 302, 328
Position channel, 193
position controls, Modeler viewport, 6
positioning
bones, 317, 322
objects, 258–261, 264–265
particles, 288
Powergons, 26
pre- and post-behaviors, 205
Preferences panel, 79–81
Display Options, 79–80
General Options, 80–81

Preset Shelf
prebuilt surfaces in, 90
saving surfaces to, 90, 109
storing surfaces in, 88
Presets folder, 90
preview window
Surface Editor, 89
VIPER tool, 96, 98
previews
EdgeBevel tool, 233
particle animation, 281, 283, 284
Render Options panel, 139
Surface Editor, 89, 96, 103
VIPER window, 96, 98
Primitives category, 16–17
Probability setting, 298
procedural textures, 97
Procedural Type option, 97
processing power, xix
project files on DVD, xx–xxi, 360
projection images, 135–137
creating, 135–137
explained, 135
tips for using, 137
Projects folder, xxi
Properties panel
Bone, 317, 318, 322, 324, 330–331
Cameras, 144
Light, 121, 211

Q

quad view, 220
quality settings, area lights, 140, 141
Quantize dialog box, 301
QuickCut command, 263, 264
QuickTime movies, 147, 347
QuickTime player, 360

R

radiosity, 127–128, 131, 132
Radius setting, 275
Radius/Level setting, 279, 298, 304, 307
RAM. *See* memory
Random Points tool, 250
range finders, 162–163
range-type rendering, 341–342
Ray Recursion Limit setting, 345
Ray Tracing + Spherical Map option, 107
Raytrace Reflection option, 105, 345
Raytrace Refraction option, 345
Raytrace Shadows option, 139, 345
Raytrace Transparency option, 345
ray-traced images
reflections, 93, 105, 108, 345
shadows, 138, 139, 345
ray-tracing process, 93
ReadMe file on DVD, 360
Real Lens camera, 170
Realistic Render Mode, 345
Reconstruction Filter, 157
Redo command, 56, 331
Reduce category, 21
reference materials, 356–360
audiovisual resources, 357
book resources, 356–357
companion DVD, 359–360
Web resources, 358
Reflection Blurring control, 94
Reflection control, 92, 104
Reflection Map control, 94, 107
reflection mapping, 93
Reflection Options control, 94, 105
reflections
applying to surfaces, 100–103
ray-traced, 93, 105, 108, 345
surfacing for, 103–108
Refraction Blurring control, 94
Refraction Index option, 92
Refraction Map control, 94
Refraction Options control, 94
removing
backdrop images from Modeler, 222
channels from Curve Bin, 195
See also deleting
Rename command, 89
Rename Skelegon command, 336
renaming. *See* naming/renaming
Render category, 76

Render Display options, 129
Render End Beep option, 345
Render Globals panel, 75, 144, 340–341
  Auto Frame Advance option, 345, 348
  Camera Properties panel and, 144, 146, 340–341
  Enable Radiosity option, 131, 133
  Filtering tab, 343–344
  Global Illumination tab, 126–127
  Image Viewer setting, 106, 129, 139, 345
  Limited Region setting, 151–153
  Motion Blur setting, 344
  Output tab, 346–347
  Preview setting, 139
  Raytrace Reflection option, 105, 345
  Raytrace Shadows option, 139, 345
  Resolution option, 343
  Segment Memory Limit option, 153–154, 343
  Shutter Efficiency option, 344
Render Mode setting, 345
Render Options panel, 106, 139
Render SubPatch Level setting, 317
Render tab, 74–76
rendering, 339–349
  batch, 348
  defined, 146
  frames, 146
  general-purpose, 342–346
  LightWave engine for, 340
  plug-ins for, 354
  range-type, 341–342
  saving renders, 346–347
  selected objects, 348
  setting up for, 341–342
  single-frame, 342
  speeding up, 284
  thoughts on, 349
RenderQ control, 348
Repeat setting, 205
Replace category, 68
repositioning particles, 288
Reset setting, 205
Resistance setting, 309
resizing. *See* sizing/resizing
resolution
  display options and, 218
  pixel aspect ratio and, 150, 151
  setting for cameras, 146–147, 343
  system memory and, 153
Resolution Multiplier, 147, 343
resources. *See* reference materials
Rest Length setting, 317–318
reversing layers, 250
Rewind button, 48, 179, 185
right bracket key ( ]), 240
right mouse button
  Mac computers and, xv, 34
  moving and rotating with, 259
Right view, 5
Roll option, 295, 307, 309
Rotate button, 53
Rotate category
  Layout, 68
  Modeler, 18
Rotate tool
  Auto Key feature and, 178
  bone positioning and, 317
  manual keyframing and, 184, 185
  right mouse button and, 259
  still-life modeling and, 241, 259, 262
rotating
  bones, 320–321, 322, 323
  lights, 123–124
  wind effectors, 275
Rotation channel, 193
Rotation tab, 309
Roughness setting, 298
RTV file format, 346
rule of thirds, 165–166

S

S button, 40
safe areas, 149
Save All Objects command, 67, 88
Save Animation option, 346–347
Save command, 88
Save RGB button, 347
Save Scene As command, 55

Save Scene command, 88
Save Scene Increment feature, 55
Save Surface Preset command, 90
saving
  Alpha channels, 347
  backdrops, 219
  fonts, 223
  incremental, 220
  keyboard shortcuts, 58
  objects, 67, 108
  renders, 346–347
  Skelegons, 332, 336
  surfaces, 90, 109
scalar connections, 114
Scan Directory option, 355
Scatter option, 298
scattering effect, 273, 298
Scene button, 182
Scene Editor, 64–66
  Dope Sheet in, 66
  editing lights in, 124
  exercise on working with, 64–65
  recoloring bones in, 316, 320
Scene list, 191–192
scene master plug-ins, 354
scenes
  exporting, 352
  loading, 55–56, 67, 182
  packaging, 352–353
Segment Memory Limit setting, 153–154, 343
segmented box modeling, 299–300, 302
Sel Object option, 348
Sel Switch command, 234, 236, 245
Select category, 77–78
Select Connected command, 252
Select Loop option
  dynamics modeling and, 300
  still-life modeling and, 240
selecting
  cameras, 154
  channels, 193
  curves, 200
  layers, 13, 14
  lights, 125
  polygons, 302
  surfaces, 108
Selection modes, 32–35
  Action Center, 36
  exercise on using, 32–34
  Lasso mode, 33–34
  Points mode, 32–33
  Polygons mode, 33
  Symmetry mode, 35
Selection Set option, 40, 312
Selection Sets category, 30
Selection tab, 29–30
selections
  deselecting, 33, 35
  hiding/unhiding, 31
Self Interaction drop-down, 307
Set Value dialog box, 236, 256, 257
Setup tab
  Layout, 72–73
  Modeler, 26–27
Shaded Solid option, 320
shaders, 104
Shading tab, 283, 285
shadows
  ray-traced, 138, 345
  shadow maps, 131
shattering glass, 303–309
Show Handles option, 181
Show Motion Paths option, 180, 184
Show Safe Areas option, 148–149
showing. *See* displaying
Shutter Efficiency option, 344
Simple Wireframe Points option, 250
Simply LightWave Web site, 358
single-frame rendering, 342
single-point polygons, 268, 269
Size tool, 235, 237, 251
Size Variation setting, 283
sizing/resizing
  area lights, 140, 141
  bones, 317–318
  Graph Editor, 194
  limited regions, 152
  particles, 283, 285
  Surface Editor, 102

Skelegon Tree panel, 335, 337
Skelegons, 332–337
  creating, 332–336
  deleting, 335
  explained, 26, 332
  naming/renaming, 335, 336
  Numeric panel, 334
  saving, 332, 336
  splitting, 336
  tips about, 336–337
  using in Layout, 337
  weight maps, 336, 337
  See also bones
Skelegons category, 27
Sketch tool, 222
slash key (/), 33, 35
slices, 283
Sliders tool, 71
smoke
  simulating with particles, 270–274
  surfacing particles for, 282–284
smoke effector, 278
Smooth Threshold option, 93
Smoothing option, 93, 104
snapping keyframes, 51
Soft Filter option, 158
soft-body dynamics, 309–312
SoftFX dynamics panel, 290, 311
Solid Drill tool, 221
Specialty category, 30
Specularity setting, 92, 103–104
Sphere setting, 296, 297
spherical lights, 121
SpinQuad Forums, 358
Spline Control tool, 71
Spline Draw tool
  still-life modeling and, 256
  text/logo creation and, 222
splines, 22, 23, 206–208
  Bezier splines, 207–208
  controlling in Graph Editor, 206–208
  Hermite splines, 207
  TCB splines, 206
Split Skelegon option, 336
spotlights, 121
sprites, 281–282, 283, 286
Stam, Jos, 36
Start By Collision option, 299, 306
Statistics panel, 37
  bone weights and, 328
  glass window modeling and, 302
stepped transitions, 208–209
stereoscopic rendering, 160
Stick setting, 298
still-life modeling, 231–265
  fruit, 231–255
    bananas, 232–243
    grapes, 249–255
    oranges, 243–248
  fruit bowl, 256–261
    filling, 258–261
    modeling, 256–257
  positioning objects in, 258–261, 264–265
  tablecloth, 261–265
Stop By Collision option, 299
Stretch Direction setting, 283, 285
Stretch tool, 240, 249
studio lighting, 128–132
styles, Modeler viewport, 7–8
Subdivide tools, 20
subdivision methods, 239
SubD-Type options, 36–37, 239, 255
Subpatch mode, 36, 239, 255
Subtract option, Bone Weights panel, 327
Surface Baking camera, 171
Surface button, 38, 224
Surface Editor, 60–61, 83–110
  accessing, 84
  Basic tab, 91–93
  commands, 88–90
  Edit By modes, 87–88
  Environment tab, 93–94, 105
  Filter By modes, 88
  Node Editor and, 84, 110
  Pattern field, 88
  Preset Shelf, 88, 90, 109
  previews, 89, 96, 103

Surface Editor *(continued)*
- resizing, 102
- Surface Name list, 85–87
- VIPER tool and, 94–99
- VPR feature and, 99, 100

Surface Editor button, 224
Surface Name list, 85–87
surface normal, 220
Surface Preset panel, 90
surfaces, 84
- color settings, 102–103
- copying/pasting, 109
- glass, 103–106
- lights and, 119, 141
- metallic, 106–108
- naming/renaming, 102, 112
- Node Editor and, 110–118
- organizing, 85–87
- particle, 281–284
- prebuilt, 90
- reflections applied to, 100–108
- saving to Preset shelf, 90, 109
- selecting existing, 87–88, 108
- setting up, 91–94
- Surface Editor and, 83–110
- text, 224–226
- working with, 88–90

SVGA mode, 146
SWXGA mode, 146
Symmetry mode, 35
system requirements
- for Lightwave 10, xviii–xix
- for using the DVD, 360

T

T button, 39, 61
Tab key, 239
tabs
- Layout, 67–79
  - Items tab, 67–68
  - Modeler Tools tab, 78–79
  - Modify tab, 68–72
  - Render tab, 74–76
  - Setup tab, 72–73
  - Utilities tab, 73–74
  - View tab, 76–78
- Modeler, 15–32
  - Construct tab, 20–22
  - Create tab, 16–18
  - Detail tab, 22–24
  - Map tab, 24–26
  - Modify tab, 18–19
  - Multiply tab, 19–20
  - Selection tab, 29–30
  - Setup tab, 26–27
  - Utilities tab, 28
  - View tab, 30–31

Tarantino, Quentin, 171
TCB settings, 71, 188–189
TCB spline controls, 206
technical support, xx, 359
telephoto lens, 156
television monitors, 149
Template Drill panel, 221
tension, 188
text and logo animation, 215–229
- backdrop images, 217–222
  - building elements over, 219–222
  - hiding/displaying, 221
  - saving, 219
  - setting up, 217–219
- general overview of, 216–217
- importing EPS files, 228
- Layout setup for, 228
- lighting for, 228
- motion graphics and, 215
- setting pivot points, 227–228
- text development, 222–226
  - creating text, 222–223
  - surfacing/beveling text, 223–226

Text category, 17
Text tool, 222–223
Texture category, 25
Texture Editor, 61, 97–98
Texture mode, 39
Textured Shaded Solid option, 139

textures
  lights and, 119, 141
  node-based, 110
  procedural, 97
  See also surfaces
Thomas, Frank, 357
three-point lighting, 131
Threshold Value setting, 327
Tilt Shift camera, 171
timeline, 45–46
timing adjustments, 194–198
title-safe area, 149
Toggles category, 78
toolbars, hiding, 100
tools
  deformation, 314
  Layout, 27, 70–72
  Modeler, 15, 78–79
  vertex map, 39–40
  See also specific tools
Tools category, 70–72
Top view, 5
Torque values, 296, 307, 309
Transform category
  Layout, 68
  Modeler, 19
transitions, stepped, 208–209
Translate category
  Layout, 68
  Modeler, 18
translations, 18, 68
Translucency control, 93
Transparency control, 92
troubleshooting DVD problems, 359
Tunnel operation, 221
Tuong-Phong, Bui, 104
Turbulence option, 97, 284
tutorials
  audiovisual, 357, 359–360
  DVD-based, 360
  Web-based, 358
two-button mouse, xv, 34
type animation. *See* text and logo animation
Type drop-down list, 297

U

Undo command, 56, 331
undo operations, 41, 56–57, 81, 331
Unweld command, 303, 336
Use Global option, 146, 159, 340, 343
Use Threshold setting, 327
Utilities category, 76
Utilities tab
  Layout, 73–74
  Modeler, 28
  plug-in options, 355

V

Vaughan, William, 332
vector connections, 114
Velocity setting, 272, 273–274
vertex map tools, 39–40
vertical FOV setting, 156
vertices, 235
VGA mode, 146
Vibration setting, 273
video memory, xix
video tutorials, 357, 359–360
video-safe area, 149
View category, 31
View Layout category, 77
View tab
  Layout, 76–78
  Modeler, 30–31
viewing options
  for bones, 317
  for object layers, 14
  for viewports, 51
  See also displaying
viewports
  Layout, 51–54
    movement controls, 53–54
    multiple viewports, 52–53
    VPR feature, 52
  Modeler, 4–8
    customization, 7–8
    position controls, 6
    styles, 7–8
    views, 5, 7

Viewports category
Layout, 76–77
Modeler, 31
VIPER button, 95
VIPER tool, 76
particle surfacing and, 283, 284
preview window, 96, 98
Surface Editor and, 85, 94–99
Texture Editor and, 97–98
tips for using, 99
tutorial on, 95–99
VPR feature vs., 76
virtual cameras, 176
Virtual Studio, 63
VisualParticle movie, 278, 280
Volumetric Antialiasing option, 284
volumetric effects, 269, 354
volumetric lights, 126
Volumetrics tab, 282
Vortex setting, 275, 276
VPR feature, 52
particle surfacing and, 283, 284
Surface Editor and, 85, 99
tips for using, 100
VIPER tool vs., 76

W

W button, 39
WaveCycle setting, 311
WaveSize setting, 311–312
Web animation, 153
Web resources, 358
Weight category, 25
weight maps, 325–326
bone, 326–331
Skelegon, 336, 337
Weight Shade mode, 330
weights
bone, 325–331
assigning, 330–331
creating, 328–330
settings for, 326–327
hard-body, 295, 307
particle, 274
Weights tool, 39
White, Tony, 357
wide-angle lens, 156
wind, particle, 274–278
Wind Effect setting, 296, 309
wind effectors, 275–278
Wind Mode options, 275
windows
modeling for dynamics, 299–303
shattering, 303–309
Windows drop-down menu
Layout, 60
Modeler, 10

X

X, Y, and Z axes, 3
XVGA mode, 146

Z

Z-axis bones, 314
Zoom button, 53
zoom factors, 154–156